Beyond the Neon Lights

Beyond the Neon Lights

Everyday Shanghai
in the Early Twentieth Century

HANCHAO LU

University of California Press

BERKELEY   LOS ANGELES   LONDON

University of California Press
Berkeley and Los Angeles, California

University of California Press, Ltd.
London, England

Library of Congress Cataloging-in-Publication Data

Lu, Hanchao.
    Beyond the neon lights : everyday Shanghai in the early twentieth
century / Hanchao Lu.
        p.   cm.
    Includes bibliographic references and index.
    ISBN 0-520-21564-8 (alk. paper)
    1. Shanghai (China)—Social life and customs—20th century.
2. Shanghai (China)—Social conditions—20th century.   3. Shanghai
(China)—Economic conditions—20th century.   I. Title.
DS796.S25 L8   1999
951'.132—dc21   98-31298
                                                           CIP

Manufactured in the United States of America

08   07   06   05   04   03   02   01   00   99
10   9   8   7   6   5   4   3   2   1

The paper used in this publication meets the minimum requirements of
ANSI /NISO Z39.48-1992 (R 1997) (*Permanence of Paper*).

Parts of the following chapters are revised versions of materials published elsewhere: chapter 3: "Creating Urban Outcasts: Shantytowns
in Shanghai, 1920–1950," *Journal of Urban History* 21, no. 5 (July
1995): 563–96; chapter 6: "Away from Nanking Road: Small Store and
Neighborhood Life in Modern Shanghai," *Journal of Asian Studies* 54,
no. 1 (February 1995): 92–123. These revised portions appear here by
permission.

To the memory of my parents

Contents

Illustrations

Tables

Acknowledgments

For help with a book about the lives of ordinary people in old Shanghai, my first and foremost thanks go to numerous veteran residents of the city for providing me with rich and graphic information about life in the pre-revolutionary era. I am particularly thankful for their enthusiasm and good humor: while I often inquired in some detail about their lives in the "old society," a topic sometimes at the edge of the taboo in the People's Republic of China not too long ago, virtually no one asked me the potentially embarrassing question of why a returned student from the United States had become so inquisitive about some seemingly trivial matters of the past. In Chinese academia, I benefited greatly from being associated with the Shanghai Academy of Social Sciences (SASS). I am especially indebted to Xiong Yuezhi of the Institute of History of SASS and Lu Hanlong of the Institute of Sociology of SASS for their support over the years, ranging from facilitating access to library and archival materials to arranging surveys and interviews. Song Zuanyou was extremely helpful in giving me valuable research assistance even when I was not in China. I also thank Chen Zhengshu, Feng Shaoting, Li Tiangang, Luo Suwen, Pan Junxiang, Shen Zuwei, Tang Zhenchang, Xu Min and Zhang Jishun for their support of my research in Shanghai.

Joseph Esherick, Kenneth Pomeranz, and David Strand carefully read the manuscript and offered insightful and detailed comments that greatly helped refine the theme of the book. I am particularly happy to acknowledge my gratitude to them. I am also deeply in debt to David Buck, Sherman Cochran, David Faure, and William Rowe, who have given me sound advice on some chapters of the book.

I would like to thank Linda Grove for encouraging me to advance my studies in the United States when I was an academic vagrant in Japan. Without her vision I may never have written this book. My greatest intellectual debt goes to Philip Huang, who ushered me into the vigorous field of Chinese socioeconomic history and constantly showed his confidence in my work. Kathryn Bernhardt, Deborah Davis, Benjamin Elman, Eric Monkkonen, Fred Notehelfer, Douglas Reynolds, and Richard J. Smith have been valuable sources of inspiration in the writing of this book. I particularly wish to thank Perry Link and Jonathan Spence; their encouragement and support of this research have meant a great deal to me.

Over the years of research and writing I benefited from discussions with many scholars. I offer my thanks to Ronald Bayor, Marie-Claire Bergère, Robert Bickers, Francesca Bray, Wellington Chan, Clayton Dube, Mark Elvin, August Giebelhaus, Noriko Kamachi, David King, Chi-Kong Lai, Chang Liu, Tao Tao Liu, Stephen MacKinnon, Brian Martin, Andrea McElderry, Kerrie McPherson, Geoff Millar, Zane Miller, Susan Naquin, Matthew Somer, Stephen Usselman, Xi Wang, Xiaoping Ye, and Zhang Zhongli (Chung-li Chang) for their comments and help that contributed to my research on various occasions. I thank Ming-te Pan for always being cheerfully available for discussion, Jiahua Lu for sending me books from Princeton, and Songhua Shi and Wei Ding for solving crises in computer word processing and drawing. I also thank Sheila Levine, Laura Driussi and Rachel Berchten of the University of California Press for handling the manuscript with care and efficiency. I owe a double debt to Robert Hawkins, Robert McMath, and Gregory Nobles for their support of this project and for their leadership at Georgia Tech in creating a rich and supportive research environment for the humanities and social sciences. For financial support, I am grateful to the Henry Luce Foundation, China Times Foundation, Georgia Tech Foundation, and Shanghai Research Center for grants that made my annual summer trips (1993–97) to China possible.

Romain Rolland once said that human gratitude is like the fruit on a tree: it decays if not picked in time. I would like to alter the metaphor and give it a more optimistic tone by saying that if the fruit is made into wine, it mellows with age. For over a decade, Richard Gunde has most generously lent me his expertise and, in particular, shared myriad thoughts with me about this book. To him, I am profoundly grateful.

One of my mentors in China, a renowned author and in many ways a quite "Westernized" individual, once expressed his disapproval to me of what he believed to be an unnecessary, or even affected, practice among *yangren* (foreigners) of thanking one's *laopo* (wife) in a book acknowledgment. He implied that a spouse is an all too natural part of an author's life to be acknowledged in public. Cultural shock, one might say. Yet I cannot help but be a rebellious student—my final thanks go to my family: to Lin-lin for her love, to Freddy and Jeffrey for being adorable children. Their childhood constantly reminds me of my own and hence of my loving parents, to whose memory this book is dedicated.

Notes on Chinese Currency and Romanization

The symbol "$" and the word "dollar" in the text refer to Chinese silver dollars (*yinyuan*; used before November 1935) and Chinese yuan (known as *fabi*, or "legal currency"; used after November 1935); the two were roughly equivalent.

The silver-copper exchange rate fluctuated constantly and varied by region. In Shanghai in the early 1930s the exchange rates were 1 silver dollar to about 300 to 330 coppers, and 1 copper to 10 cash (*wen*).

Based on the degree of purity, silver dollars were categorized into "big dollars" (*dayang*) and "small dollars" (*xiaoyang*). In the early 1930s, 1 small dollar equaled about .76 big dollar. Unless otherwise indicated, dollars quoted in the text were big dollars.

Chinese currency in the 1940s was unstable and chaotic both in name and in value. In order to avoid confusion, 1940s prices mentioned in the text represent, wherever possible, conversions of the yuan (*fabi*) according to its value just before the war (1936–37); the main criterion for conversion is the price of rice.

I have used pinyin romanization with a few exceptions for originally romanized street names (such as Nanking Road instead of Nanjing Road) and conventional romanization for people's names (such as Ah Q instead of A Q).

Introduction

The history of modern Shanghai has in recent years received an extraordinary amount of scholarly attention both in the West and in China. In the West, readers have been struck by the variety as well as academic depth of the literature on Shanghai that has appeared since the early 1980s. Studies on the city's history touch upon a wide range of topics in the political, economical, social, and cultural realms: from the indigenous growth of pre-treaty-port Shanghai to the presence of the West in the city, from the Qing "circuit intendants" (or Daotai) to the "Mixed Court," from traditional merchant organizations to modern entrepreneurship, from public health to higher education, from the police establishment to the underground, from labor strikes to student protests, from native-place associations to social biases, from the divisions among intellectuals to the taxonomy of prostitution, and so on.[1] Like any high-quality research that focuses on a regional topic, most of what has been published has aimed at and, to different degrees, successfully brought out broader issues whose significance reaches beyond that of a single city.

It is a blessing to scholars outside China that a similar efflorescence of research on the history of Shanghai appeared almost simultaneously in the city itself. Starting in 1978 as part of a nationwide program to revive the Chinese tradition of writing local history, or *fangzhi*, researchers in Shanghai made great efforts to continue the work of an official Shanghai history writing group known as Shanghaishi tongzhiguan (Institute for the History of Shanghai), headed by the noted scholar-official Liu Yazi (1886–1958).[2] Under this movement, research on Shanghai has reached beyond the limits of conventional gazetteer compilation. Source materials on Shanghai of various types, including collections of historical materials on a given topic, archival materials, reminiscences, historical anecdotes, and documentary photographs, as well as research monographs and treatises, appeared in good quality and quantity.[3] More significant, research in Shanghai has been internationally oriented; although scholarly engagement based on mutual understanding of analytical theories and methodologies between researchers in and outside China still leaves much to be desired, communications among researchers of Shanghai are among the best in academia.[4]

In this rich and colorful gallery of portraits of Shanghai, what has not been adequately portrayed is the daily life of ordinary people. If human history involves primarily the people, and if what shapes people's outlook and affects their activities involves the places they live and work, then the importance of daily life in historical research needs no further explanation. The purpose of this book is to portray the quotidian aspects of the lives of the people of Shanghai in the first half of the twentieth century, with particular attention to everyday life in the city's residential quarters.

A city as large and complex as Shanghai—indeed, it has been one of the world's largest and most cosmopolitan metropolises—contains within it an incredibly wide variety of people. Although in most years less than 3 percent of the city's population was foreign born, this portion of the population came from virtually everywhere in the world and, as far as social composition is concerned, included an impressive array, from vagabonds and prostitutes to diplomats and parvenus. The Chinese residents of Shanghai were, in a sense, also foreigners: they came from all provinces in the nation. The majority were rural folk who flocked to the city looking for a better life.

The most numerous of the Chinese immigrants were of two major groups: the little urbanites (*xiaoshimin*), as they have been called, and the urban poor. About three-quarters of the city's dwellings consisted of a single type called *lilong* (alleyway or lane) houses: these were the homes of the average city people (the little urbanites) for about a century following the 1880s. A close look at alleyway-house neighborhoods—where well over half the residents hailed from the countryside—reveals how life was lived in the world of the middle and lower-middle classes of Shanghai. This forms the subject of most of this book. As for the poor of Shanghai—who, like the xiaoshimin, were almost entirely from the countryside—most ended up in the many shantytowns that sprang up across the city. I will also explore life in these hovels.

The experiences of the xiaoshimin and the urban poor reveal the interplay of the customs, habits, and traditions that these "peasants of yesterday" brought into the city with the new, modern, and Western aspects of urban life. With this focus in mind, I have aimed to delineate the daily life of the city's ciphers and nonentities—at least that is what these people were in the eyes of the city's elites, whose life, in turn, receives the least attention in this study.

As my research for this study unfolded, three major issues emerged. Although the research is entirely locally focused, the issues it bears on are national in scope. By the end of my study, these issues had become the themes into which I had woven bits of empirical evidence and against which I had tested theoretical assumptions. The first issue is the character of urban-rural relations in modern China: while the Chinese people rapidly cast off the notion of cities as uninteresting or dangerous and came to think of them as superior to the countryside, was a metropolis like Shanghai in fact so modern, so sophisticated, so Westernized, and in other ways unique that it was alien to hinterland China? How did Shanghai's commercial culture contribute to the sense among outsiders that the city was somehow alien, somehow not quite Chinese? Derived from this issue is the question of how the people of Shanghai identified themselves: what did it mean to them to be a Shanghairen (a Shanghai person, or Shanghainese), and what sense of community, if any, emerged from living in tightly packed neighborhoods? Finally, as part of the issue of modernity and identity, there is the question of how appropriate Western-derived assumptions are to plumbing daily life in a Chinese city.

Urban-Rural Relations: A Continuum or a Gulf?

Researchers of Chinese urban history have argued that there is a striking difference between traditional China and medieval Europe in regard to urban-rural relations. Whereas European cities stood out as islands of culture in a sea of rural backwardness, Chinese cities were integrated with their surrounding rural villages in all political, cultural, and socioeconomic dimensions. One of the central themes that G. William Skinner and his colleagues present in the monumental volume *The City in Late Imperial China* is the urban-rural continuum in traditional China. China up to the nineteenth century was a harmonious landscape in which cities and villages at various administrative and commercial levels as well as in different geographic regions were integrated with each other. Accordingly, there was no sharp contrast or gap between city and country, particularly in the social and cultural realms. Even obvious landmarks like city walls did not set the city apart from the countryside.[5]

As a result of the urban-rural continuum, the sense of urban superiority commonly associated with Western cultural tradition did not prevail in traditional China. The reasons for this are multifaceted. First, Chinese elites were landed gentry-literati whose essential socioeconomic base was in rural communities rather than urban centers. The elites who resided in the city, as well as a large number of people who pursued occupations that kept them away from their rural home, always retained their ties to their native place: it was there that they maintained their formal place of residence and their *hengchan*, or permanent property (i.e., land), and it was there that their family tomb and lineage temple were to be found—in short, their roots and identity were still rural.[6] Also, Chinese cultural life did not fall into two widely divergent spheres or display characteristic dichotomies between the urban and the rural. For one thing, Chinese cities were not necessarily cultural preserves and religious centers, as they were in Europe. Like men on a chessboard or stars in the sky, cultural and religious sites spread across China without any clear-cut division into urban and rural settings, thus denying the notion that the city (perhaps with a few exceptions, such as the capital city) was culturally superior to small towns and villages. Furthermore, unlike European cities Chinese cities did not possess a corporate identity, civic monuments, or "citizens" that set the city apart from its surrounding rural areas. Between towns and villages, frequent communication of various sorts and a flow of population in both directions integrated rural and urban areas in a way that made a sense of urban superiority groundless.[7]

In fact, quite the opposite social sentiment could be detected: the city in traditional China often had a negative image. Before the Song dynasty (960–1279), Chinese cities were predominately administrative centers, inextricably associated with government yamen, taxation, the corvée, criminals, and lawsuits. Its political function tended to make the city a place held in awe, at least by peasants. The commercial character of Chinese cities in the post-Song era did not improve the peasants' overall image of the city. The vicious reputation of merchants and the stubborn social bias against commerce in Chinese society only added to their original awe of the city, the place where the yamen was located: they also came to see it as the place where cunning prevailed. Mark Elvin once observed, "The city was in some respects feared by peasants. One Ch'ing [Qing] official wrote that 'country-folks are terrified to enter their country capital, dreading the officials as if they were tigers.' The city was a place where taxes and rents were often paid, and where lawsuits were tried. It was the haunt of criminals such as the 'market bullies' who were experts at victimizing peasants. In times of famine, it was in the city that farmers sold starving children whom they could no longer feed."[8]

Not only the peasantry (who were, of course, the overwhelming majority of the population) but all of society to some degree viewed the city as an abomination. In a nation that highly valued its system of rule—an enormous body of peasants governed by a scant elite of scholar-officials—it is understandable that ideal society would be that in which people lived contentedly in the countryside. The great Chinese historian Sima Qian (c. 145–90 B.C.) wrote of men aged sixty or seventy who had never visited towns as evidence of peace, order, and prosperity.[9] Such thinking endured. As the eminent seventeenth-century thinker Gu Yanwu (1613–82) commented, "If people live in the country, the society will be in order; if people live in the city, the society will be in turmoil. People living in the country results in reclamation of land and the peace of farms; people will inevitably have a permanent faith [*hengxin*]. People living in the city results in onerous corvée and frequent lawsuits; it will be impossible to expect people to have a permanent faith."[10] This is a succinct statement of the mainstream view on urban-rural relations in traditional China.

The twentieth century saw a dramatic change in this age-old value system. Although distrust of the city lingered on in some respects, modern, industrialized, and highly commercialized cities came to be seen as better places than small towns and villages. This sweeping reassessment was chiefly brought on by the economic opportunities cities presented. The rural deterioration that paralleled the industrialization of the city in the early twentieth century accelerated urban-rural differentiation and sharpened the gap between city and country—the urban-rural continuum was gradually replaced by an urban-rural gulf. That this occurred in the turbulent age of twentieth-century China itself would have brought a wry smile to the face of Gu Yanwu, inasmuch as his viewpoint had, unfortunately, been confirmed.

In trying to fathom the depth of the urban-rural gulf, one constantly comes up against the inescapable reality that hundreds of thousands of rural immigrants in urban areas lived a life of bare subsistence yet fiercely stuck to the city. These rural immigrants formed the majority of the urban poor in Shanghai. By virtue of their poverty, they were denied access to most of the facilities and conveniences a modern city offers and suffered social discrimination. Yet all the hardship and disadvantages did not drive them out of the city. On the contrary, where possible they brought their families from the villages to the city.

In Republican-era Shanghai, two groups of urban poor best reflect the lure of the city: rickshaw pullers and street beggars. Both were multitudinous and ever present. In his renowned novel *Camel Xiangzi*, Lao She describes his protagonist, a former farmer lured by opportunity to Beijing in the 1920s, where he made a living as a rickshaw puller: "The city gave him everything. Even starving he would prefer it to the village. . . . Even if you begged in the city you could get meat or fish soup. In the village all one could hope for was cornmeal." Citing Lao She's unadorned words, David Strand comments, "Because of the great disparity in urban and rural incomes, even a 'lower class' occupation like rickshaw pulling might satisfy a peasant's ambition for a better livelihood." [11] This was certainly so in Republican Shanghai. Close to 100,000 public-rickshaw pullers labored in Shanghai in the late 1930s, competing for about 25,000 rickshaws for hire in the city. Two shifts around the clock yielded about 50,000 jobs for pullers. Fifteen to sixteen shifts per month was considered a normal, full-time workload for a puller. In addition, there were thousands of men hired to pull private rickshaws.

The overwhelming majority of this army of rickshaw pullers were peasants who had come directly from the poverty-ridden villages to the city seeking opportunity. Many of them, in fact, could not survive in their native villages, which had been devastated by natural disasters, banditry, and war. They came to the city for bare subsistence. For them, the move was not necessarily a search for a better life but for *life* itself. Merely to survive in the city was a powerful measure of the economic opportunity they found there. Although the majority of them lived in sheer poverty, survival itself was reckoned to be success. As a popular Chinese saying put it, "A bitter life is better than a comfortable death" (*haosi buru ehuo*).

There was another group of former peasants whose experience in the city fit, unfortunately but perfectly, the philosophy expressed by this proverb: beggars. Shanghai in the 1930s had about 20,000 to 25,000 professional beggars who were, like the rickshaw pullers and most of the other urban poor, refugees from rural poverty. Of all the 360 callings (*hang*) that the Chinese used as an analogy for all walks of life, mendicants were the lowest. As another Chinese saying goes, in a human life "there is no catastrophe except death; one cannot be poorer than a beggar" [12] (*chu si wu da'nan, taofan zai buqiong*).

However, an exploration of the beggars' world in Shanghai reveals that mendicancy was not necessarily, as generally thought, a downward movement in social status, a mark of improvidence, or the outcome of individual failure. In Republican Shanghai, mendicancy was a highly organized profession and one that not every newcomer could easily enter. For rural immigrants in the city, mendicancy was sometimes a preferred livelihood, and one that denoted privilege. A popular Chinese saying dramatizes the preference for begging: "Having been a beggar for three years, one would decline an offer to be an official." [13] This truly happened in some cases. A beggar in Guangzhou once declined an offer from his brother-in-law to serve as an official in a county office, saying that he would rather "be accompanied by the Five Hundred Monks [i.e., his fellow beggars] than bow himself down for the Five *dou* of Rice [i.e., a salary]." [14] With all its myths, tactics, and organizations, begging became an urban "job" option and a part of the lure of the city in modern China.

As I have suggested, urban poverty was more a result of rural crisis than a product of urban growth. The lure of the two lowest urban occupations (one, pulling a rickshaw, was described as a job that literally entailed "running like oxen and horses" [*niu ma zou*] and the other, begging, was mournfully paired with death) reveals more than anything else the depth of the urban-rural gulf in modern China. Since urban poverty in twentieth-century China was primarily the result of rural depression that made the city a symbol of opportunity for the impoverished and desperate masses of the countryside, any means that promised bare subsistence was taken as a straw to be grasped before drowning in an ocean of destitution.

Shanghai in its heyday was notorious as a city where, in famine years, police and charities had to pick up thousands of corpses. Most of the victims were new arrivals from the countryside and the abandoned infants of the poor.[15] One may argue that a city like this can hardly be described as a paradise for the poor. Truly it was not. However, in comparison with the wretched who died on the streets and the much more numerous victims of famine and war in the villages, the destitute survivors in Shanghai—of which rickshaw pullers and beggars were the most visible—could justifiably be regarded as the lucky.

The idea of the superiority of the city has been criticized as "a cliché of our Western cultural traditions," and one that does not fit traditional Chinese society.[16] But by the early twentieth century this Western cliché had clearly captured the imagination of the common people of China. Rural people clinging to the city for sheer survival gave substance to the notion in a down-to-earth and unadorned way. It also showed that the concept was not imported but was a product of Chinese social reality and a summary of ordinary people's life experiences. The economic opportunities, convenience of daily life, and richness of cultural and social life in the city, all granted incomparable and irresistible advantages to the city over the country. As twentieth-century China's most modernized city, Shanghai concentrated and highlighted the attractions of an urban life, giving birth to the boastful saying "East and West, Shanghai is the best."[17] This sense of Shanghai's superiority is also apparent in a folk song that mocks the vanity of a country girl:

> A country girl wants to imitate the manners of Shanghai.
> Desperately trying, with all her strength, she still cannot get it.
> Ah! she is now a little bit closer
> —but fashions in Shanghai have already changed.[18]

What we see here is not just a satirical sketch of an innocent country girl, but an allegory of the backwardness of the countryside.

The City and Modernity:
The Making of a Commercial Culture

Although the old negative image of the city faded, it did not entirely disappear. While the city was generally seen as a better place to live than the country, many (and not only the peasantry and earthbound gentry class) continued to despise the city as somehow irrational and dangerous. By the twentieth century, judgment on the city was not single-minded but had become a mixture of contradictions, with admiration, envy, fear, and contempt all mixed together. Although sentiment for the city became increasingly positive, some measure of the old awe lingered even after the Communist revolution.

This contradiction became something people were aware of, and it was often revealed in satirical literature written by socially sensitive writers. Lu Xun (1881–1936) epitomized peasant mentality in his famous character Ah Q, a day laborer in Wei village who always thought well of himself. At the top of Ah Q's "list of prides" was that he had been to town a couple of times.

> Yet he could be contemptuous of townsfolk too. For instance, Wei Villagers called a seat made from a three-foot plank a longbench and so did Ah Q, but the townsfolk called it a stickbench. "That's not right, that's flatass dumb!" he thought to himself. And how about fish? When frying bigheads, Wei Villagers would toss chopped scallions into the pan, but the townsfolk always used shredded ones. "That's not right, that's flatass stupid!" he thought to himself. "On the other hand, I gotta remember that next to me, Wei Villagers are just a bunch of hicks. They've never even seen how bigheads are fried in town."[19]

Naturally, if the object of attention were not a nearby town but a great metropolis like Shanghai, this mixed feeling toward urban life would be still more drastic and dramatic. Indeed, mixed or contradictory sentiment was a frequent topic in popular fiction in early-twentieth-century Shanghai. Bao Tianxiao's *The Countryman Revisits Shanghai*, which was serialized in Shanghai's leading newspaper, *Shenbao*, is a good example. Bao described the unpleasant but comical experience of a hayseed in Shanghai in the early thirties. From the countryman's point of view, Shanghai is "expensive, foreign, irrational, petty-minded, impersonal, depraved, and chaotic." The obstinate man dislikes virtually everything he sees in the city: from the name of railway station tickets, the classes of streetcars, and the arrangement of shops to the distant relations of the people, the calculating character of society, the shamelessness of prostitutes, and so on. However, while the city's moral decay is most evident in the case of a village girl lured to the city to be a prostitute, even this old peasant realizes that the city is a place where great money can be made: "Did not even this poor lost daughter send enough money back to the countryside to build a fine cement house for her parents?"[20]

Two years after Bao published this piece, Mao Dun in his classic *Midnight* started with the dramatic death of old Mr. Wu, a wealthy member of the gentry who arrives in Shanghai to visit his elder son, a modern entrepreneur. Sitting in a motorcar of the latest design, holding an ancient classic, and observing the street scene of the "Sinners Paradise," the old man is overwhelmed by the frenzy of the city. He is shocked when he sees "a half-naked young woman sitting up in a rickshaw, fashionably dressed in a transparent, sleeveless voile blouse, displaying her bare legs and thighs." In the old man's eyes, the countless lighted windows of the towering skyscrapers gleam like the eyes of devils and the traffic becomes a snakelike stream of black monsters, "each with a pair of blinding lights for eyes, their horns blaring, [which] bore down upon him, nearer and nearer!" All this causes him to close his eyes tight in terror, and tremble all over. The first thing that the old man seizes upon when he recovers from his dizziness is the ravenous way his younger son had gazed at the half-naked woman from the car window, accompanied by his daughter's complaint that "father would not like me to dress pretty!" The overwhelming contrast of what he saw upon entering the city, and the constant thought that "of all the vices sexual indulgence is the cardinal; of all the virtues filial piety is the supreme" drumming in his mind, bring on a fatal stroke the very evening of his arrival at his son's luxurious modern home.[21]

In some way Mao Dun's novel reflects the feeling of alienation and disorientation experienced by many people who came to the city from a rural or less urban background, including the author, who himself grew up in a Jiangnan rural town and came to Shanghai to work as an editor at the Commercial Press. While Mao Dun delineated alienation and disorientation through a fictional figure, his contemporary Yu Dafu (1896–1945) was forthright in expressing his own feelings. Born and raised in a small town in Zhejiang, where his neighbors included firewood choppers and vegetable peddlers, Yu Dafu noted that his first impression of Shanghai was of "being surrounded by women's pearls and make-up, smelling their perfume, and living in the shadow of the hairs on their temple; all of these almost made a newly arrived country youth like me out of breath. I felt that I was going to fall into a coma." Yu described city life as "perverted and decadent," characterized by a "scramble for money, openness of crime, waste of spirit, and rampage of carnality"; he asked, "after all, was this the goal of mankind?" [22] His diaries, particularly those written in Shanghai, were full of sad and depressed sentiments over things urban, yet without the city, he proclaims, his life would have been meaningless.[23] Yu was known for portraying sensational female characters, and his personal love life and marriage were much publicized. His female protagonists were remarkably consistent: all were urbane, charming, novel, yet full of temptation and danger—like the city itself.[24]

Perry Link describes the popular mentality toward the city (in particular, Shanghai) as "anxious ambivalence." [25] Other scholars of Shanghai have made a similar observation: the city's "everyday life was suffused with ambivalence." [26] But, why was there this ambivalence? Why was it not limited to outsiders who lived in the country (whose complaints about the city might be dismissed as "sour grapes"), but felt as well by those who lived in and apparently benefited from the city?

The ambivalence was arguably derived from the gulf between the countryside—which, with some noticeable exceptions, was bound by tradition, largely untouched by modernity, and conservative—and the city, which was less concerned about tradition, more open to modernity, and progressive. Like many commonly used but loosely defined terms, both "tradition" (or "traditionalism") and "modernity" invite broad and sometimes divergent interpretations. In modern China, traditionalism was frequently associated with things indigenous and an attitude of looking back in time. Modernity, however, was associated with things foreign and an attitude of looking forward.[27] This is particularly true in the case of Shanghai: the city was the nation's leading treaty port, its largest commercial center, and its most Westernized metropolis. Ambivalence toward the city in general and Shanghai in particular reflected earthbound China's contradictory feelings towards things new, unorthodox, and foreign.

From the late Qing through the socialist era, the Chinese have seen Shanghai in many different ways, but in the final analysis there are only two views that count: the city is a symbol of economic opportunities to be seized, or it is a trap of moral degeneration (including the triumph of Western imperialism) to be shunned or condemned. One might think that strong, contradictory views like these could easily divide people into opposing groups. But in Shanghai these views were by no means divisive. Rather, it was clear that any individual could hold both views and not feel ridiculous about doing so.

Criticism of the city came from not only the conservative, Confucianism-minded moral camp but also the progressives. From Wang Tao (1828–97), one of the nation's pioneer reformists in the late Qing, to Chen Duxiu (1880–1942), the Communist radical, writers portrayed Shanghai as an evil empire where human dignity was crushed by greed and lust, and Chinese pride was trampled by barbarian foreign devils (or, to use a later term, Western imperialism).[28] Even the terminology used to convey the image of Shanghai was consistent across ideological lines and time periods. From the late Qing to the era of the People's Republic, *da ran'gang,* or a gigantic dye vat, was one of the most popular metaphors used to describe Shanghai, implying that the "spiritual pollution" (to borrow a recent political neologism) of the city was so contaminative and inevitable that anyone who lived there might be unconsciously and indelibly "dyed." As a local saying put it, "One could not clean oneself even by jumping into the Huangpu River" (*tiaojin Huangpu jiang ye xibuqing*).[29]

As an essentially rural-based movement, the Communist revolution inevitably inherited the ambivalence toward Shanghai. The city's solid industrial and financial base and fine workforce that were built in the prerevolutionary period have been generally recognized to be invaluable national resources. For decades, the city's contribution to China's national revenue was incredibly high, far beyond any conceivable normal share of a single city in a country of China's size.[30] But Shanghai's economic contributions did not prevent the regime from sticking to its preconceived prejudice, which was of course based on an all too important ideology, that the city had been an evil bridgehead of foreign encroachment and the supreme headquarters of domestic reactionaries and therefore should be condemned.

The story of the "Good Eighth Company on Nanking Road" (*Nanjing*

Lu shang Haobalian), a People's Liberation Army unit stationed in downtown Shanghai, offered a national role model in the 1960s. The promotion
of the Good Eighth Company preceded and then paralleled the political-
moral campaign to "Learn from Comrade Lei Feng" personally trumpeted
by Mao Zedong. It dramatized the official, orthodox, negative view of
Shanghai. At his post on Nanking Road, a soldier of the Eighth Company
sighed to his fellow soldiers that "even the wind on Nanking Road smells
good." This unadorned expression of feeling was taken as a dangerous sign
of the corrosive influence of bourgeois ideas, of which Shanghai (and, in
particular, Nanking Road) was a symbol. The entire story of the Eighth
Company involved a single theme: how to resist such influences. The Good
Eighth Company on Nanking Road, which was the official honorary title
the unit earned in 1963, became a national role model simply because
the unit, established in rural north China during the Civil War, was able
to maintain an essentially rural lifestyle while stationed in the midst of
Shanghai's urban dissipation.[31]

No wonder stories such as the following were propagated. A soldier of
the Good Eighth Company was reluctant to see his wife, who had cheerfully come from their home village to visit him in Shanghai. After having
experienced the dazzling city life, the soldier disdained the woman's rough
and rustic manner. Like the exclamation "Even the wind in Nanking Road
smells good," the soldier's "deviation" was treated as an indication—an
even more serious indication—of the corrosive effects of the city. After
much political education (or brainwashing, one might say), the soldier
was back to "normal." The happy ending, as it was plotted into a drama
named *Sentries under Neon*, was that once the deviant soldier took off his
leather shoes and put on cotton-cloth shoes (handmade by his wife), and
once he and his wife together enjoyed their "down home" food—*wowo-
tou* (steamed buns made of maize or sorghum)—things were once again
right.[32]

The assumption here, as well as what lay behind feelings of "anxious
ambivalence," was that Shanghai was different from the rest of China: the
city represented a modernity that was alien to the nation. But the question
remains, how sound was the assumption? Or, to put it more precisely, how
modern were the city and its people? If modernization is, by one definition,
"the process by which societies have been and are being transformed under
the impact of the scientific and technological revolution," we encounter two
different images of Shanghai.[33] One is a metropolis that was a gigantic re-
ceptor of modern technological development. Running water, gas, electricity, telephones, streetcars, automobiles, air-conditioning—all appeared

in Shanghai soon after they were introduced in the West. Nanking Road and the Bund featured imposing Western-style office buildings, including East Asia's tallest edifice (the Garden Hotel) and "the most sumptuous building from the Suez Canal to the Bering Sea" (the Hong Kong and Shanghai Bank), and modern facilities such as China's first Otis escalator (in the Daxin Department Store) and the world's longest bar (in the Shanghai Club).[34] In addition to Shanghai's unquestionable position as the nation's first modern industrial, commercial, and financial center, the city was also known for its cultural sophistication—for its prosperity in literature and the fine arts (the first female nude model for painting stunned the nation in 1913), for its initiatives in Western-style higher education, for its development of modern media and the press, for its concentration of China's finest movie studios and theaters (which earned the city the appellation "Hollywood of the East"), for its leading role in fashion, and so on.

But if we step away from the fashionable boulevards and look into the back alleys where the majority of the people of Shanghai lived, we witness another image—a less publicized but perhaps more realistic picture, and one that may be regarded as *not* modern. Calling it an urban village with a small-town type of life would be a more appropriate way to describe the scene. The majority of Shanghainese lived in two- or three-story brick attached houses built row upon row in the narrow alleyways that sprawled all over the city. A typical day in these neighborhoods started with the rumble of the two-wheeled nightsoil cart rolling along the back alleys. The din of the nightsoil man pulling his cart was always the first sound to break the stillness of the dawn. Chickens, commonly raised in these neighborhoods, bestirred themselves; the cockcrow echoed the nightsoil man's yelling for people to bring out their nightsoil to be collected. This daily collection of human waste was followed by the daily chore of lighting a gasoline can–sized coal stove; coal was the only source of cooking energy in the kitchen of the average Shanghai family.[35] Wastepaper and wood chips were used to kindle a fire that in turn ignited egg-shaped briquettes of compressed coal. Wisps of smoke rose slowly into the air, painting streaks of gray against the whitish morning sky. This scene, viewed from a distant building on the Bund, was not unlike what one might see when viewing a rural village from a nearby hill: the smoke from the kitchen chimney of ordinary peasant households is a symbol of a lively community in rural China.

But to see such a scene in Shanghai was odd in the sense that this was the first city in China to have piped gas and a modern sanitary system. But irony can be found in many aspects of the daily life of the city people. While Shanghai has the reputation of having a diverse and rich cuisine, the standard breakfast fare for the people of Shanghai was, and remains, tasteless *paofan* (made by reheating leftover cooked rice) and pickles.[36] In high fashion, the city led the nation ("the Paris of the East"), but ordinary people seldom purchased clothes off the rack at a fashionable shop. What most Shanghainese wore was made either by the handy housewife (as most of them were) or a Ningbo or Suzhou tailor, whose shop most likely sat right on the corner of the alley. It was also not unusual to see residents returning from a visit to the countryside carrying bundles of clothing with them.[37] While automobiles were found in abundance on the streets of Shanghai, most people had never taken a taxi; for the majority, to ride in a sedan would have been considered a once-in-a-lifetime experience. The two-wheel rickshaw might be considered by some to be a symbol of Oriental backwardness, but it was an improvement over the wheelbarrow popularly used from the late Qing well into the Republican period. By any standard, the city had excellent means of public transportation, but it was not uncommon to see people commuting, sometimes for miles, by the inborn means of transportation: walking, a practice known in jest as taking the "Number Eleven Bus."[38] The scene in the city's shantytowns was even more rural and primitive. Most of the residents there were denied access to the basic facilities that any modern city offers: electricity and running water. Using a pail to lift water from a nearby creek or crude well drilled by the residents and lighting a kerosene lamp were the ways these people got water and light. Paved roads were rare in these areas, not to mention sewers and regular garbage collection. One of the reasons that squatters' neighborhoods often sprang up along the banks of a river or a creek was that these places readily served as both a source of water and a dumping ground. The shantytowns of Shanghai were not just an example of the usual "urban problem" associated with any big city. They were an integral, fundamental part of the city and the home of a good part of the city's population. By the end of the Republican period, nearly 1 million, or about one-fifth, of the city's people lived in shantytowns.

Overall, as far as daily life was concerned, Shanghai can be seen as a honeycomb consisting of numerous small cells—the compact, even crowded, and multifunctional neighborhoods—where people conducted most of their daily activities. For most people these were carried out in an area that at most stretched just a few blocks from their home. Almost all daily needs could be met within walking distance. Public transportation was utilized mainly for commuting to work. Taking a bus to go shopping or for other purposes was seen as a significant event. Of course, the living quarters of shopkeepers in the neighborhood served as workplace too, not unlike the peasant's home and farm rolled into one. Also, most children went to school within a few blocks of their home or even in the same alley. The city therefore was fragmented into numerous small communities wherein a life of moderate comfort could be obtained and maintained without venturing into the outside world—just a few blocks away. To many residents the few blocks around their homes were what the "city" meant to them, and most of the city's much publicized modern amenities were quite irrelevant to their daily lives.

However, this provincial or urban-village type of lifestyle, so to speak, did not prevent Shanghainese from being viewed, in the eyes of Chinese outside the city, as the most cosmopolitan and urbanized people of China. An old Shanghailander (an old-fashioned way of saying "a person of Shanghai," one that often refers to Shanghai's Westerners) could fastidiously point out the distinctions between a person from the so-called "higher corner" (or *shang zhi jiao*, referring to the city's fine neighborhoods) and a person from the "lower corner" (or *xia zhi jiao*, referring to the city's poor neighborhoods), but such distinctions were too subtle for non-Shanghainese. For them, all Shanghainese seemed to share, among other things, a most distinctive characteristic that one needed to take precautions against: astuteness. This characteristic was, on one hand, associated with being calculating, fastidious, quick-witted, and, if necessary, with benefiting oneself at the expense of others. On the other hand, it was not necessarily associated with bargaining over trivial matters, and certainly not with being niggardly. Rather, it implied a style or a boldness of vision in life to have the daring, as a Chinese saying put it, to look to the long term by "casting away gold like throwing out dirt" (*zhi jin ru tu*). In the twentieth century, all across China "Shanghainese" and "astuteness" became inseparable like body and shadow.

It is more meaningful, and perhaps also less conjectural, to explore the origin of any stereotype than to discuss its legitimacy. In looking at the source of this stereotype—and perhaps all the characteristics of Shanghai's people mentioned above—one inevitably encounters a powerful fountainhead, namely, commerce. One may imagine a "typical" Shanghainese, as envisioned by many Chinese, to be rather like Shakespeare's merchant of Venice but with a breadth of spirit and "merchants' ways" that were veiled with the kind of sophistication tempered only by living in an extremely cosmopolitan and complex city. In other words, Shanghainese were far from philistine, and their "merchant character" was often implicit and diluted with the higher culture that the city generally represented. Nonetheless, underneath it all nothing could change the fact that the essence of being "Shanghainese" derived from commerce.[39]

As is now common knowledge in the field of Chinese history, commerce and commercial culture were age-old and widespread phenomena in China; in particular, late imperial China witnessed vigorous commercialization in the lower Yangzi delta region, of which Shanghai was a part. Nevertheless, modern Shanghai possessed a more densely clotted and highly localized commercial culture than the nation had ever seen before. Here in a riverside city of little more than a dozen square miles gathered millions of people; each came cherishing a dream, each ventured into this strange land in search of survival or success; and in the process each had become a merchant of a sort. Here, in some way everybody was a commodity and everything was for sale: from the flesh and blood of a newly arrived country girl to the muscle of a simple coolie, from auspicious words uttered by a street urchin to monopolistic protection provided by notorious gangsters, from missing national art treasures to recycled opium dregs, and so on. Such commercialization may well be an inevitable part of modernity—it was certainly not seen as too extravagant in the capitalist West during the Industrial Revolution—but it was novel and peculiar to most Chinese in the early twentieth century. It was therefore all too natural that the Chinese perceived their compatriots in Shanghai as a group of anomalous people immersed in a distinctively commerce-derived culture that somehow differed from the rest of the country; hence they looked askance at Shanghainese.

One is easily tempted to look for Shanghai's commercial culture in the city's bustling, prosperous commercial centers that featured modern, multicolored business mansions, department stores, entertainment centers, theaters, hotels, restaurants, and ever-changing neon lights and commercial advertisements of all sorts.[40] All of these are certainly important components of commerce and commercial culture, and all are present in modern cities elsewhere. This study, however, chooses to focus on something less conventional but more characteristic of a Chinese city with a unique commercial culture rooted in everyday life: the commerce in the back alleys where most people lived. The purpose of this focus is to witness the human drama of everyday life. Here we see how commerce was not limited to just the city's commercial districts but rather was an everyday matter carried out in the narrow paths between residential houses, at the back doors of common households, in people's living rooms, and even in the inner chambers of ordinary homes. It was in this extraordinary mixture of residence and commerce that a vibrant commercial culture was born: commerce was made such a vital part of life that, we may say, one had to commend one's soul to it in order to survive.

How "China-Centered" Are We?

In the half century since the end of World War II, Western scholarship on the history of late imperial and modern China has in a broad sense moved toward a "China-centered" approach that has gradually replaced, or in some ways remedied, the "Western-impact/China-response" model.[41] This movement has been stimulated by a younger generation of researchers well trained in the Chinese language, and by political changes in China since the late 1970s that have allowed a better research environment, including access to archival materials and local records previously closed to researchers and the possibility of field studies.

The more profound reason, of course, has to do with a change in philosophy: the internal dynamics and logic of a non-Western nation have come to be seen as a more powerful force than a strong but external impact. Applying this outlook to modern Chinese history, scholars have convincingly demonstrated that in some dimensions of Chinese life traditional social and institutional practices continued into the modern era, that modernity in China in some respects had Chinese roots and was not something entirely transplanted from the outside, that some social and political aspects of late imperial China were comparable to those of "early modern" Europe, that the Communist revolution may have carried out programs that had started a century earlier,[42] and so on. Overall, discontinuities and stimulus from the West have come to be seen as less important than the continuation of Chinese tradition and indigenous development. The history of modern Shanghai has been taken as a showcase to demonstrate both perspectives. For decades under the "impact-response" model, the city was seen as the "key to modern China," as representing the path that the rest of China should have taken.[43] This view has been much modified by more recent scholarship, but to see Shanghai as an unusually important city (whether "key" or not) remains unquestioned. This surely is one of the reasons for the boom in Shanghai studies in recent decades. Little explanation is required for the view that a history of the Chinese labor movement, a history of the Chinese bourgeoisie, or a history of modern Chinese literature, among many other subjects, would be unthinkable without research on Shanghai.[44]

Although modern Shanghai was far from being firmly in the grip of

Westernization—as its image of "China's most Westernized city" often conveys—an awareness of the Chinese character of the city should not lead to underestimation of Western influences. In fact, the old "impact-response" model is perhaps more relevant in Shanghai than in any other place in the nation. Most of the changes that occurred in the city after 1843 (when Shanghai was opened as a treaty port) were an obvious consequence of the Western impact or were associated with the West. Indeed, the persistence of tradition in the life of the people of Shanghai is only more striking if we are fully aware that such continuity existed despite the formidable forces that worked to cut Shanghai off totally from the past. In other words, an underestimation of the Western influence on the city—something that a "China-centered" approach could easily lead to—would not only introduce a bias that is opposite on the surface but similar in nature to that of "Western impact," but also prevent us from full appreciation of the tenacity of Chinese traditionalism.

Nowadays an emphasis (or overemphasis, as critics would say) on the Western impact on modern China is vulnerable to criticism—if it is not seen as too hackneyed even to be worth criticizing. But, ironically, the new breed of China-centered studies may not be immune from the dangers of a Euro-centered bias. In analyzing a historical phenomenon in China by examining it from "within" (which is what the China-centered approach attempts), we must choose whether to view that phenomenon as something essentially Chinese in a Chinese context or perspective, or to view it as a *Chinese counterpart* of things Western. The latter has the obvious merit of putting Chinese history in comparative perspective and, for a practical purpose, making things Chinese easier to understand. One may also add that, in the final analysis, all human societies share something in common; thus a counterpart-hunting approach is not altogether inappropriate.

However, such an approach runs the risk of conceptualizing Chinese history based on Western experience or of distorting it to fit Western-derived theoretical models. In analyzing what he has called "the paradigmatic crisis in Chinese studies" (in particular, in social and economic history), Philip Huang points out: "Our field has far too long borrowed analytical concepts entirely from Western-derived schemes, attempting in one way or another to force Chinese history into the classic model of Smith and Marx."[45] Indiscriminately applying Western models to Chinese realities encompassed Chinese Communist orthodoxy that had long declared Marxism to be a theory that "fits well everywhere" (*fang zhi sihai er jie zhun*). Regardless, the counterpart-hunting approach in the field of Chinese history could fall back into the trap of the much criticized Euro-centered perspective on Chinese history, although this time the trap would be better hidden and, consequently, more dangerous.

These thoughts occurred to me as I tried to employ some frequently applied analytical concepts in the field, some of which seem inevitable tools in my research on neighborhood life in Republican Shanghai. I found the tools blunt and unable to cleanly dissect the empirical material that I have gathered in my research. Neighborhood life is by any definition part of *society*. Thus with such a topic an application of the "state-society relations" approach seems almost imperative. While any research on neighborhood life cannot completely ignore that angle, such an approach produces a rather indistinct and insipid picture in which the neighborhood ("society") is largely free from governmental and political intervention.

A few examples, beginning with the *baojia* mutual responsibility system, may make the point clearer. The Chinese state had a long tradition, or at least a consistent intention, of exerting control down to the urban neighborhood. The baojia system was the most notable, institutionalized, and protracted effort in this regard. The system can be traced back to at least the Song period (960–1279). In the Qing (1644–1911) its importance was frequently emphasized by the imperial court, and the system was refined to an unprecedented degree of sophistication. Nevertheless, in all accounts the baojia turned out to be more an intention of the state rather than a reality in society; it existed largely on paper or was more a matter of form than substance. Even at its zenith in the Qing, it was far from being completely carried out nationwide.

Later, the Nationalist government tried to reestablish the baojia system but achieved no more success than its Qing predecessor. In Shanghai, the regime only followed the same track of drawing up the blueprints with much fanfare, but never really got the institution built. The only time that Shanghai residents felt political control from the above was during the Japanese occupation, when a wartime baojia system was indeed enforced. But the system was brief, incomplete, and taken as a wartime emergency measure.[46] It was not until after the Communist revolution that the people of Shanghai were, in the span of a few years (1950–54), incorporated into a neighborhood organization system unprecedented in Chinese history.[47]

Thus, prior to the early 1950s when a three-tier system of urban neighborhood organization was built nationwide, neighborhood life was essentially free of state intervention. In the saying "Heaven is high and the Emperor is far away," one finds a reflection not only of the peasants' view of state power but of that held by the ordinary city people of Republican Shanghai. Here, the analytical model of state versus society is still useful in framing the picture (in the sense that it brings out the issue), but in large measure it is irrelevant to the content of the picture.

One of the issues regarding state-society relations that has been the subject of lively and thought-provoking discussions in recent years involves the question of civil society and public sphere in China. Developed by the German thinker Jurgen Habermas in analyzing late-seventeenth-century Great Britain and eighteenth-century France, the public sphere–civil society construct has become a favorite analytical framework for China scholars who are interested in testing whether notions and institutions similar to those that pervaded Great Britain and France may have existed in late imperial and twentieth-century China. Such scholars often bring in the Chinese notion *gong* as the best available equivalent to the "public sphere." Elite and mass participation in local affairs has been interpreted as a form of local autonomy, an expression of society (in contradistinction to the state), and a harbinger of democracy: all are the essence of civil society or, to carry the argument further, signs of modernity.[48] Such arguments have achieved remarkable successes in Chinese urban history, most importantly in William Rowe's study of Hankou in the late Qing and David Strand's study of Beijing in the early Republic. Their works demonstrate the sophistication of city people (in particular, the nongovernmental elite) in dealing with various political, economic, and professional issues. Many practices were Chinese innovations that had developed in the nineteenth century and continued into the twentieth century and that may bear some similarities to the European experience in the eighteenth and nineteenth centuries.[49]

But if we were to look for local autonomy, the expression of public views, or a sense of community in the homes of Republican Shanghai, we would be in some degree disappointed; at the very least, we would meet forms of "public sphere" and "civil society" very much unlike those in Western Europe. A typical residential neighborhood in the city was a walled and gated compound consisting of several rows of identical attached houses. Each house was, more often than not, subdivided, with its rooms rented to different families, many of which lived under the same roof for decades. Living cheek by jowl with one's neighbors did not create a strong sense of community, contrary to what one might expect. There was no regular or usual neighborhood organization like the *chōkai* (neighborhood associations) that flourished in Japan in the same period.[50] Occasionally, tenant committees cropped up in Shanghai, representing residents fighting rent increases or renovation plans (that would force residents to move out). These committees were loosely organized, occasional and temporary in nature, formed by a few volunteers, and only lukewarmly supported by those who had an interest in the negotiations; often they ended in failure.

Of course, neighbors were not totally alienated from each other. News and gossip were circulated and spread among neighbors through casual chatting at alleyway corners, in daily morning shopping at a neighborhood food market, in the "enjoying the cool" summer-evening gatherings, or at the hot water service and snack store combination that could be found in most residential neighborhoods. Love affairs and marriages among neighbors were uncommon. Disputes among neighbors over trivial matters, however, were frequent, and sometimes physical fights broke out, but more serious violence was rare and disputes seldom found their way into a court of law. Serious disputes were almost always mediated by neighbors, although no formal institution for that purpose existed prior to the Communist revolution.

Scholars are now well aware—or should be—that our knowledge of the public sphere in China is still limited.[51] This limitation springs from our incomplete, and in some areas superficial, knowledge of the warp and weft of everyday life in China. We need a more detailed and nuanced picture of the life of the ordinary people before we can say that any theoretical construct has meaningfully framed the nature of Chinese history.

PART 1

IN SEARCH OF
AN URBAN IDENTITY

CHAPTER 1

Going to Shanghai

The writer Aldous Huxley (1894–1963), who traveled the world extensively, exclaimed in 1926 that none of the cities he had ever seen so overwhelmingly impressed him with its teeming humanity as Shanghai. "In no city, West and East," Huxley wrote, "have I ever had such an impression of dense, rank, richly clotted life. Old Shanghai is Bergson's *elan vital* in the raw, so to speak, and with the lid off. It is Life itself."[1] This spirited life Huxley observed in the Chinese section of the city was just part, perhaps the less vigorous part, of modern Shanghai, a city that in the span of a century grew from a muddy town on the Huangpu River to a booming metropolis of 5 million people. The city drew its inhabitants from all over the country (indeed, all over the world) and from of all walks of life; most were peasants who flocked to the city in pursuit of the dream of a better life.

Like many phenomena in modern China, modern Shanghai's birth was attended by the West. This was not merely in the sense that the modern city grew out of the treaty port classification imposed by the West, but that its origins lay in a somewhat bizarre system, in which a settlement deliberately designated for the British ended by being inhabited overwhelmingly by Chinese, who lived side by side with foreigners of all stripes. It was precisely this unexpected and unintended mixture that eventually turned Shanghai into the single most cosmopolitan city of China.

From Segregation to Mixed Residence

THE BIRTH OF A CITY

Shanghai has been the largest metropolis in twentieth-century China, and one of the five or six biggest cities in the world. Its actual area, however, was small in the middle of this century: the city proper (i.e., urban districts, excluding rural counties under the Shanghai municipality) was 31.8 square miles (82.4 square kilometers), and the main part of the city, the former foreign concessions where modern Shanghai arose, was barely 13 square miles (33 square kilometers). The core of the city virtually coincided with the 1848 boundaries of the former British Settlement, an area of about 470 acres (.7 square mile).[2] In Shanghai's heyday in the Republican period, if one walked from Nanking Road or the Bund—the prosperous commercial heart of downtown Shanghai—in any direction for a distance of about 5 miles, one would find oneself in the midst of fields of cotton and rice. If one departed from the Bund by ferry and crossed the Huangpu River—a trip of less than ten minutes—one would land in an almost untouched, traditional bucolic setting.[3]

Thanks to the more than two decades of rigorous research on the commercialization of Ming-Qing China, especially in Jiangnan and the lower Yangzi delta region, nowadays few scholars would still say that pre-treaty-port Shanghai was but a fishing village.[4] Early in the nineteenth century, the walled town of Shanghai was ranked as a so-called third-class county seat. This placed it under the provincial capital of Nanjing and the prefectural capital of Songjiang, but still accorded it some prominence for its commercial prosperity, based primarily on a booming cotton trade in the Qing period.

However, the northern outskirts of the city, where the future International Settlement and the French Concession were to be located, was truly rural in November 1845 when Gong Mujiu, the Shanghai Daotai, or circuit intendant, assigned the first piece of land there to the British: the landscape was dominated by cotton and rice fields, uncultivated fields of reeds, and winding footpaths for towing boats along the waterways.[5] What was to become the famous Bund was then just one of the footpaths near the waterfront at the confluence of the Huangpu River and Suzhou Creek. The walled county town, in spite of its prosperity before the mid-nineteenth century, formed only a small portion of modern Shanghai, about one-twentieth of Shanghai proper in the Republican period. In that sense, the modern city of Shanghai did spring from obscure rural origins.

In population, too, Shanghai grew from an insignificant beginning. The population of all of Shanghai county reportedly reached 540,000 in the mid-nineteenth century, about half of whom lived in the walled county seat and its immediate outskirts and the rest in villages and small towns scattered throughout the county. The northern suburbs of the town, where the International Settlement later appeared, had merely five hundred inhabitants. The population there was so sparse and considered so insignificant that contemporary surveys of Shanghai simply ignored it.[6]

However, half a century later, the population in this part of the city had skyrocketed to half a million residents. Another half century later, the population of Shanghai reached more than 5.45 million. In other words, Shanghai experienced a tenfold growth of population in a span of a century. Equally significant was the tremendous concentration of the population: the overwhelming majority were not dispersed throughout old Shanghai county, but densely packed into what had previously been the northern suburb of the county seat. This was one of the world's most densely populated places: average population per square kilometer was 43,570 in 1930, 50,032 in 1935, and 76,880 in 1940–42.[7]

By the mid-nineteenth century, Shanghai had exceeded Guangzhou in population and become China's leading treaty port.[8] The rapid growth of Shanghai could be measured by economic data such as shipping volume in and out of the port of Shanghai. In 1844, the first year after the port was open, a total of 44 foreign ships (together carrying 8,584 tons) entered Shanghai; in 1849 a total of 133 ships (52,574 tons) entered; and in 1863 a total of 3,400 foreign ships (964,309 tons) entered, and a total of 3,547 foreign ships (996,890 tons) departed. The staples of this busy trade were (among imports) opium and (among exports) tea and silk.[9]

The dynamic of development in modern Shanghai fundamentally diverged from that in traditional Chinese cities. Scholars in China view the development and prosperity of modern Shanghai as a result of Western imperialism and the exploitation of the hinterland by the treaty port.[10] In the final analysis, such a view is not substantially different from the Western interpretation of Shanghai as a proud product of Western sophistication or as a city literally built on the notorious opium trade.[11] Putting moral concerns aside, views on both sides of the Pacific share the common ground that the city was nurtured by the commercial vigor and entrepreneurship brought by the West. Although Shanghai had been a busy commercial center prior to its opening to the West, the new dynamic brought by the Westerners meant that traditional commerce, such as the cotton trade, was largely irrelevant to the modern development of Shanghai.

The composition of the people of modern Shanghai also differs from that of the old city. Researchers have shown that pre-treaty-port Shanghai was by no means a city inhabited only by local people. For instance, the role in the city's commercial life played by so-called guest merchants (*keshang*)—who came from a variety of places ranging from the southern provinces of Guangdong and Fujian to Anhui in the Yangzi River valley and the provinces of north China—was vitally important.[12] Still, the population of Shanghai, like that of other county seats, was overwhelmingly local. In contrast, the great majority of the inhabitants of modern Shanghai came from elsewhere. From the late nineteenth century to the mid-twentieth century, immigrants consistently made up about 80 percent of the city's population.[13]

So here we have a city that was *new* in three basic senses: it sprang from pastoral farmlands, but quickly overshadowed the old walled county town; its population consisted overwhelmingly of newly arrived immigrants; and it was spiritually stimulated and driven by Western commercial values and vigor, something that was novel to China. All of these changes began with a system of residential segregation.

THE FOREIGN SETTLEMENTS

The foreign concessions, the focus of growth in modern Shanghai, were originally designed in 1845 to be settlements reserved exclusively for Westerners. Except for a handful of farmers already living there at the time the settlement was created, Chinese were banned from purchasing and renting land within the boundaries of the settlement, either for residential or commercial purposes. The segregation was terminated in 1854 and thereafter could not be restored. Except for a few years during the Pacific War, the foreign population in Shanghai had never exceeded 3 percent of the city's total population.[14] The residents of Shanghai's foreign settlements (namely, the International Settlement and the French Concession) were overwhelmingly Chinese. Shanghai, in spite of its heavy foreign accent, remained predominately a Chinese city.

There was virtually no justification in treaties for the legal status of Shanghai's foreign settlement. The only document that can be considered as possibly providing a legal basis is an agreement known as the Land Regulations, signed in 1845 by Gong Mujiu, the Shanghai Daotai, and George Balfour (1809–94), the first British consul in Shanghai. The agreement allowed British subjects to rent property in a designated area in the northern suburb, outside the walled Chinese city. This area, later to become the core of the International Settlement, covered an area from the Bund in the east to Boundary Road (today's Henan Road) in the west, and from Lijiachang (at the confluence of the Huangpu River and Suzhou Creek) in the north to Yangjingbang Creek (today's Yan'andong Road) in the south, a total area of about 830 Chinese *mu* (138 acres). According to the Chinese notion that "all the lands under heaven belong to the emperor" (*putian zhi xia, mofei wangtu*), foreigners were in theory not allowed to purchase land within the area but were permitted to permanently rent real property there. This is an early example of how the Chinese saved face while granting privileges to foreigners.[15]

The French Concession was bounded by the walled Chinese city in the south and the newly created British Settlement in the north—as a result of a lengthy negotiation in 1849 between the French consul Louis Montigny (1805–68) and the Shanghai Daotai, Lin Gui.[16] The American Settlement in Hongkou, located on the north side of Suzhou Creek about five miles northeast of the Chinese city, was more a fait accompli presented by a concentration of property purchased (or permanently rented) by the American Church Mission than an officially designated area for the Americans. As Hosea Ballou Morse (1855–1934) put it, "The American Settlement was not created, but 'just growed.'"[17] In 1848, Bishop William J. Boone (1811–64) got oral agreement from the Daotai Wu Jianzhang that Hongkou was to be an "American Settlement." The official boundary was settled in June 1863 by the American consul George Frederick Seward (1840–1910) and Shanghai Daotai Huang Fang. Three months later, on September 21, the British and American Settlements were formally amalgamated. The resulting concession was known (especially after 1899) as the International Settlement. Thus, by the end of the 1840s, three major powers all had settlements in Shanghai.

The land regulations prohibited Chinese from renting property within the International Settlement and the French Concession. Chinese inhabitants of the area were to be gradually evacuated, and eventually the area was to become completely segregated. By the end of the 1840s, even a casual visitor could observe that the Chinese who lived within the settlement "generally left of their free will and were liberally remunerated for their property by foreigners." These natives "were moving gradually backwards [i.e., westward] into the country, with their families, efforts, and all that appertained unto them" including their family tombs.[18]

This system of segregation was not entirely imposed by the West. Rather, at the beginning, it was a mechanism that the Qing authorities adopted to limit foreign influence and minimize disputes between local people and the "barbarians." According to the Bogue (Humen) Treaty, which was signed October 8, 1843, as a supplement to the Treaty of Nanjing, local Chinese authorities in concert with the British consul in the five

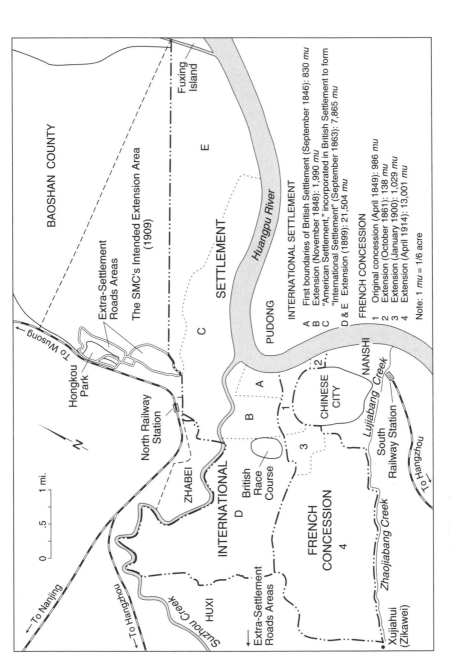

Map 1. The growth of Shanghai, 1846–1914.

BAOSHAN COUNTY

To Wusong

Hongkou Park

Extra-Settlement Roads Areas

The SMC's Intended Extension Area (1909)

Fuxing Island

N

0   .5   1 mi.

To Nanjing

To Hangzhou

Suzhou Creek

HUXI

North Railway Station

ZHABEI

INTERNATIONAL

D British Race Course

FRENCH CONCESSION

4

Extra-Settlement Roads Areas

Xujiahui (Zikawei)

Zhaojiabang Creek

To Hangzhou

South Railway Station

Lujiabang Creek

NANSHI

CHINESE CITY

1

3

B

A

C

SETTLEMENT

PUDONG

Huangpu River

E

INTERNATIONAL SETTLEMENT

A   First boundaries of British Settlement (September 1846): 830 *mu*
B   Extension (November 1848): 1,990 *mu*
C   "American Settlement," incorporated in British Settlement to form "International Settlement" (September 1863): 7,865 *mu*
D & E Extension (1899): 21,504 *mu*

FRENCH CONCESSION

1   Original concession (April 1849): 986 *mu*
2   Extension (October 1861): 138 *mu*
3   Extension (January 1900): 1,029 *mu*
4   Extension (April 1914): 13,001 *mu*

Note: 1 *mu* = 1/6 acre

treaty ports of China were to designate a limited zone within which foreigners could travel, as well as an area where British subjects could reside.[19] This was considered a victory by the Qing, as can be seen from the correspondence between Qiying (1790–1858), the imperial commissioner who negotiated and signed the treaty, and Emperor Daoguang (1782–1850). Qiying reported to the emperor that, by signing the supplemental treaty, he had successfully arranged that in the treaty ports "the boundaries of an area should be designated which foreigners are not allowed to exceed" (*yiding jiezhi, buxu yuyue*). The Chinese version of the Bogue Treaty actually carried this wording, but the tone was not clearly reflected in the English version.[20] The Qing rulers, by confining the "barbarians" to an officially designated special zone, apparently hoped to resurrect the old Canton system, that is, a system that strictly confined foreigners to a segregated zone in the treaty ports.[21]

Locally, in his first announcement of the opening of Shanghai to foreign trade dated November 14, 1843, George Balfour, the British consul in Shanghai, informed the British subjects in the city that "arrangements are in process for selecting a suitable site for dwelling and store-house for settling by assay."[22] In order to ensure that things went smoothly, the Daotai or one of his officers always went in person to Chinese landowners to negotiate the sale of land to the foreigners. This proved a difficult task. Frequently, the owners simply refused to "rent." In one case, an old lady "went so far in her opposition to all proposed bargains, that, after pouring on the head of the party a torrent of colloquial Billingsgate, she actually . . . spat in the Taotai's face and declared that she would never sell her patrimony to foreign devils!"[23] Such things would not have happened to a *huiguan* (guilds) merchant who came from another part of the country. Also, it was never a problem for Chinese "guest merchants" to establish guild houses in the walled city. For the British, however, this was the foremost difficulty that they encountered in Shanghai. At the beginning, Balfour could not even find a house for the consulate.[24] The intention of the Chinese officials was clear: to keep the foreigners out of the city. The British finally decided to located themselves in the northern suburbs and asked the Daotai to designate an area there as a segregated British settlement. This dovetailed with the mandarin's intentions.

For a decade after 1845 this segregation continued without much difficulty. In 1848, with the permission of the Manchu Daotai Lin Gui, the British Settlement was expanded westward to Nichengbang (lit., Muddy Town Creek; later filled in and transformed into Tibet Road) and northward to the southern bank of Suzhou Creek. This rural area was soon inhabited by an increasing number of foreigners, as the following statistics on the foreign population in Shanghai show:[25]

1844	1845	1846	1847	1848	1849	1850	1851
50	90	120	134	159	175	210	265

The total population in the settlements in 1852 was about 500. This means that foreigners were gradually coming to outnumber the local Chinese residents.[26]

This was the dawn of what was to become a great city, although few at that time would have predicted greatness for Shanghai.[27] For the Western adventurers in Shanghai, life was enjoyable and placid. By 1850, a public park, a race course, and amateur theater clubs were founded in the foreign community. On summer evenings, Westerners driving ox carts relaxed in the breeze on the broad waterfront of the Bund, the business center of the settlement and site of much new construction.[28] A new term, "bunders," was coined to refer to these Westerners, and the Bund was often poetically associated with, in the words of an insider, "its gossip, its cool evening breezes, its ever-changing outlook, its pleasant promenades, its reminiscences of valued friendships, its pensive regrets."[29] The availability of a variety of wild game (mainly birds) in the region and the peaceful nature of the local people made hunting a real pleasure for the Europeans.[30] Shanghai was, as a British botanist who traveled extensively in China at that time exclaimed, "one vast beautiful garden, by far the richest which I have seen in China."[31] This pastoral, even romantic, life was perhaps typical of what Western sojourners enjoyed in Asia. Similar lifestyles could be found in the early colonial history of other Asian cities such as Calcutta and Yokohama.

But the foreigners in Shanghai would soon face an unexpected event that would dramatically bring to an end the tranquillity of their life and, much more important historically, change the course of the development of the city.

THE END OF RESIDENTIAL SEGREGATION

On the morning of September 7, 1853, an uprising organized by the Small Swords, a Fujian-based secret society headed by the Cantonese vagrant Liu Lichuan (1820–ca. 1855), killed the Shanghai county magistrate at the site of an ongoing annual ceremony at the city's Confucian temple.[32] The rebels then took the county seat and declared the establishment of the "State of Great Ming" (Da Ming Guo). This event was the beginning of seventeen months of warfare in Shanghai and its vicinity. Two days after their success in Shanghai, the rebels marched to attack other county towns near Shanghai. In ten days, Baoshan, Nanhui, Chuansha, and Qingpu were under the control of the Small Swords. Jiading, a county seat twenty-five miles northwest of Shanghai, was occupied by the rebels prior to the Shanghai war. In the turmoil of the fighting, thousands of refugees, mostly from the county town of Shanghai but also from other occupied towns, poured into the foreign settlements, which were within walking distance of the war-torn city.[33] The population of the combined British and American Settlements jumped from 500 in 1853 to more than 20,000 in 1855.

These refugees encountered two different attitudes in the settlements. Foreign merchants saw them as an opportunity to make a fortune: the quickest way to get rich was to build dwellings for the refugees. Rows of simply constructed, single-story wooden houses appeared literally overnight along the Bund, in the northwest part of the British Settlement, as well as on the banks of Yangjingbang, the creek that separated the British and French settlements.[34] Many of the refugees were well-off merchants and landlords who could afford the prices that the foreigners asked.[35]

Another group of Westerners, however, was more concerned about the comfort and safety of the foreign community. This group was represented by the British consul, Sir Rutherford Alcock (1809–97), who in January 1855, after consulting the Shanghai Daotai, ordered "the removal of objectionable natives and demolition of objectionable tenements." Alcock's order left thousands of Chinese homeless in the bitter cold of winter.[36] This action sparked some antiforeign sentiment among the Chinese, but from the viewpoint of the British authorities, such a move seemed necessary if the idea of segregation from the Chinese was to be preserved. Shortly after the rebellion, the British Settlement, according to one observation, had been transformed from "a purely foreign reservation" into a "native Alsatia, the southern portion being blocked with abominably overcrowded and filthy hovels, fraught with the danger of fire and pestilence, rife with brothels, opium shops, and gambling dens."[37]

The debate over whether to continue accepting Chinese refugees was therefore a burning topic in the foreign community. The foreign settlement was at a crossroad. But no one could have predicted the impact that the ultimate decision would have on the fate of the city. Thus, when an outspoken British merchant approached Alcock to express his views, he was quite unaware that his words would result in a milestone for the city:

> No doubt your anticipations of future evil have a certain foundation, and, indeed, may be correct enough, though something may be urged on the other side as to the advantages of having the Chinese mingled with us, and departing from the old Canton system of isolation; but, upon the whole, I agree with you. The day will probably come when those who then may be here will see abundant cause to regret what is now being done, in letting and subletting to Chinese. But in what way am I and my brother landholders and speculators concerned in this? You, as H.M.'s Consul, are bound to look to national and permanent interests—that is your business; but it is my business to make a fortune with the least possible loss of time, by letting my land to Chinese, and building for them at thirty or forty percent interest, if that is the best thing I can do with my money. In two or three years at farthest, I hope to realize a fortune and get away; and what can it matter to me if all Shanghae [Shanghai] disappear afterward in fire or flood? You must not expect men in my situation to condemn themselves to years of prolonged exile in an unhealthy climate for the benefit of posterity. We are money-making, practical men. Our business is to make money, as much and as fast as we can; and for this end, all modes and means are good which the law permits.[38]

The view expressed here was no doubt representative of the majority of foreign merchants in Shanghai. Alcock was "quite convinced" by this lecture and the warning that he "was losing time in any efforts to stem the tide of land-jobbing and house-building for Chinese tenants"; thus he ended his struggle to keep the Chinese out of the settlement.[39] It is doubtful that even if the British authorities had continued to forbid renting houses to Chinese tenants, they would have been able to stem the tide of refugees flooding the foreign settlement. As Alcock admitted, to insist on a purely foreign settlement in Shanghai under these circumstances was "too evidently hopeless."[40] The official abandonment of segregation by the British consul, who was the most influential if not the most authoritative leader in Shanghai's foreign community, cleared the road for creating a mixed settlement of Chinese and foreign residents. In this regard, the combination of the Small Sword Uprising and Alcock's decision was a turning point in the development of Shanghai.

This decision was soon legalized, at least from the viewpoint of the Western powers. In July 1854, Alcock, together with the American consul, Robert C. Murphy, and the French consul, B. Edan, signed a new set of Land Regulations. Although this document was never approved or signed by the Chinese authorities, it was nevertheless proclaimed as a revision of the 1845 Land Regulations, and on July 11 it was passed in a public meeting of foreign residents in the settlement. After that, the Land Regulations served as the fundamental law, or "constitution," for Shanghai's foreign settlement until the settlement was abolished in 1943.[41]

A number of important institutions set up by this law dominated the fate of Shanghai for almost a century. In September 1869, the Land Regulations were revised and approved by the European envoys in Beijing to create the Shanghai Municipal Council (SMC, which replaced the former Executive Committee of the settlement),[42] which would govern the International Settlement until 1943. The 1869 Land Regulations also served as the legal basis of the merger of the British Settlement and American Settlement, although for practical reasons (such as policing) the latter already had been under the administration of the British Settlement since September 1863. Officially, the French insisted on having a separate concession in Shanghai. The French Concession was therefore governed by a separate municipal council headed by the French consul-general and was not subject to the Land Regulations. In reality, however, much of the administration of the French Concession duplicated the regulations and practices of the International Settlement.

The new regulations also deleted the segregation provision of the 1845 regulations, although officially Chinese were still not allowed to acquire land in their own name within the Settlement. At this stage the Chinese government was still unwilling to see mixed residence in Shanghai. According to a proclamation issued by Daotai Lan Weiwen in 1855, "No Chinese subject can acquire land, or rent, or erect buildings, within the Foreign Settlement, without first having obtained an authority under official seal from the local Authority, sanctioned by the Consuls of the three Treaty Powers."[43] When the foreign consuls wrote a letter asking the Daotai to take care of health and moral conditions in the settlement, the Daotai responded with a complaint rather than a solution: "According to the original land regulations, native domicile was interdicted within the settlement; now, however, tenements were built by foreigners to accommodate natives, regardless even of the risk incurred in harbouring people of bad character indiscriminately, and of the difficulties this unregulated state of affairs would entail in criminal cases."[44]

Despite the opposition of the Daotai, by the late 1850s there was no doubt that the concessions were no longer a reserved area for foreign residents, but rather were a special district mostly populated by Chinese but governed by Europeans. The suppression of the Small Sword rebellion in

1855 did not end population mobility into the foreign settlement. The Taiping Rebellion, which was most violent and destructive in Jiangnan, continued to drive refugees to Shanghai. In 1860–62, the Taipings several times attempted to seize Shanghai; this created even more panic among the people of the region, and, consequently, refugees continued to pour into Shanghai's foreign concessions for protection. By 1865, the population of the British-American settlement had increased to 92,884. At the same time, almost 50,000 Chinese moved into the French Concession. By the end of the Taiping Rebellion, well over 110,000 Chinese had moved into the foreign settlements.[45]

From the "Five Lakes and Four Seas"

The opening of Shanghai in the mid-nineteenth century, first to "barbaric" foreigners and then to a great variety of Chinese refugees from outside the Shanghai area, represented the continuation of a local tradition of easy acceptance of outsiders. Traditional Chinese writers, including the compilers of local gazetteers (*fangzhi*), often described the people of Jiangnan as *rouruo* (soft and weak).[46] The tradition of ready acceptance of outsiders was seen as part of this "soft and weak" nature. In the mid-nineteenth century, when Shanghai was a hot spot in Sino-foreign relations, the Qing court frequently cautioned officials to beware of the "soft and weak" nature of the Shanghai folk when dealing with "barbarian affairs" (*yiwu*).[47] Lin Yutang (1895–1976) once contrasted the "simple thinking and hard living" northern Chinese and the "progressive and quick-tempered" southerners with the people of Jiangnan, who were, Lin claimed, "inured to ease and culture and sophistication, mentally developed but physically retrograde, loving their poetry and their comforts, sleek undergrown men and slim neurasthenic women, fed on birds'-nest soup and lotus seeds, shrewd in business, gifted in belles-lettres, and cowardly in war, ready to roll on the ground and cry for mamma before the lifted fist descends."[48] Such views added up to a stereotype, of course, and in any case might have applied more to the upper classes than to working people, but, like many stereotypes, there was some truth to these words.

There was also a more charitable interpretation of the "soft and weak" nature of the people of Shanghai that emphasized their virtues of openness, amiability, tolerance, flexibility, and so on.[49] The commercial boom of Shanghai in the Qing period was initially led by the "guest merchants," who came from nearby places as well as from remote provinces to conduct business in Shanghai. The influence of these merchants, particularly those of Guangdong and Fujian, was strong prior to the treaty-port era. Apparently, prosperity created by the "guest merchants" eventually led to a proclivity to value commerce and easily accept outsiders and outside influences. Such a tendency was, even by the modest standards of the time, viewed as a departure from orthodoxy and, therefore, was condemned as evil.[50] But it was precisely because of this heterodoxy that Shanghai rose above the horizon of a vast conservatism and became a great, modern city.

FOREIGN ADVENTURERS

This tradition of openness was even more characteristic of Shanghai during the treaty-port era. By the late nineteenth century, Shanghai was an exceptional place where the natives welcomed sojourners, while elsewhere in the country the normal pattern was the reverse. As an indicator of its openness, a variety of Chinese dialects could be heard in the streets and neighborhoods of the city; everyone lived side by side, seemingly without fear of discrimination. Indeed, Shanghai seemed most receptive to those who spoke a Western language, because people who spoke a foreign tongue could, as a late-nineteenth-century poem put it, "do as they please."[51]

At the beginning of the treaty-port period some Westerners had apparently bought into the stereotype of the "soft" Shanghainese. A British Royal Navy commander who traveled extensively along the China coast and lived there for five years immediately after 1842 wrote:

> The English merchant at Canton is almost a prisoner in his house; he has only a few streets open to him for the required recreation, even for the benefit of exercise, and then with the probability of insult. Experience has taught him that even his own house may be a very unsafe refuge from a furious and ignorant mob; any excitement, from whatever cause it originates, is sure to vent itself on the unfortunate foreigners, and, perhaps, bring the building about his ears with very small chance of redress. On the other hand[,] at Shanghae [Shanghai], he is surrounded by a peaceable and hospitable community, where crime is a matter of such rare occurrence, that His Excellency Kun Mŭkiŭ [Gong Mujiu], the civil governor, said in my presence that, during his government of so large a population, which had lasted, I believe, nine years, one execution only had taken place. . . . Besides the absence of crime in Shanghae, the city is always open to the foreigner equally with the native; and I have had several years' experience to ground my statement on, that insults or annoyance, of every kind, are less frequent to strangers than in any part of the world.[52]

Although the rise of modern Shanghai must be explained from a multifaceted analysis—including the favorable geographical location of the city, sitting as it does at the middle of the nation's lengthy coastline facing the Pacific to the east and the Yangzi Valley to the west—the "soft" nature of the Shanghainese no doubt played an important role. To put this softness into a broader and perhaps philosophical perspective, one may relate it to the value of liberalism. A Chinese author who tried to analyze the nature of the people of Shanghai from a historical perspective argued that the "strongest psychological character of Shanghai civilization was tolerance and coexistence based on individual freedom." [53]

Be that as it may, unquestionably liberalism contributed to the cosmopolitanism of the city. In few Asian cities could foreigners feel as at home as in modern Shanghai. By the twentieth century, "Shanghai became a legend. No world cruise was complete without a stop in the city. Its name evoked mystery, adventure and license of every form." [54] Going to Shanghai was a classic adventure for Westerners and a solution for many who had problems in their homeland. Shanghai was thus a city of dreams and a city of escape. In the Republican period, its foreign population included people from more than twenty European nations, a sizable community of Japanese, Indians, Vietnamese, and Koreans, and citizens from Middle Eastern and South American nations—as well as the nationless. [55]

The largest foreign contingents were, of course, the British, the Americans, and the French, whose respective concessions formed the heart of the city. The European-style office buildings on the Bund and the sumptuous and secluded residences on the west side of the city were constant reminders of the foreigners' status as masters of the city. By the twentieth century, despite the decline of the British Empire, old Shanghai residents still put the British ahead of other Western nationals, and even ahead of all other Anglophones: witness the word order in the term "British-American people" (YingMeiren). [56] Despite whatever privilege the sentiment might have accorded the British, all foreigners in Shanghai had reason to feel at home. "To be a Shanghailander—whether British or American, whether stateless Jew or Russian refugee—had always seemed an honoured privilege. Shanghai was a city of homes, not a city of transients. Young people might in the first instance be posted by a trading house to work there for a few years, but often as the moment of transfer approached, they begged to stay. People of every nationality settled there, married, raised children." [57] The following missionary report tells of a vivid street scene in the downtown area in 1909:

> Shanghai, with its mixture of races, with its national antipathies and jealousies, is indeed one of the most attractive but strangest towns in

the whole world. Every race meets there; and as one wanders down the Nanking Road, one never tires of watching the nationalities which throng that thoroughfare. There walks a tall bearded Russian, a fat German, jostling perhaps a tiny Japanese officer, whose whole air shows that he regards himself as a member of the conquering race that has checkmated the vast power of Europe; there are sleek Chinese in Western carriages, and there are thin Americans in Eastern rickshas; the motorcycle rushes past, nearly colliding with a closely curtained chair bearing a Chinese lady of rank, or a splendid Indian in a yellow silk coat is struck in the face by the hat of a Frenchman, who finds the pavements of Shanghai too narrow for his sweeping salute; one hears guttural German alternating with Cockney slang; Parisian toilettes are seen next to half-naked coolies; a couple of sailors on a tandem cycle almost upset two Japanese beauties as they shuffle along with their toes turned in; a grey-gowned Buddhist priest elbows a bearded Roman missionary; a Russian shop where patriotism rather than love of gain induces the owners to conceal the nature of their wares by employing the Russian alphabet overhead, stands opposite a Japanese shop which, in not too perfect English, assures the wide world that their heads can be cut cheaply.[58]

In later years, the cultural shock suggested in this report became attenuated, but the cosmopolitanism of the city lasted well into the 1940s.[59]

Not all Westerners played the role of "master" of the city. About 25,000 to 50,000 White Russian émigrés arrived in Shanghai in the Republican period.[60] Although most of them were poor—Russians were the only Westerners to include a sizable number of prostitutes and beggars—the businesses they opened along Avenue Joffre (now Huaihaizhong Road) in the French Concession helped create an elegant European atmosphere on the street.[61] The concentration of Japanese in North Sichuan Road in Hongkou caused the area to be known as Little Tokyo. The city's traffic was largely directed by Sikh policemen, nicknamed "Turbaned Number Three" or "Number Three Redhead" (*hongtou asan*), whose presence in the streets became a feature of the city.[62] The success of Jewish merchants in Shanghai is an often-told story. Real estate magnates such as the Sassoons and Silas Hardoon (1847–1931) contributed to the "get-rich quick" reputation of Shanghai, and their grand office buildings and extravagant homes were proud landmarks of the city. Partly because no visa or papers of any sort were required to enter the city, during World War II Shanghai hosted about 20,000 Jewish refugees who had escaped the Nazis and made the arduous journey across the hemisphere. Most of them lived in the alleyway-house (*lilong*, or lane) neighborhoods in Hongkou in the northeast section of the city. Half a century later, although practically all of the Jews had gone elsewhere (particularly to the United States), most of their former homes remained little changed and became sentimental relics for those who returned to visit.[63]

Despite Shanghai's wide-open cosmopolitanism, some foreigners may well have had reason to feel that they were "strangers always," as the title of Rena Krasno's memoirs of Jewish life in wartime Shanghai suggests. Yet loneliness, or perhaps homesickness, never prevented foreigners from coming to Shanghai and making a living, if not a fortune. In the early 1930s a Shanghai writer listed the reasons foreigners of various nationalities came to the city:

> Shanghai's foreigners pack together in the city for the same reason our Chinese do: they could not make a living in their home country and came to Shanghai in search of a livelihood. Japanese prostitutes come to Shanghai to make a living by selling sex.[64] The White Russians, who are anti-Red, came to Shanghai to make a living by begging. The over-bearing British toughs came to Shanghai to make a living by running the police department. The bored Spanish came to Shanghai to make a living by playing tennis [*huiliqiu*]. The nationless Jews came to Shanghai to make a living in real estate. The merchants of American trust companies came to Shanghai to make a living by selling gasoline. The French, who love a life of ease, came to Shanghai to make a living by selling cosmetics. The oppressed Indian and Vietnamese came to Shanghai to make a living by working as policemen, and so on and so forth— there are just too many such cases to give a complete account of the subject.[65]

By the thirties, many foreigners considered the city their permanent home (see Fig. 1). As a Britisher indicated on the eve of the Japanese attack on Shanghai in 1937, "It is time the old idea that foreigners come to Shanghai for a few years and then go away with a fortune was abandoned. This is a place of permanent residence for most of us."[66] The Japanese attack on Shanghai in 1937, and their occupation of the whole city after the outbreak of the Pacific War in December 1941, cast a shadow over the Western presence in the city. But it was really not until the victory of the Communist revolution in 1949 that the century-long golden age of the Westerners came to a close.[67]

CHINESE IMMIGRANTS

Despite the seeming ubiquity and importance of foreigners in Shanghai, the growth of the modern city lay not in its attraction for foreigners but,

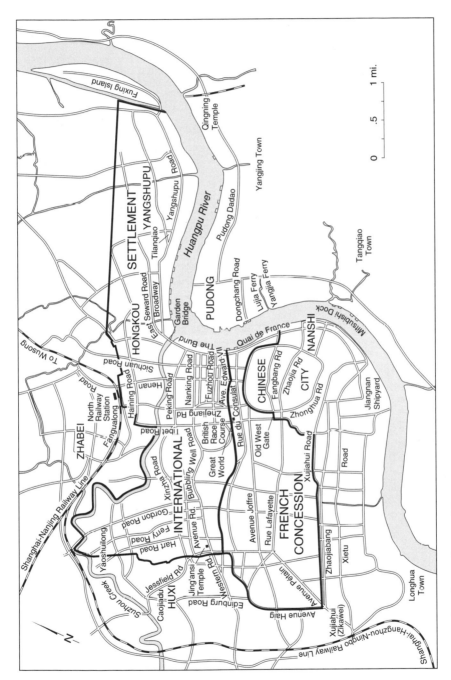

Map 2. Shanghai in the Republican era.

Fig. 1.   This bird's-eye view of where Suzhou (Soochow) Creek joins Huangpu
River was photographed in 1937. The right (i.e., southern) side of the creek is the
core of the International Settlement, with Garden Park (across from the British
Consulate) at the northern end of the Bund. Nanking Road is just one block out
of the scene, to the right. The 350-foot-long Garden Bridge was Shanghai's first
iron and concrete bridge, built in 1906–7; it is one of the symbols of modern
Shanghai. Across the bridge to the north is the New Broadway Mansions, built
in 1934. The area behind the mansion is Hongkou, where residential neighborhoods featured alleyway houses mixed with consulates, warehouses, and bars in
the Broadway area. The second bridge in the picture is the Zhapu Road Bridge,
built in 1927. The area across this bridge to the north consisted mainly of lilong
neighborhoods. Courtesy of Shanghai Municipal Archive.

essentially, in its attraction for the Chinese. Ever since the end of the system of residential segregation, the overwhelming majority of the people of
Shanghai had been Chinese immigrants. In the span of three-quarters of a
century (from 1855, when the segregation ended, to 1930, when the city entered its heyday), the population in the core of the city, the International Settlement, had increased about fiftyfold, and about 97 percent were Chinese.[68]
By 1937 and the end of the Republican period, the city's total population
had increased at least tenfold, or possibly twentyfold in the city proper.[69]

The administrative area of Shanghai did not significantly expand in the century prior to 1949; rather, such rapid population growth was the result of immigration. Modern Shanghai attracted and absorbed immigrants from everywhere in the nation. From the late nineteenth century to the late 1920s, non-Shanghai natives consistently made up about 85 percent of the city's population.[70] During the Nanjing decade (1927–37), the percentage of non-Shanghai natives dropped slightly, possibly because after a few generations of migration some people born in Shanghai considered themselves Shanghainese and reported their native place as Shanghai. But the outbreak of the Sino-Japanese War in 1937, followed by the Civil War (1946–49), brought new tides of immigrants to the city. By the end of the Sino-Japanese War, nonnatives still accounted for 80 percent of the population; in January 1950, the percentage of nonnatives had increased back to 85 percent.[71]

Most of these immigrants came from the provinces of the lower Yangzi delta (in particular, Jiangsu and Zhejiang) and from Guangdong in southern China. In the early 1930s, the five provinces from which Shanghai drew most of its immigrants were Jiangsu (53 percent, including 20 percent of local Shanghai origin), Zhejiang (34 percent), Guangdong (5 percent), Anhui (3 percent), and Shandong (1 percent).[72] This pattern continued up to 1950.[73] To apply a Chinese expression, modern Shanghainese came from the "Five Lakes and Four Seas" (*wuhu sihai*), that is, everywhere in the nation.[74]

Immigrants came to the city for their own individual reasons and purposes, and included everyone from multimillionaires who came to pursue an extravagant yet secluded lifestyle that could hardly be found in other Chinese cities, to the absolutely destitute who roamed the city's streets in search of bare survival; from political dissidents who fled to the "safety zone" of the foreign concessions, to criminals who came to join the nation's largest underground; from modern women (or flappers) who found in this city the freedom they sought, to innocent rural girls who were inveigled by labor contractors to come work in the city but who ended up being sold to brothels. Yet virtually all who came to Shanghai had a simple, shared goal: to find a better life.

In the winter of 1928, the Shanghai Municipal Bureau of Social Affairs conducted a survey of homeless people in seven public shelters. The 1,471 vagrants surveyed were all recent immigrants to the city, and they hailed from all eighteen provinces of China proper and from Manchuria. These people listed more than forty previous occupations, but the largest group (310) were jobless. There were 138 demobilized soldiers who were supposed to return to their home villages, but who decided to stay on in Shanghai although they had no job. In response to the question "Why did you come to Shanghai?" 586 replied, "To look for a job." Another 354 said they came to Shanghai to look for relatives or friends. For most of these people, the purpose of visiting a relative or friend was to connect with someone who could help them find a job. Thus, virtually 64 percent of the respondents were motivated by the job opportunities to be found here.[75]

This survey was echoed by a 1989–90 survey of residents in seven neighborhoods who were immigrants in the Republican period. About 70 percent of the male interviewees gave "to look for a job" as the main reason for coming to Shanghai. In this they were successful. The percentage of employment among these immigrants increased from 46.6 before coming to Shanghai to 75.3 after arrival. The survey also found immigrants to Shanghai had a great variety of occupational backgrounds. More than half (56.4 percent)—by far the largest group—had been farmers; almost all found a job in the city, mostly in manufacturing and commerce. The remainder of those surveyed had come from diverse occupational backgrounds. This is consistent with another aspect of their background: half of the immigrants (50 percent) had come directly from the countryside, 21 percent from small rural towns, 15.3 percent from county seats, 11 percent from medium-size cities, and about 2.7 percent from large cities.[76] Shanghai's immediate "radiation zone" for attracting immigrants included its suburban rural areas and the more distant lower Yangzi delta counties. People in the nearby countryside looked upon Shanghai as a place to get ahead. "Where is the market for agricultural and handicraft products? Shanghai. Where is the place for people to seek an occupation? Shanghai." The gazetteer of Chuansha, a rural county adjacent to Shanghai, exclaimed: "Overpopulation? Move to Shanghai! Unemployment? Look for opportunities in Shanghai!"[77] It is probably the case that most rural immigrants came to Shanghai looking for factory work, for in the late nineteenth and early twentieth centuries, Shanghai grew to be the nation's largest industrial center.[78]

The recruitment of workers from nearby villages for Shanghai's industries started as early as in the 1870s. Shanghai's earliest workshops were the Western-run shipyards in the Hongkou area (along the northeast banks of the Huangpu River).[79] The shipyards at first hired skilled Cantonese workers. By the late 1870s, as the industry grew, workers from Nanjing, Ningbo, and local villages gradually outnumbered the Guangdong workers, for the obvious reason that local residents were closer and easier (and cheaper) to recruit. But, unlike the Guangdong workers, who were experienced artisans, workers from Jiangnan were mostly peasants and hence started their careers in industry as apprentices.[80]

A veteran worker in the machinery industry, Qian Rendao (born 1881), recalled that his grandfather was a local farmer who only had two or three mu of land planted in vegetables. Since it was difficult to support a family on such a small farm, the grandfather went to the International Settlement in search of a job and became a porter in the Hongkou dock area. Apparently he still kept his vegetable farm; thus his son (Rendao's father) as a child worked as a vegetable peddler to earn extra money to support the family. But the family had already become urban oriented. When Rendao's father grew up, he became an apprentice in the Chinese-owned Fachang Machine Factory. After serving out his apprenticeship, he entered the British-owned Xiangsheng Shipyard (Boyd and Co.) with the help of his wife's brother, Song Milong. Song also had been a vegetable farmer in his youth. He used to sell vegetables to the Fachang Machine Factory, which is how he got to know the people there; through this connection he later found a job in the factory as an apprentice. After his apprenticeship, he transferred to the Xiangsheng Shipyard in 1880 and worked as a coppersmith. His skill and performance got him quick promotions. He became a section chief a few years later and served in this position until 1905. Having an uncle like Song Milong in the factory, Rendao entered the Xiangsheng Shipyard as an apprentice at age eighteen and became a second-generation coppersmith.[81] Stories such as this were by no means uncommon. In 1960–62, when veteran workers in the machine industry were interviewed by a group of historians, the interviewees recalled that their experiences were similar to those of the Qian and the Song families.[82]

The same pattern of securing labor from nearby villages obtained in the textile industry, the largest industry in modern Shanghai.[83] A 1920 investigation into the life of textile workers in Shanghai found that all had been farmers from nearby areas.[84] The experiences of these workers reveal in a number of ways the process by which peasants sought an urban life in this still-fledgling stage of China's industrialization. Even after moving to Shanghai, many of this group continued to maintain land and houses in home villages where their families had lived for generations; some even still lived in the village while working in a factory.[85]

The 1920 survey found that workers known as *kemin* (guest people)—who hailed from the three counties of Nantong, Chongming, and Haimen, all near the mouth of the Yangzi River—did not become factory workers immediately upon arrival in Shanghai. Instead, they worked as tenants or farm hands in villages near Shanghai; in other words, they replaced the labor of local peasants who had gone to work in the city's factories. Land in Shanghai was much more fertile than the saline-alkali soil in their native places, so to farm land near Shanghai was already a move upward for these peasants. Their ultimate goal, however, was not to farm but to work in a factory. After settling in villages near the city, many of them managed to get acquainted with people in cotton mills and eventually found jobs there (Fig. 2).[86] This pattern of urban-rural transformation continued into the 1930s. As the sociologist H. D. Lamson reported in 1931, villages near Yangshupu, just northeast of Shanghai, served as stepping stones into the city for those from more distant regions. "Families move into our villages from such places as Tsung Ming [Chongming] Island," Lamson wrote, "remain some time, and perhaps eventually some or all of them move into the city itself."[87]

Compared to peasants from outside the region, local farmers were sometimes less enthusiastic about new industries invading their homeland and upsetting their peaceful rural life. When Nie Zhongfu established the Hengfeng Cotton Mill and Sheng Xuanhuai established the Sanxin Cotton Mill—both were among Shanghai's earliest modern textile mills—nearby farmers saw the plants as strange creatures and called cotton looms "the deity's vehicles"; few wanted to work in the factories.[88] When the Jiangnan Shipyard, one of China's earliest and largest modern enterprises (in 1894 it alone employed about 4 percent of all of China's industrial workers), opened in Gaochangmiao in suburban Shanghai in 1865, rumors spread among local peasants that the factory recruited workers to be "thrown into the chimney" and that workers would be "smashed by the machines." For a while the situation was so unfavorable that the shipyard had to recruit apprentices from the local orphanage. The peasants also had another reason to resent the factory. Veteran worker Qian Haigen recalled that his grandfather was a farmer of Gaochangmiao whose land was taken over by the Jiangnan Shipyard to build the factory. Qian refused to work for the new factory and instead made a living by selling green onions. He even established a family rule that none of his offspring or their descendants should work for the shipyard. However, facing the much stronger trend of industrialization, neither the rumors nor the old farmer's resentment could count for much. Barely two decades later, the Jiangnan Shipyard had become a highly desirable place to work. The Qian family, after the grandfather died, ignored his behest and entered the shipyard.[89]

The job opportunities in the city included much more than just employment in the mills. In a suburban village of Pengpu, women commonly worked in textile mills and men earned a living as peddlers in the city.[90]

Fig. 2.   The artist and writer Feng Zikai (1898–1975),
a native of Zhejiang but a lifetime resident of Shanghai,
was known for his unique style of plain ink drawings on
subjects of everyday life, an approach similar to that of
Norman Rockwell. This drawing dates to about 1932:
a farmer and a boy watch a passing train. The caption
reads, "[This train] is heading for Shanghai." In an
implicit but sprightly way, the cartoon expresses rural
people's general longing for Shanghai. From Feng Zikai,
Feng Zikai wenji.

Peasant women from Fengxian county, which was close to the southern
boundary of the city, made matchboxes for Shanghai's factories. Also making matchboxes were peasants in other nearby villages, as well as in Pudong (east of the Huangpu River).[91] The 1922 gazetteer of Fahua, a tiny
town southwest of Shanghai, reported that, in addition to its farmers becoming mill workers, the men also worked in Shanghai as gardeners, road
construction workers, cart drivers, and unskilled workers of all sorts, while
the women earned a living by making lace trimmings, hair nets, paper
yuanbao (joss money to be burned for the dead). They also worked as do-

mestic servants, a popular occupation among peasant women (Fig. 3).[92] As early as the Guangxu period (1875–1908), women from Shanghai's neighboring counties, such as Qingpu, were described as "going after the job [of domestic servant] like a flock of ducks." Some even abandoned their families to live in the city.[93] The popularity of domestic service never faded. The number of servants in the city increased in parallel with the general population: Shanghai in 1930 had about 50,000 servants; by 1950 the size of this army had almost doubled.[94]

A DUAL IDENTITY

A popular saying in Shanghai had it that "having explored up to the edge of the world, one could not find a better place than the two sides of the Huangpu River."[95] Other local sayings expressed the same sentiment, declaring, for instance, "what a great fortune for a person to live in this colorful and dazzling world [of Shanghai]" (*ren zhule huahua shijie, dayou fuqi la*) and "Shanghai is a mountain of gold and silver" (*Shanghai jinyinshan*).[96] For most people the very word "Shanghai" provoked excitement, stimulated the imagination, and raised hopes. "So this is Shanghai!" was a usual exclamation of newcomers, both foreigners and the Chinese.[97] After being absent from the city for eight years and having lived in many places in the hinterland during the Sino-Japanese War, Wang Xiaolai (1886–1967), one of Shanghai's leading entrepreneurs (he originally came from a village in Zhejiang), returned to Shanghai on September 8, 1945. He wrote of his feelings as the airplane was about to land: "I see about 40 percent of the red-tiled houses in Huxi [west Shanghai] are newly built. Nanshi and Zhabei [the Chinese districts] have declined and show little vigor, but the former foreign concessions look like before. The happy lot of Shanghainese is indeed great. To compare Shanghai with the hinterland is to compare paradise and hell."[98]

Almost as a rule, a new immigrant to the city would soon be proud of being not just a city person but a "Shanghai person," or Shanghairen. Along with the rise of Shanghai as China's number one city, Shanghairen were popularly associated with sophistication, astuteness, and a certain degree of Westernization. The writer Zhang Ailing (Eileen Chang) wrote in 1943, "The Shanghainese are not only traditional Chinese but are tempered by the high pressure of modern life. . . . Everybody says that Shanghainese are bad, but they are bad with a sense of propriety. Shanghainese are good at flattering, good at currying favor with the powerful, and good at fishing in troubled waters. However, because they know the art of conducting oneself in society, they play along without overdoing it."[99]

Fig. 3.   In an alleyway, a newly arrived country woman carries her children and belongings in two rattan baskets. Immigrants like this often ended up living in a squatters' area but made a living in the city's better-off alleyway-house neighborhoods, working as domestic servants, street hawkers, tinkers, itinerant artisans, or the like. From R. Barz, *Shanghai: Sketches of Present-Day Shanghai.*

While the people of Shanghai were proud to call themselves Shang-hairen, they were not always ready to totally identify themselves with the city. Since the people of Shanghai were mostly immigrants, ties to one's native place were acknowledged as a social norm. The statement "I want to be buried in my hometown" was, for example, commonly included in wills, and virtually all children, not necessarily only those who were filial, carried out this wish. One of the major functions or services of the city's numerous "native-place associations" (*tongxianghui*) was to send the dead to their hometown for burial. Consequently, for many Shanghainese it was routine to go back to their home village or town to visit the family tomb—a practice known as "sweeping the graveyard" (*saomu*), which usually involved a ritual ceremony for the dead and cleaning of the family graveyard. Leave for this purpose was sometimes part of employees' benefits. For instance, up to 1924 all employees of Nanyang Brothers Tobacco Company had a month's leave with full pay solely for the purpose of "sweeping the graveyard."[100]

One's hometown or village was not only a place to be buried but also a place that modern Shanghainese, as well as others, regarded as a home to which one could return. This tie to one's native place was frequently utilized to solve social problems. For instance, one of the conventional methods adopted by the Shanghai Municipal Bureau of Social Affairs to deal with unemployment was to send the unemployed back to their home villages at the government's expense (*ziqian huanxiang*).[101] At the nongovernmental level, laid-off employees commonly received travel expenses (*chuanzi*), based on the assumption that people who lost their job would return home. Sending people back to their native places was also a mechanism for dealing with wartime crises in the thirties and forties, and in fact was the principal solution adopted by government and charities for the crush of wartime refugees in late 1937 and early 1938.[102] The Communists not only inherited this mechanism but used the power of the state to make it more effective. Mobilizing the people of Shanghai to go back to their hometowns or villages (*dongyuan huixiang*) was frequently integrated into the political campaigns of the 1950s and 1960s.[103]

While the authorities used native-place ties for their own purposes, the poor looked upon strong ties with their hometown or village as a necessity. Rickshaw pullers, port coolies, unskilled casual laborers of all sorts, the unemployed, and vagabonds tended to return to their home villages if life in the city became too difficult or their city job could provide only part of their livelihood. Some of the urban poor still had land or were tenant farmers in their home village.[104] The sociologist Lamson observed during his in-

Table 1. The Overlap of Native Place and Trade in Republican Shanghai

Native Place (xiangbang)	Trade (yebang)
Shandong	silk cocoons
Huining	tea, timber, ink sticks, pawnshops
Jiangxi	Chinese medicine, chinaware, paper, cotton cloth, Sichuan Chinese medicine, wax
Wuxi	silk, pork, preserved pork
Jinhua	ham
Qianjiang	silks and satins
Shaoxing	wine, coal and briquettes, dyeing, traditional banking (qianzhuang)
Ningbo	cotton cloth, groceries, coal and briquettes, fish, Chinese medicine
Fujian	timber, lacquer, tobacco
Guangdong	silk cloth, groceries, sugar, Cantonese food
Suzhou	fans, tea and snack bars
Wenzhou	mats, umbrellas

SOURCE: Shen Bojing and Chen Huaipu, *Shanghaishi zhinan,* 347.

vestigation of working-class families in the Yangshupu area in 1929–31, "Sometimes people are unsuccessful in business ventures or become unemployed and move back to the rural regions."[105]

Better-off people and those who had firmly settled in the city also had their reasons to value native-place ties. Businesspeople found that networking based on native-place origins was one of the most convenient and reliable ways to conduct business in this sojourners' city. Table 1 shows some samples of the overlap between native place (*xiangbang*) and trade (*yebang*) in the city. The phenomenon of certain trades being dominated by people of certain native origins had its roots in the pre-treaty-port era. Traditional trade organizations such as guilds were formed either according to the merchants' native place and named after it (such as the GuangZhao gongsuo, or the Canton guild), or according to the product or service provided and named after that (such as the *douye gongsuo*, or the bean guild). Thirty native-place trade organizations could be found in Shanghai prior to 1842. These institutions did not fall into desuetude after the coming of the West, but instead flourished along with the rise of modern Shanghai. By 1911, at least 108 such organizations were operating in the city.[106] The overlap of trade and native place was such common knowledge in the city that an average resident might be able to give a list of the overlap in a casual conversation, reporting, for example, that the Cantonese were known for trading in tobacco, opium, and foreign groceries, Anhui merchants in tea and silk, merchants from Jiangsu, Zhejiang, and Shanxi in banking and finance, and so on. At a time when industries were developing in the city, local origins divided not only business owners but their employees as well. Examples of such divisions were everywhere (although they were not necessarily rigid): silk weaving, printing, and dyeing were mostly done by people from Shenxian, Dongyang, Xinchang, Hangzhou, Shaoxing, Huzhou (all countries in Zhejiang province), and Changzhou; flour milling and oil pressing were done by people from Wuxi, Haimen, Ningbo, Shaoxing, and Hubei; shipping was the business of people from Guangdong, Tianjin, and Ningbo; and the ranks of the police force were filled with natives of Hebei and Shandong.[107]

In industries, business owners tended to recruit employees from their native places. Mu Ouchu, an America-educated entrepreneur whose investment in textiles represented an early Chinese effort to promote modern industry, began to recruit workers from his native province of Hunan for his Shanghai cotton mills in 1919.[108] A recruiting poster read: "Since Hunan has frequently suffered from war, the life of people there, especially of women, is difficult. So, a portion of the hiring quota in my factory in Shanghai is reserved for Hunan women in order to promote the idea that women can earn a livelihood by themselves, to train skilled textile workers, and to prepare for the growth of the textile industry in Hunan in the future."[109]

Recruitment policies such as this became almost a standard. Liu Hongsheng, one of the best-known entrepreneurs of twentieth-century China, had his enterprises recruit workers from his home county of Dinghai in Zhejiang for more than a decade, beginning in 1936. Liu himself decided on this policy.[110] A less well known capitalist, Wang Daban, who started as a shop assistant in Ningbo and later came to own five factories in Shanghai and Ningbo, also favored hiring people from his native Ningbo. When Wang established a new printing and dyeing factory in Shanghai in 1935, the first bunch of workers were all from his hometown; the Ningbo *bang* (Ningbo group) formed the backbone of Wang's enterprises.[111]

Native-place ties were perhaps even more central in the Fufeng Flour Mill, the first Chinese-owned modern mechanized flour mill. Its owners, the Sun family of Anhui, came to Shanghai to establish a mill in 1898. By 1937, the factory they had established was known in the trade as "number one in the Far East." But the management of this enterprise was rather provincial. For half a century, chief executives and management personnel were, with only one exception, all members of the Sun clan from Anhui. About 90 percent of the employees were of Anhui origin, and many had been directly recruited from Sun's hometown, Shouzhou, and its vicinity. These employees were not only "peasants of yesterday"; they were to some extent still regarded as peasants by the Suns: while they worked in the Suns' mill, many of them kept their families back in their native village as tenant farmers of the Sun family.[112]

Native-place ties between employers and employees provided a natural linkage between the two and made for easier management: the owners felt comfortable and safe having *tongxiang* (fellow villagers or townsmen) wield the hammers in the workshops while the employees were grateful to their boss for giving them a job. But native-place ties in business and work were not simply a matter of practicality; they were also a matter of emotion. They reflected the dual identity of the people of Shanghai, who, while they happily saw themselves as Shanghainese, also liked to maintain every possible tie with their native place. This is not unlike an ethnic group in the United States that tries to preserve some degree of its culture. As most of the people of Shanghai were immigrants, only about 10 percent of the entries in a typical *Who's Who of Shanghai* would be identified as natives of the city. Although all people in such publications were supposed to be Shanghairen—since they were listed as "Shanghai celebrities" and the publications customarily bore titles such as *The Celebrities of Shanghai's Enterprises and Commerce* (Shanghai gongshang mingren lu), *Pictorial Biographies of Shanghai's Celebrities* (Shanghai mingren xiangzhuan), and so on—a native place was always put before the person's name. Thus, one reads of "Yuhang (native place) Zhang Taiyan," "Wuxing (native place) Chen Qimei," "Foshan (native place) Wu Yanren," and so on.[113] These people were Shanghainese because they lived in the city, had careers there, and perhaps would stay in the city all their lives. But at the same time they identified themselves by their native origins, just as contemporary Americans are sometimes distinguished as "Irish American," "Jewish American," "Chinese American," and so on.

Among all the factors that immigrants identify with or assimilate from a new culture, language is perhaps the most essential and profound. The historian Xiong Yuezhi points out that the first criterion for distinguishing a "Shanghai person" was the fact that the person spoke the Shanghai dialect. Without speaking the standard Shanghai dialect (that is, the dialect as spoken in the city proper), he asserts, one could hardly be recognized by one's peers as Shanghainese.[114] This statement is more applicable to contemporary Shanghai, where the strictly imposed urban household registration system has produced at least two generations of Shanghai-born people who speak the pure Shanghai dialect, while reducing immigration to an insignificant level, than to pre-1949 Shanghai, when immigrants poured into the city, bringing with them all sorts of local tongues. Moreover, the Shanghai dialect itself has undergone some changes directly caused by the impact of dialects spoken by the immigrants.

The Shanghai dialect was originally a branch of the Songjiang dialect. At late as the third quarter of the nineteenth century it was still the language commonly spoken in the city. The phonetics of the Shanghai dialect recorded by the Sinologist Joseph Edkins (1823–1905) in the mid-nineteenth century, for instance, were those of the Songjiang dialect with a slight Pudong accent. In other words, in the first few decades of the treaty-port era, the Shanghai dialect essentially retained its original form.[115] To this day this dialect is still spoken by people in the vicinity of Shanghai, especially in the counties of Shanghai, Fengxian, Nanhui, and Songjiang.

The modern Shanghai dialect, the one spoken in twentieth-century Shanghai proper, diverged from its source by absorbing influences from the Suzhou and Ningbo dialects. Obviously, this was because immigrants from these areas were numerous in the late nineteenth century. The Shanghai dialect is perhaps the youngest in China: it was gradually formed at the turn of the century, and in the early Republican period it became distinguishable as the dialect of Shanghai proper. In 1916, when the philologist Gilbert McIntosh published his book on the Shanghai dialect, he had to include many new expressions and idioms, which suggests that the dialect was absorbing new blood.[116] In the Republican period, the original Shanghai dialect, the one with a Songjiang or Pudong accent, gradually came to be regarded as the language of the country folk (*xiangxiaren*), and the new dialect prevailed as what might be called urban speech. Indeed, the Shanghai dialect had a very limited "speech zone," literally only the city proper. It was the dialect spoken in the foreign concessions and their immediate vicinity, that is, an area of about 60 square miles. To the east, across the Huangpu River, the accent was slightly different, but different enough so that a Shanghainese from the west side of the river felt he was in the country.[117]

It is ironic that the Pudong, or Songjiang, accent, the original Shanghai dialect, came to be regarded as countrified speech, while in this city of immigrants, accents of all sorts were generally seen as normal. People who spoke the Shanghai dialect with an accent were sometimes nicknamed, according to their native origin and age, as "Little Shaoxing," "Old Guangdong," "Little Suzhou," "Old Ningbo," and so on, but this was customarily regarded as a cordial form of address, and there was little or no sense of discrimination or prejudice involved.[118] Like many immigrants in the United States who speak a foreign tongue at home, it was common for people in Shanghai to speak the dialect of their native place as well as the Shanghai dialect.[119]

Dragons and Fishes Jumbled Together

By the 1930s, Shanghai was a city of 3 million strangers, each of whom, it may be presumed, had his or her own reasons for living in this metropolis. For the privileged—the wealthy, the politically powerful, the intellectually outstanding—the city was a foundation for their elite status. For the poor, the city was a fragile life buoy. And for those in between, the city was the substance out of which the dream for a better life might be spun. While every city is a mixture of types and classes, and Shanghai may have had its share of the universal social stratifications, it also was unique.

So far I have reckoned the diversity of the people of Shanghai horizontally, by observing the various races and nationalities of the foreigners who lived in the city as well as the variety of native-place origins among the Chinese residents. Now let us turn to a vertical reckoning in order to uncover the social and economic strata of modern Shanghai.

THE ELITES

Shanghai's commercial prosperity and security (assured by the foreign powers) made the city a real paradise for wealthy Chinese. From the early twentieth century on, bureaucrats, warlords, politicians, landowners, literati, and magnates of all sorts came to the city seeking a life of comfort and luxury.

During and after the Taiping Rebellion, many of those who fled to Shanghai were wealthy landlords, merchants, and literati from Jiangnan. These well-to-do immigrants were generally of two types. One took advantage of the favorable commercial environment of the city by investing in various types of businesses and, generally, got richer. It was from this type that the compradors and China's modern entrepreneurs sprang, as discussed below. The other type consisted of those who lived in Shanghai chiefly for the comforts and freedom that it afforded. In time, retreating to Shanghai became popular among the rich and the celebrities of China. The epithet "Mr. Hermit" (*yugong*) was applied to those whose goal seemed to be a comfortable exile in the city, free of responsibilities and concerns. Needless to say, not every Mr. Hermit was a real recluse, and it was not unusual for politicians to retreat to Shanghai as a strategy for restoring their prestige or staging a comeback.[120]

In any case, these celebrities left a legacy to the city in the form of the grand houses and gardens they built. The late Qing reformist Kang Youwei (1858–1927), for instance, spent his later years in Shanghai. From 1914 until his death, Kang had three spacious homes in Shanghai. The site of one of his residences in the International Settlement was big enough, after he had moved out, to build first a Buddhist temple and, later, a pharmaceutical factory (which is still there today). Another of Kang's residences was demolished in 1930 and replaced by a residential compound of twenty-nine three-story alleyway-houses (with a garage on the first floor) that, in 1988, housed 222 households, or 828 residents.[121] The bureaucratic bigwig Sheng Xuanhuai (1844–1916) also lived in Shanghai after the 1911 revolution: his luxurious Western-style residence is now the consulate general of Japan.[122] Even many busy politicians who never had time to be a "Mr. Hermit" maintained villas in Shanghai. Li Hongzhang (1823–1901), for instance, had a villa for his concubine, Dingxiang. The villa is preserved to this day as a resort known for its combination of charming traditional Chinese garden and chic European architecture.[123] High-ranking politicians of the Nationalist regime almost without exception kept a residence in Shanghai. The quiet tree-lined avenues on the west side of the city were dotted with the residences of many major political figures in the Nanjing government.[124] Shanghai proved to be a better place to settle complicated and subtle political issues than the capital city of Nanjing. It was said that after 1927 the capital was the stage where political drama was performed, while Shanghai was the backstage.[125] The relationship between Nanjing and Shanghai was rather like that, in contemporary China, between Beijing and the summer resort of Beidaihe, which has been the favorite site for secret gatherings (and sometimes formal meetings) of top Communist leaders.

Not only was Shanghai the place where big political deals were arranged; it was also where big business deals were made. And, at least in the nineteenth century, big business deals were rarely cut without the intervention of middlemen known as compradors. These men served as agents for foreign firms. They were generally quick-witted, spoke a foreign tongue—most often pidgin English—and had some knowledge of foreign customs and business norms. Without them, foreign companies would have found it difficult, if not impossible, to do business in China. In the middle of the nineteenth century, few Chinese spoke a Western language, and few Westerners spoke Chinese. Furthermore, Western businesspeople had at best an imperfect knowledge of the Chinese market and Chinese ways of doing business. Finally, many Chinese merchants simply would not deal directly with foreigners. Compradors were thus crucial to conducting business, and consequently they were well compensated: their high salaries and commissions (which were usually much higher than the salary) soon made them China's foremost nouveau riche in the second half of the nineteenth century.[126]

Compradors in Shanghai were almost exclusively immigrants from Guangdong and a few Jiangnan cities such as Ningbo and Suzhou. In the latter half of the nineteenth century, Russell and Company (American, founded 1846) employed ten compradors in Shanghai, Jardine Matheson and Company (British, founded 1843) employed fifteen, and Dent, Beale and Company (British, founded in 1843), six: none of these compradors was a native of Shanghai.[127] Compradors of foreign banks were mostly Ningbo and Suzhou natives. These men were usually from well-to-do families that had moved to Shanghai late in the nineteenth century. They learned English in their youth and entered a foreign firm, sometimes first as a clerk and then, later, as a comprador. Compradors of foreign banks often had experience in a traditional Chinese bank (qianzhuang) before entering a foreign bank. The position of comprador was often passed down from generation to generation, and thus by the turn of this century so-called comprador clans (maiban shijia) had emerged.[128]

Most compradors simultaneously had their own businesses in addition to working for a foreign firm. Thus after the 1920s, when the role of the comprador declined, these people managed to remain the richest class in Chinese society. The Communists labeled them the "comprador-capitalist" class and made them a chief target of the revolution. Indeed, many successful capitalists in the city, especially the biggest industrialists, had been compradors. This is reflected in the membership of the Shanghai General Chamber of Commerce (Shanghai zongshanghui), which was founded in 1902 and became the city's most influential business organization in the early twentieth century.[129] In 1925–26, 45 percent of the chamber's board of directors and 22 percent of its members had a dual identity: as both comprador and business owner.[130]

No matter what kind of trade or business the entrepreneurs of Shanghai followed, the majority of them were not local people but immigrants. In 1923, 86 percent of the members of the Shanghai General Chamber of Commerce were from Zhejiang. Of the thirty-five members who served on its board of directors in 1924, only four were natives of Shanghai.[131] Of

69 Chinese banks, or qianzhuang, in 1921, only 7 were run by Shanghai natives; by 1933, out of 72 qianzhuang in Shanghai, only 3 were run by natives.[132] In 1944, of the 177 real estate companies in the city, only 35 (one-fifth) were run by natives.[133]

Shanghai was the capital of modern Chinese industry, and in the early twentieth century the capitalists of Shanghai were, as Parks Coble has pointed out, "the most powerful native economic group in China."[134] Prior to 1927, more than one-fifth of the nation's industrial enterprises (exclusive of mines) were located in Shanghai; more than a quarter of the country's industrial capital was concentrated there. In 1932–33, half of China's 2,435 modern factories (defined as mechanized and employing at least 30 workers) were in Shanghai.[135] Thus any serious study of the Chinese bourgeoisie must begin with Shanghai. As Bergère has indicated, this is not just because the Shanghai bourgeoisie "are the easiest to find out about; it is also because, of all the [Chinese] entrepreneurs, they were both the most active and the most numerous. Furthermore, most of the entrepreneurs, in their ordinary activities, always appear to function as a group at an essentially local or regional level. To disregard their geographical anchorage would [lead] to the empty categorizations characteristic of a familiar kind of Marxist analysis."[136] One may add that the Shanghai bourgeoisie was not really "Shanghai," or local. The diverse native-place origins of Shanghai's capitalists and the reach of their activities beyond the boundaries of the city (the former often contributed to the latter) greatly increased the significance of this class at the national level.

Turning our scan from businesspeople to educated modern professionals, we find another elite, which included doctors of Western medicine, executive managers, accountants, attorneys, engineers, and other higher professionals who were either employed in the modern sector (industry, banking, transportation, and communications) or were self-employed. Although these people constituted less than 1 percent of the population of Shanghai, Shanghai had more of them than any other Chinese city.[137] Many professionals were also investors of sorts; thus they were not merely white-collar workers but capitalists as well. All had received a higher education, often in mission schools and universities; some were so-called returned students, who had been educated overseas. Professionals appeared in public in Western attire, socialized with foreigners, and (some at least) spoke fluent English. They lived in quiet and comfortable areas in west Shanghai, typically in what were called garden alleyway-houses (*huayuan lilong*) or in detached houses (*yangfang*). The western part of Bubbling

Well Road (today's Nanjingxi Road), Zhaofeng Road (today's Yuyuan Road), and the so-called extra-Settlement roads (*yuejie zhulu*, lit., "roads that exceed the boundaries")—areas that were immediately west of the foreign concessions—were known for their concentration of elegant homes.[138] Many of the residents had private cars (or rickshaws), kept servants, and were avid club-goers. In the eyes of their fellow countrymen, the west-end residents were a different kind of Chinese: a "superior Chinese" (*gaodeng Huaren*).

Another elite included writers, actors, painters, musicians, movie stars, and so on—what might be called the cultural elite. This group gave birth to and nurtured the so-called Haipai (Shanghai school) culture, which became locked in battle with the Jingpai (Beijing school) tradition. The division between the two started in the late nineteenth century over differences in painting styles, but later spread to other cultural dimensions such as theater and literature. Eventually, the contest (at least in the eyes of the Haipai) became one between a vibrant, liberal culture centered in Shanghai and a conservative, traditional culture symbolized by Beijing.

In the Tongzhi period (1862–1874), among the immigrants to Shanghai from the Jiangnan region were professional and amateur painters, many of whom were traditional "men of letters" (*wenren*). Instead of following the regular, orthodox track of pursuing a career in the imperial government, these people chose to live in the foreign concessions and make a living by selling their artistic works. Inasmuch as polite society had always considered the purpose of painting to be self-cultivation, the commerce-driven paintings done in Shanghai were regarded as vulgar.[139] Later, this same tendency toward commercialism was also found in theaters. "Peking opera" as played in Shanghai was known as the southern style or simply the Shanghai style; it had a reputation of emphasizing—for the purpose of attracting a large audience—lavish and sensational effects (such as costume and stage sets) over skillful performance.[140]

By the Republican period, the word "Haipai" also came to be associated with literature. The so-called Mandarin Ducks and Butterflies fiction can be regarded as the first "Shanghai-style" literature. This writing took entertainment to be the purpose of fiction; plots were dominated by sensational and often tragic love stories, although a sober-minded reader might still find social and moral value in these stories.[141] In the early Republican period, the Mandarin Ducks and Butterflies school dominated the literary world of Shanghai: about half the literary magazines published in China in the second decade of the twentieth century were published in Shanghai, and most of them were works of this school. In the three decades between 1908 and 1938, 180 newspapers and magazines of the Mandarin Ducks and Butterflies type were published in Shanghai; the year 1914 alone saw 21 new newspapers and magazines of this type founded in Shanghai.[142]

But this was just one type of publication. Modern Shanghai was China's publishing center. From the late nineteenth century to 1956, when private ownership was transferred to state or collective ownership, about six hundred presses (not including newspaper and magazine publishers) opened in the city, most of them during the Republican period. The concentration of bookstores in Fuzhou Road and Henan Road in the International Settlement made these "cultural streets" famous nationwide.[143] No city in Republican China enjoyed more freedom of the press and cultural prosperity than Shanghai.

The city therefore attracted, or produced, China's most predominant intellectuals. Hu Shi, the hero of the New Cultural Movement, recalled that it was his early education (from 1904 to 1910) in Shanghai that made him an enthusiastic follower of Charles Darwin (1809–82) and Thomas Huxley (1825–95) and a pioneer advocate of the vernacular language.[144] A galaxy of twentieth-century China's outstanding writers, such as Lu Xun, Mao Dun, Yu Dafu, Xia Yan, and revolutionary intellectuals, such as Chen Duxiu and Qu Qiubai, all lived in Shanghai for a substantial period of time and published there. None of them was a native of Shanghai. All sojourned in the city; its dazzling life inspired and stimulated them to create works fated to become classics of an era.

Financially, these intellectuals occupied the lower rungs of the elite group. In wealth, they simply could not be compared with the city's capitalist bigwigs. But their incomes allowed them to live comfortable lives. A productive writer of popular fiction in the second decade of the twentieth century, for instance, could earn as much as $300 per month. The writer Bao Tianxiao got $120 a month in 1907 by writing three hours in the morning for a fiction magazine and spending afternoon and evening hours writing for a newspaper.[145] Working as an editor of the Commercial Press, Mao Dun earned a monthly salary of $100 in 1921; Yu Dafu's wife recalls that in the late 1920s, every month she collected $100–200 in royalties for her husband.[146] By comparison, a skilled worker's monthly salary in 1926 was $30–40; that was sufficient to support a family of five.[147] Still, given Shanghai's congested living conditions, the income of a writer typically allowed him or her to rent a house in an average alleyway-house neighborhood, next door to, say, a skilled worker or a shop clerk. But the differences were still there. Many a writer (including such luminaries as Lu Xun, Mao

Dun, and Yu Dafu) was able to rent a whole alleyway-house, while his neighbors shared a house with other tenants.

These well-off and popular writers were the top of the heap that included many young intellectuals who had come to Shanghai to make a living as freelance writers. Economically, these junior writers may or may not have been part of the elite. In any case, their income from selling their works was not necessarily greater than that of an average mechanic or shopkeeper. Many struggling writers rented a little "pavilion room" (*tingzijian*) in the city's common alleyway-house neighborhoods (discussed in detail in chapter 4) and lived among the populace while maintaining the mentality of an elite. Indeed, these intellectuals in Republican Shanghai bore some similarities to the French writers and poets who worked during the time of the rise of French industry after the Napoleonic Wars, as well as to American writers of the 1920s who escaped to Europe in search of a better environment for self-expression. Cowley's description of American writers in Paris in the twenties could also apply to intellectuals who sojourned in Shanghai in roughly the same period (the 1920s and the 1930s): "Some of them became revolutionists; others took refuge in pure art; but most of them demanded a real world of present satisfactions, in which they could cherish aristocratic ideals while living among carpenters and grisettes."[148]

THE PETTY URBANITES

"Petty urbanite," or *xiaoshimin* (translated in this book as "little urbanite"), was a blanket term popularly known and liberally used to refer, often with condescension, to city or town people who were of the middle or lower-middle social ranks. Like most conventional labels for a social class or group, xiaoshimin was never precisely defined. It was less clear who should be included in the category than who should be excluded. The elite at the top and the urban poor at the bottom would never be referred to as xiaoshimin. It was the people who stood in between who were called "petty urbanites."

The liberal use of the term contributed to its vagueness. Although people who used the word—which was almost everyone—certainly knew what it meant, nowhere in Chinese sources is the term adequately analyzed and carefully defined. In the West, Chinese petty urbanites have been discussed mostly in connection with the readership of twentieth-century Chinese fiction and periodicals. Perry Link, who is the first scholar in the West to have taken up the issue of xiaoshimin in academic research, applies an annotation from a Chinese dictionary to explain that xiaoshimin refers to "the middle class or the petty bourgeoisie." Links points out that "the term is taken to include small merchants, various kinds of clerks and secretaries, high school students, housewives, and other modestly educated, marginally well off urbanites." These people were the major audience of the Mandarin Ducks and Butterflies novels of the second and third decades of the twentieth century.[149] According to Frederic Wakeman and Wen-shin Yeh, in the Republican era the petty urbanites "constituted a huge new urban audience for periodicals like *Shenghuo* (Life)." These people were "literate clerks and apprentices in trade, manufacturing, the professions, the public and private service sectors, as well as among elementary and normal school teachers."[150]

While the term "middle class" often does not convey the precise character of a social group and sometimes is even misleading (because of, among other things, our contemporary stereotypical notion of this category), the xiaoshimin of Shanghai in some ways resembled the Kleinburger of early modern Germany. Like the xiaoshimin, the Kleinburger were "socially and economically as distinct from capitalist bourgeoisie as they were from the propertyless proletariat." They were predominantly craftspeople but also shopkeepers, petty traders, and minor officeholders, men with a "narrow, particularistic outlook on life." These words precisely describe the mentality of the Chinese xiaoshimin (as we shall see in later chapters). The historian Christopher Friedrichs has selected "lower middle class" as the best available translation of "Kleinburger."[151]

It seems to me that the approaches to defining xiaoshimin have paid attention only to occupational or vocational criteria; none has focused on what made these people a community. In fact, the expression itself has a connotation associated with community. From a purely terminological point of view, the word "xiaoshimin" consists of two parts: *xiao* (little) and *shimin* (urbanite). Here, "urbanite" stresses one's residential orientation (i.e., city people, not country people), and "little" stresses one's social standing (i.e., a small potato, not a big shot). Combining these two parts of the expression, the term xiaoshimin has strong implications for one's community background. When people used the term "xiaoshimin" to describe an individual, it was often with the idea of "a person from a common neighborhood." In premodern times, there was a similar term to describe townspeople, that is, *shijing zhibei* (a fellow from the marketplace). Thus the image of "petty urbanite" carries implications for social rank based on community, and it is the residential community that is being emphasized. When people used the term, the first thing that came to mind was usually a type of person whose outlook was limited by the community in which he or she lived.[152]

In modern Shanghai, the xiaoshimin were identified with a type of residence known as the *shikumen* house. Emerging in the late nineteenth century, shikumen houses were first a type of dwelling for well-to-do families. Later, the structure of the shikumen underwent a number of simplifications, mainly a downsizing of the house and a reduction of its cost. By the early twentieth century this type of house had become the single most common form of residence in the city, and those who lived in these houses were mostly middle- and lower-middle-income people. In other words, the shikumen were the homes of Shanghai's petty urbanites. The expression "the petty urbanites of the shikumen neighborhood" was common in the city.[153]

One of the major constituents of Shanghai's petty urbanites, as well as one of the primary residents of the shikumen neighborhoods, was so-called *zhiyuan*, a broad social category chiefly composed of office workers, clerks, all types of white-collar workers, and shop assistants. According to one definition, zhiyuan were "service personnel who work in economic, cultural, and political offices or institutions."[154] Table 2 lists various types of zhiyuan in Shanghai in the 1930s. By the late 1930s, there were about 250,000 to 300,000 people in this category in the city.[155] Zhiyuan and their family members numbered no fewer than 1.5 million persons, or about 40 percent of the city's population in the middle thirties (when Shanghai had 3.5 million people).[156]

Another major group of petty urbanites was factory workers. In discussing industrial workers in modern China, scholars both inside and outside China have often resorted to broad generalizations and even stereotyping. Inside China, this was largely because official ideology needed to forge an image, however distorted, of a unified proletariat as the leading class of the revolution. Outside China, scholars simply lacked information that would have made possible a nuanced picture. This latter weakness has been significantly remedied by recent research on Chinese labor, which sees industrial workers as a highly stratified social group divided by local origins, type of work, and gender.[157] But it is also important to examine the residential patterns of factory workers. Where workers lived and what type of house they lived in was not only a measure of their economic status but also, like the role played by the workplace, a vital influence on their outlook.

Surveys conducted in the early 1930s found that Shanghai's factory workers lived in three major types of houses: alleyway or shikumen

Table 2. Zhiyuan (White-Collar Employees) in Republican Shanghai

Year	Trade or Institution	Number of Zhiyuan
1934	Stores (old type)	82,900
1936	Six major department stores	3,000
1936	Hardware stores and Western-type pharmacies	9,200
1936	Banking and finance	10,000
1936	Schools and colleges	13,500
1933	Media	15,000–17,000
1934	Postal service and transportation	10,000
1937	Foreign firms	45,000
1936	Municipal Council of the French Concession	1,400
1936	Municipal government	2,100
1938	Factory office and other office workers	80,000–100,000

SOURCE: Zhang Zhongli, ed., *Jindai Shanghai chengshi yanjiu,* 724; Zhu Bangxing et al., *Shanghai chanye yu Shanghai zhigong,* 701–2.

houses, old-style one-story houses (*pingfang*), and straw shacks. Of 76,218 houses inhabited by workers, 37 percent were alleyway houses, that is, the typical type of house in Shanghai's petty urbanite neighborhoods. These houses were found virtually everywhere in the city; they were the homes of about half of Shanghai's factory workers and their families.[158]

The surveys found that the distinction between so-called workers' zones and nonworkers' zones was by no means rigid; families of industrial workers were frequently found in areas quite distant from factories, intermixed with white-collar households.[159] In other words, a considerable part of Shanghai's industrial workers lived side by side with people of many other social types. Factory workers in these neighborhoods were mostly skilled or semiskilled men (and some women) who had a relatively stable or long-term (in contradistinction to casual) job in an industrial enterprise. These workers and their families who lived in shikumen houses were quite distinct from their "class brothers" who lived at the bottom of society: casual workers, day laborers, and unskilled coolies of all sorts. The latter group was driven by poverty to the squatters' areas on the outskirts of the city proper and were despised by the contented petty urbanites in shikumen—let alone the aloof elites in the city's wealthy neighborhoods—as rustic coolies or simply country bumpkins.[160]

THE URBAN POOR

It is understandable that most people in Shanghai tended to see shack dwellers as hayseeds. The urban poor were overwhelmingly former peasants. They may have migrated to the city but they were not quite urbanized, if one defines urbanization as primarily involving having a stable job and place of residence in the city. These people lacked any of the three basic conditions that allowed a newcomer to find a fairly desirable and relatively stable job: skill, money, and a good social network.

First, most peasant immigrants were illiterate and unskilled. Their opportunities were further blocked by the fact that they could not afford the lump sum payment or nonrefundable "deposit" (which was virtually a payment) required by many trades in Shanghai for obtaining a starting position or an apprenticeship. The amount of the deposit varied by trade (or individual enterprise); commonly, it was equivalent to two months' salary in the trade in question.[161] The poor simply could not afford such a large payment; hence they could not take the first step toward a permanent job. Finally, poor rural immigrants usually did not have connections in the city that would have helped them find a good job. The best networking connection they might have was a relative, a fellow villager, or an acquaintance who had come to Shanghai earlier. But these earlier arrivals themselves were, more often than not, at the bottom rung of society and could hardly offer much assistance. At best, if connections ever worked, they only helped the newcomer find a place in the ranks of Shanghai's poverty-stricken multitudes.[162]

On one hand, the growth of Shanghai's modern industries during and after World War I, and the urban development that paralleled it, resulted in countless job opportunities, as well as all the amenities and accoutrements of modern urban life; this proved to be a powerful attraction. On the other hand, in the countryside economic and social deterioration, wars, banditry, and natural disasters that frequently marked the Republican period created an army of uneasy peasants who imagined the city to be a refuge. Thus, the city and an army ready to surrender to its attractions met in early-twentieth-century Shanghai. The result was an onslaught of rural poor who stuck to the city for sheer survival.

The most sizable groups of the urban poor in Republican-era Shanghai were rickshaw pullers, dockworkers, street beggars, and countless casual workers—and the unemployed. In the mid-1920s, there were about 62,000 rickshaw pullers, 22,000 wheelbarrow and handcart operators and carriage drivers (*mafu,* or "grooms"), and 35,500 dockworkers in Shanghai. In the late 1920s, there were about 50,000–60,000 dockworkers; in the mid-1930s, 20,000–25,000 street beggars; and in the late 1930s and early 1940s, 100,000 rickshaw pullers.[163] These figures do not include the army of casual factory workers and the unemployed. By the end of the Republican period, close to 1 million people like these lived in the city's shantytowns.

Although, as noted above, not all factory workers were necessarily among the urban poor, many of them were. While some skilled and semi-skilled workers obtained stable positions in factories, lived in average lower-middle-class alleyway-house neighborhoods, and therefore ascended to the ranks of the petty urbanites, casual workers (*linshigong*) descended to the bottom of society. Available statistics do not give us the number of casual workers in Shanghai in any given year, since the category "factory worker" in all statistics does not distinguish casuals from long-term workers (*changgong*). According to official statistics, Shanghai in 1920 had 181,485 factory workers; the number increased to 223,681 in 1928 and reached 394,654 by January 1950.[164] Although these statistics give us no hint of the relative proportion of long-term and temporary workers, hiring of casual workers was increasingly common in Shanghai's factories through the Republican period. It is therefore safe to say that a sizable portion of the city's factory workers were casual or day workers who were poorly paid and under constant threat of unemployment.

By the end of the Republican period, these temporary laborers, vagabonds, the unemployed and underemployed, and the like, plus their families, made up nearly one-fifth of Shanghai's 5 million people.[165] Like the disadvantaged in any society, they were despised and discriminated against by the city's general public; but they could not be ignored.

The importance of these people in the life of the city lies not only in their large number but also in their backgrounds. The poor moved to the city for virtually the same reason that most of the city's better-off people did: to find a better life. Thus the overwhelmingly rural backgrounds of the urban poor reflected a profound social phenomenon in twentieth-century China: for millions of peasants, an urban life, no matter how arduous and difficult, meant a better life. The world of rickshaws, with its everyday presence in the city, provides a powerful and illuminating example of such pursuit.

CHAPTER 2

The World of Rickshaws

In July 1926, Hu Shi (1891–1962), while visiting Harbin, the metropolis dubbed the "Shanghai of North China" by virtue of its foreign concessions and foreign (in this case, Russian) influence, was struck by the difference between the former Russian concession, where (as a legacy of foreign administration) rickshaws were not permitted, and the Chinese district, where rickshaws still operated in abundance.[1] Hu Shi declared that he had found "the boundary between Eastern and Western civilizations." That dividing line was, he later concluded, "precisely the boundary between the rickshaw and the automobile civilizations."[2]

In the early twentieth century, the rickshaw was a symbol of the backwardness of Chinese cities, and the rickshaw coolie remained "the classic example of his class."[3] Shanghai would have been a totally different city had there been no rickshaws. The importance of these conveyances lay not just in their role in the city's transportation system nor in their contribution to the exotic appearance of the city. More significant, rickshaws were the means of livelihood for thousands of people.[4]

The story surrounding this simple vehicle is a richly multifarious one. The rumble of the rickshaw reflected the rhythm of life in the city, not in the sense that the din of the rickshaws' wheels as they rolled over the city's asphalt streets literally contributed to the hubbub of the city but in the sense that the rickshaw trade, or "racket," was part of the city's commercial culture. The rickshaw puller was certainly exploited and oppressed, but at the same time he also saw his opportunity to survive by playing his role in the trade. Just as the "backwardness" of the rickshaw was relative, the plight of the pullers also had its context.

Rickshaws

The rickshaw, like many other things introduced to modern China via Shanghai, had a Western connection. In the spring of 1873, a French merchant named Menard came to Shanghai from Japan with the idea of opening a business in imitation of the lucrative rickshaw business in Japan.[5] Early in June, he petitioned the municipal council of the French Concession for a patent right to run "hand-pulled vehicles" for ten years. The request was discussed by the council, which then consulted the municipal council of the British Settlement. The councils denied Menard's request for a patent but agreed to permit the business in both concessions on the grounds that the operation of such vehicles would improve the flow of traffic and increase revenue. The councils planned to allow up to 1,000 rickshaws to operate in the two concessions (500 in each) that year. Twenty licenses, each for 25 rickshaws, were issued in the French Concession. As a courtesy to Menard, he was granted 12 licenses to run 300 rickshaws.[6]

The news was soon publicized. In August, Shanghai's major Chinese newspaper, *Shenbao*, reported the forthcoming arrival of rickshaws and indicated that the vehicles would be brought from Japan by Western merchants.[7] On March 24, 1874, Menard registered the first rickshaw company in Shanghai. The next three-quarters of 1874 saw another 9 rickshaw companies opened in Shanghai, all owned by Westerners. At the end of that year, these 10 companies had about 1,000 rickshaws in operation.[8]

The term "rickshaw," or "ricsha," was originally derived from the Japanese term *jinrikisha*, meaning "man-power-vehicle,"[9] which also became the formal Chinese name of the vehicle (pronounced *renliche* in Chinese). But the latter name was never popularly used in Shanghai. In this city, the rickshaw was at the beginning known as *dongyangche*, meaning, "East-foreign-vehicle," or rather, in an alternative but perhaps more accurate translation, "Japanese vehicle," a name that reflected the origin of the conveyance. By 1913, the SMC issued a regulation that all public rickshaws be painted yellow in order to more easily distinguish them from private rickshaws, and after that, rickshaws were commonly called *huang baoche* (lit., yellow private vehicle). This became the most popular name for the vehicle.[10]

Once introduced, rickshaws steadily gained in popularity. In 1882, 1,500 rickshaws were in business in Shanghai's foreign concessions; by 1914, the International Settlement alone had 9,718 public rickshaws.[11] The merits of the rickshaw as a means of urban transportation were obvious. In comparison with the old single-wheel wheelbarrow, which was a major conveyance in nineteenth-century Shanghai, the rickshaw was comfortable. Technical improvements of the rickshaw through the decades after its introduction made it even more fit for travel. These included discarding the original iron-shod wooden wheels in favor of solid rubber tires, then pneumatic rubber tires, adding a backrest for the comfort of the passenger, replacing the flat, hard seat with spring cushions, adding lights, and so on.[12] Rickshaw fares were within the means of the common people of the city. A ride of a mile or so—the most common distance for which a rickshaw was hired—cost less than 20 cents in the late 1920s and the early 1930s (see Table 3). That was about as much as the average tip that a passenger gave a taxi driver at the time.[13]

The most important appeal of the rickshaw, however, was its flexibility. Without awkward jostling, the rickshaw could easily gain access to literally every corner in the city's numerous winding and narrow streets and alleyways, something no motor vehicle could do (Fig. 4).[14] The rickshaw was also flexible in the sense that it was available at any time and stopped anywhere the passenger wanted, unlike the bus or tram, which had regular schedules and set stops. "When the typhoon season came around," one Westerner wrote, "the rickshaw coolie would cheerfully carry you pickaback from front door to rickshaw, or vice versa, to keep your feet dry."[15]

By the end of the nineteenth century, rickshaws were already the most common conveyance in the city.[16] Of Shanghai's three administrative jurisdictions, the International Settlement, the core of modern Shanghai, accounted for most rickshaws. In 1900, there were 4,647 rickshaws for public hire in the Settlement. By 1907, the number had increased to 8,204.[17] By the 1930s, there were more than 23,000 registered rickshaws in operation in Shanghai's streets for public hire, for an average of 1 public rickshaw for every 150 people.[18]

In 1899, the same year that the Willis Bridge survey was conducted, the SMC started to issue licenses for private rickshaws (*baoche*).[19] In 1907, 5,625 private rickshaws were registered in the International Settlement.[20] By 1924, of the 19,882 rickshaws registered in the Settlement, 9,882 were private (see Table 4).[21] These private rickshaws were sometimes casually referred to, like public rickshaws, as huang baoche (yellow private vehicles), but they were actually painted black. Although public and private rickshaws were the same type of vehicle, it was certainly easy to tell which was which. Rickshaws for public hire were not only yellow but looked, in general, shabby and tumbledown, although they seldom broke down in the

Fig. 4. Rickshaws literally provided door-to-door service. Here rickshaw men are waiting for fares in front of an alleyway entrance. Inside the arched portal are rows of attached houses. A grocery store with a huge cotton cloth sign is on the right of the alleyway entrance and a tailor's shop is on the left. As a rule, stores were lined up side by side on both sides of the alleyway entrance. In neighborhoods such as this, shopping and transportation were always available a few steps away from home. From R. Barz, *Shanghai: Sketches of Present-Day Shanghai.*

street. Commenting on these dilapidated-looking conveyances, a foreign observer in Shanghai satirically said that "this [the broken-down appearance of public rickshaws] must not intimidate the nervous, for the stranger will not be long in China without seeing a miracle, that things Chinese (including the government) when in ruins ought to go to pieces, but somehow never do."[22] Invariably, it seemed, private rickshaws were always shiny, were carefully maintained, and sported "a spotless white upholstered double seat, a clean plaid for one's lap, and a wide protective tarpaulin to protect the passenger (or passengers, since sometimes up to three people rode together) against the rain."[23]

While owning a private automobile and employing a driver was an exceptional luxury limited to the wealthiest, to own a private rickshaw and employ a puller for it (or, the equivalent in the late 1940s, to own a pedicab and hire a driver) was a luxury enjoyed by many upper-middle-class families.[24] More commonly, well-off families (both Chinese and Western) had a favorite public rickshaw puller whom they would hire on a regular basis

Table 3. Rickshaw Fares in Shanghai, 1917–1937

Engaged by Distance	
First mile or less	10 cents
Each subsequent ½ mile or less	10 cents
Engaged by Time	
One hour or less	50 cents
Each subsequent hour or less	40–50 cents

SOURCE: Fang Fu-an, "Rickshaws in China," 800; Darwent, *Shanghai*, xiv.

NOTE: These were official fares determined by the SMC but never strictly enforced. Actual fares were usually higher; rickshaw pullers and their would-be passengers commonly bargained over fares. In the rickshaw dispute of 1933–34, many people did not even know there were official rates. See Guo Chongjie, "Shanghaishi de renliche wenti," 19–20; Darwent, *Shanghai*, xiv; Pal, *Shanghai Saga*, 168–70.

Table 4. Public Rickshaws in Shanghai, 1934

Area	*Rickshaws*[a]	*Rickshaw Firms*	*Rickshaw Pullers*
Hubei[b]	2,900	805	8,700
Hunan	6,014	1,292	18,042
Huxi	3,124	1,215	9,372
Pudong	1,078	180	2,156
Wusong	200	175	400
International Settlement	9,990	1,148	39,960
Total	23,306	4,815	78,630

SOURCE: Shanghaishi chuzu qiche gongsi, *Shanghai chuzu qiche renliche*, 75.

[a] Shanghaishi gongyong shiye guanliju, comp., *Shanghai gongyong shiye*, 250, gives a slightly different total number of rickshaws in Shanghai in the mid-1930s: 23,335. Other sources (Tim Wright, "Shanghai Imperialists versus Rickshaw Reforms"; Perry, *Shanghai on Strike*, 266) also gives 23,335 as the number of rickshaws in the Chinese districts.

[b] Hubei (North Shanghai) mainly consisted of Zhabei. Hunan (South Shanghai) included the French Concession and Nanshi (the old Chinese City and its vicinity). Pudong included four towns: Yangjing, Tangqiao, Gaoqiao, and Luhang.

for certain purposes, such as taking children to and from school, shopping, and other regular, short trips.[25] Running rickshaws was a highly profitable business. According to one report, in the late nineteenth century a rickshaw made in Japan sold for $15, and the daily rent for a rickshaw (paid by the puller to the owner) was 400–600 *wen*, which was about one-thirtieth the cost of the rickshaw itself.[26] This means that by renting out a rickshaw for a month, the owner could recoup his investment; after that, the profits rolled in.[27] Such quick profits soon aroused the interest of Chinese in the business. After the 1880s, the Chinese were able to make their own rickshaws, and the market price for the vehicle began to fall. In 1898, Chinese started to run businesses (called *chehang*, lit., "vehicle firms") that rented out rickshaws for public hire in the walled Chinese city. From 1910 on, Zhabei, the newly developed Chinese-administered area, also started to have rickshaw firms. Later on, rickshaw firms were established in suburban areas like west Shanghai (Huxi) and Pudong.[28]

However, up to the early twentieth century, foreigners still dominated the rickshaw business in Shanghai. The names of large rickshaw companies owned by Westerners—such as Nanhe, Feixing, Huifang, Jicheng—were familiar to Shanghainese. These companies rented rickshaws directly to Chinese contractors, who then sublet the rickshaws to pullers. In this way, of course, the foreign owners were saved the trouble of dealing directly with numerous pullers—"dirty work" in their eyes—and did not have to face the language barrier.[29] The Chinese contractors, known as *baotou* (subletting heads), were mostly members of gangs or otherwise had some sort of disreputable background. Often, after they had contracted for rickshaws with their foreign owners, they sublet the vehicles to other, minor, middlemen who then sublet to individual pullers. Sometimes more than one layer of middleman was involved; hence names such as "second middleman" (*erbao*), "third middleman" (*sanbao*), and so on became part of the jargon of the business.

From about the early 1920s on, the Chinese contractors gradually purchased the rickshaws from their foreign owners and took over the companies, although some foreigners still remained the officially registered owners of the vehicles. By the late 1920s, Chinese had purchased most of Shanghai's rickshaw businesses. The Nanjing decade (1927–37) saw the peak of the history of rickshaws in Shanghai. By then the business, from owners to various layers of middlemen to pullers, was purely Chinese. By the late 1930s, the Chinese could declare that "the rickshaw business is 100 percent ours."[30]

By the 1920s and 1930s, the rickshaw business had become one of Shanghai's notorious rackets, especially in the International Settlement. The SMC, out of concern about traffic congestion, pursued a policy of limiting the number of rickshaw licenses. In particular, licenses for public rickshaws were strictly controlled. Between 1917 and 1934, the number of public rickshaws in the Settlement was almost frozen.[31] From September 1924 on, the SMC set a cap of 10,000 licenses for public rickshaws, and the cap was kept in place into the 1930s.

The limit on the number of licenses and other administrative peculiarities (such as automatic renewal of licenses) created a highly complex "license hierarchy" in the trade. At the top of the hierarchy were the official license holders, a total of 144 individuals or companies in the 1930s who registered 9,900 public rickshaws in the Settlement.[32] These license holders paid a nominal fee of $2.00 per month to the SMC (which was increased slightly to $2.20 in the late 1930s), but the actual market value of a license in the 1930s ran as high as $750.00.[33] Since licenses were legally not transferable, many license holders sold or rented their licenses but remained officially registered owners and received regular payments from the license purchasers. According to an investigation conducted by the SMC's rickshaw committee in 1933–34, only 34 percent of the license holders actually owned and managed the registered vehicles; the rest of the rickshaws were either partially or totally rented out or virtually sold.[34] The average annual net profit from the racket of renting or selling licenses ranged from 100 to 300 percent, depending on how many middlemen were involved. By simply renting out the SMC-issued enamel license (which was kept in the vehicle), the profit was 100 percent.[35] Thus the business of running rickshaws in the International Settlement, from the SMC office down to the actual pullers in the streets, involved multiple layers of license holders, rickshaw owners, contractors, and middlemen, each profiting to varying extents from the racket of renting and buying and selling licenses.[36]

At the bottom of the hierarchy were, of course, the thousands of pullers (Fig. 5). According to the Shanghai Municipal Bureau of Social Affairs, the city had about 80,649 public rickshaw pullers in the early 1930s, each of whom on average supported a family of 4.23. Thus it was that the rickshaw provided a livelihood for more than 340,000 people, or about 10 percent of the city's population.[37] A more moderate estimate of the SMC indicated that in 1934 in the International Settlement alone about 140,000 people depended on the rickshaw for a livelihood. No wonder the term *huangbaoche fu* (rickshaw puller) was almost a synonym for the poor.[38]

Fig. 5. Rickshaw men were not always poorly clad and seedy looking. Work uniforms were sometimes provided, and the Shanghai Municipal Council had decreed that pullers must be "decently clad," although the rule was not strictly enforced (Gamewell, *Gateway to China*, 94–95). It was not uncommon to see rickshaw men like this one, who is waiting on the Bund wearing a Western-type shooting cap, heartily smiling as he faces a camera held by an inquisitive journalist or a curious tourist. Courtesy of Shanghai Municipal Library.

Rickshaw Pullers

In the English-speaking world, Chinese rickshaw pullers were made known, vividly and in some detail, by the translations of Lao She's classic novel, *Camel Xiangzi*, and, more recently, by David Strand's scholarly work, *Rickshaw Beijing*. Both books are based on the life of rickshaw pullers in Republican Beijing. Shanghai rickshaw pullers no doubt shared many characteristics with their Beijing counterparts. But there were also some notable differences. The major difference lay in the origins of the pullers. Unlike the rickshaw pullers of Beijing, who were mostly natives of that city (less than one-quarter of them came from the countryside),[39] almost all rickshaw pullers in Shanghai came directly from the country-side, particularly from the rural areas of Subei (also known as Jiangbei, the northern part of Jiangsu province), the source of Shanghai's poorest immi-grants.[40] An article in the popular magazine *Dongfang zazhi* used a straightforward title to indicate that the so-called rickshaw pullers' prob-lem was a "direct result of rural bankruptcy."[41]

The rural origins of Shanghai's rickshaw pullers were revealed in a num-ber of surveys conducted in the 1930s. A 1929–30 study of 100 rickshaw pullers in Yangshupu found that only one was Shanghai-born. Of the oth-ers, 85 had been farmers who came to Shanghai during famine in their home villages, 9 had come as children with parents who left their villages for the same reason, 2 were former soldiers, and another 2 had come to Shanghai in order to escape gambling debts.[42] A report on the former occupations of Shanghai's rickshaw pullers based on an investigation con-duced by the SMC in 1934 found that pullers had left the following oc-cupations (number of pullers is in parentheses): farmer (30), cotton mill worker (6), peddler (3), coolie (4), night watchman (4), fisherman (1), boat-man (1), carpenter (1), teacher (1).[43]

Clearly, the great majority of pullers were former peasants. In addition, those who declared their former occupation to be factory worker, peddler, coolie, night watchman, and so on were often of rural origins. Sometimes peasants who came to Shanghai looking for a livelihood had tried other jobs before they became rickshaw pullers. The main qualification for pulling a rickshaw was, of course, muscle. For the immigrants, pulling a rickshaw was usually not their first choice. Most of the pullers of Shanghai were from the poorest counties of Subei, such as Dongtai, Yancheng, Funing, Gaoyou, and Taixian. Immigrants from the better-off counties of Subei, such as Nantong and Haimen, were a minority among Shanghai's rickshaw men.[44] One author wrote satirically in 1934:

> The destitution of the countryside forced farmers to put down their hoes and plows and turn to the city—Shanghai. But the only skill these people had is farming. Shanghai is the so-called golden land. It is not easy to find a square foot of soil in the city's asphalt streets and cement courtyards. Here, farm hoes and plows were simply junk. So peasants who arrived in Shanghai could not find a [suitable] occupation.
>
> The only solution for these people was to pull a rickshaw. There was little skill needed in this calling: one needed only to know [what] the red and green traffic lights [mean], how to get up and down street curbs, and some simple traffic regulations about making a right or left turn.[45]

Nonetheless, there was competition for this occupation. So many peasants had poured into the city that many of them could not find anything that resembled a job.[46] Few rickshaw men were able to own a rickshaw; most pullers rented rickshaws on a daily basis from a rickshaw firm, and there were always many more pullers available than rickshaws. In the Nanjing decade, the situation was consistently such that 4 or 5 pullers competed for each rickshaw, leaving the majority of the pullers under constant threat of unemployment.[47]

To take 1934 as an example, in that year in the International Settlement there were 1,009 rickshaw firms, which owned a total of 9,990 rickshaws; at the same time, there were 40,000 rickshaw pullers in the Settlement. Thus on average at least 4 pullers shared each vehicle.[48] There were two shifts in the rickshaw-pulling business in Shanghai: the first from 3 P.M. to 5 A.M. (14 hours), and the second from 5 A.M. to 3 P.M. (10 hours).[49] If each rickshaw was rented 24 hours every day, the maximum number of pullers who could get access to a rickshaw would be about 20,000. This means that at any given moment about half the rickshaw pullers in Shanghai were unemployed.

This situation worsened in the late 1930s. In 1939, fewer than 20,000 rickshaws were in operation for public hire, while about 100,000 people were working as rickshaw pullers; thus on average 5 pullers shared each rickshaw.[50] An investigation found that a "full-time" rickshaw puller on the first shift could work only 15 days per month, while the second-shift pullers, 20 days.[51] Naturally, limited work days substantially limited the pullers' income. According to two studies on rickshaw pullers sponsored by foreign and Chinese authorities (SMC's rickshaw committee and the Shanghai Municipal Bureau of Social Affairs, respectively) in 1934, the average monthly income of pullers was $9.[52]

Surveys conducted by the Shanghai Municipal Bureau of Social Affairs found that the monthly earnings of male factory workers averaged $20 in 1928, and $25 in 1933.[53] In other words, on average a rickshaw puller's income was less than half that of a factory worker. If factory workers, particularly unskilled casual laborers, are regarded as the prototypical urban poor, then rickshaw pullers would seem to have been impoverished. This is in contrast to the rickshaw men of Beijing who were, Strand argues, "poor but not impoverished."[54]

However, the real life of Shanghai's rickshaw pullers was more complicated than the statistics suggest. In the struggle for a livelihood in Shanghai, a rickshaw puller was always ready to try other jobs. Therefore, surveys that put a person in one occupational category or another could be arbitrary, and income figures based on the category of "rickshaw puller" may not have been entirely reliable. First of all, a puller could always have a second job (*fuye*), or, in some cases, pulling a rickshaw itself was his "second job."[55] Moreover, if a rickshaw man had a family, it was not unusual for the wife and children to work; their earnings could be a significant part of the family's income. This situation was similar to that of some factory workers in Tianjin who, as Gail Hershatter describes it, "had no fixed occupation, but squeezed themselves into whatever economic niche they could construct, and diversified their source of income by sending almost everyone out to work, or bringing in work to those who remained at home."[56] For instance, some rickshaw pullers in Shanghai had a regular factory job, and every day after factory hours they pulled a rickshaw to earn extra money. This practice, colorfully known as "pulling the buttocks of the rickshaw" (*la chepigu*), was particularly common among casual workers for the simple reason that the income from their factory job was insufficient to support a family.[57]

Although a factory job was regarded by most people as better than pulling a rickshaw, not all rickshaw pullers agreed. In response to surveys regarding job preferences, some rickshaw men indicated that rickshaw pulling had certain advantages over factory work: first, factory jobs involved long hours (usually 12 hours a day or longer) and the work hours were strict, while a rickshaw puller's work hours could be shorter and flexible. The night shift was long, it is true, but it was often shared by two pullers; the second puller was the one who "pulled the buttocks of the rickshaw."

Second, the type of job that an unskilled laborer could expect to get in a factory paid about what a man could earn by pulling a rickshaw, that is, about $0.40 a day in 1930. This meant that a puller could earn about the same income as an unskilled factory worker, but in less time. Moreover, by the nature of the job, a rickshaw puller could always expect a lucky day when business was especially brisk or when a generous customer paid especially well. On such days, a puller's takings might be double or triple his usual earnings.[58] Obviously, these opportunities did not exist in a factory. Peng Fuyang, a forty-four-year-old rickshaw man, told an investigator in 1930, "I don't want to work in a mill where I can earn only 40 cents a day. I earn more by pulling a rickshaw, and the earnings are not set—if I am lucky I can earn more. In the factory you can never expect more than 40 cents a day."[59] Some of the rickshaw men surveyed had actually given up a factory job in favor of pulling a rickshaw.[60]

In a typical pattern of migration from rural areas to Shanghai, young male members of a peasant family went to the city first to test the waters, so to speak. If everything went well, it usually took a young man a year or so to settle down in the city. Then he might be in a position to bring the rest of his family. But some immigrants were never able to do so and remained single throughout their sojourn in Shanghai. This contributed to the persistently uneven sex ratio in modern Shanghai. The male-to-female ratio in pre-1937 Shanghai was more than 130 to 100; by the late 1940s, the ratio was still more than 120 to 100.[61] Lower-class laborers often could not afford to maintain a family in the city. Many of them were simply unable to marry at all and remained, in the common term, "single sticks" (guang-gun).[62] A popular song vividly described the life of a "single stick":

> Mai mi yi ding mao (To buy rice, his cap is the container),[63]
> Mai chai huai zhong bao (To buy firewood, his arms are the container),
> Zhu de mao cao wu (He lives in a straw hut),
> Yue liang dang deng zhao (The moon is his only lamplight).[64]

A strikingly high proportion of rickshaw pullers were unmarried. It was estimated that in 1939 there were about 100,000 of them working in Shanghai's foreign concessions, of whom more than 60,000 were unmarried or had left their families back in the village.[65]

One Shi Zhilin, a thirty-six-year-old rickshaw man who hailed from Yancheng in northern Jiangsu province, typified three aspects of Shanghai's rickshaw pullers: their origins, the pattern of their migration, and their strong family ties back in the village. Shi told his story in 1929:

> Two years ago because of a lean year in my home village, I came to Shanghai. My parents have five sons; I am Number Two. My elder brother works in an electric lamp factory [in Shanghai]. Both my

Number Three and Number Five brothers are farmers in Jiangbei [northern Jiangsu]. My Number Four brother is also a rickshaw puller in Shanghai. The five of us have already divided the family property [*fenjia*]. Each of us got 13 mu of land. But because of the lean years in Jiangbei, I worked as a rickshaw puller in Shanghai, leaving my wife home to take care of our land. My folks are supported by all five of us. This year the famine in Jiangbei is extremely bad, so my wife has recently come with our [six] children to join me in Shanghai. Our land is farmed by my brothers to support my parents and to help with my brothers' expenses. I do not want the output of the land, but if my parents die I would take the land back.[66]

For those who brought their family to Shanghai, making a living was a collective effort of the household. In 1933–34, the Shanghai Municipal Social Bureau conducted a survey of 291 rickshaw families, with a total of 1,230 people. It reported that "except for some feeble persons and little children, most family members have some sort of work to do." Based on this survey, the bureau interviewed a sample of 57 families (245 persons) in detail about the types of work they were doing. The jobs they reported, with number of working persons in parentheses, were rickshaw pulling (71), straw shoe making (23), toothbrush making (12), yarn spinning (16), peddling (9), sorting chicken feathers and fleece (4), gleaning rubber balls to sell (5), laundering (3), gleaning charcoal (1), working in a cotton mill (1), unskilled laboring (3), selling foreign goods (1), weaving (1), and vehicle attending (2).[67]

This rather diverse list suggests the hardship of, as well as the opportunities for, rickshaw families. On one hand, the variety of the jobs reveals that life was a cooperative, family-based venture for these rural immigrants: every mouth needed to be fed and every possible person had to work. Some of these jobs, such as "gleaning leather balls," were most likely done by children.[68] On the other hand, almost all the jobs were not available in the villages. In other words, the variety of jobs suggested opportunities available only in the city. Even by picking up trash to sell, a child could significantly supplement the family income. It was reported in 1936 that 20,000 people in Shanghai worked at "picking up trash" (*shihuang*). More than 5,000 of these trash pickers were children aged seven to fourteen; daily earnings from selling trash ranged from 100 to 500 wen.[69] No matter how low these jobs might have been in the eyes of the city's better-off people, they provided the opportunities that lay at the heart of the city's attraction.

The most common combination of occupations in Shanghai's poor working-class families involved the husband working as a rickshaw puller and the wife as a textile mill worker. As we have seen, many factories, especially those in the largest industry in Shanghai, textiles, tended to hire women (and girls) for unskilled work.[70] This pattern was significantly different from that in more tradition-bound cities such as Beijing, where women's major occupations were still sewing and washing, and family income was basically whatever the husband earned.[71] A folk rhyme, the "Song of Women Filature Workers" (*Sichang nügong qu*), poignantly portrayed the difficult life of the woman who was wife, worker, and mother:

> I rushed out of bed, dressing in the gray dawn.
> Holding the mosquito net, I turned to see my child:
> "Oh, baby, you look pained when mother must go out to work."
>
> Having just served tea to my father-in-law,
> I heard the mill whistle blowing.
> With disheveled hair I wasn't in the mood to do anything,
> but carrying a round bamboo basket [i.e., lunch box] I hurried to work.
>
> It was lucky that the jail gate [i.e., the factory entrance] wasn't
>   closed yet.
> I rushed to the silk reeling workshop where the hot air stings one's skin
> —Who would come if not for the sake of money?
>
> I worked till noon and fed myself cold rice.
> I lowered my head and thought of my husband,
> who, at that time, must be pulling the rickshaw;
> he must be dripping wet with sweat.
>
> My hands never stopped working in the boiling water.
> The afternoon passed, twilight passed;
> when I got off work,
> the street in front of the factory was in deep darkness.
>
> I hurried back home and heard my child crying.
> "Oh, sweetheart, don't ask mama to hold you—
> Mama's whole body aches unbearably.
> Is Daddy back home from rickshaw pulling?
> Mama can cook if he brings rice home."[72]

Some rickshaw pullers were among those immigrants who remained part-time farmers. Men often came to Shanghai and pulled a rickshaw during slack seasons, and then, in busy seasons, went back to their village to farm.[73] They were, as Elizabeth Perry pointed out, "true peasant-workers who kept one foot firmly planted in the countryside while the other ran through the city streets in search of a fare."[74] Mary Gamewell, a foreign resident in Shanghai who wrote about life in the city in the second and third decades of the twentieth century, told of rickshaw coolies "who come to the city in winter from farms and return to them in the spring."[75] These people were mostly from poor Subei counties such as Yancheng and Funing, who had easy access to Shanghai by boat via the Grand Canal.[76]

The 1929–30 investigation into rickshaw pullers in Yangshupu found that the farm back in the home village was one of the three major sources of income for Shanghai's rickshaw families (the other two being, of course, the puller's earnings and the earnings of other family members). Some rickshaw men in the survey had as many as 7–8 mu of land at home, and some had left their family, including wife, children, parents, and siblings, back in the village.[77] Naturally, these pullers had close ties with rural life. As Tim Wright has indicated, "Although [by 1934] many Shanghai rickshaw men had been pulling for ten years, such workers were still not entirely divorced from agriculture, and the supply of labor was often seasonal, reflecting the rhythm of rural life."[78] If the rather vague occupational lines among the urban poor in Shanghai, in which a rickshaw puller could, for instance, simultaneously be a dock coolie and a casual factory worker or vice versa, reflected the struggle of rural immigrants to eke out a living in the city, then the strong rural ties of these rickshaw men indicate that the struggle to become urbanized could be long and arduous. People like this might best be described as semiurbanites.[79]

The Other Side of the Coin

The plight of rickshaw men was an oft-told story. Working the streets no matter what the weather, dressed in rags, shod in straw sandals or sometimes simply barefooted, rickshaw men looked to be not better off than beggars. Much of Shanghai's foreign community believed that "pulling a rickshaw is so strenuous that no puller ever reaches the age of fifty and is past his prime at thirty!"[80] It was also rumored among the Chinese that as a rule rickshaw men were short-lived and would "definitely die after seven years of pulling."[81] A doctor in charge of a missionary hospital where many sick coolies were sent reported in the second decade of the twentieth century that "a large number of the cases brought in are in a state of collapse due to malnutrition and the bad hygienic conditions of their life superadded to the strenuous spasmodic strain they undergo."[82]

A life insurance foundation was established by the Shanghai (Rickshaw) Pullers' Mutual Aid Association (PMAA, or *Renliche huzhuhui*) in 1936 to provide life insurance and disability insurance. Table 5 is based on the report of the first five months of this insurance program. More than 95 per-

Table 5. Insurance Report of the Pullers' Mutual Aid Association of Shanghai, May 1, 1936, to September 30, 1936

	Disability	Death
No. of claimants	5	107

	Age at Time of Death						
	25–29	30–34	35–39	40–44	45–49	50–54	Other Ages
No. of deaths	13	13	12	19	23	12	15

	Causes of Death		
	Contagious and Epidemic Diseases	Digestive Disease	Other Causes
No. of deaths	59	18	30

SOURCE: *Shanghaishi nianjian,* 1937:O:36–37.

cent of the claims were for death, and two-thirds of the dead were middle-aged. According to the report, the average life span of Shanghai's rickshaw pullers was about forty-three years.[83]

The report of the insurance program for the fiscal year August 1936 to July 1937 listed a total of 240 deaths. The causes of the deaths, shown below with the numbers of deaths given in parentheses, in a sense add up to a profile of the lives of Shanghai's rickshaw pullers: enteritis and gastritis (37), cardiac-renal (6), pulmonary disease, and tuberculosis (58), specific infection (61), eye, ear, nose, and throat disease (1), skin and other pyogenic maladies (6), venereal disease (4), wounds and injuries (9), suicide (4), and miscellaneous (54).[84] The most common causes of death—contagious and epidemic diseases—were prevalent in Shanghai's slums. Most of the rickshaw pullers who had their families with them in the city lived in miserable shantytowns located on the immediate outskirts of the International Settlement. Indeed, rickshaw pullers and their families constituted a major part of Shanghai's shantytown dwellers.[85] Pullers who had left their families in the villages usually lived in dormitories provided by rickshaw firms. These were perhaps the most crowded places in this most crowded city of China. A single, cramped loft often housed twenty to fifty men.[86] Digestive disease was another main cause of death, no doubt the result of irregular eating occasioned by the nature of the job and poor diet, which a SMC report described as "extremely bad and rough, without much nutrition, and tasteless."[87] For the fiscal year 1936–37, the PMAA received 5,499 relief cases; 4,925, or about 90 percent, of these cases were caused by sickness or wounds and injuries. The number of relief cases dropped slightly the next year to 5,271; still, about 85 percent (4,504) of the cases were disease and injury related. The most common diseases reported in the PMAA files were similar to the diseases that caused death listed above.

But all the miseries of rickshaw men—the backbreaking work, poor diet, disease, and even the presumably short life—did not prevent peasants from pouring into the city and joining this already much oversupplied labor force. In the short span of five years, from 1934 to 1939, for instance, the number of registered rickshaw pullers (excluding many part-time pullers) in Shanghai increased from fewer than 70,000 to more than 100,000; and this was at the time when rickshaws increasingly became a target of social criticism for being "inhuman" and were increasingly restricted by the authorities who wished to limit the use of these "backward conveyances."[88] The lure of rickshaw pulling reflected the social and economic deterioration of the countryside. As a contemporary author wrote in 1935, "Unemployed peasants abandon the countryside; smiling, they run into the city looking for a rickshaw pulling job thinking they are entering a happy land."[89] For Shanghai's rickshaw men themselves, the "better livelihood" in the city was quite evident.

"PHEASANT RICKSHAWS"

Available sources of information on the lives of Shanghai's rickshaw men are mostly social surveys conducted in the 1930s by the authorities (both the SMC and the Chinese Municipal Social Bureau) and individuals who sympathized with these unfortunate men.[90] Reports of these investigations tended to paint an entirely negative picture of the men's lives. This is largely because of two subjective factors. First, the surveyors were motivated by compassion or by a sense of duty to arouse social concern in order to generate some sort of solution.[91] This led to the second factor: the surveyors (who were officials and intellectuals) tended to look at the pullers' lives from the point of view of the social elite. Unconsciously perhaps, they reported on the rickshaw world in a tone of sympathy mingled with a sense of superiority; the lives of rickshaw men in their descriptions were entirely miserable. If these investigations had been conducted by someone from the villages these pullers had left, the perspective would have been quite different.[92] Still, parts of these reports, especially some original interview records, present information from the other side of the coin and unintentionally explain why countless rural immigrants endured the "miseries" of the rickshaw men's world.

Chen Caitu, a sixty-seven-year-old rickshaw-puller, came to Shanghai in 1895 after a lean year in his home village of Yancheng of Subei. Chen, then in his early thirties and married, left his wife in the village. He first worked as a porter transporting rocks for a while and then, with the help of a friend, got a job pulling a rickshaw. According to Chen, the job, which was not too physically demanding, was a turning point in his life: "From then on my life was better every day. I saved some money, and two or three years later I was able to bring my wife to Shanghai." His misfortune seems mainly to have begun with the family reunion. His wife had bound feet and could not find a job. The couple began a family, and eventually had five sons. Chen could barely feed his family. One by one the children came down with various illnesses and died.[93]

The thirty-six-year-old rickshaw puller Shi Zhilin also hailed from Yancheng. Shi was fortunate to have a wife who worked for the Tongxing Cotton Mill, where she earned 14 silver dollars a month. All six of his children were healthy and helped supplement the family income. His eldest son, fourteen, worked as a floor cleaner in the Tongxing Cotton Mill, earning 10 silver dollars a month; his second son, twelve, was a floor cleaner in the Yihe Cotton Mill, and earned 6 silver dollars a month. To feed these mouths, the family needed 150 *jin* (165 pounds) of rice per month, which cost them 15 silver dollars. Thus the earnings of the two boys were sufficient to cover the cost of this staple. The family knew how to save every cent. Younger children often went out with their mother to pick up firewood chips for cooking and thus saved the expense of fuel. At the time of the interview, Shi Zhilin was quite confident about the future. He planned to send all his children to work in cotton mills when they grew up, except for his fourth son, who was, as the proud father said, "extremely smart" and would be sent to school.[94]

This kind of optimism was not uncommon among Shanghai's rickshaw pullers. It made them appear to be, according to Rena Krasno, who lived in the city in the early 1940s, "a noble breed: uncowed, independent, deriding Fate with gumption." [95] In answer to a curious passenger's question about how a rickshaw man might be successful in Shanghai, a puller replied that there were a number of ways to rise from being a coolie to being comfortable financially (*xiaokang*): "but in the end," the puller said, "the key lies in two words: hard work and thrift." [96] One thing that many desired was to be hired as the puller of a private rickshaw. This usually required a reliable sponsor to reassure the hiring family or the master (*dongjia*) about the puller's background and character. Once hired, the family provided room and board for the puller, plus a monthly wage, which was 5–7 silver dollars late in the second decade of the twentieth century and 10 silver dollars in the early 1930s. This was about equivalent to the wage of a shop clerk. Tips depended on the family's financial situation or goodwill, but there were always some. Work clothing, including a raincoat, were also provided by the employer. Furthermore, traffic tickets were paid by the employer.[97] As mentioned earlier, in the early 1920s there were about 15,000 such private rickshaw pullers in Shanghai.[98]

By virtue of "hard work and thrift" (as the rickshaw man commented), plus knowing and practicing certain tricks of the trade, many pullers of private rickshaws eventually managed to buy a rickshaw or even an entire rickshaw firm (*chehang*). One of the best-known ways for rickshaw men to make the leap from "rags to riches" was to pull a so-called pheasant rickshaw (*yeji che* or *yeji baoche*). In Shanghai slang, anything inauthentic or fraudulent may be called "pheasant" (or "wild chicken," *yeji*).[99] Pheasant rickshaws referred to those registered as private vehicles but actually plied for public hire. In a year or so a shrewd rickshaw puller might be able to save 40–50 silver dollars, enough to purchase a used rickshaw that he might register, often under a false name, as a private vehicle. Since there was risk of being caught by the police, these pullers liked to solicit customers in areas where business offices or brothels were located: they could pretend they were private pullers of wealthy businessmen and were awaiting their masters. Since Shanghai policemen tended to carefully check up on public rickshaws but paid only scant attention to private rickshaws, thousands of men in Republican-era Shanghai made their living as pheasant rickshaw pullers.[100]

It was said that Shanghai's prostitutes used pheasant rickshaws in particular. By hiring a pheasant rickshaw, a prostitute might wander the streets, disguised as a proper lady, which gave her a better chance to watch out for a wealthy customer. Once an ideal customer was "caught," the prostitute let the man sit in "her" rickshaw, and she herself hired another rickshaw to follow. This way the customer was "safely" conveyed (it was not easy for him to run away if he changed his mind) to the brothel or wherever the prostitute resided. As a rule, she paid the puller generously. Prostitutes in Shanghai were nicknamed "pheasants"; thus the term "pheasant rickshaw" connoted the nature of not only the vehicle but its riders as well.[101]

As mentioned earlier, in the International Settlement, where most of the city's rickshaws plied their trade, the SMC restricted the licensing of public rickshaws out of concern for traffic congestion (Fig. 6). In 1934, when registered public rickshaws in the Settlement numbered 9,990 and private rickshaws 12,751, it was estimated that about 20,000 pheasant rickshaws illegally worked the streets.[102] It was common for pullers of private rickshaws to rent out the rickshaw license to the owner of a pheasant rickshaw. Someone who could afford to have a private rickshaw and hire a puller usually did not pay attention to this kind of trifle. Even if by chance a private rickshaw was caught in the street without its license, the master paid the fine and the puller excused himself by saying he had forgotten to bring the license with him.[103]

The next step up from owning a pheasant rickshaw was to own a rickshaw firm. Indeed, for most rickshaw men this was considered the pinnacle of success. According to one investigation in 1934,

> Pulling a pheasant rickshaw, a man can earn an average of $1.50 a day, or $40.00 to $50.00 a month. He pays a license fee of $3.00 and spends $7.00 for food; thus [at the end of the month] he has about $30.00 in his pocket, which is about an elementary schoolteacher's salary. After two or three years' hard work, he can save $1,000.00, or $500.00 at the least. He can then purchase a number of used rickshaws and rent them out at a monthly rate of $6.00. Now the puller himself can relax. Dressing in a long gown and short waistcoat [the traditional attire of a gentleman], he is no longer a laborer but can assume the airs of a capitalist.[104]

This picture is by no means unrealistic. Gu Zhuxuan (1885–1956), a boss of the Green Gang, Shanghai's biggest underworld organization, started his career as a rickshaw coolie. A native of Yancheng, Subei, Gu came to Shanghai at the age of sixteen. For seven years he worked as a rickshaw puller—first for a wealthy family and then on his own as a puller of a rickshaw for hire. By 1918–19, he had saved enough money to buy some rickshaws to rent out. His brother, Gu Songmo, also started his life in Shanghai as a rickshaw puller, and later became one of the ten major contractors (*baotou*) for the French-owned Flying Star (Feixing) Rickshaw Company, which controlled 350 rickshaws.[105] It was contractors like Gu Songmo who later purchased foreign rickshaw firms in the 1920s and turned the rickshaw trade into a Chinese preserve.

Although, as noted earlier, in the official records of the foreign settlements rickshaw licenses were held by only a few firms, in actuality they

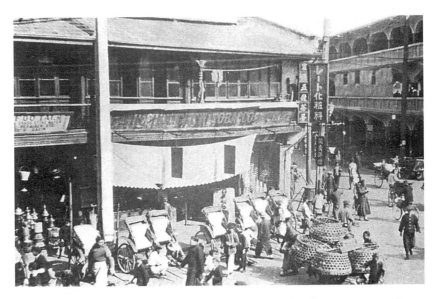

Fig. 6. A rickshaw station on a back-street corner in Hongkou in 1923 stood across the street from the Sanjiaodi Food Market (on the right), Shanghai's largest indoor food market, built in 1916. Note that within this small section of the street are shop signs in Chinese, English, and Japanese. The big bamboo cages on a cart contain domestic fowl for sale; these were usually shipped directly from nearby farms. From R. Barz, *Shanghai: Sketches of Present-Day Shanghai.*

were owned by numerous small rickshaw concerns. In the mid-1930s, Shanghai had 23,306 public rickshaws and 4,814 rickshaw firms, for an average of fewer than 5 rickshaws per firm. In the Chinese districts, the average was fewer than 4 rickshaws per firm. Even in the Settlement where rickshaw firms were in general bigger, the average number of rickshaws per firm did not reach 9.[106] That firms were so small reveals that the owner required little capital. Owners of rickshaw firms, as noted, were often former pullers. They were usually "hard working and thrifty" (*qinjian*) and knew the tricks of the trade. Although not many pullers eventually became owners, still, the success of those who did suggests that there was a degree of social and economic mobility. If the goal of most pullers to become an owner of a rickshaw firm was a dream, a more realistic goal was to hold a "big license," that is, an SMC license. As the playwright Yu Ling, who lived in Shanghai in the 1930s and 1940s, recalled, as long as a puller was able to have (or more accurately, to rent) a rickshaw license for the International Settlement, his income would be much higher than that of an average schoolteacher. This perhaps explains why after the outbreak of the Sino-Japanese War in 1937 some white-collar workers eked out a living by pulling a rickshaw.[107]

EDUCATION: A RAY OF HOPE

As one would expect, rickshaw pullers as a group had little or no schooling. The investigation of 100 rickshaw men in Yangshupu in 1929–30 found none could read; the only literate person was Zhang Baoding, a rickshaw company owner.[108] In another, citywide, survey of 304 rickshaw men, 26 (8.55 percent) were classified as "able to read quite well," 120 (39.47 percent) as "literate," and 158 (51.98 percent) as "illiterate."[109]

The low rate of literacy in no way made rickshaw pullers unusual in a nation that had hundreds of millions of illiterate citizens. Official statistics showed that in 1936–37, China had a population of 286,332,536 illiterates; the proportion of the literate, even by a generous definition that included "all those who had been enrolled on schools at one time or another regardless of the length of attendance," was merely 23.4 percent of the total population.[110]

Yet the great esteem that Chinese society has for education was also a part of the rickshaw pullers' culture. Shi Zhilin's plan of having his favorite son receive a school education reflected the mind-set of rickshaw pullers in general. Ying Wengao, another puller who lived in Yangshupu, expressed great regret for being illiterate. At age forty-three, this rickshaw man still spoke with resentment about his deceased father, an opium addict who sold all the family property for drugs and never provided schooling for his children. Ying was determined to have his children educated, and had managed to send his eldest son to school for a few years.[111] Men like Shi and Ying can be seen as a representative of the deeply rooted tradition that values education as the most important (if not the only) way to climb up the social ladder. And in both cases, the men gave hope to the younger generation.

Here, the city stimulated and supported such hope. A favorite plot in Chinese literature and popular drama was the (ultimately successful) struggle of a son of a poor family, who, by studying hard, passes the imperial civil service examinations and goes on to win a higher degree.[112] But such romantic stories rarely had a peasant as hero. Rural life in general provided little stimulus for the ambition, or, perhaps more likely, such ambition was defeated because it was too remote to be achieved.[113]

In any case, once in Shanghai, poor immigrants found that their views on education and life began to change. The city placed opportunities—almost flaunted them—right before their eyes. But to seize these opportunities usually required some sort of education or skill; hence these former peasants felt the pain of illiteracy, something they had never felt before, or at least not to such a degree, in the villages. Indeed, these rural immigrants ended up pulling a rickshaw precisely because they were uneducated and unskilled, as virtually all social surveys on Shanghai's rickshaw pullers revealed.[114] This naturally provoked the desire for education—in particular, education for the younger generation in order to break this "karma of poverty."[115]

The city not only provoked bitterness for being illiterate; it also offered opportunities for learning that the villages simply could not provide. In a cosmopolitan city like Shanghai, an illiterate rickshaw puller would usually learn to read at least some street signs and numbers, both the Arabic and traditional Chinese numbering (immeasurably useful for recognizing addresses), and pick up some pidgin English (useful when dealing with foreigners).[116] But the opportunities went beyond that.

The Pullers' Mutual Aid Association of Shanghai, founded in 1933, provided educational facilities for its members, all free of charge.[117] The PMAA sponsored seven schools for children of rickshaw pullers and adult school for the pullers themselves. Each branch office of the PMAA had a reading room that subscribed to most major newspapers and pictorials. As a rule, a tea room for relaxation was connected to the reading room. The PMAA also had mobile libraries, each with more than five hundred books.[118] These facilities were well used. In 1937–38, the reading rooms were visited 273,592 times by patrons, and the libraries 101,503 times, for a daily average of 750 patrons for the reading rooms and 278 for the libraries.[119]

In short, rickshaw pullers enthusiastically received these services. No official enrollment figures were recorded for the schools, perhaps because many students attended irregularly. But monthly attendance was impressive: a total of 4,744 attended in August 1937, just before the outbreak of the Sino-Japanese War, which devastated Zhabei and Nanshi, where a number of these schools were located. The enthusiasm for education, moreover, was not extinguished by the war: three schools inside the International Settlement continued classes during the war, with 400 students regularly enrolled. By July 1938, class attendance reached more than 8,000, almost double the prewar level of attendance.[120]

Such enthusiasm for education was actually a tradition among the pullers. In 1927, when for the first time Shanghai's rickshaw pullers organized their own union, which attracted more than 300 members in a few months, the organization set itself the goal of providing its members with a basic education. By that, the organization meant members would learn to read (*shizi*).[121] In the late 1940s, when the PMAA had deteriorated significantly, it was still operating four schools for the children of pullers, with more than 500 students and eleven teachers. Ironically, in the mid-1930s, when the plight of rickshaw pullers had drawn much public attention, the welfare dispensed by the PMAA was criticized for being insufficient; in the postwar era, the PMAA's programs, which had largely disappeared, were nostalgically recalled as part of the "good old days," and the PMAA, with its once-vibrant school system and other services for pullers, was regarded as "the best of Shanghai's labor unions" prior to 1937.[122]

"BEASTS OF BURDEN"

Pulling a rickshaw has been described as "running like cows and horses" (*niu ma zou*).[123] Naturally, the muscle and energy demanded by the job favored the young and healthy. The investigation conducted in 1934 by the Shanghai Social Bureau found that 71 percent of the rickshaw pullers surveyed were between the ages of 26 and 45; the average age was 35.5.[124] Another survey, conducted in 1930, found that 94 percent of the pullers were between the ages of 20 and 40.[125]

However, pullers over the age of 50—sometimes considerably over that age—were also fairly common in Shanghai. For instance, Chen Caitu was laid off at age 59 by the rickshaw company for which he had worked for twenty-seven years. But he still managed to rent a rickshaw from a fellow from his hometown (*tongxiang*), Zhang Dingbao, who owned a rickshaw company and continued this "running like cows and horses" work into his sixties.[126] Another rickshaw man had just started his "urban career" at the time of his interview in 1930—at the age of 62:

> I am now 62 years old. My native place is Yancheng, Jiangsu. My family had five or six mu of land, but all of this land was on the coast of the East [China] Sea. It is now all inundated with the salt water of the ocean.
> In Jiangbei [Subei], I was a tenant and also farmed my own land. But this year there is a famine there, so I, together with my wife, son, and daughter, came to Shanghai looking for a livelihood. Because of my age I could not find a suitable job. I asked Zhang Baoding, who is my tongxiang and an acquaintance, to let me pull a rickshaw, and he agreed. If the policemen see me they would not let me do the work. I therefore have to work in the evening pulling a pheasant rickshaw, which means that each time other pullers are going to end their shift, I go ahead and talk nicely with a puller and ask him to do me a favor by let-

ting me pull the rickshaw for two to three hours, usually from 9 P.M. to midnight, and this way I do not have to pay any rent [for the rickshaw].

When I pull a rickshaw, I wear a big black cap which covers my face leaving only my two eyes uncovered so that I can see the road. Disguised in this way, policemen and customers cannot figure out my age. Each evening I can earn .20 to .30 *xiaoyang* ["small dollar"]. If I earn some money, we can eat rice, otherwise we can only have gruel.

My wife is too old to work. My daughter, who is only ten, is too young to work. My son is fifteen. He is still too young, but, since every mouth in the family needs to be fed, I have sent him to work as an apprentice with a bricklayer—no pay, merely free board.

The house where I am now living belongs to somebody else. The landlord is sympathetic because of my age and lets me live there for free.[127]

The age of 60, known in China as reaching the "cycle" (*huajia*), was considered very old in those days.[128] Yet, in 1955, when Shanghai's rickshaws were finally eliminated, the average age of pullers was 55–60, and the oldest pullers were 77. Some had been rickshaw pullers for more than thirty years, which meant they started pulling in the 1920s.[129] At the other extreme, child rickshaw pullers were also frequently found on the streets. In 1935, this became such an issue that the Shanghai Public Safety Bureau banned the practice for the sake of the "health of children and safety of passengers."[130]

In another depressing case, a one-armed man had made a living in the Settlement pulling a pheasant rickshaw. The son of a rickshaw puller, this unfortunate lost his right arm at the age of nine. Wrestling with his playmates one night, he fell down and broke his arm. Bungled treatment by Chinese physicians brought no relief of the pain and eventually led to the amputation of the fractured arm in "a hospital of the 'redhaired man' type" (that is, a hospital run by foreigners, most likely a missionary hospital). As an adult, despite his handicap, the man still had to work to live. Following in his father's footsteps, he took up rickshaw pulling. By 1934, he had already pulled a rickshaw for eight years.

According to L. Z. Yuan, a columnist for the *Shanghai Evening Post and Mercury*, "Mr. Single-Armed Puller," as Yuan called the man, "has adjusted himself to his calling in a perfect manner." The puller had worked out his own technique for managing a rickshaw: he grasped the left shaft with his left hand and tied a cord fastened to both shafts around his waist, which helped him pull the vehicle. He usually worked after dusk in the so-called amusement park rush so that his handicap might go unnoticed by discriminating patrons who might otherwise turn away. Yuan found the puller "quite willing to talk. In fact, he is proud of himself" for being, as he claimed, the only one-armed rickshaw puller in Shanghai, if not the whole country.[131]

The SMC's new rickshaw puller's licensing legislation, which went into effect on March 1, 1934, was ominous news for Mr. Single-Armed Puller. The legislation required the 40,000 pullers plying the Settlement to be registered in the SMC office (and to pass a physical examination and have their photograph taken) in order to obtain a license.[132] The one-armed puller made no attempt to hide his anxiety over the new regulations. "But he still is plucky," Yuan observed. "The world is never too small for a man who is willing to work, he declared. There you have thousands of cities in China where one may pull a ricsha to earn a living, he said. His immediate plan is to work in Chapei [Zhabei], Nantao [Nanshi] and [the] French Concession[,] where a pullers' license is not necessary—if he is not allowed to work in the International Settlement."[133]

To be sure, it was a callous society that pitied the weak and disadvantaged but did not help them. In fact, Yuan's story was sensational and seemed calculated more to entertain the reader than to arouse compassion. But the fact that the aged and even the handicapped were, no matter how reluctantly, able to pull a rickshaw for a livelihood for a number of years raises the practical question of just how debilitating this job was. Recall that it was widely believed that the rickshaw puller faced not just a miserable life but a short one. In fact, the "professional" life of a rickshaw man, it was said by one source, did not last more than five years.[134]

The idea that pulling a rickshaw was a death sentence sprang mainly from the everyday image of a ragged, sweat-soaked coolie pulling a corpulent, richly dressed customer. This slavelike image was particularly offensive to the eyes of the "gentlemen" who came fresh from the West with the notion that the rickshaw was the classic example of the backwardness of the Orient. Mary Gamewell described how rapidly this fastidiousness disappeared. "It is interesting," Gamewell wrote, "to see how quickly a fresh arrival from the West accustoms himself to ricsha riding. At first he is apt to inveigh against man-drawn vehicles, or if he gets into a ricsha, to sit lightly on the seat, with perhaps one foot hanging out at the side, with the idea of helping the coolie along, but presently he abandons himself to the enjoyment of the little, easy-running carriage, or as one enthusiastic woman described it[,] 'a grown-up's perambulator,' and almost ceases to think of the puller as a human being."[135] When it came to concern for the poor rickshaw puller or saving a few cents, most people were not bothered about being a little hypocritical. Wang Yingxia, wife of the well-known writer Yu Dafu (1896–1945), recalled that her frugal husband preferred to hire a human-drawn vehicle, either a rickshaw or a wheelbarrow, because they were cheap. Yu particularly liked to hire aged pullers, believing that old men knew that they were physically weak and thus would not overcharge the passenger.[136]

For many years there had been talk about the rickshaw being an "inhuman" and "backward" vehicle, and that it should be eliminated.[137] But such talk concerned mostly the "uncivil street scene" that revolved around the rickshaw, with little real care about the pullers or the pragmatic problem of what to do about the thousands of men who would have been put out of work if the rickshaw were banned. Without a real solution for the livelihood of the thousands of pullers, calls for abolishing rickshaws can only be regarded as cheap talk. In fact, in spite of the song and dance, the rickshaw competed with motorized vehicles and served as one of the major means of public transportation in Shanghai for well over half a century.[138] The decline of the rickshaw in the 1940s was essentially not the result of social reform but of a technological innovation: the advent of the pedicab. The pedicab appeared on the streets of Shanghai in 1942 and by 1946 or 1947 had pretty much replaced the rickshaw.[139]

Among the many reasons accounting for the persistence of human-drawn vehicles in Shanghai was that the physical demands on the puller were in fact not overwhelming. Indeed, pulling a rickshaw was less physically demanding than many other forms of coolie labor such as cargo loading and unloading (especially on the docks), brick or rock transporting, boat towing, and many others. Shanghai's dock coolies, for example, commonly carried about 200 pounds of cargo on their shoulders.[140] And pulling a rickshaw was less physically demanding than manhandling other human-drawn vehicles common in Shanghai. A handcart coolie, according to the Shanghailander John Pal, "most of the time, is called upon to put about four times the poundage per square inch into his daily toil than required of a rickshaw coolie when plying for hire. The wheelbarrow-pusher, on his part, raised steam to the tune of six or seven times that of the rickshaw coolie."[141] One must also bear in mind that, as noted earlier, rickshaw pulling was not necessarily a heavier job than farming. Lai Qigeng, a former rickshaw puller, said that he considered rickshaw pulling a light job because in his home village in Taixing, Subei, he used to carry a 250-jin (276-pound) load on a bamboo pole balanced on his shoulder, as he hobbled along the narrow ridges between fields.[142]

While some foreigners—and Chinese too—were uneasy about riding in a rickshaw, more sober-minded ones shared the point of view of the journalist Ernest Hauser, who observed that "pulling a rickshaw, in itself, is not a hard work. Rickshaws are constructed cleverly. They have a built-in balance that takes care of the puller's weight from the waist up whenever he pulls a normal-sized passenger. That gives the legs a lot of independence and, on a downhill pull, the coolie's feet seem hardly to touch the ground." [143] John Pal had even tried pulling a rickshaw himself:

> To rickshaw-runners of quite ordinary physique, trundling a rickshaw offers very little hardship. It is merely a matter of "balance", as I have tried and discovered. I once lost an election wager and by way of payment had to drag a newspaper colleague the full length of Nanking Road by rickshaw in broad daylight, wearing an opera hat and holding a twelve inch cigar in my mouth all the way. Once the shafts have been raised, the weight of a passenger is transferred to the wheels and, after a good heave and a trot, the rickshaw runs itself on level ground. And in most of China's great cities, particularly the treaty ports, the ground is very level. Shanghai's highest "hill" was merely an arched stone bridge in the centre of the city across the celebrated Soochow [Suzhou] Creek, where there were always strong Chinese urchins waiting to grasp the shafts and help haul your rickshaw over the hump for a couple of coppers.[144]

Perhaps such accounts can be dismissed as mere anecdotes. But not the research of Adolph Basler, the director of the Physiological Institute of Sun Yat-sen University in Guangzhou. Basler undertook meticulous research on the energy expended by the rickshaw man and published the results in New York–based *Science* magazine. Based on his observations on rickshaw locomotion in busy streets and his application of mechanics to the observations, Basler found that when pulling a rickshaw under normal street conditions, the double step of a puller was from 4 to 6.5 feet and the number of paces per minute varied between 76 and 87. Basler pointed out that the design of the rickshaw was such that during motion the center of gravity was over the axle, which required the puller to exert no force upwards, but allowed him to apply all his power to pulling. Thus, once inertia was overcome and the rickshaw was rolling on level ground, the puller needed only to overcome the resistance of friction. In line with other data on frictional resistance, pulling an occupied rickshaw required overcoming a resistance of 4 to 11 pounds, depending on the nature of the ground. Basler concluded that both the amount of external work per minute and the duration for which it could be maintained were the same as if the puller were drawing a cord over a pulley, the end of which was fastened to a weight of 4 to

11 pounds, which required exertion "less than that of the Egyptians who lift water from the Nile, while themselves standing still, or that of French navies ascending a ladder."[145]

These observations, no matter how solidly based they were, could easily run the risk of being criticized as unsympathetic, or, in the Maoist idiom, as "bourgeois anti–working class nonsense."[146] A Chinese proverb, "There is no light load if one has carried it for a hundred paces" (*baibu wu qingdan*), may also be quoted to justify such criticism. But two facts must be noted here. One is that most rickshaw pullers did not work every day but every other day; thus each day of labor was balanced by a day of rest. The other is the generally short distance of the typical rickshaw trip.

As we have seen, the limit on the number of licensed rickshaws made fifteen or sixteen shifts per month the normal full-time work load for a puller. And on average, "pulling a rickshaw for one day earned two days of livelihood."[147] Although, as we have also seen, sometimes factory casual workers pulled the "leftover" shift or "the buttocks of rickshaw" to supplement their income, all of the intensive surveys on rickshaw pullers conducted in the 1930s mention nothing about pullers getting other unskilled work during their off hours.[148] Practically speaking, this every-other-day work schedule allowed a puller to rest and get ready for the next shift.

As for the typical trip by rickshaw being quite short, this was related to the layout of the city and the availability of a good system of public transportation for longer trips. In particular, after the introduction of trams, trolleys, and buses early in the twentieth century, rickshaws were mainly used to get to places not easily accessible to mechanized conveyances.[149] Given the physical layout of Shanghai, many destinations were located in small, winding streets and narrow alleyways. The International Settlement covered only about 8.7 square miles (22.60 square kilometers). The French Concession was merely 3.9 square miles (10.22 kilometers).[150] From the Bund at the east end of the Settlement to Bubbling Well Road on the west end was barely 3 miles. Most rickshaw trips were less than this distance.[151] From the North Railway Station in Zhabei to any part of the city was considered a long-distance trip, and many rickshaw pullers were unwilling to take a customer that far, although from the railway station to most parts of the city was less than 3 miles.[152]

The divided city administration of Shanghai made long-distance trips impossible for many pullers. There were three types of licenses for public rickshaws in Shanghai. The first type was obtained by registering in the Settlement. As mentioned earlier, the SMC restricted the number of licenses to a total of 8,000 in 1920 and 9,990 in the 1930s. Those who possessed an SMC license had the privilege of paying additional fees to obtain licenses permitting the rickshaw to ply the French Concession and the Chinese districts. Pullers commonly called these "big licenses" (*da zhaohui*).[153] The second type (known as "small licenses," *xiao zhaohui*) permitted the rickshaw to work in both the French Concession and the Chinese areas but not in the Settlement. There were 1,800 rickshaws with such licenses in 1920, and 6,014 in 1934. The third type was valid in Chinese-administered areas only. Two thousand rickshaws had such licenses in 1920 and 7,302 in 1934.[154] The Chinese licenses were further divided into those valid in Zhabei only and in Nanshi only; additional permission and fees were required for plying the railway station. Thus most rickshaws in Shanghai operated in one or two areas. If the passenger's destination was in another area, he or she would have to alight from the rickshaw at the boundary and find another, suitably licensed, rickshaw. For example, if a passenger hired a rickshaw (with a small license) in Avenue Joffre in the French Concession and wanted to go to Nanking Road in the International Settlement, upon arrival at the Great World (Shanghai's most popular entertainment center) the passenger had to alight and find a rickshaw with a "big license" to take him or her the rest of the way. This of course inconvenienced the passenger but helped ensure that most rickshaw trips would be short.[155]

Those who investigated the living conditions of rickshaw men complained of the difficulty of interviewing pullers since it was hard to find them at home. From what we have seen, we know this was definitely not because pullers worked inordinately long hours. On the contrary, most pullers found themselves with ample free time on their hands. When not working, rickshaw men often went out to teahouses or bathhouses for relaxation, dropped by neighbors' homes for a chat, or simply stayed home and slept.[156] Gambling was the foremost popular entertainment for rickshaw pullers. A card game known as *puke* (a name derived from poker) and mah-jongg were especially popular. These games could be played anywhere, but most often were enjoyed with a few neighbors or friends gathered in one's home.

Outside the home, the teahouses frequented by rickshaw pullers offered a relaxed place to chat, gamble, or listen to Suzhou storytellers.[157] Opium addiction was also common among rickshaw pullers, partly because, it was said, they needed the drug to unlock the energy required in their job. Cheap and inferior opium was always available for sale in many of the city's back alleys.[158] The squalid opium dens that peppered rickshaw pullers' neighborhoods were usually full of men sleeping off the effects of their indulgence.[159] It was estimated that in the second decade of the twentieth century 20 to 30 percent of Shanghai's rickshaw pullers were opium addicts, and that they typically spent 70 to 80 percent of their earnings on the drug.[160]

A variety of entertainments for the poor was also available literally on the street corners. For instance, a homesick puller could easily cheer himself up by attending Jiangbei opera, which was often performed in open spaces in the city's back streets. Shanghai was crawling with itinerant entertainers of all sorts; in the popular parlance, such people made their living by "eating the rice of the rivers and lakes [i.e., they were vagrants]" (*chi jianghu fan*) or "eating rice by opening the mouth" (*chi kaikou fan*). Their audiences were of course any passersby, but most were laborers who found street entertainment to be to their taste, available anytime, and affordable—no ticket was needed and the entertainers only collected donations after the show. Although itinerant entertainers could be found anywhere in the city's busy commercial districts and crowded working-class neighborhoods, they gathered at a few popular spots in particular.

The entertainers who regularly performed on the Rue Hennequin (An'-nanjin Road) in the French Concession, for example, caused the place to be nicknamed "The Great World of Subei" (*Jiangbei dashijie*), a name suggesting that this was the "Great World" (*Dashijie*) (Shanghai's foremost popular entertainment center; see Fig. 9 in next chapter) of the poor.[161] Also in the French Concession, a few blocks southeast of the Great World and the Bridge of the Eight Immortals (*Baxianqiao*), was perhaps the largest open-air entertainment area in Shanghai. Streets running off the Rue Soeur Allegre, the Rue de Peres, the Rue de Saigon, Ningpo Road, and others were full of many different types of popular divertissements.[162] One could find monodrama (*dujiaoxi*), comic dialogue, storytelling, Chinese and Western magic shows, conjuring, sleight of hand, sung stories accompanied by a drum (*dagu*), flower-drum songs (*huaguxi*, a popular north China form), stunt cycling, modern drama (*huaju*), peep shows (*Xiyangjing*), puppet plays, sword play, tightrope walking, animal fighting, fortune-telling (*shuo yinguo*), qigong (breathing exercise) shows, sword swallowing, fire eating, monkey shows, freak shows, and various types of "talking and singing" shows (*shuochang*). Almost all types of entertainment offered in the more fashionable amusement centers in the city could also be found here, as well the "lower-class" type of diversions that were unavailable elsewhere. And, just as some commercial streets in the city specialized in a certain product or service, popular entertainments were clustered by type in one or another section of a street, making a tour of a few streets very much like wandering in the Great World.[163] Every day from noon to late evening, such places were full of working-class people or, as they were called by a more bookish but fashionable name in the 1930s, the *puluo* (proletariat).[164]

In sum, the design of the rickshaw, the puller's limited working hours (which allowed rest and recreation), and the short-distance service in one way or another explain why many rickshaw men could work for decades without collapsing and why some aged men were still able to pull a rickshaw for a living. The relatively manageable physical demands of pulling a rickshaw and the little skill required may also explain, at least partially, the lure of this calling for the tens of thousands of unskilled rural immigrants who flooded into the city. These factors may provide a context for appreciating some street scenes described by contemporary witnesses, which were not entirely gloomy but somewhat upbeat. "The green light is switched on," an author wrote of an everyday street scene in Shanghai in about 1940. "The rickshaws start dashing on like Marathon runners. They try frantically to beat the motorcars by a length before the next red light stops them again. Often they succeed, winding their way through the traffic that handicaps the bigger vehicles in their progress. That is the coolies' fun— then they can laugh and joke and tease the uniformed conductors of official traffic."[165]

Was this observation a rare scene portrayed by an indifferent bystander? It seems not. Rena Krasno, a Russian Jew whose family had lived in Republican Shanghai for many years, recorded in her diary in March 1944 an almost identical and even more cheerful picture of rickshaw pullers: "Before the [Pacific] War, rickshaw men often laughed, joked, and dashed like marathon runners, surging forward when the traffic light turned green. They had fun trying to outwit bicycles, motorcycles, and carriages and concentrated their strength upon moving swiftly forward, weaving cunningly through Shanghai's disorganized traffic."[166]

FLEECING THE CUSTOMER

Rickshaw pullers' fleecing of passengers was a classic example of the cheating and extortion that prevailed in modern Shanghai. According to a popular, if not universal, stereotype, rickshaw pullers often cheated or overcharged customers, especially those who did not know the city well. The fleecing of passengers, or in Shanghai slang, *qiao zhugang* (lit., knocking with a bamboo stick), was an all-too-common tale. On one hand, since the great majority of pullers came from Subei, this stereotype reflected the general bias against Subei people in Shanghai.[167] On the other hand, that fleecing was in fact common may well have contributed to the bias against Subei people in the first place. Virtually all guidebooks on Shanghai published in the 1930s, if they had a section on rickshaws, warned readers of devious rickshaw pullers.

In due time, the stereotype of the dishonest puller became a part of the city's culture—like the multilayered crime, vice, shady deals, and gangsterism that made modern Shanghai world famous as a city of sin. Like taxi drivers in many cities of the world who unconsciously serve as a window through which new visitors get their first impression of the people of the city, the thousands of rickshaw pullers who plied Shanghai streets day and night were one of the most visible incarnations of the city's culture.

A sophisticated Shanghailander, or what was known as an "old Shanghai hand" (*lao Shanghai*), having a sound knowledge of the streets and the structure of fares, was unlikely to be cheated. But fledgling riders and newcomers who did not know Shanghai well were ripe for the picking. By a customer's accent a rickshaw puller could easily identify who had long been in Shanghai and who had not. In spite of their rural origins and ties, and although many of them were often regarded as "country bumpkins," rickshaw pullers were snobbish toward newcomers from the hinterlands. Pullers tended to disdain "hinterlanders" (*waidiren*) or simple "country folk" (*xiangxiaren*), disregarding the fact that many were not from a rural background at all.[168] The common and uncomplicated ways of cheating were exactly what one might imagine. A rickshaw puller might charge double or triple the normal rate, or he might intentionally take an unnecessarily roundabout route in order to secure a higher fare. Since by custom the fare was paid at the end of the trip, when the customer wanted a round-trip a puller might agree to a low fare at the start, but at end of the trip insist that the fare be doubled because, he would say, the price he gave was for a one-way trip, only the customer had misunderstood him.[169]

Even after paying, a passenger might still be swindled. A trick known as the "switch" (*diaobao*) or "shifting money" (*diao yuanbao*) was one of the commonest flimflams. Rickshaw pullers sometimes carried a counterfeit silver dollar made of copper with silver-plating. When a passenger paid the fair and was about to leave, the puller quickly switched the counterfeit coin for the passenger's authentic silver dollar. The puller would then shout, "Hey, the dollar you gave me is a fake." The real coin was hidden in the puller's jacket, which had a cleverly hidden hole underneath the third button. If a suspicious passenger questioned the puller's honesty, the puller would unbutton his jacket and ask the customer to search him as he pleased. But no one could ever find the hidden coin: as the puller was opening his jacket with one of his hands, he naturally grasped the garment right over the spot where the coin was hidden. Pullers might also hide money in the tarpaulin or the sidelights of the vehicle. If a rickshaw puller was lucky, he could use this ruse to "shift" as many as twenty dollars a day. Few customers knew the trick and, since counterfeit money was quite common, they tended to accept the puller's claim.[170]

It was also inescapable that rickshaw pullers took advantage of certain situations to charge unreasonable fares. For instance, it was customary that at the end of a visit, a hospitable host would hire a rickshaw as a courtesy for the guest, especially if the guest was a woman or was elderly. Unless the host had negotiated a fare out of the presence of the guest, the puller would always ask for a higher price because he knew very well that a host would not want to haggle in front of a guest. Often the guest would insist on paying, and the host and guest would then politely "struggle" over who would pay. On such occasions, naturally the puller would eagerly demand a high fare.[171]

In other ways, too, pullers took advantage of the customs of polite society. One writer described what happened to him when he disembarked from a ship at the dock of the Chinese Bund in the Nanshi district in autumn 1937.[172] The "petty bourgeois," as the author derisively called himself, could not find a taxi, and although he had only a small suitcase, he knew that it was improper for a gentleman to trudge down the street carrying a bag. The rickshaw pullers knew this too. The traveler approached one of them:

> "Rickshaw! To the French Concession!"
> "Three dollars!" the rickshaw puller answered in a snobbish tone as if he were insulted by being hired. He then told [the traveler] that a war was going on, clearly implying that he would take advantage of the situation. No matter what the destination, "three dollars" was the minimum. Why should you expect him to be fair? In Shanghai, the hooligan's world, nothing is fair.[173]

A Chinese author, using the pen name Biweng, exclaimed that the "pure and innocent" nature that pullers brought with them from the countryside was distorted by the prosperity of Shanghai. For instance, a customer who needed a rickshaw urgently (because of, say, a medical emergency) or who had heavy luggage rarely escaped the clutches of the unscrupulous puller. By the same token, rainy days were always good business days for pullers. "Rickshaw pullers," Biweng wrote, "are always soliciting your business, but when it is raining, it is perhaps your turn to solicit them. In that event, the puller may ignore your call, lowering his head, pulling an unoccupied rickshaw and pretending he doesn't hear you. This is their tactic—after this pretense you won't be able to negotiate the fare. When you loudly call him back, he first glances to see if you are wearing leather shoes or have an umbrella. If you don't have either, it is time for him to fleece you and demand what fare he will." [174]

Knowing how to negotiate a rickshaw fare was virtually a must for the people of Shanghai. As a rule, before climbing into the rickshaw, the would-be passenger "had to state his destination almost to the exact yard, and sometimes the travelling directions required plenty of clarification before the puller would commit himself. He required a clear mental picture of the spot where his fare intended to alight. Having got this he then named his fare, and the next few moments generally developed into a walking argument along the curbside until one or the other gave way. Only then did the journey begin." [175] Invariably it seemed, pullers asked an unreasonably high take and passengers retaliated by "chopping the price in half" (*sha banjia*); that is, the passenger's first offer was only half of what the puller asked. From this bottom line the fare was negotiated. But even after the two parties reached an agreement, the journey did not always end without further arguments over the fare or destination. The puller might stop a few yards or a couple of blocks short of the destination and say that this was where he thought the customer wanted to go. Whether this was the result of a misunderstanding or a deliberate trick on the part of the puller, or of the passenger, an argument might ensue. John Pal, a longtime resident of Shanghai, graphically portrayed what could happen next: [176]

> "You said this is where you wanted to go," he would say to the fare, emphasizing the remark by dropping the shafts of the rickshaw to the ground.
>
> The fare most probably countered by retorting: "You're mistaken. It's another couple of blocks further on."
>
> "I'm not mistaken," the coolie would splutter back. "You cheated me."
>
> "I didn't cheat you. You're probably some country bumpkin who doesn't know this city very well."
>
> "I'm a third generation rickshaw-runner in this place and I don't like being cheated."
>
> "You're a fool. No one is trying to cheat you. You haven't yet reached the place I told you."

"Don't call me a fool! This is as far as I'm taking you for the twelve
coppers we agreed upon. So hand me money and let me get about my
business, or shall I call a policeman?"

"I'll pay you when we reach the place I said."

"Well, I'm not taking you a yard further for twelve coppers. If you
want to pay fourteen coppers I'll take you two more blocks. If not, pay
up and let me go."

Such arguments were likely to end up in victory for the puller: the fare either paid the difference or got off the rickshaw and walked to his or her destination. Even if the argument proceeded to the point of bodily assault,
which was not uncommon if the fare was a man, a third party would always
come out to mediate, saying something like one should not get into a hag-
gling match with a coolie, or other words intended to make peace, and to
end the unpleasantness the passenger would pay up.[177]

Disputes like these seldom occurred if the customer was a foreigner. As
a rule, foreigners (or more accurately, Westerners) paid more than Chinese
did,[178] not just because they "leaned to the side of mercy" but also because
in general they were heavier than Chinese and usually asked the puller to
run faster than did Chinese.[179] The Shanghai rickshaw man usually did not
negotiate the fare with a foreigner in the first place. All he needed to know
was "Where go, marster?"[180] The author Biweng complained that in the
busiest commercial sections of Nanking Road or in front of theaters, "you
can never hire a rickshaw unless you pretend that you are a rich man (*kuo-
lao*) who will ride without negotiating the fare. But if you happen to be
walking with a foreigner, your chance of getting a rickshaw is even smaller,
because [the coolie's] whole attention is concentrated on the hope of pulling this foreign God of Wealth (*yang caishen*)."[181] Foreigners also noted
the pullers' preference for Western customers. "Time and again when on
the lookout for a public rickshaw I came upon one in the throes of arranging a contract with a Chinese," Pal wrote. "In a flash all negotiations were
broken off and the rickshaw placed at my feet with a grin and a 'Where to,
marster?'"[182]

But to the pullers' dismay, there were different kinds of *waiguoren* (foreigners). Worthless (*xialiu*) foreigners sometimes paid little or even nothing, rushing into a foreign-owned firm, hotel, bar, dance hall, home, or
other place where a fierce and arrogant doorman or policeman would bar
the desperate puller's way.[183] As early as December 29, 1874, only a few
months after rickshaws had started operating in Shanghai, two foreigners
took a rickshaw to Sanyangjing Bridge at the northern boundary of the

French Concession and left without paying; when the puller tried to collect his fare, one of them threatened him with a knife.[184] This was just the earliest instance of foreigners' bullying of pullers in Shanghai. Most of those who refused to pay were foreign seamen. In a number of cases reported in the 1930s and 1940s, pullers who insisted on getting their fare were brutally beaten or even killed; without exception the bullies were seamen from England, Spain, Italy, and America.[185]

The most publicized case involved Zang Dayaozi, a forty-three-year-old rickshaw man who, on the night of December 22, 1946, took a Spanish seaman on a five-mile ride from Hongkou to the former French Concession. The sailor refused to pay; when Zang insisted on his fare, the seaman's companion, an American bluejacket, struck and killed Zang. The incident quickly became headline news nationwide, especially since it symbolized the Nationalist government's impotence in dealing with Western outrages in China.[186]

Zang Dayaozi was one of the few rickshaw men who had the nerve to argue with foreign toughs. Zang actually waited for hours in front of the Anlegong (lit., palace of peace and pleasure) dance hall where the Spaniard had entered, and approached him after he had had enough fun and was drunkenly staggering out of the building. But in this treaty-port city, Zang's nerve and anger only led to his tragic death, after he had pulled a rickshaw in Shanghai for twenty years.[187] Most pullers did not dare insist on their fare from a foreign tough who refused to pay—most likely they would do no more than spit or curse. This was partly because of the language barrier no doubt, but even more because of the general awe with which foreigners were regarded. Biweng once nastily denounced what he believed to be rickshaw pullers' blind worship of foreigners: "Their knowledge is so superficial that they only know that all foreigners are rich. They can't even tell who are the Jews (who are much stingier than the Chinese) or the White Russians (who do not have a nationality and are even poorer than the Chinese). They treat them all like people from England and America. They are so silly that they just bend down in front of the foreigners like a hen trying to mate! They are full of pidgin English—nonsense like Mai-da-mu [Madame], Mai-si-dan [Master], li-ke-xi [rickshaw]. It just makes you laugh."[188] Since the majority of Shanghai's rickshaw pullers came from Subei, Biweng's attack can be seen as part of the popular prejudice against Subei people; or, conversely, the concentration of Subei people in rickshaw pulling and their everyday presence on the streets can be seen as contributing to such prejudice.[189] In all fairness, revering the West, or *chongyang* (worshiping things foreign), was part of the city's culture; rick-shaw pullers' preference for foreign customers was just an undisguised part of that culture.

To some extent rickshaw pullers were not ignorant but well informed. Plying the streets of the "Paris of the East," they witnessed a great many aspects of life in the city and daily heard its rhythms. Their job involved dealing with a variety of people: negotiating to rent a rickshaw from an owner or a middleman, bargaining with customers, arguing with the police, chatting with friendly or talkative customers along the way. Pullers were, as a local saying had it, people who "know the market and situation" (*ling shimian*),[190] and they were much more cosmopolitan than, say, factory workers, who in their twelve-hour daily shifts were confined to a dark workshop and probably talked with no one.

That Zang Dayaozi had the gumption to demand his fare from a for-eigner was perhaps related to the deterioration of the position of the for-eign powers in this treaty-port city: first as a result of the Japanese oc-cupation of the International Settlement and the French Concession in December 1941, which was followed by the abolition of the foreign con-cessions in 1943; and second, as a result of Japan's defeat, which occurred only a year before Zang's murder. Biweng's indignant comment on rick-shaw pullers' blind subservience to all foreign passengers might have been well grounded in December 1940, but it became less accurate after the out-break of the Pacific War. In March 1944 a Russian Jew commented that "rickshaw coolies are insolent, aggressive, almost threatening, knowing full well that foreign customers are powerless today. The few that still lord it over the rest—the Germans and other Axis members—are usually suf-ficiently well off to use chauffeured motorcars. In any case, after years on the streets the coolies can quickly differentiate between foreigners, know-ing almost instinctively whom they can harass without fear of retribu-tion."[191] This comment and that of Biweng were written only three years apart, but they convey startlingly different images. While subjectivity (if not bias) to some extent always enters into observations such as these, the differences in this case may also reflect the fact that rickshaw pullers in Shanghai were not as ignorant and benighted as commonly thought, but were informed and quick to size up the situation.

Rickshaw men were compelled to "know the market and situation" in order to survive. In this regard they were not different from any other so-cial type in the city—say, the astute businessman whose plush offices over-looked the famous British Race Course at the center of the city or the shrewd street peddler who regularly set up his stand in a corner of the old

Temple of the City God in Nanshi. The most significant aspect of the story of the rickshaw was that this simple vehicle had transformed peasants into "petty traders" who, with their muscles as their only commodity for sale, daily involved themselves in endless marketing (soliciting customers in the streets) and bargaining (over the fares with customers and over the rents with rickshaw owners). Like anyone else who entered the market for business, a rickshaw man was compelled to play his role actively, seek his opportunities wherever they lay, and stand firm for his rights. He had to deal with people of all walks of life in a "cash business" every day. In his home village he might have been a tenant farmer, selling labor to a landlord. In the rickshaw business, however, the intense bargaining, the diversity of the clientele, and the frequent business opportunities were beyond the wildest imagination of a rural inhabitant. Thus the former peasant had to quickly shed his simplicity in order to become part of the challenging yet promising urban life. In short, in this highly commercialized urban society, rural immigrants were made into petty traders of all sorts. In turn, these "small potatoes" became the true brickwork of the commercial world and its culture we call "Shanghai."

PART 2

A PLACE TO STICK AN AWL

CHAPTER 3

Escaping the Shantytown

Modern Shanghai was often described by romantic sobriquets such as "the Paris of the East," "the bright pearl of the Orient," and "a paradise for adventurers."[1] The stylish architecture on the famous Bund and Nanking Road served as a proud symbol of this great metropolis. Much less noted was another, darker and less romantic, aspect of urban growth in modern Shanghai: that is, the countless filthy straw huts chaotically thrown together into dozens of shantytowns. From the plate glass windows of the skyscrapers in the bustling downtown area, virtually wherever one looked one's eyes fell on "the Orient's most scrofulous slums."[2] It is proper to say that, like the Bund skyline, the shantytowns were a symbol of modern Shanghai, or, as Emily Honig has put it, "another of Shanghai's distinctive worlds."[3]

By 1950 Shanghai's squatter areas were home to roughly one-fifth of the city's population. The overwhelming majority of the shanty dwellers were rural immigrants who, in the sense that they now lived in the city and eked out a meager existence by various callings that were available only in the city, had become urban. But the incredibly congested and miserable living conditions of the city's shack settlements and the high unemployment and underemployment rates there made their inmates, in the eyes of other people of the city, "urban outcasts," in the sense that they were unsettled rural immigrants. For these people, factory jobs were highly coveted but almost beyond reach. Industrial workers, who are generally regarded as constituting the majority of slum residents in modern industrial cities, formed merely a minority of Shanghai's shantytown dwellers.

Why were the large shantytowns of China's largest industrial city not predominately inhabited by industrial proletarians? This question leads us to the matter of the social stratification among Shanghai's factory workers.

While temporary employment in the form of a low-paid factory job could not save a rural immigrant from the fate of squatting in a shack neighborhood, those who managed to obtain stable and better-paid factory jobs fled the shantytowns and settled in the city's "average" neighborhoods, where the middle and lower-middle classes lived. Thus, the search for one's niche in the urban structure—or, as the Chinese put it, the search for "a place to stick an awl" (*li zhui zhi di*)—resulted in comparatively unusual residential patterns. The patterns of where people lived, and the contours of their material, social, and cultural lives, render the conventional category "industrial worker," or proletarian, a gross oversimplification.

A Museum of Global Architecture

Modern Shanghai was a city rich in architecture style. Not surprisingly, imposing Western-style edifices made up some of the city's most eye-catching landmarks. Merely a decade after the city's opening as a treaty port, the Bund featured a mile-long string of European-style buildings. By the 1920s, the influence of British, American, French, German, Russian, Italian, Spanish, Norwegian, and Dutch architecture on Shanghai architecture was obvious. Imitations of European architectural styles ranged from Roman classic, baroque, and Renaissance to modern and contemporary designs. The urban landscape was further embellished by Japanese-style structures and even by a few Islamic-style buildings. Many of these imported styles were modified by or integrated with elements of traditional Chinese design, making eclecticism the order of the day. At the same time, traditional Chinese architecture survived. Less than a mile south of the Bund were the authentic Chinese structures of the old city, as well as the classic Ming-dynasty garden, Yuyuan, completed in 1577 by the Confucian scholar Pan Yunduan for entertaining his parents (Fig. 7).[4] "A museum of global architecture" (*Wanguo jianzhu bolanguan*)—another epithet applied to Shanghai—well matched the reality.[5]

When it came to housing, a wide variety of types was available, depending on one's tastes and pocketbook. Like most places in the world, the neighborhood in which one lived, and even the style of one's residence, reflected one's status. In general, residential dwellings in Shanghai can be divided into three broad categories: Western-style houses, alleyway houses, and shanties. Each category subsumed a variety of types (or subgroups) that differed in one way or another from each other but nevertheless shared some common distinguishing characteristics.

Western-style, or foreign-style, houses (*yangfang*), as the name implied,

Fig. 7.   This teahouse at the center of the old Chinese city was
built in 1784. Known among the Chinese as the "pavilion in the
middle of a lake," and among Westerners as the "willow-pattern
teahouse," this edifice and its zigzag bridge have together been a
symbol of Shanghai's old Chinese city since the late nineteenth
century. From R. Barz, *Shanghai: Sketches of Present-Day
Shanghai.*

referred to European-style detached, multifloor homes with a front garden. Hence this type was also known as a "Western-style garden house" (*hua-yuan yangfang*).[6] This was by far the most luxurious type of housing in Shanghai; many such houses were truly extravagant even by Western standards of the time, and, like extravagant homes elsewhere in the world, they often served as proud symbols of the city. They were, however, largely irrelevant to the lives of ordinary people.

The second category consisted of a sort of terraced house known as the alleyway house (*lilong*), the homes of the majority of Shanghainese. From the early 1870s to the late 1940s, alleyway houses were built in abundance all over the city. The quality of any particular house depended on how much skill and money the builders wished to invest, and over the years the design was modified in various ways, but the essential characteristics of the lilong—a row house that combined both European and Chinese features, usually situated within a gated compound—remained unchanged. Most of the alleyway houses built before 1935 were known as *shikumen* (roughly translatable as "stone portal," a name derived from the design of its front door; see for example the design of the front door of the pawnshop shown in Fig. 8). Shikumen are the single most common residential housing type in twentieth-century Shanghai.[7]

Competing with shikumen were the so-called new-style alleyway houses (*xinshi lilong*), which came on the market in the early 1920s and soon made shikumen old-fashioned (hence the latter also came to be known as the "old-style alleyway house"). Most of the new-style alleyway houses were built between 1924 and 1938. One of their most distinguishing features was that the front door could have a variety of patterns and often reflected European taste, so to speak. This was in contrast to the plain (and somewhat monotonous) front door of shikumen, which was always two planks of wood set within a stone or concrete framework. Inside, the new type of house had sanitary fixtures (such as bathtubs and flush toilets), which most shikumen houses lacked. The new-style alleyway house also usually had steel-sash windows and polished (waxed) wooden floors; these could not be found in the shikumen house, which made do with wooden sash windows and floors painted in deep red or dark reddish brown. Thus, in time the new-style alleyway house came to be known as *gangchuang ladi* (steel-sash windows and waxed floors).

Some alleyway houses featured a tree-lined front garden and a garage at the back lane and were regarded as a type of yangfang (foreign-style house); these were known as "garden alleyway houses" (*huayuan lilong*).

Fig. 8.   This shikumen housed a pawnshop named "Perpetual Prosperity." The gigantic characters on either side of the entrance read *DANG* (Pawn), a standard pawnshop sign in Shanghai, usually painted in black on a white wall. People commonly pawned clothing and jewelry, but a sign on the wall shows that this pawnshop also accepted high-quality wooden furniture. Courtesy of Shanghai Municipal Library.

These exquisite homes were definitely the elite of alleyway houses. Yet another type of elite home, known as "new-style apartments" (*Xinshi gongyu*), referred to either buildings with large, multistory apartments, or new-style houses built as flats. Often, in a compound of new-style alleyway houses, the front row facing the street was built in the apartment style, and the inside rows were built in the alleyway-house style. Many of these luxurious homes were erected in the 1940s as a result of Shanghai's wartime prosperity.

The third category of Shanghai dwellings consisted of bungalow-type, single-story houses (*pingfang*) and straw shacks. The single-story house originated in the countryside (and it remains the most common type in rural China). In Shanghai such houses were built to serve as factory dormitories or dwellings for the poor. The inferior structure of these houses did not allow construction of a second floor, and the houses often lacked running water and electricity. Most of them were composed of a single room or, sometimes, a single room divided into a few compartments by wooden boards. If the structure allowed, a loft might be built under the roof. These houses were found particularly in Yangshupu, Zhabei, and Caojiadu, that is, the industrial areas of the city. They were also found in large quantity in Pudong (on the east side of the Huangpu River).[8]

Mixed with the single-story pingfang in poor neighborhoods were straw shacks. A single-story house was made of brick nogging (a rough brick infill within a wooden frame) and had a tile roof, while a straw shack was a thatched hut constructed of no more than bamboo, straw, and mud. But both types were considered inferior and no more than slum dwellings.

All these different types of residential housing intricately coexisted in this metropolis. Although there were no rigid boundaries between the areas in which each particular type of housing was found, a general picture of the distribution of housing in the city can be drawn.

The west and southwest corners of Shanghai contained the city's best residential areas. Most of the yangfang and new-style alleyway houses were found here. Along Bubbling Well Road (today called Nanjingxi Road), the major thoroughfare in west Shanghai, and stretching all the way to Yuyuen (Yuyuan) Road and up to Jessfield Park (today's Zhongshan Park) on the northwest edge of the city, there were numerous new-style alleyway houses and high-quality shikumen. To the south of Bubbling Well Road, along the tree-lined Rue Lafayette (today's Fuxingzhong Road) and Avenue Petain (today's Hengshan Road), and in their vicinity, were gathered most of the city's yangfang. These areas were part of the International Settlement and the French Concession. Foreign control gradually spilled over the boundaries of the two concessions and extended into the adjacent Chinese-administered areas, creating so-called "extra-Settlement roads" (*yuejie zhulu*), in which fine homes were built. One of these areas was in Hongkou north of Szechuan (Sichuan) Road, where numerous new-style alleyway houses were built in the 1930s and 1940s. At the same time, luxurious Victorian and Spanish-style villas and cottages spread out westward in the extra-Settlement areas toward the suburb of Hongqiao.

The eastern district (west of the Huangpu River and east of Tibet Road) encompassed the commercial areas of the city. Together with tall buildings and large mansions built mainly for business purposes, many residential buildings (mostly shikumen houses) were built here, forming a jagged, interlocking pattern of residence and commerce (Fig. 9). This was the core of the city: much of Shanghai's political and commercial culture emerged here.

The northeast (mainly Yangshupu), the north (mainly Zhabei), and the northwest (mainly Caojiadu) areas of the city were industrial zones. Here were found a mixture of shikumen houses, single-story houses, and straw

Fig. 9.   The Great World, Shanghai's most popular amusement center, was established in 1917. This four-story structure with a European-style tower was a remodel of the center undertaken in 1929. It housed ten multifunction theaters, an
open-air central stage primarily for acrobatics, a dancing hall, and a skating rink.
It also had a variety of bars, teahouses, shops, corridors, and gardens. Although
people of all walks of life found this place entertaining, most of its patrons were
"little urbanites." The Great World attracted fifteen thousand to twenty-five
thousand customers daily and was the largest amusement center in Republican
China. A few blocks beyond the Great World, street entertainers performed before pedestrians. From R. Barz, *Shanghai: Sketches of Present-Day Shanghai.*

shacks. In the southern part of the city, mainly the old town seat of Shanghai county and Nanshi (lit., Southern Market), there were some traditional Chinese-style houses left from the last century, straw shacks, and
single-story houses, but most of the residential structures were of the
shikumen type.

   In short, with a few exceptions, the distribution of the types of dwellings
in Shanghai followed a pattern: the best housing (Western-style houses
and apartments, and new-style alleyway houses) was in the western part of
the city, and the poorest housing (single-story houses and straw shacks)
was in the peripheral areas, while the middle-level housing (the shikumen
or old-style alleyway houses) was spread all over Shanghai proper.[9]

   Despite this variety, finding a place to live remained the foremost problem for a newcomer. One old Shanghailander, Cheng Guohua, who came

with his uncle in 1933 from their hometown of Taicang, Jiangsu province, to Shanghai to "learn business" (*xue shengyi*), was quite lighthearted about the situation. "The most pressing thing for us was, upon stepping off the train at the Northern Railway Station, to find a place to stay," Cheng recalled. "When you walked on the streets, there were houses of every type everywhere, but we could not afford to rent a single room in an ordinary house. After a few weeks searching in vain for an affordable home (meanwhile we stayed with a relative), I wished I had just been a snail carrying its shell on its back, so I could roll myself up in there at night. Probably many people felt the same way. Eventually my uncle managed to rent a pavilion room [a small room above the kitchen of an alleyway house] in Nanshi, and I was hired as an apprentice in a hardware store that provided lodging—just a loft above the shop, where I always had to be careful not to hit my forehead on the rafters."[10] The Chengs were among the myriad people who ventured into the city in search of a livelihood, but they were far from being unfortunate. For many, as we will see, the "shell" in which to roll up in at night in this "museum of global architecture" was no more than a filthy shantytown straw hut.

Shantytowns

Unlike the slums of twentieth-century America, which have been associated with the inner city, slums in Shanghai were all peripheral, often located along the boundary of the city's foreign settlements.[11] Imagine the British Race Course (now People's Square) as the center of an oval stretching 5,000 meters (about 3.1 miles) east to west and 3,000 meters (about 1.9 miles) north to south. Virtually all of the city's shanty dwellings could be found on the circumference of that oval.[12] Their peripheral location reveals what we might call the superfluous nature of the slums and their occupants. At least from the viewpoint of the majority of Shanghai urbanites who were settled in more "decent" areas of the city, the shantytown dwellers were uninvited outsiders and the outskirts they occupied were a blight on the city.[13] Likewise, the shantytown inhabitants felt that they were denied entrance to the life of the inner city.

To some extent, it is more accurate to describe those who lived in Shanghai's shantytowns as homeless people rather than as ghetto dwellers. Although there is no complete agreement on the definition of "the homeless," most would agree that someone who is "on the street" or in temporary emergency shelters is homeless.[14] By these criteria, the shantytown occupants were a Chinese version of the homeless. The Shanghai po-

lice forces, which were composed of four different foreign and Chinese authorities, pursued an injunction against the "loafer" population in order to
keep the city "clean."[15] To the authorities in Shanghai, only beggars were
street people. In the early 1930s, when the city had a population of more
than 3 million, according to one report there were barely 3,000 homeless
beggars in Shanghai.[16] At the same time, the city generally lacked public
emergency shelters. But there was no lack of homeless people. They were
simply driven out of the inner-city streets to squat on the immediate
outskirts of the urban areas. The shacks there could barely be called
"homes." As Peroff points out, "In less developed countries, sizable seg-
ments of the population live in permanent conditions that are much less
adequate than the living conditions provided in the emergency shelters of
the United States."[17] Shanghai's shantytowns were, in that sense, the home
of the homeless.

But there is always the danger of drawing a forced analogy when one
tries to find a Western counterpart for a Chinese social phenomenon. In
twentieth-century America, unemployment has been the primary cause of
vagrancy, living as a tramp, and social deviance—the conventionally recognized types of homelessness.[18] In China, however, unemployed people
huddled in shantytowns. The great emphasis in traditional Chinese culture
on the family and home probably reduced the number of people who truly
lived on the streets. More important, however, are the causes behind the
scene. Unlike homelessness in America, which has been mainly a social
problem associated with America's ethnic heritage, the shanty squatters in
Chinese cities reflected something quite different: the gulf that separated
rural from urban China.

Moving from a rural community to urban society, especially to a large
metropolis like Shanghai, was (and still is) most widely considered by the
general public in China as a form of upward social mobility.[19] "To go to
Shanghai" was analogous to the pursuit of the "American dream" by immigrants to the United States. Although hundreds of thousands of "Shanghai dreamers" ended in crude shacks, the allure of the city never faded.[20]
The majority of the shantytown residents, in spite of their poverty, at least
survived in the city. Their fate had they remained in the villages—in times
of famine and war—may have been worse. Without the Communist takeover in 1949 and the forceful policies prohibiting migration afterward,
shantytowns in Shanghai would most likely have continued to grow.[21] The
existence of the numerous and teeming shantytowns in modern Shanghai
therefore illustrates the coexistence of two sharply distinctive worlds—
rural and urban China—in a single Chinese city.

YAOSHUILONG: THE EMERGENCE OF SHANTYTOWNS

Scattered shack settlements could be found in nineteenth-century Shanghai, mainly in the suburbs along the Huangpu River.[22] Large shantytowns were a later phenomenon: they began to appear on the immediate outskirts of the city late in the second decade of the twentieth century, in conjunction with Shanghai's industrialization during World War I, and spread quickly thereafter.[23] As noted in chapter 1, immigrants to Shanghai in the second half of the nineteenth century were, generally speaking, mostly well-off merchants, absentee landlords, frustrated bureaucrats and literati, skilled workers, and adventurers.[24] The tidal wave of rural immigrants to Shanghai, which gave rise to large shantytowns, was a twentieth-century phenomenon. By the end of the 1940s, the whole city was encircled by numerous clusters of straw-hut settlements. In order to gain a clear picture of how these shack areas grew and evolved, let us begin by examining Yaoshuilong (lit., Lotion Lane), Shanghai's largest shantytown.

Yaoshuilong was located on what had been a desolate field on a bend of Suzhou Creek, about five miles northwest of the Bund and Nanking Road, the commercial heart of the city. Beginning in 1920, a slum gradually formed around a lotion factory, which gave the place its name.[25] During and after World War I, many textile mills, chemical factories, machinery factories, and kilns were built in Huxi (west Shanghai) where Yaoshuilong was located. The proximity of these factories made this once-deserted riverside an ideal spot for a compact residential community of factory workers and urban poor. At the end of the 1930s, Yaoshuilong already had about 5,000 households, or 10,000 inhabitants. By the end of the 1940s, it encompassed almost 1.4 million square feet (about 130,000 square meters); there were 16,000 residents living in 4,000 dwellings, most of which were straw shacks.[26]

Most pioneer residents of Yaoshuilong, like virtually all other slum dwellers in Shanghai, were from the countryside. The difficult experience of these people who sought to settle in Shanghai can be traced by what we might call their "housing solution" in this area. Usually, immigrants from the countryside passed through three stages in their struggle to find shelter in the city. The emergence of Shanghai's shantytowns paralleled the struggle.

Numerous peasants came to Shanghai via the Grand Canal on small wooden boats commonly known as *maomaochuan* (lit., capped boats).[27] These wooden boats with reed roofing crowded along the banks of Suzhou

Creek. Many were berthed for years on the river and served as homes for these newcomers in their first stage of becoming "urbanites" in Shanghai.

When a boat became too decrepit to stay afloat, the family that lived aboard would pull the leaking craft onto the river bank, thus beginning the second stage of their residence in Shanghai. They would either live in the grounded boat, or sometimes, when the boat was simply too far gone to serve as shelter, they would use material from the old boat's roof to set up a hut on the muddy ground of the bank. These dilapidated and shabby huts were known by a most romantic name: *gundilong* (lit., rolling earth dragons). Probably this name arises from the Chinese homophones "dragon" (*long*) and "cage" (*long*), since the huts were virtually cages for human beings. These dwellings were so crude that it is hard to classify them into shapes. Roughly speaking, there were two types of gundilong. One was formed by bending reed mats from an old boat roof to form a semicircular hut; the other was formed by tilting together a bunch of thin bamboo strips or mats to form a triangle. Since the huts were made of these insubstantial materials and their owners could not afford to erect posts or walls within them, neither of the two types of gundilong could be larger than a king-size mattress or taller than an average human being.[28] Nevertheless, it was just these kinds of tiny "rolling earth dragons" that sheltered thousands of the new immigrants in the city.

For these squatters, a straw shack (*penghu*) was a great improvement and was, moreover, perhaps the best type of dwelling they could reasonably expect to acquire.[29] After years of hard work, a family might be able to save up a bit of money and build a straw shack. The average cost of materials for a typical straw shack in the 1930s was about $20, which was equal to about 135 pounds of rice, enough to feed a family of five for a month, or about one month's wage for an average semiskilled factory worker. A shantytown family could not afford to hire a carpenter, but had to do all the construction work by themselves; at most they might get some help from neighbors. A shack could be erected in two or three days. The difficult part was to manage the cost of materials, which was often met through loans. It was a happy moment when a rolling earth dragon was torn down and a thatched shack built in its place.

A straw shack usually consisted of a single room, about 12 feet wide by 24 feet long. But straw shacks less than 10 feet square were also very common.[30] Bamboo was most commonly used for the main structure. The posts were bamboo; the walls were bamboo wattle plastered with mud. The roof consisted of a few bunches of straw. A piece of lumber salvaged from a wooden boat often served as the door, but sometimes the "door" was merely a straw curtain or a ragged piece of cloth. Straw shacks were built directly on the muddy ground, which served as the floor. Glass for windows would have been considered the height of luxury, and many straw shacks had no windows at all.[31] A survey of housing conditions in Yaoshuilong in 1951 found that among the 4,191 houses investigated, 1,020 — about a quarter of the total—had no windows.[32] For the residents of these shacks, the usual solution to the need for a window was to knock a hole in the wall. This was presumably easy to accomplish since the walls were very thin. However, the primitive structure of a straw shack more often than not did not allow such "construction work" because it might lead the already weak wall to collapse. So, many straw shacks did not even boast a hole for ventilation. The shack thus was inevitably dark and damp and stank of mildew. Even on clear days no light was admitted if the door was closed; during the rainy season the interior was nearly as wet as the street outside.

There was, however, hardly any place within the slum that could be properly called a "street." Yaoshuilong, like all other slums in the city, was a crowded place full of grounded boats, rolling earth dragons, and straw shacks. The houses, if they can be called that, were built without control, and since the slum became more and more crowded in the 1930s and 1940s, any space that could hold a straw shack was soon occupied. The remaining spaces served as lanes that were often so narrow as to barely allow two men to pass shoulder to shoulder. Moreover, many straw shacks were so decrepit that they had to be leaned against one another in order to avoid collapse. Thus, walking through the slum was rather like negotiating an obstacle course. As one walked, one would have to bend down to pass under low eaves, and jump dozens of bumps and potholes. No matter what the weather, it was impossible to pass through a slum without muddying one's shoes.

Conditions in Yaoshuilong were typical of those in the city's shack settlements. In 1932 some sociologists investigated an unidentified slum in Yangshupu and reported conditions that in all aspects were familiar to Yaoshuilong residents:

> In the housing study we included a number of huts of the very poor which are made of very inflammable materials such as matting, straw, bagging, old boards, and the like. . . . These dwellings are not rain-proof nor wind-proof, and therefore are not sufficient protection from the rigors of Shanghai's variable climate. After a heavy rain, the inmates may be observed walking about in water perhaps up to their knees, while children are placed on the bed in order to keep them out

of the water. Even after the sun comes out, the inside of the dwelling remains wet for many a day. Mud walks are built up outside and finally in some instances the level of the floor is lower than the land outside the hut. Sanitary conditions are bad, garbage and sewage being left uncovered. No public facilities are used by these dwellers, even though on a main road a few yards away there may be a sewerage system and garbage collecting service. Many of these dwellers in huts of straw are fond of keeping pigs as an investment, pig-pens being placed right next to and adjoining the huts. Chickens are prevalent and at night sleep under the beds. Odors of decaying garbage, excreta of pigs, or dirty dampness pervade the atmosphere in the vicinity of these human habitations.[33]

As this statement suggests, scarcely any public utilities were available in Shanghai's shantytowns. Although the inhabitants of Yaoshuilong lived in close proximity to the luxurious and modern facilities of this great metropolis, they were separated from water and power services. No electric service was available in any of the slums in Shanghai. Just as in the villages, kerosene lamps were still the only source of artificial light. Also, it was difficult for the slum residents to get access to running water. Where potable water was available, it was often controlled by thugs and became a source of income for them. In Yaoshuilong there were only two public water taps, which were shared by more than 10,000 of its residents. The taps were controlled by a handful of local gangs popularly known as the "ten shareholders of running water" (*zilaishui shidagudong*). These gangs raised the water price several times higher than market price; thus the majority of the Yaoshuilong residents could not afford running water.[34] Fire hydrants on the streets at the margin of shantytowns were usually objects of contention. Having thousands of people forced to share one fire hydrant led to daily disputes and violence over access to the water.[35] As late as the 1960s, when all the major slums of the city had been renewed under government programs, the polluted and noisome Suzhou Creek still served as the main source of water for the daily needs of some of the remaining slum dwellers—drinking, washing, and cleaning chamber pots, all were done at the same riverside.[36]

FANGUALONG AND ZHAOJIABANG: SHANTYTOWNS CREATED BY WAR

The formation of squatter communities in Shanghai was directly associated with population growth. In the decade after 1927, 1.2 million people were added to the population of Shanghai; most of this growth was accounted for by immigration from the countryside.[37] The population continued growing during the Sino-Japanese War (1937–45) and the Civil War (1946–49) as refugees from virtually everywhere in the nation poured into Shanghai, a wartime safety zone. As a result, in the 1930s and 1940s straw-hut slums mushroomed and, at the same time, housing conditions there worsened.

In the immediate neighborhood of the North Station (Beizhan), Shanghai's primary railway station, was a large shantytown known as Fangualong (lit., Melon Alley), which might be considered typical of the slums created as a result of wars. Fangualong covered some 18 acres (about 70,000-odd square meters) immediately south of the railway line between the North Station and the East Station (Dongzhan, which was about half a mile east of the North Station). About 20,000 people lived in this area in the late 1940s. The average living area was only 4.1 square yards (3.5 square meters) per capita.[38]

The rise of Fangualong was directly related to the fate of Zhabei, where the slum was located. The first three decades of this century saw the growth of Zhabei, a new and moderately prosperous district often cited as evidence of Chinese capability to create and govern a modern urban area in this largely foreign-controlled city.[39]

The ongoing boom in Zhabei, however, was nipped in the bud by the two wars waged by the Japanese in 1932 and in 1937. On January 28, 1932, Japanese troops attacked Shanghai, starting a month-long battle generally known as the Song-Hu War (i.e., the Wusong and Shanghai War). Since the central part of Shanghai (i.e., the foreign settlements) was under the protection of the Western powers, the war was fought in the north and northeast suburbs of Shanghai, which were under Chinese jurisdiction. Zhabei became the main target of the Japanese troops. For two weeks after the battle started, Japanese bombers attacked Zhabei almost daily. Thousands of bombs pounded it into ruins. It was estimated that 68 percent of the total loss suffered by Shanghai in this battle occurred in Zhabei. In the whole of the district, according to a field report immediately after the war, there was not a single house that survived unscathed.[40] Zhabei was never to recover, although some efforts at "urban renewal" were made by the Chinese government. A second blow dealt by the same enemy extinguished any hope for the revival of Zhabei. On August 13, 1937, Japanese troops attacked Shanghai again and, after two months, finally occupied the whole city except for the International Settlement and the French Concession. For the second time, Zhabei was severely bombarded by Japanese aircraft and artillery. This time, fighting raged for more than two months.

Thereafter the Japanese army, when it occupied Zhabei, set fire to whatever structures remained standing. Zhabei was thus thoroughly devastated.[41]

The Fangualong slum appeared between these two wars. Although it was located in this war-ravaged area, Fangualong still had some attraction for the urban poor. First, it was, as noted, in the immediate neighborhood of the Shanghai Railway Station, which, for decades after it was established in 1908, was the main entrance to Shanghai. The area directly surrounding this railway station became a sort of a dumping ground on which were cast the teeming crowds of newcomers who sought shelter in this strange city. Furthermore, Fangualong, like any area near a railway station that serves as a key entrance to a great metropolis, provided a number of job opportunities (as porters, rickshaw pullers, and other types of coolies) for unskilled and newly arrived immigrants.

Also, Fangualong was located in an area just outside the northern boundary of the International Settlement and was only loosely controlled by the local Chinese authorities. This situation created a sort of administrative vacuum which, to some extent, was conducive to the appearance of a slum. In addition, the bombs of 1932 had created a wasteland; with landmarks gone, it was often difficult to tell where one lot began and the next ended. Ownership of real property, in other words, became unclear, making it relatively easy for poor people to squat without permission or paying rent. Not only in Fangualong but elsewhere on the periphery of Shanghai, poor immigrants just squatted on tiny scraps of land and erected their huts.[42]

In general the rent for a piece of land on which to erect a straw hut was relatively easy to manage, which was the primary reason that poor immigrants could at least hang on in the city without being literally homeless. In most cases, land was jointly rented by a number of dwellers. A typical contract surviving from the early 1920s describes terms for one piece of land: for leasing a half mu (one-twelfth of an acre), the tenants paid $200.00 annual rent; the land was leased by twenty-one households to erect huts that would house about one hundred people. This meant an average monthly rent of $0.79 for each household.[43] In the 1930s, the normal rent for about 4 square yards (3.3 square meters) of land, the size needed to build a straw shack, was $1.00 per month; sometimes the tenants could even obtain free rent.[44] Since straw-hut slums were often built on deserted spots, one reason why some landlords allowed land to go for low rents, or even asked no rent at all, was that once the land was densely populated, its value increased. "Usually the owners of such land," a report on housing of laborers argued, "do not care much for the amount of rentals, as they gain by the fact that the real estate they own would become more attractive and grow in value by being inhabited."[45] Another report on housing credited squatters with contributing to the real estate market in the city: "These coolies are in fact pioneers in expanding urban markets in Shanghai. In general, wherever they gather gradually flourishes and the value of real estate increases. Then, they are driven out of the area and to remoter places. The urban growth of Shanghai in recent years is the result of such changes."[46] The issues surrounding land use were, however, not always so smooth. More often than not, quarrels over ownership or rent rights broke out in the squatter areas, and some became violent.[47]

The general deterioration of the rural economy in the late 1920s and the early 1930s and the Sino-Japanese War severely affected the hinterland of Shanghai, particularly northern Jiangsu and Anhui provinces. The war made the already bad situation in the countryside even worse. Thousands of refugees from rural areas around Shanghai flowed into the city. Those areas of Zhabei close to the railway station and covered with nothing but piles of rubble were convenient spots for squatters. In 1935, an *Evening News* reporter took a trip through the straw huts located a few blocks away from the railway station and wrote the following account:

> There you can discover shoulder high huts with any odds and ends
> such as broken pieces of wood, grass, reed or discarded iron sheets serv-
> ing as tile for the roof; for windows there are little holes in the mud
> wall; rain or shine, summer or winter, the same darkness, dampness
> and dirty smells prevail. Some have a few pieces of broken-down fur-
> niture coated with slimy dust so that one cannot tell the material of
> which it is made, some even without what could be called a chair[,]
> for the occupants not only sit on the ground but sleep on it as well!
> On the little narrow paths there are always puddles of muddy water;
> here men, women, children, pigs, dogs, chickens and ducks move and
> live. It is difficult to pick one's way through the dirt.[48]

In fact, just as in Yaoshuilong, so too in Fangualong straw shacks were considered relatively good housing; the majority of dwellings in this slum were the so-called rolling earth dragons. But even the inhabitants of these hovels might have felt fortunate compared to those who lived in Zhaojia-bang, another large slum in the southern suburbs of Shanghai.

Zhaojiabang was originally a creek about 98 feet (30 meters) wide and 10–13 feet (3–4 meters) deep. Its upper reaches connected with the water system in the Xujiahui area in west suburban Shanghai and wound 5.6 miles (9 kilometers) eastward to flow into the Huangpu River.[49] In the nineteenth century it was a picturesque waterway where nearby villagers fished and netted crabs. Although it was a small creek and not well maintained, it actually carried water until 1937. The creek finally silted up after the Japanese occupied the city: the occupation force in Xujiahui constructed military roads, cutting off the creek's source. It gradually became the trash dump for factories and residences along its banks. Stagnant water in the creek joined by polluted water from nearby factories plus a daily in-pouring of garbage soon made Zhaojiabang a stinking sewer. At the end of the Sino-Japanese War, the silted-up creek became home to thousands of migrants who swarmed into the city from the countryside because of the Civil War (1946–49). After 1945, the central stretch of the creek, about 2 miles long, quickly became crowded with poor people. During 1946–48, the numbers of households along Zhaojiabang rapidly increased from several dozen to 2,000, with a population of about 8,000, making Zhaojiabang one of the largest slums of Shanghai.[50]

All kinds of crude dwellings found in the other slums of Shanghai sprang up in Zhaojiabang: the grounded boats, the rolling earth dragons, straw shacks, and mud huts. But the majority of the dwellings in this new slum were what was called *shuishang gelou* (lit., lofts on the water). As the narrow waterfront became crowded with factories, straw shacks, and gundilong, the newcomers had to build right over the creek itself. This was done by driving a few bamboo or timber poles into the silted-up creek bed as posts on which a straw hut could be built, with one end resting on the bank and the other end on the posts. In this way space was "borrowed" from the creek. This was the worst type of dwelling imaginable: the dark, smelly water and mud of the dead creek were right under the floor, which was made up of merely a few broken boards with large cracks between them. It was a pestilential hellhole full of flies, mosquitoes, and other vermin. On rainy days the so-called lofts *on* the water became lofts *in* the water (*shuizhong gelou*).[51]

If Yaoshuilong, which was formed in the early 1920s, was representative of the first slums in Shanghai, then Zhaojiabang, formed in the late 1940s, was representative of the later slums in the city; and Fangualong, formed in the 1930s, can be considered an example of the slums that were somewhere in between. In comparing these three major slums in Shanghai, we see that the rude straw shack had become a "high-class" form of dwelling. By 1949 most of Yaoshuilong's 4,000-odd dwellings were straw shacks; in Fangualong, straw shacks were considered good housing, for most of its 20,000 residents lived in rolling earth dragons; and in Zhaojiabang, not only were straw shacks rare, but 2,000 families did not even have enough ground on which to set up a rolling earth dragon. They had to build their houses on the dead creek bed.[52]

The policy pursued by China's post-1949 authorities in slum clearance programs strengthens this classification or "grading" of these three major slums. Zhaojiabang, the poorest of the three, was given top priority in these programs. Construction work in Zhaojiabang was listed among the key projects under the First Five-Year Plan in Shanghai. The slum was demolished in 1954, and a beautiful avenue was built on the site in 1956. The major part of Fangualong was not completely renewed until 1964, when ten five-story apartments were built there. Indeed, these two slum removal projects became a favorite topic in the Party's political propaganda. Yaoshuilong, graded the "best," was not favored with any large-scale renewal program. The dwellings there were much improved after 1949, although some straw shacks remained as late as the 1970s.[53]

In a word, during the period 1920–1950, housing conditions in each new squatter community in Shanghai were worse than in the communities that preceded it. Late in the period, even Zhaojiabang did not look so bad compared to the "living arrangements" which sprang up here and there in the city. For instance, in 1948 a slum near Luban Road was said to contain "the city's most miserable dwellings": the so-called *yaopeng* (lit., kiln hut). These were less than 3 feet high and had a floor area of less than 18 square feet. In such a hovel one could scarcely sit upright; there was barely room enough to permit three people to sleep together.[54] But there was worse housing still: in the dock areas along the Huangpu River, one encountered straw lean-tos built against the walls of public toilets. These uninvited neighbors of public toilets sometimes simply slept inside the lavatories. For example, Liu Zhikang, a dock walloper, had slept in a public toilet for four years, from the age of twelve to sixteen.[55]

Shantytown Dwellers

It was estimated that in 1926 the city had more than 50,000 straw huts housing about 200,000 to 300,000 people.[56] A survey sponsored by the Shanghai Municipal Government in 1936 found that in the city's Chinese district alone there were more than 20,000 households, with a population of 100,000, living in squatter settlements. According to a district-by-district survey conducted in 1948, the slums of Shanghai contained about 70,000 households, or more than 300,000 inhabitants, that is, about 10 percent of the city's total population.[57] These figures might be considered conservative since the slums were scattered over much of the city, and as one can imagine, conditions in squatter communities were such that it was difficult to get an exact count of households.[58] A more systematic survey conducted in the early 1950s estimated that there were about 180,000 to 200,000 households living in 130,000 straw shacks of various types in Shanghai's shantytowns.[59] The total population of the slums was close to 1 million, or about one-fifth to one-sixth of the city's total population.[60]

Who were these shantytown squatters?

A depiction of the slum dwellers in contemporary Calcutta may be borrowed here to describe the shanty squatters in Republican Shanghai: "These people began their lives, without exception, in the villages. They came here lured by the city's gold, and this was the end of their rainbow. They have adopted a curious mixed, half-urban life-style. They illustrate a special history and a special social mobility."[61] The growth of Shanghai and the success stories it generated spread illusions about life in the city, and, even for those who were not driven by the desire to get ahead but merely to survive, Shanghai nevertheless seemed the logical place to go. As a folk song sung in the rural area of Wuxi, Jiangsu, goes:

> Two swords weigh on the shoulder[s] of the peasant:
> High rent and interest.
> Three roads are open to him:
> First, escape;
> Second, prison;
> Third, to hang himself.

Here, escape was the first choice for the peasant, and the reference to "escape" pointed right at Shanghai.[62] For many of the immigrants, a relative, neighbor, or friend who had earlier gone to the city and settled there was an inspiration, or at least permitted the hope or expectation that a friendly, or even helpful, reception awaited. They came to Shanghai, cherishing the hope of a fresh start; it must have been a rude shock to find that life in Shanghai was much harder than they had anticipated. To get a factory job was the usual goal for these former peasants. But once they arrived in Shanghai, they discovered that factory work was not easy to find. As noted earlier, to obtain even an entry-level factory job, one first needed strong recommendations, and, second, one had to give some gift to the factory foreman; in some cases, there were educational requirements or skill tests to be passed.[63] One can imagine the difficulty that poor newcomers had finding any kind of personal connection in this strange land. In addition, newcomers often found that their relatives, friends, and acquaintances ac-

Fig. 10. On a winter afternoon curious shantytown dwellers, mostly children and young adults, crowd around to see foreign visitors, an apparently unusual adventure in this squatter's area. Note that a number of children are eating from bowls. On a warm day, the lane would be livened up by residents who liked to have their supper in the public space outside their hovels. Courtesy of Shanghai Municipal Archive.

tually could not help much, since they themselves were usually desperately poor. As a Chinese saying put it, "A mud Buddha can hardly protect himself when he crosses a river" (*ni Pusa guojiang, zishen nanbao*).[64] Thus, countless newcomers without skills in demand in modern factories, without personal connections, and without money drifted to squatter areas (Fig. 10).

One author who visited several slums along the banks of Suzhou Creek near Caojiadu (the Cao family ferry) and Fanhuangdu (the Buddha ferry) was saddened by the conditions there and asked the dwellers a question, knowing that his question might seem naive or offensive to them: "Why don't you stay in your home village and farm rather than come here and suffer?" One of the residents, an old man in his sixties who looked experienced and knowledgeable about life, answered, as if he were lecturing someone on a belabored topic: "Farm? Nowadays you can't make a living from farming!" He then spoke of the disaster-ridden life in the countryside—most residents had come from the villages of Yancheng and Gaoyou and nearby counties in Subei—and concluded that for them coming to Shanghai was virtually a case of "fleeing for one's life." The visitor observed that almost all the residents' belongings were things they had brought from their home villages, yet other than a kerosene oven and some cooking utensils, he could see virtually nothing in the shacks. "Haven't you brought anything else from your old home?" he asked. "Yes, we have," a dweller answered with a wry smile: "We have all brought a mouth to be fed!"[65]

The story of Zhang Kouzi, a fifty-year resident of Yaoshuilong, illustrates how difficult it was for those who came to Shanghai from a poor rural area to get a steady job to "feed the mouth." Very often the only migrants who could get factory jobs were children. Zhang was a son in a poor peasant family in Subei. In about 1924 a natural disaster led the family to lose their only property—their house—and they became homeless. Zhang's parents managed to obtain a small boat, on which the whole family came to Shanghai along the Grand Canal. They anchored the boat on the bank of Suzhou Creek near Yaoshuilong, where the family (Kouzi, his parents, one younger brother and one younger sister) commenced to live. Seeking a factory job, the Zhangs sought help from a relative who had come to Shanghai several years earlier and who was working in a Japanese cotton mill. Being a poor worker himself, the relative was unable to help them to get into the mill. In any case, the mill did not need adult male labor, so Kouzi's father became a rickshaw puller. Kouzi's mother, who then was in her thirties, was considered too old to be a mill worker. After the family sent a gift to the foreman, Kouzi alone, who at that time was thirteen, was hired as a laborer in the mill.[66] However, the combined income of a rickshaw puller and a child laborer was not sufficient to support the whole family. Therefore, the mother sent the two younger children to roam the streets scavenging trash to sell. Needless to say, the family lived in dire poverty. After many years the Zhang family moved from the boat, which was now too decrepit to live in, to a gundilong. Kouzi's younger brother and sister did not survive the hardship, both dying in childhood.[67]

The experience of the Zhang family was in many ways typical for the shantytown squatters in Shanghai. For example, in 1926, a petition to the local authorities presented by thousands of slum residents in east Shanghai (Hudong) said that all the petitioners were from villages in northern Jiangsu province. An investigation of Beipingmincun, a straw-shack slum in the southwest of the city, indicated that 60 percent of the residents there had migrated to Shanghai directly from rural areas.[68]

In terms of origin, immigrants from Subei (or Jiangbei, mainly those areas of Jiangsu province north of the Yangzi River) formed what we might call the stereotypical body of slum residents in Shanghai. As Honig observes, "So close was the association of Subei people with the slums that they were often referred to as 'Jiangbei shack settlements,'" and these areas "became a central arena in which the category Subei people was constructed and imbued with symbolic meanings."[69] If there was an "official" language in the slums, it was not the Shanghai dialect but the Subei dialect, which until the 1980s was still commonly spoken in the area where the former slums were located.[70] An investigation conducted in 1936 estimated that of Shanghai's nearly 100,000 shantytown residents, 70 percent were Subei natives; Hubei natives and Shanghai locals made up 10 percent of the population each; Shandong natives accounted for 5 percent; and another 5 percent were people of other native origins.[71] Although a lack of detailed statistics makes it impossible to tell the precise numbers of Subei people in Shanghai's shack settlements over the years, it is unquestionable that residents of Subei origins constituted the majority of the population.[72]

The occupations of the Zhangs were also rather typical for slum residents. Adult males usually found work where muscle was the only qualification, hence the large numbers of rickshaw pullers, coolies, and dockworkers who inhabited the shantytowns. Adult females, if not fortunate enough to find a job in a factory, often became street peddlers, carrying a bamboo basket with small items such as sesame cakes and fried dough sticks, the most common breakfast food of Shanghai's urbanites; or green onions and ginger roots, the favorite spices in Chinese kitchens; or some other tiny, cheap items. Some, like Kouzi's mother, were too poor to buy anything to resell, and thus they could only roam the streets picking up trash to sell. Part of the trash they picked up, such as discarded vegetables, became food for their families. Quite a number of slum residents had simply no livelihood but begging.

A 1939 investigation reported that all of Yaoshuilong's residents were rickshaw pullers, coolies, small peddlers, or mill workers.[73] The last were a large occupational group, perhaps in part because this slum was adjacent to the major cotton mill district of the city. The occupational composition of the residents of Yaoshuilong was confirmed in a survey made in the early 1950s at the same location. The survey revealed that 40 percent of the residents were factory workers, while the remaining 60 percent were rickshaw pullers, pedicab drivers, or peddlers.[74] In fact, because of its close proximity to the Huxi industrial district, Yaoshuilong had the largest proportion of factory-worker residents among the three major slums discussed; hence it was often called an "industrial slum." If factory workers were only a minor component of the Yaoshuilong population, then, it is safe to say that factory workers were far from being the major inhabitants of the city's shantytowns.

Factory Employment: A Shantytown Dream

Modern industrial workers have been commonly viewed as the lower class or, to use a Marxist expression, the most exploited class. But in Shanghai, any adult who could find and keep a stable factory job was definitely not on the lowest rung of the social ladder.

There were two notable surveys on the living standards of Shanghai industrial workers made during the Nanjing decade (1927–37). One was jointly conducted by the Shanghai Bureau of Price Investigation (*Shanghai diaochahuojiaju*) and the Peking Institute of Social Investigation (*Beiping shehui diaochasuo*) in 1927–28, with Tao Menghe as the program director.[75] The other was conducted by the Bureau of Social Affairs of the City Government of Greater Shanghai (*Shanghai shizhengfu shehuiju*) in 1929–30, with Cai Zhenya as the program director.[76] Tao's survey investigated the families of 230 cotton mill workers in Caojiadu, Huxi. Cai's survey was more diverse. It surveyed 305 working families of various occupations and districts in Shanghai, including the foreign settlements and the Chinese districts.

As far as housing patterns were concerned, the results of these two surveys showed that most industrial working families in Shanghai did not live in straw shacks. In Tao's survey, 95.7 percent (220 households) resided in two-story alleyway houses, and 4.3 percent (10 households) resided in bungalow-type, single-story row houses; no family in the survey resided in a straw shack.[77] As noted, all the households in this survey were headed by a cotton mill worker. Such workers were among the lowest paid of Shanghai industrial operatives.[78] Therefore, if, as this survey showed, cotton mill workers were not residents of straw shacks, it is reasonable to assume that the majority of Shanghai industrial workers were not residents of the straw-shack slums.

Cai's survey reinforces this conclusion. In his study, which covered not only industrial workers but also some other occupations such as transportation worker, service worker, and so on, 61 percent (185 households) resided in two-story row houses, 34 percent (103 households) in one-story row houses, and only 5 percent (17 households) in straw shacks.[79] Since Cai's survey was more diverse than Tao's, both in area as well as in occupations covered, it must be considered the more representative of the two.

Even though Cai provided no detailed information on the occupations of the 5 percent who lived in straw shacks and we do not know if they were factory workers, the results of his survey reinforce the conclusion that most industrial workers did not live in straw-shack slums.

H. D. Lamson, a professor at the University of Shanghai and one of the few contemporary sociologists to have paid attention to the slums of the city, conducted a detailed study of 23 households in Yangshupu in 1932. Lamson reported, "Where occupations were stated, the men were employed as follows:—farmers (8), wheelbarrow coolie (5), coolie (3), road building work (2), and factory work (1). This suggests that these straw hut occupants are not predominantly mill operatives. As to the occupation of the women, there are nine classed as farmers, two as factory workers; two do washing, one is a street peddler. The children either do nothing, peddle small things in the streets, or pick up things from rubbish dumps."[80]

Two things are especially notable about Lamson's report. First, although Yangshupu was the largest industrial district of Shanghai, factory work was nevertheless the least prevalent occupation among the slum dwellers Lamson studied. Of course, slums that were not so close to factories were likely to have an even lower proportion of factory workers.

Second, those who stated their occupation to be "farmer" were actually unemployed or virtually unemployed. Yangshupu in the 1930s was already a well-established industrial area where little land was available for farming. As early as the beginning of this century, rural life started to disappear in this area, and many villagers, in part as a result of the lack of available land, gave up farming in favor of some type of urban employment.[81] As Lamson wrote, "Most of the people living in these miserable huts are 'kiang-pei' [Jiangbei] or 'kompo' [Jiangbei in the Shanghai dialect] people from north of the Yangtze River. Having no friends or relatives, and being without means, these laborers have drifted to the big city to seek opportunities for employment." The "farmers" of Lamson's study were most likely former peasants but currently jobless in the city.

A large portion of shanty squatters were unemployed. An investigation conducted by the Bureau of Social Affairs of the Municipal Government of Greater Shanghai in 1928 of ten different labor and trade unions found that of 155,069 union members, 10,009 (6.45 percent) were unemployed.[82] In Cai's survey of Shanghai working families in 1929–30, the unemployment rate was 8.74 percent.[83] Unemployment in the shantytowns must have been much higher than the city's average unemployment rate. During the Civil War period (1946–49), for example, Shanghai's unemployment rate was about 5 percent, while in Yaoshuilong it was 17.5 percent.[84] Another survey, of Fangualong, discovered something rather amazing: in 1949, 45 percent of the total households in this slum were without a single employed family member, and 51.5 percent had only one family member employed.[85]

This survey of 202 households in Fangualong found that among 404 "adults" between the ages of 16 and 45, 142 (35 percent) were unemployed. Of those who had a job, 186 (46 percent) were rickshaw pullers, pedicab drivers, or street peddlers; only 76 (19 percent) were factory workers.[86] Another survey, conducted in the early 1950s in Yaoshuilong, found that factory workers made up 39.2 percent of the adult population (above 15 years of age).[87] A third survey, conducted at the same time, of a sample of 547 households in Yaoshuilong, including 1,223 adults, revealed that 53.7 percent of the adults were employed; among those who were employed, factory workers constituted 37.1 percent; rickshaw pullers and pedicab drivers, 24.4 percent; peddlers, 20.3 percent; and others, 18.2 percent.[88] Given the fact that this slum was located right in the Huxi industrial district, where cotton mills and many other factories were concentrated, the percentage of factory workers among the employed adults can only be considered fairly small; if we add in the unemployed, the percentage of factory workers among all adults was even smaller.

One author explained that the rural refugees who came to Shanghai cherishing the hope of finding a factory job were thrown into the gigantic army of urban unemployment before they even had a chance to step into the gate of a mill, so the slums were the only place they could hang on in the city.[89] The problem goes beyond that. Even if one did get a factory job, in most cases life still remained uncertain because most jobs available in factories were of a casual and part-time nature, with little job security. Throughout the Republican period, employers in Shanghai preferred hiring temporary, casual workers. The resulting fluidity of the labor market had two important implications. On one hand, hiring casuals suggests that job openings were frequent and plentiful, and this in turn means that there were opportunities for newcomers. A peasant who came to the city without any training may have realistically hoped to find a temporary, unskilled or semiskilled job in a mill that changed its labor force frequently. On the other hand, the practice of hiring casuals indicates the difficulty of maintaining a stable job in the city. And, for an immigrant from the countryside, not having stable employment in the city meant one was unsettled—living in a straw hut was just the most visible symbol of the tenuous existence of rural immigrants.

According to official statistics, in 1928 the textile industry employed

76.5 percent of all industrial workers in the city, and textiles remained the most important industry of the city through the Republican period.[90] A notable feature of the textile industry was the fact that women and children formed the majority of its workers. Throughout the 1920s, the number of male laborers in the textile industry decreased dramatically. Largely because of the availability of female workers, textile mills laid off male workers at a startling rate in the late twenties. For example, in 1928 about 40 percent of the 4,000-odd employees of the Shenxin Number Seven Cotton Mill, one of Shanghai's early textile factories, were male; only a year later, in May of 1929, the percentage had dropped to 1 percent.[91] At the same time, indentured female workers became the industry's main source of labor.[92] Many women workers started their careers in textile mills as children. By 1930, 66.5 percent of Shanghai's textile workers were women, and 9 percent were children; male workers made up less than a quarter of the workers.[93] The Rong family, which owned a number of conglomerates in the textile and flour trades and was regarded as the Rockefellers of China, set a hiring policy in 1931 that "anywhere women can do the job, they shall be hired." In 1933–35, 93–98 percent of the new hires in the textile mills owned by the Rongs were female.[94]

But this does not mean these workers obtained stable jobs. Quite the opposite; a major reason for hiring female workers was the fact that they were supposedly easier to manage and easier to lay off than male workers. When business was slow, many woman workers lost their jobs. In the Yong'an Cotton Mills, one of the largest conglomerates of its kind, from 1932 to 1935 about 42 percent of the workers (mostly women) lost their jobs.[95]

A few more examples underscore this point. In the Zhanghua Woolen Textile Company (owned by the industrial magnate Liu Hongsheng), long-term workers were issued red identification cards while casuals were given blue ones. Switching from a blue card to a red one required passing a technical proficiency test; success in the test was considered a big step up.[96] In the Hengfeng Printing and Dyeing Mill, worker status was divided into three types: long-term, casual, and probationary. There were very few long-term workers; most employees were casuals and probationary workers. After the Sino-Japanese War, casuals in the mill were called by different names, such as term workers (*dingqi gong*), preferential workers (*zhaogu gong*), and probationary workers (*shiyong gong*). Most casuals were recruited when business was good and laid off when it was slow. Casuals might work for just a week, and no longer than three months. Sometimes they might work only half a day: in the afternoon when fewer workers were needed, they were immediately sent home.[97]

Unlike in the textile industry, workers in the mechanized flour milling industry, which ranked next to textiles in economic importance in Republican China, were all males.[98] But this does not mean workers were secure there. Production in flour mills was largely seasonal, fluctuating with the availability of wheat. Consequently, employment was also seasonal. Every year around the time of the Chinese Dragon Boat Festival (Duanyang, the fifth day of the fifth lunar month, which usually falls in June)—which coincides with the wheat harvest—when production in flour mills went full tilt, many workers were recruited. But around the Double Ninth Festival (Chongyang, the ninth day of the ninth lunar month, which usually falls in October), when the wheat was used up, these workers were terminated. Thus, flour mill workers were nicknamed "two-*yang* workers" (*liangyang gongren*; the two "yangs" being the Duanyang and the Chongyang). In the flour industry many porters were hired to work outside of the workshops carrying heavy bags of wheat and flour. These porters too were all two-yang workers.[99]

Qiao Zongyuan, a senior worker in Fuxin Number One Flour Mill, recalled that every year around the Duanyang festival many workers, most of them casuals, were recruited into Fuxin. Those who had been terminated the previous autumn might be called back at that time. But in September and October, when the off-season arrived, at least half of the workers were laid off. Usually, skilled workers were kept to maintain the equipment. For laid-off workers who had land in their home village, going back to the village was the best option; otherwise, they had to roam the streets and face hunger, like all who had no land to farm in the countryside. Ming Changmei, a casual worker in Fuxin Number Two and Number Eight Flour Mills, said that in off-seasons he went from place to place in search of a job. He worked as a porter in factories in Nichengqiao near the Nanking Road area and in the Yangshupu industrial area, and also as a coolie on the docks along Yangjiadu (lit., the Yang family ferry) in Pudong.[100]

In a city where the rent for a 107-square-foot (10-square-meter) room in a working-class neighborhood could easily exceed half of a worker's income, casual workers and the unemployed almost inevitably turned to shantytowns to find a home. Casual workers in cotton mills were typical of factory workers who lived in shanty areas. According to a 1936 report on nearly 100,000 straw-hut dwellers in the city, dockworkers, night soil collectors, and coolies each made up 15 percent of the shantytown population; 5 percent were rickshaw pullers. The other half of the population consisted of the unemployed (30 percent, which included beggars) and casual cotton mill workers (20 percent). Most of the mill workers were women and children, and most of those, at the time of investigation, worked only one shift in three or four days. In fact the line between these casual workers and the unemployed was difficult to draw. With an extremely uncertain job, and hence uncertain income, these people understandably gravitated to Shanghai's shantytowns.[101]

Since the poor desperately sought any means of livelihood, one would expect to find them drawn to those places that offered even minimal means of eking out a living. Thus, a slum's location often gives a clue to the occupations of its residents. For instance, many porters lived in the slums close to the Shanghai Railway Station in Zhabei, where daily thousands of passengers came and went. Also, most dockworkers lived in the slums along the Huangpu River, while few lived in the western part of the city where scarcely any major docks were located. Factory workers were most likely to be found in the slums of the Huxi and Hudong industrial districts. In the shantytowns in the southern district of the old county town, one could find another occupational group: handicraftspeople. Their concentration there might have been a heritage of the traditional handicraft workshops that had been located in the nearby county seat.[102]

By the same token, rickshaw pullers (and in the late 1940s, pedicab drivers) could be found in every slum of Shanghai. The nature of their work—they operated everywhere in the city—made the location of their residence relatively immaterial.[103] In September 1950, the municipal government conducted a citywide survey of slums, classified by the occupation of the household head, and found that rickshaw pullers were the single largest occupational group in all slums: 37 percent of Shanghai's shantytown families were headed by rickshaw pullers, compared to 17 percent by street peddlers (the second-largest group) and 16 percent by other unskilled laborers (the third).[104]

Likewise, beggars were another ubiquitous group in shantytowns. Shanghai in the early 1930s had about 20,000 professional beggars, all of whom lived in shack settlements or straw huts scattered in back alleys.[105] The public so closely associated these slums with beggars that all the shack settlements in the city were simply referred to as "beggar villages" or "beggar huts"; and the capped boats on Suzhou Creek that housed the poor were labeled "beggar boats," regardless of who really lived there.[106]

On the walls at the entrance of a typical alley in shanty areas one could always see signs in big characters handwritten in limewash or white chalk. These were usually wishful blessings for life, such as "All Is Well" (*renkou ping'an*) or "Four Seasons in Peace" (*siji taiping*). Some signs, however, served a more practical purpose, such as "Public Toilet Inside This Lane" or

"For Defecation, Please Walk In." In time, these signs became a symbol of Shanghai's slums.[107] In some way they expressed a more human touch than some printed signs often found in the city's other neighborhoods, such as those reading "No Posting!" or "Any Poster Will Be Torn Down at Once!"[108] But the blessings for life revealed precisely the fragility and uncertainty of life inside these lanes. Ironically perhaps, the ultimate goal of the dwellers there was to escape the neighborhoods that were protected by nothing more than a few wishful limewashed signs.

Most workers in higher-paid industries and trades lived in the city's average residential dwellings, that is, alleyway houses. On average a working-class family in pre-1937 Shanghai spent 6–9 percent of its income on housing.[109] For a household with a monthly income of around $30.00—about average for the family of an unskilled laborer in the 1930s—a monthly rent higher than $3.00 would have been more than it could afford. According to an SMC report, the monthly rent for rooms in squatters' huts in the Settlement in the mid-1930s varied from $0.40 to $3.00. This was, of course, the lowest rental that one could find in the city, and it suggests that a family with a monthly income of around $30.00 could hardly escape the fate of living in shantytown.[110]

In the same time period, the rent for a simple row house (a single-bay alleyway house; see chapter 4) in an average neighborhood varied from $10.00 to $30.00. While this rent would be unthinkable for an unskilled laborer, it was manageable for a postal worker, a transportation worker, a skilled machinist, and the like. For instance, the monthly rent for a house in Jiahe Li, an alleyway-house compound located just across the street from the British-owned tram company on Hart Road, ranged from $8.00 (without a courtyard) to $12.00 (with a courtyard) in the late 1920s. Many similar alleyway houses around this area in west Shanghai—many were owned by the real estate magnate Silas Aaron Hardoon (1847–1931)—were rented by employees of the tram company.[111]

These workers, and workers elsewhere in the city, might not have been able to rent a whole house but had to be content with one or two rooms for the entire family, a situation that was common among Shanghailanders, and not only working-class families. Alleyway-house compounds therefore housed people from all walks of life except those who were extremely poor or dazzlingly rich. Thus it is to alleyway-house neighborhoods—where working-class types rubbed shoulders with teachers, artists, writers, shop clerks, office workers, small business owners, prostitutes, and priests—that one must turn to witness how most people of Shanghai lived.

CHAPTER 4

The Homes of the Little Urbanites

The lilong, or alleyway houses, in spite of being everywhere in the city, might have easily been overlooked. This is not only because they were usually located in back alleys behind commercial enterprises but also because, paradoxically, their very commonness made them blend into a backdrop against which other urban structures stood out. Visitors were often struck by Shanghai's modern skyline along the Bund and Nanking Road, or impressed by its European-style villas in the city's western suburbs; more social-minded observers were perhaps stunned by the abject poverty of the city's squatter shacks, described in chapter 3. But few people (including scholars) paid attention to the lilong. As for local residents, lilong were merely the place most people called home and were nothing special. The lack of attention to this common architecture was simply a matter of, as a Chinese proverb describes, "turning a blind eye to a familiar sight" (*shu shi wu du*).[1]

But this neglect must be corrected. No social or cultural history of Shanghai would be complete without an examination of this particular architecture and the neighborhoods it fostered. And, given the importance of Shanghai in twentieth-century China, it is no exaggeration to say that the same statement applies to modern Chinese urban history. This chapter provides details on the lilong houses (in particular, the shikumen) and their social implications, which involve primarily the housing market that operated at the rental and subletting levels and its impact on the life of ordinary people. The lilong neighborhoods, where commercial enterprises and residential premises mixed, played an decisive role in creating modern Shanghai's commercial culture.

The Rise of the Modern Real Estate Market

Shanghai's modern real estate market originated in two wars that occurred near the city's foreign settlements in the mid-nineteenth century: the Small Swords Uprising and the Taiping Rebellion. As noted in chapter 1, from September 1853 to February 1855 the walled county seat of Shanghai, whose northern gates were located only a block south of the French Concession, was occupied by a rebellious band known as the Small Swords, or the Triads. Their fight to seize the county seat brought the first tide of refugees into the foreign settlements, which, in spite of the ambiguities of their legal status, had been until then reserved for Westerners only. By early 1854, more than 20,000 refugees from the county seat had entered the foreign areas. Later, the number of refugees reached 80,000.[2]

As we have seen, in the face of this crisis, Shanghai's foreign community debated whether to expel the Chinese and maintain segregation or to build housing for the refugees (to be rented to them for, it was hoped, a profit). Eventually, the idea of continuing segregation was overridden by the undisguised wish to make money by renting land and buildings to the Chinese. But whatever the result of the debate, the dismantling of segregation was soon to prove inevitable: the Taiping Rebellion (1850–1864)—the capital of the Taipings was Nanjing, two hundred miles northwest of Shanghai—drove thousands of Chinese in the Jiangnan region to flee to Shanghai and seek safety under European rule. In particular, in 1860–62, when Taiping troops marched toward Shanghai several times, it was reported that refugees in Shanghai's foreign settlements reached half a million.[3] Given the geographical size of the foreign settlements at that time, this might be an exaggerated estimation. More reliable sources reported that by 1865 the population of the British and American Settlements (later known as the International Settlement) had increased to 92,884. Most of the population were Chinese from the vicinity of Shanghai. At the same time, about 50,000 Chinese had moved into the French Concession. By the end of the Taiping Rebellion, well over 110,000 Chinese had moved into Shanghai's foreign settlements.[4]

In spite of the unhappiness of both the British consul and the Chinese Daotai over the problem of crime and the threat to public health caused by the refugees, the business of building and renting houses to the Chinese boomed.[5] From September 1853 to July 1854, more than 800 two-story row houses were built on Guangdong Road and Fuzhou Road in the British Settlement; still more houses were scattered in the northwest part of the Settlement, as well as on the Bund and along the Yangjingbang Creek, which separated the British Settlement from the French Concession. By 1860, there were 8,740 houses in the British Settlement, mostly owned by Britishers and Americans but inhabited by Chinese. Clusters of houses continued to be built on Hankou Road, Jiujiang Road, and further north to Nanking Road and up to the south bank of Suzhou Creek.[6]

These new clusters did not merely change the landscape of Shanghai, but, more significant, they marked the beginning in China of a modern real estate market. In traditional China, residences were usually built as individual, free-standing structures. A row of houses was usually formed without plan by a gradual accumulation of structures built at different times and in different styles.[7] In that sense, the houses built in Shanghai's British Settlement in the 1850s and 1860s were new to the Chinese, for these houses were built in batches of identical units and were, as a modern developer would say, built on speculation (that is, built for the market). The difference in design, arguably, was derived from the difference in purpose: traditional Chinese houses were constructed individually because they were mostly built by or for owners for their personal use, while the row houses in the foreign settlements were constructed solely for commercial purposes. In Shanghai in the mid-nineteenth century, both the design and purpose of these houses were European innovations. Of course, land and housing had been commodities in China long before the coming of the West. At least from the eleventh century on, house purchasing and leasing were already common in Chinese cities.[8] But these commercial activities were usually conducted on a small scale. House purchasing and leasing were primarily a matter of what might be called self-consumption (e.g., building a home for oneself), of convenience (e.g., renting a house for a sojourn away from home, or selling a house when one relocated), or of a shift of wealth (e.g., selling a house to pay debts, or purchasing a house in order to have *hengchan*, or permanent property). To build identical houses on a large scale solely for the market, as Western merchants started to do in Shanghai in the middle 1850s, was something that the nation had never before seen.[9] In that sense, it could be argued that China's first modern real estate market was born in the gun smoke in Shanghai, or more specifically, on the blocks of Nanking Road. In the climate of continuing Western encroachment in the late nineteenth century, the modern real estate market was destined to have a profound impact on the life of the Chinese residents of the city.

The end of the Taiping Rebellion brought a temporary decrease in the population of the city in the late 1860s, but the real estate market remained steady. According to a British merchant, by renting land or a house to the Chinese, foreigners in Shanghai could make a profit of at least 30 to 40 percent.[10] A contemporary commented in the early 1870s that renting out houses was the "most profitable business" in Shanghai, a business that until then had remained predominately foreign-run.[11]

By the 1870s the wartime speculation had died away and a more regulated real estate market began to emerge in Shanghai. As we have seen, in September 1869 the Land Regulations, regarded as the constitution of Shanghai's foreign settlements, was revised and approved by the European envoys in Beijing to create the Shanghai Municipal Council to govern the International Settlement, the core of modern Shanghai. One of its first orders of business was to levy a tax on real property. The rate was set at 3 percent of estimated land value in 1874 and gradually increased to 7 percent by 1919. In 1869 taxes levied on houses were set at 8 percent of the rent for Chinese-style houses and 6 percent for Western-style houses. By 1919, taxes for both Chinese and Western houses were levied at a rate of 14 percent. Furthermore, mainly for purposes of taxation, the International Settlement was divided into four districts: the Central, the North, the East, and the West, and periodically all real property was reassessed.[12] A brochure indexing land value and tax was issued by the SMC, in which landlords could easily find the standard taxes for their property. In the period 1869–1933, at least nineteen assessments of property value were conducted by the SMC; in other words, on average there was a reassessment every three to four years.[13]

Initiated by Westerners, Shanghai's real estate market was also dominated by them. All real estate magnates in late-nineteenth-century Shanghai were Westerners. Among them we find the names of such well-known China adventurers as Edwin Smith, Thomas Hanbury (1832–1907), Henry Lester (1840–1925), the Hogg brothers (William, James, and E. Jenner), the Sassoon family, and Silas Aaron Hardoon (1847–1931). From 1869 to 1933, the top three real estate magnates—whose holdings fluctuated to include from 36 percent to more than 60 percent of the real estate along Nanking Road—were all foreigners. In the early 1930s, close to half the real estate along Nanking Road, the most expensive area in the city, was under Hardoon's name.[14]

However, shortly after foreigners launched the real estate market in Shanghai, Chinese merchants started to join the adventure. Among the refugees who came to Shanghai during the Taiping Rebellion were many wealthy landlords and bureaucrats. Some of them soon found that speculation in urban real estate was a much more profitable business than renting out farmland in the countryside. Among the Chinese real estate owners were four families—surnamed Zhang, Liu, Xin, and Peng—known as the "Four Elephants," who owned many shikumen compounds in the Nanking Road area. These four families had a few things in common. They all hailed from Nanxun, Zhejiang province, and all owned a great amount of land and controlled the silk and tea markets there. Having come to Shanghai, they continued their silk and tea businesses but shifted the bulk of their capital to real estate.[15]

By the end of the 1940s, Shanghai had more than 3,000 Chinese who were qualified to be called great real estate investors (*fangdichan dayezhu*), an epithet commonly applied to anyone who owned more than 10,760 square feet (1,000 square meters) of real property in the city. About 160 of this group owned more than 100,000 square feet (10,000 square meters) of real property; 30 owned more than 300,000 square feet (30,000 square meters).[16] Many Chinese real estate investors were compradors.[17]

Both Chinese and foreigners invested in not only commercial property but also residential houses in the Nanking Road area.[18] From 1910 to 1940, most old houses along Nanking Road left from the previous century were remodeled into alleyway (lilong) houses.[19] This type of dwelling was derived from the two-story houses built in clusters during the Taiping period but rebuilt with a new and more sophisticated design in the early 1870s (discussed below). First built in the Nanking Road area, alleyway houses soon appeared in other parts of the city and, toward the end of the nineteenth century, they had become the predominant type of housing in Shanghai. By the end of the 1940s, seven decades after the emergence of alleyway houses, more than 72 percent of the city's dwellings were alleyway houses, and about three-quarters of these were shikumen houses.[20] To the present day, more than a century since the first shikumen was built, alleyway houses remain the predominant type of housing in the city.[21]

Shanghai's real estate market, therefore, was launched with the construction of alleyway houses, and much of the market remained connected with the evolution of these houses in the late nineteenth and early twentieth centuries. What was important to the everyday life of the people of Shanghai was of course not the operation of the market at the level of the real estate magnate (whether foreign or Chinese), but its operation at the grassroots level.

Let us now look into how the alleyway houses and the housing market changed to meet the needs of ordinary people, and, in turn, how the daily life of the ordinary people of Shanghai was profoundly shaped by changes in the housing market.

The Evolution of Alleyway Houses

The row houses built during the refugee tide of the 1850s and 1860s were constructed in a rush and, since all were made of wood, by the 1870s many of them had become dilapidated. In addition, wooden houses built in rows were particularly unsafe in case of fire. Thus, newly built houses in the early 1870s were constructed of brick, wood, and cement. These houses were still built in rows, and a few rows were marked off by surrounding walls to form a residential compound. Paved alleyways between the rows were built within the walled compound, a necessity for access, light, and ventilation. Hence the name for this type of dwelling: *lilong fangzi* or *longtang fangzi,* meaning alleyway house. Later, alleyway houses evolved into a number of different styles, but the term "lilong," or "longtang," continued to be used to describe all types of alleyway houses in the city.[22]

NAMING THE ALLEYWAY HOUSES

The earliest as well as the most common type of alleyway house was known as shikumen, a name descriptive of the main entrance of the house. The origin of the term is obscure and needs some explanation. Although virtually everybody in twentieth-century Shanghai knew the word "shikumen," few could explain its meaning and origin. Literally, it means "a stone warehouse door," an interpretation that does not help us understand the character of the house itself. The main entrance of shikumen houses was a wooden door of two planks painted black, with two bronze knockers, one in the middle of each plank. The door was placed within a stone framework; hence the term "shikumen" can mean "a wooden door within a stone frame" (Fig. 11).[23]

In her recent research on Shanghai's alleyway houses, Luo Suwen gives a historical and literary interpretation of the term. Luo found that it was associated with the names for entrances of palaces in ancient China. In ancient China, the standard design of the entrance to an emperor's or king's palace consisted of five layers of gates, and the design of the entrance to a prince's or duke's palace, three layers of gates. Each of the gates bore a special and literary name, but the outermost gate for both emperor-kings' and prince-dukes' palaces shared the same name: *kumen.* Thus the name of Shanghai's alleyway houses means a "stone *kumen.*"[24]

Given the fact that the main entrance or the front door of the house was stone-framed, this interpretation is illuminating. This line of thinking, however, suggests that the outermost door (i.e., the kumen) referred not to the front door of individual houses inside the compound but instead to the

Fig. 11.   In the early 1990s the Chinese postal service issued a series
of stamps depicting people's dwellings (*minju*). Each stamp in the
series bore an image of one or another type of traditional house that
best represents ordinary dwellings of a given locality (provinces and
municipalities). For Shanghai, the alleyway house was chosen as the
archetypal dwelling. The stamp depicts a cluster of shikumen homes.
The four-character caption at the lower right reads *Shanghai minju*
(People's dwelling of Shanghai). The stamp can be seen as an official
recognition of the status of the shikumen house in Shanghai. Photo
property of the author.

entrance of the compound itself. Since a typical alleyway house was always
built inside a walled compound that had a stone-framed main entrance, it
seems more likely that the word "kumen" originally referred to the gate of
the compound. A newspaper advertisement for shikumen houses, which is
among the earliest pieces of information about this type of house, corrob-
orates this. It describes the advertised premises as being "inside a shikumen," revealing that the name referred to the entrance of the compound.[25]

This discussion of the term "shikumen" is not offered as textual criticism, but to suggest an important social change that occurred in Shanghai
in the second half of the nineteenth century. After the turmoil of the 1860s,
newly built alleyway houses were no longer temporary dwellings for refugees but stable homes for newcomers. Two decades or so after the deseg-
regation of Chinese and Europeans, the foreign concessions in Shanghai
gradually gained a reputation as the "model settlements" of East Asia, and
the Chinese started to see the settlements as their "happy land" (*letu*).[26] To
call the main entrance of these residences "stone kumen" was to imply that
these new homes built predominantly in the foreign settlements were as

comfortable as a palace. At the beginning this may well have been commercial puffery, but it was also an instance of the Chinese practice of praising favorite objects with exaggerated artistic or literary expressions.[27]

This love-of-home sentiment was further evidenced in the practice of
giving each alleyway-house compound a distinctive name. All of the names
contained the word "li" or the like (most commonly "fang")—words that
in ancient China referred to the basic urban neighborhoods, which varied
in size from 25 to 100 households.[28] The use of these words, therefore, indicated that the Chinese sojourners in the foreign settlements had started
to see these alleyway-house compounds not as temporary lodgings but
settled neighborhoods. The word "li" was so commonly used for naming alleyway-house compounds that, by the twentieth century, it became
equivalent to "alleyway house."[29]

A typical name for an alleyway-house compound consisted of two characters plus "li" or "fang."[30] Names were selected by various methods. An
alleyway-house compound could be named after its owner, or things related to the owner (such as the owner's hometown), or local features (such
as an old tree), or something that was significant to the owner, and so on.
But by far the most common way of naming an alleyway-house compound
was to use words considered auspicious or words with good connotations.
Among the most common were *fu* (luck), *bao* (treasure), *fu* (wealth), *gui*
(noble), *qing* (celebration), *rong* (glory), *an* (tranquillity), *chang* (prosperity), *ji* (auspiciousness), *shan* (kindness), *de* (virtue), *he* (peace), *kang*
(healthiness), *xing* (flourishing), *xiang* (auspiciousness), and others. Sometimes a character like *yong, heng, jiu,* or *chang* (all of these characters
mean "permanent," "forever," or "long") was combined with a lucky word
to express the wish for everlasting happiness. For example, a popular name
for an alleyway-house compound was Yongxing Li, meaning "Neighborhood of Perpetual Prosperity." A survey found that the names of 230
alleyway-house compounds that started with the character De, 279 with
the character Fu, and 365 with the character Yong.[31]

It was also popular to name alleyway-house compounds with words containing moral meanings, such as expressions from the Confucian classics.
For instance, "*mingde*" (bright virtues or "to understand virtue"), a phrase
from the Confucian classic *The Great Learning* (Daxue), was borne by
seventeen alleyway-house compounds scattered all over the city.[32] Among
other popular names in this category were Airen (love and benevolence),
Hengde (lasting virtue), Huaide (cherishing virtue), Huairen (cherishing
benevolence), Rende (benevolence and virtue), and so on.[33]

To give a fine name to an alleyway-house compound was a matter of

adding a touch of elegance, bestowing a blessing on a new home, and, practically, establishing an everlasting advertisement. The names were inscribed and sometimes painted in red on a horizontal stone installed above
the often arched entrance of the alleyway-house compound. The characters
were written in regular script by a fine calligrapher. Each character was
about two feet by two feet and could be seen from a distance (Fig. 12). The
names were also a must for postal service. Every house inside an alleyway-
house compound was numbered, but the compound itself was not. Instead
the name of the compound was an essential part of the address. A standard
home address in pre-1949 Shanghai read, in order, "name of street, plus
name of alleyway-house compound, plus number of house."[34] This administrative use of alleyway-house names further strengthened the status of
the compound as a residential unit or a community.

One might think that a walled alleyway-house compound with an elegant name inscribed at its entrance would help create a sense of community
among its residents. Such a sense would perhaps be more likely to develop
if the alleyway houses had a stable group of residents who came from similar social backgrounds or places of origin. But history did not give much
time for alleyway-house residents to build up such a feeling. In the first
half of the twentieth century, old shikumen houses underwent a number
of changes, stimulated mostly by the goal of meeting the needs of residents increasingly diversified in character. New designs of alleyway houses
appeared; these new designs did not replace the shikumen but made it
outmoded.

FROM MULTI-BAY TO SINGLE-BAY HOUSES

Figure 13A shows the floor plan of an early alleyway house built in 1872.
While the general layout of Shanghai's alleyway houses—i.e., they were
built in a row—revealed the influence of the West, the interior layout was
obviously derived from the traditional Chinese house known as the *si-
heyuan* (courtyard house or quadrangle house).[35] The alleyway house consisted of a two-story central part, which contained a living room on the first
floor and a master bedroom on the second floor, and wings on each side—
a floor plan that could house a large family (parents with their married children) fairly comfortably. A paved and walled courtyard was located in front
of the living room between the two wings, providing some space for outdoor activities. A kitchen, a servants' room, and rooms for miscellaneous
purposes were located in a single-story detached structure at the back.
A flat roof fenced with wooden rails was built on the top of the kitchen

Fig. 12.   Alleyway-house compounds were commonly given auspicious names, like this shikumen alley built in 1917 on Xinzha Road. The name of the alley, Fukang Li (Alley of Fortune and Good Health), is inscribed above the arched entrance. Fukang Li was a multilane compound, with each lane opening directly on Xinzha Road. More rows of houses were built in Fukang Li in 1934. The two smaller characters on top of the name indicate that this was the "second lane" of Fukang Li. Note that inside the alley was a well topped with a wooden lid. Although running water was always available in lilong neighborhoods, a well was often sunk inside an alley to supplement the water supply. From Luo Xiaowei and Wu Jiang, comps., *Shanghai longtang.*

Fig. 13. Alleyway-house floor plans came in three styles: *A*, a multi-bay, U-shaped shikumen house built in 1872 in Xingren Li (Alley of Prosperity and Benevolence); *B*, a "two-bay, one wing" shikumen house built in 1924 in Huile Li (Alley of Joint Pleasure); *C*, a "single-bay" shikumen house built in 1930 in Jianye Li (Alley of Establishing Careers). The transformation from the multi-bay to the single-bay design reflected the changing real estate market, which through the years had to cope with mounting pressure on housing. Partly because of the housing problem, multigeneration families also declined in favor of nuclear families, which found the single-bay comfortable and economic.

and/or the servants' room for drying clothes. In between the two-story front part and the single-story back part of the house, a back courtyard (a long and narrow open-air space) provided some privacy on both sides of the residence.

These multi-bay, U-shaped shikumen houses were built mostly in the late nineteenth century, although a few were constructed early in the twentieth century. One of the earliest multi-bay shikumen compounds survived until the early 1980s. Known as Xingren Li (Alley of Prosperity and Benevolence), it was built in 1872 and located at the core of the British Settlement in Ningbo Road, one block north of Nanking Road and two blocks west of the Bund. The shikumen complex occupied about 3.3 acres of land. The houses were not well maintained, and in the early 1980s the whole complex was torn down to make way for new construction.[36]

Anyone who is interested in the history of Shanghai may have reason to regret the disappearance of the oldest alleyway houses from the city, but practically speaking this type of house was out of date as a result of mounting pressure by the city's population. The design of the alleyway house—as row houses with contiguous walls—remained in use, but the original design was changed in various ways to meet the increasing demand for housing in the limited space of the foreign settlements and their adjacent areas. The U-shaped alleyway house became unpopular in the early twentieth century because it required much space, an important consideration in view of Shanghai's crowded and expensive land. Instead, newly built alleyway houses in the early twentieth century were smaller. The most common way to reduce the size was to remove one of the wings. These single-wing alleyway houses were called "two-bay, one-wing" (*liangjian yixiang*) houses (see Fig. 13B), in order to distinguish them from the old U-shaped, two-wing houses, which by then were known as "three-bay, two-wing" (*sanjian liangxiang*) houses or, in case of a three-story structure, "three-up and three-down" (*sanshang sanxia*). The open space between the main building and the kitchen annex was eliminated. The kitchen was connected directly to the back of the house and became known as the "draping room" (*pijian*) or "draping kitchen" (*zaopijian*); the latter is still the word for "kitchen" in the Shanghai dialect. Furthermore, from just before 1920 on, in many newly built houses wings were totally absent, and what had been originally the central part of the house was built as a single unit known as a "single-bay" (*dan kaijian*), or "one-up, one-down" (*yishang yixia*), house (the latter because most were two stories). From then on, newly built alleyway houses in the city were mostly two-story, single-bay houses (see Fig. 13C).[37]

Not only were the wings removed and the central part made into a single unit, but compared to the U-shaped shikumen the overall size of the single-bay house was reduced. An average two-story, single-bay house occupied a lot of about 13 by 46 feet (4 meters by 14 meters). Each floor was about 13 feet (4 meters) high. A number of alleyway houses built in the 1920s and 1930s were below these standards. Sometimes the lot was reduced to about 11.5 by 21 feet (3.5 meters by 6.5 meters), and the front courtyard was deleted. The height of the first floor was reduced to 10.8 feet (3.3 meters), and the second floor to 9.8 feet (3.0 meters).[38] These small and lower-ceiling alleyway houses without a yard were called "Japanese houses," a name apparently derived from the notorious Chinese image of the Japanese as "dwarfs."[39] But the name also was connected with the fact that these houses were favorite residences for the Japanese in Shanghai. Many of these houses were built in Hongkou, the center of Shanghai's largest Japanese community. There was yet another name for these structures: "Cantonese houses." It was said that these houses resembled those of Canton, perhaps because, like the Japanese, many Cantonese immigrants in Shanghai lived in this type of alleyway house in Hongkou.[40]

However, not all changes in alleyway houses represented a deterioration of standards. Simultaneously with the appearance of single-bay alleyway houses late in the second decade of the twentieth century, some newly built alleyway houses featured modern amenities, mainly sanitary fixtures (bathrooms with a bathtub and flush toilet) and a gas supply for cooking and hot water. These houses were called "new-type alleyway houses" (*xinshi lilong*) in order to distinguish them from the old alleyway houses (i.e., the shikumen), which usually did not have modern sanitation or gas.[41] These houses were still built in rows and belonged to the general category of alleyway houses (lilong). But they were usually three-story houses with a front gate of iron plate, a feature that differentiated them from the "wooden door within a stone framework" type. Some were built in such a style that, in the eyes of average Shanghainese (who were, typically, residents of the old-type alleyway houses), they were not exactly an "alleyway house" in its classic meaning (i.e., the shikumen) but rather were associated with yangfang (foreign houses or Western-style houses). These new-type alleyway houses were of higher quality, with a reinforced concrete structure (shikumen houses were of wood and brick), steel-sash windows, waxed hardwood floors, gates of wrought iron, and a small front garden, in addition to sanitary fixtures and a gas supply. Garages were also built in the better new-style alleyway-house compounds, indicating that some of the residents had private automobiles. Consequently, the main lane in such compounds was widened to at least 19.5 feet (6 meters), and the branch lanes to about 11.5 feet (3.5 meters).[42] Some of these houses had two bays or two and a half bays to meet the requirements of well-off tenants or buyers, but most had a single bay and were designed to house a single nuclear family.[43]

The shrinkage of alleyway houses indicated an important social change. Although available demographic data on modern Shanghai do not contain precise details on the composition of residents in terms of occupation, there is little doubt that immigrants to Shanghai in the second half of the nineteenth century were mostly well-off merchants, absentee landlords, frustrated bureaucrats and literati, skilled workers, and adventurers.[44] It was estimated that in 1860–62 at least 6.5 million taels of silver were brought by Chinese immigrants into Shanghai's foreign concessions.[45] Shanghai at that time was seen as a place primarily for business and pleasure. The tide of immigrants who flooded into the city looking for jobs (in particular, factory jobs) had not yet come.

Well-off immigrants who came to Shanghai with family in tow required large dwellings. As extended families were common in China, it was usual for these people in their hometowns to live in multigeneration households in big houses with courtyards or, for better-off families, in private garden-houses (*tingyuan*). After moving into Shanghai's foreign settlements, these people were no longer able to have such spacious homes. But the U-shaped alleyway house was an ideal substitute for the traditional dwellings they used to live in, and it allowed them to continue in some ways their traditional family life in this "foreign barbarians' area" (*yichang*), as the concessions were called in those days. For an extended family, the wings of an alleyway house could accommodate the married sons in such a way that the young couples could live under the same roof with their parents while still having some privacy. Some earlier alleyway houses, such as those in the Xingren Li compound, had double wings on each side, a backyard, and several annexes behind the backyard that allowed the residents to keep domestic servants.[46] While a well-off family that moved from a traditional town in Jiangnan to a Shanghai shikumen might miss the elegance of their private gardens, they could take comfort in the notion that the alleyway house was a comfortable and pragmatic urban alternative.[47] The resemblance of the early alleyway house to the traditional courtyard house was an architectural invention that catered to people's reluctance to abandon a traditional way of life.

But changes in housing patterns were inevitable when land values skyrocketed in the twentieth century.[48] As noted, Shanghai's real estate dealers soon found that the U-shaped shikumen was less popular than the two-bay, one-wing house, and the latter was in turn less popular than the single-bay house. By early this century, U-shaped alleyway houses had largely been eliminated from the foreign settlements. Alleyway houses built after the second decade of the twentieth century were mostly single-bay structures. The lot of an average alleyway house in the 1930s had shrunk to about one-fourth of that of U-shaped houses built in the 1870s.[49]

Simultaneously, alleyway-house compounds were getting larger. A typical compound in the late Qing contained 20–30 units, although some had fewer than 10 units. By the 1920s, it was not uncommon to see alleyway-house compounds with more than a hundred houses. The construction of the largest alleyway-house compound in Shanghai, Siwen Li (Alley of Gentleness), was completed in 1921. It was composed of more than 700 houses in a single, walled compound.[50] Any sizable alleyway-house compound always had a main lane no less than 13 feet (4 meters) wide leading to several branch lanes, each about 8 feet (2.5 meters) wide—wide enough for a rickshaw to pass. As the city was always short of land, developers limited the width of alleys as much as possible. It was not uncommon to see some back alleys that were only about 5 feet (1.5 meters) wide. Narrow alleys were dubbed "one thread of sky" (*yi xian tian*), after famous Mount Lingyan of Suzhou, where a narrow chink between two precipitous peaks leaves the sky looking like a piece of thread (Fig. 14).[51]

Let us step back in time and look at an average single-bay alleyway house, the place called home by the majority of Shanghainese in this century. In 1937, a housing committee of the SMC surveyed Chinese houses in the International Settlement and gave the following description in its report on its "inspection of typical premises":

> It is the "li" or alleyway house that is the unit in the Chinese housing system in the Settlement, and it is this type of housing that constitutes the dominant problem. This type of house has a frontage of about 12 feet, and a depth of about 40 feet, or a ground area of about 500 square feet including yard space. Thus, there approximates 12 to 13 house to the mow [mu, or one-sixth of an acre]. Roughly described, passing through the door in the outer wall is found a small courtyard designed to admit a certain amount of light and air. From the courtyard the main room is entered, which occupies the full width of the building, that is about 12 feet, and it is about 15 feet deep. A door at the far end leads to a wooden stairway. . . . Beyond the stairs there is a kitchen and a small back yard. Over the main front room is an upper room of similar size. There is a small back bedroom over the kitchen, and above this

Fig. 14. A bird's-eye view of Xiafei Fang (Joffre Alley) shows a new-style alleyway-house compound built on Avenue Joffre in 1924. Note the small, walled, flat roofs at the back of each unit (on top of the "pavilion rooms"). These were designed for drying laundry and outdoor activities such as *taiji* exercising in the morning and "enjoying the cool" on summer nights. Note also that a few flat roofs were covered, indicating that the residents had turned the area into a small room to gain more indoor living space. From Luo Xiaowei and Wu Jiang, comps., *Shanghai longtang.*

> again an open space intended for use as drying stage and reached by a steep stair.[52]

Half a century later, houses of this type had deteriorated because of age and generally poor maintenance, and in the building frenzy in Shanghai in the 1990s they were torn down on a wide scale. Still, today it would not require a thirty-minute walk from any place in the city to find such a house, although to locate a well-maintained alleyway-house compound in its original form would be more difficult. In the recent building binge, the city government decided to preserve a few authentic shikumen house compounds as relics of the type of dwelling that once housed most Shanghailanders. These protected structures have been declared off-limits to builders. Among these compounds is Jianye Li (Alley of Establishing Careers), a shikumen compound constructed in 1930 in the French Concession

(Fig. 15).⁵³ This is a sizable compound, with 260 units lined up in 22 rows and with three major entrances from the street. Our tour could start from any one of these entrances. On the stone arch spanning the entrance were inscribed three big characters: Jian-Ye-Li. Stepping inside, we find ourselves in the main alleyway, about 16.5 feet (5 meters) wide, which runs directly from the entrance. The length of alleyways varied greatly according to the size of the compound. Some compounds had just a single lane. But more commonly a compound had a main alleyway plus a number of branch alleyways stretching from both sides of the main lane, thus forming an insulated residential compound. Since houses in Jianye Li are identical, we could walk into any unit and quickly get a sense of what all the others are like.

Walking through the two-plank shikumen door of a typical unit, we first come to an open space called the *tianjing* (lit., heavenly well), which is a paved, walled, and almost square courtyard. Courtyards varied slightly in size from compound to compound; in Jianye Li, they are about 108 square feet (10 square meters). The tianjing was a place for drying clothes and for other outdoor activities. Often flowerpots stood in the yard. Sometimes a flower bed occupied a corner. The plants in the yard were perhaps the only greenery that an average Shanghai resident could enjoy on a daily basis in this urban jungle of cement. Stepping forward, through the front yard, we come to a French window, beyond which lies the rectangular living room (*ketang*) of about 215 square feet (20 square meters), one of two major rooms in the house. At the far end of the living room is a stairway, located between the living room and the kitchen, which is at the other end of the house. The kitchen is about 108 square feet and can also be entered through a back door.

Directing our feet up the stairs, on the second floor we find a bedroom of exactly the same size as the living room right below it, that is, a rectangular room of about 215 square feet, with front windows facing to the south, overlooking the courtyard. Builders of some stylish alleyway houses constructed after the early 1920s replaced the front windows with French doors through which one could walk onto a small, half-roofed or open-air balcony to get a good view, but Jianye Li was not among them. Retracing our steps to the stairs, we find, halfway down the stairs, a room right on top of the kitchen. This room was known as the *tingzijian* (pavilion room): a den, or a place for study, or a room for miscellaneous purposes. A flat roof with waist-high walls was built on top of the pavilion room and served as a deck for drying clothes. If this were a three-story house (which was not too common among shikumen), the third floor would consist of a bedroom

Fig. 15.   Inside Jianye Li (Alley of Establishing Careers) in the
French Concession, this 187,000-square-foot alleyway-house compound (built in 1930) had three main lanes, each of which led to several branch lanes on both sides. Inside the lanes were 260 shikumen
houses built in twenty-two rows. Numerous stores operated in the
forty units facing Rue J. Frelupt (today's Jianguoxi Road). Courtesy
of Lu Hanlong and Hu Sen.

the same size as the living room and a pavilion room the same size as the kitchen, and the flat roof would be built on top of the third-floor pavilion room.[54]

The shift in popularity from multi-bay to single-bay alleyway houses was also a reflection of changes in the composition of immigrants to the city in the early twentieth century: from a larger number of the social-elite type of immigrant, such as rich landlords, merchants, literati, bureaucrats, and the like, to a larger number of commoner type of immigrant such as shop assistants, clerks, schoolteachers, artisans, and the like. In view of Shanghai's increasingly expensive housing market, the latter could not afford to have several generations living under one roof. The majority could afford to keep only their immediate family with them in the city. Indeed, as noted earlier, it was not unusual for a person to leave his or her entire family back in the village and come to the city alone to pursue the "Shanghai dream." For these people, the single-bay house was a more practical and affordable proposition than the multi-bay house. Furthermore, along with the broader social changes in China brought by the New Cultural Movement and the May 4th Movement (multifaceted and far-reaching nationalistic upheavals late in the second decade of the twentieth century and in the early 1920s that aimed to sweep away the old and modernize China), of which Shanghai was a powerhouse, the nuclear family became more common in the city than the multigeneration household. But the housing situation in Shanghai involved more than a change in the composition of the household. In the twentieth century, in the face of a mounting demand for housing, the single-bay house was soon subdivided into small rooms for rent.

COMPARTMENTALIZING THE SHIKUMEN

All types of alleyway houses were designed to accommodate one family per house. Such a house, even the single-bay house, was a cozy home for a couple with unmarried children. Usually the parents occupied the bedroom on the second floor, and the children slept in the pavilion room or, if it was a three-story house, the third-floor bedroom. There was no dining room in a single-bay alleyway house; the family dining table commonly sat in the kitchen or living room.

However, because of the shortage of housing in Shanghai, alleyway houses were often not occupied as their designers intended, but instead commonly housed more than one family. Many houses were remodeled to create more rooms and increase floor space to accommodate tenants. These newly created rooms had their own particular names, which were such common knowledge in the city that it would be hard to find a single Shanghai resident ignorant of the terms. Following is a list of the reconstructions most commonly found in shikumen houses: [55]

1. The living room was extended to engulf what was formerly the front courtyard.

2. The living room was divided into a front living room (*qian ketang*) and a back living room (*hou ketang*).

3. The ceiling of the back living room was lowered to allow an additional room to be created between the back living room and the bedroom on the second floor. This addition was called the second loft (*er ceng ge*).

4. Like the living room, the bedroom on the second floor was divided into a front bedroom (*qianfang*) and a back bedroom (*houfang*).

5. The ceiling of the second floor was lowered to make room for a so-called false third floor (*jia san ceng*) or third loft (*san ceng ge*).

The floor area of a single-bay alleyway house that underwent such remodeling could be increased 50 percent, and a house originally designed for a family of no more than 8 or 9 could be remodeled to accommodate 15 to 20 persons, or 4 to 9 families.[56] A 1936–37 survey of housing in Shanghai conducted by the SMC found that virtually every house surveyed had undergone some sort of remodeling. The following account from the SMC report provides a graphic description of how a single-bay shikumen house with a floor area of 718 square feet and 8,077 cubic feet of space housed eight families with twenty-four persons:

> The courtyard has been covered in. The main ground floor [living room] has been cut in two by a partition, and a passageway with a storage loft [the second-floor loft] over made at the side. In the front part [the front living room], about ten feet square, live the lessor [the "second landlord"] and his family, five persons in all. He customarily pays the rent of the whole house to the landlord, letting out the rest to subtenants ["third tenants"]. In the back portion [the back living room], about 10 ft. by 8 ft., live three persons. The kitchen has been sectioned off and three more live in a 9 ft. x 9 ft. room. Upstairs, the large front room [bedroom] has been divided into two. The front part [the front bedroom] is the best in the house for it has light and air and runs the full width of the house—it is occupied by two persons. The back part [the back bedroom], smaller by reason of the passage, is home to three persons. The room over the kitchen [the pavilion room] has its advantages because it is secluded; this also is occupied by two persons. This

was originally a two storeyed house, but two lofts [the third-floor lofts] have been made in the slope of the roof. The front one has a height of only 5 feet in front, 7 ft. 6 in. at the apex of the roof, and is about eight feet deep; it shelters two persons. The back room, about 10 sq. ft., is right under the roof slope, is only 3 ft. high at the back and is occupied by a single person. What was the drying stage [platform] has been enclosed, and two more people live in it—about 9 sq. ft.[57]

The subdividing described in this report was typical in Republican Shanghai. Investment in old-type alleyway houses stagnated after 1935; in the city's most desirable areas few new shikumen compounds were built.[58] Instead, developers built the new-type alleyway houses mentioned earlier (with steel-framed windows, waxed floors, modern sanitary facilities, and a small front garden). But the population continued to increase and the majority of people could not afford the new type, and so shikumen houses were still in big demand (Fig. 16). The solution to the limited availability of and continuing demand for the old-type alleyway house was subdivision, and more and more residents came to live in compartmentalized rooms within a single shikumen. According to the 1937 SMC report, in the International Settlement where most of Shanghai's alleyway houses were located, the numbers of families per house were:

14,310 families living one family to a house;
12,874 families living two families to a house;
18,945 families living three families to a house;
22,764 families living four families to a house;
15,435 families living five families to a house;
14,028 families living six families to a house;
7,840 families living seven families to a house;
3,824 families living eight families to a house;
2,061 families living nine families to a house;
and 1,305 families living more than nine families to a house.

The report indicated that in some cases a single alleyway house accommodated as many as 15 families. A concentration of 4 families, or 24 persons, per house was the rule in these neighborhoods, which gives an average 30 square feet or 337 cubic feet per person.[59]

The crowding within shikumen became a favorite topic of literature. A local farce, "The Seventy-two Tenants," played by the well-known comic actors Yang Huasheng and Lu Yang, tells of the life of tenants in a shikumen house. The farce was so well received that the term "seventy-two tenants" became a synonym for sharing rooms in the crowded shikumen

Fig. 16. This late-style shikumen house on Avenue Foch was built in 1937. Each wing had a balcony with a wrought-iron railing. Between the wings, behind the front door, is a small yard. Residents usually came and went through the back door. An old woman sitting on a bamboo chair is washing food in a basin, a morning chore for almost every family. Residents took advantage of this sunny winter day to hang out their bedding. Because the sun's warmth inflated the quilts and left them fresher smelling, that night's sleep would be particularly comfortable. Courtesy of Lu Hanyi and Li Jin.

houses of Shanghai.[60] The plots of a number of Chinese movies produced in the late 1940s that later became classics, such as *Wanjia denghuo* (Lights in Thousands of Families) and *Wuya yu maque* (The Crow and the Sparrows), were based on neighborhood life in crowded shikumen houses.[61]

Second Landlords

Rooms in a compartmentalized shikumen house were not rented out by owners but sublet by tenants. Standard lease contracts in Shanghai had a clause prohibiting subletting without the owner's permission, but this rule remained largely on paper only.[62] After a tenant rented a house from the owner, as long as the tenant paid the rent there was little interaction between the landlord and tenant. There was no manager or leasing office on the premises; an owner might simply hire a gate guard whose main responsibilities were to sweep the alleyway and collect rent. Nobody was on the site acting on the landlord's behalf to watch for subletting. Actually, subletting without the lessor's consent was permitted by law. According to code 312 of the Civil Law of the Shanghai Mixed Court: "If during the term of the lease the lessee sub-lets the leased thing to a third party, he must (first) obtain the consent of the lessor, unless there is any custom to the contrary."[63] In other words, *custom* prevailed.

Subletting was not a controversial issue in landlord-tenant relations in Shanghai prior to the end of the 1920s. By the early twentieth century subletting was already a common practice, and the expression "second landlord" (*er fangdong*), which referred to tenants who sublet rooms to others, was already in common use. Bao Tianxiao, a well-known journalist and writer, came to Shanghai from his hometown of Suzhou in 1906. Since he planned a long stay, he started to look for a house. He spent three days looking along the newly constructed roads (today's Huanghe Road and Fengyang Road) toward the west end of Nanking Road, where a number of shikumen compounds had recently been built, and finally came across a shikumen compound with a notice pasted on the entrance announcing a room for rent. Bao walked into the alley and found the house:

> I knocked at the door and stepped in. I saw an eighteen- or nineteen-year-old girl sitting quietly in the living room making shoes. I noticed that she was a pretty girl (and according to psychologists, this very first impression indicated that things were moving forward favorably). I explained my purpose and an old lady came out to greet me. She took me upstairs to look at the room. This was a two-bay, two-story house, and the room for rent was the wing on the second floor. Because this was

a new house the walls were clean. The wing faced east and had a window at the back, which made the room cool in the summer. Everything looked fine and I felt satisfied.

When I asked about the rent, the old lady, who was the second landlord, at first did not answer. Instead, she asked me questions about my family, occupation, native place, and so on, and I answered accordingly, which seemed to satisfy her. She told me her family had five members. She and her husband had a daughter, who was the girl I had just seen, and they also had a son and a daughter-in-law. Although their native place was Nanjing, they spoke the Suzhou dialect because their in-law was a native of Suzhou. She said, "We like a quiet life. Tenants with a big family would bring bustle and we would decline them. You, sir, are an intellectual, and you are a native of Suzhou. I therefore would not ask for an unfair price—the monthly rent is $7." I agreed with the rent immediately. I paid $2 as a deposit and asked them to remove the "for rent" notice right away.[64]

A few important points can be gleaned from this account of renting a dwelling in early-twentieth-century Shanghai. First, it seems that subletting was an accepted and common practice. Bao was looking to sublet rather than to rent an entire house directly from the owner. The fact that the Cai family (i.e., the second landlord) posted an ad at the entrance of the compound where they lived indicated that they did not scruple to publicize the subletting in the neighborhood, which further suggested that subletting was not regarded as an infringement on the owner's rights; otherwise the Cai family would at least have tried to post the ad somewhere else. In fact, to post a for-rent sign was the most common way of finding a tenant in Shanghai. Such an advertisement, known as a "call for rent" (*zhaozu*), was customarily a piece of red paper, equivalent to about one quarter of a sheet of 8.5" x 11" paper, on which the location and size of the available rental were written by brush. Such notices were often posted at the entrance of the lane, or on the telephone poles in the streets nearby.[65]

Bao regarded the $7.00 rent as reasonable, although it almost equaled a month's income for an average factory worker. The range of monthly wages for workers in one of the major flour mills in Shanghai at that time, for example, was $7.50–$10.00.[66] In some less desirable areas outside the central part of the International Settlement, such as Hongkou, the rent for a house let directly by an owner averaged $3.00–$4.00 a month in 1906.[67] The Cais' shikumen house, although new, was not located in the best residential area of that time. The rent that the Cai family asked for must not have been merely a share of rent but had to include a profit. In other words, subletting in early-twentieth-century Shanghai was already a profitable business.

The Cai family's preference for a Suzhou tenant showed that native place or local origin (*jiguan*) played some role in choosing one's neighbors and tenants. In this story, the fact that the Cais, who hailed from Nanjing, adopted their daughter-in-law's Suzhou dialect suggests a social favoring of people of Jiangnan origins, in contrast to the bias against Subei people that developed in the city at a later time.[68] But the preference for having neighbors with the same local origins was never strong enough to create native-place-based segregation among alleyway-house neighborhoods. Some districts of Shanghai were known for some degree of concentration of people who came from similar native places. For instance, North Sichuan Road in Hongkou was known for its Cantonese residents. But many others, including Japanese, also lived in the same area. Segregation by local origins (mainly segregation of Subei people) could be found in the city's peripheral shantytowns,[69] but it never existed in the city's vast alleyway-house neighborhoods. Researchers of modern Chinese socioeconomic history have in recent years paid increasing attention to the role of local origin in Chinese society (in large cities in particular). But in an important dimension of social life in Shanghai—choice of place of residence—local origin was insignificant, at least for the majority of the people. It was rare to see a single alleyway house—much less a whole alleyway-house compound—inhabited by families of the same local origin.[70]

One thing that caused people of different local origins to live together was that, in an environment of mounting population pressure, most Shanghai residents simply could not afford to pick and choose their neighbors on the basis of local origins. The first three decades of the twentieth century saw the most rapid population increase in the city's history. At the turn of the century, Shanghai's population had not reached 1 million; by 1930, more than 3 million people lived in the city, mostly in the foreign concessions.[71] These three decades were the golden age for Shanghai's shikumen houses. Among the 108 shikumen compounds located in the core of the Nanking Road area (today known as the Nanjingdong Road Ward), where the first shikumen were built, 98 were constructed between 1902 and 1931.[72] But, as I have suggested, the availability of housing lagged far behind demand, and consequently subletting became common.[73] By the late 1920s, second landlords had gradually become the major players in leasing dwellings in the city, and they continued to be so in the 1930s and 1940s, as shown in Table 6. As a result, a tenant leasing a room from a

Table 6. Subletting in Republican Shanghai
(Samples from an Early-1950s Survey)

	Time of Leasing		
	Before 1938	*1938–45*	*1948*
Number of tenant households	383	1,198	568
Number of tenant households leasing as "third tenants"	258	910	482
Percentage of "third tenants"	67	76	85

SOURCE: Adopted from Yu Shan, "Er fangdong yu dingfei yazu."

second landlord was known as the "third tenant" (*san fangke*) and the owner of the house was called the "big landlord" (*da fangdong*). By the early 1930s, these appellations had already become popular, and they remained what an informant called a "Shanghai specialty" (*Shanghai techan*) through the Republican period.[74]

A key element that contributed to the rise of subletting was the appearance of the so-called takeover fee (*dingfei*) as a requirement for renting. The fee was originally compensation paid by a new tenant to a previous tenant who had left some fixtures or furniture in the house. Because these things were useful to a new tenant but cumbersome for an old tenant to have to move, the payment was a mutually beneficial arrangement welcomed by both parties. The fee was supposedly voluntary and was usually less than half the original price of the materials left behind. This custom probably started in the late nineteenth century, when renting (rather than purchasing) a house had become common in the city. But the nature of the fee gradually changed. By the late 1920s, this kind of courtesy between tenants had already become something belonging to the "good old days," and takeover fees became a standard and nonrefundable charge for renting.[75]

To rent a shikumen house in the early 1930s a tenant had to pay the landlord a takeover fee that usually equaled about two to three months' rent. A shrewd tenant saw the fee as an investment, because the rental was not only his or her own residence but also a business opportunity. After renting the house, he or she could sublet rooms, and out of the rents collected from the subletting could soon recoup the takeover fee. After that, the difference between the rent paid to the "big landlord" and the rent collected from the "third tenants" was a constant source of income. Being a second landlord was therefore a popular business in Republican-era Shanghai.

In addition to the ambiguity of the legal codes regarding subletting in Shanghai's real estate market that I have mentioned above, the city's special situation as a treaty port also contributed to the second landlord practice. According to an early agreement between the Shanghai Daotai, Gong Mu-jiu, and the British consul, George Balfour, rental contracts in the foreign settlement had to be registered with the consulate and endorsed (sealed) by the Daotai, hence the name *daoqi* (title deed sealed by the Daotai).[76] Before 1890, only foreigners were permitted to hold title. Thus, a Chinese who wished to purchase land in the settlement had to go through a foreign registrant. Later, the provision was abolished but Chinese land buyers still preferred to have their property registered in the name of a foreigner in order to avoid exposure to the corruption and legal ambiguities that frequently occurred under the Chinese authorities. The result was a booming business run by Shanghai's Westerners acting as registrants for real estate actually owned by Chinese. These Westerners, known as "foreign registration merchants" (*guahao yangshang*), charged ten taels of silver as an annual fee. As a result an alleyway-house compound often had two owners: one, the registered owner, that is, the foreigner under whose name the daoqi was issued, and the other, the "beneficial owner" who was the real, Chinese, owner.[77] The ambiguity of ownership made it almost impossible for the real owner to sue because of subletting, for ownership itself may have been legally in doubt. Furthermore, an alleyway-house compound had only one title deed, in spite of the fact that it may have contained dozens of houses. To purchase an individual house within an alleyway-house compound involved the compound owner issuing a "certificate of ownership" (*quanbing dan*) indicating that the house was registered as part of the compound but was actually owned by the purchaser. This type of transfer of ownership was widely practiced during the Sino-Japanese War, but, since it often involved the foreign registration merchants acting on the behalf of Chinese absentee landlords who had left Shanghai at the beginning of the war, it further complicated the issue of ownership.[78] But the most important reason for subletting without interference from the owner was that the takeover fee continued increasing in the Republican era and by the early 1940s was close to the purchase price. Once the tenant paid the fee it was mutually understood (without being spoken and never put in writing) that he had the privilege (if not the right) to sublet the house at a profit.

The subletting boom brought brokers into the business. Brokers earned commissions by introducing house owners and renters. Brokers' main interest, however, was not to earn a commission based on the monthly rent but to get a commission on the takeover fee. Brokers in this business were called "termites," an epithet reflecting exactly how people felt about them. Advertisements by *dingwu gongsi* (companies for "taking over" houses) appeared every day in Shanghai's newspapers in the 1940s. Such companies amounted to no more than an office (often rented rather than owned), a telephone, and a notebook to record information about clients. But companies like this were by no means the most obscure ones in the business. In fact, the majority of the "termites" were, to use a popular term in present-day China, "go-it-alone, individual enterprises" (*dan'gan geti hu*). Most "termites" conducted their business in teahouses. Two of Shanghai's famous teahouses, Tongyuchun on Nanking Road and Chunfeng Deyi Lou in the Yu Garden of the old Chinese city, were particularly favored by brokers. A Shanghai resident recalled, "Every day when dawn broke and the city was still asleep, these teahouses were already full of customers. The great majority of these customers were the 'termite' type of rental brokers. They came here every day, just like workers go to their early shifts. Over a cup of tea and a piece of cake, they exchanged information with each other. In the conversations they all attempted to gain as much information as they could and grudgingly gave information to others. But as long as there were no conflicts of interest they liked to exchange information, because more information meant a better chance to have more business, and more business meant a lot of commissions."[79]

The speculation in subletting was greatly stimulated by the wars that occurred in Shanghai and its vicinity in the Republican period. The Wusong-Shanghai War of 1932, commonly referred to by Shanghai residents as the "128" war (January 28, read as "1-2-8"), brought a tide of refugees to Shanghai and contributed to a boom in the subletting business. As one author commented in 1933, "Last year when the January 28 War occurred in the Chinese districts, the Special Districts [i.e., the International Settlement and the French Concessions] ordered a reduction of rents for three months [in order to guarantee affordable housing for refugees]. The 'big landlords' were like 'a dumb person tasting bitter herbs' [i.e., unable to complain]. But the 'second landlords' beamed with a smile—'A Pavilion Room for Rent for $20 a Month,' 'A Third Floor Loft for Rent for $18 a Month'—the paste underneath these posters had not yet dried before these rooms were already gone!"[80]

This wartime housing crush was repeated, with even more severity, in the 1940s. The Sino-Japanese War of 1937–45 and the Civil War of 1946–49, although each at the beginning brought a temporary setback to commerce in the city, did not end the prosperity of Shanghai. Quite the opposite; the so-called Solitary Island (*gudao*) period (1938–1941) and the mid-1940s were periods in the city's history when it flourished best. A huge population, rich and poor, poured into Shanghai from everywhere, seeking a relatively safe haven. Most of the new alleyway houses with modern facilities were built in the late 1930s and the 1940s, but their numbers were far from sufficient to meet the demand for housing. As mentioned earlier, these new-type alleyway houses were mostly rented or purchased by well-off families. Very few old-type alleyway houses were built after 1940, which meant that the majority of the population—which by 1949 was close to 5.5 million—had to jam into the shikumen houses built before 1935. The second landlord business boomed. It was in the 1940s that the takeover fee was no longer equivalent to a few months' rent but was close to the purchase price.[81]

A researcher examining Shanghai's real estate pointed out in the early 1930s that "the biggest creditors in the market are landlords, and the most serious debts are rents. In our people's daily life, the number one expense is rent for housing."[82] For the common people, the biggest creditors were the "second landlords" rather than the "big landlords." It was estimated that in working-class shikumen neighborhoods, second landlords controlled 99 percent of the rentals.[83] An average factory worker or shop assistant paid 20 to 40 percent of his or her income to rent a kitchen, a pavilion room, or a loft of about 108 square feet (less than 10 square meters): in a single room such as this the whole family lived.[84] Because of the extreme shortage of housing in wartime Shanghai, Shanghai's second landlords exhausted virtually every possible way to subdivide and compartmentalize rooms for renting. Remodeling, such as adding a number of lofts underneath the roof, was common everywhere in alleyway-house neighborhoods. Even a few pieces of tinplate could form a room on the flat roof above a pavilion room. In some extreme cases second landlords rented their lofts by the bunk (or berth) space, as if running a little inn.[85]

For the majority of the people of Shanghai, who could not afford to rent a whole house, the second landlord was a person they generally disliked but could not avoid in their daily life. A comment on second landlords made by a journalist perhaps represented the general sentiment of Shanghai residents: "If you want to know who are the most scheming people in Shanghai, they are the second landlords."[86] In spite of second landlords' bad reputation, money still mattered, and many tenants found that being a second landlord was an attractive way of making money. Toward the end of the Republican period, when the Civil War drove hundreds of thousands of people into Shanghai, even "third tenants" tried hard to sublet their rooms. According to *Shenbao*, it was not unusual in the late 1940s for a third tenant who lived in a wing to divide the room into three parts (a "front wing," "middle wing," and "back wing"). Typically, the third-tenant family lived in the front wing and sublet the middle and back wings. No wonder that in these years when people paid a New Year's visit to friends and relatives (by custom, after exchanging greetings people wished each other well for the New Year), they commonly offered the felicitation "May you become a second landlord this year!" [87]

The Shikumen Mélange

A MIXTURE OF RESIDENTS

Although second landlords were often only grudgingly accepted by the general public and were criticized by some indignant intellectuals as an "exploiting class," they were indeed no more than a group of "little urbanites" (xiaoshimin) who sacrificed the comfort of their homes to offset some of their rent, supplement the family income, or make a living. [88] Their financial situation was not necessarily better than that of the third tenants who rented rooms from them. It was common for second landlords and their families to live in the less desirable (if not the worst) part of the house (such as the kitchen, loft, or back room) in order to rent out the better parts of the house (such as the front bedroom, front living room, and pavilion room). [89] There was no clear line of class or social rank dividing these landlords and their tenants.

Indeed, shikumen residents came from all walks of life and had widely different backgrounds. Sociologists may have some difficulty in trying to classify them according to conventional sociological criteria. In post-1949 China, the Communists' labeling of these residents according to the party's standards of social class was purely for the purpose of orchestrating political campaigns, and in no way reflected objective reality. [90] It was precisely the differences among these people (whether differences in class, occupation, local origin, or anything else) and the similarity of their residences that characterized Shanghai's alleyway-house neighborhoods. These neighborhoods may not have been a melting pot, but they were certainly, to use another figure of speech, a Chinese wok ideal for stir-frying—a place where a great variety of people were tossed together to produce a sauté (*chaocai*): it is this I call "the shikumen mélange."

Xia Yan's classic drama, *Under the Eaves of Shanghai* (*Shanghai wuyan xia*), which describes the lives of a group of shikumen residents in the 1930s, is a vivid showcase of the shikumen mix. A typical single-unit shikumen house located in east Shanghai (Hudong) is the setting of this three-act tragicomedy. According to the author, the drama was based on his personal experience in Shanghai's shikumen houses. He himself had lived under "these kinds of eaves" for more than ten years before he wrote the story in the spring of 1937, intending to tell of the "grief and joy of those small figures in this abnormal society of Shanghai."[91] The author's familiarity with the lives of the characters he created and his intention to reflect real life in Shanghai make this celebrated work realistic and, therefore, worthy of discussion in the context of historical analysis.

The inhabitants of the house in Xia's story are a microcosm of Shanghai's shikumen residents. Lin Zhicheng (aged thirty-six), the "second landlord," who lived with his wife, Yang Caiyu (aged thirty-two), in the living room, was a clerk in the payroll office of a cotton mill. An elementary schoolteacher, Zhao Zhenyu (aged forty-eight), lived in the kitchen with his wife (aged forty-two) and two children (a thirteen-year-old son and a five-year-old daughter). The pavilion room (tingzijian) was rented by a twenty-eight-year-old college graduate, Huang Jiamei, and his twenty-four-year-old wife, Guifen. Huang had been an office worker in a foreign-owned company but had recently been laid off. The bedroom, which was the main room of a shikumen house, was rented by a seaman's wife, Shi Xiaobao (aged twenty-seven or twenty-eight). Her husband's occupation often kept him away, and the lonely young woman supported herself as a "half-open" prostitute (or, to use a euphemism applied to this kind of prostitute at that time in Shanghai, a "modern lady"). She occupied the best room of the house for the convenience of her clients. A dark loft underneath the bedroom (the so-called second loft) was the home of a newspaper seller, Li Lingbei (aged fifty-four), who was single and an alcoholic.[92]

Such a variety of residents in a single shikumen house was not merely the result of the exercise of artistic license but reflected real life in Shanghai's alleyway-house neighborhoods. Within about 540 square feet (50 square meters) of floor space, dwellings like this normally housed three to five families, or about a dozen residents of all sorts of backgrounds.[93] Mixtures of residents in single alleyway houses were evident everywhere in the city, but particularly in shikumen neighborhoods. A year after Xia Yan wrote his drama, a schoolteacher published an essay describing what he called "ten views from a loft": ten households that lived in a compartmentalized single-bay shikumen similar to that portrayed by Xia Yan. Using a plain style of writing, the author offered a sort of record of "all mortal beings" in Shanghai's alleyway-house neighborhoods. Here is a sketch of the residents by the order of the rooms they occupied:

1.   Front living room: a policeman with his wife and two teenage daughters. The policeman, a Shandong native, was also a moneylender; most of his clients were peddlers who lived nearby.

2.   Back living room: a couple with three children. The couple were teachers in an elementary school inside the alleyway (a so-called alleyway school). They became romantically involved when the wife was a student of the husband. But the romance was ruined by being "married, with children." The author complained that the couple often quarreled, the wife cursed and cried, and the children made all sorts of noise.

3.   Second-floor bedroom: shared by two dancing girls and a tourist girl (a guide). They stayed home in the morning and worked afternoons or nights. Sometimes they came home after midnight or at dawn. The author admitted that he often felt aroused by his young female neighbors who lived so close to him in the same house: "Every time I saw them walk up and down the stairs, their breasts and hips undulating like waves, my heart beat faster."

4.   Second-floor loft (between the back living room and the second-floor bedroom): a cobbler and his wife, both from Subei. Every day the cobbler shouldered his bamboo carrying pole and walked to nearby alleyways to ply his trade: repairing and making shoes. His wife just loafed or played mah-jongg with neighbors. She was quite unaware that her idleness had become a topic of discord for her neighbors, the schoolteachers who lived downstairs in the back living room. The teacher's wife blamed the husband for failing to give his wife a better life, saying the cobbler had a low-class occupation but he nevertheless was able to let his wife enjoy her life.

5.   Third-floor bedroom: a woman in her early thirties who had a full-time live-in maid cum companion. The woman was an opium addict, stayed home most of the time, and supported herself by being a mistress.

6.   Kitchen: the second landlord, a man in his fifties, and his wife, who was in her late twenties. The wife, a Suzhou native, was a shrewd woman who dominated their household. The man seems to have spent his leisure time at a Suzhou storyteller's theater every day.

7.   The flat roof: a single man who was a proofreader for a newspaper.

8.   Third-floor pavilion room: a Suzhou native in her twenties who was a stage actress (of modern dramas, *wenming xi*) and her husband, an opium addict who idled about and was supported by his wife.

9.   Second-floor pavilion room: four young men who were waiters in a Western-style restaurant. They often dressed in white Western suits and boasted that their work clothing was "better than what university students wear." These young men and the second-floor girls often teased and flirted with each other in the pavilion room.

10.   Third-floor loft: the author, a schoolteacher who lost his job when the elementary school where he taught was bombed by the Japanese during the August 13 incident of 1937. He moved into this shikumen house in the International Settlement and worked as a freelance writer to support his family.[94]

Shikumen houses like this could be found in most parts of the city but they were particularly common in the central and northeastern parts of the International Settlement, which included the busy commercial center of the city around Nanking Road and the factory and dock areas in Yangshupu northeast to the Huangpu River (see Map 2 in chapter 1). In these areas and elsewhere in the city, factory workers lived in shikumen neighborhoods. As noted earlier, the majority of Shanghai's factory workers (aside from casual employees) resided in shikumen houses, not in the city's squalid shantytowns. Shanghai's industrial areas like those in Yangshupu and Huxi (west Shanghai) had some concentration of factory-worker residents, but even there factory workers lived in shikumen with people of various other callings.[95] Elsewhere in the city, shikumen houses were the most common residence of factory workers of all sorts.[96] Pavilion rooms, for instance, were popular among factory workers because of their relatively low rent and secluded position in the house.

Pavilion rooms in some way were a symbol of life of Shanghai. This small room of about 108 square feet (10 square meters) was sometimes jokingly referred to as the "immediate supervisor" (*dingtou shangsi*) of the kitchen, for it was always built above the kitchen. As in all Chinese houses, the front rooms of an alleyway house (i.e., the first-floor living room and the second-floor bedroom) were designed, wherever possible, to face the south so that the main rooms would be warm in winter and cool in summer and have ample light. Thus, the pavilion room at the back of the house often faced the least favorable direction, the north, and could enjoy sunlight only on steamy hot summer days. But the room was located right off the middle landing of the staircase towards the second floor, had its own entrance, and was not adjacent to other rooms. For roughly the same rent—$7–8 in a moderately desirable neighborhood in the thirties—most tenants would choose a pavilion room over a back living room or back bedroom. Consequently, pavilion rooms were known for the diversity of their dwellers in these already diverse neighborhoods. One could find in them office clerks of all sorts, factory workers, apprentices, college and high school students, freelance writers, and what might be called "intellectual vagrants" of all types, such as unemployed or self-employed artists, dramatists, musicians, and so on.[97] The very name "pavilion room" seems to suggest a room small but cozy, like a pavilion in a traditional Chinese garden.

This type of room in particular was home to many of Shanghai's educated single youths, who were typically from small rural towns and who sojourned to the city looking for careers (mostly in literature, journalism, and education). Their small incomes limited them to renting pavilion rooms. One such sojourner recalled that during the eight years he had lived in Shanghai, except for two years when he lived in a dormitory provided by his employer, his home was always a pavilion room. He seemed to miss his life there, not only because the pavilion room was the place where he entertained his lady friends but, more memorably, because of the numerous evenings he spent with young men like himself:

> After supper a group of my friends who were lonely would come over to my place to chat. The little room would be full of people—chairs and my tiny iron-framed bed were occupied by one buttock after another. We smoked cigarettes, laughing and wrangling. Every one felt free, being unrestrained and undisciplined. The topics we talked about were even more unlimited: from the Three and Five Emperors in remote ages to the decline of Xuantong [the last emperor of the Qing]; from Mr. Sun Yat-sen's revolution to the treason of Chen Jiongming; from Mussolini and Hitler to Stalin and Roosevelt; from "Manchukuo" to the Japanese warlords. If we tired of current political affairs, we would shift the subject to the life and folk customs of various places, from Beiping to Nanjing, from Shanghai to Guangzhou, from Hangzhou to Hong Kong, from Suzhou to Yangzhou. And, inevitably, the topic shifted to women. Starting with female students, we would go all the way to concubines, social butterflies, dancing girls, massage girls, prostitutes, waitresses, and country girls. Along this line, the topic would become the "wife issue," and all of us would join in the debate about one's taste in choosing a spouse. Or we might sigh, stroking the beard on our chin, and feel full of self-pity.

But these young men also felt burden-free, being single as they were in Shanghai. Without a family around, the happy gathering often went on till after midnight. On a fine night, they would take a stroll in the streets and alleyways nearby and then go back to the pavilion room, and the talking would continue. Whenever their pocket money allowed, drink and a pot-luck meal crowned these gatherings.[98]

It was from this kind of lifestyle that came some of Republican China's finest "literary youth" (*wenxue qingnian*). Recalling them and some of their seniors is like entering a gallery of twentieth-century China's most prominent writers: Lu Xun (1881–1936), Mao Dun (1896–1981), Ba Jin (1904–), Yu Dafu (1896–1945), Liang Shiqiu (1903–1987), Zou Taofen (1895–1944), and so on. All had lived and written in a pavilion room. The room was small and, as one writer put it, "if these people sit and talk in the same room they end up breathing the carbon dioxide that comes out of each other's mouths";[99] it was nevertheless a happy nest for many intellectuals. In 1933, Qu Qiubai (1899–1935), the Communist intellectual and leader, lived in a pavilion room in Number 12 Dongzhao Li (Alley of Eastern Lights), within walking distance of Lu Xun's home in Number 9 Dalu Xin-cun (New Village Continent). Qu's wife, Yang Zhihua, recalled that her husband's friendship with Lu Xun was forged in a pavilion room: "Almost every day Lu Xun paid us a visit. He chatted with Qiubai on various sub-jects—politics, current news, and literature—and we enjoyed having him as if he were fresh air and warm sunlight in a boundless world. Qiubai was a quiet person, but every time he saw Lu Xun his mood immediately changed. They talked happily and sometimes laughed heartily, enlivening the stuffy pavilion room. We were always reluctant to let Lu Xun leave, but after every visit, his laugh, happiness, and warmth remained in our little room."[100] Lu Xun himself was part of this pavilion-room type of life. All his residences in Shanghai, with one exception, included a pavilion room. He worked the fanciful name of his study in his Hongkou residence, Qie-jieting, meaning the "Semiconcession Pavilion," into the title of three of his best-known books (that is, collections of his essays).[101]

Although Lu Xun and other famous twentieth-century writers lived in pavilion rooms and wrote some of their best pieces there, the writers' pres-tige eventually set them apart from the image of a pavilion-room dweller usually conveyed. Shanghai's pavilion rooms had been so powerfully asso-ciated with the image of the urban petty bourgeois writer in the Republi-can period that "pavilion room writer" (*tingzijian zuojia*) and "pavilion room man of letters" (*tingzijian wenren*) became stock phrases. These au-thors were, typically, sensitive and self-esteemed, scornful of the world and its ways but always part of it, hard working but never quite successful—not unlike those frustrated garret writers and artists in Balzac's world. From this group emerged radical youth who eventually left Shanghai for

Yan'an and became Communist revolutionaries. They had such an effect on intellectual life in the heart of the Communist revolution that, in a speech in Yan'an in 1938, Mao Zedong mentioned the divisions they caused among revolutionary intellectuals in the Communist-controlled areas. In a humorous tone but apparently addressing a serious issue, Mao spoke of "men from a Shanghai pavilion room" as representative of urban-based intellectuals who had newly come to Yan'an and "men from the hilltops" (i.e., intellectuals with a rural background), and urged these two groups to know their own limitations and respect each other.[102]

MIXING RESIDENCE WITH COMMERCE

The mix in alleyway-house neighborhoods was a matter not only of the social composition of the residents but also of the coexistence of residences and various types of businesses. The front row of houses in an alleyway-house compound faced the street and was used primarily as premises for business, mostly small shops serving the neighborhood.[103] But various businesses other than small neighborhood stores were also found there. Even in predominately residential areas, businesses were often mixed with residences. Shanghai residents were so familiar with these enterprises in their neighborhoods that "alley factory" (*longtang gongchang*), "alley school" (*longtang xuetang*), "alley store" (*longtang shangdian*), and so on were standard terms in the local dialect.

The *Social Daily News* (*Shehui ribao*) once published an essay entitled "Inside Our Alley—a Survey Table of Residences," which was actually not a "table" but a description of seven houses, numbering from 24 to 36, in a shikumen lane. The author explained that the people in this little lane had "extremely different backgrounds, which is a token of the complex and mixed conditions in the world's sixth largest metropolis." This lane, for our purposes, serves as an example of how residence and commerce were mixed in alleyway-house neighborhoods. In addition to residences, one could find in this short lane (approximately 100 feet long) a tailor shop, a textile mill, a warehouse, and a dormitory for an amusement center.

A couple named Li with three children—the eldest was eleven or twelve—lived in House Number 24. Li, a Suzhou native, obviously had a good income since he worked for the Maritime Customs—any position there was regarded as one of the best in town or, as it was said, was like having a "golden rice bowl." Neighbors noticed that the family spent a lot of money to have the house painted when they moved in. Li impressed them as a sweet talker and a "perfect philistine." The "sweet talk" part was linked with a stereotype in Shanghai about Suzhou people, who were generally thought to have a "sweet mouth"—Suzhou cuisine is known for being sugary and the Suzhou dialect sounds soft and sweet.

Next door, House Number 26, was the shop of tailor Zhao Shentai. The owner, a native of Changshu, and his wife, a Wuxi native, seemed to have very different personalities. The man was a quiet and private person, seemingly always at work at his tailoring table inside the home; he seldom talked with neighbors. The wife, however, was fond of gossip and she often, even while in the sixth or seventh month of pregnancy, went to neighbors' houses to chat, something considered slightly outrageous in those days. Next to the tailor shop, in House Number 28, was a little textile mill making rayon socks. The factory ran day and night and employed both men and women: men worked in the second-floor workshop and women worked downstairs. The neighbors naturally complained of the noise of machines, but they were bothered as well by the noise of the workers, who either hummed various ditties or flirted loudly with each other through the workshop's floor/ceiling that separated them.

House Number 30 was considered a mysterious nest. Only two women lived there. The younger was sixteen, and she called the older woman, who was only about twenty-six or -seven, "Mom." Every night the two women donned provocative clothing and went out. Neighbors could not figure out if they were dancing girls or prostitutes. A woman in her late twenties and her elderly maid lived in House Number 32. A man who looked like a banker regularly paid the young woman a visit once or twice a week. Neighbors gossiped that Number 32 was but a "little house" for a mistress. As was common in Shanghai, the gossip went, the man probably first met the young woman in a brothel, then fell in love and eventually paid off the madame to get his favorite. But it looked like the woman was quite discontented with the lonely life in the "little house": she often stood at her back door gazing around, as if trying to seduce young men. Ironically, all the neighbors next door in House Number 34 were women. These women seemed to dress in the same sort of modern attire, but in a style that was out of date. Their occupations were unclear. They might be a group of waitresses at an amusement center or nightclub, although they seemed never to have to work and played mah-jongg all day long.

House Number 36, at the end of the lane, had been used as a storehouse by an electric lamp store that had recently closed. The owner of that store, a successful young businessman, had recently appeared in the newspaper in the "local news" column: his runaway mistress had sued him for mistreatment. Before the lingering lawsuit had reached a conclusion, the young man, badly upset and frustrated, went out for a drive and died in an accident. At the time the essay was published in the *Social Daily News*, the electric lamp store had a new owner and House Number 36 was vacant.[104]

The various nonresidential institutions in shikumen neighborhoods included many local schools. Elementary schools located in alleyway compounds were popular because they were convenient for children—the schools were always located within a safe walking distance from home, and students usually did not need to cross the street to get to them. In these schools, the shikumen living rooms and bedrooms were turned into classrooms, and the kitchens and pavilion rooms into offices. The front courtyard might be too small to serve as a playground, but outdoor activities could always extend into the alleyway. A three-bay shikumen house could be transformed into six to nine classrooms, each with twenty to thirty seats. Sometimes walls between a few contiguous shikumen houses were removed to form a sizable school.[105]

"Alley schools" also included institutions of higher education. Shanghai's earliest Chinese-run private university, Datong University, was founded in 1912 in a shikumen compound named Nanyang Li (Alley of the Southern Sun) in Nanshi.[106] Another school, Daxia University, was founded in 1924 in a shikumen house in Meiren Li (Alley of Beauty and Benevolence), located a few yards south of Avenue Joffre in the French Concession. One of the founding faculty members recalled that the university office was in a single-bay shikumen inside the compound. A sign posted on the front door read, "Please Use the Back Door." This was because the landlord lived in the living room on the first floor, and so to enter the house from the front meant one had to pass through his room.[107] Shanghai University, known for its sociology programs as well as its Communist inclination, was also set in an alleyway-house compound. The writer Mao Dun called Shanghai University "a veritable 'alleyway university'" because it was located in an alleyway-house compound (Qingyun Li [Alley of Meteoric Rise] on Qingyun Road in Zhabei). It was briefly relocated to Ximo Road in the Settlement in 1924, and then it moved to Shishou Fang (Alley of Teachers' Longevity), another alleyway-house compound on Qingyun Road. The school "had no gate, no sign board, and, of course, no auditorium. The assembly hall was formed by merging two rooms together by removing the wall."[108]

Bookstores and printing houses were also set up in shikumen neighborhoods.[109] In Fuzhou Road, Shanghai's famous "cultural street" (*wenhua-jie*), numerous bookstores were located in alleyway houses, side by side with ordinary residential homes and shops that specialized in selling the "four treasures of a study" (*wenfang sibao*): writing brushes, ink sticks, ink stones, and paper. By 1949, when Shanghai's bookstores were generally in decline, there were still 114 bookstores on Fuzhou Road in the two blocks (about a quarter mile in length) between the intersections of Henan Road and Fujian Road.[110]

The Neishan Book Store in Hongkou, which gained its fame from the patronage of Lu Xun, Yu Dafu and other illustrious Japan-educated Chinese intellectuals, also operated in alleyway premises. Owned by a Kyushu merchant, Uchiyama Kanzō (1885–1959), the store was located in Weisheng Li (Alley of Prosperity), a small shikumen compound on North Sichuan Road that had only seven houses.[111] In 1917, Uchiyama, who first came to Shanghai selling medicines, rented two adjacent houses to the right side of the entrance of the lane. He removed both the wall between the two living rooms and the wall between the front courtyards, covered the courtyards with a glass roof, and thus formed a quite sizable bookstore with natural light. Uchiyama, as Yu Dafu later commented, was a man who "knew his business well and acquired the Chinese habit of doing things for the sake of friendship."[112] He operated his bookstore in a Barnes and Noble–type fashion: the bookstore was fitted with full-wall open stacks and a set of seven or eight rattan-framed sofas and chairs encircling a small table known as the "chatting corner" (*mantanxi*), and free tea was served. A tired customer or anyone who liked to pass the time in a bookstore could sit there browsing, sipping a cup of tea, and chatting.[113]

In his memoirs, Zhu Lianbao, a publisher who had worked in various presses in Shanghai for half a century (1921–70), recorded the details of about six hundred printing houses and bookstores in pre-1949 Shanghai, of which more than half were set in alleyway houses, mostly in shikumen houses.[114] Shikumen compounds housed some of China's best-known presses and newspapers. Li Boyuan, who was regarded as the forefather of Shanghai's tabloids, founded *Fanhua bao* (*Prosperity*) in April 1901. The office and print shop of the tabloid were located in Yixin Li (Alley of Boundless Good Fortune) on Nanking Road.[115] The largest press in modern China, the Commercial Press, started business in 1897 in Dechang Li (Alley of Virtue and Prosperity) on Jiangxi Road in the Nanking Road area. The next year, the press moved to Shunqing Li (Alley of Smoothness and Celebration) on Beijing Road, still another shikumen compound.[116] The Liangyou Press, publisher of the most popular pictorial in Republican China, *Liangyou* (*Fine Companion*), which was published for almost two decades and had a circulation of forty thousand, started in 1926 as a small printing house in Hongqing Fang (Alley of Great Celebration) on North Sichuan Road.[117] In 1929, the Settlement police raided the press of a communistic newspaper, the *Red Flag*, which was produced in an ordinary alleyway house. The living room on the first floor had been turned into a print shop and the rooms on the second floor were used as a dormitory for the printers. This arrangement was seen as perfectly normal in alleyway-house neighborhoods. The underground Communist Party thus took advantage of the anonymity of shikumen compounds to produce secret publications.[118]

The Shanghai Bookstore, the Chinese Communist Party (CCP) press from 1923 to 1926, was in Zhenye Li (Alley of Promoting Careers) in the Little North Gate (Xiaobeimen) district of Nanshi, in the midst of a densely clotted alleyway-house neighborhood. At the same time, the Mingxing (Bright Star) Printing House, a mill that produced numerous Communist publications including the noted journals *New Youth* (*Xin Qingnian*), *Chinese Youth* (*Zhongguo Qingnian*), and *Guide* (*Xiangdao*), operated downtown in a shikumen house in Xi Fuhai Li (Alley of an Ocean of Fortune, West) near the well-known Garden Hotel. Its warehouse was yet another shikumen house across the street, in Sande Li (Alley of Three Virtues). From 1927 to 1932, the CCP's masthead journal, *Bu'ershiweike* (*Bolshevik*) was located in Hengchang Li (Alley of Prosperity) in Yuyuan Road.[119]

In other ways as well, the Communists skillfully used Shanghai's alleyway-house neighborhoods for their revolutionary agenda. The concessions proved to be a relatively safe place for underground activists because, of course, the Chinese police could not operate openly there. Inside the concessions, the mixed alleyway-house neighborhoods, especially with their many schools, printing houses, and bookstores, were ideal for underground Communist activities. In a residential neighborhood where people of all walks of life lived side by side with businesses of all kinds, whatever the Communists did was unlikely to draw attention. To begin with, the First National Congress of the Chinese Communist Party, which proclaimed the birth of the CCP, was held in a shikumen house in the French Concession on July 23–30, 1921 (Fig. 17). The house, 106 Wangzhi Road (today the address is 76 Xingye Road), was an ordinary two-story shikumen house located in the middle of a five-house row built in 1920. Number 106 was the home of Li Hanjun, one of the founding members of the CCP; his elder brother, Li Shucheng, a follower of Sun Yat-sen who helped found the Tongmenghui (or United League, the forerunner of the Guomindang, or Nationalist Party), lived next door, in Number 108. The congress, described by the Communists as an event that "turned heaven and earth upside down," took place in the living room of Li Hanjun's home. This 194-square-foot (18-square-meter) room is now a sacred place in

Fig. 17.   This alleyway runs next to the shikumen house where the Chinese Communist Party had its first national congress in July 1921. Although the site has been a sacred relic in China since 1952, in the Republican period it was a typical and undistinguished alleyway-house neighborhood. The stone-framed entrances with their carved ornaments on top are characteristic of shikumen. The structure on top of the arched lane entrance is a so-called *guojielou*. Photo property of the author.

China. As early as September 1950, this relic was placed under official protection and completely restored. Today the five houses on Wangzhi Road are the best-preserved shikumen in the city. Number 106, the birthplace of the CCP, is adorned with a signboard bearing Deng Xiaoping's calligraphy identifying it as the museum of the First National Congress of the Chinese Communist Party.[120]

About 328 feet (100 meters) north of 106 Wangzhi Road, at 389 Rue Eugene Bard (today the address is 127 Taicang Road), was the Bowen Women's School, founded in 1917 and moved to this location in 1920. The whole school was located in a three-bay, two-story shikumen house. The school was used to lodge those who attended the CCP's first national congress. Classrooms were turned into temporary dormitories. On the second floor, Mao Zedong and He Shuheng (representatives of Hunan Communists) slept in the west wing, and Dong Biwu and Chen Tanqiu (representatives of Hubei Communists) in the east wing. It was not unusual for a school to be used as a dormitory in the summer—in fact, the whole group was lodged there as a "group of teachers and students of Beijing University on a summer excursion."[121]

The CCP's Second National Congress also took place in a shikumen-house compound. In July 1922, the congress convened in Number 30 of Fude Li (Alley of Guided Morals) on North Chengdu Road, a compound of fifty two-story shikumen houses built in 1915. A few steps away, in House Number 42, was the Pingmin Women's School, which had a communist-sponsored work-study program in 1922–23. Students supported themselves by making socks, sewing, and taking in laundry. The CCP held yet another national congress in a shikumen house. The Fourth National Congress was held in January 1925 in a three-story shikumen house located on the north edge of Hongkou. The meeting took place on the second floor, and participants slept on the third floor. According to Zheng Chaolin, a veteran Communist who was the congress secretary, the house was made to look like an English language school, an institution not likely to arouse suspicion in an alleyway-house neighborhood. Every participant had an English textbook ready: if an uninvited visitor came in, they could claim that an English class was in session.[122]

If one goes back in time a bit to the New Cultural Movement period (1915–1920), when the Communist ideology was in a ferment in China, one can find more relics of this kind in Shanghai's alleyway-house neighborhoods. In 1920, House Number 2 of Yuyang Li (known as old Yuyang Li, Alley of Gaining the Sun) on Route Vallon (today the address is 100 Nanchang Road, #2), a single-bay, two-story shikumen house, was the home of Chen Duxiu, the most renowned Communist radical at that time, as well as the editorial office of the famous journal he edited, the *New Youth*. Chen and his wife, Gao Junman, lived on the second floor and used the living room on the first floor as the editorial office. It was in this shikumen that Chen and like-minded intellectuals such as Li Da, Li Hanjun, and Chen Wangdao formed the nation's first so-called Communist group (*gongchan zhuyi xiaozu*). The editorial office of a monthly journal of the group, the *Communist*, was also located in the house.[123]

In that year, if one took a stroll from Yuyang Li north to Avenue Joffre and then turned eastward on Avenue Joffre, one could see an alleyway-house compound that bears the same name: Yuyang Li. The three black characters, Yu-Yang-Li, were inscribed right on the entrance—as if to show that there was no copyright on names of alleyway-house compounds. Customarily, local residents called this alleyway-house compound "new Yuyang Li" in order to distinguish it from the old one on Route Vallon. Co-incidentally, new Yuyang Li is another important relic in the history of Chinese Communism. Inside the compound, in front of House Number 6 there was a wooden board about one foot wide and three feet long inscribed with five characters: *wai guo yu xue she*, "foreign language school." If one checks the September 30, 1920, issue of *Minguo ribao* (*Republic Daily*), one can find this school advertising its Russian and French programs. However, this alleyway school was in fact a Communist stronghold. Most of the students—the highest enrollment was about sixty—were not recruited via commercial advertisements but through connections with Communist comrades. Among the students one can find the names of many who later became top Communist leaders: Liu Shaoqi, Ren Bishi, Ke Qingshi, Xiao Jinguang, and so on. Their purpose in learning Russian and French was to read Marxist works and prepare for further training in the Soviet Union. In spring 1921, the school sent three batches of students to Moscow.

This two-bay, two-story shikumen house looked identical to the other thirty-two in the compound, but it seemed destined to become a historical site. The house was first rented by Dai Jitao (1890–1949), a follower of Sun Yat-sen and a high-ranking official in the Chiang Kai-shek government. In March 1920, when Dai was going to move out, he happened to know that his friend, Chen Duxiu, was looking for a house, so he notified him of the forthcoming vacancy. Chen's purpose was to rent a house for Communist activities, since a Comintern representative was in touch with him in Shanghai at that time and they were preparing to found the Chinese Communist Party. The house was rented in the name of Yang Mingzhai, an interpreter for the Comintern. In addition to housing the foreign language school, Number 6 served as the headquarters of the Socialist Youth League (later known as the Communist Youth League) and as the office of the Sino-Russian News Agency (Hua E tongxunshe). The wings on the first floor became classrooms. When enrollment increased, the living room also functioned as a classroom. On the second floor, the front bedroom served as the office of the Youth League, and the back bedroom and wings as a student dormitory. The pavilion room was Yang Mingzhai's bedroom as well as the office of the news agency.[124]

Since 1950 most of these Communist-related alleyway houses have been well preserved and restored as relics of the revolution. Unintentionally, this has also helped preserve a slice of city life in the Republican period. However, cultural institutions such as schools, presses, and bookstores were a less important part of the businesses established in Shanghai's residential alleyway compounds. Most alleyway businesses were purely commercial, such as stores, workshops, warehouses, opium dens, brothels, and other small enterprises. For instance, from the late nineteenth century on, the shikumen compound of Furun Li (Alley of Wealth and Profit), located a few yards from Nanking Road, was known for its "three abundances" (*san duo*): an abundance of shops, workshops, and warehouses.[125] Another well-known compound, Baxian Fang (Alley of Eight Immortals), contained seventy-one shikumen houses. Rooms on the first level were mostly used for businesses, not as residences. Pawnshops alone occupied six of the houses. These businesses were interspersed with the dwellings of Baxian Fang residents, most of whom were street peddlers, small merchants, artists, prostitutes, magicians, and other entertainers.[126]

In the Nanking Road area, both modern, Western-type banks and *qianzhuang* (traditional Chinese banks) were found in shikumen compounds. In the Republican period, Qingyuan Li (Alley of Purity and Remoteness) and Ruyi Li (Alley of Doing As One Wishes), among the earliest shikumen compounds in Shanghai (both were marked on a map published in 1876), were distinguished by a number of financial institutions mixed in with residences.[127] Western-type banks were found in Qingyuan Li along its rows facing Beijing Road; qianzhuang were located in the rows inside the compound. In Ruyi Li, banks and business offices actually outnumbered residences.[128] The same was true of Xingren Li, another of the oldest shikumen compounds in Shanghai, located a block north of Nanking Road. Of the twenty-four houses of Xingren Li, twenty functioned as qianzhuang. A single family from Ningbo, the Fangs, once owned three banks inside this compound.[129] Obviously, these shikumen neighborhoods became favorite places for banks and qianzhuang because of their convenient proximity to the major commercial and financial centers in the Nanking Road area. Visitors to Shanghai were impressed by the European-style bank buildings along the Bund; few would have noticed these small institutions set in the back alleyways. But these small banks, numerous as they were, certainly contributed to Shanghai's status as China's foremost financial center.

Shikumen also housed entertainment establishments. In shikumen compounds in the city's busy commercial areas (especially the Nanking Road area), opium dens, gambling houses, and brothels were plentiful. It was estimated that by the mid-1860s, when Shanghai was just emerging from under the Taiping threat and was not yet a great metropolis, there were already 1,500 brothels in the city.[130] By the early 1930s, according to Gail Hershatter's estimate, one of every thirty Shanghai residents sold sex for a living.[131] The vast majority of Shanghai's brothels operated out of ordinary shikumen houses. For half a century, from 1860 to the end of the Qing dynasty, Baoshan Jie (Street of Treasure and Mercy), a street four blocks south of Nanking Road, and its vicinity, was the center of prostitution. This part of the Nanking Road area continued to be a red-light district (*hong-deng qu*) or "decency district" (*fenghua qu*) in the Republican era. Shikumen compounds on Baoshan Jie, such as Gongxing Li (Alley of Collective Prosperity), East Gongxing Li, Gongshun Li (Alley of Collective Smoothness), and—best known of all and perhaps most appropriately named—Huile Li (Alley of Joint Pleasure), were full of brothels.[132] Huile Li, a compound of 14,500 square feet (4,420 square meters) originally built at the end of the nineteenth century, boasted a main alleyway 15 feet (4.6 meters) wide and about 280 feet (85 meters) long, four branch alleyways, and, after a remodel in 1924, twenty-eight three-bay, two-wing shikumen houses.[133] The compound was built in a moderately tasteful style: each house had a spacious front courtyard, those houses facing the main alleyway had a balcony, and arches stood at the main entrance as well as at the entrances of branch alleys, with stone inscriptions indicating the direction and number of the branches (such as "East First Branch Alley," "West Second Branch Alley," etc.). Although it was not deliberately built to accommodate brothels, by the late 1920s the compound had become a favorite site for Shanghai's higher-class prostitution.[134] By 1949, twenty-seven of the houses in Huile Li functioned all or in part as brothels; the only house that was not a brothel was a pharmacy, which perhaps primarily served those suffering from sexually transmitted diseases.[135] This shikumen compound was so well known for its prostitution that the name Huile Li was virtually a synonym in Shanghai for "whoring" (Fig. 18).[136]

Shikumen compounds housing brothels could also be found in many

Fig. 18.   Above Huile Li (Alley of Joint Pleasure), one of Shanghai's notorious red-light alleys, were hung lanterns of various shapes marked with the "professional" names (known as the "artistic" names) of various prostitutes. These names were always suggestive, such as Aroma (*xiang*), Dazzling (*yan*), Red (*hong*), Orchid (*lan*), Jade (*yu*), Gorgeous (*li*), and so on. By January 1949, 171 brothels (or about a fifth of Shanghai's registered brothels) operated in this alleyway. Courtesy of Shanghai Municipal Archive.

other areas of Shanghai. Along Tibet Road, from its northern end in the International Settlement down to the southern end in the French Concession, many shikumen compounds accommodated various types of businesses dealing in vice. For instance, by the late 1930s in Xiande Li (Alley of All Virtues), a compound on Tibet Road built in 1910, 20 percent of its fifty-two houses were used as brothels, and many others served as opium dens. Mixed in together with these businesses was a variety of residents, including some Moslems from various places, who hailed from many places: Yangzhou in Subei, Ningbo in Jiangnan, Guangdong.[137] Another shikumen compound in Tibet Road, Taiyuan Fang (Taiyuan Alley), built in 1929 and close to the famous Shanghai entertainment center, the Great World (Dashijie, built in 1917), housed numerous brothels, opium dens, and inns with shady reputations. Four adjoining shikumen houses inside the compound were remodeled into theaters specializing in Yangzhou opera.[138] A few blocks south, in the so-called Great Road of the French Concession (Fa Damalu), was a shikumen compound known as Shengping Li (Alley of Peace), built in 1925, where ten houses out of thirty-two served as opium warehouses.[139]

These are merely a few examples of the rather creative use of alleyway houses for nonresidential purposes. One could add to the list. By the late 1940s, about half Shanghai's total of 250 hotels were located in alleyway houses. In 1947, seven of the city's forty-five broadcasting stations occupied alleyway-house compounds.[140] Chen Guhai, a veteran journalist, recalled that the China United Broadcasting Station, a radio station quite active in Shanghai in 1946–47, actually broadcast from his home in an alleyway house in New Dagu Road; the broadcasting booth sat right in his bedroom for nine months.[141] Early in 1931, the CCP's central broadcasting station was set up in Number 11 Xingqing Li (Alley of Joy and Celebration) in Moulmein Road; the same house also contained the transmitter.[142] In 1933, the CCP even had an underground radio center in Number 20 Heqing Li (Alley of Joint Celebration) on Dagu Road to communicate with Moscow. During the Civil War, the CCP radio station was located in yet another alleyway house: Number 15 Lane 107 Huangdu Road, in Hongkou. Li Bai, the radio operator, secretly worked on the third floor of that house for three years, until he was arrested on the spot in December 1948.[143]

All sorts of wholesale offices, public bathhouses, fortune-tellers, restaurants, clinics, lawyer's offices, and sometimes even government bureaus could be found in the alleys. A local saying described the multifarious use of alleyway houses as "performing a Buddhist [or Daoist] rite inside a snail shell" (luosi ke li zuo daochang).[144] This was sometimes not a metaphor but virtually a reality: According to a directory of the Shanghai Buddhist Association (Shanghaishi Fojiao hui, founded in June 1929), by the late 1940s many of the city's 285 Buddhist temples were located in shikumen alleys.[145] With the addition of a few religious statues and a table for joss sticks and candles, a living room or wing room of a shikumen could be transformed into a Buddhist temple where worship and rituals were conducted in all their proper forms.

PART 3

UNDER THE EAVES OF SHANGHAI

CHAPTER 5

Behind Stone Portals

No place can one get a better image of daily life in Shanghai than in the alleyway-house neighborhoods that spread across the city. As we have seen, these neighborhoods were the homes of the great majority of the people. For them, these back alleys were not only where they lived but also where they worked, entertained, socialized, and conducted most of their daily transactions—in short, the neighborhood was the city to these people. In contrast to some highly publicized images of the city that represented neither daily life nor activities relevant to the common people, life in the back alleys of Shanghai embodied the real world for most of Shanghai's people. One may see this world in two closely related parts, divided physically (but not culturally) by the entrance of the alleyway-house compound. Behind the entrance, within the homes in the alleyways, was the private (and sometimes not so private) world of Shanghai's common people. Outside, in the nearby streets, lay an extension of everyday life.

The Men Who Woke Up a City

In stark contrast to Shanghai's reputation in the first half of the twentieth century as one of the world's most modern cities was the pedestrian reality that most of its people did not have sanitary fixtures at home. Shanghai was among the first cities in the world to have electricity, gas, telephones, and other modern facilities, but even at the city's peak in the 1920–40s, the family toilet for most people was a simple wooden nightstool, basically little different from that used in any remote hinterland village. Emptying and cleaning the nightstool was not only a daily household chore that few families could avoid but also a morning overture to life in the city (Fig. 19).

All nightstools in the city were similar if not identical: a wooden,

Fig. 19.   This row of shikumen houses built in 1919 stood in Nanshi, near Old West Gate. The iron bars protruding from the walls were for resting bamboo poles for air-drying laundry (the other ends of the bars were built into the wall of the opposite row of houses, which cannot be seen in this photograph). A nightstool leaning against the door reveals that the houses lacked modern sanitary fixtures, which was common in shikumen neighborhoods. The lid of the bucket rests ajar, showing that the bucket had been emptied and washed and was set out to dry in the morning sun. Customarily, residents took their nightstools back inside before noon. Photo property of the author.

drum-shaped bucket about sixteen inches high and a foot in diameter, with a one-and-a-half-inch-wide wooden ring on the top as a seat, an iron or brass handle fixed to the body, and a round wooden lid on which were routed two semicircular grooves by which one could grasp the lid and lift it off. A coat of tung oil was applied to both the inside and outside of the bucket to make it waterproof and durable; then it was painted purplish red or golden yellow.[1]

Because it was a daily necessity, the nightstool was customarily associated with women as a part of their dowry. In this regard, it was equivalent to the color television in the dowry of present-day Shanghai brides but was, of course, more indispensable.[2] When a nightstool was included in a dowry, red-dyed eggs were placed inside the nightstool to serve as a symbol or wish for the birth of a child (particularly a son).[3] Exquisite nightstools were encircled with rings painted in gold and had dragon-and-phoenix pictures painted on both the body and the lid. Nightstools of such quality sometimes became a target of theft.

The nightstools used in the city were about two-thirds the size of those used in the countryside. The reduction of size was obviously related to the crowded living conditions in the city.[4] Alleyway houses without sanitary fixtures (i.e., the old-type lilong houses) had neither a room nor a space designed for placing a toilet. Thus the family nightstool had to be small and light to allow flexibility. Most families put their nightstool wherever they could manage to find space in their congested dwelling. The most common place was the back corner of a room, curtained off with a cotton drape for privacy, or behind a piece of furniture. Sometimes, the triangular space underneath a stairwell was used as a "toilet room."

If a public lavatory was available nearby, men tended to use it, a practice very similar to that in rural areas.[5] But public lavatories in most cases were not conveniently nearby, and so the small wooden bucket had to be used by everybody at home. An important household chore was to put the family nightstool outside the back door late at night, so it could be emptied by the nightsoil man, who usually came before daybreak, around 4 or 5 A.M., when most people were still asleep. The nightsoil man, pulling a black, two-wheeled cart with red wheels, entered every lane and yelled, "Empty your nightstool! Here comes the nightsoil man! Empty your nightstool!"[6] Sometimes he also rang a little copper bell. The sound broke the stillness of the alleyway and often stimulated the cockcrow (Fig. 20).[7]

By municipal regulation, the nightsoil cart was the only place residents could pour their nightsoil.[8] Although most families had two nightstools, for use on alternate days (thus one was kept empty and clean at all times),

Fig. 20.   This Feng Zikai cartoon dated 1934 depicts a
nightsoil cart rumbling through a shikumen lane. Collecting nightsoil was an everyday service provided all
year round. The caption, which reads "The Men Who
Don't Know New Year's Day," divulges the artist's sympathy for and appreciation of the hardworking nightsoil
workers. From Feng Zikai, *Feng Zikai wenji.*

missing the nightsoil man on his daily rounds meant a family either had to
use yesterday's nightstool or had to keep two dirty nightstools at home, an
obviously uncomfortable and unhealthy nuisance, especially in Shanghai's
steaming hot summer. A considerate nightsoil man recognized this and
would sometimes give a final shout before leaving the alleyway compound:
"[I am] Leaving! Won't be back!" It was then that one often saw a sleepy
housewife, still in her night attire, pop her head out of the door and re-
spond, "Hold on a second!" Then in a rush she would pull her bucket to the
nightsoil cart.[9]

Some half a century ago an author described the sight in a jocular tone: "Nightstools of every type and of every household are higgledy-piggledy placed in alleyways and lined up like dismissed soldiers. What a great view: this is just like having a 'nightstool exhibition.'"[10] Ernest Heppner, a resident of wartime Shanghai, recalled this part of life in Shanghai during World War II: "Few houses in Hongkew [Hongkou; which then had a large Jewish community living side by side with ordinary Chinese] had a toilet; close to the entrance of most houses was this ubiquitous bucket with a seat on top. Every morning a coolie would go noisily from door to door with a pushcart and empty the smelly buckets, the contents to be sold as fertilizer."[11] In fact, residents of shikumen houses in the 1980s could tell virtually the same story about nightsoil collection in the neighborhoods as that told by people who lived through the Republican period, for the simple reason that, for about 1 million households in the city, the family toilet was still the "honey bucket." Of this part of city life, a person born in the sixties or seventies saw virtually the same alleyway scene that his or her grandparents had witnessed a half century earlier.[12] A resident of Shanghai in the late 1980s jokingly used the term "grand sight" (*zhuangguan*) to describe the scene: hundreds of nightstools placed in zigzag lines from the end of each alleyway all the way up to the entrance. Those who lived in the row facing the street simply put their nightstools on the street, under a dim road lamp.[13]

Collecting nightsoil was "the lowest business in reputation, with the highest profit."[14] The monthly fee for the service was $0.20.[15] This was collected as a tip at the end of each month by the "Emptying Master" (*dao laoye*), as the nightsoil man was jokingly called. The nickname reflected, naturally, an ambivalence toward this stinking but important figure who appeared at the back door every morning. But it was also derived from the competition for the trade. In order to be an "Emptying Master," a man needed about $100.00 for fees to be paid to the "Head of Nightsoil" (*fentou*), who did the hiring. Once hired, the man would be given a nightsoil cart, with a proper license, and told to empty nightstools in an assigned area. A monthly wage, which was much less significant than the tips, was also paid by the boss. As long as the nightsoil man did not violate regulations, of which the most important ones were not to collect nightsoil after 8:00 A.M. and not to work in unassigned areas, his job was secure and normally would not be affected by a change of the Head of Nightsoil; in fact, he could even pass on his position to his son and grandson.[16] But the real profits belonged to the boss. All nightsoil carts were wheeled to the docks, where the contents of every cart were mixed with a like volume of water.

The resultant sewage was sold to farmers at $1.00 per cart.[17] In China, nightsoil has long been considered the best fertilizer. Early each morning, hundreds of farmers steered their boats to Shanghai. "Every day the boats carried their liquid cargo from the city to some little country creek where a farmer waited for his manure, to be stored in huge earthenware jars until it was time to spread it on his crops," a caption of a photo of the "nightsoil jetty" in Hongkou reads. "Shanghai nightsoil was particularly welcome, considered superior and especially fertile thanks to the rich diets of the people."[18]

There were a number of nightsoil docks in Shanghai (Fig. 21). The one serving the International Settlement was in Caojiadu, northwest of the city; the Dapuqiao dock in the south took care of the French Concession. Both docks were operated by gangs. In the French Concession, a moll known as Sister Ah Gui and her son, Ma Honggen, were the "Royalty of Nightsoil" for many years after the second decade of the twentieth century. They owned four hundred nightsoil carts, which were the fixed capital they needed. After pledging $14,000 to the French Concession authorities, they hired hundreds of men to collect nightsoil in the Concession. The profits from this business amounted to about $10,000–12,000 per month. Sister Ah Gui was a paramour of Huang Jinrong (1868–1953), one of Shanghai's three top gang bosses in the twenties and thirties. This connection allowed her to monopolize the business, and although very few people knew her real name, her nickname, Sister Ah Gui, was well known among Shanghai residents.[19] For them, the fact that someone could make a fortune from the "filthy" business of collecting nightsoil was seen as a powerful "footnote" to the legend of Shanghai as a city where "gold covers the ground" (*biandi huangjin*).[20]

Most residents were perhaps not interested in knowing who the nightsoil magnates were or where the nightsoil was taken. But they were certainly familiar with the shout of "Empty your nightstool!" that reverberated in the alleyways early in the morning all year round. Like rickshaw pullers, dock coolies, and other manual laborers, nightsoil collectors were almost exclusively immigrants from Subei. Undoubtedly, this contributed to the public's disdain of Subei people. Yet the work was not as simple as it might have looked. Indeed, it required a pair of dexterous hands. Yelling "Empty your nightstool" off and on, the collector had to stop his cart every few yards—a distance that was convenient for him to pick up the nightstools that lined both sides of the lane. Then, he stooped to lift a bucket using his right hand, and, halfway through, with his left hand he quickly took off the lid and put it against the bottom of the bucket. With his right hand

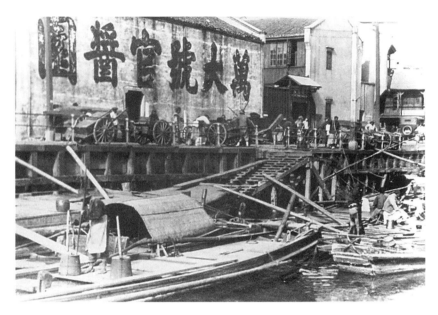

Fig. 21. Nightsoil carts are lined up on a dock near the southern boundary of the French Concession waiting to unload their contents. On the streets of the French Concession alone, more than four hundred carts operated every morning before 8:00 A.M. The boats are waiting to ship the excrement to the countryside, where it will fertilize fields. The big characters on the wall announce a sauce and pickle shop that has an entrance facing the dock. Shops such as this manufactured their own condiments and wholesaled them to smaller retail stores. From R. Barz, *Shanghai: Sketches of Present-Day Shanghai.*

he lifted the bucket further up to reach the mouth of the tank, which was on the top of the cart, and simultaneously, using his left hand, pushed the bucket with the lid and thus dumped the contents into the tank. In this maneuver, his hands touched only the handle and lid of the nightstool, and thus the collector minimized the chance of soiling his hands.[21] He then dipped a ladle into a pail hanging on the cart and put a scoop of water into the nightstool. He sloshed the water around the bucket once or twice before pouring it into the cart. The purpose of this action was not to clean the bucket but to wash out any contents that might be stuck inside the bucket.

A nightsoil man proficiently repeated these actions hundreds of times every morning. Usually in less than ten minutes he could finish his work in an alleyway of about thirty households. The city authorities would not allow nightsoil carts to run in the streets after 8 A.M., so the nightsoil man was always in a hurry.[22] He sometimes had a helper; when he did, it was usually his wife. An experienced nightsoil man might be relaxed enough to exchange greetings with residents or even have a casual chat with a maid of his acquaintance, who was always awakened in the morning by the shout of the collector and thus started her morning chores. Indeed, nightsoil collectors awoke not only maids and housewives: they were virtually the alarm clock of the neighborhood (if not the whole city). A writer described the morning scene with prankish humor:

> The sun gradually rises above the horizon, as if it were forming the beautiful, dreamlike view known as "The East Sea Bathing in the Sunshine." When the brilliant rays reach the Shanghai coast, the city takes off her night clothes and starts to get dressed for the morning! . . . But the first thing displayed on Miss Shanghai's dressing table is the "perfume of sweet-scented osmanthus," which, according to our investigation, is not made in Paris but is an indigenous Chinese product—What on earth are you talking about?!
>
> In Shanghai in the morning, the first one who mounts the stage of city life is the "Emptying Master." . . . At a time when nine out of ten streets are still very quiet, there is hustle and bustle in every alleyway. The "Emptying Master" and the "Emptying Mistress" push the "tank"—the nightsoil cart—and raise their voices sounding like a broken bamboo pipe: "Hi! . . . Empty your nightstool!" The husband yells like he is exercising his voice, while the wife quietly immerses herself in the work—"whiz! whiz!" This is really putting into practice [the Chinese saying] "While the husband is singing, his wife follows" [*fuchang fusui*]. Facing this picture, should not divorced men and women be shamed to death?! [23]

After the nightsoil cart had gone, and the empty nightstools lined the lanes, there came a major morning chore: cleaning the bucket. For this unpleasant job, the housewife wielded a scrub brush made of a bunch of two-foot-long split bamboo sticks, which were readily available at neighborhood stores or from peddlers. Washing the nightstool, which was done in the alleyway, was exclusively a preserve of the female members of the family, usually the mother or grandmother. Unmarried daughters would try to avoid it if they could. A resident recalled that only on one occasion had she ever seen a man cleaning a nightstool. It was a day during the Chinese New Year holidays when the only woman in the family of old Grandpa Li Xikang, his daughter-in-law, had gone back to her native village in Jiading to visit relatives. Unexpectedly, she did not come back that night.[24] The next morning, the family got up in a panic: who would clean the nightstool? It was unthinkable that the middle-aged father or any of the three teenage sons would clean a nightstool in public. The aged grandfather seemed more pragmatic than his offspring, and he was ready to do the job. However, just as he started, a neighbor, Mrs. Peng, offered her help. Obviously she thought it improper or even pitiable to let a man clean a nightstool. In fact, for about one dollar a month a family could hire the services of a maid who helped clean nightstools for several neighbors, but such service was usually available only on a monthly basis.[25]

Cleaning a nightstool required some strength to scrub the material that stuck inside the bucket. Water was frequently poured in and splashed out of the bucket in the process of scrubbing. Sometimes a cleaner used a bowlful of clam shells inside the basket to function as scrubbers to make the bamboo brush work more efficiently. Residents knew that the best time to wash a nightstool was before the excrement became dry and stuck in the bucket. Thus, right after the nightsoil cart left the alleyway all the families started to wash their nightstools, usually in an open-air space near a sewer outside the back door. The alleyway filled with noise, which in Shanghai was jocularly dubbed "the cantata of our alleyway." To this day the scene of women diligently scrubbing nightstools is encountered all over the city. As one writer noted in 1994: "Early every morning, 800,000 nightstools are scrubbed in the alleyways, composing the special tune of Shanghai's morning song."[26] After cleaning them, residents leaned their nightstool against the foot of a wall to air dry. Often in less than half an hour all the residents had finished this morning chore.

By that time daylight filled the alleyway. This was the time for the residents to light their coal stove, go to the nearby food market to purchase the makings for the main meal of the day, and go to a sesame cake store to buy breakfast (see chapter 6). In the meantime, peddlers and vendors of all sorts started to arrive in alleyways; the parade of peddlers did not end until after midnight. The nightsoil cart thus served as the vanguard of daily life in the city's residential neighborhoods. A folk song popular in Shanghai in the 1940s described a typical morning in the city's alleyway-house neighborhoods:

> The nightsoil cart is our morning rooster:
> What a great variety of noise follows it!
> In the front lane, a vegetable peddler is yelling;
> In the back lane, a rice peddler is shouting.
> From the front room comes the deafening cry of the neighbors'
>   little boy;
> From the second floor comes the stomping noise of the young couple
>   there.

The smoke of the coal stove brings tears to my eyes: this is our
  "stove-opener" in the kitchen;
A ragged bed sheet is fluttering in the wind, just like our national flag:
This is the greeting from the flat roof—
Such is our everyday life: always like this![27]

This song expressed a "life goes on, do what one may" feeling toward
everyday life in the city's jammed residential neighborhoods, a feeling that
was shared by most residents. Literature on Shanghai's neighborhood life,
found in local newspapers and small, incidental journals and magazines,
was often written by authors who themselves were part of the bubbling life
in the alleyway compounds. These intimate observers of the real life of ordinary people did not appeal to the refined taste of some of their contemporary readers; moreover, what they turned out was not regarded as "real"
literature. As a result, these authors often adopted a sort of "poking fun at
oneself" or satirical attitude toward their subjects, as in some of the examples quoted above.

Shanghai residents might well have reason to smile wryly at the morning scene in the alleyways: they were in the nation's most modern city,
the city known as the "Paris of the East," the "Chinese New York," the
"world's sixth greatest city," and so on.[28] Residents of alleyway houses
might well be regarded as the "middle class" of the city, especially in comparison with the hundreds of thousands of shantytown squatters. Still, in
daily life they could not avoid using a small wooden nightstool, the same
article that had been used by millions of peasants in the countryside for
centuries.

However, the scene in the alleyway after the nightsoil cart had gone was
a reminder of the prosperity of the city, the relative wealth of its people,
and the convenience of life there. Street peddlers—in particular, those who
sold edibles and provided various services—started to walk through the alleyway entrance and conduct their business in a vigorous and characteristic style—the peddlers painted another picture of daily life in Shanghai.

Peddlers

EATING WELL IN SHANGHAI

Yimi xingren lianxin zhou (porridge made of the seed of Job's tears,
  apricot kernel, and lotus seeds)
meigui baitang lunjiao gao (steamed rice cakes made of rugosa rose
  and white sugar)

xiarou huntun mian (shrimp-dumpling-and-noodle soup)
wuxiang chaye dan (eggs stewed in tea leaves and five spices) [29]

These were the chants of peddlers in Shanghai's lilong neighborhoods as recorded by Lu Xun (1881–1936) at the beginning of his essay "The Past and Present of Alleyway Businesses," written in 1935. Shanghai residents were perfectly familiar with these cries because peddlers hawked their goods from lane to lane every day in their neighborhoods. As we have seen, Lu Xun lived his last ten years in Shanghai, mostly in alleyway houses. The residence where he spent the last three years of his life, now a well-preserved relic, was an ordinary new-style lilong house in Hongkou.[30] On a number of occasions Lu Xun recorded, with his celebrated sharpness and insight, aspects of life in Shanghai's neighborhoods in his famous *zawen* (short essays on miscellaneous topics) style. Here he discusses hawking: "If one kept a record, [one would find that] from morning to evening there were probably twenty to thirty hawkers of edibles who came to these alleyways. It seems that residents were really good at spending their pocket money and having between-meal snacks, for they often gave the peddlers some business. The yelling stopped from time to time, which meant that the peddler was taking care of his customers." [31] Peddlers were among the most active players in the drama of alleyway life in the city. Those who sold staple foods such as rice and vegetables came early in the morning, right after the nightsoil cart. After that, hawkers of different sorts of edibles and snacks roamed back and forth all day long in the city's alleyways, making Shanghai a place where getting something to eat could not have been more convenient. Food hawkers were so ubiquitous that even visitors to the city easily noticed them. Only a few days after she arrived in Shanghai in 1935, an American correspondent observed that "there is some appropriate sort of food for any time of the day. Besides breakfast and lunch and dinner— the Shanghai Chinese eat those meals as we do, though the Cantonese have only two large ones, at eleven and four—you can have your elevenses at any hour of the morning: boiled or fried noodles with ham or tiny shrimps or shreds of chicken. Or you can eat sweet almond broth. For afternoon snacks there are endless sorts of sweet or salty cakes stuffed with ground beans or minced pork or chopped greens." [32] Edibles like these were also served in restaurants, in the so-called puluo (proletarian) restaurants, or in small neighborhood establishments such as sesame cake stores.[33] But the most popular and innovative form of food selling involved portable kitchens carried on a street peddler's shoulder pole (Fig. 22). Food sellers toting their kitchens were found everywhere in the city; as the writer

Harriet Sergeant puts it, these hawkers "turned snacking into a Shanghai institution."[34] Food peddlers of course went to where their customers were: not Shanghai's major thoroughfares but the back streets and alleyways where most of the city's people lived.

Old Shanghailanders, after the 1949 revolution, often recalled the "good old days" when street peddlers provided an ever-needed service (namely, filling one's stomach) and formed an integral part of the dynamic street scene in residential neighborhoods. Shanghainese who left the city may well have missed the great variety of what the Chinese called the "little eats" (*xiaochi*), which were always available within walking distance, and the street songs of hawkers.

Tie Min (Tim Min Tieh, born in 1905), a Shanghai native who lived for many years in Europe and America, became homesick in the fall of 1940 when he recalled the sound of Shanghai's street peddlers as he was waiting in Lisbon for passage to America from war-torn Europe. He had taken up residence at Rossio in the heart of the city. "The Portuguese chauffeurs were fond of tooting incessantly even when the street was perfectly clear," Tie wrote. "As I sat in front of my window, evening after evening, compelled to listen to the distracting noises, I could not but notice with regret the sharp contrast between those noises and the melodious street songs which the peddlers used to sing in the streets of Old Shanghai during my boyhood days."[35] Tie began to write an essay, "Street Music of Old Shanghai," to ease his homesickness. The writing was soon interrupted and the essay left unfinished. But his memory of Shanghai's street melodies remained unfaded. Forty years later, when Tie accidentally found his old manuscript, he was able to resume writing and complete the essay. The essay was circulated among his young students who knew little about life in old Shanghai. When I interviewed Tie in the summer of 1993 he was eighty-eight years old and blind, but was still working at home as an English tutor. His memory of life in old Shanghai was remarkably fresh and detailed. He was among the most brilliant conversationalists I encountered in Shanghai. The following paragraphs aim to convey some of the rich and graphic information that Tie recounted about peddlers in Shanghai's alleyways.

The great variety of edibles sold in Shanghai neighborhoods reflected the rhythm of the seasons as well as of the day. Seasonal edibles were brought to the alleyway just in time to satisfy residents' desire to taste the season's foods as soon as they came on the market. Many of the edibles sold by street peddlers were not available in stores or food markets. When new

Fig. 22. Shanghai's street food sellers like the one pictured here were able to carry a movable kitchen on a single bamboo shoulder pole. This stand was ingeniously designed, with a boiler on top of a wood stove at the front and a cupboard at the back. The cupboard drawers were filled with noodles, dumpling skins, a plate of ground pork or shrimp, and various herbs and spices. In a matter of minutes the peddler could offer his customers a steaming bowl of fresh noodle soup or won ton dumplings. The posters on the wall advertise *rendan*, a Chinese-Japanese patent herbal medicine for treating minor heat prostration. Courtesy of Shanghai Municipal Library.

sweet corn had just been harvested, for example, the corn seller—toting ears of corn kept hot in a brightly painted, lined basket covered with quilts—came to the alleyway and made himself or herself known by shouting "Pearl-grained corn; hot pearl-grained corn!" The corn was of an excellent variety, tender, juicy, and sweet.

Another popular seasonal food was sour plums, picked in late spring or early summer when they were still green. The appearance of sour plums in the alleyway was a sign of the coming of Jiangnan's rainy season, known as the "yellow plum rainy season" (*huangmei tian*). A kind of frosty sugar coating was put on the plums to counteract in some measure the sourness; the result was a delightful sweet-and-sour flavor. The mere thought of sour plums could make an old Shanghailander's mouth water. The fruit easily met the three standards for good food in China: good color, aroma, and taste. It was even described as "Snow White," a name that revealed the influence of Western popular culture in the city.[36] A resident recalled with regret that this fruit, which had been a seasonal favorite in the city for many years, at least from his youth in the 1930s up to the late 1950s, became scarce in the 1960s when official policy dictated "taking grain as the key link" (*yi liang wei gang*). This policy resulted in greatly reduced fruit planting in most parts of the Jiangnan region where the plum had been grown.[37]

The sour plum was not the only item to disappear from the neighborhoods after Liberation or, even more drastically, after the Great Leap Forward that diminished the diversity of agricultural products. Ginkgo nuts were another loss. Roasted ginkgo nuts had been sold in the alleyways of Shanghai in autumn, right after the nuts were harvested. Hawkers often appeared in the early afternoon, each carrying a little iron pan with a curved bottom, heated by a crude stove underneath it. The peddler turned and shoveled ginkgo nuts together with bits of porcelain into the pan. The porcelain bits ensured that the nuts were evenly roasted and produced a rattling sound, which advertised his approach. As he turned the nuts, the peddler sang out:

> Hand-burning hot ginkgo nuts,
> Every one is popped, every one is big.
> Should you want to eat hot nuts,
> Each cash will bring you three.
> And three cash will bring you ten.
> Ah, sweet smelling,
> Soft, and delicious![38]

Children, and adults too, were attracted by the rattling at a distance and then by the pretty little song that followed. They hastened to get their money ready. As soon as the peddler rested his load in the street or alley-way, crowds gathered to buy the roasted nuts, kept hot in a padded bag.[39]

To compete with this vendor who peddled just one commodity, another dealt in sundry snacks. His song was just as attractive as that of the ginkgo-nut vendor and his business was no less prosperous. As walked down the lane he sang briskly:

> From the east side of the [Huangpu] River,
> Beans of five-fold flavor,
> And sweet, Oh dear me!
> Stewed plums besprinkled
> With liquorice powder,
> *Huanglian* [the rhizome of Chinese goldthread] shoots,
> Specially flavored dry turnips,
> Only ten pennies a package.[40]

The shouts of hawkers were loud, melodious, and to the ears of some Shanghailanders, "rich in artistic appeal."[41]

In summer, hawkers selling ice products and watermelons added a new vitality to the year-round, brisk neighborhood life. Ice was often sold by a teenager with an insulated bucket swinging at his side. In a high soprano he sang, "Oh, so cold! Buy your ice! Ice, ice, buy your ice!" It was impossible for him to carry big twenty-pound chunks of ice in his bucket, but the average Shanghai resident was not a great consumer of ice. Most people just wanted a few small pieces to put in their tea or in the mint-flavored sweet-green-bean soup that was a popular cold drink in summer.[42]

Then, here came another lad with the same kind of bucket but different contents. He belonged to a later date, for he was selling ice cream. "Top-notch stuff! Sold at only ten-cash a cup," the peddler hawked. Ten cash was a small sum, but the peddler did not worry, for the cup was a very small one, no larger than a liqueur glass. No matter; most people bought that little cupful of ice cream more to satisfy their curiosity about this foreign snack than to appease their stomach. Nevertheless, ice cream was one of the most popular snacks in Shanghai, and the trade was brisk in summer, as those in charge of public health examinations complained to the Shanghai Municipal Council: "In the summer so many very small establishments commence the manufacture of this product that it is extremely difficult to keep track of all of them and still more to examine samples from each bacteriologically."[43]

Inadequate inspection of ice cream products was not a big public health problem, partly because iced drinks and ice cream were never able to compete with the watermelon demanded by thirsty Shanghai residents on hot summer days. Fruit stores were found on virtually every block in residential areas. In the summer, residents bought watermelons in lots of hundredweights. Children in the family awaited with great eagerness the assigned time, usually after dinner, for the opening up of one or more of the melons. They would, long before the happy hour arrived, take great pains to imitate their elders in thumping each melon to ascertain which was ripe. Hawkers also sold cut watermelon, sliced on a crude collapsible table under the shade of a tree or a huge parasol. The vendors were great masters of the art of slicing the melons into uniform pieces of the smallest actual size with the biggest appearance. As he did the cutting, the hawker sang at fortissimo: "Fresh, cold, and sweet! Ten-cash apiece!" The price underwent great and rapid change according to the supply of melons, but for decades the same song was sung by nearly all the thousand and one watermelon vendors of Shanghai.

Street peddlers were talented advertisers. Some edibles were believed to possess mild medicinal properties or to be especially nutritious. Reed root, for instance, was believed to prevent certain maladies, especially those prevalent in summer. These qualities were advertised in the tune of the reed root peddler: "Ah, if reed root is used as a beverage as tea is, it has the wonderful effect of brightening one's eyes! When it is used by a babe or a child in midsummer, he will be free from all kinds of skin disease."[44]

Another edible, pear syrup candy (*ligaotang*), was a Shanghai specialty that had been popular since the Xianfeng period (1850–61). Shanghai residents were familiar with the song of pear syrup candy sellers, who came to the alleyways singing in the Subei dialect: "*Wuya wuli kuangya, liya ligaotang ya*—Grandpa eats my pear syrup candy: he sleeps soundly to sunup; Grandma eats my syrup: she keeps her good hearing and won't get 'dizzy sighted.'"[45] Such a ditty, sung to the accompaniment of an accordion, always following the same tune, could be worded in a variety of ways. The song usually went on to advocate the specific advantages of eating the candy for people of different age groups and professions, as well as the disadvantages of not eating it.[46]

These peddlers gained a nickname, "little craze" (*xiaorehun*), which initially referred to pear syrup candy sellers and their songs, but later was applied to many other street peddlers who also sang songs to advertise their goods. "Little crazes," who combined the business of hawking and free entertainment, became very popular. Street scenes such as the following were common all over the city: a crowd standing in a semicircle partly blocks the sidewalk, engrossed in something; passersby curiously ask, "What's that?" and are told, "It's a 'little craze' show."[47]

These street shows included storytelling, and peddlers were often gifted storytellers. Their shows were enchanting and invited audience involvement. Their subjects ranged from the plots of classic novels and popular dramas to contemporary romance; sex was always an enticing part of the show. George Wang, a Shanghai native born in 1927, recalled that in his home neighborhood near Nanshi, on warm evenings after supper there was always a peddler-storyteller standing on a stool with a high-legged box beside him for a table. Night after night people came to listen to the man's never-ending story. When Wang was eight or nine, he went to listen to the show nearly every night. Wang retrieved the scene in a memoir in English:

> This man talked in Shanghai dialect, suiting his voice and hand gestures to each character in turn, and periodically rapping a small block of wood on his table to draw the audience's attention. Like the puppeteer, he used vocal sound effects to represent a galloping horse or the boom of a cannon, but he did them much better. When he came to the sexy part of a story, his voice changed. In low, mysterious tones, he described every detail, every movement, and this always caused laughter in the audience. I didn't always understand what he said or what he meant, and I was too busy listening to turn around and look at [the audience], but their enjoyment was clear. Then, when the story reached a really exciting point, we knew what he would say:
> "If you want to know what happened, listen to the next chapter. But first, let me invite you to taste my ligao tang." And he would open his box and bring out his pear syrup candy to sell.[48]

With his "little urbanite" audience, this "stay tuned" tactic was usually effective, and the candies sold well, for the show was apparently a daily treat that many residents eagerly awaited. And for the children, this bit of street culture, which included commerce and sex, served as part of their primer for the world.

Seasonal edibles were only additions to a great variety of foods available all year round. Among these regular offerings were sweet-scented osmanthus, red bean soup, fried beancurd, fermented glutinous rice, breads, sesame cakes, pastries, and many others.[49] Fried beancurd was particularly popular. Beancurd was fried in a potful of boiling vegetable oil. The seller dipped a pair of long chopsticks in the boiling oil to turn the beancurd until it became yellow and crispy outside while the interior remained white and soft. If the customer came with a plate, the peddler would put the beancurd on it; if one came empty-handed, the peddler would furnish a bit of clean, dry straw on which he strung together pieces of fried beancurd, as a fisherman does with his catch. The beancurd was hot and tasty; but one had to take care not to burn one's tongue with it. This snack was perhaps the most savory food sold by street peddlers. The aroma that wafted down the lane signaled from a distance that the fried beancurd seller was in the neighborhood. The snack had a funny name: smelly dried beancurd.[50]

In the dead calm of night in winter, peddlers were still at work bringing favorite edibles to their customers. A typical night snack was fresh green olives. The fruit had a slightly alkaline taste that soon turned into a mild sweetness with a pleasant, refreshing, and invigorating effect. It was believed that the fruit could help one through the cold of night; it was a favorite of many who had learned to enjoy it. Wang vividly recalled from his childhood the olive peddler who regularly hawked on winter nights: "Late at night, if I was still awake, I could hear peddlers' cries from several streets away. 'Ta-an sia-ang ganlan, mai ganlan! Cri-isp spi-cy olives, buy my olives!' This man carries a basket hoisted over his shoulder on a rope, the fresh green olives covered over with a wet towel. He sells his olives by the piece, at three prices: fat, thin, and brownish. The last are yesterday's stock."[51]

Another popular night repast was *zhou,* a porridge or sweet thick broth resembling a thin, fluid pudding and made of glutinous rice and lotus seeds. The latter was believed to be very nutritious and to have a tonic effect. *Zongzi,* a pyramid-shaped dumpling made of glutinous rice wrapped in fresh reed leaves; *tangtuan,* dumplings made of glutinous rice flour and stuffed with ground meat, sweetened red bean paste, or ground sesame, served in soup; and won ton soup were also among the common night edibles sold in the alleyways.[52] The seller kept his commodities steaming hot over a portable stove. His song broke the still of the cold night: "Ham *zongzi,* ah! White sugared lotus seed porridge, ah!" Old customers had been anxiously expecting the seller for some time. As soon as they heard him, they lowered a basket with money and a bowl in it from the second-story window, as it was not quite pleasant to run right out into the cold wintry air in person.

These nighttime edibles were peddled in most seasons of the year; in fact, they were sold virtually every night except those following a few really hot days in the summer when fruits and watermelon dominated the market. In 1933, when the novelist Zhang Henshui lived in Shanghai, his study was a pavilion room in an alleyway house in Tianjin Road. Because of the popularity of his novel *Tixiao yinyuan* (Fatal Love), first published in installments in Shanghai's *Xinwen bao* (Daily News) in 1932–33, Zhang was in demand as a writer; indeed, at that time he was writing novels for ten publishers simultaneously. Social engagements often kept Zhang busy during the day, so he used to write at night, in his study. The arrival of the zongzi peddler signaled Zhang's regular midnight break. Zhang's wife, before she turned in, would not forget to remind him: "Listen for the sound of the zongzi hawker. When he comes to the alleyway, be sure to buy a couple of ham zongzi for me" (Fig. 23, top left).[53]

Lu Dafang, a writer and an old Shanghailander, recalled how a bowl of won ton soup from an alleyway peddler one night served as the "drug" that launched him on the way to a dissipated life in Shanghai in the late 1930s. As Lu described that fateful night, he and his young friends were enjoying a happy gathering in an alleyway house, a typical salon in "old Shanghai." The gathering was in fact so happy that it was already the middle of the night when the participants noticed the time. "We were hungry, and heard the sound of '*dou dou*' in the alleyway," Lu wrote. "It was a won ton peddler. To save us the trip downstairs, the girls took off their silk stockings and tied them together into a rope; we attached a basket to one end, and from the third floor we lowered the basket down to the alleyway. Egg-flavored won ton soup, one bowl after another, was lifted to our rooms on the third floor. We all ate with great relish." The hot and delicious soup, Lu recalled with humor some forty years later in Hong Kong, led to his first sexual experience that night, with a girl in the party (Fig. 23, top right).[54]

Lu Dafang's tidbit gives zest to what was a rather common business in Shanghai's residential areas. Alleyway trade such as Lu described occurred on such a regular basis that customers and peddlers gradually built a relationship of mutual trust. Every day, the food peddlers' punctual appearance in the alley made them part of the residents' quotidian life. Almost all won ton peddlers, for example, conducted their business from 8 P.M. to about 1 A.M., and they followed a certain route from lane to lane in residential neighborhoods; thus in any given alleyway the peddler would appear at roughly the same time every day.[55] Upon hearing the sound, *pu pu pu* or *dou dou dou*, depending on the type of bamboo clappers the peddler used, regular customers put a container and money in front of the door or hung a container with money from a window. In a few minutes, the peddler collected the money and filled the container with steaming hot won ton soup. The dumplings were made of very thin wrappers—so thin that after cooking they became transparent: the meat filling (pork or shrimp) was pink,

Fig. 23. Four sketches by Feng Zikai capture some sidelights of Shanghai's alleyway life. *Top left:* Lowering a basket down to the alley to purchase zongzi from a hawker (1923–25). *Top right:* A won ton seller with his kitchen on a shoulder pole (1934). *Bottom left:* A peddler selling straw mats, a necessity for every family in the summer (1934). *Bottom right*: A street barber cleaning his customer's ears, an after-haircut treat provided by the barber as a courtesy (1934). From Feng Zikai, *Feng Zikai wenji.*

in contrast with the green onions, brown dried mushrooms, yellow egg sheets, and hot pickled mustard tuber, all sliced into little pieces into the soup. For many people, this became an irresistible late-night snack.

Shanghai was "a city without night" (*buyecheng*). Although most people could not afford the nightlife in Nanking Road and other commercial areas—and, of course, were not writers like Lu Xun or Zhang Henshui, who produced their best pieces in the middle of the night—the average Shanghai family went to bed late. In contrast, a Li family who owned a coal store on Hart Road in the 1940s maintained much of the lifestyle they had brought with them from their native place of Shaoxing, including turning in early. The Lis went to bed before 9 P.M.; neighbors thus jokingly called the family "country folk."[56]

A story goes that a young couple who lived in a pavilion room in a shikumen neighborhood used to spend their evening together at home, where by the light of a desk lamp the husband read and the wife sat knitting until the middle of the night. When the sound of the won ton peddler was heard in the alleyway, the wife tied a pair of stockings together as a rope to lower a bamboo basket from their window down to the alleyway to purchase some soup. Inside the basket were money and a sauce pot. In due time this became a happy routine in their night life; the customers and the peddler conducted their business without saying a word or even seeing each other for years. Unfortunately, the young man died at an early age. His widow, lonely and heartbroken, affectionately continued buying won ton soup for another two years—in the memory of her husband, but also because she did not want to disappoint the peddler—until the peddler found out what had happened and did not have the heart to continue the business.[57]

SERVICES TO THE DOOR

Selling snacks was by far the most common alleyway business in the city's residential areas, but there were many more peddlers who brought their commodities and services into the alleyways. Among these peddlers were those who sold newspapers, flowers, fresh vegetables, rice, salt, needles, thread, socks, handkerchiefs, towels, soap, cigarettes, mats, bamboo poles (for hanging out clothes to dry), toys, and many other things. Like the hawkers who sold edibles, these peddlers also had their songs, which they often sang in set, particular tunes to draw people's attention (Fig. 23, bottom left). Daily the sock peddler, for instance, walked into the lane singing a song in praise of the durability of his socks. Sometimes two cotton fabric sellers alternately sang a song to praise the low price of their goods. Singing, they entered the alleyway, went all the way to the end of the lane, then walked back and left the alleyway, still singing.[58] Newspaper peddlers also came twice a day. In the morning, they were among the earliest peddlers of the day. At about seven or eight, riding bicycles, they were already busy selling newspapers, and in the late afternoon they reappeared, selling evening newspapers.[59] Since the publication of the *Da wanbao* (Great Evening News), whose first issue was circulated on February 12, 1932, reading newspapers twice a day had become a custom in the city.[60] Many newspaper peddlers were poor children whose daily appearance in the streets and alleyways made them a topic of folk songs and cartoons. The figures in these songs and cartoons epitomized the poor and wandering children in the city.[61] Services needed in daily life, such as the repair of household items, blacksmithing, coppersmithing, fortune-telling, dentistry, barbering, and so on were also provided by petty traders and handicraftspeople whose business was chiefly in residential neighborhoods. These tradesmen and -women either roamed the neighborhood soliciting customers or set up shop in a fairly regular spot in an alleyway-house compound. Heppner recalled that, compared with the busy scene on the streets of Shanghai, "it was even more crowded in the lanes, where cobblers would make a new pair of shoes for a customer in less than a day, and locksmiths a new set of keys while customers waited. Discovering that many European refugees were destitute, some Chinese invented several trades appealing to them. Craftsmen plied the lanes calling: '*Kaputie — ganz machen,*' which, translated from German slang, meant that they would fix whatever was broken."[62]

A barber's stand set up on a street corner or at an alleyway entrance was among the most common sights in Shanghai (Fig. 24). This was no more than a wooden stool or chair and a bamboo stand with two shelves: on the top shelf lay a basin for shampoo and on the bottom rested the barber's tool kit. If the barber's stand was close to a wall, the barber might hang a mirror or set up a curtain for privacy, but such fastidiousness was rare. A barber like this could easily carry all his equipment on a shoulder pole and wander around looking for customers. But most barbers had a regular location, which was always close to a hot water shop where the barber could purchase water for shampooing and preparing a hot towel for shaving. The convenient location and low cost of haircuts—usually 25–30 percent less than in a regular barber shop—attracted residents, and the barber usually had a fairly regular clientele in the neighborhood. An adult might, however, feel a little uncomfortable about having a haircut in public; besides, haircuts at these stands were believed to be less stylish. Thus the majority of the customers were children and oldsters; women customers were rare.

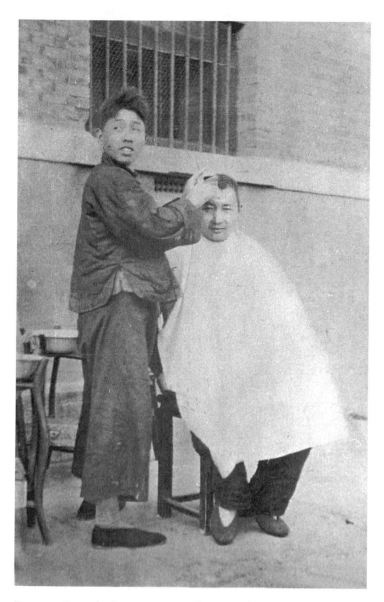

Fig. 24. Street barbers were virtually everywhere in Shanghai. The
stand was portable, but each barber usually had his regular spot, which
could be either on a quiet street corner or in the midst of bustling
traffic. This photograph was taken in the early 1930s; as documented
by the photographer, in addition to a washbowl, soap, brush, and
blades, these street barbers even provided a full-length drape, quite
in the manner of a fashionable barbershop. From R. Barz, *Shanghai:
Sketches of Present-Day Shanghai.*

An informant told me that he had his hair cut at a neighborhood barber stand from childhood up to age 21, when he felt a little embarrassed sitting on the barber's stool while some of his acquaintances passed by. Thus he started going to a barber shop for haircuts. An elderly resident said he missed this old-fashioned service, particularly because the barber he patronized for decades gave such a good massage and, he added, "nowadays people don't do it anymore." Customarily, if asked, a barber would provide services such as cleaning the customer's ears or massaging the customer's shoulders and back for a few minutes for free as an after-haircut treat (Fig. 23, bottom right).[63]

Another feature that appealed particularly to children was the traveling libraries found in alleyways. These lending libraries consisted of a few portable bookshelves, each about six feet tall, and one or two benches. By paying one cent, a customer could rent one to three books, depending on the popularity of the book, to be read right on the spot. Overnight rental was not a regular feature, although a good customer might occasionally ask for the favor of taking books home for a night or so. These libraries might be set up anywhere in the alleyway, but the most common places were the roofed entrance of a lane, known as *guojielou* (overhead floor spanning a lane)—such a spot allowed the library to operate on rainy days—or an alleyway corner where a wall was available for the bookshelves to lean against and the light was sufficient. Usually, a resident who lived right in the neighborhood operated the library. Thus, he or she could, with relative ease, move the library (bookshelves, books, and benches) from home to alleyway in the morning and back home again after dusk (Fig. 25). The books for rent were mostly novels and other types of fiction and children's books. Picture storybooks (*lianhuan hua*), which were standardized at about four by six inches in size and had an illustration (often by skillful artists) and a caption of two to three lines on each page, were among the most popular books in the libraries. In fact, these picture storybooks were popular among all sorts of readers, regardless of age. Many children got their first exposure to classic novels such as *The Romance of the Three Kingdoms* (Sanguozhi yanyi), *The Water Margin* (Shuihu zhuan), *The Record of a Journey to the West* (Xiyou ji), and *The Deities Conferred* (Fengshen bang) through picture storybooks.[64]

The seamstress was another regular vendor in the neighborhood. Women who did sewing carried a bamboo basket with cotton patches, needles, thread, a tape measure, and scissors and canvassed customers in relatively poor neighborhoods. Their clients were mostly factory workers, shop assistants, apprentices, and bachelors of all callings.[65] Shanghai

Fig. 25.   Portable libraries like this were part of everyday life in the city. While children most enjoyed the street libraries, grown-ups were also patrons. Many picture-storybooks on the portable shelves were adapted from China's rich historical works, classic novels, fables, and dramas. For instance, many people had read the cartoon version of *The Romance of the Three Kingdoms* or *The Dream of the Red Chamber* before they were able to read the original. Street corner readings therefore served as a primer of history and literature for the average person. From R. Barz, *Shanghai: Sketches of Present-Day Shanghai*.

was full of men who were single or had left their families back in their hometown. The male-female ratio in Shanghai was constantly more than 130:100 during most of the Republican period (1912–1949). In 1935, for instance, it was as high as 141:100.[66] It was the custom in China, as perhaps in other parts of the world as well, for men other than professional tailors to do no needlework. As a Chinese proverb goes, "A man who does needlework is going to be poor all his life" (*nan zuo nügong yishi qiong*).[67] One of the stereotyped merits of having a wife was that she could do the man's sewing. A popular song, "Old Wang Number Five" (*Wang Laowu*), pokes fun at single men: "Oh, Old Wang Number Five, you have wasted your time living to the age of thirty-five, and you still don't have a wife, your clothes are worn—nobody to help patch them up."[68] Thus seamstresses had good business.

While needlework was exclusively a women's occupation, most other services in alleyway compounds were provided by men (Fig. 26). Shanghai residents could easily list the services provided literally at their door: men,

Fig. 26.   A tinker specializing in bamboo ware mends a basket in an alleyway in the International Settlement. Note that tools and materials are hung on the tinker's shoulder pole leaning against the wall near the door of a home; most likely the man is repairing an item for this household. The round panels on the shoulder pole are parts of bamboo food steamers, used as a sort of "microwave oven" in every Shanghai household in those days. Itinerant handicraftspeople of all kinds were available literally right at one's door. These artisans were an indispensable part of the life of the city. Except when confronted by the occasional local thug, they were largely free from outside intervention and taxation. Courtesy of the Shanghai Museum.

and occasionally women, came to repair enamelware, aluminum utensils, leather shoes, rubber products, umbrellas, nightstools, water buckets, bathtubs, rattan work, bamboo ware, *zongbeng* (a wooden bed frame strung with crisscrossed coir ropes, the most common type of bed in Shanghai), straw mats, clocks, wooden furniture, and many other household items.[69] Locksmiths, with their equipment hung on both sides of a bike, came to the alleyways on a regular basis. The repairing of rubber shoes—rubber-soled shoes and galoshes were the most common footwear in Shanghai after the first British rubber products were imported to Shanghai in 1866[70]—was a common service in the alleyways. The repairman carried a little wooden box with his "means of production": sandpaper, a file, glue, and a few pieces of rubber from used rubber shoes. He squatted anywhere in the alleyway to do his job: he cut a piece of rubber of the desired size and abraded it and the hole that needed to be repaired, before gluing the rubber on top of the hole. In a few minutes, the customer could walk back home with mended shoes.[71]

Some of these craftspeople, such as umbrella repairers, also purchased used or broken household items from residents, repaired them, and sold them in the alleyways. An umbrella repairer often carried dozens of umbrellas made of tarpaulin or colored oil paper for sale. On the shoulder pole of a nightstool repairer, a few repainted used nightstools were always available for sale. A great many vendors accepted trade-ins. Such businesses were not only convenient but low priced, and the profits were sufficient for the peddler to make a living, usually a good enough living to support a family (Fig. 27).[72] These small and brisk businesses, this mingling of commerce with residence, made Shanghai a much easier place to live than many smaller cities, to say nothing of rural towns and villages.

Ironically, perhaps, a lower-class opium business conducted in Republican-era Shanghai is a particularly revealing example of the mutual benefits to the parties involved. Shanghai's coolies, drained of energy by their daily backbreaking work, sought opium for stimulation.[73] But opium, even that of inferior quality, was expensive. A business arose to meet the need. In Shanghai's alleyways, residents often encountered men with a straw bag in their arms, soliciting for what was called "faucet dregs" (*longtou zha*), the dregs left by the opium addicts of well-off families. Instead of throwing opium dregs into the trash bin, servants of these families collected their masters' leftovers and sold them to the solicitors to earn some pocket money. Sometimes, they also sold broken opium pipes and trays, since opium paraphernalia used for years contained a rime of opium. For a few pennies the solicitor purchased the opium dregs, then took them to a quiet

Fig. 27. An old woman baby-sits her grandson while running a petty gambling game. The round table set on an upside-down rattan basket with a moving "candy picker" in the middle is divided into a number of folding-fan-shaped spaces, where candy, snacks, or sometimes tiny toys could be placed. The player flicked the picker with a finger, causing it to spin; the player won the prize located where it stopped. Since most of the prizes were worth less than the cost of playing the game, the vendor was sure to make a profit. Courtesy of the Shanghai Museum.

lane entrance where he had set up a coal stove to boil the dregs with water. He sold the result, called "faucet water"—which implied that this liquid was as cheap as tap water—to coolies, rickshaw pullers, beggars, and other addicted poor people who could not afford regular opium. The user decocted the water to extract the opium for smoking. The opium rime on broken pipes and trays could also be dissolved for this purpose.[74]

This business was beneficial to three groups of people. First of all, hundreds of the faucet water dealers made a living by selling the concoction. The trade was so profitable that it became a daily business in many of Shanghai's alleyway-house compounds. Second, from the customers' point of view, this business provided an affordable luxury—opium. By paying three to four copper coins, a person could get a wine pot full of faucet water, which was quite sufficient to keep a coolie vigorous for a few hours.

A medium-size pot of the liquid sold for four copper coins, and a large pot, six copper coins. The daily cost for a hopeless addict was therefore no more than fifteen or sixteen copper coins.[75] It was reported that in the 1930s the business had about 20,000 to 30,000 customers, ranging in age from twenty-five to seventy.[76] And, finally, numerous domestic servants and maids happily got pocket money by selling what would otherwise have been trash. Wang Zhiping (born in 1918), a former head of the Zhabei district, recalled that at age thirteen he was an apprentice in a small leather shop on Sixth Road (today's Beihai Road) in the downtown area. The store owner, Lin Sanyuan, was a heavy opium addict and a skillful opium maker (processing raw opium into a form ready for smoking). One of Wang's daily duties was to process opium for his boss to smoke at night; Wang kept the dregs to sell to a peddler the next morning.[77]

In the 1920s, an average monthly wage for a domestic maid was about four to five silver dollars, less than half the income of an average factory worker. But the maid got free room and board and her duties were relatively light, mainly needlework, combing out her mistress's hair, and serving as a companion.[78] In addition, the maid pocketed whatever she got by selling the discards from her employer's household. Opium dregs were only one of many castoffs for which there was a market. Other items included newspapers, bottles, broken glass, cans, rags, old clothes, worn shoes, inkfish and turtle (both were favorite dishes) bones, and so on. The junk man, toting a big bamboo basket or carrying a pair of square-bottomed bamboo baskets hung from a shoulder pole, was a common figure in the alleyways. He hawked the items that he collected, from old clothes, little metal objects, old watches and clocks, and bric-a-brac to furniture made from padauk trees (*hongmu*, or red wood).[79] Sometimes for a mere pittance he purchased a rare curio of immense worth from an owner who did not know its real value. But, of course, to be a really successful dealer in old things one had to be a connoisseur and a shrewd tradesman in one. Most junk men were just petty peddlers. In recent interviews, old Shanghai residents could still recall the songs of junk men that reverberated in the alleyways all over the city. When I interviewed four old Shanghai residents in different lilong neighborhoods, one informant imitated the song of the junk man who came to his alleyway every two or three days. The other three smiled because they had heard exactly the same tune in their neighborhoods, obviously sung by different hawkers: "*A-hu-a*, come out to sell your junk! Foreign bottles and broken glass can be exchanged for matches!"[80]

Neighbors

Any discussion of relations among residents in Shanghai's crowded alley-way-house neighborhoods must take into account three elements: first, the baojia system, a failed attempt of the government to interject itself into neighborhood life; second, ad hoc and sporadic citizen organizations, mostly for the purpose of negotiating rent; and third, the spontaneous and multifarious reactions of one human to another—in other words, conventional human congeniality and discord among neighbors. While the first two were brief and feeble, the third was derived from the quotidian aspects of life and made up "politics" understood by the people themselves.

"HEAVEN IS HIGH AND THE EMPEROR IS FAR AWAY"

For centuries, the Chinese state dreamed of extending political control from the national capital down into the neighborhoods where ordinary people lived their everyday lives. The state's most obvious effort in this regard was the baojia system of neighborhood watch and mutual responsibility. In Shanghai, the baojia system was established as early as 1648, only four years after the founding of the Qing dynasty (1644–1911). However, as elsewhere in the country, in Shanghai the system existed merely as a formality.[81] Although the authorities in Beijing emphasized the importance of the baojia off and on, local officials either ignored orders or followed them dilatorily, fearful of the difficulties of carrying out the program. The system, in short, had not been strictly applied in the Qing as it was originally designed.[82]

The Nationalist regime nevertheless viewed the system as a useful means of exerting state control over society. The Nanjing government officially adopted the baojia system in the provinces of Henan, Hubei, and Anhui in August 1932 and extended it nationwide in November 1934.[83] Probably because of the strategic importance of Shanghai, a plan to establish the baojia in Shanghai was proposed as early as 1927, immediately after the formation of the Shanghai Special Municipality (*Shanghai te-bieshi*), a name deliberately designed to refer to the whole of Shanghai, including the foreign concessions.[84] The proposal aimed to establish a three-layered neighborhood organization under the administration of *qu* (districts), in which five households (*hu*) would form a basic neighborhood unit known as the *lin*, five lin would form a *lü*, and twenty lü a *fang*. It appeared that an average hu was reckoned to contain eight "mouths"; a municipality of 1 million people would thus be organized as follows: 1,000,000 people = 125,000 hu = 25,000 lin = 5,000 lu = 250 fang = 25 qu.[85]

The plan remained on paper in the Nanjing decade, partly because of the complexity of implementing the program even in the city's Chinese sections alone, and partly because the fighting with Japan in 1932 and 1937 made any major administrative reorganization impossible. While the Nationalists were unable to build their own baojia system, in some areas the city authorities had to rely on the personnel of the old local system, such as the *dibao* (a local constable or land warden), to carry out administrative duties such as measuring land, stamping deeds, and reporting property value.[86] At the same time, the idea of establishing a complete baojia system in Shanghai had not been given up. This can be seen in the Nationalists' attitude toward the wartime baojia system established in Shanghai by the puppet city government under Japanese control. By the end of the war, not only did the Nationalists have no intention of abolishing the system, which could justifiably be seen as a wartime evil imposed by the occupation forces and their collaborators, but moreover they wanted to strengthen it. Under rigid Guomindang ideological control and bureaucratic screening procedures, an intensive training program with five classes for "local self-government" cadres was carried out in 1947–48. This was intended to prepare the ground for an overall reconstruction of the baojia system in the city.[87] The efforts ended up being in vain, with the collapse of the Nationalist regime in 1949.

Thus, the only time in the Republican era that the people of Shanghai really felt that the baojia system was part of their lives was during the Japanese occupation (1938–45). It took the Japanese and their puppet city government about five years, from September 1938 to late 1943, to build the baojia system in Shanghai, including the foreign concessions.[88] The basic unit of the system was the household; ten households located in an immediate neighborhood formed a *jia* and ten jia formed a *bao*, with a registered head at each level.[89] A "household" was not necessarily defined as a natural family of kinship but could be a bunch of families that lived in the same house. In fact, the hu unit often consisted of all the residents of an alleyway house, and the landlord or the second landlord was registered as the household head (*huzhang*) of his tenants.[90] This was because of Shanghai's crowded living conditions, in which, as we have seen, it was common for half a dozen families or so to live in a single shikumen house. Apparently, the occupation authorities felt it would have been pointless to try to break down the household unit into natural (biological) families.

The primary purpose of the wartime baojia was to build a system of mutual responsibility (*lianbao lianzuo*) among residents to prevent expressions of anti-Japanese sentiment and anti-Japanese activities. If there was any "crime" against the Japanese in a neighborhood, the household head was held responsible and all the neighbors within the jia would be involved.[91] The occupation forces, via their puppet city government, also used the baojia system to levy taxes, assign community services, and impose rationing. From July 1942 on, rice was rationed to individuals (*jikou shouliang*) instead of to households (*jihu shouliang*), and an individual's residential status had to be verified by both the head of household and the head of the jia. Although the authorities were never able to complete the rationing system and the insufficient amount and inferior quality of rationed rice drove people to buy rice on the black market—which thrived throughout the city during the entire wartime period—the rationing of food grain was the only part of the baojia system that really mattered to most people.[92]

But perhaps it was because the system was imposed by an occupying force as a wartime measure that it never functioned well. From the very beginning, the mobility of the people of Shanghai in an uncertain, wartime situation, their jammed residential neighborhoods, and their general dislike of the Japanese made establishment of the system and its operation extremely difficult. Residents of Shanghai were generally uncooperative, if not openly resistant. Indifference to the baojia responsibilities, abuses in its operation, and corruption of baojia personnel were widespread.[93] Prior to the outbreak of the Pacific War, the Japanese were unable to set up the system in the city's core, the International Settlement and the French Concession. By late 1943, when the system had just spread to more or less the whole city, it had been in operation less than two years and it operated badly. In the summer of 1945, the Municipal Baojia Committee, the chief administrative organ of the system, complained in its semiannual report that no district, except for two in rural Pudong, had submitted monthly household statistics and other routine reports and that the system was virtually at a standstill.[94]

In spite of the Nationalists' effort to revive the system during the Civil War period, on the eve of the Communist takeover the baojia in Shanghai existed in name only. The Communists, who understood better than anyone else in Chinese history the importance of political control at the grassroots level, were careful not to attack the system rashly. Instead of adopting the usual hackneyed tone to condemn the baojia, as the Communists did regarding almost everything else the previous regime had done in the city, the Communists publicly acknowledged the usefulness of the baojia. In an open letter to "the people of Shanghai" dated May 3, 1949, the Communists called for a unification of residents to maintain order and public safety: "The people of Shanghai seldom unite, but now they are all facing the catastrophe [of war] and feel it is necessary to unite for self-defense. It shall be very easy to take the lilong as the basic unit of organization. This can be done by centralizing around the heads of the baojia and other individuals who have broad contacts with the residents."[95] In another letter, to "the personnel of Guomindang offices and the baojia personnel," dated April 29, 1949, one month before the takeover, the Communists lectured the receivers that "in particular, you baojia personnel should save the household registration books in your hands, report saboteurs, and immediately organize the alleyway residents. . . . Do not worry about your jobs and livelihood in the future. The policies of New Democracy are to ensure that everybody has a job to do and rice to eat. As long as you are determined to serve the people, the new government is committed to placing you properly and employing you according to your ability."[96]

These promises to the old Guomindang personnel were not necessarily fulfilled after liberation. But the Communists did commit themselves to establishing a vigorous neighborhood control system in the country; China's largest city was at the forefront of this effort. Shanghai was among the first cities to establish neighborhood organizations. In June 1950, a year after its liberation, the city already had established 102 "offices of takeover commissioners" (*jieguan zhuanyuan banshichu*), which were an embryonic form of the so-called street offices (*jiedao banshichu*), directly under the administration of the city's twenty districts.[97] This was five years before the three-tiered neighborhood organizations (from the bottom up: the resident group, the residents' committee, and the street office) were established nationwide.[98]

Thus prior to the Communist era, the state had little presence in neighborhood life. When asked to discuss governmental presence in the neighborhoods before Liberation, a group of longtime Shanghai residents dismissed the idea, saying that there was in general no such thing in their neighborhoods. Some even implied that it was only because of the forty-year experience with the Communists' "residents committees" (*jumin weiyuanhui*) that one might possibly imagine that "politics" (*zhengzhi*) existed in the neighborhoods before 1949. These aged residents mentioned an old Chinese saying that they thought aptly described life in Shanghai's lilong before Liberation: "Heaven is high and the emperor is far away" (*Tian gao huangdi yuan*).[99]

The residents' general unawareness of governmental intervention in their daily life should not lead to the conclusion that Shanghai's residential neighborhoods were a Land of Peach Blossoms, totally cut off from politics or government.[100] It is better to regard this unawareness as the result of the impotence of, rather than absence of, governmental intervention. The fact that the city was mostly under foreign administration contributed to the weak presence of Chinese state power. The concessions themselves were not a laissez-faire kingdom, but had their measures to regulate society within their boundaries. For one thing, as far as the neighborhoods were concerned, both the International Settlement and the French Concession had rules and regulations in meticulous detail on the construction and maintenance of dwellings, including things like construction materials, the size of alleys, the sewer system, street lighting, and so on.[101] These rules were certainly a form of governmental control. However, following them was regarded as the business of the builders or real estate developers who owned the property. An average resident lived in a lilong compound for years without even being aware of these regulations. Since the authorities took no measures beyond issuing the regulations, residents naturally felt that life in their neighborhood was largely free of governmental intervention.

A "MOTLEY CROWD"

By the same token, relations among neighbors themselves (which may be seen as a horizontal relationship versus a vertical state-society relationship) concerning public affairs in the neighborhoods can be characterized this way: there was little evidence of a sense of community based on the lilong, but residents, at least some "public minded" ones, occasionally worked together on matters of mutual concern.

In a nation where most people lived in a community for generations without moving, the people of Shanghai were seen by some hinterlanders as peculiar because, like urbanites elsewhere in the world, they frequently changed their place of residence. It was believed that the general, mutual indifference among neighbors in Shanghai was the result of the fact that people "liked to move." [102] But the people of Shanghai were mobile only in comparison with people who lived under the same roof for generations. An investigation, conducted in 1990, of residents in seven lilong communities found that 87 percent (381 out of 438 residents) had moved at least once before settling in their current address. Even so, 79 percent of the residents had been living in the same house since the early 1950s, in other words, for nearly four decades. Furthermore, of that 79 percent, more than half had moved into the neighborhood in the early 1940s and stayed put.[103]

Another survey, conducted in 1995, found much the same (see Table 7).

Table 7. Residents in Zhengming Li, Shanghai, 1933–51

House No.	Family Name	Occupation of Male Head of Household[a]	Move-in Date	Place of Origin
2	*You	Lilong compound guide	1933	Ningbo (Z)
4	Lu	Photographer	1941	Shunde (G)
6	Wu	Proofreader	1938	Changzhou (J)
8	Zhu	Accountant	1935	Ningbo (Z)
	Deng	Trolleybus driver	1938	Wuxi (J)
10	*Zhao	Unknown	1939	Jinan (S)
	Han	Bus conductor	1945	Yangzhou (J)
12	Lu	Factory manager	1937	Jiangyin (J)
14	*Jiang	Factory manager	1937	Ningbo (Z)
16	Hong	Unknown	1946	Chaozhou (G)
18	Sun	Press editor	1946	Ningbo (Z)
	Shen	Supervisor of conductors	1947	Ningbo (Z)
20	Zhao	Lawyer	1936	Suzhou (J)
22	Xi	Cotton mill office worker	1935	Nanhui (SH)
24	Deng	Tram driver	1950	Ningbo (Z)
	*Zhao	Peddler	1951	Pudong (SH)
26	Sun	Office worker	1947	Shaoxing (Z)

SOURCE: Author's fieldwork, carried out in collaboration with the Institute of Sociology, the Shanghai Academy of Social Sciences, August 2–11, 1995.

NOTE: All families, except those marked by an asterisk, were current residents of Zhengming Li at the time of investigation in August 1995. Residents who moved into the compound after 1951 are not included. Abbreviations: (Z) = Zhejiang, (G) = Guangdong, (J) = Jiangsu, (S) = Shandong, (SH) = Shanghai.

[a]The column "occupation of male head of household" shows occupations before 1949.

Most of the residents of Zhengming Li (Alley of the Upright and Honest), a typical shikumen compound in west Shanghai, had lived there for decades since the Republican era. The majority (12 of 15) of the families who had moved into this alleyway-house complex in the late thirties and the forties were still there in the early nineties. Of these 12 families, 3 had moved in during the first decade following the lilong compound's construction. Some early residents had died, but their offspring were still living there.

There are various reasons for this stability. Partly it is a result of the government's household registration system pursued after the mid-1950s, which almost ended all immigration into the city and made changing one's residence within the city a complex and bureaucratic nightmare.[104] But even before Liberation, when people were entirely free to change residence, in reality moving was so costly and hectic that they would try to avoid it if possible. During most of this century, housing in Shanghai was in short supply, and the choice of dwellings for rent limited. Residents who had a house or room in a shikumen neighborhood might well have thought themselves lucky and would not have been eager to, or could not afford to, move somewhere else. Finally, the Chinese notion of "being content with the land and cautious about moving" (*an tu zhong qian*) also played some role.[105]

Shanghai alleyway-house compounds to some extent resembled China's villages, where farmers lived in the same "insular, and perhaps also solidary [*sic*], community" for generations.[106] However, while a sense of community may grow among villagers tied together by bonds of residence, workplace, and, sometimes, kinship, such a sense rarely grew among the city people, who were never tied together by production or kinship and who merely happened to live within the boundaries of the same alleyway-house compound. Here and there were some concentrations of residents who worked for the same, nearby company. For instance, many employees of the British Trambus Company lived in the lilong compounds along Hart Road, where the company was located, and the lilong compounds along Hengbang Road in Hongkou had many residents employed by the Commercial Press. But since a complex body of residents lived in these neighborhoods, such gatherings of a certain type of worker were still dispersed and far from being powerful enough to forge a bond or a sense of community.[107]

In short, the people of Shanghai did not develop a sense of identity based on the alleyway compound or, in a broader sense, based on the neighborhood.[108] If there was a sense of community or sharing derived from residence, it was no more than a casual mentioning, in greetings or other social conversations, that one lived in the same li or fang as the other party. Neighborhood relations in alleyway houses fit the pattern described by the Daoist forefather Lao Zi: namely, that neighbors could hear each other's chickens and dogs but would not bother to pay each other a visit even once in a lifetime.[109] Despite having lived in the same lane for decades, many residents in Zhengming Li never had even a casual conversation with one another. Usually, they just smiled or nodded when they ran across each other in the alleyway. Here, the bond of neighbors was situational: they were people jammed together because they lived in an extremely crowded city.

The way that neighbors addressed each other also reflected the casualness of relations. Commonly residents in an alleyway-house compound did not know each other's given name, despite the fact that they might have lived in the same compound or even the same house for decades. People usually addressed their neighbors as "the Mother of the Zhang Family," "the Uncle of the Li Family," and so on. Children's names were frequently employed in addressing their parents, since children often played in alleyways and their given names were easily known among neighbors. Thus adults were known as "Xiaolin's Mamma," "Daguo's Dad," and so on. It was also not unusual for neighbors to live in the same compound for years but not know each other's name at all (not even the family name, which in China was socially more important than one's given name). Customarily, a combination of what might be called the "age and sex typing" of a person with the type of room she or he lived in resulted in a form of address, such as "the Grandma of the Front Living Room," "the Sister-in-Law of the Pavilion Room," "the Aunt on the Second Floor," and so on. A woman in Zhengming Li was called by her neighbors "the Bride," because she was a bride at the time she moved into the neighborhood; but some thirty years later, she was still "the Bride" (with reason, some called her "the Old Bride"). Few people in the neighborhood knew her real name.[110]

Yet, residents were not totally isolated from each other. Although the baojia system was imposed only briefly as a wartime emergency measure and Shanghai residents never had neighborhood organizations such as the *chōkai* of Tokyo, when tenants and landlords (not including the second landlords) had disputes, tenants selected (often on a volunteer basis) a committee to negotiate with the landlord.[111] In the last quarter of 1929 alone, for instance, there were three major tenant-landlord disputes in shikumen neighborhoods in the downtown area: one in Yude Li over a 40 percent rent increase,[112] one in Fuxing Li (Alley of Fortune and Prosperity) over an early termination of leases in conjunction with an unexpected demolition of the whole compound to make way for new construction, and one in Chunhua Li (Alley of Spring Flowers) over a new leasing procedure caused by a change of ownership. In each case tenants organized a "tenant association" (*fangke lianhehui*) to negotiate with the owners.[113] Such tenant organizations also existed in some residential compounds for the purpose of maintaining neighborhood safety and cleanliness. But most associations were very loosely organized, for a temporary purpose (primarily, for negotiating rent). None were officially registered, and the representatives or members of negotiating committees were not elected but formed by a few "public minded" tenants who volunteered. These organizations often ended up, as a researcher on the housing of Shanghai put it, as no more than an inefficient, "motley crowd."[114]

But it seemed that occasionally the "motley crowd" was able to make a major noise, as in the case of a citywide rent reduction movement in 1934. The source can be traced back two years earlier, to the Wusong-Shanghai War of January 28, 1932, when Japanese air raids destroyed much of Shanghai's Chinese district (especially Zhabei) and dealt a major blow to the city's real estate market. On one hand, houses continued to be built on a wide scale in the early 1930s despite the war. In 1930, 2,792 new houses were built in Shanghai; in 1932 the number increased to 4,895; the next year it jumped to 9,585—more than triple the 1930 figure.[115] But on the other hand, the construction boom was only a false sign of prosperity in the real estate market. While the city was teeming with new houses, the real estate market was declining rapidly, as revealed by the total trading volume of real estate in the early 1930s: in 1931 the trading volume was $183,000,000, and the next year, it dropped to $25,175,000—an obvious aftermath to the war earlier that year. The trading volume bounced back to $43,130,000 in 1933 but dropped again in 1934 to a record low of $12,990,000. During the remainder of the decade, the trading volume of Shanghai's real estate market never exceeded $14,460,000.[116] The stagnation of the market was also evident in the vacancy rate in residential houses. According to a survey conducted in the spring of 1933, 12.8 percent of the city's Western-style residential houses (including the new-style alleyway houses) were vacant, a record high since 1910, and 4.4 percent of Chinese-style dwelling houses (mainly the shikumen) were vacant, more than in the previous five years.[117] In the International Settlement in 1930, only 2 percent of Chinese houses were unoccupied; by 1935, vacancies had increased to 8.5 percent. The Settlement alone had about 5,000 unoccupied Chinese houses in 1934 (and 5,517 in 1936), a startling figure considering the sardine-can-like living conditions in most of the city's densely populated neighborhoods. One obvious reason for this anomaly was the rental rate: while the prices of 260 items used in daily life had dropped 20 percent since 1930, rent had increased 12 percent by 1934.[118]

This was the background to the citywide rent-reduction movement that arose in 1934. In Shanghai, complaints about high rents had been a conventional topic of conversation—something like talking about the weather—for years. This gave birth to the expression *Shanghai ju, da buyi* (It is difficult to live in Shanghai), which derived from the ancient saying *Chang'an ju, da buyi* (It is difficult to live in Chang'an).[119] By the end of 1933, in the International Settlement the City People's Association

(Shimin Lianhehui), an organization sponsored by middle-ranking merchants, proposed in the daily *Shenbao* a citywide rent-reduction campaign to "reduce the people's burden and maintain social peace and stability." The association then held a meeting on January 6, 1934, at which it was resolved to solicit the support of other organizations in the city. On January 16, representatives of more than a hundred organizations of various types, including the Chamber of Commerce (Shanghui), the City People's Association, the General Labor Union (Zong Gonghui), and a variety of trade unions (*tongye gonghui*) and native-place associations (*tongxianghui*), held a joint meeting in the assembly hall of the Chamber of Commerce. At the meeting the establishment of a "Rent-Reduction Committee of Shanghai Municipality" (Shanghaishi Jiandi Fangzu Weiyuanhui) was proclaimed. The joint convention issued nine "Organizational Rules" and fifteen "Organizational Regulations" to govern the Committee, and it selected an executive committee of thirty-five members; nine members of the executive committee formed a standing committee to handle daily operations. In a few months the Committee established five branch committees citywide: in the First Special District (i.e., the International Settlement), the Second Special District (i.e., the French Concession), Nanshi, Zhabei, and Pudong. Subbranch committees were also formed in a number of alleyway-house neighborhoods. Starting in June the Committee published a newsletter. By the summer of 1934, the campaign had drawn support from some concerned foreigners of more than a dozen nationalities. Although most of these foreigners just lent moral support, Russian, Indian, and Japanese merchant organizations did apply to join the Committee.

The campaign achieved some scattered results. News about monthly rent reductions in some alleyway-house neighborhoods—the amounts varied from a couple of dollars to several dozens—was reported, and occasionally stories about landlords volunteering a rent reduction were circulated. But rent reduction was far from widespread in the city. The campaign's greatest success was in the Nanshi, Zhabei, and Hongkou area, and to some extent in the semirural Jiangwan area. In the core of the city—the foreign concessions—where the issue was most pressing and where the campaign began, there were few reductions. Although the campaign had a social basis (i.e., the general complaints about high rent), it was largely a top-down movement dominated by the merchants who believed that high rent was an important source of the recession in Shanghai after the January 28 War. The Committee was financially sponsored by the city's trade organizations, and it relied on the donations of Committee members who were the leading figures in these organizations. Although the active life of the Committee was only a few months, its bureaucracy was unrealistically colossal. The executive committee had its "special committee," "secretariat," "standing committee," "general affairs section," "finance section," "organizational section," "investigation section," "public relations or propaganda section," "mediation section," "legal consultant section," and so on. This bureaucracy soon led to financial problems, and in July the Committee had to modify its own regulation of "no membership fee" and start demanding contributions and volunteer services of members. By the fall of 1934 the movement had already become a spent force, or, as the *Social Daily News* put it, "a show of martial arts," implying that the movement could only make threatening gestures. Organizations like this may have created a sense of unity at a time of crisis but they could hardly contribute to an enduring sense of community comparable to that—weak as it was—based on living for years in the same residential compound.[120]

With regard to public matters, the superficial and loose relations among the residents of Zhengming Li were, evidently, typical for neighborhood compounds all over Shanghai. Zhengming Li had sixty-five two-story shikumen houses lined up in four lanes, each separated by additional lanes, and had its own entrance leading to Hart Road near Bubbling Well Road, in the west end of the International Settlement.[121] Table 7 provides information about the residents in one of the four lanes of Zhengming Li. This was the only lane that did not have typical shikumen but instead boasted dwellings with fashionable front facades: each house had a wrought-iron gate set before a little front yard, a sizable balcony on the second floor, and an arched front wall decorated with cobblestones—all were imitations of the new-style alleyway house. Perhaps this design was too costly, for the houses in the other lanes in Zhengming Li were built in the typical, nondescript shikumen style. This was a quite stable neighborhood: as mentioned earlier, most of the residents who moved in during the late 1930s and the 1940s were still there in the 1980s and 1990s. According to the residents, because most houses in this lane were occupied by one family, neighborhood relations were simple. If there was an issue that concerned all the residents in the lane, a few families would play a sort of senior's role among the neighbors of this lane. On that occasion, the male household heads of the families Wu (House Number 6), Zhu (House Number 8), Lu (House Number 12), and Xi (House Number 22) would have a meeting, usually in Mr. Wu's house, to discuss the issue or, should it be necessary, to work out a solution. But such occasions were rare. As far as Mr. Xi and Mrs. Zhu (the widow of Mr. Zhu) could recall, in the late forties there was only one occasion that these four families had an informal meeting in Mr. Wu's house to discuss how to negotiate with the landlord (a flour mill company) concerning a rent increase. The negotiations did not result in a solution and lingered on until Liberation.

The only person who played a connecting role among the neighbors in Zhengming Li was Mr. You (House Number 2), a man who worked for the landlord cleaning the alleyway and collecting rent. House Number 2 was not a regular house but rather was built on top of the alleyway entrance, with a stairway set on one side of the entrance. This structure, known as a guojielou (overhead floor spanning a lane), was designed to accommodate an alleyway gate guard. Gate guards worked without pay usually, but received free or reduced rent (see Fig. 17).[122]

Residents in Zhengming Li believed that, as was common among alleyway guards, You had some sort of connection with local gangsters. Although no one could tell the exact details of such connection, it was generally felt that an alleyway guard had to have a certain gang background so that he would be tough enough to get rid of nuisances in the neighborhood such as beggars or rowdies. Residents recalled that overall You was innocuous, except that he occasionally overcharged for the alleyway cleaning fee, which he collected door to door every month. In some ways he respected the residents who lived in the regular house units from number 4 to 26 and looked upon them as more upstanding residents than himself, a man who swept the lane and lived in a guojielou.[123]

EVENING CHATS

According to the occupations of its residents and the essentially one-house-per-family living arrangement, Zhengming Li may be regarded as a comfortably well-off, although not wealthy, neighborhood. In more crowded neighborhoods, residents tended to build closer relationships and know each other better. In most lilong neighborhoods, where house touched house and row paralleled row and people lived in compartmentalized rooms, the physical closeness naturally led to neighbors' communications other than political ones like those that took place in the rental disputes. As a general rule, neighbors in shikumen houses had closer relations than their counterparts in the new-type alleyway houses. The higher the quality of the house, the less communication among its dwellers.

A densely populated lilong compound was sometimes a tiny community within which residents had few secrets from their neighbors. In these neighborhoods, as two historians have observed, whenever someone had a guest, neighbors would come to say hello. If a family had difficulties, others would come to help. The sorrows and joys of any family were shared with the neighbors. Even when a family made won ton or *jiaozi*, for instance, the family would take some of the delicacy in person to their neighbors to share. One could truly be relaxed when one was at work: should it rain unexpectedly, the next-door grandma would help bring in the clothes that had been hung out to dry. Nor need one worry about thieves breaking in; neighbors all kept an eye out for trouble. As a Shanghai folk saying put it, "Neighbors are better than relatives." [124]

For people who formerly lived in more private surroundings, neighborhood relations like these could be irritating, for they often infringed on privacy. But once a resident left the community, that person may well have missed the warmth of human relations found in these neighborhoods. In post-1949 Shanghai, residents were often reluctant to leave their crowded old alleyways and move into more spacious new apartment complexes assigned to them by their work units (*danwei*). There were various reasons for this, but missing old neighbors often played an important role.[125] An alleyway resident who had moved to a new residence complained in an article he wrote for a local newspaper that in his new apartment complex, "finding a neighbor to chat with was a forlorn hope." Looking back nostalgically, he expressed a feeling of loss, recalling how in his old neighborhood, Red Bean Lane, neighbors used to get together in a small courtyard on summer nights to chat and enjoy the cool of the evening.[126] "Although many of the neighbors spoke vulgarly or even rudely," the author wrote, "the cooling time was full of frankness, friendliness, and humor. . . . Once one stepped into the small courtyard, one forgot the sweltering, hot weather. Every summer night the little courtyard was full of joy and laughter." [127]

Enjoying the coolness in the alleyway on a summer evening was a custom that brought neighbors together for relaxation and camaraderie. The three hours from supper time—around 6 P.M.—to around 9 P.M. (the sun set around 8 P.M. in July and August) were known as *cheng fengliang* (enjoying the coolness). Residents came out of their hot and suffocating homes, bringing small stools, fans, mats, and sometimes beverages (green tea made of chrysanthemum was popular) and fruits (watermelon was popular) and sat in the alleyway and chatted with each other. These were the "happy hours" of the alleyway, when neighbors told stories, exchanged gossip, discussed news or current affairs, and got to know each other. This was often the only time an aloof neighbor might come out to talk with others. The writer Mao Dun recalled that he started his writing career in the summer of 1927, when he lived in Jingyun Li (Alley of Rosy Clouds), where "after supper, neighbors in the alley all came out to enjoy the cool outdoors: men and women, elders and children, laughs and cries, all came to-gether to make a great bustle." [128]

Lu Xun's masterpiece, "Outdoor Chatting on Language and Literature" (*Menwai wentan*), was said to be a result of summer evening chatting in his residence in a Shanghai alleyway, in 1934, hence the title. The preface to this work begins with the following words:

> It is said that the hot weather this year in Shanghai has broken a sixty-year record. In the daytime I went out to make a living. Lowering my head, I came back home in the evening. But the room was hot, and there were mosquitoes. At that time, the only paradise was outdoors. Perhaps because Shanghai is on the ocean there is always a breeze, and I did not have to fan myself. People who lived in the lofts or pavilion rooms nearby came out of their rooms and sat outside. These neighbors knew each other a little but did not see each other often. Some of the neighbors were shop assistants, some were proofreaders in publishing houses, and some were skilled workers who were really good at draft-ing. Tired out by their daily work, they were complaining. But, any-how, this was a time of leisure, so neighbors were also chatting. The topics of the chats were by no means narrow, but included the drought, prayers for rain, the flirt, the [so-called] three-inch dwarf, exposed thighs, as well as ancient Chinese prose, vernacular, the language of the masses. [129]

All of these topics, except language and literature, appeared in Shanghai's newspapers that summer. Summer evening chats of this sort were typical in the alleyway-house neighborhoods. Another author described summer evening life in alleyways that apparently were poorer than Lu Xun's, but otherwise the descriptions were almost identical:

> The sun was gradually setting in the west, and an evening breeze flowed through the alleyways. This was a time when poor people could enjoy their life a bit. Men wearing only shorts came out of their homes in the third floor loft or pavilion room and sat in the alleyway with a palm-leaf fan in hand. The Eldest of the Back Room, the Grandma of the Kitchen, and others came out too. Having gathered, the Eldest, to-gether with Number Three and Number Four, started their great chat. Their topics could include, on the top, the Jade God sending his assistant god down to the world for the salvation of all mortal life; in the middle, how General Chen Jitang's plane had crashed; and, at the bottom, gos-sip about a domestic maid of a family in the neighborhood who was meeting the chauffeur of another family in a hotel room. [130]

Since the topics of conversation included not only gossip but also current political affairs, there may have been a link between this form of communication among neighbors and the political demonstrations and strikes that marked the city's history in the Republican era. Certainly such communications played some role in the flow of information basic to any political activity.

Chatting was not the only outdoor activity in these hours. Residents also enjoyed popular forms of entertainment such as poker, mah-jongg, and chess. Residents were quite creative in making a temporary site in the narrow alleyway for these games: a broken mat, a few stools, and a wooden board (used for washing laundry) could make an instant game table. These games always attracted a number of bystanders, who formed a circle around the players. Sometimes the bystanders themselves became so immersed in the game that they could not help exclaiming or breaking the rules by providing uninvited advice to one player, to the annoyance of the others. Mao Dun recalled that the excitement of the poker players and their sudden exclamations sometimes gave him a start. But the hubbub in the alleyway did not bother Mao Dun as much as it bothered Lu Xun, who in 1927 lived in the same alleyway—Jingyun Li—because Mao Dun used to write during the day, when the alleyway was relatively quiet, but Lu Xun was accustomed to writing at night, when the din usually peaked.[131]

Neighbors also played musical instruments, of which the *erhu* (a two-stringed fiddle) was the most popular, on summer nights in the alleyways. The music was often accompanied by song, sung either by the player or a companion. Bystanders often clapped their hands and echoed the amateur musicians, making the alleyway a place of noise, joy, and excitement.[132] Summer nights like this were a golden opportunity for peddlers who, as noted earlier, came to provide instant goods and services, from snacks to newspapers. Watermelon peddlers illuminated the alleys with their stands, which often had an electric lamp hanging in front; they drew customers who dug through the hundreds of melons piled on the ground, looking for one that was "just right." All of these activities continued until well after midnight. On some exceptionally hot summer nights, a few residents slept overnight in the alleyway on a bamboo chair or a canvas cot.

Summer nights were no doubt the most lively time in the alleyway-house neighborhoods. But in all seasons the alleyways bustled with activity. Women and domestic servants liked to do their household chores at the back door of the house, which was the only spacious place close to the kitchen and sink, where most of the household duties, including laundry, were done. The alleyway, especially at the entrance of a lane, was a convenient place for residents to have a casual chat. These were some of the most common scenes in the neighborhoods: in the morning a few neighbors sat together on stools in the alleyway, sorting through various types of vegetables for meals (vegetables from food markets or peddlers always needed cleaning to get rid of withered parts or weeds); on a sunny afternoon, neighbors enjoyed the sunlight while stretched out on armchairs, or they put their bedding or heavy winter clothes in the alleyway to take advantage of the sun (that night, their bedclothes would be warmer and fresher smelling than usual; also people believed that sunlight was the most effective way to kill bacteria); and on a summer evening, as we have seen, the alleyway was usually full of residents who sought the cool night air. In such a situation, strangers or anything unusual easily caught the eye of the residents. Here, "neighborhood watch" was not an organized action but a situation. For decades, some families in Zhengming Li used to leave their back doors unlocked during the day, and it was said that not a single thing was stolen.[133] Thievery was rare in the neighborhood, partly because most families had someone—wives, maids, grandparents, children—at home at all times, and partly because of the ever-present activities in the alleyway.[134]

INTIMACY AND ROMANCE

Residents might well have felt secure living in an alleyway house neighborhood like this. The other side of the coin was, however, that their own lives might also be closely watched. Not only were things like who visited whom today, what food one had on the dining table, who often went shopping by rickshaw, and so on easily known by neighbors, but love affairs and adultery could not easily be kept secret from neighbors for long. Indeed, it sometimes seemed that what these "little urbanites" (*xiaoshimin*) enjoyed most of all was uncovering sexual affairs among their neighbors. If, as scholarly research has indicated, Shanghai's little urbanites were the major audience of works of the "Mandarin Ducks and Butterflies" school, a school of popular literature centered in Shanghai but also with a strong, nationwide influence in the early twentieth century (especially in the 1920s), then, to the residents of alleyway houses, neighborhood love affairs were living replications of the love stories they read.[135] A schoolteacher who lived in a shikumen house once described how he discovered the secret of one of his neighbors on the third floor of the same house:

> She looks like a fashionable woman of middle age (about thirty). Her only companion is a young maid. At first I could not figure out what she was doing. She might be, say, a business woman, but she stays home most of the time. She has no male visitors except a dark-skinned man dressed in a Western business suit who comes every two or three

days. The "Western-suited friend" is about forty and doesn't look like
a Shanghainese. He sometimes stays overnight in the woman's room,
sometimes not. Obviously, she is his mistress. One day, I suddenly saw
a monk dressed in Buddhist *kasaya* and shoes walk into the house and
go straight upstairs to the third floor. I could not help being astonished:
was this woman also secretly having illicit relations with a monk? In
great curiosity, I waited for the monk to come out in order to see what
he looked like. At night, the monk came out of the room and walked
downstairs. I looked at him and suddenly saw the light: he was none
other than her "Western-suited friend" who came every two or three
days. Because he always wore a basin-shaped cap [Panama hat], one
could not see his shaved head. At this point, I had fully discovered the
woman's secret: she was none but the mistress of a monk! [136]

The tone adopted in this paragraph is typical of Shanghai's little urbanites:
inquisitive about other people's affairs and delighted to talk about clan-
destine things. The scandals dug up were surely dished out as the food
for chitchat in the alleyway. Another piece of writing dated some twelve
years earlier shared a similar tone. After talking about food and clothing
in Shanghai in 1926, the author started to describe housing and quickly
shifted attention to his neighbors:

As for my neighbors in the back bedroom, they are simply annoying
as well as funny. They are a couple who may or may not be officially
married. According to my observations, he seems to work in a factory.
Every day he leaves home early and comes back late, quite enjoying his
job. But his "she" is an unusual woman. Always, after her husband
comes back home, she makes all sorts of odd noise without pausing for
a second. One night the noise from their room suddenly diminished.
Nevertheless, since their room and my room were separated only by a
wooden board, no matter how subtle the sound was, one could understand what was going on. In the middle of the night, I was awakened by
someone knocking on the back door. I listened intently and found it
was the Back Bedroom husband who was knocking. I became curious—
didn't I just hear the couple go to bed together a moment ago? Why
had he gone out and come back? I heard a sound of panic coming from
the back room, and then the woman said, "I'm coming." I heard two
persons walk downstairs. Further, I heard they were going not to the
back door but the front door. Upon opening the front door, the woman
said loudly, "Hi, where are you?" She repeated that a couple of times
before the husband walked around from the back door to the front
door, and then the couple went upstairs to their room. Gentlemen,
please think about it: Why was the sound from the back bedroom lower
than usual? Who had slept with that woman? Who walked downstairs

with her? Why did she go to open the front door while it was clear that someone was knocking at the back door?—That is the end of this peculiar drama.[137]

In crowded alleyway houses it was not unusual for adultery to be observed by neighbors who lived in the same house or even the same room, as this author did—although few people put their observations into writing. A Shanghai "bamboo branch poem" (*zhuzhici*, an occasional poem in the classical style devoted to local topics) of the twenties reveals the crowded situation in what the author described as the city's "lower-middle-class" neighborhoods:

> A small house of a half rafter shared by numerous families
> —as if a thousand hooves form a crowd.
> This is the most incredible thing:
> You wake up from an idle dream in the middle of the night,
> only to hear neighbors' moans of ecstasy—
> to the ear, it is simply intolerable.

An annotation was attached to the poem: "[In an average home in Shanghai] even the hallway and kitchen were full of people. Such living arrangements were surely economic, but day and night neighbors touch each other's hands and feet. In this extremely jammed situation, a little infringement of privacy or a breach of etiquette would not be seen as a fault."[138] This was echoed by Heppner's description of life inside the alleyway houses in Hongkou in 1938–48: "The walls were paper thin, and you whispered unless you wanted the whole house to hear what you were saying. Standards of etiquette were impossible to maintain when men and women were forced to meet in the narrow hallways at all hours of the day or night, in all stages of undress, on their way to or from the 'honey bucket.'"[139]

Love affairs among young and unmarried neighbors also occurred in alleyway houses. A Shanghai guidebook offered a variety of advice about love in the city; finding a girlfriend or boyfriend from among one's neighbors was one of the "ways" of love. If a young man found himself smitten by a girl in the neighborhood, he was advised to often stand at his shikumen, looking out on the alleyway as if he had time on his hands, which was quite common among Shanghai's shikumen residents. The purpose was to let the girl know that there was such a person in the alleyway, so she would not be caught by surprise when he struck up a conversation with her. When your face became familiar to her, the advice continued, you could say hello and get acquainted with her. Or, for a more conservative girl who seldom left home or stood at the doorway, one way to start a conversation was to borrow a household item from her, which was common among nearby neighbors.[140]

Sometimes these affairs resulted in marriage, known as "claiming alleyway kinship" (*pan longtang qin*).[141] More often, however, love affairs ended unhappily and served as food for gossip among neighbors. Sometimes love affairs among young neighbors developed into a legal case. In one example, a young man named Xiang Shanbao, a shop assistant in a fruit store on Pushi Road in the French Concession, fell in love with a sixteen-year-old girl, Sheng Xingzheng, who lived in the alleyway house behind the fruit store. As was common among shop assistants, Xiang was lodged in a room on the store's second floor. The two young people were therefore close neighbors and saw each other every day, as described in a love letter that Xiang wrote to his girlfriend: "I lay on my bed and miss you. In the morning I wait on the deck to see you opening the door. I am very happy to catch a lovely glimpse of you." At last the two lovers eloped. In anxiety, Sheng's foster father found the love letter in her room, which led to the arrest of Xiang, who was accused of kidnapping the girl.[142]

It may not have been easy for a humble shop assistant like Xiang to have a happy ending to his love affair in the alleyway, but for a local tough, things were different. Cai, a gangster in Nanshi in the early twentieth century, fell in love with a carpenter's wife who lived in the same alleyway. Cai spent five hundred dollars to force the carpenter to divorce his wife, and then took the neighbor's wife as his third concubine. Since the woman apparently took the initiative in the affair, the husband, although he was unhappy, accepted the money and divorced his wife. There was no legal dispute involved in this case.[143]

Cai's was a case of naked bullying, something that few people in Shanghai emulated. However, for well-off people an alleyway neighborhood was an ideal place to house a secret mistress. This was by no means an occasional arrangement but a common practice and was known as having a "little house." The word "little" indicated the nature of the mistress—a "little wife" (*xiao laopo*, or concubine)—rather than described the house, for the "little house" could be as large as a three-up, three-down alleyway house that had enough rooms to house a multigeneration family. Although not all "little houses" were necessarily in alleyway-house neighborhoods, most of them were. It was said that the "little house" institution was initiated in the late Qing by a young man in the family of the high-ranking bureaucrat Sheng Xuanhuai (1844–1916). The junior Sheng fell in love with one of the best-known courtesans in Shanghai, Lin Daiyu,[144] and since it was not proper for a young master in a family of Sheng's standing to marry a courtesan, he simply purchased a shikumen house in Burkill Road (today's Fengyang Road) near the British Race Course (today's People's Square) as a "little house" in which to hold his trysts. Later, keeping a "little house" became a popular form of seeking pleasure outside of one's regular marriage, and many alleyway houses surrounding the downtown area became love nests.[145] The prevalence of unofficial marriages and "living together" in this crowded city was incisively described by a local proverb, which, with pardonable exaggeration, described the city as a place where one "lives without the bond of marriage and dies without a place to be buried" (*sheng wu jiefaqi, si wu zangshendi*).[146]

However, considering the crowded living conditions and the physical closeness of residents in Shanghai's alleyway houses, intimacies and love affairs among neighbors could not be described as having run rampant. In the neighborhoods where one family per house was the general pattern, love affairs and adultery were rare. In Zhengming Li, residents could not recall a single affair among the neighbors. The reason, as explained by one resident, was: "We Chinese believe that 'a rabbit won't eat the grass that grows near its lair.' Even thieves usually won't steal from their next-door neighbors. It is shameful if things don't come out well and one becomes the topic of gossip. In old Shanghai there were plenty of places for fun. Why should one have *those things* among neighbors? Only country bumpkins would be interested in looking around for a partner (*duixiang*) from among their neighbors."[147] Confucian ethics, the concerns about one's reputation or "face," the aloofness of relations among neighbors (especially in well-off neighborhoods), and the availability of diversion all over the city all played some role in limiting the incidence of love affairs and sexual peccadilloes in alleyway-house neighborhoods. Shanghai's landlords often put the words "no tenant without a family" (*wu juan mo wen*, or "don't ask for a rental if you don't have a family with you") on rental ads. This suggested not merely a pro-family sentiment but the assumption that a person with a family was less likely to make trouble (including adultery) in the neighborhood.[148]

In more crowded neighborhoods where shikumen houses were shared by a number of tenants, intimacy among neighbors was more likely to occur. One of the most shocking murder cases in Republican-era Shanghai— a thirty-year-old housewife used a kitchen knife to kill her husband and then cut the corpse into sixteen pieces, which she put in a suitcase—suggests that adultery may not have been rare in those neighborhoods but was only covered up or not recorded in the written record. The site of the murder was a common two-story shikumen house: 85 Jiangyuan Long (Alley of the Sauce and Pickle Shop), Xinzha Road.[149] On March 20, 1945, around 6 A.M., the second landlord of that house, Wang Xueyang, a blind fortune-teller, and his wife were awakened in their pavilion room by shouts of "Help!" Wang thought it was his apprentice who had gotten an electric shock, and asked "What happened?" Zhou Chunlan, the woman who lived in the back bedroom on the second floor answered from her room: "It was Fatty talking in his sleep." "Fatty" referred to her husband, Zan Yunying, a pawnshop clerk. Not at all suspicious of this explanation, the Wang couple went back to sleep. It was not until about 8 A.M., when Mrs. Wang got up and went downstairs to the back living room (which was where Wang received his customers), and found blood dripping from the ceiling (i.e., the floor of the back bedroom), that the murder was discovered.

The murder created a furor in Shanghai. It turned out to be a case of wife abuse: Zan Yunying had severely mistreated Zhou Chunlan for nine years since their marriage in 1936. It was said that finally, at time of the murder, she had become insane. But an adulterous relationship between Zhou and "Pockmarks He," the man living in the front bedroom, also contributed to Zhou's extreme reaction to the abuse. Living virtually in the same room—it was divided only by boards—Pockmarks He witnessed the suffering that Zhou had endured over the years: Zan started an affair only two months after their marriage and continued to go out with various "guide girls" (*xiangdaonü*, a kind of semiprostitute) through the years; he beat his wife at will and forbade her to work (Zhou had once worked in a tobacco factory), believing that she would "steal a man" (that is, have an affair) if she had a job outside the home. For his part, Zan was addicted to gambling, hung around in various nightclubs, and was seldom at home, leaving his wife to starve without financial support. In desperation, Zhou often had to borrow money from the sympathetic Pockmarks He. Frequently, she was unable to repay the loans and felt guilty about it. She and Pockmarks He first had sexual relations when He had lost his job and was at home—his wife was away, having gone back to her native village for the Chinese New Year. The affair arose partly out of the loneliness of the two and partly out of Zhou's sense of obligation to her benefactor. Although He was not involved in the murder, his relationship with Zhou, perhaps unconsciously on both sides, made Zhou even more resentful of her abusive husband.[150] Obviously, a love affair like this could have gone on without leaving any trace if the murder had not been committed.

ALLEYWAY ROWS: SQUABBLING OVER TRIFLES

A quite different kind of neighborhood relation—quarreling among residents—was much more open than love affairs. Sometimes verbal quarrels escalated into physical confrontations. But such disputes were most likely to be mediated by neighbors and bystanders on the spot and seldom escalated into violence. Almost all alleyway quarrels that broke out were over trifles. For example, a fight between two children who were playmates might result in the mother of each child blaming the other child for starting the fight. If a quarrel ensued over such a matter, it might be worsened if fathers or other adults in the family became involved. Or, if the Zhang family hung out their laundry to dry and the clothes or bedsheets blocked the sunlight from the windows of the Li family, who then removed the bamboo clothes pole without consulting the Zhangs, a quarrel might follow. In crowded neighborhoods, where typically three to five families shared a single shikumen, rows were more likely to occur among neighbors who lived in the same house. Irritating things such as noise coming from the back room, water dripping from the second floor, or a dispute over use of the common area (such as sundry items piled along paths or stairways, clothes drying on the roof, etc.) were often causes of quarrels.[151] Wrangling among neighbors sometimes involved some physical insult, such as pushing and shoving, but it rarely developed into serious fighting and was even less likely to end up in court. Usually when things developed to the point where neither side could compromise without losing "face," a neighbor, or several neighbors, would come out to mediate on the spot, saying that since they all lived in the same alley, "if you don't see the other party while you hold your head high, you nevertheless see them when you lower your head" (*taitou bujian ditou jian,* that is, you run across each other all the time), "it is not wise to make an enemy of each other," and so on. Sometimes, the Confucian notion of *lirang* (comity) was brought out as a rationale for compromise. Mediation like that may not have solved the problem altogether, but in most cases it eased the tensions.

Bao Tianxiao, a writer well known for his intimate observations of common people's lives in Shanghai in the early twentieth century, described a spat that typified the type of wrangling that often erupted in alleyway neighborhoods.[152] A fop, Zhang Dakui, and a tailor shop owner, Lu Rongbao, were neighbors in a shikumen compound. One day, Lu's apprentice blew ashes from a flatiron into the alleyway, and the wind carried the ashes into the Zhangs' house, where the Zhangs were having dinner.[153] A quarrel ensued. Zhang, who knew exactly where the ashes came from, cursed loudly, "Which short-lived tailor shop is blowing flatiron ashes? Why don't you open your doglike eyes to see that the ashes are coming into other people's houses?"

An accusation like this was not likely to win an apology. The tailor shop owner retorted, "Even if my apprentice carelessly blew flatiron ashes, you should have spoken to us kindly. Why do you open your mouth to curse people? We are blowing ash in the alleyway, not in your house. It was the wind that blew it into your house. We can't control the wind. If you act like this, you'd better live in a single family village." The quarrel did not lead to fisticuffs only because neighbors came out to mediate.[154]

But the discord between the Zhang and Lu families worked its way to the surface on other occasions. It was a widely practiced custom to discard dregs of a decoction in the street to let them be tramped by pedestrians. This was a superstition (but the doctor who prescribed the medicine often advised people to do this): the more people who stepped on the dregs the better the patient's chances for recovery. This practice was banned by the SMC for the obvious reason that it was unclean and unhealthy. Since one couldn't dump dregs in the street with impunity, narrow alleyways in residential areas, especially alleyway entrances, became the favorite place for superstitious residents to discard dregs.[155] On one occasion Zhang's wife was sick, and she dumped her dregs in front of Lu's store, believing the store entrance would have more foot traffic than the path in front of an ordinary residence. Lu's wife, regarding the dregs as a symbol of bad luck, was offended and took a broom to sweep the mess back in front of the Zhangs' door—again, a quarrel broke out.[156]

In crowded neighborhoods the alleyway often served as a place to do various sorts of household chores—light up a coal stove, clean a nightstool, wash and dry clothes, sort through food, dust things like bedclothes or mats, and so on. Residents sometimes also did handiwork such as carpentry, painting, and repairing in the alleyway. There was no clear line between using an alleyway space for individual household needs and infringing on other residents' rights as a result of such use. In most cases, temporarily using the alleyway for household chores was virtually a custom, and even if such use caused inconvenience to other residents, it was often tolerated. But tolerance could be interpreted either as a courtesy extended by one's neighbors or as a privilege of the resident who used the alleyway, and the line between the two was, if ever drawn, a matter of common sense, not regulation. At times when common sense did not prevail, disputes such as in the Zhang-Lu quarrel arose. Given the crowded living conditions and lack of community regulations, it is remarkable that disputes among neighbors did not develop into serious social problems. Quarrels and fights among neighbors were seen as disgraceful and "low-class" behavior, and most residents would try their best to avoid disputes in public. Quarrels were thus often associated with housewives and maids who were at home all day long and could not easily avoid friction with neighbors. Lu Xun once described a woman named Ah Jin, the maid of his neighbor across the alleyway—from his window he could see her room. Ah Jin was a typical troublemaker: she liked to talk loudly in the alleyway, spread rumors among neighbors, and provoke fights:

> [In the alleyway] there was an uproar as usual; and the uproar became disturbing and spread out: Ah Jin and the old woman of the tobacco and paper store on the other side of the road started fighting, and men were involved. She had a loud voice, and this time it was louder than usual. I was sure that she could be heard some twenty houses away. Soon a crowd gathered [to watch the spectacle]. It was all too natural that at the end of the quarrel things like adultery [*touhan*, or "stealing a man"] and the like were mentioned. I did not hear what the old woman said, but Ah Jin's answer was: "Nobody wants you, old bitch! But somebody wants me!"
>
> This was probably true, and it looked like the bystanders were mostly sympathetic to her. The old bitch "nobody wants" was thus defeated. At that time a foreign policeman, with his hands crossed behind his back, strolled up. Having looked for a while, he drove the bystanders away.[157]

Lu Xun concluded the essay by saying, "I hope Ah Jin is not the model of Chinese women." In the postscript of *Qiejieting zawen* (Essays Written in the Semiconcession), which included "Ah Jin," Lu Xun satirized the Guomindang authorities' censorship of this essay, saying that he was puzzled by the censoring of a piece that was "indeed no more than a casual chat."[158] In all fairness, Ah Jin was a figure less well known than many of Lu Xun's other protagonists. But this petty character had caught the attention of the "greatest leader," Mao Zedong, who remained a loyal reader of Lu Xun all his life. Mao's personal physician, Li Zhisui, recalls that in the summer of 1967, at the peak of the Cultural Revolution, Mao was still reading Lu Xun's works—as he read he usually reclined on his specially constructed, huge wooden bed, of which half was stacked with books: "One day while we were still at Meiyuan guest house in Wuhan and Mao was reading some short stories by Lu Xun, he suddenly looked up and began talking about one of the least likable of Lu Xun's female protagonists, a promiscuous maid named A Jin [Ah Jin], whose many boyfriends were always making noise, getting in trouble, and picking fights. A Jin was a woman who enjoyed making trouble for others. 'Ye Qun is just like A Jin,' Mao said, referring to Lin Biao's wife. 'So is Jiang Qing.' " [159] This is an intriguing portrait in which a petty and quarrelsome maid who lived in a Shanghai alleyway-house neighborhood in the "old society" (as the pre-1949 society is referred to in the PRC) is made to resemble two female communist revolutionaries who, via their marriages to Lin and Mao, were (once upon a time) the most powerful women in the "new China." Of course, the resemblance, as Lu Xun hoped, should not be interpreted to mean that Ah Jin epitomized Chinese women. But Lu Xun, with his extraordinarily sharp eye and bitter sarcasm, did sketch the character of troublemakers in Shanghai's alleyway-house neighborhoods who might well find their counterpart in any rank of the social hierarchy.

CHAPTER 6

Beyond Stone Portals

A walled, gated residential compound naturally gave its residents some sense of privacy, security, and comfort. Although this rarely developed into a sense of community, the residents did consider the entrance of the alleyway-house compound a demarcation line in their daily life. As described in chapter 5, life was lived inside the compound, which the residents usually referred to as *longtang li* (inside the alley), as distinct from *longtang wai* (outside the alley). Daily activities took most residents beyond the compound, into the immediately adjacent streets, which were always a walker's delight. One could easily spend the bulk of a day browsing through the countless establishments along tree-lined avenues: restaurants, tailor shops, open-air food markets, bathhouses, and all other sorts of businesses that provided the goods and services needed for everyday life. For the people of Shanghai, what mattered most in daily life was the petty but vigorous commerce and activities conducted in an area within walking distance from home, not the dazzling life symbolized by the Bund and Nanking Road.

Commerce in a Living Room

Lilong compounds, as shown in Figure 28, always had a front row (or, in some cases, a few front rows) of houses facing the street. Unlike the units inside the compound, which had a front yard and a yard through which one had to pass to enter the living room, the front-row units usually did not have a yard. In other words, the living rooms of these front-row units could be entered directly from the sidewalk (Fig. 29). These living rooms were often used for business purposes rather than for housing; most often they functioned as small stores or shops.

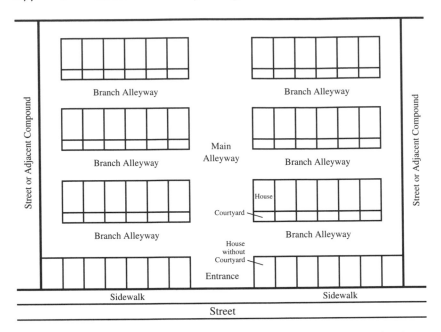

Fig. 28. Although alleyway-house compounds varied greatly in size and style, their layout was fairly consistent. This diagram provides a glimpse of the general arrangement of Shanghai's alleyway-house compounds. The main alleyway of a typical shikumen compound was about seventeen feet wide, and the branch alleyways about ten feet wide. The new-style compounds usually had wider alleys. Some lilong compounds had several entrances, so that branch alleyways were directly accessible from the street.

Establishing a store in a lilong neighborhood usually followed a pattern: a man (store owners were mostly men) managed to save or borrow enough money to rent a front unit in a lilong compound; he would then move his family into the second floor and turn the living room into a small store. As Shanghai's population consisted mainly of immigrants from other parts of the country, this living arrangement was obviously efficient: it simultaneously solved the problems of residence and employment.[1]

The rent for a lilong house varied according to neighborhood and the quality of the house itself. And although the front units had the advantage of being suitable for use as a store or shop, rent for such houses was sometimes only a little higher (by 10–20 percent) than for units inside the compound.[2] The reason for the small disparity in rent was that front-row houses were less comfortable to live in. Not only did units facing the street

Ground Floor   Second Floor

Fig. 29.   Except for a type of lower-cost lilong house known as a "Japanese house," virtually all lilong houses had a cement-paved front yard measuring about a hundred square feet (see Fig. 28). Yards were, however, often omitted from front-row houses facing the street. Without a front yard, the living room of a front-row house opened directly on the sidewalk, as shown in this diagram. This design allowed the family the flexibility to use the living room as a store if desired.

have no yard but they suffered from noise and dust from the street and were easy targets for thieves and burglars. In a way, the owners of these stores tolerated a less comfortable life in order to earn a living. Yet, being without a living room was not considered a big deprivation in Shanghai. To this day, to use the "living room" as a living room is still considered a luxury.[3]

These were small stores in every sense: a normal living room in a lilong house occupied about 215 to 320 square feet (20 to 30 square meters) of floor space, although a few adjacent living rooms were sometimes put together (i.e., the walls between the rooms were dismantled) to make a fairly large store.[4] The stores were, of course, open to anyone who walked in, but since they were located in residential areas the majority of the customers were local people. In fact, a great many of the customers were people who lived on the same block where the stores were located.

Among the most common stores in these neighborhoods were those that sold grain, coal, cotton fabric and goods, groceries, hot water, condiments, snacks, fruit, wine, meat and vegetables, and other products. Other shops offered such services as tailoring, barbering, repair of household items, and currency exchange, and there also were laundries, teahouses, public bathhouses, and so on. In short, in Shanghai's lilong neighborhoods the merchandise and services most closely related to daily life could be purchased within a block or so of one's residence.[5]

For instance, the neighborhood shops along a section of Hart Road (today's Changde Road) between the intersections of Bubbling Well Road (today's Nanjingxi Road) and Avenue Foch (today's Yan'anzhong Road) (see Table 8), included everything from a dentist to a blacksmith to a wineshop.[6] In this typical lilong neighborhood with several lanes, each leading to an entrance to a compound, residents could do virtually all their shopping for daily necessities within a few steps of their homes, without even having to cross the street.[7]

The vital importance of these stores can be summarized in a single Chinese proverb, which some sixty years ago a journalist cited to describe a neighborhood store: "One cannot live without this gentleman for a single day" (*buke yiri wu cijun*).[8]

RICE STORES

Rice is, of course, the staple food in south China. Although modern Shanghainese came from everywhere, for almost everyone rice was the principal food in their diet. According to one investigation, in 1933 (when Shanghai had a population of 3,133,782) only 92,126 people, who were originally from north China and Manchuria, ate wheat as their staple food. In other words, rice was the staple food for 97 percent of Shanghai's people. It is estimated that an adult male in Shanghai annually consumed 2.74 *dan* (453 pounds) of rice, and an adult female 2.01 dan (332 pounds). Shanghai in the 1930s thus needed about 1 billion pounds (6 million dan) of rice annually to feed its people.[9]

Although the overall volume of the rice business was very large, individual rice stores were usually quite small. There were two types of rice businesses in Shanghai: *mihang* (rice companies) and *midian* or *mihao* (rice stores). The mihang were wholesale stores but they also had an

Table 8. Neighborhood Stores on Hart Road, 1940s

> *Intersection of Bubbling Well Road*
> *Entrance of Lane 109*
> fabric store
> towel store
> butcher
> soy sauce store
> blacksmith
> **wineshop
> **sesame cake store
> **hot water store (*laohuzao*)
> **sesame cake store
> *Entrance of Lane 81*
> *pharmacy (traditional Chinese medicine)
> **rice store
> *plumber
> *butcher
> *Entrance of Lane 63*
> **grocery store (Southern China products)
> *barber shop
> towel store
> *Entrance of Lane 53*
> *dentist
> fruit store
> **coal store
> **tobacco and paper store
> *Entrance of Lane 43*
> *tailor shop
> *coffin shop
> *bottle store
> *cotton fabric store
> *Entrance of Lane 33*
> *rattan work and bamboo-ware shop
> **tobacco and paper store
> **soy sauce store
> *Entrance of Lane 15*
> *Intersection of Avenue Foch*

SOURCE: Author's field study conducted in March 1989, verified by Informants I-9, I-10, I-11, I-12, I-13, I-15, I-16, and I-17.

NOTE: Residences and other buildings not used for businesses are omitted. The lane numbers are the present-day street numbers. An asterisk (*) indicates stores open until the 1960s; two asterisks (**) indicate stores still open in the 1980s. The length of the road between the two intersections was about 273 yards (250 meters). All stores listed were located on the west side of Hart Road. The east side was bisected by Annam Road (the whole road was an open-air food market), which formed a T-intersection with Hart Road. In the late forties, on the east side of Hart Road north of Annam Road, there were a restaurant, a rice bowl store, a coal store, a grocery store, a cotton cloth store, a tobacco and paper store, a bucket and tub repair shop, and a rice store. South of Annam Road a British-owned tram company occupied the whole section. This company was founded in 1908 and has operated most of the city's tram lines to the present day.

Fig. 30.   In an ordinary rice store in 1937–38, shop clerks are busy weighing rice. In a part of the room used for storage, gunnysacks of rice are piled up to the ceiling. This shop is under contract to the (Rickshaw) Pullers' Mutual Aid Association. Note the crowd with coupons in their hands: these were pullers (or members of their families) who belonged to the PMAA and were too sick to work and temporarily entitled to receive free rice as a PMAA benefit. From Pullers' Mutual Aid Association of Shanghai, *Annual Report*, 1938.

attached retail store as part of the business. These rice companies often specialized in a particular product. For example, some stores specialized in rice from certain provinces (e.g., Jiangxi) or foreign countries (e.g., Thailand), while others specialized in trading wheat, beans, or *zaliang* (miscellaneous food grains), or other products. Because of their size and amount of capital these businesses were generally regarded as the leading participants of the rice business in Shanghai.

However, for ordinary Shanghai residents, the midian, which were exclusively retail stores, were the place to go for rice (Fig. 30). The Shanghai Rice Guild had 1,544 members in 1930; the population of Shanghai at that time was about 3,100,000;[10] thus, on average a rice store served about 2,000 residents. The actual number of people shopping at any single rice store must have been lower, because some rice stores were not members of the guild.[11]

Only 5 percent of Shanghai's rice stores were classified as "large stores," most of which were retail stores attached to mihang. The "medium stores," which had only one-tenth the capital of the large stores, accounted for 30 percent. Most of the rice stores (65 percent of Shanghai's rice stores) were small businesses, with an average of only $200 of capital. To estimate the value of $200 in the 1930s, consider the fact that the average wage for an unskilled factory worker was about $20 per month, and it was not uncommon for a skilled worker in some industries (e.g., silk weaving) to earn more than $50 a month.[12] Thus, the capital of these rice stores was equal to merely a few months' wages for a factory worker.

Both the small capital and the limited space of the typical store constrained the amount of rice the shop could keep in storage (which was in the back half of the "living room"). The normal inventory ranged from five to ten days' sales; rarely did the inventory exceed half a month's sales.[13] Improper storage easily resulted in moldiness, especially in Shanghai's rainy season of May and June. The shop owner paid the cost of shipping rice from the wholesaler to his shop, a cost that varied with distance and method of transportation—boat, truck, or rickshaw. Rice from the wholesalers might not be ready for sale but in need of screening to get rid of sand, small stones, and crushed rice. Since rice was a daily necessity, people were still lured into the business in spite of these difficulties, especially in the early 1930s, when the population was rapidly growing.[14]

COAL STORES

Shanghai was one the world's first cities to have a gas supply. In 1865 the city built its first gasworks, and from 1882 on, gas was increasingly used for household heating. From 1926 on, people in the new-style lilong houses and Western-style apartments cooked and heated with gas.[15] But a gas supply was never common in the homes of most of Shanghai's people. Up to 1949, only 2.1 percent of Shanghai's households had gas stoves in their kitchens.[16] For the majority, a gas supply was something related to the elite and therefore associated with luxury.

Up to the early thirties, firewood was still the major fuel for most households. As in the countryside, cotton stalks, straw, reeds, and bean stalks also fueled cookstoves in working-class households. Such fuel could be purchased from a firewood store or, more commonly, from street peddlers.[17] From the mid-1930s on, most households switched to coal to fuel their stoves. A coal stove was usually a square or round tube made of tin-plate, about eighteen inches high, and ten inches on each side (if it was square) or one foot in diameter (if it was round), with a cone-shaped furnace in the middle, insulation materials (such as coal cinders) stuffed between the furnace and the tinplate edges, and handles. For decades, a coal stove like this was the only energy source for cooking and heating in ordinary Shanghai households; and about 98 percent of Shanghai's inhabitants could not live without it. As late as 1983, about 51 percent of the households of Shanghai were still using coal stoves as their only cooking and heating appliance.[18] It was reported that in 1990, 1.04 million coal stoves were being used by the residents of Shanghai,[19] a fact that contradicts the popular image of the modernity of China's leading treaty port.

Because of the ubiquity of coal stoves, shops sold coal everywhere in the city. These were originally firewood and charcoal stores (*chaitan dian*), but as coal became the most common fuel, these stores switched to selling coal, particularly egg-shaped briquettes. Hence their new name: "egg-shaped briquette stores" (*meiqiudian*). But coal stores also sold charcoal, firewood chips, and other fuels, such as kerosene. Even after egg-shaped briquettes replaced firewood as the staple fuel, firewood chips remained a daily necessity. Most households extinguished the coal stove every night before going to bed and first thing in the morning rekindled the stove with waste paper and wood chips.[20]

All the coal store shopkeepers lived upstairs, above the shop, and tended to business all day long. Usually the male head of the family was the owner and manager of the store. He might hire one or two shop assistants, who were, more often than not, relatives or fellow townsmen. His wife and adult children often worked as helpers when needed. One coal store owner on Hart Road, for example, employed his nephew as counter clerk (also as bookkeeper) for seventeen years (1936–53), and his eldest son as shop assistant for nine years (1938–47). In 1947 he opened another coal store a few blocks from the first one and had his eldest son run the new store. His daughter-in-law became the counter clerk and bookkeeper of the new store.[21]

TOBACCO AND PAPER STORES

Stores popularly known as *yanzhidian* (lit., tobacco and paper stores) were actually variety stores. The name described the two major commodities sold: cigarettes and toilet paper. It was said that at a typical store, early in the morning when it opened its doors, the first customer was the "little cobbler" of the next lane who came to buy three pieces of toilet paper (for one *wen*, or cash) and two cigarettes (also for one cash). The cobbler then went to a public lavatory. Small transactions like this made up most of the morning business of the store. But the name was merely suggestive: in addition to cigarettes, the "tobacco" (*yan*) category included cigars, cut tobacco and pipe tobacco, plug tobacco, and other related items such as tobacco pipes, pipe racks, cigarette cases, ashtrays, and matches; in addition to toilet paper, the "paper" category included stationery, brown paper, wallpaper, mounting paper, and so on.[22]

The owner of one such store, Liu Xiangyu, had run a variety store since 1942, when he inherited his father's barbershop on Hart Road. He soon turned the barbershop into a yanzhidian. Like rice and coal stores, tobacco and paper stores were family-run businesses but smaller in scale. Few of them were larger than a single living room. Usually, like Liu's (see Table 8, the tobacco and paper store at lane entrance 43), the tobacco and paper store was merely the front half of a living room facing onto the street, with the back half used by the family for household needs. In some cases, the whole store was no more than a shop window, with no space for customers to walk into; in such stores, all business was conducted over a counter set on the shop windowsill. Owners of these stores could not afford to have helpers other than family members; hence these stores were nicknamed "husband and wife stores" (*fuqi laopo dian*),[23] similar in meaning to America's "mom and pop stores."

No matter how small these businesses were, tobacco and paper stores enjoyed great popularity among Shanghai people. It was estimated that in the early 1930s Shanghai had at least 1,500 such stores; it was said that "typically every entrance of a lilong has a tobacco and paper store."[24] This was probably the fastest-growing trade in Republican-era Shanghai. In 1937, there were 3,400 tobacco and paper stores and their wholesalers in the city; the number increased to 8,495 by April 1943 and 8,600 by May 1949.[25] Their sundry goods were the small items needed by every household: in addition to the tobacco and paper products and matches already mentioned, they sold bottled beer (but no other alcoholic beverages), needles, thread, soap, incense (for religious worship), candles, mosquito coil incense, cooling ointment, envelopes, pencils, rubber erasers, pins, paper clips, batteries, hairpins, string, shoelaces, toothpaste, candies, cookies, crackers, dried fruit, Ping-Pong balls and paddles, toys, playing cards, kites, calendars, and Chinese New Year's pictures (Fig. 31). In fact, the list could be doubled or tripled because in many cases there was a selection of items in each category. These goods were neatly displayed on the congested store shelves inside the shop window and on the walls. In addition, currency exchange, postal service (stamps and postbox only), and a public telephone were available in these stores.[26]

Fig. 31.   On the shelves of a neighborhood store like this one located on the corner of an alley, a Shanghai resident might find anything fit to be sold. This store, like other tobacco and paper stores, sold bedbug killer (see the poster to the left) and Chinese patent medicines and balms popularly taken for relief from headaches, diarrhea, heat prostration, and minor ailments (noted on the wooden signboard at top right). The store also sold a variety of housewares, hardware, toys (note the dolls at the bottom of the display case), and bric-a-brac. Tobacco and paper stores usually provided a currency exchange service: for example, big silver dollars in exchange for small silver dollars or copper coins. Some also collected the government stamp tax. Stores like this were considered an interesting, even picturesque local feature, especially among Shanghai's foreign community. This particular image appeared on an early-twentieth-century postcard captioned in English "Chinese Hardware Store" (Hans-R. Fluck, Barbara Böke-Fluck, and Zhu Jiahua, eds., *Souvenir from Shanghai*, 129). Courtesy of Shanghai Municipal Library.

TAILOR SHOPS

In China a conventional description of the essence of daily life is contained in a list that combines four basic necessities in a plain and orderly fashion: "clothing, food, shelter, and transportation" (*yi-shi-zhu-xing*). At first glance the order of the four items may seem problematic: How can "clothing" go ahead of "food," since it is common sense that eating is more crucial to life? Apparently, the order is not random.[27] Another Chinese expression, "Parents of clothing and food" (*yishi fu-mu*), referring to sources of livelihood such as one's customers, patron, or employer, has the same order. It reflects, in a broad sense, the great weight given in Chinese culture to the Confucian notion of *li* (proper behavior and civility). Of the four necessities, clothing is the only one that decisively distinguishes humankind from animals. In this regard, the order makes perfect sense. No wonder the worst kind of censure in Chinese is to call a person "a beast in human attire" (*yiguan qinshou*).[28]

In Shanghai, the importance of clothing is particularly related to snobbishness. A popular saying in the city describes the tendency of society to "recognize attire only, not the human being" (*zhi ren yishan bu ren ren*).[29] Lu Xun sharply commented on this custom: "To live in Shanghai, it is better to be fashionably attired than to wear rude clothing. If you dress in old clothes, the trolleybus driver will not stop where you ask him to, the guide at a park will check your entrance ticket in a particularly careful manner, the doorman of a large mansion or apartment will not allow you to enter the building through the front door. That is why some people can tolerate living in a small room and literally feeding their bodies to bedbugs. Such a person, nevertheless, must put his Western-style pants underneath his pillows every night so that every day he will have creases in his trousers."[30] People described such vanity as "A beggar dressing in Western clothing but cooking his own rice" (*Yangzhuang biesan, ziji shaofan*).[31]

Of many fields in which modern Shanghai led twentieth-century China, fashion was an obvious example. Terms like "headquarters" and "authorities" were frequently used to describe the city's influence on the nation's clothing. Two major types of twentieth-century Chinese attire, the *qipao* for women and the *Zhongshan zhuang* (best known in the West as the Mao suit) for men, were born in Shanghai in the early Republican period. The qipao (lit., Manchu gown), as the name suggests, was originally a Manchu dress for women. From the early 1920s on, it gradually spread to Han Chinese women and by 1926 had became popular nationwide, probably because the Northern Expedition (1926–28) helped its spread. But by then the qipao was quite different from its Manchu original. Shanghai played a leading role in transforming it. The modern qipao had a high-neck, single-breasted top that buttoned on the right, a slim waistline, a long skirt extending below the knees with slits on both sides, and a variety of sleeve styles (ranging from long sleeves to midlength or short sleeves to sleeveless). There were numerous variants; all differed significantly from the cumbersome Manchu dress.[32] The Zhongshan zhuang, or "Zhongshan suit," named after Sun Yat-sen (1866–1925, best known in China as Sun Zhongshan), was based on a Japanese military uniform that Sun brought to the Rongchangxiang Wool Fabric and Western Suit Shop on Nanking Road (founded in 1903). Sun and the shop owner, Wang Caiyun (1880–1933), who was a skillful tailor as well as a shrewd businessman, collaborated in altering the uniform into a civilian men's suit. Some of the design was Sun Yat-sen's idea and had political implications. The flaps of the four pockets on the jacket were shaped like a Chinese pen holder,[33] symbolizing the importance of intellectuals (who were customarily called "the shaft of the pen") in the revolution. The jacket had five buttons down the front, symbolizing the "five powers" (legislation, administration, judicature, examination, and supervision) in Sun's political theory, a modification of the three-power structure in the West.[34] Soon after Sun's death in 1925, the Zhongshan suit became popular in Shanghai, especially among students, and thereafter spread nationwide. More significant, after the Communist revolution, while the qipao became associated with the "old society" and gradually disappeared, the Zhongshan suit, which had undergone some moderate changes and had a few slightly different variants, enjoyed great popularity. It virtually became the standard men's suit in the PRC for about four decades.

These are just two obvious examples of how Shanghai led the nation in fashion. The city provided a constant model for the rest of the country to follow. Aside from major innovations in clothing like the qipao and the Zhongshan suit, new styles or fashions often involved technically minor but sensationally effective changes, such as adding a button on the cuff or a slit on the skirt, double stitching seams, shortening the skirt, trimming a skirt with lace, lowering a collar band, and so on. These types of small refinements here and there cost little (or sometimes they lowered the cost) but provided a fresh impression or made clothing more comfortable. The quality of the materials was not necessarily the best, but the style, the design, and the match of color had to be just so to ensure an appropriate and neat appearance. Hats, shoes, scarves, gloves, and other accessories were also part of the competition among designers and patrons. Therefore, "dressing well in Shanghai" became words of praise.[35] For simply dressed people in the hinterland, these types of minor but sensational innovations powerfully enhanced the stereotype of the people of Shanghai, or Shanghairen, as shrewd and sophisticated. Of all things that contributed to the city's reputation as "the Paris of the East," fashion and clothing were perhaps the most relevant.[36]

But, whence came fashion and clothing? There was, of course, no lack of elegant fashion shops in Shanghai. Famous shops on Nanking Road, such as Pei-Luo-Meng (founded in 1934) for men's suits, Hongxiang (founded in 1914) and Bong-Street (founded by a German Jew in 1935; its Chinese name is Pengjie) for women's clothing, enjoyed a nationwide reputation—the mere mention of these names suggested quality and elegance. These names were ignored after the Communist revolution and eventually were discarded during the Cultural Revolution (1966–1976). But this did not prevent them from reemerging in the midst of the economic reform of the eighties, via a practice known as "restoring famous-brand stores" (*mingpai shangdian*). In fact, the gold-painted store signs of these old shops among the jungle of newly erected neon in downtown Shanghai in the 1990s symbolizes the eagerness to use past glories in the present money-making frenzy. The glories of these old shops ranged from Madame Sun Yat-sen's special praise written in an inscription in 1935, to an embroidered robe made as a special gift for the British queen Elizabeth II for her wedding in 1946. Celebrities of all kinds were loyal customers of these stores.[37] This no doubt contributed to Shanghai's reputation as the fashion capital of China and, to some extent, fashions designed in these stores influenced, if not set, clothing styles in the city.

But for most people the names of these stores, while familiar, remained but names, remote from their daily life. In terms of clothing, what was relevant to the daily life of most of the people of Shanghai was not the fashionable shops on Nanking Road but the small tailor shop on the corner of the alleyway where they lived. Typically, these small shops were owned by an experienced tailor who employed one or two assistants or trained a few apprentices. Like the tobacco and paper stores, some of the tailor shops were "husband and wife" businesses; that is, the tailor had no assistant other than his wife—although sewing was regarded as women's work, tailoring was considered primarily a man's profession. Tailor shops that specialized in Chinese attire were known as "Su-Guang" tailor shops, recalling the legacy of an old-time notion that the styles of Suzhou and Guangzhou (or Guangdong) were fashionable. In the late nineteenth century, tailors who specialized in Western-type attire (mainly men's suits and women's overcoats) were called by their fellow tailors "barbarian-type masters" (*Fanbang shifu*). But by the Republican period such tailors became known as "Ningbo tailors" (*Hongbang caifeng*), because of the dominance of Ningbo immigrants in the trade.[38] A tailors' union founded in January 1946 claimed to have 3,050 members who worked in more than 420 tailor shops that specialized in Western men's suits. The members of the union excluded the owners of these shops, who themselves were usually tailors. If the owners (assuming one owner per shop) were added to the members of the union, that would make an average of 8 to 9 tailors per shop. The Chinese-type Su-Guang tailor shops were usually smaller than

Western-style tailor shops. Most of these shops had only a single master tailor and 1 or 2 assistants or apprentices. It was estimated that at that time Shanghai had about 40,000 Su-Guang-style tailors who either worked for about 2,000 Su-Guang tailor shops or were self-employed. This business provided a livelihood for about 200,000 people (i.e., tailors and their families).[39]

The Su-Guang tailor shops were the place where most people went most often to have their clothing made. A woman who did not make clothes herself would send her orders to a Su-Guang tailor shop, except on those infrequent occasions when she purchased a ready-made Western-style coat in a dress shop or ordered one from a Hongbang tailor. The qipao could be purchased from a department store or a dress shop. But buying ready-made clothing was more expensive than purchasing fabric and having it made into clothing at a tailor shop. As for men's attire, there were basically two types in the Republican period: the Chinese-style gown and the Western-style suit, both of which were standard men's outer wear and appropriate for all occasions. But a Chinese gown was only 40 percent of the cost of a Western suit. Needless to say, tailor shops in alleyway-house neighborhoods were mostly of the Su-Guang type.[40]

To order clothes, customers usually went in person to a tailor shop, which was always within walking distance of home. Occasionally, a tailor would walk through the alleys soliciting orders, a custom inherited from the late Qing period. Prior to the early 1920s, few tailor shops were located in residential areas. Tailors, like the peddlers described in chapter 5, went from neighborhood to neighborhood soliciting business door to door. Sometimes tailoring was done at the customers' home, but more often the tailor brought back measurements and material and worked at home. When an order was placed, customers provided their own materials, including sometimes buttons and thread. The desired style was discussed and measurements were taken on the spot. Often, old clothes were provided as a sample for duplication or were presented for alteration. In a few days the tailor would deliver the completed clothing. Thus the tailor always needed to carry a cotton cloth bag in which to put the order (i.e., the fabric, buttons, etc.) as well as the finished clothing to be delivered. Hence tailors were called "Bag-Carrying Masters" (*lingbao shifu*).[41]

Along with the increase of population and the prosperity of the city in the Republican period, these bag-carrying tailors gradually settled down in residential neighborhoods for business, and thousands of tailor shops were opened in the city. Not only were these small shops most relevant to people's needs for clothing; they were indeed the incubators of many prestigious dress shops. For instance, Hongxiang, Shanghai's first and one of its best dress shops, was founded in 1914 by the brothers Jin Hongxiang and Jin Yixiang (the store was named after the elder brother), both of whom started their careers as Bag-Carrying Masters. Wang-Rong-Tai, a tiny tailor shop near Yixin Li (Alley of Boundless Good Fortune) on the corner of Zhejiang Road and Tianjin Road was owned by Wang Caiyun's father. It was in this store that Wang was taught Western dressmaking by his father. Later Wang opened his own shop, Rongchangxiang, the best Western-type tailor shop in early-twentieth-century Shanghai, and the one that designed the first Zhongshan suit.[42]

Although tailor shops were available everywhere in the city, ordering clothing from a tailor shop, even a small one set in an alleyway, was for most people something they considered expensive. Buying ready-made clothes in a dress shop was most expensive, having clothes made in a tailor shop was less expensive, and making one's clothing oneself was still less costly. A survey of how common people obtained clothing in pre-Liberation Shanghai found that out of 436 people surveyed, well over half (257) stated that mainly they purchased material in a fabric store and then they (or a member of the family) did the actual tailoring at home. Less than a quarter (104) of those surveyed had clothing made at a tailor shop; still fewer—46 persons (about 10 percent)—said that most of the clothes they wore were brought from their hometown in the countryside.[43]

These rather frugal patterns of obtaining clothing contradicted the "fashion capital" image of the city, but obviously they reflected the real life of the people. For an average Shanghai family, it was important to save every penny. Their thinking was simple and practical: ready-made clothing was most expensive because the seller made a profit on both the materials and the labor; clothing from a tailor shop, when the customer provided the fabric, saved the customer the part of the profit the tailor would otherwise make on the materials; and homemade clothing eliminated both profits. If cotton fabric was brought home from one's village, one even saved the cost of purchasing material at a fabric store.[44] Here "self-consumption" was not just a matter of the persistence of the so-called small peasant mentality; in this metropolitan environment it was more a way of coping with the cost of life in the city.

An additional benefit of making clothes at home was that one did not have to worry about the tailor cheating. Tailors were generally seen as hard-working people, always bent over their sewing table (which could be as simple as a large board put on a set of folding legs), immersed in the tedium of cutting and sewing. It was said that tuberculosis was the disease of their profession. In many a tailor shop, one would find a scroll on the wall bearing a rhyming couplet written by a calligrapher (who might well be a satisfied customer): "It is against my will to see people suffer from cold. It is my wish to see everybody in warm clothes." Kind tailors! On the other side of the coin, however, people believed that few tailors would not cheat on materials; that is to say, that they would not deliberately overestimate materials and keep the offcut. For example, a tailor might ask a customer to buy seven *chi* (one chi was slightly more than a foot, or one-third meter) of fabric for a shirt that actually needed only five and a half chi. The tailor's object was to embezzle the excess. As a popular saying put it, "The tailor won't steal cloth, but every three days he gets a pair of pants," implying that the tailor could frequently make new clothes just by using the offcut embezzled from his customers.[45]

The common practice of making clothes at home meant that the city had hundreds of thousands of "amateur tailors." Except for Western-style men's suits and overcoats, which were considered complicated attire that had to be made by a professional tailor, the people of Shanghai bravely applied scissors to fabric and eventually ended up with homemade clothing of all kinds that they wore with pride. The majority of these amateur tailors were women; indeed tailoring was so common among Shanghai women that most of them, from all walks of life, had some knowledge of dressmaking. The ability to make clothes was valued not just for pragmatic reasons (to save money) but also because it was thought to exhibit a woman's skill. Go-betweens said things like "She is good at making clothes" when they tried to arrange a marriage (or, more accurately, to urge a man and woman to start dating). It was not at all unusual to meet a housewife who was able to make various articles of clothing—from shirts, skirts, and pants to qipao for formal occasions—for everybody in her family. A less skillful woman might demurely claim, "I know nothing about tailoring," but one could not take her words at face value, for most women could at least make underwear.[46] In Lu Xun's family, his wife, Xu Guangping, made most of their son's clothes by herself, although Xu herself was an intellectual and, according to a stereotype, this type of woman was not good at "women's work."[47]

An even more common, almost universal, skill among women (and one that excluded men) was knitting. Knitting was seen more as a way to while away leisure time than "work." These were everyday scenes in Shanghai: a woman standing in an alley and enjoying an afternoon chat with her neighbors, all the while knitting; or, in a Suzhou storyteller's theater, middle-aged women sitting in rattan armchairs, moved to tears by the heartbreaking love stories (which were a usual theme), but their hands never stop knitting, except occasionally to dab their wet eyes with a handkerchief.[48]

Fashions in clothing in Shanghai, especially women's fashions, were constantly changing. The qipao, for instance, changed almost every year from 1926, the year it became popular, to the 1940s. If one were to line up the "fashionable qipao of the year" for every year from 1926 to 1941, the length of the skirts would make a perfect up-and-down curve.[49] On one hand was what might be called a middle-class dilemma: the sensitivity and snobbishness of the general public toward attire made people careful and self-conscious about their clothing when they appeared in public; yet the average Shanghai family could not afford to continually buy clothes from a dress or tailor shop to keep up with fads. One solution to this dilemma was to be an amateur tailor. On the other hand, this "mass tailoring" by amateurs stimulated the tides of fashion that engulfed the city. In a way the advantage of homemade clothes was not just economic. It was the amateur tailor's pleasure to browse in various fabric shops, taking pains to compare the color, design, quality, and price of a dazzling array of fabrics and, often after a somewhat fussy deliberation, choose the right type of material for the clothes in mind. Meanwhile, the sales clerks often gave helpful advice, as they were trained to do, about the quantity of the material needed so that offcut could be minimized. Back home, the amateur tailor might consult a pictorial or a fashion magazine or even recall a few Hollywood movies that she (most of these amateur tailors were women) had seen to get a sense of attire in the West. Then, spreading the fabric on the dining table, she carefully but confidently applied chalk and scissors.[50] Innovations in clothing in this fashion capital thus cannot be attributed solely to the professional designers in a few of the city's noted fashionable shops; they also belonged to the tailors in the hundreds upon hundreds of small shops set in back alleys, as well as the tens of thousands of amateurs in common Shanghai households.

PROLETARIAN RESTAURANTS

For most families, making clothes was not an everyday affair, but, needless to say, eating was. Restaurants were much more numerous than tailor shops, both in the city's major commercial areas and in residential neighborhoods. What was most relevant to most people was not the restaurants that featured famous cuisine but small "rice" restaurants. Unlike big restaurants that provided not only fine cuisine but also an elegant setting (such as stylish tables, chairs, and rooms) for entertaining and ceremonial purposes, the function of these small restaurants was simple and primitive: to fill an empty stomach. Because of their popularity, these simple restaurants gained an interesting name: *puluo guan* (proletarian restaurants). "Puluo," was a pidgin English term (a shortened pronunciation of "proletarian") that not did not necessarily mean "proletarian" but more often was used in a broader sense to refer to things common and popular. Its opposite was another pidgin English term, *bu-er-qiao-ya* (bourgeois), a word that connoted "noble and Western."[51]

One could easily identify a puluo restaurant by its signboard out front. A big or classy restaurant usually had a refined and well-phrased name that ended with the character *lou* ("tower"; sometimes *jiulou*, lit., wine tower). This name was proudly and prominently displayed on a gold-colored sign on the facade. The puluo restaurant, however, had a simple name plainly displayed: a wooden board with the big character RICE on it, hanging at the front of the restaurant. This single character had three functions: it was a store sign, an advertisement, and the main menu of the restaurant. Most of the customers who walked into this type of restaurant were looking for one or two bowls of rice, which was served with meat, vegetables, or bean products. Prices at the rice restaurant were affordable: 6 coppers per bowl of rice (two bowls were enough for an adult male); and 7 coppers each for two pork cutlets served with greens known as "chicken feather cabbage" (small Chinese cabbage sprouts, which look like green chicken feathers). The restaurants served the greens underneath the pork with no additional charge. There were a variety of substitutes for the greens, such as soft beancurd, green bean noodles, bean starch sheets, bean sprouts, solidified chicken blood, and so on. The total cost was 28 coppers, including a tip of two coppers. If one ordered only vegetable dishes, a meal would cost less than 20 coppers. A regular puluo restaurant patron wrote, "If you have twenty coppers in your pocket and you are starving, you can enter this type of restaurant with ease. After being seated, just ask the waiter to give you a dish of bean sprouts or fresh soybeans, or some other type of vegetable. With the vegetable, you can have two full bowls of steamed rice and your stomach will be full. All types of vegetables cost only six coppers per dish." A gluttonous customer might satisfy himself or herself by ordering other dishes on the menu such as stir-fried fish, salted pork, steamed eel, and so on, but dinner for one person at a puluo restaurant would never exceed .20 small silver dollar (about 46 coppers).[52]

If one preferred other sorts of food in an inexpensive restaurant, one had a variety of choices. There were three types of puluo restaurants, each specializing in a particular kind of food: porridge, noodles, or "vegetable rice." A customer could walk into a porridge restaurant, where a bowl of porridge consisting of a mixture of rice, meat, seafood, vegetables, and a variety of spices cost only 4 coppers, and, after enjoying two bowls, walk out with a full stomach. Side dishes were available: 4 coppers for a plate of pot-stewed, spiced dry beancurd or 5 coppers for a plate of fried (Spanish) peanuts. Porridge restaurants were the only type of eating establishment in Shanghai open twenty-four hours a day. Sometimes homeless people took advantage of this. A customer having a meal in a porridge restaurant after midnight (and, to be on the safe side, after 2 A.M.) was allowed to occupy a seat and snooze at the table. Such a privilege, however, was given to frequent patrons only. A first-time "lodger" might ask for the favor by paying an extra tip to the waiter. Once one got acquainted with the waiters, one didn't need to ask for permission each time but could just take the liberty of passing the night in the restaurant.

At a noodle restaurant, a bowl of noodle soup known as "spring noodles" (*yangchunmian*), which consisted of freshly made noodles spiced with sesame oil, soy sauce, green onions, sliced egg sheet, and dried shrimp, was enough to satisfy an empty stomach; it cost 16 coppers. A meal in a vegetable rice restaurant cost more, for it offered a combination: one bowl of vegetable rice (rice steamed with peanut oil and a variety of vegetable bits), two pieces of pork spareribs (patrons could substitute stewed pork, duck liver, chicken leg, stewed egg, and so on for one piece at no extra charge), plus a bowl of soup—all for .20 small silver dollar (46 coppers). Customers also had the flexibility of having more rice and a smaller piece of meat, or vice versa. An experienced customer knew how to use a four-character expression to tell a waiter his preference: "Light rice, heavy top" (*qingfan zhongjiao*) or "Heavy rice, light top" (*zhongfan qingjiao*).[53]

Wine was not served in restaurants, but customers were welcome to bring their own bottle. If one wished to purchase liquor in a wineshop nearby and needed a container, a small metal can would be provided by the restaurant. Shanghai had thousands of small wineshops that sold a variety of alcoholic beverages: from bottled beer to cooking wine, from low-alcohol fruit wine to *shaojiu*, a type of spirit like whisky. There was always a wineshop near every restaurant, if not next door.[54] These shops retailed all types of liquor from big jars; the minimum purchase could be as little as one *liang* (50 grams), but customers had to provide their own containers. If a customer was not in the mood to make a trip to the wine shop, the restaurant waiters were expected to run over and buy liquor for the customer if so asked.[55]

The phrase "puluo," as mentioned earlier, suggested something common, popular, and widespread rather than "proletarian." As a Shanghai guidebook indicated, these restaurants were "the places for meals of ordinary people."[56] Although not a perfect equivalent, these eating places, found all over the city, were a Chinese type of McDonald's. In alleyway-house neighborhoods, puluo restaurants were located in one or two facing-to-street living rooms. Some were found right inside alleyways; thus the smell of food pervaded the alleyway, and neighboring residents could hear the sound of stir-fry from the restaurant kitchen. In working-class neighborhoods in Yangshupu and Zhabei, one could find restaurants set in tents along streets or alleyways. The cost of a meal there was very low: 4 coppers for a bowl of rice, 8 coppers for beancurd soup, and 5 coppers for a dish of dried beancurd stir-fried with spicy sauce and pork. Even in the Nanking Road area right behind the city's most modern department stores, puluo restaurants found a place. Some of these establishments, when they were located in two-story shikumen houses, were called "semi-puluo restaurants": the first floor was the "puluo" section, serving working people or the "short shirts" (i.e., people who were not formally attired in a long gown; equivalent to "blue collar" in English); on the second floor were the "elegant seats" (*yazuo*), where a meal could cost $5–10.[57]

No matter where a puluo restaurant was located, for most people it was affordable. If, say, a decent meal in a puluo restaurant in the early 1930s (which is the time when all the above prices were current) was 28 coppers including a tip, and the daily earnings of a semiskilled worker in Shanghai at that time amounted to about $0.70 (or 210 coppers at the minimum exchange rate at that time: $1.00 = 300 coppers), then a meal at such a restaurant was about 13 percent of that worker's daily wage.[58] In other words, even if the worker had all three daily meals at a restaurant, the cost would be less than 40 percent of the worker's daily earnings. This, of course, does not mean that the worker could afford to have every meal in a restaurant, since he or she might have a family to support. Rather, the cost of eating in a restaurant was not at all high, especially considering that working-class families in Shanghai, who seldom ate at restaurants, normally spent 53–56 percent of their budget on food.[59] In this regard the word "puluo" matched the reality. All types of "short shirts" could enjoy meals frequently in puluo restaurants.

But these restaurants had a diverse clientele beyond the "short shirts" alone. White-collar workers, writers, students and schoolteachers, small business owners, and people of other callings sat side by side with rickshaw pullers and coolies. One office clerk who earned 20 silver dollars per month in 1926 by working six hours a day in a foreign firm—definitely a highly desirable job—said his daily breakfast was a bowl of spring noodles that cost him 10 copper coins: obviously he ate in a puluo restaurant.[60] Another salaried man, who identified himself as "lower middle class," explained in detail that a meal for 30 coppers in a puluo restaurant could include steamed rice, stir-fried pork and vegetables, beancurd soup, plus a can of 120 proof spirits served with fried peanuts or soybeans, a meal he regularly ate at such restaurants several times a month.[61]

TIGER STOVES AND SESAME CAKE STORES

Since most lilong houses did not have hot water facilities, the household heated water itself in a kettle or bought hot water at what Shanghai people called the "tiger stove," that is, a professional hot water service. Tiger stoves were among the most common stores in Shanghai's residential areas. The hot water store (*laohuzao*), by not only providing hot water but also acting as a teahouse and bathhouse for residents, as well as being located adjacent to a snack shop and, sometimes, a wineshop, often served as a kind of community center.

The laohuzao was a small store facing the street or an alleyway. Inside was a huge stove (the so-called tiger stove) that heated water twenty-four hours a day, seven days a week. Perhaps the laohuzao were the only stores in Shanghai that year round never closed their doors. Every household in the neighborhood was a customer; especially in Shanghai's bone-chilling winter, people flocked to the laohuzao and in the evening often formed a queue in front.

Since hot water was in constant supply, by placing a few tables and benches next to the tiger stove, a simple but convenient tea room could be easily set up. In the evening, just by stacking the tables and benches in a corner of the room and putting out a few wooden bathtubs and a cotton curtain, the tea house could be quickly turned into a crude but convenient bathhouse.[62]

Hot water stores spread all over Shanghai and enjoyed an increasing popularity in the Republican period. In 1912, there were 159 hot water stores in Shanghai; by 1928 there were 1,123; and by 1936, well over 2,000.[63] The stores were particularly common in the lilong neighborhoods. The Western-style houses of the city often had heating facilities at home, so laohuzao were less common in those neighborhoods. In straw-hut shantytowns, the ramshackle condition of the dwellings did not allow building tiger stove facilities.[64]

The teahouse service of these stores deserves some further discussion. The teahouse has long been associated with traditional Chinese urban life. Although the importance of teahouses varied by location and social group (or class), the teahouse is without doubt one of the most characteristic features of Chinese culture.[65] In Jiangnan, for example, it is not unusual for a medium-size town with a few thousand households to have close to a hundred teahouses.[66] But in Shanghai it has long been thought that teahouses were in decline in favor of a great variety of restaurants, wineshops, bars, and what might be called refreshment stores, of national renown. A 1933 Shanghai guidebook provides a fourteen-page list of Shanghai's major restaurants, but uses barely five lines to list teahouses, most of which were located in Shanghai's old Chinese city and the downtown areas. According to the editors, "Teahouses in Shanghai are not flourishing."[67]

But did teahouses gradually vanish in Shanghai? Was the city so thoroughly modernized or "Westernized" that this traditional form of business for refreshment and social contact was discarded? The laohuzao story tells us that the answer is no. The teahouse not only survived but, to some extent, enjoyed a special revival. Indeed, from the 1940s on, the various types of teahouses in Shanghai increased in number, and among them, as one report indicated, were "laohuzao teahouses on small streets, with one or two tables; their patrons were the working people in the neighborhood."[68] Up until the 1960s, it was still not difficult to find the laohuzao-teahouse combination in Shanghai's narrow streets and alleyways.[69]

Another reason for the popularity of hot water stores was that they were always located next to a snack store commonly called a "sesame cake store" (*dabing dian*). These stores had long service hours, usually from 4 A.M. to midnight, and some were open twenty-four hours a day. The major business was breakfast, both "sit-down" and "take-out." The food served included sesame cakes, fried dough sticks, steamed bread, fried bread, glutinous rice cakes, noodle soup, won ton (dumpling) soup, and soybean milk. All were popular breakfast foods in Shanghai (Fig. 32).[70] Like other neighborhood stores, each sesame cake store was originally a living room or, at most, two connected living rooms. Although there were tables where customers could sit and eat, most customers felt more comfortable taking the food back home, just a few yards away.

Every day from 6 A.M. to 8 A.M. was the rush hour for these stores. Often working people queued up in front, awaiting their turn to buy a fast-food breakfast before rushing off to work. Housewives came to buy sesame cakes, fried dough sticks, and soybean milk—the three most popular types of breakfast food—for their families. During morning hours, sesame cake

Fig. 32.   A sesame cake store like this could be found on literally every block
in the city's average residential areas and was patronized by every family in the
neighborhood. The man in the middle of the picture is tending sesame cakes baking in a barrel-like coal oven. Two customers, one dressed in a good middle-class
gown and the other in a working-class short shirt with a hat, are waiting for the
fresh-baked cakes while chatting with the baker. Behind the baker, a cook pre-
pares steaming hot noodle or dumpling soup for a woman customer. The man
in front with a cigarette in his fingers may also be a customer waiting for his
order. From R. Barz, *Shanghai: Sketches of Present-Day Shanghai.*

stores were certainly the most crowded stores in the city. The late morning
and early afternoon were slow times, but from 3 P.M. on, business was brisk
again as afternoon refreshments were served.[71]

Although sesame cake stores were busy year round, the laohuzao had a
slow season. But the business of the laohuzao always seemed to match the
needs of their customers. Song Aling, a native of Ningbo who had run a hot

water business for forty years, explained that in summer, when hot water was less in demand, the store was busy with bathhouse business. At those times, part of the store was turned into a bathroom. Right behind the tiger stove of Song's store was a small room that could scarcely accommodate six wooden bathtubs at the same time. But Song said this was fine with his customers, who were drawn by the cheap price and convenience the store provided. Customers paid only 6 coppers for a bath, while the lowest charge in a regular public bathhouse was 15 coppers.[72] Perhaps the convenience of the laohuzao was more attractive than the low price, for all the customers were residents who lived within walking distance. In fact, most of the customers were people who lived on the block and did not even need to cross the street to get to the store. In summer when twilight approached, the front of the laohuzao would be lit by a lantern made of transparent oilpaper bearing four big, brush-written characters that could be seen from a distance: *qing shui pen tang,* or "pure hot water tubs."[73] After dinner, with soap and towel in hand, a man (this type of bathhouse was exclusively for men) could take a stroll to the tiger stove and there enjoy a relaxed bath. After the bath he might sit in the store and enjoy a cup of tea and idle chatter with other customers, or he could walk next door for a bowl of won ton soup.

Public bathing establishments like the tiger stoves or the regular bathhouses (*yushi*) were an enduring feature of residential neighborhoods. Only a few yards behind Song's store inside Jiahe Li (Alley of Fine Grain) was a standard public bathhouse that served the neighborhood in all seasons, beginning in 1933.[74] This was a two-story house, with the first story devoted to what might be called the economy class and the second story to the luxury class. Each floor was divided into two sections. One was a room furnished with beds or deck chairs for changing and relaxation. Before and after a bath customers could loll on a bed or deck chair, sipping a cup of tea, reading a newspaper, chatting, or simply doing nothing. Clothes and personal belongings were hung on a long towel rail suspended from the ceiling, putting them out of reach of thieves. The bathroom attendant used a long bamboo pole to hang up or to take down the clothes, something that required some skill. The other section was the bathing room itself, where the main facility was a tile bathtub that looked rather like a wading pool (about twenty-five feet long, twelve feet wide, and three feet deep). Set into the floor, it occupied almost the whole room, leaving only a narrow path around the walls. A few sinks were installed on the walls. The big bathtub was used for relaxed soaking; bathers were supposed to soap themselves down and rinse off at the sinks, not in the tub.

Bathhouses like this obviously needed more capital than tiger stoves did;

thus they were less numerous but still by no means uncommon.[75] Public bathhouses, including the tiger-stove type, were a usual feature of Chinese cities. No later than the thirteenth century, sizable public bathhouses, which also served tea and provided massages, were widespread in Jiangnan cities like Hangzhou.[76] Such bathhouses prospered for centuries, and they were reincarnated in Shanghai's foreign concessions. Robert Fortune described a bathhouse near his residence in the walled city of Shanghai in 1844. This bathhouse resembled in almost every detail the one at Jiahe Li a century later: "There are two outer rooms used for undressing and dressing; the first, and largest, is for the poorer classes; the second, for those who consider themselves more respectable, and who wish to be more private. . . . [The bathing room] is entered by a small door at the farther end of the building, and is about 30 feet long and 20 feet wide; the water occupying the whole space, except a narrow path round the sides. The water is from 1 foot to 18 inches deep, and the sides of the bath are lined with marble slabs, from which the bathers step into the water, and on which they sit and wash themselves." Fortune went on to describe the steamy scene when the bathhouse was full of customers: "In the afternoon and evening this establishment is crowded with visitors, and on entering the bath room, the first impression is almost insupportable; the hot steam or vapour meets you at the door, filling the eyes and ears, and causing perspiration to run from every pore of the body; it almost darkens the place, and the Chinamen seen in this imperfect light, with their brown skins and long tails, sporting amongst the water, render the scene a most ludicrous one to an Englishman."[77] The scene may have been ludicrous to a European of that time, but it was perfectly normal and obviously pleasant for the people whom Fortune observed. Fortune himself realized that the bathhouses of China "must be of great importance as regards the health and comfort of the natives." By the late nineteenth century, public bathhouses known as "bathtub cubicles" (*pentang*, lit., hot water tubs) were already a regular feature in Shanghai's foreign concessions.[78]

A century after Fortune, a Chinese author describing the public bathhouses of Shanghai reported a scene almost identical to the one Fortune saw, but the tone he adopted was joyful: "When you open the door of a bathhouse, what greets you is an enshrouding mist—gentle and soft steam. Especially in the winter, once you enter the room it makes you feel as warm as if it were spring. After you lie down on a sling chair anywhere you please, a steaming hot towel is brought to you together with a cup of tea, which is your favorite type of tea, the type you asked for. Without the slightest effort your clothes are off and you are back to nature." The author went on to describe the pleasure of chatting with follow bathers, reading newspapers, munching snacks, and luxuriating in services such as "body brushing," "back massages," and "foot cleaning," all common services in any public bathhouse and available for a very reasonable price.[79] Indeed, some of these services were a sort of physical therapy. In "foot cleaning," for instance, the attendant wielded a tiny knife to pare toenails, calluses, and corns after a bath. It was not in hospitals or clinics but in bathhouses that thousands of people with foot ailments—such as corns, warts, ring-worm of the toenails (onychomycosis), and fungus—found a cure.[80] An old Chinese saying humorously conveyed the pleasure of the teahouse and bathhouse in daily life: "In the morning, water inside the skin; in the evening, skin inside the water" (*zaoshang shui pao pi, wanshang pi pao shui*).[81] The two sideline services of the tiger stove—serving tea and pro-viding baths—readily met both needs.[82] If Fortune had survived into the Republican period, he could have witnessed countless tiger stoves and bath-houses that duplicated in every detail the scene he had reported a century earlier in the old walled city—the only difference, perhaps, was the disap-pearance of the "tails."

The "Little Food" Markets

The sesame cake store and tiger stove combination was often located near an open-air food market known as the *xiaoce shan* (little-food market) in the Shanghai dialect or *xiaocai chang* in Mandarin Chinese. Here the ad-jective "little" described the type of food sold, not the size of the market. The term "little food" (*xiaoce*), of Suzhou origin, included virtually every-thing—meat, eggs, fish, bean products, and vegetables—that could be served with the staple food, rice. The term also connoted that these were "daily home-cooked foods," as distinct from "restaurant foods." Finally, when this Suzhou term was absorbed into the Shanghai dialect (much of the Shanghai dialect vocabulary has a Suzhou origin), it gained a new meaning that, in a small way, reveals the "worshiping-things-foreign" mentality in modern Shanghai: "xiaoce," or "little foods," meant home-made Chinese food as distinct from Western types of food, which were called *dhace* (*dacai* or *dacan* in Mandarin, meaning grand food). In the eyes of the people of Shanghai, Western foods were associated with things chic and elegant, and Chinese foods with quotidian life. Hence, the latter were "petty."[83] In any case, like the rice store and the coal store, the little-food market (henceforth referred to simply as the food market) was an inevi-table part of daily life. Moreover, because of the custom of shopping at the market for fresh food every day (it was not unusual for people to go out to purchase fresh food for every meal), the food market was the place that some member of every family visited at least once a day.

The history of Shanghai's food markets parallels changes in the diet in the city, as reflected by what was served on the average family's dining table: from relatively simple, rice-and-vegetable-based daily meals to a very diversified menu. Although Shanghai had been a prosperous county town prior to modern times, the daily diet of ordinary people was far from indulgent. Zhang Chunhua, a collector of Shanghai folklore, observed in the Daoguang period (1821–50), "Our county borders on the sea so the folk are thrifty," alluding to the fact that seaside land is not prosperous farmland, and the people must necessarily be careful with their money. Similar observations were also recorded in local gazetteers.[84] Meat dishes were not everyday food for most people. In common families, meat and fish were served about four times a month: usually on the second, the eighth, the sixteenth, and the twenty-third day of each lunar month. These days were known as *dang hun* (having meat or fish). On other days, vegetable and bean products were the main accompaniments to rice.[85] Simple and vegetable-based foods made traditional Shanghai cooking insignificant compared to the prestigious Chinese schools of cuisine, each of which originated in a specific region, such as the well-known cuisines of Canton (Guangdong), Szechwan (Sichuan), and so on.

Even when Shanghai boomed in modern times, the reputation of its cooking did not rise parallel with its fame in other areas. The Shanghai kitchen was still regarded as peripheral to or even entirely out of place in the nation's splendid cooking tradition. However, the prosperity of modern Shanghai and the fact that its people had immigrated from all over the country meant that virtually all major cuisines were brought to the city; in fact, diversity became the outstanding feature of the food in Shanghai, much like the situation in contemporary America: while the fast food at McDonald's (if we may take it as representing American cuisine) may not be appreciated as among the world's best cuisines, anytime people in any major U.S. city wish, they may treat themselves to a great variety of restaurants serving food in a plethora of styles. Insofar as diet is concerned, the most meaningful change in twentieth-century Shanghai, of course, was not what was served in restaurants but what was put on the dining table in the average household. One of the most obvious changes in the diet of common people was that food made of *hun* (a term for all kinds of meat, fish, eggs, seafood, etc.—as opposed to *su*, or vegetables) became the main course. By early in the twentieth century, it had become the norm that average Shanghai families had "no meal without meat dishes" (*wu hun bu chifan*)—vegetables had become side dishes.[86] In the Republican period, food in Shanghai—both what was served in restaurants and what was made at home—was perhaps the richest and the most diversified in the nation.[87] Meat, fish, and seafood freshly cooked in a variety of styles and methods (frying, stir-frying, steaming, stewing, roasting, etc.) were daily fare; a meal with only vegetables, bean products, or preserved foods was considered a symbol of a poor diet. So-called coolie food in Shanghai, for instance, consisted of "plain dishes of bean sprouts and salt fish and ordinary cabbage and that sort of thing."[88] A rickshaw puller's diet, which was typical of coolie food and considered by others in the city as "extremely cheap and coarse," included green vegetables, potatoes, dried bean curd, soft bean curd, salted fish, and fresh fish, in addition to rice, noodles, sesame buns, and *zongzi* (pyramid-shaped dumplings).[89] A Shanghai folk song simulating the whining of a spoiled child revealed how finicky people had become:

> Whenever I am starving,
> I pick up a pair of chopsticks
> and rush into the kitchen.
> Let's see what we have today.
> Oh, again, green cabbage stir-fried with beancurd.
> How can I eat rice with dishes like these?[90]

When vegetables and bean products were still the main course, people got these items, as well as their rice, from door-to-door peddlers, who were mostly farmers from nearby villages. Shops selling meat, chickens, ducks, eggs, fish, and bean products were found in the walled city and its immediate vicinity known as Nanshi (lit., the southern market), but not in residential neighborhoods. There was no regular food market in the foreign concessions.

Thomas Hanbury (1832–1907), a Britisher who made a fortune in Shanghai real estate and who arranged Shanghai's first cable service with London, thought that it might be profitable to furnish peddlers with tents and stalls so that they could sell their goods at a regular spot—a regular spot near his property, which of course would increase in value with a market nearby.[91] In a petition to the French Municipal Council, Hanbury and his partners proposed that such a food market could yield five hundred taels in taxes every year and that after ten years the council could own the market for free. The council approved the petition, and in December 1864 a few tents were erected along Ningxingjie (lit., Road of Peace and Prosperity). Built in 1863, Ningxingjie was a narrow street south of the Yangjingbang

Creek in the French Concession, where Hanbury and his partners owned property. The council posted notices in the concession announcing that from January 1, 1865, on, all food peddlers must sell their goods in the Central Food Market, as the Ningxingjie market was named. However, the notice was generally ignored and the market did not last long, mainly because at a time when people's diet was simple, customers seemed to be satisfied buying from door-to-door peddlers. The council for its part did not intend to create a monopoly by driving all peddlers to the Central Food Market. By April 1865, three months after its opening, the market had closed.[92]

However, the Ningxingjie food market did leave a legacy. The street had gained some fame because of Hanbury's food market, and over the years butcher shops, poultry and egg shops, and so on opened along Ningxingjie. By the 1930s, on this 1,720-foot- (525-meter-) long street were dozens of stores and over a thousand food stalls. More than seven hundred different kinds of food, which were categorized into twenty-five types (vegetables, fruit, meat, etc.), were sold there. By that time few people referred to the street by its formal name; rather, most knew it as Food Market Street (*caishi jie;* today's Ninghaidong Road). The name is still used by the residents in the area. The name matched reality well.[93]

More significant, the Ningxingjie market was the first food market open daily where residents could purchase the "little foods." In fact, only a few years after the Ningxingjie market opened, similar markets were established in other spots in the International Settlement and the French Concession: one opened in Baxianqiao (Bridge of the Eight Immortals) in 1871; the next year, another opened in Wufulong (Alley of Five Fortunes) near Nanking Road; and in 1879 one opened on Nanking Road, followed by another in 1884. The Wufulong food market was initiated by a local merchant, Yang Zhijing, who donated money to erect tents to shelter the peddlers who regularly gathered in Wufulong for business. Later, the Shanghai Municipal Council took administrative responsibility for the market and levied a monthly fee of two to three dollars on each stall. The food markets in the International Settlement were operated in the same fashion.[94] Regulations on food markets were issued by the city's Chinese authorities in 1930, suggesting that food markets had become a regular and standard establishment in the city.[95]

Unlike the first Ningxingjie market, which was planned by Hanbury and his partners, most of Shanghai's food markets were not *built* but simply *grew,* like the later Ningxingjie market. Like traditional markets in Chinese towns, food markets in Shanghai often started on a spot, usually along a roadside, where peddlers set up their stalls on a fairly regular basis. Gradually, an open-air market emerged and stores opened in the surrounding area.[96] Such food markets, naturally, were always close to a densely inhabited area or in many cases were right in the midst of a populous residential neighborhood.[97] By the twentieth century, some food markets operated in multistory buildings sponsored by private entrepreneurs (many of whom were British) and the municipal authorities. Most of these buildings were erected in the two decades prior to the outbreak of war in 1937, in response to the increasing congestion in the city (in particular, in the foreign concessions [Fig. 33]). They were, nevertheless, often built on a spot where food peddlers regularly gathered. For instance, the three-story Sanjiaodi food market, Shanghai's largest (78,500 square feet [7,300 square meters] in 1986), was built in 1916 precisely on the spot where an open-air market had first appeared in 1891.[98] The Ximo Road Food Market, famous for its Western-type food (especially beef, bacon, foreign ham, butter, and cheese), was built in 1929 to cater to the growing population of well-off residents along the west end of Bubbling Well Road. Fruit and flowers, which were uncommon in other food markets, were available at the Ximo Road Food Market to meet the demand of the residents of this "upper corner" (*shang zhi jiao*) residential area.[99] Other major food markets, such as the Taipingqiao (Peace Bridge) Food Market (built in 1917, also known as the Ximen [West Gate] Food Market), the Tilanqiao (Bamboo Basket Bridge) Food Market (built in 1934), and the Baxianqiao Food Market (built in 1871), were all located in the city's most densely populated areas.[100] Shanghai's foreigners also shopped at the markets, some of which were associated with particular foreign communities. For instance, the Beibu Food Market (built in 1939) had more than two hundred food stalls operated by Japanese peddlers to serve the Japanese community in Hongkou, and in the early 1940s, when Shanghai had more than twenty thousand Jewish refugees, some Jews made a living by selling canned food and bread in the Tilanqiao Food Market, which was near the city's major Jewish community in Hongkou.[101]

However, food markets housed in permanent buildings were an "elite." By August 1937 Shanghai had forty-nine major food markets, most of which were open-air; markets newly opened after 1937 were all open-air and remained so after 1949.[102] A typical open-air food market occupied a section of a street (a block between two intersections), which was closed to vehicular traffic in the morning hours, when the market was busiest. In any case, most markets sprang up on back streets that were near residential neighborhoods but had light motor traffic. Open-front tents made of bamboo sheets were put up on the sidewalks on either side of the street for

Fig. 33. An indoor food market, which occupied a four-story building built by the Shanghai Municipal Council in 1930, covered almost 25,000 square feet on the corner of Fuzhou Road and Zhejiang Road and cost 73,000 taels of silver. Courtesy of Shanghai Municipal Archive.

the peddlers to set up shop. Customers thus walked in the street rather than on the sidewalk. Unlike most streets of Shanghai, a typical food market street was not paved in concrete or asphalt but was covered by fist-sized irregularly shaped rocks. It was said that this kind of rugged pavement had its merits: because the road in a food market was always wet, a rough surface prevented slips, slowed down vehicles, and reduced the need for maintenance.[103]

As mentioned earlier, although traditional Shanghai cooking was not regarded as among the best cuisines of China, modern Shanghai was a city of immigrants, and cooking in an average Shanghai household was, as one might say, "a true melting pot."[104] Satisfying every palate was almost a standard requirement for being a housewife. "In the old days, it was not easy to be a daughter-in-law in the 'shikumen,'" one writer recalled. "Shanghai was a community of immigrants, its residents coming from everywhere. Usually after a few generations of marriage, a family would be composed of people of different native origins. Father-in-law might be a Subei native and mother-in-law a Ningbo native, while the daughter-in-law's mother was Cantonese, and her father Sichuanese—this was a rather common family. Still, the daughter-in-law was able to arrange fine food for everybody in the family." [105] Her secret was the so-called daily dishes in the Shanghai style (*Haipai jiachang cai*), which referred to the dishes commonly served in ordinary Shanghai families. These daily dishes fell into three categories. First were local specialties, such as Shaoxing's "pork stewed in soy sauce with dried vegetables and bamboo shoots"; Ningbo's "steamed eel," "dried eel stewed with ground pork," and "salted cabbage boiled with fresh soybeans"; Subei's fried meat balls (known as "lion heads"); Guangdong's "tender beef in oyster sauce"; Sichuan's "spicy garlic pork" and "mapo bean curd"; Hangzhou's "West Lake fish cooked with vinegar," "Dongpo pork" (named after a famous man of letters, Su Dongpo, 1037–1101), and "water shield soup"; Shanghai's "mixed eight treasures [meat, dried beancurd, peanuts, bamboo shoots, etc.] stir-fried with hot sauce," "sliced pork and beancurd custard"; and so on. Second were dishes that imitated those served in restaurants. All major schools of Chinese cuisine had their "lunch special" types of dishes that did not require complicated cooking procedures or special cooking equipment (such as a big stove or a huge pot) and hence could be cooked at home. Most of these were stir-fry dishes. Stir-frying was in fact the favorite cooking method of the people of Shanghai. [106] Therefore, stir-fried sliced pork, sliced fish, diced chicken, shrimps, finless eel, peas, dried mushrooms, bamboo shoots, and many other foods often graced the family dining table. Other restaurant dishes such as "shrimp with cashew nuts and green peas," "pork with green onions," "spareribs in sweet-and-sour sauce," "soup of three delicacies," and so on were also known as *jiachang cai* (common home dishes). Finally, many daily dishes were not derived from any established recipe but were creations of the "family cook," who tried to use whatever materials were available in the kitchen. Occasionally, Western-style cooking methods were imitated, such as putting lemon on steamed fish, adding butter to beef soup, serving dishes with coriander, and so on. One type of soup that was quite popular (especially in the summer) was made of cabbage, tomatoes, potatoes, carrots, and beef and known as "Luosong soup" (Luosong is an "out of tune" pronunciation of "Russian" in the Shanghai dialect). [107]

Dishes such as these were the usual fare in most Shanghai families. Eating well or at least eating diversely was something shared by most people in the city, including working-class families. An investigation into working-class life in Shanghai, which recorded the daily expenses of 305 working-class families for an entire year, from April 1929 to March 1930, found that the sample families consumed a great variety of food: 22 types of cereals and cereal products, 12 types of bean products (not including beans themselves), 66 types of vegetables, 55 types of meat, fish, and eggs, 20 types of fruit and dried fruit, and 14 types of condiments. These were all common foods; less common foods were categorized as "others" and not counted.[108] In general, Shanghai workers had better nutrition than their counterparts in other Chinese cities. A comparative study conducted during 1940–42 on workers' nutrition in Beijing, Shanghai, and Chongqing found significant differences between these cities. For instance, workers in Shanghai got 13.2 percent of their nutrition from meat, fish, and eggs, while Beijing workers received only 3.2 percent from these foods; 22.7 percent of Shanghai workers' nutrition came from miscellaneous types of food (i.e., food other than grains, vegetables, and meat), but this was true of only 7.7 percent of Beijing workers. On average, workers' families in Chongqing spent only 45.7 percent of what Shanghai workers' families spent for food.[109]

The local food market was the place that made the great variety of "daily dishes in the Shanghai style" possible. Or, it could also be said that these dishes were everyday fare that made it necessary to have a food market within walking distance of home. In 1940, a special report by the Chinese Medical Association revealed that of the 526 common types of food consumed in the city, about half were available in the food markets.[110] One of Shanghai's largest markets, the Baxianqiao Food Market, was originally called the Huayang (Chinese and Foreign) Food Market because the wide variety of foods it sold attracted both Chinese and Westerners. Since the building that housed the market was remodeled in 1929, the market has been known as the "Great World of Nonstaple Foods" (*fushipin dashijie*)—not just because the market was located a few blocks southwest of the well-known Great World (*dashijie*) amusement center but also because it offered a magnificent selection of foods: more than 2,700 different types by one count.[111] An average food market, of course, could not compete in terms of the diversity of foods, but it usually had all of the ingredients for popular dishes that were available in the Great World of Nonstaple Foods.

By the Republican period, although peddlers still walked from one alleyway to another selling their goods (mainly rice and fresh vegetables), for most of the residents of Shanghai, buying food from peddlers had become supplementary. Every morning, in virtually every household someone (a member of the family or a maid) took a bamboo basket in hand and walked to the nearby food market to purchase the ingredients for the meals of the day. Should people meet in the alleyway in the morning, they would often greet each other with the words "Have you bought the little foods yet?"—words that in significance and function were something like the conventional customary Chinese greeting "Have you eaten yet?" [112]

Shopping on the Block

The great variety of Shanghai's small neighborhood stores, shops, and markets made it possible to do all of one's shopping virtually within a single block. Although the people of Shanghai considered Nanking Road the center of the city, they rarely felt the need to visit there for the simple reason that they could get most of what they required for daily life without crossing more than one or two streets. The center of their daily shopping and, to some extent, socializing and entertainment was on the corner of the street, or literally at the place where the laohuzao and sesame cake store were located. In a way, these stores were, to use Skinner's term, the "standard market town" of the Shanghainese, while Nanking Road was the "provincial metropolis." Indeed, Shanghai's neighborhood stores bear some similarities to the shops described by Skinner in his model of the standard market town:

> Even though most sellers at any standard market are likely to be itinerants, the standard market town normally has a certain minimum of permanent facilities. These typically include—in addition to the socially important tea houses, wineshops, and eating places—one or more oil shops (selling fuel for wick lamps), incense and candle shops (selling the essentials of religious worship), and at least a few others offering such items as looms, needles and thread, brooms, soap, tobacco, and matches. Standard market towns normally support a number of craftsmen as well, including most typically blacksmiths, coffin makers, carpenters, and makers of paper effigies for religious burning. [113]

If the "standard market town" adequately met the needs of Chinese peasants, so too the small neighborhood stores and food markets met the needs of the common people of Shanghai. A survey of seven neighborhoods located in four different areas of the city found that on average, 82 percent of the residents did most of their shopping at neighborhood stores. Even in Baoyu Li (Alley of Treasure and Abundance), a lilong compound located between the commercial centers of Nanking Road and Avenue Joffre and no more than a ten- to fifteen-minute walk from either, only 5 percent of the residents reported that they did most of their shopping on Nanking Road or Avenue Joffre. [114] One reason for this shopping pattern was that, like the shikumen mix discussed in chapter 4, Baoyu Li was itself also a mini commercial center. On either side of the main alleyway of Baoyu Li, which was 410 feet (125 meters) long and 15 feet (4.6 meters) wide, were numerous small businesses, including tobacco and paper stores, a sesame cake store, a tailor shop, a shop selling ham, a coal store, a hardware store, a foreign sundry goods store, restaurants, and a fabric store. A small inn, a sock factory, a clinic, and an elementary school were also located in Baoyu Li.[115]

Since early in this century, Shanghai has been providing its customers with the nation's best and greatest variety of goods (including luxurious foreign merchandise). Even today, from the capital to obscure rural towns, commercial signs making statements such as "Made in Shanghai" and "In the Shanghai Style" can often be seen on the street, revealing the prestige of the city's products in the Chinese consumer's mind. But for the common people of Shanghai, neighborhood stores seemed quite adequate for most of their needs, and they seldom went elsewhere to purchase fashionable goods. It was therefore quite common for Shanghai people to visit Nanking Road and the Bund only once or twice in many years, although from most parts of the city good transportation was available. One informant told me that in the previous fifty years she had visited Nanking Road only three times: once for sightseeing when she first arrived in Shanghai, once to buy gold rings for her son's wedding, and another time to see fireworks on National Day (October 1).[116] When asked why people did not frequent Nanking Road, since it was famous nationwide for shopping, a group of lifetime Shanghai residents said, "We have nothing to buy there." To the question "Why don't you go there to window-shop?" they responded, "We rarely have leisure time to wander about the streets window-shopping."[117]

Still, "strolling around the streets" (*guang malu*) was a popular way of whiling away time. Nanking Road, as the center of the city, and Avenue Joffre, with its European exoticism, were the two best-known spots in Shanghai for "strolling around." Each of the streets was about a mile long and seventy to eighty feet wide (including sidewalks).[118] Even if most of the city's residents only occasionally shopped or window-shopped on these streets, since the city contained 3 million inhabitants in the early thirties and 5 million in the late forties—not to mention thousands of tourists and visitors on any day, on whose itinerary these spots were a must—the streets were always full of pedestrians.

Most people, however, if they wanted a greater selection than that offered by neighborhood stores or if they wished to spend an hour or so "strolling around the streets," turned to a regional shopping center. Such spots, usually centered on a busy intersection, were within a ten- or fifteen-minute walk of almost any residential area. In the present-day administrative vocabulary these are called "district-level commercial centers," of which there are twenty-five in Shanghai, with an average of seventy stores per center, altogether representing about 10 percent of the city's retail stores.[119] In the hierarchy of commerce in Shanghai, these centers may well be described as analogous to the "intermediate market towns" in Skinner's model, standing in between the "standard market town" (i.e., the blocks where neighborhood stores were located) and the "provincial metropolis" (i.e., the Bund and Nanking Road). Most of these commercial spots were developed since the late nineteenth century and many have an interesting history to tell.

Jing'ansi, or Temple of Peace, can be traced back to A.D. 247, during the Three Kingdoms period. It has occupied its present site since 1216, but the structure standing there now is a late-nineteenth-century reconstruction. From an unknown date a natural well (probably a spring) in front of the temple has been bubbling water day and night. Local villagers dubbed it "the bubbling well" or "the eye of sea," believing that the well would never dry up because it was connected to the Pacific Ocean. In 1862, in expectation that the Taipings might attack Shanghai, a two-mile-long military road was constructed from Nanking Road to the temple. Later the road was officially named by the SMC "Bubbling Well Road" (or Jing'ansi Road in Chinese), and still later it became an elegant street in west Shanghai. The temple was remodeled and expanded in 1880 and again 1894; in 1874 the well was surrounded with a protective marble fence and graced with a stone tablet proclaiming it to be the "Number Six Spring under Heaven." From 1881 to 1961, an annual temple fair was held for a few days around the eighth day of the fourth month of the lunar calendar to celebrate the birthday of Sakyamuni. On these occasions, the streets near the temple were filled with tents and stalls; in some years the fair reportedly attracted more than two hundred thousand people.[120]

Xujiahui, or the Village of the Xu Clan, was the hometown of Xu Guangqi (also called Paul; 1562–1633), the Ming grand secretary (a position equivalent at the time to prime minister). The name of the village became famous because of Xu's conversion to Christianity and, later, because of the Jesuit presence in the area. A Catholic church was founded in Xujiahui in 1847, barely four years after Shanghai was opened as a treaty port, while the place was essentially rural. The village was located at the confluence of three creeks. The only commercial establishment there in the Xianfeng period (1851–61) was a rice shop run by Xu Jingxing, a member of Xu family, in three thatched-roofed bungalows facing the east end of Dong-sheng Bridge, which spanned the creeks. In the late nineteenth century, as the population of Shanghai expanded, this area gradually became inhabited by a mix of people. By 1914, when the French Concession officially extended its boundaries to the eastern edge of Xujiahui, the area had already become a fairly busy commercial spot. In character, however, it remained mainly church related. In 1910 a Gothic cathedral was built a few yards north of the tomb of Xu Guangqi. Since then the towers of the cathedral have been a prominent landmark in the area. Other churches and church-sponsored schools, libraries, museums, presses, charities, and an observatory were developed in the area, making Xujiahui the most prominent center of Catholicism in Shanghai, if not all of China.[121]

Caojiadu, or the Cao family ferry, was located about two and a half miles northwest of the old county seat. A stele dated 1762 reveals that a ferry was run by a local Cao family (whose ancestors had come from Anhui late in the sixteenth century) to help farmers cross Suzhou Creek, hence the name. At the end of the nineteenth century, the area was still rural and some Westerners had built villas there to enjoy the pastoral surroundings. In 1892, Caojiadu's status was raised to that of administrative market town (*zhen*), and three years later silk filatures appeared in the area, followed by cotton mills, flour mills, leather factories, lightbulb factories, and many other industries. Wholesale firms dealing in agricultural products were also opened there to take advantage of its convenient location on the banks of Suzhou Creek, which led to the rich agricultural areas of Jiangnan, especially the Lake Tai region west of Shanghai. By the early 1920s, Caojiadu had already become one of Shanghai's major industrial areas, and a few "extra-Settlement roads" were built to connect the area to the western part of the International Settlement. Thus, the area became merged into the city proper. The center of Caojiadu, located at the intersection of six streets, became known as Five Points Square (Wujiaochang). In addition to industry and commerce, the area was also home to people from many different places in China, including Wuxi (in Jiangsu province), Hubei, Ningbo (in Zhejiang province), and Subei (northern Jiangsu), and to foreigners such as the Japanese, British, and Italians. The prestigious St. John's University and the famous Jessfield Park (today's Zhongshan Park) were located within walking distance of Caojiadu.[122]

Beizhan, or Northern Station, derived its name from the city's major railway station. The station, where the Shanghai-Nanjing and Shanghai-Wusong railways intersected, was completed in 1909. Because of its favorable location on the northern boundary of the International Settlement, the area around Beizhan soon became a center of Zhabei. In spite of two devastating bombings by the Japanese in 1932 and 1937, Beizhan survived and served as the (land) gateway to Shanghai for more than seventy years, until a new railway station was built to its west in 1987. In the Republican period, Beizhan and its vicinity were considered the most developed area in Shanghai under Chinese administration.[123]

Tilanqiao, or Bamboo Basket Bridge, was a busy commercial area in Hongkou in northeast Shanghai. The area was a market town that dated back at least to the Jiaqing period (1796–1820). An oral tradition of the area presented Tilanqiao as a typical, picturesque Jiangnan small market town: a wooden bridge thirty-three feet (ten meters) long and six and a half feet (two meters) wide was built across the Xiahaipu, a creek that flowed into the mouth of the Yangzi River. The surrounding area was punctuated by paddies and crisscrossed by waterways.[124] Nearby was an ancient temple named after the river, the Xiahai Temple, that attracted crowds of pilgrims. On market days farmers, peddlers, pilgrims, and others thronged the streets around Tilanqiao. The growth of the foreign concessions south of Tilanqiao made this place busier than ever because for the people in the northeast suburbs, the bridge was the only surface route into the city. A bamboo ware store near the east end of the bridge was well known for its fine bamboo baskets, hence the name of the bridge as well as the area.[125]

Laoximen, or Old West Gate, was one of the six portals of the old, walled county seat. The wall itself was built in 1553 to protect the city from Japanese pirates (known as Wokou, or "dwarfs"). Each gate had an official, refined name, which was etched in stone on top of the gate. But these names were perhaps too elegant for the common people, who instead tended to refer to them simply by their location. The West Gate was officially the "Gate of the Ritual Phoenix" (Fengyimen), but because it was on the west side of town, people simply called it the "west gate." In 1906, when another gate was constructed in the west section of the wall in order to improve the flow of traffic, people started calling the Gate of the Ritual Phoenix the "old west gate." Laoximen was close to the foreign concessions and hence a busy commercial area. It faced the French Concession, and in 1912–14 when the wall and all its gates were torn down, the area was merged with the French Concession. Nonetheless, the name has survived until the present.[126]

In a way the small neighborhood stores and these regional centers made Shanghai a walking city. Either in a lethargic mood or in high spirits, on a sunny spring morning or a breezy summer evening, a resident might walk

out of the stone-framed wooden gate of a lilong compound and take a stroll
in the streets nearby. On the way, he or she might nod to an acquaintance,
say hello to a neighbor, or greet a friend and soon end up in a nearby commercial center. It seems that the streets of Shanghai could never bore a
stroller. Wang Yingxia (1907–) recalled that early in her marriage to Yu
Dafu the two of them often strolled through west Shanghai. In 1928, the
young couple rented a house in Jiahe Li (Alley of Fine Grain) on Hart Road,
one block south of Bubbling Well Road. Wang nostalgically recalled more
than half a century later, "We often took a stroll beneath the parasol trees
along Avenue Joffre. Walking towards the west, we could soon see the
double spires of the Catholic church of Xujiahui. If we were not tired at that
point, we might continue walking to Longhua. The pagoda of the Longhua
Temple was a place we often visited. This was the itinerary that Yu Dafu
and I often took while strolling in those days. It was quite a distance to
cover on foot. After the trip we were not weary but that night we would
sleep soundly." [127] On another occasion Wang said, "Yu Dafu was fond of
walking. Being young and innocent, I was obedient to his will and always
accompanied him. Thus for five or six years we walked through Shanghai.
Now I am over eighty but can still walk without a cane—Yu Dafu should
be credited for that." [128] In Shanghai walking for pleasure and relaxation
was common, particularly in the western district of the city, where streets
were graced with large sidewalks and trees. Song Qingling (Madame Sun
Yat-sen) also recalled that she and Sun liked to stroll on Yuyuan Road
(northwest to Bubbling Well Road) in Sun's later years. [129]

But what was more relevant to everyday life was shopping for daily necessities at the stores near home. For most of Shanghai's families this was
not a once-a-week-or-so task, but a daily activity. The daily shopping of
Mrs. Chen Yuehua, wife of a trolleybus driver and mother of four children
(three daughters and a son), illustrates the importance of the neighborhood
stores and the little-food markets in the daily life of Shanghai's people.
From 1939, for more than half a century, the Chen family resided in
Zhengming Li (next to Jiahe Li, where Yu Dafu and Wang Yingxia lived in
the late twenties) on Hart Road. That part of Hart Road was an ordinary
lilong neighborhood with numerous small stores along the front rows of a
number of lilong compounds (Table 8). The following account, mainly provided by Chen and verified by a number of other informants, pieces together what we might call a "typical" daily shopping pattern for Shanghai
families over the span of a few decades.

Chen was usually the first person in her family to rise in the morning.
She might only have time to dress and brush her teeth before rushing to

an open-air food market across the street where she would buy fresh vegetables, fish, and meat. The market, which was on Annam (an outdated name for Vietnam Road, today's Anyi Road), a small street between Hart Road and Hardoon Road (today's Tongren Road), was only one or two minutes from her front door. The entire street, about 865 feet (264 meters) long and 65 feet (20 meters) wide, was closed to traffic in the morning, when the sidewalks were covered with stalls.[130] Although the market was open all day long (from 6:00 A.M. to 7:00 P.M.), vegetables were usually sold only in the morning. Many residents liked to go to the market early in the morning, when the food was freshest and the widest variety was available.[131] Wang Yingxia recalled that she usually shopped at the Annam Road Food Market, across the street from Jiahe Li. But Yu Dafu was, as she put it, a gourmand (*meishijia*) who liked "to have a different food with every meal." Yu thought the market across the street was not good enough, so Wang Yingxia often had to walk along Bubbling Well Road to the Ximo Road Food Market, where a larger variety of foods was available. The trip took about fifteen minutes.[132]

To return to Chen: Back home from the market (usually around 6:30 – 7:00 A.M.), Chen lit a fire in the coal stove. This was done in three steps. First, she lit a piece of newspaper or other wastepaper in the bottom compartment of the stove. Then she put wood chips on the fire. Finally, when all the wood chips were afire, she put coal briquettes on the chips. All day long, every hour or so, she added coal briquettes to keep the stove hot. This work might remind her that her supply of wood chips or coal briquettes was almost used up and that she needed to go to the coal store when it opened (at 7:30 A.M.).

Although most families did not go to the coal store every day, it was still a place Shanghai people frequently visited. Coal briquettes are bulky and demand storage space, and because of Shanghai's crowded living conditions most families could manage to store briquettes for only about a week's needs. To keep a coal stove lit for the entire day, say from 6 A.M. to 9 P.M., as most families did, required about 276 pounds (125 kilograms) of coal briquettes a month. As noted, to light a coal stove in the morning required wood chips; these could be bought only at the coal store. In the afternoon, most families did not need to keep the stove going at full strength but had to keep the fire alive to use the stove for preparing supper in the evening. They used coal dust paste (coal dust mixed with water) to seal the fire temporarily. Moist coal dust paste was placed on top of the stove so that the briquettes beneath would burn slowly. Once the paste was removed, the fire would rekindle. Some families also used this method to keep the fire alive overnight so they would not have to light the stove in the morning. Thus, coal dust was another item people needed from the coal store.

Coal stores were always close to any lilong neighborhood where a gas supply was not available. Nevertheless, coal briquettes are heavy and hard to bring home without some sort of carrier. The stores usually provided customers with bamboo shoulder poles and bamboo baskets to carry the coal home. In Shanghai's residential areas it was common to see men using a bamboo shoulder pole to carry two baskets of coal briquettes (each containing fifty-five pounds [twenty-five kilograms] of coal briquettes) from the store to home. This might be the only occasion in which city people ever needed a bamboo shoulder pole, which was (and still is) the most commonly used carrying tool in rural China. Some coal stores also provided a four-wheel, rent-free cart for their customers' convenience, but a coal store usually could not afford to have more than one cart, so bamboo shoulder poles were used quite often.[133] That this rural carrier never completely vanished in modern Shanghai is another indication of the persistence of tradition in this Westernized city.

After lighting the stove, Chen would next go to the sesame cake store to buy soybean milk, fried dough sticks, and other breakfast foods for her family. For most families in Shanghai, breakfast could be as simple as paofan (gruel made by reheating cooked rice, usually leftover from the previous supper, in boiling water). This was the most economical and, to many Shanghainese, the most convenient breakfast. After eating hot rice gruel, together with a few side dishes such as pickles, fermented beancurd, dried meat ("pork sung"), salted eggs, and thousand-year-old eggs (preserved eggs), one would feel fresh enough to go to work. A 1991 survey of Shanghai people's breakfast habits found that paofan was the favorite breakfast: 66 percent of the people surveyed said that paofan with pickles was their regular breakfast.[134]

But paofan is hardly a hearty meal and before noon one might feel hungry again. Thus foods such as sesame cakes, steamed bread, fried dough sticks, or soybean milk—all available at sesame cake stores—were often served as supplementary breakfast dishes and afternoon snacks. Needless to say, buying ready-to-eat foods from stores cost more than making paofan at home. Most families in Shanghai (not only those who lived in lilong houses) had paofan for breakfast and let employed or senior members of the family eat the food from the sesame cake store. For example, according to 76-year-old Wu Tianming, one of the reasons for his mother's longevity (she was 104 years old at the time of the interview) was that for decades he and his wife had only paofan for breakfast but managed to let grandma have *dianxin* (dim sum) from the sesame cake store.[135] This, obviously, is an example of traditional filial piety, but it also reveals the role of the sesame cake store in the daily life of the people of Shanghai. In fact, four standard foods from the sesame cake store—sesame cakes, fried dough sticks, glutinous rice cakes, and soybean milk—were popularly referred to as the "four Buddha's warrior attendants" (*si da Jin'gang*). Not only were these foods (plus paofan) the staple of Shanghainese breakfast; they also became an indispensable part of people's lives. An old Shanghailander who has lived in the United States for twenty years once sighed to a friend that these were the foods he missed most abroad. The friend, a historian, commented on the nostalgia: "In the mindset of this fellow, things like sesame cakes, fried dough sticks, and paofan were part of the notion of Shanghai."[136]

This is one of the ironies of the Western influence in China. Shanghai has been noted for its famous Western restaurants and, in particular, for its Russian-style baking tradition: the city has been "the focus for the diffusion of bread, cakes, pies, candy, and many other Western snacks through much of China during the last century."[137] However, this influence was largely limited to Nanking Road and Avenue Joffre (today's Huaihai Road), where most of the city's Western restaurants were located; it extended little into the daily life of the ordinary people of Shanghai. For the latter, paofan and pickles or food from the sesame cake store made up the breakfast on their dining table.

Chen used to cook twice a day (midday and evening) to give her family hot meals, which usually consisted of rice, three to four dishes, and soup. But for families without a person at home to cook during the day, noodles or won ton soup were common fare for lunch. Uncooked noodles, won ton, jiaozi skins (wrappers), and bread—all of which were sold in rice stores—had to be fresh, that is, made on the same day that they were sold. If kept overnight, they were not considered fit to eat. This meant that many residents needed to visit rice stores on a daily basis.

For daily cooking, an important store was the so-called soy sauce store (*jiangyou dian*) or pickle shop (*zaofang*).[138] These stores sold several varieties each of cooking oil, soy sauce, salt, vinegar, wine, spirits, fermented bean curd, pickles, and other items. Often, more than a dozen different types of pickles and fermented beancurd were available. Even cooking oil had some varieties: peanut oil, soybean oil, rapeseed oil, coconut oil, sesame oil, and lard. In the 1940s, an average soy sauce store was run by two to three persons; more than two thousand soy sauce stores "spread across the whole city like sesame seeds."[139] Chen visited the soy sauce store fre-

quently. Fermented beancurd, preserved vegetables, and pickles often accompanied the rather flat-tasting paofan breakfast, and cooking oil, salt,
and other seasonings were used daily by every family in Shanghai.

Shanghai families usually did not buy these necessities in large quanti-
ties; rather, they preferred to shop frequently to ensure freshness, assuming that food from the stores was always fresher than foods that had been
kept at home for days. Some cooking sauces, such as hot pepper sauce and
thick broad-bean sauce, were considered perishable. Whatever was not consumed within a day or so was discarded.[140] What made this practice convenient, or at least possible, was the close proximity of stores; one could easily pick up a fresh supply of condiments from the neighborhood store. In a
way, shopping frequently and buying fresh foods were luxuries enjoyed
particularly by the urban Chinese. China's rural population usually lived
some distance from major commercial centers or towns, and so were denied
this luxury, as are modern Westerners (whose major supply of "fresh"
food comes from the family refrigerator). According to Chen, it was often
the case that she sent her child to the soy sauce store to buy one cent's
worth of hot pepper sauce or two cents' worth of vinegar to add to the stir-
fry dish that she was cooking on the coal stove.

For those who were not away at work, early afternoon was a quiet and
relaxing time. Unlike the morning, when the object was to quickly purchase fresh food for the day's meals, the afternoon was a time for doing
things less pressing. One might go to the nearby commercial center to run
some errands or simply take a stroll. Chen often went to Jing'ansi on Bubbling Well Road, where she could get virtually anything that might not
have been available at a neighborhood store. Or, if her object was not shopping, she might walk into the Temple of Peace to burn a bundle of joss
sticks to secure the goodwill of Buddha, although she did not see herself as
a very religious person. For her, going to the temple was more a folkway
than anything else—in any case, it was merely a five-minute walk. Occasionally, on leisurely afternoons housewives got together to play mah-
jongg, but an industrious person found this was a good time for sewing and
mending or dressmaking. Fortune-tellers (who were mostly blind men)
knew this was the best time of day to solicit patrons. So they paced up and
down in the neighborhood, playing the *sanxian* (a three-stringed, plucked
instrument) to announce their presence.[141]

After dark most neighborhood stores were closed. Tobacco and paper
stores usually stayed open until 9 P.M. or later, especially in the summer, to
serve the needs of residents and passersby. For Chen, the tobacco and paper store was a place she might visit any time of the day: to buy matches to

light the stove in the morning, to get a needle for sewing in the afternoon, or to purchase a cake of soap for washing in the evening. The store was also a place her husband often visited because he was a habitual cigarette smoker. Tobacco and paper stores were also a favorite place for children; there, children often got their first toy and spent their pocket money. Indeed, children were regular and important customers for candy and treats, of which there were many types primarily for children, and which were available in tobacco and paper stores only. Candied fruits, such as Chinese olives, hawthorn, salted jujubes, and dried radish, were standard children's snacks in these stores. In a lilong neighborhood one could see children playing in an alleyway while nibbling candied fruits from a tobacco and paper store. Such a store might well have been where a child got his or her first experience with commerce (and learned the value of money).

At night in Shanghai's residential neighborhoods the lights burned bright in the hot water and sesame cake store "combination." Both stores kept the longest hours in the city. Hot water stores were usually busiest from late afternoon and into the evening, when hot water was needed for the whole family, especially in winter. Chen said that she usually prepared hot water on the coal stove for drinking (such as for tea), but for washing and bathing she often went to the tiger stove. The family's coal stove simply could not produce enough hot water at the time everyone in the family needed it. On any evening around twilight, people with thermos bottles and kettles in their arms would rush along the narrow alleyways between their homes and the store. Bringing bottles of hot water home from the tiger stove might be the last bit of shopping in a family's daily activities unless someone craved the Shanghai equivalent of a midnight snack and ran out for a bowl of won ton or noodle soup from the sesame cake store. When the lights of the sesame cake store and laohuzao were finally extinguished after midnight, it was the end of daily shopping in the neighborhood and the streets at last became quiet.[142]

The Politics of Intervention

Internally, family businesses that were operated from the home had little trouble with such management tasks as arranging shifts and allocating payments. Labor disputes were extremely rare. Externally, neighborhood stores were, in various ways and to various extents, subject to the intervention of guilds, the government, and local toughs. Outside intervention was, however, never strong enough to fundamentally shape the character of small business. Nonetheless, shopkeepers' responses to outside forces can provide insight into tradition-bound state-society interactions.

GUILDS

Two neighborhood-store guilds can trace their history back to the nineteenth century. The Shanghai Rice Guild was founded in 1867 as the Hall of Fine Grain (*Jiagu tang*), and it was registered in the Shanghai county yamen in the mid-1870s as an officially recognized guild for retail rice stores (*midian*). From the Qing to the Republican period, the nature of the guild changed little: it remained a loosely organized trade association providing a modicum of coordination among its members. From 1867 to the 1930s even the guild office itself remained in an old building on a narrow street inside the old Chinese city. The guild, or hall, began as a temple dedicated to the God of Agriculture (Shennong), as well as a place to honor deceased rice store owners. The funds for such activities were provided by well-off store proprietors. Later, monthly membership fees were charged to maintain the hall and a regular office. The guild's regulations called for "philanthropic acts" (*shanju*), including providing medical care, compensation for bereaved families, relief for poor members, and so on. But a dearth of funds ensured that the "benevolence" remained largely on paper.[143]

A guild of hot water stores known as the Hall of Retained Benevolence (Cun Ren Tang) was established in the Xianfeng period (1851–61) and registered with the county yamen in the Guangxu period (1875–1908), and it continued into the Republican period. This guild seems to have been effective. At the very beginning the Hall of Retained Benevolence appeared to be a sort of rule-making organization. The trade regulations it made included a definition of the business, rules on prices, standards of containers, monthly "contributions" (membership fees), and most important, a rule on opening new stores. According to the last, no new store would be allowed to open within a distance of forty-eight *zhang* (seventeen yards) of an existing one.[144] Initiated in the late Qing, these trade regulations remained unchanged in the early Republican period. In 1919, 202 members of the guild met to issue "new" regulations whose fourteen clauses were in fact basically a restatement of the older, perhaps unwritten, guild rules (*hanggui*). According to the 1919 rules, licenses (*hangdan*) were to be issued by, and valid only with, the signature and stamp of the guild head, whose status was acknowledged by the Shanghai county authorities, since the guild was an officially registered organization.[145]

Many types of stores had no guild at all until the Republican period.

Tobacco and paper stores did not establish a guild until June 1925; the guild was reorganized in May of 1930.[146] Sesame cake stores had a short-lived guild known as the Association of Steamed Breads, Sesame Cakes, and Dough Sticks, founded in 1936.[147] In some trades, wholesalers that sold the small neighborhood stores their goods had a guild, but such guilds did not include retail stores. For instance, *jiangyuan*, shops that made and sold seasonings, had a guild that began in 1895. But retail stores—soy sauce stores—were not members of the guild.[148]

The jiangyuan guild did not deny membership to retail stores; it simply could not attract them. In 1920, the guild could claim only forty-eight stores among its members, which represented less than a third of Shanghai's jiangyuan.[149] Indifference toward guilds was common. The Shanghai Rice Guild was one of the few well-established guilds among small stores, but it could not claim even half of the city's rice stores as members during the second decade of the twentieth century. By 1928, more than 30 percent of Shanghai's rice stores still had not joined the guild.[150] In 1936, when the guild of sesame cake stores was founded, most people in the business clearly indicated that they would not join it.[151]

Small store owners tended to like being left alone and doing business without interference from outsiders. Mao Zedong in 1926 described the so-called petty bourgeoisie, of which small traders were the main component: "People of this sort are timid, afraid of government officials."[152] While, as we shall see, government had little impact on these businesses, many shop-keepers saw guilds as being much like officials (*guan*) who sought to check up on them. For instance, in the hot water trade, the guild's right to issue licenses and impose a limitation on opening new stores gave it a para-official status in regulating the trade. Another important function (if not a right) of this guild, as well as of guilds in other trades, was to set retail prices, which naturally was of vital concern to store owners.[153] The reason that the majority of those in the sesame cake business refused to join the guild was that they believed that the purpose of the newly established guild was to raise prices, and in this they did not concur.[154] While having a guild to moderate competition and to protect trade might have been welcomed by storekeepers, many felt guilds were manipulators more than protectors.[155] A coal store owner who never joined a guild said he believed that guilds were for larger businesses, and since his store (*dian*) was "little more than a stall (*tan*)," he could do business well enough without the help of any group. As he put it, in running his business he preferred that "everybody shovel snow in front of his own door and not bother to look after the frost on the roofs of others."[156]

GOVERNMENT

William Kirby has suggested that the twentieth century saw increasing governmental intervention in private economic activities.[157] Recent research by Christian Henriot also shows that in the Nanjing decade (1927–37) the state's effort to regulate various sectors of society was more effective than has usually been thought.[158] While governmental intervention in small neighborhood stores was not entirely absent, such intervention was, on balance, of little importance. The small neighborhood stores of Shanghai occupied the lowest level of commerce in the city, with only street peddlers below them. From this sprang the primary reason for the weakness of governmental intervention. As the coal store owner indicated, many neighborhood stores were little more than stalls. Both Chinese and foreign authorities had many more pressing things to deal with than regulating these obscure businesses. While regulating bigger businesses (which was the object of William Kirby's research on company law) was an important matter for the national economy, and, as Frederick Wakeman and Gail Hershatter reveal, "licensing leisure" (including prostitution) was an important aspect of controlling social vice, small stores possessed no particular importance in the eyes of government.[159]

In addition, even if authorities had the will to penetrate society it was difficult for political power to reach into the lower levels of urban commerce in the circumstance of a city divided among different administrations and without a highly developed and unified legal system. The city government even had difficulty levying regular business taxes on shopkeepers. It sometimes (e.g., in 1932) could collect no more than one-sixth of the anticipated tax from shopkeepers.[160] Since refusal to pay tax was widespread, even among larger stores on Nanking Road, more often than not small neighborhood stores were simply beyond the reach of taxation. In many cases the authorities did not even know of the stores' existence. As the owner of one sesame cake store put it, "You have a room that faces onto the street, you manage to get some goods, then you open a store. Period."[161]

The limitations on government intervention can perhaps be best appreciated by looking at what were arguably the most important small neighborhood stores, the rice stores. In the Chinese saying "The masses see food as Heaven" (*min yi shi wei Tian*), the word "food" (*shi*) mainly refers to food grains or, more specifically in Shanghai, to rice.[162] The vital importance of rice should have made the stores vulnerable to government intervention. However, the government usually did no more than set up a committee to try to regulate prices in times of rampant speculation. Even emergency measures of this kind were often no more than hollow rules on paper; to implement its wishes the government was usually "forced to depend on the merchants' goodwill and low-key intervention by the foreign authorities."[163]

The impotence of governmental intervention in the rice business led to the notation in an official document in 1942 that the Chinese government had long pursued a laissez-faire policy in the food grains market.[164] During Shanghai's so-called solitary island period (1938–41), when rice was in severe shortage and speculation was savage, major efforts to ease the crisis were made not by officialdom but by the Shanghai Coordination Council of People's Food, a merchant organization sponsored by Yu Qiaqing and other bigwigs.[165] Small rice stores had not been seriously affected by the wartime situation until after the outbreak of the Pacific War, when the Japanese occupied the whole city. Rationing of rice imposed by the Japanese led to an order in January 1942 to reduce the number of retail rice stores through merger. In the International Settlement, rice store numbers were cut from 700-odd to 250, and in the French Concession to 150, and only officially designated stores could sell rice at par price.[166] This was the only substantial government intervention in rice stores during the Republican era. But it was imposed by an occupation force in wartime.

The Guomindang government, however, did try to put guilds under some sort of control. The most obvious efforts in this direction were made early in the Nanjing decade. An Industrial and Commercial Trade Associations Act was issued by the Guomindang government on August 17, 1929. The next year, seventeen regulations on how to implement the act were issued by the Ministry of Industry and Commerce. Accordingly, the city government of Shanghai issued regulations on the city's trade associations in June 1930. The act and regulations aimed at unifying names for trades and guilds and regularizing application and registration procedures. All existing guilds (*gongsuo*) were required to be registered as trade associations (*tongye gonghui*), and new guilds were not to be established without prior official approval.[167] These regulations applied to all trades and stimulated the emergence of a number of new trade associations among small businesses such as tobacco and paper stores, sesame cake stores, hardware stores, and general stores (*baihuo dian*).[168]

The purpose of regulating guilds was to promote a more systematic organizational network to mediate trade issues, rather than to promote direct governmental involvement in trade. Such an approach to regulation was a long-established tradition. As Bergère points out, the Chinese state often felt a need to lean on social intermediaries to put its plans into operation, and "when these intermediary partners did not exist, the State created them."[169] In this regard, the guild was an ideal and ready-made intermediary for the state. But leaning on guilds or their like reveals the lack of an alternative course for state penetration. The ineffectiveness of the state in collecting tax in the 1930s, for example, arose from the dependence of the government on the General Chamber of Commerce via its affiliated guilds to levy tax. But only half the shops were affiliated with a guild. When shopkeepers refused to fill in tax return forms, the state simply lacked the means to impose its will.[170]

In the hot water business, disputes over the right to open a new store outside the forty-eight-zhang area without permission from the guild led to the issuing of licenses by the Shanghai Bureau of Social Affairs beginning in 1928. During 1928–30 about a third of the applications for opening a tiger stove were rejected by the bureau for the reason that these applicants did not have facilities that met safety requirements.[171] But many tiger stove shops merely ignored the rules and operated without a license.[172] In the concession areas, in spite of the apparent importance of hot water service to people's daily life and health, these shops largely escaped the attention of the authorities. As one writer complained, "The authorities have paid much attention to the hygiene of restaurants and the like, but in sharp contrast, there has not been a single effort to regulate the filthy tiger stove shops—this can be counted as an oddity in the concessions!"[173]

Unconcern with governmental regulations was also common among tobacco and paper stores. For instance, in contravention of the official exchange rate between old silver dollars (*yinyuan*) and newly issued legal currency (*fabi*), which was issued after the 1935 currency reform, tobacco and paper stores, acting on their own, deducted 1 percent from the official exchange rate and pocketed the difference.[174]

In theory, tiger stoves were not allowed to conduct businesses other than selling hot water. In reality, there were the three additional businesses commonly associated with these stores. Government regulations issued in 1947 gave official sanction to hot water stores to also operate as teahouses. But this was a case of the government accommodating itself to a fait accompli, for hot water stores had also been acting as teahouses for decades. Nowhere in the regulations was there mention of the public bath service, which, as we have seen, was just as common as the teahouse service.[175]

The third service often provided by hot water stores—so-called night tea (*ye cha*)—was actually the provision of lodging, similar to the custom in "proletarian" restaurants mentioned earlier, but in the case of hot water stores was a formal part of the business. Late at night, after the sale of hot water had ended for the day, another tea service, which lasted until 6 A.M., began. The real purpose of customers who availed themselves of this service was not to have a hot drink but a place to stay overnight. The fee for this service was very low: 2 copper coins in 1916, and two decades later, 10– 12 copper coins. One witness observed, "When a customer steps into the room, admission must be paid in cash without exception. Then, a pot of hot tea will be served. You can sit there reading a newspaper, nodding, chatting, or you can spread a newspaper on the floor and sleep on it—no one will interfere with you as long as you leave by six o'clock in the morning!"[176] No lodging facilities other than a chamber pot were provided by the shop. Yet, "night tea" was popular among those who could not afford better overnight shelter in this "golden land" of Shanghai.[177]

LOCAL TOUGHS

While small businesses could often ignore hollow government rules, it was not always easy for them to deal with intervention from another quarter: disturbances such as theft, extortion, and vandalism perpetrated by local toughs. Harassment from this quarter was often trivial and occasional but nonetheless could be irritating, since troublemakers were on the spot and not easily ignored. Liu Xiangyu, the tobacco and paper store owner mentioned above, once made himself a disciple's disciple (*tusun*) of Wu Shibao, one of the major gang bosses in Republican Shanghai. For this Liu was labeled a "bad element" and punished during the Cultural Revolution. But, according to Liu, establishing this relationship was simply his way of protecting his business from harassment.[178]

Liu's explanation can be verified by a 1936 report that many tobacco and paper stores in Shanghai were bullied into selling groceries smuggled from Japan during a time when there was nationwide sentiment to boycott Japanese goods. "Tobacco and paper storekeepers are senseless people and all timid as mice," a reporter said with scorn. "Being intimidated by bully-boys by beatings and other kinds of harassment, none of them would dare to say 'no' and they all ended up accepting these goods."[179] Hot water stores, especially those that engaged in the "night tea" business, were especially vulnerable to such harassment. Many of these stores were run by people who had some sort of underground background.[180]

Shanghai's gangs and their bosses, as Brian Martin reveals, had a complicated relationship with both the Guomindang and foreign authorities.[181] The harassment that small stores encountered did not emanate from the gang bosses such as Huang Jinrong or Du Yuesheng but from lower-level local hoodlums whose low social status matched that of the people who ran these businesses. This was why Liu could only be a "disciple's disciple" of Wu Shibao and not Wu's disciple. Bigger gangsters were not interested in picking up a few crumbs from these stores. A storekeeper recalled that she used to pay a quarterly "cleaning" fee to a petty gangster neighbor who helped clean the alleyway. She said she did not really need such a "service" but neither did she mind paying a little money to keep her store free from disturbance.[182]

A similar motive can be seen in the operation of the so-called beggar tax (*qigaishui*). Beggars in Shanghai always had a clear idea of where they could beg and would not infringe on the "territory" of others. Many beggars had an income from stores that paid them on a regular basis. Twice a year (in spring and fall) beggars went to stores to collect the "beggar tax." Once the "tax" had been collected, the beggars would give the store a "receipt" consisting of two pieces of colored paper that the store owner would post in a conspicuous place in the store. One was a diamond-shaped, green, glazed piece of paper with the big character KAN ("look" or "attention") on it. The other was a red, rectangular, glazed paper with a notice reading, "All beggars and tramps: No begging!" Stores that posted these "receipts" were exempt from further begging and soliciting. The "beggar tax" varied from a few dollars to $20, depending on the size of the store. Most store owners felt it was worth paying a few dollars twice a year to avoid repeated encounters with beggars. Some even paid as much as $80 a year to the beggars in exchange for their services as night watchmen.[183] That shopkeepers had to rely on their own wits rather than on the legal or administrative system (e.g., the police) to maintain a minimal level of social order necessary for conducting business once again reveals the weakness of governmental intervention in neighborhood life.

Conclusion

In modern Shanghai, urbanization, modernization, and Westernization were inextricably linked. Since Shanghai was populated mostly by rural immigrants, its rapid rise early in the twentieth century from a county town to one of the world's great metropolises inevitably involved a vigorous urbanization of its people. As China's foremost cradle of new ideas and innovations, the city itself was a product of modernity. And finally, because it was a leading treaty port with countless ties to the West, urbanization and modernity in Shanghai always involved a certain degree of Westernization.

Yet in looking at the everyday life of the people of Shanghai, one repeatedly encounters the past, the persistence of tradition, and reminders of things indigenous. While the influence of the West could be found virtually everywhere in the city, in some quotidian aspects of life the West seemed to be absent. When the Communists came to power, they paid special attention to Shanghai: the city lay at the intersection of the past and the West; both were to be swept away by the revolution. But thirty years of Communist "ground cleaning" did not completely uproot tradition. Rather, decades after the supposed break with the old world the past endures with remarkable tenacity.

While these broader categories—urbanization, modernization, and Westernization—are intricately linked, one certainly should be cautious not to equate them. It is now an accepted fact that the vigorous commercialization (and hence some degree of urbanization) in late imperial China demonstrates that social transformation in modern China had its own, indigenous, roots and was far from being a matter of foreign influence. One may also add that for any nation the criteria of modernization are relative: they have their historical context and do not always need a foreign reference. To emphasize the perdurability of Chinese tradition, therefore, is to correct some thinking in the field that tends to overemphasize the "modern" and "Western" aspects of the treaty-port cities in general and Shanghai in particular. But this should not be interpreted as a call to emphasize the other side of the somewhat hackneyed dichotomy of "tradition" versus "modernity" or "Chinese" versus "Western."

Quite the opposite, our stories of daily life in Shanghai suggest how sophisticated were the common people of China in adaptation and integration. As we have seen, the basic setting for the daily life of most people of Shanghai, that is, the lilong house, was itself a half-breed, incorporating both Western and Chinese architectural features. Or, to take another example, the Zhongshan suit, which could serve as a standard man's suit for all occasions, was itself an amalgam of the Chinese long gown and the Western suit. Shanghai's food markets were yet another instance in which a Western initiative was adapted and imbued with Chinese characteristics. Such cases, described by a Chinese idiom as "a jade combining Chinese and Western parts" (*ZhongXi hebi*), are too numerous to list: they are ubiquitous in Chinese life.

For years, the Communists in China declared that feudalism (a synonym for tradition in Maoist terminology) and imperialism (a synonym for the West) were the chief targets of the revolution.[1] Ordinary people, while their lives were greatly affected by the revolution that was essentially made of this ideology, saw the ideology itself as largely an empty cannon.[2] Is our approach to the history of modern China, at least sometimes and to some extent, an inherited empty cannon? If we go farther down this line of thinking, we may find that even notions such as "compromise" and "integration" have the lingering weakness of tending to observe the world in a binary fashion. Was this also the way that the people who lived in Chinese society saw their own lives and lifestyles? Or, is it more our habitual practice in academia?

For ordinary people, the dominant way of thinking was pragmatism, a pragmatism of incorporating whatever was appealing and available to make life better (or in some cases to make life possible). This does not imply that people had a narrow outlook, lacked imagination, or were absolutely unconcerned about ideology. Rather, it suggests that the ways that common people coped with the epic changes in modern China were much more sensible, multifarious, and substantive than generally thought. People of all walks of life in China cite a folk adage to justify their pragmatism: "It is all too natural that man goes to a higher [better] place, just like water flows to a lower place."[3] In the first half of the twentieth century, when thousands upon thousands of people moved to Shanghai, they were going to a "higher" place, and they did so in part to survive in an age full of uncertainties and calamities. The story of daily life in Shanghai is as a tale of how the little people, in their own creative ways, lived through the gigantic changes in modern China.

In this process, ideology was often too luxurious for, if not irrelevant to, daily life. People stuck to some old ways of living not because of any serious concerns about keeping "tradition," and even less for the sake of patriotism, but because they felt comfortable with old ways or because it was economically beneficial to do so. And, whenever prudent or necessary, they would not hesitate to shun the old and take up the new—or more commonly, people happily adopted or absorbed whatever they felt was good for them in order to create multifaceted lifestyles, which cannot easily be framed by any dichotomy. The writer and artist Feng Zikai (1898–1975) once observed with admiration what he believed to be a Chinese peasants' invention: using Chinese chopsticks to eat European food. This had the merit of letting one enjoy exotic cuisine without the trouble of wielding the knife and fork that many Chinese felt clumsy using; at the same time, European-style meals avoided the Chinese way of sharing dishes directly with each other, a custom Feng (and many other Chinese as well) regarded as "unhealthy."[4] There may have been an economic reason too: Western-style tableware was often much more costly than chopsticks and usually not readily available, so why not employ something more comfortable, handy, and less expensive? Examples such as this may be trivial but they are certainly not insignificant, for "trifling matters" in daily life often reveal certain plain truths that more sophisticated or abstruse theories fail to convey.

The Past

Just as the city's innumerable alleyway houses were overshadowed by its skyscrapers, so too the lives of ordinary people were often obscured by the dazzling light cast by the city's elite. But it was Shanghai's multitudinous yet obscure "little urbanites" who wove the most colorful part of the warp and weft of the city. In the early twentieth century, changes in life in Shanghai were obvious and predictable—in the final analysis, the rise of Shanghai from a relatively obscure county seat to the nation's first city was itself a powerful manifestation of change. But Shanghai's image as modern China's showcase of Westernization often overshadowed the persistence of the past in the daily life of the "little people." While things Western were literally a daily part of life (although they were not necessarily exploited by every person every day), the people of Shanghai comfortably kept and adapted many old customs and lifestyles. Though the influence of the West was readily apparent on the city's major thoroughfares and played up by the Chinese upper classes, in the narrow alleys that crisscrossed the city tradition prevailed. Moreover, changes often had to coexist, integrate, or intertwine with continuities. If Shanghai was a place where two cultures— Chinese and Western—met but neither prevailed, it was not because the two were deadlocked but because both showed remarkable resilience. It was precisely in this conjunction that, for many, lay the charm of the city.

To conclude this point, I choose not to elaborate on a purely conceptual discussion that might easily slip into abstraction or even emptiness. Rather, my disposition is to let the empirical evidence unbosom itself, so to speak. I will examine, among other things, two seemingly contradictory phenomena of life in the city: namely, how traditional festivals were popularly celebrated at a time when the Western calendar had been officially adopted as the national calendar, and how some "outmoded" conveyances such as the sedan chair and wheelbarrow continued to ply the streets at a time when Shanghai had already become a motorized city. Again, the vitality of tradition in Chinese life should be seen as an indicator of the elastic or even buoyant nature of the people in their way of coping with a rapidly changing world.

FESTIVALS AND THE LUNAR CALENDAR

After the 1911 revolution that brought an end to more than two millennia of imperial rule, the new republican government abolished the traditional Chinese calendar and adopted the Western Gregorian calendar as China's national calendar (*guoli*).[5] To show a break with the past in this regard, for a few years immediately after the revolution the traditional calendar was called the "abolished calendar" (*feili*). Gradually, however, the term disappeared; instead, the Chinese calendar came to be referred to as the "old calendar" (*jiuli*), the "agricultural calendar" (*nongli*), the "lunar calendar" (*yinli*), or the "Xia calendar" (Xiali, referring to the then still legendary first dynasty in Chinese history). The changes in name had their reasons. As Richard J. Smith has indicated, "Neither the feeble government in Beijing, nor local provincial officials, could eradicate centuries-old traditions by decree."[6] The Chinese calendar was in fact not abolished after the revolution but remained in use in various aspects of life. For instance, in the countryside the twenty-four solar periods on the Chinese calendar continued to be the most relevant benchmarks for events during the year. In the cities too the old calendar far from disappeared.

In Shanghai, popular beliefs such as the idea that a thunderstorm prior to Jingzhe (the Waking of Hibernation, third solar period) foretells a bad year, eating many watermelons after Liqiu (the Beginning of Autumn, thirteenth solar period) may cause typhoid, tonics are most efficacious if taken after Dongzhi (the Winter Solstice, twenty-second solar period), and so on remained powerful in the twentieth century. By the same token, the three most important festivals in Chinese life—the New Year (known also as Chunjie, or the Spring Festival), the Dragon Boat Festival (Duanwu or Duanyang), and the Full Moon Festival (Zhongqiu, or "middle autumn")— remained the most important days on the Chinese calendar.[7] Customs related to these three festivals, such as paying off debts before New Year's Eve and using the three festivals as occasions for laying off or hiring new workers, especially in the retail trade, remained unchanged.[8] Also unchanged was the way people reckoned their age. Virtually all the people I interviewed in Shanghai counted their age and celebrated their birthday according to the Chinese calendar, although their birthday in official documents, such as the household registration book (hukoubu), was reckoned by the Western calendar.[9]

The clearest example of how the old calendar continued as an indispensable part of Chinese life was the fact that New Year's Day, the foremost event of the year in the Chinese tradition, continued to be celebrated according to the Chinese calendar, not the "national calendar." Immediately after the 1911 revolution, Shanghai's Chinese authorities ordered, as part of their effort to popularize the Western calendar, the forthcoming New Year's celebrations to be held on the first day of the new year according to the Western calendar, that is, on January 1, 1912 (Chinese New Year fell on February 18 that year). But the day passed without any spontaneous celebration. To make up for this disappointment, the authorities mobilized merchant organizations and the army to celebrate the "lantern festival" (which is traditionally the last event of the New Year's celebrations) on January 15, instead of on the fifteenth day of the first month of the lunar year. That night, the city was lit up with lanterns, and crowds of some size were drawn. But this officially sponsored event did not seem to appeal to the public. Those who were out on the streets that night lacked enthusiasm and spirit. The crowds were, it was observed, drawn not by a mood of celebration but by curiosity: people came out to watch the soldiers rather than the lanterns.[10]

After 1912, the authorities surrendered and the New Year was again celebrated on the first day of the lunar year. Indeed, during the entire Republican era the New Year season was celebrated in much the same way as it had been celebrated for centuries: as in the past, "sending the Kitchen God" (*song zaoshen*) was on the twenty-third day of the twelfth month of the lunar calendar, "ancestor worship" (*jizu*) on New Year's Eve (an event that lasted until the dawn of New Year's Day), "(Buddhist and Daoist) deity worship" (*jishen*) on New Year's Day, "receiving the God of Wealth" (*jie caishen*) on the fifth day of the first month, and the "lantern festival" (*yuanxiao*) on the fifteenth day of the first month. All of these events, which were part of a national tradition, were universally celebrated in Shanghai. Even during the Sino-Japanese War, when Shanghai was encircled with battlefields, the old New Year's celebrations and ceremonies were still undertaken in the city, following the traditional pattern in all its meticulous detail.[11]

Many minor festivals and special occasions on the Chinese calendar also continued to be part of life in the city. Except for the eleventh month, every month in the lunar calendar had some festival days, most of which were based on religious and folk beliefs and, in particular, on legendary birthdays of Buddhist and Daoist deities.[12] The absence of festivals in the eleventh month was probably for the purpose of reserving energy for the busiest holiday season of the year, that is, New Year's. These minor festivals were by no means taken lightly. On these occasions, even foreigners, and not necessarily the most perspicacious ones, "could see through the front windows of Chinese homes the front-room joss pieces, statues of the major gods or incense-burners arranged on little tables covered with embroidered cloths and set with lighted candles and dishes of sacrificial food."[13]

Sometimes activities on these occasions extended into public spaces. For instance, the thirtieth day of the seventh month was traditionally celebrated as the birthday of the God of Earth (*Dizangwang pusa*). During that night, joss sticks and candles were placed on sidewalks and on alleyways to honor the earth. Often candles and joss sticks were wedged between curbstones and in the crevices surrounding manhole covers. The flickering light from the joss sticks and candles added charm to the powerful illumination of neon shop signs and electric road lamps. The scene was an unwitting but striking microcosm of the coexistence of tradition and modernity.[14] In fact, the survival of a minor festival like this demonstrates more powerfully than the New Year's celebration the tenacity of the past. Given the importance of New Year's Day to a calendar (any calendar) and the particular prominence of New Year's celebrations in Chinese culture, it is perfectly understandable why people wanted to continue celebrating it at the time and in the manner to which they had become accustomed. But the connection to the past was certainly deeper than that.

The Midyear Festival (Zhongyuanjie, the fifteenth day of the seventh month) further illustrates the point. The holiday was also known as the "ghost festival" or the "birthday of ghosts," because it was said that hungry ghosts appear in the seventh month of the lunar year, ghosts that should be respected in some measure in order to ensure peace and prosperity in the world. This ancient festival—although unequal in importance to New Year's Day, the Qingming Festival, the Dragon Boat Festival, and the Full Moon Festival—continued to be popular and was taken seriously. Because the activities surrounding the festival lasted for a couple of weeks and involved people of all walks of life, the arrival of autumn in Shanghai was, in the words of a resident, "accompanied by an increasingly ghostly bustle in the city. No matter where one goes one feels a ghostly atmosphere." On street corners and at alleyway entrances, everywhere one turned were posters that read "The King of Ghosts," "Make a Fortune Wherever You Look," or "Peace on Earth." These posters were hung together with various articles of clothing, shoe-shaped gold or silver ingots, and various types of furniture and household items all made of colorful paper. Early in the evening, on stages circled with colored lanterns and ribbons set up at the entrances of lilong compounds, Buddhist monks and Daoist priests chanted scriptures, sang songs, struck percussion instruments, and otherwise made all sorts of peculiar sounds. The purpose of all this activity, known as "Public Worship for Great Peace" (*taiping gongjiao*) or "Yulanpen," was to expiate hungry ghosts so that their souls could be released from purgatory or hell and peace could reign on earth.[15] There was much bustle and excitement associated with these performances and, as is generally true of festivals, plenty of commercial activity. In describing the Midyear Festival of 1933, one writer jeered:

> Among the crowd in threes and fours there is the "Shopkeeper of the Tobacco and Paper Store," the "Owner of the Hot Water Service," "Old Number Four of the Mah-Jongg Shop," "Little Number Three of the Sesame Cake Stall," and others. These people purchase yellow paper from which they make booklets to solicit signatures and donations from household to household. Having solicited one or two hundred dollars, they now can play a massive game between man and ghost.

Thanks to the king of the ghosts, these solicitors can get some extra income from the donations—what is called in Shanghai "taking advantage of ghosts"!

The "Great Gathering of Lanpen" and the "Public Worship for Great Peace" are popular not only among the lower classes but also among well-off families, store owners, and old-type gentry who are all scared of being haunted by hungry ghosts. In order to prevent themselves from being the last offspring of their family lines, they are willing to spend hundreds of dollars in the Zhongyuan Festival to hire Buddhist monks and Daoist priests to hold a large-scale ceremony, although in ordinary times these people are stingy about giving a penny to poor people.

So, in autumn, Shanghai is full of a ghostly atmosphere and one can observe people worshiping and praising ghosts in every street![16]

In contrast to this rather fervid mass undertaking during this relatively minor Chinese festival, only two major holidays on the national calendar ever caught the fancy of the public: Christmas and New Year's Day. Neither, however, was celebrated with any real enthusiasm. Once the Western calendar had been officially adopted, January 1 became the major holiday of officialdom. The city government took three days off on New Year's. It became a matter of social etiquette for officials as a group to make New Year's calls (*tuanbai*) during the holiday.[17] However, tuanbai were carried out rather perfunctorily, as a mere matter of form rather than real celebration. What is more, the public remained generally indifferent to the Western New Year, partly perhaps to reserve their energy and money for the Chinese New Year (which usually arrived a little more than a month later).

The public was still less enthusiastic about Christmas. Most people considered Christmas as a holiday for foreigners, Chinese Christians, and Western-oriented Chinese families. The last category consisted mainly of the so-called high-class Chinese (*gaodeng Huaren*). In many parts of the city but particularly in the concessions, department stores displayed Christmas trees, stockings, and lights, Christmas choirs sang in the churches, and Santa Claus was a familiar sight to pedestrians—all seemingly confirmed that the city was an authentic Westernized enclave. But a common name in Shanghai for Christmas reveals what might be called the Shanghainese "power of adaptation," as well as the public's image of this Western holiday as something alien: Christmas was known as the "Foreign Winter Solstice," referring to the twenty-second solar period in the Chinese calendar, Dongzhi (Winter Solstice), which usually falls on December 22.[18]

SEDAN CHAIRS AND WHEELBARROWS

As in other Chinese cities, sedan chairs were the main conveyance in Shanghai before the middle of the nineteenth century. The sedan chair could easily negotiate the narrow and winding streets and alleyways of the walled city. A foreign visitor described the walled city in 1897: "The streets, with houses built of slate-colored, soft-looking brick, are only about eight feet wide, are paved with stone slabs, and are narrowed by innumerable stands. Even a wheelbarrow—the only conveyance possible— can hardly make its way in many places. True, a mandarin sweeps by in his gilded chair, carried at a run, with his imposing retinue, but his lictors clear the way by means not available to the general public."[19]

A very similar scene was recorded, in intimate detail, by a Chinese resident early in the twentieth century:

> Most streets of [the old city of] Shanghai were very narrow. For example, Sanpailou [lit., the Third Decorated Archway] Road was known as the main thoroughfare of the city, but one can imagine the narrowness of this street by merely observing that residents on either side of the road could rest their bamboo poles [for drying clothes] on the eaves of the houses across the street. A permanent feature of the street was that a variety of things, from women's pants, baby diapers, to footbinding strips, were hung on these bamboo poles and waved over the street. Even worse, some lazy women hung wet clothes without ringing them out first, so water dripped on the street as if it were raining. Often, a pedestrian was "lucky" enough to be wet by the "finest cream" [the water] and scolded [the owner], and the owner scolded back, and then an endless quarrel ensued. At this moment, if the sound of gongs was heard, which announced that the local magistrate was on his way, immediately yamen runners would rush ahead to clear the street, yelling, "Take down your wash!"—in such haste as if they were on fire. People then rushed to take the bamboo poles home, picking up the clothes that dropped to the ground in a great hustle. Those who did not do it quick enough were censured in public, and thus ended the farce.[20]

Not only officials, but well-off families, too, often had a private sedan chair and carriers. A successful physician, for example, often retained three carriers for his private sedan chair. When making a house call, as Chinese doctors often did, two carriers bore the chair, while the third cleared the way or at night held a lantern to light the way ahead and, if need be, to spell the other carriers.[21]

Although most people did not own a sedan chair, and still fewer enjoyed the privilege of having lictors clear a path for them, nonetheless for centuries sedan chairs were available for rent by the public. There were a number of sedan chair stations (*jiaohang*) in the walled city where one could hire the conveyances. This service continued after Shanghai had become a treaty port. In fact, because of the commercial boom brought by the opening of the city to the West, sedan chairs were in big demand and public sedan chairs had to be registered (so they could be taxed). By the Tongzhi period (1862–74), sedan chairs were widely used in the foreign settlements. The SMC taxed each sedan chair for hire 2 silver dollars (the cost of about seventy pounds of rice) per quarter.[22] Sedan chairs with special decorations for events such as weddings and funerals were also available for rent, usually not at a sedan chair station but at the shops that specialized in "red" (wedding) and "white" (funeral) events (Figs. 34 and 35).

After the introduction of rickshaws late in the nineteenth century and trams and taxies early in the twentieth century, the use of sedan chairs quickly declined. In 1905, when rickshaws and other vehicles were already plentiful, there were still 733 sedan chairs registered in the International Settlement. By 1911, their number had dropped to 199. But the custom of using a sedan chair for weddings survived even after Shanghai became a motorized city. Even during the 1930s, many families considered it virtually essential that a bride be carried to the wedding in a sedan chair (Fig. 34). The Shanghai expression "riding a flowered sedan chair" (*cheng huajiao*) remained a synonym for (a woman) getting married. It cost 20 silver dollars to rent a sedan chair for a wedding, which was about equivalent to an average worker's monthly income at that time; taking a taxi to a wedding would have cost only 4 or 5 dollars.[23]

Another old conveyance that persisted into the modern age was the wheelbarrow. Sedan chairs were for carrying passengers only and were rather elegant, but wheelbarrows were all-purpose vehicles and purely utilitarian. The wheelbarrow was in many ways especially suitable for the city, and it continued to have a role even after the introduction of the automobile. Before the middle of the nineteenth century, transportation of goods in Shanghai was mostly by boat. A mid-nineteenth-century manuscript map of Shanghai shows a spider web of waterways that covered the landscape.[24] In contrast, there were only five roads in the walled city in the early sixteenth century, more than two centuries after it had become a county seat.[25] In 1814 the Shanghai local gazetteer recorded a total of sixty-six streets in the city, most of which were narrow alleyways no more than six and a half feet (two meters) wide.[26] These roads obviously served only as a path for residents, not for vehicular traffic. However, in the late nineteenth century, when the volume of trade in the city had increased dramatically,

Fig. 34.   Traditional bride's sedan chairs were still common in Shanghai prior to 1949. Here eight men dressed in shirts with the "double happiness" character, a symbol for marriage, carry a fully adorned bride's sedan chair through a street in the International Settlement. From R. Barz, *Shanghai: Sketches of Present-Day Shanghai.*

even the narrow alleyways were needed to supplement waterborne transportation. Thus, for about half a century after the 1860s, wheelbarrows came to be widely used.

The wheelbarrow had several virtues. Like the sedan chair, it could easily negotiate the narrow, winding streets and alleyways inside the walled city. In the foreign settlements where streets were broader, small and nimble vehicles like wheelbarrows seemed to make headway no matter how heavy the traffic. The wheelbarrow needed but one person to operate it, yet could safely carry as much as six hundred pounds of goods. In a regulation issued by the SMC in 1887, wheelbarrows were in fact limited to a load of six hundred pounds, but in reality the limit was often exceeded. Furthermore, although wheelbarrows were primarily used to carry goods, they could also carry passengers, and in fact the latter function survived the former. By the 1930s, when wheelbarrows for transporting goods had been largely replaced by other sorts of vehicles, they were still commonly in use to carry passengers.

Thus, well into the Republican era the wheelbarrow remained a familiar sight on Shanghai's streets. Its popularity as a passenger vehicle even in-

Fig. 35. While Western-style weddings sometimes caught the imagination of Shanghainese, funeral ceremonies in the city remained almost exclusively Chinese. This funeral procession of a wealthy man, featuring a huge dragon ornament and mourners clothed in traditional linen, passes through a street in the French Concession dotted with Western-style restaurants and a Christian church—an indication of the city's mixed lifestyle. From R. Barz, *Shanghai: Sketches of Present-Day Shanghai.*

creased after it was used in the concessions. In the old Chinese city, wheelbarrows were regarded as a conveyance of the working people (*yonggong*). But in the concessions wheelbarrows gradually became a popular form of public transportation. Passengers included those of the educated classes and merchants (*shishang*), reflecting a pragmatic attitude toward this convenient means of transportation.[27] A wheelbarrow could carry as many as eight passengers (Fig. 36). Often, the passengers, sitting on either side of the vehicle, enjoyed chatting with each other or with the wheelbarrow pusher. It seems that the wheelbarrow provided a rare opportunity for passengers of the opposite sex to sit together in some intimacy, an altogether unusual situation in a society that still more or less emphasized the ritual separation of men and women. It was therefore reported that "offenses against decency" occurred on these rides, and some wheelbarrows, by order of the authorities, were reduced in size to allow only one passenger to sit on each side.[28]

But wheelbarrows continued to serve as an easily accessible public conveyance at a time when Chevrolets and Austins were already a common

Fig. 36.   This ancient means of transportation continued to serve the public in Republican Shanghai. Here, six mill workers ride home on a cart capable of carrying eight. Women workers were typically the main patrons of this conveyance. Courtesy of the Shanghai Museum.

sight on Shanghai's streets.[29] The order reducing the size of wheelbarrows was not strictly enforced it seems, as it was observed in the late 1930s and the 1940s that "it was a common sight to see a long line of wheelbarrow 'taxis' transporting as many as eight plump Chinese mill-girls—four on each side—to and from work morning and evening—and glad of the business."[30] These primitive conveyances were jokingly called "fourth-class" vehicles, in reference to the automobile (number one), the rickshaw (number two), and the tram (number three). Wang Yingxia, wife of the writer Yu Dafu, mentioned in chapter 6, recalled that in the early thirties,

> often . . . when the weather was mild and flowers were blooming, Yu Dafu and I liked to take a stroll. In what was then Jessfield Road (today's Wanhangdu Road) and Yuyuan Road we were often solicited by wheelbarrow pushers who were on their way back to Caojiadu. Yu Dafu always liked to have us ride on these "fourth-class" vehicles. In the beginning I was a little embarrassed and also afraid of falling off. But once we got on and sat steadily on each side of the wheelbarrow, with my left hand holding his right hand, and the pusher behind us, and we

chatted from time to time on all sorts of topics, it became a really zestful ride. Sometimes on the way we came across our "automobile class" friends, who waved to us from their cars, and we returned their greeting by nodding, with an expression that we were quite enjoying ourselves and would ignore what others might say.[31]

If one were to take in some of the street scenes in the city—the row upon row of lilong houses, the numerous neighborhood stores of all kinds, every sort of "you name it" service shops, the bustling open-air food markets, the innumerable refreshment stands, the shouting street peddlers, the squeaking wheelbarrows, the wedding parades with their sedan chairs, the great throngs at temple fairs, the hustle and bustle of traditional festivals, the heavily trafficked bridges over Suzhou Creek with urchins at both ends helping to push human-powered vehicles over the slope, and so on—in short, if one were to take in the endless, streaming crowds and the forest of structures in the densely clotted urban setting that was Shanghai, one might well be struck by the similarity between the street scenes in this treaty-port city and those in a traditional Chinese city, such as the one meticulously portrayed in the famous Song painting *Qingming Festival on the River*. Gazing at this painting and recalling life in modern Shanghai, one may feel a certain poignancy, as if urban life in twelfth-century Kaifeng may have been recreated in twentieth-century Shanghai. In walking through the streets of modern Shanghai, one might also get the impression that Shanghai's lilong neighborhoods were not unlike "urban villages" and the residents, "urban villagers."[32]

The West

Customs or habits accumulated in daily life are perhaps the last stronghold to be conquered by change. A Shanghai resident might have participated in new realms of political or social life but at the same time might have kept his or her old habits in everyday life. A person might have been a modern union activist or a Communist intellectual or a Christian church-goer, and at the same time might have remained a loyal customer of small neighborhood stores and enjoyed chatting with neighbors while sitting beside a tiger stove or munching snacks in a sesame cake store. Indeed, hot water stores in Shanghai's working-class neighborhoods were often a favorite place for social gatherings and, during labor disputes, for organizing strikes.[33] A woman worker might have joined the YWCA, while her daily life at home (symbolized, say, by the lighting of her coal stove in the morning) remained unchanged.[34] Continuities of traditional ways in people's daily lives did not necessarily contradict (at least not immediately) changes in other dimensions of their lives.

Obviously, the tenacity of tradition in daily life was partly the result of a lack of modern amenities. The widespread availability of refrigerators or a gas supply, for instance, might have dramatically changed people's shopping behavior and made small stores irrelevant. But the dynamic of the persistence of tradition was essentially not material but cultural. Chinese institutions thus should not be measured against standards based on the "Western-derived model of urbanization" and judged backward or inferior.[35] Indeed, there is reason to believe that in industrialized societies people miss the "pastoral" style of neighborhood life. That is why, as Bestor tells us, public baths (*sentō*) in Tokyo are "still well patronized, serving as social centers for local residents, including many who could bathe at home but prefer the congenial atmosphere of public bathing." After a bath, patrons often stop "on their way back to do a bit of shopping, to chat with friends, or to have a bowl of noodles in a restaurant."[36] That is also why the anthropologist E. N. Anderson is justified in worrying about "the worst thing that could happen" to Chinese food in the new, affluent world of the future—that is, the disappearance of the great variety of so-called poverty food served in traditional fashion in "street stalls and tiny hole-in-the-wall restaurants."[37]

In spite of the overwhelming evidence that in some important respects Shanghai was home to a strong and vibrant current of traditionalism, a traditionalism that can be equated with continuity or persistence of things indigenous to the Chinese, the city has been almost invariably perceived—in the Chinese mind as well as that of the foreigner—only in its guise as a treaty port. Shanghai has long been stereotyped by Chinese of virtually all political convictions as the prime "bridgehead" for foreign encroachment on China. In the West, the city has been frequently portrayed as an alien island in the vast indigenous Chinese sea. Even rigorous scholarly work refers to the city simply as "the other China," "in China but not of it," "a foreign city even in its own country," and so on.[38]

Consistent with this image of the city as something alien to the "true" China, modern Shanghainese have been stereotyped as a people who somehow differ from their fellow citizens. Like most generalizations about a particular city's people (such as, say, New Yorkers), the image or stereotype of the "Shanghai person," or Shanghainese (Shanghairen), was well conceived and widely known but seldom articulated. Also, like virtually all generalizations about a group of people, the stereotype of the "Shanghai person" runs the risk of being biased, leading to strained interpretations or oversimplification of complexities. With this in mind, let us look more closely at the perception of the Shanghai person, a somewhat peculiar but nevertheless important subject in twentieth-century Chinese social history.

On one hand, the criteria for being categorized as Shanghainese were vague and equivocal. Being a Shanghainese was not determined by birth, nor by language—although both factors are of vital importance in defining local identity in China (perhaps also elsewhere in the world). As noted, the majority of Shanghainese were not born in Shanghai, and they spoke the Shanghai local dialect with various accents. On the other hand, the notion of "Shanghainese" could be so distinct and definite that few would mistake what it meant. To this day, many Shanghainese believe, apparently with some degree of exaggeration but also certainly with some justification, that a non-Shanghainese can be easily identified in Shanghai's streets, stores, or bus stops simply by his or her manner and mien. By the same token, a Shanghainese—even if that person had left the city for years and lived in a place thousands of miles from Shanghai—can still be readily identified and/or would self-identify as Shanghainese.[39]

Such a social phenomenon—what one might call the personified Shanghai identity—has great potential to generate studies whose significance goes beyond Shanghai. Such studies may require one to call upon historians, sociologists, anthropologists, and even psychologists to engage in interdisciplinary research to connect the Shanghai identity with other important themes in Chinese studies. For our purposes, and also to address an essential aspect of the Shanghai identity, we shall look at the role that the West played in the formation of this rich and imaginative yet concrete identity.

In an effort to answer the question "Who are the Shanghainese?" and to explicate the notion of the "Shanghai person" in a scholarly context, the historian Xiong Yuezhi wrote that one criterion for qualifying as a "Shanghai person" was "being experienced and knowledgeable. Those who raised their head to enjoy looking at a tall building, or joined a throng to gawk at foreigners on the street, or gazed at a store window with an expression of astonishment, were mostly not Shanghainese—the skyline, foreigners and foreign goods were simply all-too-familiar sights for the people of Shanghai."[40] In a well-received essay on the "Shanghai person," the writer Yu Qiuyu points out that the formation of the shared characteristics of the "Shanghai person" must be traced back into history: "Older generation rickshaw pullers were all able to speak a few English words; people as low class as they dared to take a stand against the foreigners in

the agitation of the May 30th Incident [of 1925]. There were many foreigners who lived in Shanghai's alleyway-house neighborhoods; having
been neighbors with each other for years, they adjusted their relations
[with the Chinese residents] so that they became quite ordinary. Shanghai's
shop assistants did not have much regard for foreign customers. They
would often estimate the customer's budget and make suggestions about
what to buy."[41] In her essay titled "After All, This Is the Shanghainese,"
written in 1943, the writer Zhang Ailing (Eileen Chang), who has been
praised as "the author who best catches the feeling of old Shanghai," points
out the subtleness and extraordinary sense of balance with which Shanghainese conducted themselves in society.[42] This meant, among other things,
that Shanghainese had no blind faith in any "perfect model," which included the model of the West. As for the notion of perfection, as Zhang describes it, the Shanghainese would say, "Go back to children's stories!" Perfection can only find a place for herself in the fairy tales "Snow White" and
"Glass Slippers" [Cinderella]![43]

This maturity was also reflected in the attitude of the people of Shanghai toward foreigners or, more specifically, Westerners. Shanghai was
known as a hotbed of a number of major anti-imperialism movements
in twentieth-century China, and, ironically, at the same time it was condemned for its tendency to "worship things foreign" (chongyang), which
stemmed largely from its status as China's number one treaty port. Both
images are in some way misleading. The manner that the Shanghai people
adopted toward Westerners was a more calm, balanced, and sophisticated
one than either image can convey. Having lived in a city where safety and
prosperity were brought by uninvited foreign powers, and caught in the
dilemma of nursing a wounded national pride and at the same time admir-
ing the West, the people of Shanghai somehow managed to find a comfortable, balanced point on which to stand. It was, so to speak, the Daoist "let
nature take its own course" philosophy mixed with a sense of humor that
usually characterized the Shanghainese.

Indeed, Shanghai in its heyday, from after the May 30th Incident in
1925 to the end of the war in 1945, had extraordinarily few outbreaks of
xenophobia against the West. This had to do with a number of factors, including the increasing encroachment of Japan during these two decades,
something that shaped Chinese nationalism primarily into a resist-the-
Japanese movement. But a high degree of familiarity with, and decades
of living together with, foreigners must have played some role. It would
be naive to say that Chinese and Westerners in this cosmopolitan city
achieved perfectly harmonious relations, but at least people of different

ethnic and cultural backgrounds were a familiar, everyday sight, and they adjusted to circumstances and generally lived in peace with each other.

Often, Shanghainese of Chinese origin used humor in dealing with the "Shanghainese" of foreign origin.[44] A few local expressions created with wry amusement illustrate this phenomenon. Chinese servants in foreign firms or houses were called by their bosses "boy"; the Shanghainese transformed this derogatory form of address into a somewhat comical name: 1309 (because, at least to some eyes, the handwritten English word "Boy" looks like the handwritten number 1309). Being kicked by foreigners (many a rickshaw puller was booted by foreign policemen) was known as "eating foreign ham." The term "foreign tray" (*yangpan*) means "fool," and originated from terminology used in the Shanghai Stock Exchange.[45] *Lasan*, derived from "lassie," refers to loose and frivolous girls. *Xian-shuimei* ("saltwater sister"), a transliteration of "handsome maid," referred to Chinese prostitutes who specialized in entertaining foreign clients. Since "saltwater" implies the ocean and the ocean implies foreigners, the term makes a good pun. "Gamen," an adjective in the Shanghai dialect derived from the word "German," means "indifferent and reluctant," reflecting a general impression among Shanghai's Chinese of the Germans as reserved and unexcitable. While Westerners were more or less regarded as superior, the people of Subei, whose inferior social status in Shanghai has become known in the West through Emily Honig's work, were called "the French."[46]

Local expressions like these, numerous as they are, were only drops in a deep reservoir of social attitudes toward the West. Zhang Ailing once said that because of age-old political and social controversies the people of Shanghai adopted "a laissez-faire attitude that stemmed from weariness. It is a smile on a sweating face—a characteristic of the typical Chinese sense of humor."[47] This was something widely known among the populace, deeply ingrained in its mentality, yet hardly visible in political events and seldom reflected in the literature on the city.

In any case, the balance between xenophobia and blind faith in or obsequiousness toward foreigners revealed a certain level of sophistication. To the people of the hinterland who were, by the time of the Republic, still in awe of or resentful of things foreign, it was this kind of sophistication that somehow made the Shanghainese alien. Therefore, there were two layers of elements that distanced the Shanghainese from the hinterlander: in addition to the usual type of grudge or dislike that rural or small-town people harbor for cosmopolites, it was, in whatever form, the Shanghai people's experience with and adoption of things Western that made them different.

In other words, "Shanghainese" was a dual structure: it was not just *urban* but also to some degree *Western*. The term *waidiren* (lit., an outsider, that is, a person from parts of the country other than the place from which one hails) in Shanghai implied *xiangxiaren* (country folk), regardless of whether the "country folk" might in fact come from a major city.[48] The historian Chen Xulu (1918–94) described a common notion about the magical power of Shanghai: "Having been in Shanghai for a while, the most foolish person can be smart, the most honest person can be cunning; the most odd person can be handsome. Only a few days after being in Shanghai, a slovenly girl with a running nose can become a beauty with curly hair, a woman with single eyelids and a flat nose can become a lady of dignified bearing."[49] Here, "single eyelids and a flat nose" were taken as a mark of uncouthness and reflected a general social judgment in favor of the "double eyelids and the high nose" of Westerners; "curly hair" had the same connotation. With the city's Western "ingredients," urban superiority became sublimed into the "superiority of Shanghai."

We encounter an obvious paradox: if in various ways the people of Shanghai maintained a traditional lifestyle not unlike that of the rest of China, why was the image of the city and its people so persistently different from that of other parts of the country? If in the eyes of other Chinese, modern Shanghainese were in some degree marked as "Western," then what was the essence of that imprint?

To elaborate on the subject would, as I indicated earlier, require extensive new research. However, from what we already know about the daily life of ordinary people, we may already have at least part of the answer: the extraordinary commercial character of the city, with its overwhelming Western component, contributed to the perception that the Shanghainese were fundamentally "different." Modern Shanghainese have been stereotyped as astute, resourceful, calculating, quick-witted, adaptive, and flexible (always ready to compromise but not budging an inch unless absolutely necessary). All of these are characteristics associated with commerce.

Shanghai was arguably the epitome of modern China's commercial culture, in which commerce served as the primary motor of society. It seems legitimate to name such a culture after the city, hence the term Haipai (the Shanghai school or the Shanghai type), in contrast to the supposedly rigid, tradition-bound, and orthodox Jingpai (the Beijing school or the Beijing type).[50] The Shanghai type, even in its original meaning as a school of painting and drama, was part of a broadly defined commercial culture: as

Lu Xun pointed out, "Haipai is just the helper of commerce," whereas "Jingpai is the hack of officialdom."[51]

Commerce and commerce-related social phenomena were of course not brought by Westerners. Commercialization in late imperial China, especially in the lower Yangzi delta region, predated the arrival of the West, something that has been well researched and convincingly demonstrated. But the so-called incipient capitalism (or "sprouts of capitalism") of late imperial China apparently was no match for the vigor of modern Shanghai, in which commerce was so widespread among people of all walks of life, so vital to the fate of the city, and so pervasive in every aspect of society. The role the Western powers played in the city's development in the modern era naturally marked this commercial culture with the brand of the West. The term "Hai" was not just an abbreviation of "Shanghai" but, from its literal meaning—"ocean" or "sea"—a figure of speech indicating that the culture of Shanghai was, like an ocean, boundless, all-embracing, and all-powerful.[52]

Shanghai's landscape can be seen as a powerful manifestation of the city's commercial culture. Major traditional Chinese cities, including the so-called commercial capital of Kaifeng, had been built around political or state edifices (such as imperial palaces or yamen) or religious structures.[53] Shanghai became the first major city in Chinese history that had as its paramount landmark a few blocks of commercial establishments. Nanking Road, the commercial center of the city, together with its adjacent riverside, the Bund, the site of imposing, multistory office buildings, has long been seen as a symbol of the city, in much the same way that the Manhattan skyline symbolizes New York. Nanking Road and the Bund—as the places where foreigners exercised their economic power and enjoyed special privileges, and as the places from which emanated modern, Western cultural influences—were particularly powerful symbols of the Western commercial intrusion in China.

In the vast shikumen neighborhoods beyond the Bund, the story of the daily life of ordinary people reveals the deep penetration of commercialization. It is here, in the lives of the ordinary people of Shanghai, that we can find part of the roots of Shanghai's extraordinary commercial culture. Shanghai—specifically the houses built in the city's core along Nanking Road—was the birthplace of China's first modern real estate market. In many alleyway-house neighborhoods, tenants became a type of merchant by subletting space to others. Thus, Shanghai's commercial culture was not restricted to the big enterprises in the foreign concessions where "merchants were abundant"[54] but was also found in, for instance, the so-called second-landlord practice, where a business primarily grew out of what might be called one's living arrangement. The common second-landlord/third-tenant phenomenon was a way in which people coped with life in the city, in search of either success or merely survival.[55]

It was also a showcase of Shanghai as a land of opportunity. Not all of the hundreds of thousands of poor rural immigrants made a living by begging, pulling a rickshaw, or doing other backbreaking labor; many made a living—or by certain standards, even a fortune—by simply renting out part of their dwelling. People who could not afford or were unwilling to pay the "takeover fee" could rent any size room in any type of house and thus sojourn in this "golden land" (cunjindi) in search of the "Shanghai dream." Out of these living arrangements welled a deep sense of commerce destined to shape the mind-set of the people of Shanghai. Such a mind-set was further "commercialized" by the coexistence of commerce and residence in the city's alleyways. Millions of shikumen residents lived with businesses operating literally under their very noses. These establishments—stores, workshops, factories, banks, pawnshops, opium dens, brothels, teahouses, bathhouses, inns, schools, offices, temples, and so on—were located right inside the alley, side by side with residences. In addition, peddlers of all sorts were ever present in the city, serving millions of residents in the neighborhoods as well as making a living by selling. The influence of commerce on the people of Shanghai was thus intimate, enveloping, and certain.

In a nation where commerce had long been despised, such influence was deemed to be corrupting. As early as 1861, Wang Tao (1828–97), who came to Shanghai in 1849 and worked as a translator for a British-run press for twelve years, wrote in his diary, "Shanghai is a place of corrupted social values, and the corruption is indeed due to the search for profits [lisou]."[56] Wang, one of the few reform-minded intellectuals of his time, was regarded as a pioneer in introducing Western culture to modern China, yet in private he did not hold Shanghai and commerce in high regard; we can imagine how still more unfavorable was the opinion of Shanghai and its commercial culture among the conservatives. In spite of the commerce-based prosperity of the city in modern times, business continued to be criticized as the cause of social deterioration. "In Shanghai, people only care about the value of gold and silver and do not know the origin of elegance and vulgarity." "The general social mood is so bad that everybody places great value on profit and takes personal reputation lightly. Commerce and the market are the place where the will of the people is worked out." Comments like these were frequently encountered in local newspapers and other publications, and presumably they were common in people's daily conversations.[57] By orthodox, Confucian standards, then, the city's commercial culture was corrupt and so were its people.

In condemning commerce as corrosive and degenerative, radicals and conservatives stood, ironically but not surprisingly, shoulder to shoulder. One of the founding fathers of the Chinese Communist Party, Chen Duxiu, was among the harshest critics of Shanghai; his attacks on the city bear striking similarities to those from the conservative Confucian camp. Chen, writing during the May 4th Movement, of which he was unquestionably the leading figure advocating "Down with Confucianism" and promoting "Mr. Science and Mr. Democracy" in China, proclaimed: "All these recently popularized expressions—consciousness, patriotism, devotion to the public, the Republic, Liberation, strengthening our country, hygiene, reform, freedom, the trend of new thought, new culture—once they land in Shanghai can only serve as a sharp weapon for [the advertisements of] cigarette companies, pharmacies, book dealers, and lotteries. Alas, what a society Shanghai is!" To him, "Everywhere [in the city] is the sound of the abacus and the stink of copper coins."[58]

The Communists

Chen Duxiu was later purged by his fellow Communists, but they remained firm "comrades" in denouncing Shanghai's commercial culture. The Maoist version of Communism saw Shanghai as a part of, to use Bergère's words, "the model of development inspired by the West[,] of which the city had become the symbol."[59] While the Communists were certainly right in relating Shanghai's commercialization to the West, in so doing they obviously, on purpose or not, underrated the Chinese initiative in the process. Western innovation and influence frequently provided the impetus, but later developments and innovations were almost entirely Chinese.

No doubt the revolution of 1949 brought unprecedented change to the city and to the life of its people; to use a Chinese proverb favored by the Communists in describing their revolution, it "turned heaven and earth upside down" (*tianfan difu*).[60] Yet many practices and customs in daily life deeply rooted in tradition have proved to be more durable than the sweeping changes introduced by the revolution. This study does not intend to extend its focus to the postrevolutionary era, but a few examples related to the subjects treated in this book can be brought in here to suggest that as far as daily life is concerned, the changes brought by "Liberation" may not be as thorough and fundamental as people have previously thought.

In the neighborhoods, the Communists had to cope with the existing residential patterns and housing structures in establishing their neighborhood organizations. In most cases the core of the neighborhood organizations, that is, the residents' committee, was put in charge of a few adjacent alleyway-house compounds. Each committee was named after one or another of the major alleyway-house compounds in its domain. For instance, the Zhengming Li Residents' Committee, established in 1954, had within its jurisdiction three adjacent alleyway-house compounds in Changde Road (from north to south): Jiahe Li, Zhengming Li, and Fude Fang (Alley of Fortune and Virtue). Sometimes an alleyway-house compound was big enough to warrant its own, single residents' committee; and sometimes a particularly large compound, such as Jianye Li, was too big for a single residents' committee and so was divided among a few committees. In all cases, the domains of residents' committees were carefully drawn to follow the type of housing; in other words, they were aligned with the pre-Liberation residential pattern.[61]

One should note that the city did not lack small subareas where shacks, shikumen, and new-type alleyway houses were located close enough to each other that they could have been gathered into a single residents' committee. But this seldom happened. The Street (*jiedao*), which occupied the top of the three-layered hierarchy of urban neighborhood organizations, may have included a variety of neighborhoods (or housing types) in its domain, but it usually acknowledged the existing differences by establishing residents' committees based on the type of neighborhood. For example, the Huashan Street committee administered over half a dozen residents' committees (the exact number varied with changes in the district's boundaries through the years), whose neighborhoods were diverse: the Zhengming Li Residents' Committee represented an essentially shikumen neighborhood; the Laojie Residents' Committee, an area with mostly shacks; and the rest, neighborhoods with either new-type alleyway houses or yangfang (Western-style houses). The result of this approach was that the city's residents' committees came in a wide range of sizes; even the "average" size committee ranged from 100 to 600 households.[62]

Needless to say, neighborhoods and housing patterns were based on the social and economic status of the residents. It is ironic that a revolution that claimed as its goal the eradication of social classes was actually sensitive to keeping aligned with the status quo. But this sensitivity in establishing neighborhood organizations reveals that the Communists had the sense to understand the local situation and the wisdom to compromise with it. Accepting the status quo contributed to the quick, comprehensive, efficient, and smooth establishment of neighborhood organizations in Shanghai in the early 1950s. Since the residents' committee was the basic functioning unit of the system, its old-neighborhood basis reduced the psychological impact often attendant on the imposition of a new system, and increased the effectiveness of Communist rule.

If we move on to look at commerce in the neighborhoods, again we see evidence of both change and continuity. After 1949, street peddlers were greatly reduced in number but were not completely banished, even during the Cultural Revolution. All existing food markets continued to operate in the same location and indeed became more important in daily life. Few new markets were opened after Liberation, which means people went to the same market for food as they did before the revolution. The frequent shortages of "side foods" (*fushipin*) in the sixties and seventies made the markets a morning battlefield where people vied with each other in endless lines to purchase food. Up to the recent reform that has diversified sources of food supplies—mainly by allowing farmers to enter the city to sell their products—the food market was virtually the sole source of fresh vegetables, meat, and fish. Furthermore, small neighborhood stores underwent some changes but maintained their important role in the life of local residents. Local stores and shops continued to handle the same commodities at the same locations and to serve the same customers. And, to some extent, the management too remained much the same as before the revolution.

However, most family-run small businesses did not escape the 1956 Socialist Transformation Movement, which aimed to transfer urban private enterprises to state or collective ownership. Rice stores and coal stores were all collectivized. Store owners were classified in the category "national bourgeoisie" (*minzu zichan jieji*). Some who had rather a small amount of capital and did not hire shop assistants (or more accurately, did not employ nonfamily members) were classified as "small business owners" (*xiaoyezhu*). The rice stores were turned over to the Grains and Oils Corporation, and the coal stores to the Coal and Petroleum Corporation, both of which were under the jurisdiction of the Second Bureau of Commerce of the Shanghai municipal government.[63]

Collectivization brought some dramatic changes to these stores. Down came the shop signs bearing elegant names that the owners had deliberately chosen to bless their businesses. Up went signs with the new, rather dull names consisting of a number and the relevant administrative jurisdiction, such as the "Number Six Rice Store of Jing'an District," or the

"Number Seven Coal Store of Nanshi District." Many store signs carried an "adjective" to indicate the type of collectivization involved, such as "State-Operated," "Cooperative," or "Joint State and Private Operated."[64] Still, several stores retained their old names until the beginning of the Cultural Revolution in 1966, when all the surviving old store names were criticized as evidence of the persistence of the so-called four olds (i.e., old customs, old habits, old culture, and old thinking). The names were replaced first by revolutionary names such as "The East Is Red," "Ever Red," "Proletarian Rising," "For the People," and later by the administrative numbers.[65]

Other than that, however, from local residents' point of view the change of ownership meant little more than replacement of the signboard or a few new faces (i.e., new shop assistants) behind the counter. The stores were still located in the same places and open the same hours, and were still patronized by the same customers. Former shopkeepers (now employees of the corporation) and their families still resided on the second floor above the store. Some were assigned to work in a store other than their "living room" downstairs to avoid arousing possible suspicion or "inconveniences" (*bixian*). But many others were allowed to continue working in the same store that they had previously owned. One coal store owner on Hart Road (now Changde Road), for instance, continued working in the store he had formerly owned until he retired at age eighty-one in 1964. He never had to change his residence, which was right in the house where the store was located.[66]

From the customers' viewpoint, the major change was not the switch of ownership but the nationwide rationing of grain and cooking oil that the state imposed from September 1955 on. Legal residence in the neighborhood entitled each family to obtain a grain record booklet from the Street's Grain Control Office (*liangshi guanlisuo*). This authorized the residents to receive coupons for grain, cooking oil, and other commodities every three months. To purchase the cooking oil and grain (other than rice), shoppers had to present these coupons along with cash. Rice was more strictly regulated. To purchase rice, the grain booklet had to be presented together with cash and a coupon, and the cashier had to record the amount of the purchase. Also, customers could only go to designated rice stores in their neighborhood to buy rice.[67]

But rationing was not entirely new to the people of Shanghai. During the Sino-Japanese War (1937–45), particularly after the outbreak of the Pacific War in 1941, rice was in extremely short supply in Shanghai and rationing was enforced by the Japanese occupation authorities.[68] Shanghai residents took the 1955 imposition of rationing as another wave of restrictions on this vital commodity, something they could and would cope with, just as they coped with the rest of the increasing Communist manipulation of society since the revolution.[69] In any event, there was considerable inertia in people's shopping behavior. The rationing system allowed residents to buy rice at a few different stores close to home, in consideration of providing choice and selection. Most residents, however, stuck to a single rice store, the same one where they bought rice before rationing.[70]

By virtue of the vital importance of the rice stores, state intervention after Liberation was most serious. For stores that sold goods of less importance in the economy, changes were minimal. Tobacco and paper stores are an obvious case in point. These stores, so convenient to local residents, remained essentially untouched by the nationwide socialist collectivization campaign of 1956. The stores continued to be run by their owners in the same fashion as before the revolution, and they remained one of the very few vestiges of private business in urban China after 1956. Tobacco and paper stores even survived the Cultural Revolution (1966–76), when the radicals tried to wipe out all traces of private enterprise in the country. Zhang Chunqiao, one of the "Gang of Four," who was at that time head of the Communist Party in Shanghai, declared his intention to "cut off the tail of capitalism" (*ge ziben zhuyi weiba*).[71] In urban areas, this policy aimed mainly at small family businesses that had survived the mid-1950s socialist transformation campaign. But tobacco and paper stores in Shanghai survived Zhang Chunqiao's campaign.[72]

Several factors contributed to their endurance. One was that the convenience provided by these stores could hardly be maintained by nonfamily management. Since the stores were part of the owners' home and any adult member of the family could help run the business, the stores were able to stay open long hours every day, usually from 6 A.M. to 10 P.M. Indeed, they closed only on the Chinese New Year's Day. Even after a store closed for the night, if neighbors needed something urgently they could knock at the back door of the store and get what they wanted. Had the stores been collectivized, it would have been difficult, if not impossible, to arrange shifts among the limited numbers of employees to maintain the traditionally long hours of service.

Furthermore, collectivization would have meant that the owners of these stores would become employees of state (or cooperative) enterprises, and thus the state (or the cooperative) would have borne the responsibility for employee benefits (mainly stable salaries, free medical care, and retirement pensions). Since these small stores were not profitable enough to allow establishing such a system without adding to the financial burden of the employer (i.e., the state), there was at least technically no incentive for the state to "swallow" these businesses and provide "iron rice bowls" for their owners. Thus, for decades after Liberation, when almost all other businesses in urban China had been "transformed," tobacco and paper stores continued to be run just like they had been in the so-called old society. As the tobacco and paper store owner Liu Xiangyu put it, "The state does not want us."[73]

Nevertheless, too often in the history of the PRC, economic considerations had to yield to ideological imperatives. The state never intended to let small businesses continue as private enterprises forever. Not only did the state, through its wholesale outlets, control the source of the goods that small stores sold, but from the Cultural Revolution on, the state had clearly adopted a policy of "let them perish of their own accord." Until the 1960s and 1970s, virtually all the tobacco and paper stores of Shanghai were run by aged people. Without government intervention, a family member or a relative might be able to inherit the business when the old owner died. By setting a new rule in 1968 that prohibited issuing a new license to private stores, the radical Shanghai government used a sort of laissez-faire tactic, anticipating that after the old generation passed away, these businesses would naturally "run their course" (zisheng zimie).[74]

But the course ran longer than the radicals anticipated. Developments in China since the late 1970s have reinforced, not weakened, the continuity of traditionalism. Rationing, the "revolutionary" policy that had perhaps the greatest impact on small stores, is now being dismantled in the reforms launched by Deng Xiaoping. Nationwide, grain consumption in China has steadily decreased every year since 1986.[75] In Shanghai, according to a recent report of the Shanghai municipal authorities, the average monthly grain ration is 14.4 kilograms per capita. But the actual volume sold in 1992 was only 8 kilograms per capita.[76] For the first time in Shanghai since the rationing system was set up in August 1955, people were "giving up" rationing before the system was officially abolished.

The government of Shanghai municipality announced that from April 1993 on, all rationing of grain and oil would be abolished.[77] This means that rice stores and soy sauce stores, which previously were vital to daily life, may not be so vital in the future. Another "vital" store, the coal store, had declined earlier, since piped gas had become widely available (38.7 percent of Shanghai families had piped gas in 1978 and 53.6 percent in 1987).[78]

Shanghai is only one of many Chinese cities that abolished rationing in the early 1990s. According to the official China News Agency (*Zhongguo tongxunshe*), up to May 1993, twenty-seven out of China's thirty provinces (including the municipalities directly under the central government and the so-called autonomous regions), or more than eighteen hundred of China's cities and towns that were subject to the rationing of grain and oil, had abolished the system. That leaves only Ningxia, Tibet, and Hainan still under the rationing regime.[79] The abolition of rationing should, at least to some extent, return rice stores and soy sauce stores to their prerevolution style of management. The revival of private ownership of these stores is not only possible but virtually predicable, should the reform continue.

Other less "vital" stores have already reappeared; to use a Chinese expression, they have "sprung up like bamboo shoots after a spring rain." At the end of 1987, 50,582 out of Shanghai's total of 76,743 stores were privately run. The total personnel registered for these stores was 60,700, which means that these were very small enterprises—almost all were one-person stores—which is typical of Shanghai's neighborhood businesses.[80] Many of these enterprises (10,639) were registered as "restaurants" or "eating houses" (*yinshi dian*), which is what sesame cake stores and some puluo restaurants were formally called, and as small "service shops" (19,439) that mainly sell clothing.[81]

Tobacco and paper stores have also enjoyed a renaissance. Liu Xiangyu, who owned and ran a tobacco and paper store for half a century, now could fill up his store window with whatever items he could manage to sell, free of fear of being labeled a "tail of capitalism." However, at age seventy-one in 1991, he felt the opportunity had come too late. As he complained with his usual sense of humor to a visitor who was praising the revival of his business, "'Make things alive! Make things alive!' When I am dying, they start to talk about 'make things alive'!" Still, he was happy about the situation. As he sighed to another visitor who flattered him by calling him *laoban* (boss, an old-fashioned way of addressing shopkeepers), "*Deng Xiaoping hao!*" (Deng Xiaoping is good).[82]

Perhaps, from the viewpoint of shopkeepers like Liu, the revival of private businesses should be credited to the top leaders in Beijing, particularly Deng Xiaoping. However, from a historical perspective, tradition had never been completely rooted out, neither by the revolution nor by imperialism. Once conditions permitted, tradition was easily rekindled. No wonder in the nineties, when the frenzied economic reform and building binge in Shanghai rapidly transformed the city and its urban landscape, many long-time Shanghai residents tended to view what was happening as a restoration of the past. They often sighed with deep feeling that the "old society (*jiu shehui*) is coming back," "things are not different from the old society," "forget the past sixty years—the nineties meets the thirties."[83]

In shaping modern Chinese history there were two forces, which few scholars in the China field have overlooked: namely, the Western intrusion and the Communist revolution. Shanghai has been a window through which the world could watch the actions of both of these forces. As China's leading treaty-port city, Shanghai had long been the nation's window to the outside world, as well as (to mix metaphors) the "bridgehead" for foreign encroachment on China. And, after 1949, the Communists clearly declared that their purpose for Shanghai was to purify this evil colony and transform it into a socialist city.[84] The city received a sound Communist baptism and thereafter bore the brunt of the political movements in the People's Republic. The continuous ubiquity of traditionalism in this environment is truly impressive.

Tradition has been tenacious because it is rooted neither in the Chinese superstructure, nor in an alien culture brought by foreigners, but in the quotidian life of the people. A classic Chinese poem on the hardy grass of an ancient prairie may be borrowed to describe the vitality of such traditionalism: "No wildfire can consume it completely / In the vernal breezes it once again turns the land green."[85] When the Communists finally awoke to acknowledge the importance of Shanghai and declared that the city would serve as the "dragon's head" (*longtou*) of the nation's modernization program, they were recognizing a vigorous and all-embracing culture that had been condemned and denied for decades.[86] It is paradoxical that the Communists' modernization program has greatly softened the regime's once indomitable crusade against things prerevolutionary and inevitably involves the revival of a vibrant Chinese traditionalism.

A Survey of the Origins of Shanghai Residents

From October 1989 to January 1990, in cooperation with the Institute of Sociology, Shanghai Academy of Social Sciences (SASS), and with the assistance of the sociologist Lu Hanlong, director of the Institute of Sociology of SASS, I surveyed seven residential neighborhoods in four areas of Shanghai. Five of the neighborhoods consisted of lilong compounds; the other two were a mixture of alleyway houses and single-story dwellings (pingfang). The focus of the survey was the origins of Shanghai residents and the social and economic changes immigrants underwent in the city prior to Liberation.

In order to ensure that the survey reflected the history of pre-1949 Shanghai, residents surveyed had to meet two criteria: they had to be born before 1930 (i.e., they had to be at least fifty-nine years old at the time of survey), and they had to have lived in Shanghai before 1948. I applied the latter criterion in order to exclude post-Liberation immigrants to the city, a group that differed significantly from immigrants in the prerevolutionary era. In the seven neighborhoods, 438 met the criteria. Average age of the respondents at the time of survey was 69.2.

The survey involved interviewing residents on an individual basis following the application of a prepared and unified questionnaire. On average, each interview lasted forty-five minutes. Following are other details concerning the survey.

1. Survey Spots and Number of People Surveyed, by Neighborhood

Zhabei, including Yong'an Li (Alley of Eternal Peace), Changxing Li (Alley of Lasting Prosperity), and Tongfa Li (Alley of Flourishing Together). These neighborhoods are on Tianmu Road and Shanxibei Road, Zhabei District.

107 persons surveyed (35.5 percent male, 64.5 percent female).

Downtown, including Baoyu Li (Alley of Treasure and Abundance), Beijingdong Road, Huangpu District.

101 persons (48.5 percent male, 51.5 percent female).

Huxi, or *West Shanghai*, including Wangjia Long (Lane of the Wang Family) on Zhenning Road and Jiangsu Road, both of which traversed Jing'an District and Changning District.

150 persons (47.3 percent male, 52.7 percent female).

Nanshi, including Dahua Li (Alley of Great China) and Caojia Jie (Cao Family Street, originally known as Caojiaqiao Jie or "Street of the Cao Family Bridge") on Jingxiu Road and Fuxingdong Road, Nanshi District.

80 persons (41.3 percent male, 58.7 percent female).

NOTE: The names of alleyway-house compounds are their pre-Liberation originals; at the time of the survey the names were still in use. Street and district names are the current official names.

2. BASIC CHARACTERISTICS OF THE PEOPLE SURVEYED

Total number of persons surveyed: 438 persons.

By gender: 191 men (43.6 percent), 247 women (56.4 percent).

By place of birth:

1. Shanghai-born: 41 persons (9.4 percent)
   Second-generation immigrants: 33
   Third-generation immigrants: 7
   Fourth-generation immigrants: 1
2. First-generation immigrants: 397 persons (90.6 percent) from 13 provinces and Beijing

Time of move to Shanghai (for the Shanghai-born, the time their families moved to Shanghai):

Before 1920: 106 persons (24.2 percent)

In the 1930s: 143 persons (32.6 percent)

In the 1940s: 189 persons (43.2 percent)

Age at the time of immigration:

Average: 18.21 years

Oldest: 44 years

Youngest: less than 1 year

3. TYPE OF RESPONDENT'S HOMETOWN PRIOR TO MOVING TO SHANGHAI

Type of Hometown	Number of Respondents	Percentage
Countryside	219	50.0
Rural town	92	21.0
County seat	67	15.3
Middle-size city [a]	48	11.0
Large city	12	2.7

[a] "Middle-size city" refers to cities with a population of between 200,000 and 500,000. "Large city" refers to cities that typically had a population of between 500,000 and 1 million; but here it also includes Beijing and Shanghai, each of which had a population of more than 1 million.

4. REASONS FOR MOVING TO SHANGHAI

Reason	Number of Respondents	Percentage
To attend school	9	2.1
To look for job opportunities[a]	222	50.7
To escape Sino-Japanese War	17	3.9
To escape Civil War	10	2.3
To escape banditry	3	0.7
To escape natural disasters	11	2.5
To escape family disputes	2	0.5
To seek a better life in the city	35	8.0
Other (such as family reunion)	129	29.3

[a] In the category "To look for job opportunities," 63.2 percent were men and 36.8 percent were women.

5. MARITAL STATUS AT THE TIME OF IMMIGRATION

Marital Status	Number of Respondents	Percentage
Married[a]	145	33.1
Engaged	54	12.3
Single	223	50.9
Divorced	2	0.5
Widowed	5	1.1
Unclear (unwilling to answer)	9	2.1

[a] Among the married, 16 left their spouse in their hometown (village) and 21 had children in their hometown (village).

6. LENGTH OF STAY ANTICIPATED AT THE TIME OF IMMIGRATION

Although only 44 persons, or about 10 percent of the respondents, had no immediate family member in their hometown (village), most of the immigrants intended to live in Shanghai on a long-term basis.

Intended Length of Stay	Number of Respondents	Percentage
Permanent settlement	114	26.1
Long-term stay	245	56.1
Temporary stay	14	3.2
Alternate residence between hometown and Shanghai	11	2.5
Undecided	53	12.1

7. METHODS OF OBTAINING FIRST JOB IN SHANGHAI (BY GENDER)

Method	Male	(%)	Female	(%)	Subtotal	(%)
Through relatives	82	(43.6)	39	(19.2)	121	(30.9)
Through friends	72	(38.3)	82	(40.4)	154	(39.4)

Continued on next page

By appointment	6	(3.2)	9	(4.4)	15	(3.8)
By job application	2	(1.1)	6	(3.0)	8	(2.1)
By self-employment	11	(5.9)	11	(5.4)	22	(5.6)
Other[a]	15	(8)	56	(27.6)	71	(18.2)

NOTE: The percentages reflect the employed and do not include 47 unemployed.

[a]The category "Other" includes women who had their first job after 1949.

8. LEVELS OF EDUCATION OF THE RESIDENTS

	Male	(%)	Female	(%)	Total	(%)
Illiterate	9	(4.7)	105	(42.5)	114	(26.0)
Semiliterate	14	(7.3)	36	(14.6)	50	(11.4)
Elementary school (1st to 4th grade)	36	(18.9)	46	(18.6)	82	(18.7)
Elementary school (5th and 6th grade)	56	(29.3)	31	(12.6)	87	(19.9)
Middle school graduate	53	(27.8)	21	(8.5)	74	(16.9)
High school graduate	17	(8.9)	6	(2.4)	23	(5.3)
College graduate	6	(3.1)	2	(0.8)	8	(1.8)
Total	191	(100)	247	(100)	438	(100)

9. OCCUPATIONS BEFORE AND AFTER MOVING TO SHANGHAI

Occupation or Trade	Before	(%)	After	(%)
Employed	204	(46.6)*	331	(75.3)*
Farming	115	(56.4)	2	(0.6)
Mining and lumbering	1	(0.5)	5	(1.5)
Manufacturing	22	(10.8)	153	(46.3)
Construction	1	(0.5)	1	(0.3)
Transportation and postal service	5	(2.5)	24	(7.2)
Commerce and catering	28	(13.7)	79	(23.9)
Public utilities	8	(3.9)	24	(7.3)
Health (hospital)	1	(0.5)	4	(1.2)
Education	7	(3.4)	11	(3.3)
Finance	5	(2.4)	10	(3.0)
Organization	3	(1.5)	4	(1.2)
Others	8	(3.9)	14	(4.2)
Total employed	204	(100)	331	(100)
Unemployed	234	(53.4)*	108	(24.7)*
Housewife	84	(35.9)	83	(76.9)
Vagrant	40	(17.9)	17	(15.7)
Too young to work	110	(47.0)	8	(7.4)
Total unemployed	234	(100)	108	(100)

*Percentage of the total respondents.

10. Social Mobility as Seen in the Changes of Occupation before and after Moving to Shanghai (by Percentage)

Occupation	Before (%)	After (%)	Current (1989–90) (%)
Farmer	62.1	2.9	0.3
Unskilled worker	23.1	57.2	59.3
Skilled worker	4.9	17.9	17.8
Shop assistant	3.3	11.8	6.7
Clerk	1.2	3.8	4.3
Administrator	2.1	2.6	5.9
Professional	2.9	3.2	5.1
Senior administrator[a]	0	0.3	0.3
Senior professional[b]	0.4	0.3	0.3
Total	100	100	100

[a] In the PRC, "senior administrator" officially refers to a person who holds the position of *chuzhang* (section chief) or higher.

[b] "Senior professional" refers to a person who is officially awarded a technical or professional title such as associate professor or higher.

11. Types of Dwelling New Immigrants Lived in upon Arriving in Shanghai

Type of Dwelling	Number of Respondents	Percentage
Shacks and single-story dwellings	153	34.9
Old-type alleyway houses	258	58.9
New-type alleyway houses	2	0.5
Western-type apartments	2	0.5
Western-type detached houses	0	
Other	23	5.2

12. The Frequency of Hometown (Village) Visits

Level of Frequency	Number of Respondents	Percentage
Never returned	122	31
Visited once or twice	155	39.3
Frequent visits, but fewer than one a year	88	22.3
Every year	29	7.4

NOTE: The total number of visits (394) does not take into consideration those who did not have relatives in their hometown (village). Stated reasons for hometown visits: 229 for visiting relatives; 24 for attending weddings, funerals, and other social or ritual events; 24 for celebrating Chinese New Year; and 16 for other reasons.

13. Patterns of Obtaining Clothing

Method of Obtaining Clothing	Number of Residents	Percentage
Purchased fabric for homemade clothes	257	58.9
Purchased fabric and had tailor make clothes	104	23.8
Purchased ready-made clothes	80	18.2
Brought clothes from hometown	46	10.6
Purchased second-hand clothes	16	3.7

NOTE: The methods stated are not only for the respondents but include the entire family. Each respondent could choose more than one method; therefore, the total "Number of Residents" exceeds 438.

14. Patterns of Shopping Behavior

Area	Number of Respondents	Neighborhood Stores	(%)	District Commercial Center	(%)	Nanking Road and Avenue Joffre	(%)
Zhabei	107	98	(91.6)	4	(3.7)	5	(4.7)
Nanshi	79	27	(34.2)	46	(58.2)	6	(7.6)
Downtown	97	88	(90.7)	4	(4.1)	5	(5.2)
Huxi (West Shanghai)	150	142	(94.7)	5	(3.3)	3	(2.0)
Total	433	355	(82.0)	59	(13.6)	19	(4.4)

NOTE: The "District Commercial Center" for each area is as follows: Beizhan (or Northern Station) for Zhabei, Laoximen (or Old West Gate) for Nanshi, Rue du Consulat (today's Jinlingdong Road) for Downtown, and Jing'ansi (or Temple of Peace) for Huxi. See chapter 6 for details on the city's district commercial centers.

15. The Persistence of Native Accents

Accent Level[a]	Average Age at the Time of Immigration	Years in Shanghai	1st Generation (397 Respondents)	2nd Generation (33 Respondents)	3rd and Later Generations (8 Respondents)
A	19.43	51.09	5.3%	6.1%	—
B	18.92	51.40	32.7%	12.1%	—
C	18.31	51.91	50.1%	18.2%	25%
D	15.38	61.33	11.9%	63.6%	75%

[a] Accent level A = speaks the local dialect of one's native place, B = speaks the Shanghai dialect with a heavy accent, C = speaks the Shanghai dialect with an accent, D = speaks the Shanghai dialect without an accent.

List of Informants

No.[a]	Sex	Year Born	Native Place	Born in SH	Moved to SH	Occupation[b]	Interview Location and Date
I-1	m	1929	Qidong (J)	n	1946	mill worker	Shanghai 3-16-89
I-2	m	1930	Shanghai	y	—	ferry boat attendant	Shanghai 3-16-89
I-3	f	1934	Taicang (J)	n	1939	mill worker	Shanghai 3-18-89
I-4	f	1922	Songjiang (J)	n	1938	vendor	Shanghai 3-18-89
I-5	f	1941	Qingjiang (J)	y	—	elementary schoolteacher	Shanghai 3-19-89
I-6	m	1919	Siyang (J)	n	1937	rickshaw puller	Shanghai 3-19-89 7-14-93
I-7	m	1923	Xuzhou (J)	n	1932	railway porter	Shanghai 3-19-89
I-8	m	1915	Gaoyou (J)	n	1930	rickshaw puller	Shanghai 3-19-89
I-9	m	1915	Yangzhou (J)	n	1938	store owner	Shanghai 3-20-89
I-10	f	1920	Yuyao (Z)	n	1929	store owner	Shanghai 3-20-89 3-26-89

Continued on next page

No.[a]	Sex	Year Born	Native Place	Born in SH	Moved to SH	Occupation[b]	Interview Location and Date
I-11	f	1918	Shaoshan (Z)	n	1935	housewife	Shanghai 3-20-89 3-25-89
I-12	m	1926	Shaoxing (J)	n	1938	store owner	Shanghai 3-20-89
I-13	f	1922	Nanhui (J)	y	—	store co-owner	Shanghai 3-22-89
I-14	m	1949	Ningbo (Z)	y	—	shop assistant	Shanghai 3-20-89 3-23-89
I-15	m	1920	Jiangdu (J)	n	1934	store owner	Shanghai 3-23-89 3-27-89 8-17-93 8-21-93
I-16	f	1918	Huanggang (H)	n	1942	store owner	Shanghai 3-26-89
I-17	f	1908	Shaoxing (Z)	n	1940	domestic servant	Shanghai 3-26-89
I-18	f	1950	Yuyao (Z)	y	—	schoolteacher	Los Angeles 5-17-91 5-18-91
I-19	m	1932	Changzhou (J)	n	1947	shop assistant	Los Angeles 6-29-91 6-30-91
I-20	f	1929	Suzhou (J)	n	1942	schoolteacher	Oswego, N.Y. 8-3-92
I-21	m	1917	Ningbo (Z)	y	—	small merchant	Shanghai 7-14-93 8-11-95
I-22	m	1911	Zhongshan (G)	n	1933	businessman	Shanghai 7-14-93 8-3-95
I-23	f	1919	Fanyu (G)	n	1935	office worker	Hong Kong 6-2-94
I-24	m	1921	Fanyu (G)	n	1928	doctor	Hong Kong 6-2-94

No.[a]	Sex	Year Born	Native Place	Born in SH	Moved to SH	Occupation[b]	Interview Location and Date
I-25	m	1905	Shanghai	y	—	teacher	Shanghai 7-15-93 7-16-93 7-29-95 8-2-95
I-26	f	1913	Changshu (J)	n	1938	nurse	Shanghai 8-6-93 8-17-93
I-27	m	1924	Huainan (A)	n	1936	bus driver	Shanghai 3-24-89 8-10-95
I-28	m	1918	Huzhou (Z)	n	1940	mill office worker	Shanghai 8-7-95 8-13-96
I-29	m	1916	Yuyao (Z)	n	1929	accountant	Shanghai 8-7-95 8-13-96
I-30	m	1912	Shangyu (Z)	y	—	businessman	Shanghai 8-11-96
I-31	m	1917	Shangyu (Z)	y	—	businessman	Shanghai 8-11-96
I-32	m	1917	Taicang (J)	n	1933	businessman	Shanghai 8-11-96
I-33	m	1917	Chuansha (J)	n	1925	businessman	Shanghai 8-11-96
I-34	f	1919	Zhongshan (G)	n	1939	schoolteacher	Shanghai 8-12-96
I-35	m	1922	Fanyu (G)	n	1940	photographer	Shanghai 8-12-96
I-36	f	1911	Jinhua (Z)	n	1934	office worker	Shanghai 8-18-96
I-37	f	1927	Ningbo (Z)	y	—	nurse	Shanghai 8-19-96
I-38	f	1923	Qidong (J)	n	1930	housewife	Shanghai 8-19-96

Continued on next page

No.[a]	Sex	Year Born	Native Place	Born in SH	Moved to SH	Occupation[b]	Interview Location and Date
I-39	m	1915	Tonglin (A)	n	1938	peddler	Shanghai 8-20-96
I-40	m	1927	Jiangyin (J)	n	1940	peddler	Shanghai 8-20-96
I-41	m	1925	Huzhou (Z)	n	1936	fortune-teller	Shanghai 8-21-96

NOTE: Abbreviations in the table are: m = male, f = female, (A) = Anhui, (G) = Guangdong, (H) = Hubei, (J) = Jiangsu, (SH) = Shanghai, (Z) = Zhejiang, y = yes, n = no.

[a] Informants are cited in the text by code, such as "I-1." The interviews were conducted with the understanding that names of the informants would not be released, with a few exceptions where the interviewees had no qualms about disclosing their identity.

[b] The column "Occupation" shows each informant's occupation of longest duration prior to 1949, if applicable.

Notes

1. On the indigenous growth of pre-treaty-port Shanghai, see Linda Johnson, *Shanghai;* on the presence of the West in the city, see Nicholas Clifford, *Spoilt Children;* on local circuit intendants, or Daotai, see Leung Yuen-sang, *Shanghai Taotai;* on the Mixed Court, see Thomas Stephens, *Order and Discipline;* on traditional merchant organizations, see Joseph Fewsmith, *Party;* on modern entrepreneurship both Chinese and Western, see Marie-Claire Bergère, *Golden Age,* and Sherman Cochran, *Big Business;* on relations between the capitalist class and the Guomindang government, see Parks Coble Jr., *Shanghai Capitalists,* and Christian Henriot, *Shanghai, 1927–1937;* on public health, see Kerrie MacPherson, *Wilderness;* on higher education, see Wen-hsin Yeh, *Alienated Academy,* and Ming K. Chan and Arif Dirlik, *Schools;* on the police, see Frederic Wakeman, *Policing Shanghai* and *Shanghai Badlands;* on the underworld, see Brian Martin, *Shanghai Green Gang,* and Pan Ling, *Old Shanghai;* on labor strikes and labor conditions, see Elizabeth Perry, *Shanghai on Strike,* and Emily Honig, *Sisters;* on the student movement, see Jeffrey Wasserstrom, *Student Protests;* on native-place associations, see Bryna Goodman, *Native Place;* on social biases based on native place, see Emily Honig, *Creating Chinese Ethnicity;* on intellectual life, see Poshek Fu, *Passivity;* on the world of prostitution, see Gail Hershatter, *Dangerous Pleasure.*

2. On the new county histories produced as the result of the program, see Vermeer, "New County Histories." Shanghaishi tongzhiguan had produced a number of original works (including journals, pamphlets, and annuals) that are still basic references for scholars of Shanghai. Their work was interrupted by the outbreak of the Sino-Japanese War in 1937. After August 1945, the group resumed under the name *Shanghai wenxian weiyuanhui* (Shanghai document committee) and continued to compile and publish Shanghai annuals (*nianjian*) and local gazetteers. The group finally disbanded at the end of the Nationalist regime.

3. Most noticeably, Tang Zhenchang and Shen Hengchun, *Shanghai shi* (History of Shanghai), a single-volume general history of Shanghai that covers the period from ancient times to 1949, and Zhang Zhongli, *Jindai Shanghai chengshi yanjiu* (Research on modern Shanghai City), a study of the economic, political-social, and cultural dimensions of the city from the late nineteenth century to 1949. Other major publications on the history of Shanghai include the two-volume *Shanghai jindai shi* (The history of modern Shanghai), edited by Liu Huiwu (Shanghai: East China Normal University Press, 1985, 1987), the two-volume collection of treatises *Shanghai shi yanjiu* (Research on the history of Shanghai) (Shanghai: Xuelin Press, 1984, 1988), a series called *Shanghai yanjiu luncong* (Papers on Shanghai studies), of which so far nine volumes have been published by the Shanghai Academy of Social Sciences Press, and a reminiscences series called *Shanghai difang shi ziliao xuanji* (Selected collections of materials on Shanghai local history), of which six volumes have appeared. The Committee of Shanghai Literature and History (*Shanghai wenshi ziliao bianji weiyuanhui*) has published special topic volumes in its *wenshi ziliao* (literature and history) series, including volumes on Shanghai's gangster organizations (*liumang banghui*), real estate, finance, education, and so on. A volume on social vices (*yan, du, chang,* or drugs, gambling, and prostitution) has been published by the Shanghai Institute of Culture and History (*Shanghaishi wenshi guan*). Rare historical materials have been reprinted, many under the title *Shanghai shi ziliao congkan* (Collections of historical materials of Shanghai), published by Shanghai renmin chubanshe, and *Shanghaitan yu Shanghairen* (Shanghai and the Shanghai people) published by Shanghai guji chubanshe.

4. For example, a number of symposia on the history of modern Shanghai jointly sponsored by American and Chinese institutions have been held in the United States and China. An international conference on the history of Shanghai was held at the Shanghai Academy of Social Sciences in September 1988, and the papers presented at the conference were published in both Chinese (*Shanghai yanjiu luncong,* volumes 3 and 4 under the English title, *Shanghai: Gateway to the World*) and in English (*Shanghai Sojourners,* edited by Wakeman and Yeh). In August 1993, two international symposia on Shanghai's history and economic development were held in the city, entitled respectively "Port Opening—Opening to the World: Shanghai over the Recent 150 Years, 1843–1993," and "Urban Progress, Business Development, and Chinese Modernization." From 1992 to 1995, the Shanghai Academy of Social Sciences conducted joint programs with the University of California at Berkeley and Cornell University on twentieth-century Shanghai. Sponsored by the Luce Foundation, three international conferences on the business and cultural history of Shanghai were held (convened by Sherman Cochran) at Cornell University in the summers of 1992, 1994, and 1995. A volume of papers from the 1995 conference is forthcoming from Cornell University Press.

5. Mote, "Transformation," 102–3; Skinner, "Introduction," 258–61.

6. Weber, *City,* 81–82.

7. Skinner, "Introduction," 265–67; Mote, "Transformation," 114–18.

8. Elvin, "Chinese Cities," 87.

9. Sima Qian, *Shiji*, 1243 (*juan* 25, *lushu* 3).

10. Gu Yanwu, *Ri zhi lu*, 20.

11. Strand, *Rickshaw Beijing*, 29.

12. Wang Yingxia, *Wang Yingxia zizhuan*, 201; *Shehui ribao*, August 8, 1936. For a detailed account of the beggars, see Lu, "Becoming Urban."

13. Jiang Siyi and Wu Yuanshu, *Shanghai qibai ge qigai de shehui diaocha*, 191; Siao, *Mao Tse-tung and I Were Beggars*, 77.

14. Shen Ji et al., *Zhongguo mimi shehui*, 188.

15. Isaacs, *Five Years of Kuomintang Reaction*, 62–63; Wakeman, *Policing Shanghai*, 84.

16. Mote, "Transformation," 102.

17. "*Zoujin tianbian, haobuguo Huangpujiang liangbian*" literally means "To explore up to the edge of the world, there is no place better than the two banks of the Huangpu River." See Hu Zude, *Huyan*, 52.

18. Hu Zude, *Huyan waibian*, 18; Qian Nairong, *Shanghai fangyan liyu*, 115.

19. Lu Xun, *Diary*, 108.

20. The story was published in thirty-five installments in *Shenbao*, from October 30, 1931, to December 3, 1931. It is summarized and commented on in Link, *Mandarin Ducks and Butterflies*, 225–27.

21. Mao Tun [Mao Dun], *Midnight*, 14–24.

22. Yu Dafu, *Yu Dafu wenji*, 4:27.

23. See ibid., 9:2–185.

24. Yu Dafu, *Night*.

25. Link, *Mandarin Ducks and Butterflies*, 227.

26. Wakeman and Yeh, *Shanghai Sojourners*, 12.

27. For a definition of these terms see Reynolds, *China, 1898–1912*, 207 n. 2.

28. Wang Tao, *Yingru zazhi*, 7–11; Chen Duxiu, *Duxiu wencun*, 587–996.

29. Informant I-11, March 25, 1989; I-12. (Informants are cited by code; see appendix 2 for details.)

30. Up to 1980, Shanghai accounted for one-eighth of China's national industrial production and contributed one-sixth of total national income annually; one-third of the central government's revenue came from taxes levied on Shanghai. See *Jiefang ribao*, October 3, 1980.

31. This PLA unit was formed in Laiyang, Shangdong, in 1947. For official information about the unit, see Jiefangjun wenyishe, *Nanjing Lu shang Haobalian*.

32. The drama had several slightly different versions and was also adapted into a movie by the same title. In 1963, all top Communist leaders, including Mao Zedong, saw the drama in person. Their attendance was made into much publicized events, which aimed to show the whole country the extent of official support of the drama and the moral teachings that it promoted. See Shen Xi-

meng et al., *Nihongdeng xia de shaobing;* and Nanjing shifan xueyuan zhong-wenxi, *"Nihongdeng xia de shaobing" zhuanji.*

33. Quote from Rozman, *Modernization of China,* 3.

34. The aptly named Long Bar was 110 feet in length and generally agreed to be the longest in the world. See Wright, *Twentieth Century Impressions,* 388; and Barber, *Fall of Shanghai,* illustrations after page 124.

35. In the late 1980s, Shanghai still had about 800,000 to 1 million coal stoves and nightsoil buckets in use. For details see chapters 5 and 6.

36. See chapter 6 for details.

37. Appendix 1, "Patterns of Obtaining Clothing"; I-4; I-23.

38. I-9, I-21. Getting to work on foot was common among factory workers. Sometimes a single trip to the mill took one to two hours. See Honig, *Sisters,* 137.

39. See Zhu Zijia, *Huangpu jiang,* 70–72, for a discussion of Shanghai style astuteness, in particular an insider's comparison of how business is conducted by the peoples of Shanghai and Hong Kong (or Shanghainese and Cantonese).

40. The French inventor Georges Claude invented neon lighting in 1907. In 1910, Claude demonstrated his first neon sign at the Grand Palais in Paris. Neon was soon adopted by the lighting industry for commercial use. By the late 1920s, neon lighting had already been widely used for colorful street signs and commercial advertisements. In Shanghai, the term "nihongdeng" (a semi-transliteration of "neon light") applied liberally to all city lights (or commercial lights, which included fluorescent and electronic lighting). See Claude, "Neon Tube Lighting"; "Broadway's Colors" (*New York Times,* January 23, 1929); Miller and Fink, *Neon Signs,* 1–5. See also Tang Zhenchang, *Jindai Shanghai fanhua lu,* 170.

41. See Paul Cohen, *Discovering History in China.*

42. See for instance Bernhardt, *Rents, Taxes, and Peasant Resistance.*

43. See Murphey, *Shanghai, Key to Modern China.*

44. A few works on Shanghai have been produced that emphasize the continuity of Chinese social and institutional practices. Linda Johnson's works on Shanghai from market town to early treaty port emphasize the commercial prosperity of Ming-Qing Shanghai and the perdurability of Chinese institutions in the first fifteen years of Shanghai as a treaty-port city. This conclusion is consistent with the field's broader research on the socioeconomic history of the lower Yangzi delta region in the late imperial period. Frederic Wakeman's research on Shanghai police in the Nanjing decade (1927–37) is "about connections and continuities"; it seeks to link a variety of political processes from the late Qing reforms to the Beijing Committee on State Security of 1989 (*Policing Shanghai,* xvii). In a study of everyday life in Shanghai's Bank of China, Wen-hsin Yeh shows how Confucian values continued to influence management style in a seemingly unquestionable Western-type institution: Yeh suggests that the corporate-sponsored communalism of the bank in Republican Shanghai bore similarities to the work-unit (*danwei*) system adopted

in urban China after the Communist revolution ("Corporate Space, Communal Time").

45. Huang, "Paradigmatic Crisis," 335.

46. See chapter 5 for details.

47. On urban neighborhood organizations in the People's Republic of China (PRC), see Schurmann, *Ideology*, 371–80; Whyte and Parish, *Urban Life in Contemporary China*, 22–25, 283–90.

48. See Habermas, *Structural Transformation*. For a discussion on the application of Habermas's ideas to analyzing recent Chinese history, see Rowe, "Public Sphere." The issue is further debated in a *Modern China* symposium (19, no. 2, April 1993). In Hong Kong, the *Chinese Social Sciences Quarterly* published a group of articles by both Chinese and Western scholars on "Civil Society and China" (August 15, 1993). The leading history journal in the PRC, *Lishi yanjiu* (Historical research), also devoted an issue (no. 1 [1996]) to the discussion.

49. Rowe, *Hankow*, 61–62, 136; Strand, *Rickshaw Beijing*, 167–68, 290–91.

50. Bestor, *Neighborhood Tokyo*, 66–77.

51. Lee, Introduction, 15–16.

CHAPTER 1. GOING TO SHANGHAI

1. Huxley, *Jesting Pilate*, 271.

2. This area centered on Nanking Road and was bounded by the Bund on the east, Tibet Road on the west, the southern bank of Suzhou Creek on the north, and Yangjingbang Creek (later transformed into Avenue Edward VII) on the south.

3. "Pudong" literally means "east of the Huangpu River." In the 1990s, this rural area finally caught the attention of Chinese urban planners and has become the fastest developing area of Shanghai. In 1996, the Pudong New Area (*Pudong xinqu*) was a Special Economic Zone of 201 square miles (522 square kilometers) with a population of 1.48 million. Like that of Shenzhen (in Guangdong province) in the 1980s, Pudong's development is seen as the symbol of China's dramatic economic growth and social transformation in the 1990s. For a comprehensive narrative on Pudong, see Wang Hongquan et al., *Pudong jingu daguan*.

4. However, the notion that Shanghai was virtually nothing prior to the coming of the West has lingered in some recent writings. For example, Seagrave's *Soong Dynasty* describes Shanghai thus: "In the early 1800, just before the Soongs came on stage, the old Chinese city was just a village on the muddy banks of the Whangpoo [Huangpu] River" (3).

5. The Shanghai Daotai was one of the ninety-two Daotais under the provincial government in the Qing period. On the Daotai institution in the Qing administrative system, see Leung Yuen-sang, *Shanghai Taotai*, chapter 2.

6. Zou Yiren, *Jiu Shanghai renkou*, 91.

338 / Notes to Pages 27–31

7. These statistics were calculated by the author from Hu Huanyong, *Zhongguo renkou*, 53, tables 2–11.

8. Fairbank, *Trade*, 357–61; Huang Wei, *Shanghai kaibu chuqi duiwai maoyi yanjiu*, 75–78.

9. Morse, *International Relations*, 1:356–58; Huang Wei, *Shanghai kaibu chuqi duiwai maoyi yanjiu*, 177–78, tables 25–26.

10. This is a modification of the more rigid Maoist view of treaty-port cities as entirely harmful to China. Recent scholarship in China justifies a positive assessment of the role of treaty ports by citing Engels's words that violence or "evil" forces can be revolutionary and Marx's comments on British rule in India, viz., that the Britons served as the "unconscious tool of history" in creating social revolution in India. See Tang and Shen, *Shanghai shi*, 156–57; Zhang Zhongli, *Jindai Shanghai chengshi yanjiu*, 32–33.

11. The following paragraph from a book about modern Shanghai written by an American soon after the Communist revolution typified the former mentality: "The stubborn marauders from the West dug their toes into the [Yangzi] delta and stayed: throughout the land they built great cities, of which Shanghai was the greatest. These Western conquerors could not be absorbed as China had absorbed other conquerors. They stood aloof, resisting Oriental influence, until their power weakened and they were forced to withdraw, leaving their cities, as well as their political and cultural imprints, behind them." Finch, *Shanghai and Beyond*, 3. For the latter view, see Wakeman, *Policing Shanghai*, 34.

12. Johnson, *Shanghai*, chapter 2; Goodman, *Native Place, City, and Nation*, 48–50; Lu, "Arrested Development."

13. Zou, *Jiu Shanghai renkou*, 38–41; Hu Huanyong, *Zhongguo renkou*, 49. This sometimes led to the impression that the people of Shanghai were all immigrants. An article published in the Shanghai newspaper *Shenbao* (August 10, 1900) declared that "the people of Shanghai are all sojourners, and there are no natives."

14. Calculations are based on Zou Yiren, *Jiu Shanghai renkou*, tables 1 and 46.

15. Shanghaitong she, *Shanghai yanjiu ziliao*, 1:113; Xu Gongsu and Qiu Jinzhang, *Shanghai gonggong zujie zhidu*, 19–20, 68. For the English version of the *Shanghai Land Regulations* of 1845, see *North China Herald*, January 17, 1852.

16. Maybon and Fredet, *Histoire*, chapter 2.

17. Morse, *International Relations*, 2:349–50. Morse was a commissioner in the Chinese customs service who lived in Shanghai for many years and wrote extensively on modern Chinese history.

18. Fortune, *Tea-Districts*, 2:2.

19. Imperial Maritime Customs, *Treaties*, 1:200.

20. For the correspondence between Qiying and Emperor Daoguang in this regard, see *Chouban yiwu shimo*, Daoguang Section, vols. 67, 69, 70. For both

English and Chinese versions of the Bogue Treaty, see Imperial Maritime Customs, *Treaties*, 198–207.

21. On the Qing government's intentions in this regard, see Lu Hanchao, "'Shanghai Tudi Zhangcheng' yanjiu."

22. *Chinese and Japanese Repository* 2, no. 18 (January 1865): 32.

23. Lang, *Shanghai, Considered Socially*, 22.

24. *Chinese and Japanese Repository* 2, no. 15 (October 1864): 79–88.

25. Lang, *Shanghai, Considered Socially*, 24; Shanghai Mercury, *Shanghai, 1843–1893*, 3.

26. Zou Yiren, *Jiu Shanghai renkou*, 90–91; Lanning and Couling, *History of Shanghai*, 1:292.

27. When Robert Fortune revisited Shanghai in September 1848, three years after his last visit, he was surprised by the numerous ships on the Huangpu River. He was more surprised by the appearance of the Bund: "I had heard that many English and American houses had been built, indeed one or two were being built before I left China; but a new town, of very considerable size, now occupied the place of wretched Chinese hovels, cotton fields, and tombs." *Tea-Districts*, 2:1–2.

28. Kuai Shixun, *Shanghai gonggong zujie*, 318.

29. Lang, *Shanghai, Considered Socially*, 35.

30. Dyce, *Model Settlement*, 111–12.

31. Fortune, *Three Years' Wanderings*, 114.

32. By the lunar calendar, this was the fifth day of the eighth month, the birthday of Confucius.

33. For a firsthand Western account of the rebellion, see A British Resident, *Twelve Years in China*, 187–219. A comprehensive source on the rebellion is Shanghai shehui kexueyuan lishi yanjiusuo, *Shanghai Xiaodaohui qiyi shiliao huibian*. For a well-researched history of the Small Swords, see Guo Yuming, *Shanghai Xiaodaohui qiyi shi*.

34. These houses served as the initial form of the lilong (alleyway) house, discussed in detail in chapter 4.

35. Although no exact rental or purchase prices were recorded, in general the profits from constructing houses for Chinese were 30 to 40 percent. See Zhu Jiancheng, "Jiu Shanghai fangdichan de xingqi," 11.

36. De Jesus, *Historical Shanghai*, 100; Kuai Shixun, *Shanghai gonggong zujie*, 349.

37. De Jesus, *Historical Shanghai*, 98.

38. Alcock, *Capital of the Tycoon*, 37–38. One source indicates that the merchant was Edwin Smith; see Shen Chenxian, "Shanghai zaoqi de jige waiguo fangdichan shang," 131.

39. Alcock, *Capital of the Tycoon*, 38.

40. Ibid.

41. Feetham, *Report*, 1:54–62; Xu Gongsu and Qiu Jinzhang, *Shanghai gonggong zujie zhidu*, 43–67. For a complete English version of the *Shanghai*

Land Regulations effective in the Republican period, see Feetham, *Report,* 1:68–83, Appendix 4.

42. Feetham, *Report,* 1:57–59.

43. Ibid., 1:50, appendix 2.

44. De Jesus, *Historical Shanghai,* 98–99. See also Pott, *Short History of Shanghai,* 39.

45. Zou Yiren, *Jiu Shanghai renkou,* 3–4, 90–91.

46. In the late Qing, these counties (*xian*) belonged to six prefectures (*fu*), namely, Suzhou, Songjiang, and Taicang in Jiangsu province, and Hangzhou, Jiaxing, and Huzhou in Zhejiang province.

47. *Chouban yiwu shimo,* Daoguang Section, vol. 29; *Chouban yiwu shimo,* Xianfeng Section, vol. 7.

48. Lin Yutang, *My Country and My People,* 18.

49. See, for example, *Hongzhi Shanghai zhi, juan* 1:4–5; Shanghai bowuguan, *Shanghai beike ziliao xuanji,* 38–39; Shanghai renmin chubanshe, *Qingdai riji huichao,* passim; *Tongzhi Shanghai xianzhi, juan,* 2:1.

50. Wu Guifang, *Gudai Shanghai shulue,* 81–89; Wang Tao, *Yingru zazhi,* 9–10.

51. Yi'an zhuren, *Hujiang shangye shijing ci,* 4:21.

52. Forbes, *Five Years in China,* 13–14.

53. Yu Qiuyu, *Wenming de suipian,* 201.

54. Sergeant, *Shanghai,* 3.

55. Luo Zhiru, *Tongjibiao,* 22; Zou Yiren, *Jiu Shanghai renkou,* 146–47.

56. I-21, August 11, 1995.

57. Barber, *Fall of Shanghai,* 13.

58. Gascoyne-Cecil and Cecil, *Changing China,* 104–5.

59. Abend, *Treaty Ports,* 155.

60. Power, *My Twenty-five Years,* 58.

61. Tu Shipin, *Shanghai chunqiu, xia:* 88–89.

62. The number of Sikh policemen in the International Settlement rose from 296 in 1900 to 1,842 in 1939; see Wei, *Shanghai,* 105.

63. Ross, *Escape to Shanghai,* xi; Heppner, *Shanghai Refuge,* 48. See also Pan Guang, *Jews in Shanghai.*

64. According to an investigation of the Japanese consulate general in Shanghai in October 1928, out of a total 2,178 Japanese females who worked in Shanghai, 628 (or 29 percent) were prostitutes. See *Gongshang banyuekan* 2, no. 8 (April 1930): 23–25.

65. Chunshenjun, "Zenyang weichi Shanghai de fanrong."

66. *North China Daily News,* August 12, 1937.

67. For an account of foreigners' experience at the time of the Communist takeover, see Barber, *Fall of Shanghai;* for a glimpse of the end of foreign Shanghai, see Tata and McLachlan's extraordinary photo collection, *Shanghai, 1949.*

68. Luo Zhiru, *Tongjibiao zhong zhi Shanghai,* 22; *Shanghaishi nianjian*

1936; Xu Run, *Xu Yuzhai zixu nianpu*, 295–97; Zou Yiren, *Jiu Shanghai renkou bianqian*, tables 1, 22, 50.

69. This depends on the measure one chooses. According to the most detailed demographic statistics available on Shanghai, the city's population in 1852 was 544,413 (including the rural suburban areas of Shanghai county); about a century later, in March 1949, the population of the city proper was 5,455,007 (Zou Yiren, *Jiu Shanghai renkou*, 90–91). According to Fortune, Shanghai's population was about 270,000 in 1843 (*Three Years' Wanderings*, 104). Thus, as far as the city proper is concerned, the population increased twentyfold from 1843 to 1949.

70. The native-to-nonnative ratio in the Chinese districts was slightly higher since the Chinese districts included certain rural areas where inhabitants were mostly Shanghai natives. No data on the native-to-nonnative ratio are available for the French Concession. But the 1947–49 surveys on the three districts (Songshan, Lujiawan, and Changshu) that formerly made up the French Concession found that the populations of nonnatives in these districts were as high as 90 percent of the total. See Zou Yiren, *Jiu Shanghai renkou*, 112–13, tables 20 and 21.

71. *Shanghaishi nianjian*, 1947, C:15; Shanghaishi renmin zhengfu, *yijiu sijiu nian*, 14–5; Hu Huanyong, *Zhongguo renkou*, 49.

72. Based on figures in the International Settlement in 1930 and 1935; see Luo Zhiru, *Tongjibiao*, table 43; *Shanghaishi nianjian*, 1935, G:23–24; Zou Yiren, *Jiu Shanghai renkou*, table 22.

73. Shanghaishi renmin zhengfu, *Yijiu sijiu nian*, 20–21; Zou Yiren, *Jiu Shanghai renkou*, table 24.

74. Shanghai Civic Association, *Statistics of Shanghai*, 4, table 5; Luo Zhiru, *Tongjibiao*, 27, tables 41, 43.

75. *Shehui yuekan* 1, no. 4 (April 1929): 3–5.

76. See appendix 1, "Type of Respondent's Hometown Prior to Moving to Shanghai."

77. Fang Hongkai and Huang Yanpei, *Chuansha xianzhi*, preface and introduction of *juan* 5 (Industry). Today Chuansha is one of ten counties under the administration of the Shanghai municipal government.

78. Chesneaux, *Chinese Labor Movement*, 48.

79. The workers in Shanghai's machine-building enterprises were among the earliest modern industrial workers in China. Because these workers were employed in Shanghai's foreign shipyards as early as the 1850s (Lanning and Couling, *History of Shanghai*, 1:384–91), orthodox Chinese Communist historiography regards them as China's first proletarians. The orthodox position goes on to argue that the Chinese proletariat appeared earlier than the Chinese capitalists, who were mainly a late-nineteenth-century phenomenon. Investigation of Shanghai's machine-building enterprises shows that workers in this industry hailed mainly from three areas: Guangdong province, Ningbo (in Zhejiang province), and local villages around Shanghai.

The earliest industrial workers in Shanghai's machine-building industry were mechanics from Guangdong. They were part of what Elizabeth Perry terms the "South China artisans" (*Shanghai on Strike,* 32). Since the city was becoming China's leading commercial port in mid-nineteenth century, these shipyards were designed mainly for repairing trade ships, and workers with special skills such as coppersmithing were particularly needed. The majority of these skilled workers were from Xiangshan (now Zhongshan) county in Guangdong. In the early 1860s, Hongkou (the northeastern part of Shanghai) was a spacious area where Shanghai's shipyards and docks were gathered; all the workers there were said to be Cantonese (*Shanghai xinbao,* Oct. 6, 1862). By the late 1870s, workers from Ningbo and local villages gradually outnumbered those from Guangdong (Shanghaishi gongshang, *Shanghai minzu jiqi gongye,* 1:50–70; Shanghai jiqiye gongren yundong shi, *Shanghai jiqiye gongren yundong shi,* 36–37).

80. Shanghaishi gongshang, *Shanghai minzu jiqi gongye,* 1:52, 55–56.

81. Ibid., 1:55–56.

82. Ibid.; Shanghai jiqiye gongren yundong shi, *Shanghai jiqiye gongren yundong shi,* 35–40.

83. Official statistics showed that in 1928–30, 42 percent of Shanghai's industrial workers were working in cotton mills, and 32 percent in spinning, weaving, or dyeing factories. In other words, about three-quarters of Shanghai's industrial workers were employed in textiles (Yang Ximeng, *Shanghai gongren shenghuo chengdu,* 7). This was the peak number of Shanghai's textile workers. But even after the devastating war of 1937–45 and the Communist takeover in 1949, a survey conducted in April 1951 still showed that 205,000 people worked in Shanghai's textile industries, or about 30 percent of the city's total of 750,000 industrial workers (Shanghai fangzhi gongren yundong shi, *Shanghai fangzhi gongren yundong shi,* 39; Jiefang ribao she, *Shanghai jiefang yinian,* 74–75).

84. Li Cishan, *Shanghai laodong,* 8–9.

85. For instance, workers from Pudong (a mainly rural area on the eastern side of the Huangpu River) worked in factories in Puxi (on the western side of the river) but still lived in their villages, crossing the river by ferry each day to go to work. Li Cishan, *Shanghai laodong,* 8.

86. Ibid., 8–9.

87. Lamson, "Effect," 1062.

88. Li Cishan, "Shanghai laodong zhuangkuang," 3.

89. Jiangnan, *Jiangnan zaochuan changshi,* 22–24; Shanghai shehui kexueyuan jingji yanjiusuo, *Jiangnan zaochuanchang changshi,* 86–87.

90. Huang Wei and Xia Lingen, *Jindai Shanghai diqu fangzhi jingji shiliao xuanji,* 336.

91. Ibid., 339; Shanghai shehui kexueyuan jingji yanjiusuo, *Liu Hong-sheng qiye shiliao,* 2:295.

92. Wang Zhong and Hu Renfeng, *Fahuaxiang zhi, juan* 2 (Customs).

93. Wang Wei and Xia Lingen, *Jindai Shanghai diqu fangzhi jingji shiliao xuanji*, 336.

94. *Xinwen bao*, October 30, 1930, reported that according to the Shanghai Public Bureau, there were 49,190 "servants" in Shanghai. Official statistics in January 1950 reported 94,203 "family servants" in the city at that time (Zou Yiren, *Jiu Shanghai renkou*, 111).

95. Hu Zude, *Huyan*, 52.

96. Edkins, *Grammar of Colloquial Chinese*, 181; Hu Zude, *Huyan*, 46.

97. Powell, *My Twenty-five Years in China*, 7.

98. Yang Hao and Ye Lan, *Jiu Shanghai fengyun renwu*, 324.

99. Zhang Ailing, *Zhang Ailing wenji*, 4:20.

100. Zhongguo kexueyuan Shanghai jingji yanjiusuo, *Nanyang xiongdi yancao gongsi shiliao*, 308.

101. *Shehui yuekan* 1, no. 5 (April 1929): 6.

102. Shanghai shehui kexueyuan lishi yanjiusuo, "Ba yi san," 395–416.

103. In early 1950, right after the Communists took power in Shanghai, many industries were brought to a standstill by frequent labor disputes. Sending workers back to their home villages on a rotation basis was one of the main solutions for making peace between business owners and employees (Jiefang ribao she, 1950, 62). Indeed, factory workers and other working people were often the major targets of the authorities' efforts to control the city's population after 1949. In two major campaigns of "mobilizing people to return to their homes in the countryside" in 1955–56 and 1958–62, it was mainly factory workers who were sent to their native places in the countryside or to factories in the rural hinterland. According to household registration data of the Public Security Bureau, in the single year of 1955, 847,293 people were moved out of Shanghai; among them, 779,138 were residents of Shanghai proper. See Shanghaishi gong'anju huzhengchu, *Shanghaishi renkou ziliao huibian*, 12; Hu Huanyong, *Zhongguo renkou*, 78–80.

104. See chapter 2 for details.

105. Lamson, "Effect," 1062.

106. For a complete list of these organizations see Zhang Zhongli, *Jindai Shanghai chengshi yanjiu*, 512–13, 518–22.

107. Shanghai yanjiu zhongxin, *Shanghai 700 nian*, 195.

108. Yang Hao and Ye Lan, *Jiu Shanghai fengyun renwu*, 202–9.

109. The practice, however, was criticized by the media in Hunan. Newspapers there attacked Mu for taking advantage of the cheaper labor in his native province and exploiting rural women workers. Debates on the correctness of this recruitment policy continued for more than a year and even drew the attention of Chen Duxiu, who moved this debate to his radical journal *Xin Qingnian* (New Youth) in order to draw nationwide attention to labor issues. See *Xin Qingnian* 7, no. 6 (May 1920): 1–2.

110. Shanghai shehui kexueyuan jingji yanjiusuo, *Liu Hongsheng qiye shiliao*, 2:316–18.

111. Hengfeng yinranchang, *Ranchang jinxi,* 3.

112. Shanghaishi liangshiju, *Zhongguo jindai mianfen gongye shi,* 191–93, 199.

113. See, for example, Chen Boxi, *Lao Shanghai;* and Haishang mingren zhuan bianjibu, *Haishang mingren zhuan.*

114. Xiong Yuezhi, "Zatan 'Shanghai ren.'"

115. See Edkins, *Vocabulary,* iv–vi, for rules of symbols; and Edkins, *Grammar of Colloquial Chinese,* 13–46, on the Shanghai tones and the relation of tones to accents.

116. McIntosh, *Useful Phrases.*

117. Xu Baohua and Tang Zhenzhu, *Shanghai shiqu fangyan zhi,* 3–4; Qian Nairong, *Shanghai fangyan liyu,* 73.

118. However, to call someone "Little Jiangbei" might have been considered offensive because of the general discrimination against people from Subei or Jiangbei (generally, the region immediately north of the Yangzi River).

119. In 1990 a survey of 438 Shanghai residents who had lived in the city for at least four decades found that more than half of the first-generation immigrants still spoke the Shanghai dialect with some accent, 32.7 percent still spoke with a heavy accent, and more than 5 percent simply spoke no Shanghainese at all. Even among third-generation (or later) immigrants, a quarter still spoke the Shanghai dialect with an accent, which they had picked up from their parents or grandparents. See appendix 1, "The Persistence of Native Accents."

120. Liu Meijun, "Shanghai nanzi shenghuo zhier."

121. Yang Peiming, "Kang Youwei zai Shanghai de yusuo"; Shanghaishi Changningqu, *Changningqu dimingzhi,* 146; Chen Lizheng and Yuan Enzhen, *Xinya de licheng,* 1–2.

122. The current address is 1517 Huaihaizhong Road. The Shanghai municipal government now lists the residence as a "cultural relics preservation site" (*shiji wenwu baohu danwei*). See Shanghaishi Xuhuiqu, *Shanghai Xuhui zhuzhai,* 12.

123. Shanghaishi Xuhuiqu, *Shanghaishi Xuhuiqu dimingzhi,* 345.

124. Following is a list of a few of the most dominant political figures and their residences in Shanghai:

Name	Address
Sun Yat-sen (1866–1925)	7 Xiangshan Road, Luwan District
Jiang Jieshi (Chiang Kai-shek, 1888–1975)	9 Dongping Road, Xuhui District
Song Ziwen (T. V. Soong, 1894–1971)	145 Yueyang Road, Xuhui District
Song Qingling (Madame Sun, 1893–1981)	45 Taojiang Road, Xuhui District
Jiang Weiguo (1916–)	1843 Huaihaizhong Road, Xuhui District

| Cai Yuanpei (1868–1940) | 303 Huashan Road #16, Jing'an District |
| Sun Ke (1891–1973) | 1262 Yan'anxi Road, Changning District |

After 1949, a number of private homes were turned into luxurious (and also secret) residences to house top communist leaders Mao Zedong, Lin Biao, Jiang Qing, and others when they visited Shanghai. Even in the 1990s, when Deng Xiaoping was in Shanghai, he stayed at the Xijiao Hotel, which was previously the private home of a Yao family. The images of these luxurious homes are captured in Shanghaishi Xuhuiqu fangchan guanliju, *Shanghai Xuhui zhuzhai.*

125. See Zhang Kaiyuan's preface for Yue Zheng, *Jindai Shanghairen shehui xintai.*

126. In 1878, the monthly salary of an ordinary comprador was 40 taels. Higher ranking compradors received 500 to 800 taels per month in 1932. See Hao, *Comprador,* 89–94; Wu Peichu, "Jiu Shanghai waishang yinhang maiban," 110.

127. Nie Baozhang, *Zhongguo maiban zichan jieji,* 161–64.

128. For instance, the Xi family, a well-known comprador clan, had its start on the road to wealth during the Taiping Rebellion, when Xi Pingfang moved his family from Dongshan (near Suzhou) to Shanghai. Xi went into business in Shanghai and married the sister of Shen Eryuan, a wealthy merchant and fellow Dongshan native who had moved to Shanghai earlier. Xi sent all four sons to work in Shanghai's foreign banks. By the early twentieth century, the four had become quite successful compradors. In following years, during the Republican period, Xi's grandsons, great-grandsons, in-laws, and other relatives were compradors in Shanghai. A. Wright, *Twentieth Century Impressions,* 540; Wu Peichu, "Jiu Shanghai waishang yinhang maiban," 96–109.

129. The official name was adopted after the 1911 revolution.

130. Huang Yifeng et al., *Jiu Zhongguo minzu zichan jieji,* 289–91.

131. Coble, *Shanghai Capitalists,* 24; Zhang Zhongli, *Jindai Shanghai chengshi yanjiu,* 721.

132. Zhongguo renmin yinhang, *Shanghai qianzhuang shiliao,* 770–71.

133. Wang Jishen, *Shanghai zhi fangdichanye,* 52–61. The powerful Zhejiang (or more specifically, Ningbo) presence in the formation of the Shanghai bourgeoisie has already been well described. See, for examples, Jones, "Ningpo Pang"; Rankin, *Elite Activism,* 88–89, 176–83; Schoppa, *Chinese Elites and Political Change,* 169.

134. Coble, *Shanghai Capitalists,* 27.

135. Du Xuncheng, *Minzu ziben zhuyi,* 253–54. According to an official survey conducted by the Shanghai Bureau of Social Affairs in 1929, the total number of factories in Shanghai was estimated at 2,326; see *Wages and Hours of Labor of Greater Shanghai* (1929), cited in D. K. Lieu, *Growth,* 62.

136. Bergère, *Golden Age,* 6.

137. Calculated from Xu, *State,* 45–46, 57–63.

138. Extra-Settlement roads were those constructed by the SMC and the French Concession authorities outside the official boundaries of the concessions. This had been an issue between the Chinese and foreign authorities since the early 1860s, when the latter started building "military roads and constructions" to obstruct the Taipings' several attempts to approach Shanghai. However, even after the Taiping Rebellion, the construction of roads continued for decades, mostly in the western and northeastern sections of the foreign concessions. The official expansion (i.e., sanctioned by the Chinese authorities) of the International Settlement in 1899 and the French Concession in 1914 was virtually the Chinese government's recognition of a fait accompli. But roads and houses continued to be built after the official expansions of 1899 and 1914. The legal status of these newly built extra-Settlement roads became an irritant in the Nanjing decade as the Chinese tried to recover sovereignty over these areas. Many of Shanghai's elegant homes and best neighborhoods were located along these extra-Settlement roads, most of which were in west Shanghai (Huxi) and northeast of Hongkou. See Xu Gongsu and Qiu Jinzhang, "Shanghai gonggong zujie zhidu," chapters 3 and 4; Lu Hanchao, "'Shanghai Tudi Zhangcheng' yanjiu"; Wakeman, *Policing Shanghai,* 65–72.

139. Yu Jianhua, *Zhongguo huihua shi,* 2:196–97.

140. *Shenbao,* February 28, 1925, p. 7; Xu Ke, *Qing bai lei chao,* 37:66–67.

141. See, for example, Link, *Mandarin Ducks and Butterflies,* 54–78.

142. Tang Zhenchang and Shen Hengchun, *Shanghai shi,* 504–5.

143. In 1939, for example, 92 of the city's total 245 sizable bookstores were located in these streets. Shanghai yanjiu zhongxin, *Shanghai 700 nian,* 334–37; Zhu Lianbao, *Jinxiandai Shanghai chubanye yinxiang ji,* 2, 6–7.

144. Hu Shi, *Sishi zishu,* 144–45.

145. Link, *Mandarin Ducks and Butterflies,* 154.

146. Mao Dun, *Wo zouguo de daolu,* 1:151; Wang Yingxia, *Wang Yingxia zizhuan,* 96.

147. Tang Hai, *Zhongguo laodong wenti,* 177–78.

148. Cowley, *Exile's Return,* 55–56.

149. Link, *Mandarin Ducks and Butterflies,* 5–7.

150. Yeh, "Progressive Journalism and Shanghai's Petty Urbanites"; Wakeman and Yeh, *Shanghai Sojourners,* 12.

151. Friedrichs, "Capitalism."

152. Based on a discussion with a group of sociologists and historians at the Shanghai Academy of Social Sciences, July 22, 1995.

153. I will delve into the details of shikumen communities when I discuss daily life of the common people in chapters 4–6.

154. Zhu Bangxing et al., *Shanghai chanye,* 699.

155. It has been estimated that in 1936–37, on the eve of the Sino-Japanese War, Shanghai had about 270,000 zhiyuan. See Shanghaishi zonggonghui, *KangRi zhanzheng shiqi Shanghai gongren,* 62.

156. Zou Yiren, *Jiu Shanghai renkou bianqian de yanjiu,* 26–37, tables 1, 15, and 16.

157. For research of this type on Shanghai, see Honig, *Sisters and Strangers;* and Perry, *Shanghai on Strike.*

158. About 51 percent, or 388,420 out of 759,154 inhabitants. Calculated from Bureau of Social Affairs, *Standard,* table 25.

159. Ibid., 139.

160. See chapter 3 for details.

161. Shanghaishi gongshang, *Shanghai minzu jiqi gongye,* 2:810–11; Zhu Bangxing et al., *Shanghai chanye yu Shanghai zhigong,* 241–42.

162. See details in chapters 2 and 3.

163. Tang Hai, *Zhongguo laodong wenti,* 89; Zhu Bangxing et al., *Shanghai chanye,* 647, 673; Jiang Siyi and Wu Yuanshu, "Shanghai de qigai."

164. Li Cishan, "Shanghai laodong"; Luo Zhiru, *Tongjibiao,* 72; Zou Yiren, *Jiu Shanghai renkou,* 104; Shanghai shehui kexueyuan lishi yanjiusuo, *Wusi yundong zai Shanghai shiliao,* 11, table 8.

165. See chapter 3 for details. About half of the population had virtually no occupation at all. The postrevolutionary government called the nonoccupational residents of Shanghai a "consumption population," in contrast to the "productive population" (that is, people who had an occupation or job). Rao Shushi, Shanghai's Communist Party chief and military head in the early 1950s, declared in his official address to the Shanghai Municipal Congress in August 1949 that there were about 3 million people in the city who belonged to the consumption population (Jiefang ribao she, *Shanghai jiefang yinian,* 7). Statistics also showed that in January 1950 the productive population (*zaiye renkou*) constituted 41.46 percent of the total population in Shanghai (Zou Yiren, *Jiu Shanghai renkou,* 104), which means more than half the residents of Shanghai (mostly children, housewives, and the elderly) fell in the consumption population category.

CHAPTER 2. THE WORLD OF RICKSHAWS

1. For a general history of Harbin in English, see Clausen and Thogersen, *Making of a Chinese City,* especially pages 23–52 on the Russian influence in the city.

2. Hu Shi, *Hu Shi wencun,* 3:24–25. Hu Shi had reason to be particularly sharp about rickshaws. A rickshaw-related incident dramatically changed his life (hence also affected the New Cultural Movement). In the spring of 1910, the then-nineteen-year-old Hu Shi was living in Nanlin Li (Alley of Southern Forest) on Haining Road in Hongkou and teaching Chinese at an SMC-sponsored elementary school. Being young and associated with a group of what he called "romantic friends," Hu Shi was for a while on the loose, drinking, gambling, and frequenting brothels. One night, after a bout of heavy drinking in a brothel with his friends, Hu got blind drunk and staggered from the brothel alone, hiring a rickshaw home. Once he got on the rickshaw, Hu quickly fell asleep. It was midnight and raining. The rickshaw man saw an opportunity, robbed his drunken passenger, dumped him on the street, and then

ran away. Hu ended up spending the night in a police station, charged with attacking a policeman who tried to stop him while he was staggering and acting peculiarly on Haining Road. Hu also wounded himself wrestling with the policeman on the curbstones. The next morning Hu was fined $5 and allowed to go home. That day, looking at his swollen face in the mirror, he was overwhelmed with deep regret, not just for the incident, but more for his recent dissipation in general. "Without shedding a single tear," Hu Shi recalled twenty years afterward, "spiritually I had experienced a big change at that time." He then decided to start a new life by going to study in America. See Hu Shi, *Sishi zishu*, chapter 5.

3. Hauser, *Shanghai: City for Sale*, 134.

4. As the population of Shanghai increased, so did the number of rickshaws and rickshaw pullers. In 1920, the city had about 35,000 rickshaws for public hire and 12,000 private rickshaws. By the mid-1920s, the number had increased to about 50,000 and 15,000, respectively. By the end of the 1930s, the number of public-rickshaw pullers alone reached about 100,000. See Li Cishan, "Shanghai laodong zhuangkuang," 72–74; Tang Hai, *Zhongguo laodong wenti*, 89; Cai Binxian, "Cong nongcun pochan suo jichulai de renlichefu wenti," 37; *Shanghaishi nianjian*, 1935:K71; Zhu Bangxing et al., *Shanghai chanye*, 673.

5. The invention of the rickshaw dated to 1869 and has been attributed to various people in Japan, although perhaps not all were Japanese. Credence is generally given to the claim of Izumi Yosuke, who had a workshop at the foot of Nihombashi, where he embarked on the rickshaw business in 1869 (Waley, *Tokyo*, 167–68; *Shanghai shenghuo* 2, no. 2 [July 1938]: 13). However, one author wrote, "According to the Americans, it was a missionary in Yokohama—a certain Reverend Globe—who converted a baby carriage to drag about his invalid wife in 1869 and thus produced a prototype of what soon became the popular rickshaw named in Japan *jin-rick-sha*" (Krasno, *Strangers Always*, 112). The Japan historian Seidensticker summarizes the controversy in this way: "Though the origins of the rickshaw are not entirely clear, they seem to be Japanese, and of Tokyo specifically. The most widely accepted theory offers the names of three inventors, and gives 1869 as the date of the invention" (*Low City, High City*, 42).

6. Shanghaishi gongyong shiye guanliju, *Shanghai gongyong shiye*, 248–49; Shanghaishi chuzu qiche gongsi, *Shanghai chuzu qiche renliche*, 73–74; Krasno, *Strangers Always*, 111–12.

7. *Shenbao*, August 18, 1873.

8. Shanghaishi chuzu qiche gongsi, *Shanghai chuzu qiche renliche*, 73–74.

9. Fang Fu-an, "Rickshaws in China," 796. The formal Chinese term for the rickshaw, *renliche*, has confirmed this meaning.

10. Shanghaishi jiaotong yunshu ju, *Shanghai gonglu yunshu shi*, 31; Ma Xuexin et al., *Shanghai wenhua yuanliu cidian*, 591 and 594; Zhu Bangxing et al., *Shanghai chanye yu Shanghai zhigong*, 673–74.

11. *Chinese Economic Monthly* (May 1925): 35, cited in Fang Fu-an, "Rick-

shaws in China," 798; Shanghaishi chuzu qiche gongsi, *Shanghai chuzu qiche renliche*, 74.

12. Zheng Yimei, *Shanghai jiuhua*, 17–18; Tu Shipin, *Shanghai chunqiu, zhong:* 34.

13. Regardless of the distance of the trip, in the 1920s and 1930s a taxi customer typically tipped the driver 10–20 cents; see Shanghaishi wenshi yanjiu guan, *Haishang chunqiu*, 50.

14. *China Weekly Review* (April 7, 1934): 214.

15. Pal, *Shanghai Saga*, 171.

16. According to a three-day survey in June 1889 of traffic on Willis Bridge at the confluence of the Huangpu River and Suzhou Creek, rickshaws far outnumbered all other types of vehicles combined:

Type of Vehicle	Number of Vehicles
Single-wheel carts	2,759
Carriages	1,633
Rickshaws	20,958
Lorries (goods vehicles)	22
Sedan chairs	27
Horses	38

See Wei, *Shanghai: Crucible of Modern China*, 98, and *Old Shanghai*, 57; Yang Jiayou and He Mingyun, *Ta qiao gujin tan*, 108. Willis Bridge was the main route from the Bund and Nanking Road area to Hongkou and Yangshupu. It was reconstructed in 1909 and was also known as the Garden Bridge (today it is known as Waibaidu Bridge). It was a perfect place for surveying the city's traffic.

17. Shanghaishi jiaotong yunshu ju, *Shanghai gonglu yunshu shi*, 32.

18. See Table 4. The population of Shanghai in the 1930s was about 3.5 million. See also Shanghaishi gongyong shiye guanliju, *Shanghai gongyong shiye*, 250.

19. Rickshaws for public hire were also called *baoche* (private vehicles).

20. Shanghaishi jiaotong yunshu ju, *Shanghai gonglu yunshu shi*, 32.

21. *Chinese Economic Monthly* (May 1925): 35, cited in Fang Fu-an, "Rickshaws in China," 798; Shanghaishi chuzu qiche gongsi, *Shanghai chuzu qiche renliche*, 74.

22. Darwent, *Shanghai*, 99.

23. Krasno, *Strangers Always*, 110–11.

24. Wu and Wakeman, *Bitter Winds*, 1–2; Zhang Biwu, "Zhu gongguan de baoche fu."

25. *Strangers Always*, 110–11; Wu and Wakeman, *Bitter Winds*, 2–3.

26. The regular exchange rate in the late nineteenth century was one yuan (silver dollar) = 1,000–1,200 *wen* (copper coins), depending on the quality of the copper coins.

27. Shanghaishi chuzu qiche gongsi, *Shanghai chuzu qiche renliche*, 74 and 79. Ironically, Menard, the Frenchman who introduced the rickshaw to Shang-

hai, did not make a fortune from the business. Two years after he opened the business, he became bankrupt and fled to Vladivostok. See Tu Shipin, *Shanghai Chunqiu, zhong:* 34.

28. Shanghaishi chuzu qiche gongsi, *Shanghai chuzu qiche renliche*, 74.

29. Shanghaishi gongyong shiye guanliju, *Shanghai gongyong shiye*, 252; Hauser, *Shanghai: City for Sale*, 135.

30. Zhu Bangxing et al., *Shanghai chanye yu Shanghai zhigong*, 674.

31. T. Wright, "Shanghai Imperialists," table 1.

32. Johnstone, *Shanghai Problem*, 192; Ricsha Committee, "Report of the Ricsha Committee," 59–60. Also, Krasno, *Strangers Always*, 110, reports that "only 144 people owned the total of 68,000 rickshaw licenses issued in Shanghai."

33. Ricsha Committee, "Report of the Ricsha Committee," 60–67; Guo Chongjie, "Shanghaishi de renliche wenti," 23. The $750 fee included the rent of the vehicle.

34. Ricsha Committee, "Report of Ricsha Committee," 60–63.

35. Guo Chongjie, "Shanghaishi de renliche wenti," 25–26.

36. The rickshaw racket was often in the headlines and became a hot issue in the mid-1930s when the SMC and Shanghai's Chinese municipal government tried to reform the business. For details see T. Wright, "Shanghai Imperialists."

37. The size of rickshaw families ranged from 2 to 8 persons. More than 85 percent of the households had 3–6 persons; see Cai Binxian, "Cong nongcun pochan suo jichulai de renlichefu wenti," 36–37.

38. The number of rickshaw pullers grew to about 100,000 in the late 1930s, an increase of 20,000 from the mid-1930s. Most of the newcomers were single and had no family in Shanghai. Private rickshaw pullers were not included in these statistics. According to one estimate, there were about 15,000 private rickshaw pullers in Shanghai in the 1920s. See Li Cishan, *Shanghai laodong zhuangkuang*, 74; Zhu Bangxing et al., *Shanghai chanye yu Shanghai zhigong*, 674.

39. Fang Fu-an, "Rickshaws in China," 801–2; Strand, *Rickshaw Beijing*, 29.

40. Zhu Bangxing, et al., *Shanghai chanye yu Shanghai zhigong*, 674; Cai Binxian, "Cong nongcun pochan suo jichulai de renlichefu wenti"; Shanghaishi shehuiju, "Shanghaishi renlichefu."

41. Cai Binxian, "Cong nongcun pochan suo jichulai de renlichefu wenti," 35–36. An investigation of 1,350 rickshaw pullers in Nanjing found that 1,128 (83.55 percent) were formerly farmers. The most conservative estimate was that at least 70 percent of Chinese rickshaw pullers were peasant in origin (ibid.).

42. Lei Jingdun, "Shanghai Yangshupu renlichefu diaocha," 18–19.

43. Guo Chongjie, "Shanghaishi de renliche wenti."

44. Zhu Bangxing et al., *Shanghai chanye yu Shanghai zhigong*, 674.

45. Xi Wei, "Shanghai shehui de pouxi."

46. Ibid.

47. *The Chinese Labor Year Book* (Peiping, 1928), cited in Fang Fu-an, "Rickshaws in China," 797; Zhu Bangxing et al., *Shanghai chanye,* 675.

48. *Shanghaishi nianjian,* 1935: K:71.

49. Fang Fu-an, "Rickshaws in China," 800. The shifts in the 1920s were slightly different: the first (evening) shift was from 2 P.M. to 6 A.M. (16 hours) and the second (day) shift was from 6 A.M. to 2 P.M. (8 hours). Since the evening shift was double the hours of the day shift, it was often shared by two pullers. See Li Cishan, *Shanghai laodong zhuangkuang,* 72.

50. Zhu Bangxing et al., *Shanghai chanye yu Shanghai zhigong,* 674.

51. Ibid., 675.

52. Ricksha Committee, "Report of Ricksha Committee," 66; Shanghaishi shehuiju, "Shanghaishi renlichefu," *Shehui banyuekan* 1, no. 3 (1934): 39–41.

53. Bureau of Social Affairs, *Standard of Living of Shanghai Laborers,* 3, 86; Shanghaishi shehuiju, "Shanghai de gongzi tongji," 15, 34–35.

54. Strand, *Rickshaw Beijing,* 29.

55. Lei Jingdun, "Shanghai Yangshupu renlichefu diaocha," 33–34; Shanghaishi shehuiju, "Shanghaishi renlichefu," *Shehui banyuekan* 1, no. 3 (1934): 38.

56. Hershatter, *Workers of Tianjin,* 66.

57. Shanghai shehui kexueyuan jingji yanjiusuo, *Liu Hongsheng qiye shiliao,* 1:219; Shanghaishi zonggonghui, *KangRi zhanzheng shiqi Shanghai,* 45.

58. I-6, July 14, 1993. There were, however, unlucky days when, for instance, a puller was fined for a traffic violation. Police abuse of power by seizing rickshaw licenses was common.

59. Lei Jingdun, "Shanghai Yangshupu renlichefu diaocha," 62.

60. Ibid., 21–22.

61. Zou Yiren, *Jiu Shanghai renkou bianqian,* 50, and tables 26, 27, 28.

62. Shanghaigang shihua bianxiezu, *Shanghaigang shihua,* 292–93; Chen Gang, *Shanghaigang matou de bianqian,* 38.

63. This could be interpreted as 1) a puller could not afford to buy more rice than a cap could hold, or 2) he might not have a container other than his cap, or 3) both. The same interpretations apply to the second sentence.

64. Shanghaishi chuzu qiche gongsi, *Shanghai chuzu qiche renliche,* 84.

65. Zhu Bangxing et al., *Shanghai chanye yu Shanghai zhigong,* 676.

66. Lei Jingdun, "Shanghai Yangshupu renlichefu diaocha," 55.

67. Shanghaishi shehuiju, "Shanghaishi renlichefu," *Shehui banyuekan* 1, no. 3 (1934): 41.

68. Zhu Maocheng, *Diaocha Shanghai gongren,* 3.

69. *Shehui ribao,* August 18, 1936.

70. On the hiring of female workers in the textile industry, see Honig, *Sisters and Strangers,* chaps. 3–5; Xu Xinwu, *Zhongguo jindai saosi gongyeshi,* chapter 8.

71. Gamble, *How Chinese Families Live,* 37, 317.

72. *Guohuo yuebao* 1, no. 6 (September 1924): 4.

73. Shanghaishi chuzu qiche gongsi, *Shanghai chuzu qiche renliche*, 82.

74. Perry, *Shanghai on Strike*, 228.

75. Gamewell, *Gateway to China*, 99.

76. Shanghaishi chuzu qiche gongsi, *Shanghai chuzu qiche renliche*, 82.

77. Lei Jingdun, "Shanghai Yangshupu renlichefu diaocha," 34, 55.

78. Wright, "Shanghai Imperialists," 92.

79. Philip Huang speaks of them as people who "straddled city and countryside, farming and urban work, rural and urban petty commodity production." Huang, *Peasant Family*, 334.

80. Pal, *Shanghai Saga*, 167.

81. *Shanghaitan*, 4:172; Gamewell, *Gateway to China*, 93.

82. Gamewell, *Gateway to China*, 93.

83. *Shanghaishi nianjian*, 1937: O:37. This figure may not be considered lower than the average. Life expectancy in Shanghai in 1951 was 42.0 years for males and 45.6 years for females (or an average of 43.8); see Hu Huanyong, *Zhongguo renkou*, 133–34. Zou Yiren, *Jiu Shanghai renkou bianqian*, 64, gives a slightly different average life expectancy in Shanghai in 1951: 44.6. Based on life expectancy in Nanjing in 1935, which was 38.50 years for males and 38.22 for females, Hu estimates that life expectancy in Republican Shanghai was likely lower than the 1951 figures, probably around 40 years.

84. Pullers' Mutual Aid Association of Shanghai, *Statistical Report*, "Age of Insured" and "Causes of Death and Deformity."

85. See chapter 3 for details on Shanghai's slums.

86. Zhu Bangxing et al., *Shanghai chanye yu Shanghai zhigong*, 676.

87. Guo Chongjie, "Shanghaishi de renliche wenti," 27.

88. Johnstone, *Shanghai Problem*, 191–99; Zhu Bangxing et al., *Shanghai chanye yu Shanghai zhigong*, 673–74.

89. Cai Binxian, "Cong nongcun pochan suo jichulai de renlichefu wenti."

90. The most informative reports based on these surveys are Lei Jingdun, "Shanghai Yangshupu renlichefu diaocha"; Ricsha Committee, "Report of the Ricsha Committee"; Shanghaishi shehuiju, "Shanghaishi renlichefu shenghuo zhuangkuang diaocha baogaoshu"; and Zhu Bangxing et al., *Shanghai chanye yu Shanghai zhigong*.

91. For example, most of the materials on rickshaw pullers that have been available to researchers were published in the mid-1930s, when rickshaw racketeers and pullers' lives became a headline issue in the city. The 1939 investigation into pullers' lives was part of the underground activities of the Chinese Communist Party in Shanghai; see the introduction of the 1984 version of Zhu Bangxing et al., *Shanghai chanye yu Shanghai zhigong*.

92. This hypothesis was stimulated by my spring 1989 interviews with two former rickshaw pullers in Shanghai. A relative of one of my interviewees, Pan Pinglian, a sixty-one-year-old farmer from Gaoyou, Subei, was visiting his relatives in Shanghai. Knowing that I was interested in the life of rickshaw pullers, Pan commented: "I think Shanghainese were spoilt—what in the hell

was the big deal about pulling a rickshaw? It might be humiliating to serve others, but as far as the job itself was concerned, it was not a heavy one compared to what we peasants did on the farm back in the countryside."

93. Lei Jingdun, "Shanghai Yangshupu renlichefu diaocha," 48–49.

94. Ibid., 55–56.

95. Krasno, *Strangers Always*, 110.

96. *Shanghaitan*, 4:172.

97. Ibid., 175; Li Cishan, "Shanghai laodong zhuangkuang," 73–74; Xi Wei, "Shanghai shehui de pouxi," 70.

98. Li Cishan, *Shanghai laodong zhuangkuang*, 74.

99. Up until the early twentieth century, the "Chinese pheasant," or "ringed pheasant" (*Phasianus torquatus*), a favorite game bird, was plentiful in Shanghai. The Shanghai Sportsman's Calendar marked October 1 to December 1 as the season for pheasant shooting. Younger pheasants were sometimes sold in the markets as "Shandong chickens." See Dyce, *Model Settlement*, 112–18.

100. Xi Wei, "Shanghai shehui de pouxi," 70–71; *Shanghaitan*, 4:174–75.

101. *Shanghaitan*, 4:174.

102. *Shanghaishi nianjian*, 1936: M:22–24; *Shanghaishi nianjian*, 1937: M:12, U:83; Xi Wei, "Shanghai shehui de pouxi," 71.

103. *Shanghaitan*, 4:174–75.

104. Xi Wei, "Shanghai shehui de pouxi," 70–71.

105. Wang Delin, "Gu Zhuxuan zai Zhabei faji he kaishe Tianchan Wutai," 357; Gu Shuping, "Wo liyong Gu Zhuxuan de yanhu jinxing geming huodong," 360; Shanghaishi gongyong shiye guanliju, *Shanghai gongyong shiye*, 252.

106. Shanghaishi chuzu qiche gongsi, *Shanghai chuzu qiche renliche*, 74–75; Shanghaishi gongyong shiye guanliju, *Shanghai gongyong shiye*, 250; Zheng Yimei, *Shanghai jiuhua*, 18.

107. Yu Ling, *Yu Ling juzuo xuan*, 18; Zhonggong Shanghai Hualian, *Shanghai Yong'an gongsi*, 10; Luo Suwen, *Shikumen: xunchang renjia*, 67.

108. Lei Jingdun, "Shanghai Yangshupu renlichefu diaocha," 13, 44.

109. Shanghaishi shehuiju, "Shanghaishi renlichefu," *Shehui banyuekan* 1, no. 1 (1934): 107.

110. China Handbook Editorial Board, *China Handbook 1950*, 639.

111. Lei Jingdun, *Shanghai Yangshupu renlichefu diaocha*, 51–52.

112. In stories like this, the most dramatic ending had the protagonist becoming a *zhuangyuan*, or the Number One Scholar, who was then received in audience by the emperor. For an English translation of such stories, see Birch, *Stories from a Ming Collection*, especially 19–36, 103–15.

113. In Subei, from which the majority of Shanghai's rickshaw pullers hailed, life was a constant struggle for survival. In such an environment, education was a great luxury; see Honig, *Creating Chinese Ethnicity*, 20–22.

114. Shanghaishi shehuiju, "Shanghaishi renlichefu," *Shehui banyuekan* 1, no. 1 (1934): 107.

115. Or, as the sociologist Oscar Lewis phrased it, the "culture of poverty," a term first used by Lewis in the title of his famous book (1959). Lewis later elaborated on the notion in his other publications (1965 and 1968) and developed it into a highly controversial theory.

116. Biweng, "Shanghai renlichefu"; Pal, *Shanghai Saga*, 170.

117. The membership fees were incorporated into the rents. Five cents was added to a twenty-four-hour rental. See *North China Herald*, June 27, 1934; Zhu Bangxing et al., *Shanghai chanye yu Shanghai zhigong*, 680; Johnstone, *Shanghai Problem*, 194.

118. Pullers' Mutual Aid Association of Shanghai, *Annual Report*, 4–5.

119. Ibid., 15.

120. Ibid., 4–5 and 15.

121. Zhu Bangxing et al., *Shanghai chanye yu Shanghai zhigong*, 678.

122. Chen Da, *Woguo kangRi zhanzheng shiqi*, 676–77; Perry, *Shanghai on Strike*, 232. Esteem for education can also be seen in the rickshaw men's neighborhoods, the shantytowns of Shanghai. Around 1925, five amateur sociologists explored a shantytown in northwest Shanghai, paying particular attention to education in the community. They visited three schools, all privately run, and observed some interesting and lively classroom scenes. One elementary school, which used standard textbooks issued by the Ministry of Education in Beiping (Beijing), had more than 30 students, who were "all lively and active." The observers noted that one of the schools practiced the Dalton system, which had been created only a few years earlier (in 1920) by Helen Huss Parkhurst (1887-?) in Dalton, Massachusetts. At the time of the visit, the students were discussing with their teacher Confucian doctrine on the relation between self-cultivation and statecraft. "If one compares these schools with Shanghai's commercialized colleges," one of the visitors exclaimed, "one could say the former exhibit something of the genuine spirit of education." Wang Dunqing, "You Jiangbei zhimindi ji," 17. On the Dalton system see Parkhurst, *Education on the Dalton Plan*; Dewey, *Dalton Laboratory Plan*; and Lynch, *Rise*.

123. Xi Wei, "Shanghai shehui de pouxi"; Shanghaishi chuzu qiche gongsi, *Shanghai chuzu qiche renliche*, 83. The expression "running like cows and horses" may not be as humiliating as the literal meaning suggests. The expression *niu ma zou* was customarily used as a formality in correspondence, along the lines of "Your servant" in an English letter in the Victorian era. The expression can be seen as early as the Han period in, for instance, Sima Qian's famous letter to Ren Shaoqin in *Hanshu* (The book of Han).

124. Shanghaishi shehuiju, "Shanghaishi renlichefu," *Shehui banyuekan* 1, no. 1 (1934): 105–6.

125. Lei Jingdun, *Shanghai Yangshupu renlichefu diaocha*, 17.

126. Ibid., 49.

127. Ibid., 50–51.

128. Hence the Chinese proverb *Rensheng qishi gu lai xi* (Since ancient times man has rarely lived to the age of seventy). This proverb may have

sprung from a poem by the famous Tang poet Du Fu (712–770); see *Chang-yong yanyu cidian*, 34.

129. Shanghaishi gongyong shiye guanliju, *Shanghai gongyong shiye*, 284.

130. *Shanghaishi nianjian*, 1936: O:50–51.

131. Yuan, *Sidelights on Shanghai*, 122–24.

132. Zhu Bangxing et al., *Shanghai chanye*, 680. A similar measure was taken in the Chinese districts on February 2, 1935. *Shanghaishi nianjian*, 1936: O:50–51.

133. Yuan, *Sidelights on Shanghai*, 125.

134. Thorbecke, *Shanghai*, 36; Krasno, *Strangers Always*, 111; Pal, *Shanghai Saga*, 167.

135. Gamewell, *Gateway to China*, 98–99.

136. Shanghaishi wenshi yanjiu guan, *Haishang chunqiu*, 50–51.

137. *Dongfang ribao*, December 2, 1939; Zhu Bangxing et al., *Shanghai chanye yu Shanghai zhigong*, 683.

138. Rickshaws plied the streets of Shanghai for eighty-two years: from 1874, the year the first rickshaw appeared, to 1956, the year the last rickshaw was sent to the Shanghai Museum.

139. Shanghaishi chuzu qiche gongsi, *Shanghai chuzu qiche renliche*, 75–76.

140. Zhu Bangxing et al., *Shanghai chanye yu Shanghai zhigong*, 652–53; Zhenhua, "Shanghai de matou xiaogong," 21; Chen Gang, *Shanghaigang matou de bianqian*, 27.

141. Pal continues, "No wild guesses go into that statement[,] for the evidence was always all too plain for everybody to see in the streets of Shanghai any day of the week. It was a common sight to see a long line of wheelbarrow 'taxis' transporting as many as eight plump Chinese mill-girls—four on each side—to and from work morning and evening—and glad of the business" (Pal, *Shanghai Saga*, 167). This "common sight" was captured in historical photos, such as those collected in R. Barz, *Shanghai: Sketches of Present-Day Shanghai*; Tang Zhenchang, *Jindai Shanghai fanhua lu*, 249; and Wei, *Old Shanghai*, plate 3.

142. I-6, July 14, 1993. This comment echoes Pan Pinglian's words cited in note 92.

143. Hauser, *Shanghai: City for Sale*, 136.

144. Pal, *Shanghai Saga*, 170–71.

145. Basler explained his research method as follows:

Two kinds of running can be distinguished: (1) Relatively slow running with 100 double paces in one minute and with a length of (double) step up to 210 centimeters (7 feet). The foot is posed in the same manner as in walking. The sole touches the ground completely during a short time before pushing off with that foot. (2) The second kind of running, making a possible quicker locomotion, involves contact only between the toes and ball of the foot and the ground, but this kind of running can not be continued for any length of time.

In the ricksha coolie there is a rolling motion of the foot, which is directly visible and demonstrable in photographs. It is characteristic of the first kind of running, and corresponds with the length of the step. In order to demonstrate this I marked off in a very busy street a measured distance, and from a window situated not very far from the street I counted the steps taken by ricksha coolies in covering this distance. This method has the advantage that the observed person is not aware of being observed and the length of step is that usually employed. Unlike laboratory experiments all movements are unconstrained and show no more than normal power.

Quoted in Fang Fu-an, "Rickshaws in China," 806–8.

146. Especially during the Cultural Revolution, pronouncements such as this appeared almost daily in Chinese newspapers.

147. *Renli sanlun che hangye yange* (The evolution of the rickshaw and pedicab trades), cited in Shanghaishi chuzu qiche gongsi, *Shanghai chuzu qiche renliche*, 83.

148. Wright, "Shanghai Imperialists," 92.

149. Shanghai's first tram line was opened in 1908, and its first bus line in 1922; see Shanghaishi gongyong shiye guanliju, *Shanghai gongyong shiye*, 334, 349.

150. Luo Zhiru, *Tongjibiao zhong zhi Shanghai*, 15.

151. I-6, March 19, 1989; I-22, July 14, 1993.

152. Biweng, "Shanghai renlichefu."

153. The "big license/small license" jargon was sometimes condemned as humiliating to the Chinese nation, since it suggested that the foreign (British) authorities were "greater" than the Chinese. See Wang Dingjiu, *Shanghai menjing*, section "Xing de menjing," 18–19; Xiao Lingjun, *Shanghai changshi*, 58; Yiming, *Shanghaishi*, 55.

154. Li Cishan, *Shanghai laodong zhuangkuang*, 72; Shanghaishi chuzu qiche gongsi, *Shanghai chuzu qiche renliche*, 75.

155. Shanghaishi jiaotong yunshu ju, *Shanghai gonglu yunshu shi*, 34; Yiming, *Shanghaishi*, 56–57.

156. Shanghaishi shehuiju, "Shanghaishi renlichefu," *Shehui banyuekan* 1, no. 1 (1934): 103

157. Zhu Bangxing, *Shanghai chanye yu Shanghai zhigong*, 677. Based on his own fieldwork in Shanghai in the 1940s, Chen Da (1892–1975), a pioneer Chinese sociologist, mentioned that most rickshaw pullers had the habit of spending their leisure time in the teahouse; see Chen Da, *Woguo kangRi zhanzheng shiqi*, 676.

158. *Shehui ribao*, May 11, 1937. See chapter 5 for details.

159. Shanghai Mercury, *Shanghai by Night and Day*, 86–87.

160. *Shanghaitan*, 4:173.

161. *An'nanjin* was the Chinese pronunciation of "Hennequin." The road was built in 1902 and initially named Taishan Road (Rue Tai Chan). In 1906 it was renamed after Hennequin, the vice chair of the Municipal Council of the French Concession. In 1946 the street was again renamed, this time as Dongtai Road. Dongtai is a county in Subei; thus the name was somehow related to

the street's history as the "Great World of Jiangbei [Subei]." See Shanghaishi Luwanqu, *Shanghaishi Luwanqu dimingzhi,* 173.

162. The streets in Shanghai's foreign concessions (especially the French Concession) and the so-called extra-Settlement roads were often given Western names. The Chinese names for these streets were: "Ailaige Road" for Rue Soeur Allegre (which is today known as Taoyuan Road); "Dong zilaihuo jie" for Rue de Peres (today's Yongshou Road); "Xi zilaihuo jie" for Rue de Saigon (today's Guangxi'nan Road). Ningpo Road (today's Huaihaidong Road) was so named because the well-known Siming Gongsuo, the native-place association of Ningpo (Ningbo), and its cemetery were located there. See Shanghaishi Huangpuqu, *Shanghaishi Huangpuqu dimingzhi,* 371, 383, Shanghaishi Luwanqu, *Shanghaishi Luwanqu dimingzhi,* 190; Ma Xuexin et al., *Shanghai wenhua yuanliu,* 216; Zheng Zuan, *Shanghai diming xiaozhi,* 121, 123.

163. *Shehui ribao,* February 20, 1936, and March 14, 1936.

164. *Shehui ribao,* September 12, 1934.

165. Thorbecke, *Shanghai,* 36.

166. Krasno, *Strangers Always,* 109–10.

167. Honig, *Creating Chinese Ethnicity,* 59–60.

168. Xu Guozhen, *Shanghai shenghuo,* 21, 63–64; Wang Dingjiu, *Shanghai menjing,* section "Xing de menjing," 19; I-22, July 14, 1993.

169. *Shanghaitan,* 4:178–79, 261–62.

170. See Wang Dingjiu, *Shanghai menjing,* section "Xing de menjing," 20–22. See also Xiao Lingjun, *Shanghai changshi,* 59–60; Xu Guozhen, *Shanghai shenghuo,* 64; Yiming, *Shanghaishi,* 56.

171. Yiming, *Shanghaishi,* 56.

172. The Chinese Bund lay on the banks of the Huangpu River, outside the old walled city, to the south of the Bund in the International Settlement. It was a bustling place with various shops and markets extending from the east side of the Chinese city to the Huangpu River. Local people usually called it Shiliupu (lit., sixteen shops), the name of a major dock there. See Shanghai Mercury, *Shanghai by Night and Day,* 58.

173. Lu Fen, *Shanghai shouzha,* 28–29. Three dollars was exorbitant since the regular taxi fare at that time was one dollar to anywhere inside the city proper; rickshaw fares were normally less than half of taxi fares. See Ni Xiying, *Shanghai,* 43, 142–43.

174. Biweng, "Shanghai renlichefu," 60.

175. Pal, *Shanghai Saga,* 168–69.

176. Ibid., 169.

177. Biweng, "Shanghai renlichefu," 60–61; Pal, *Shanghai Saga,* 169.

178. Gamewell, *Gateway to China,* 95; Darwent, *Shanghai,* xiv; Pal, *Shanghai Saga,* 168.

179. Darwent, *Shanghai,* xiv.

180. Pal, *Shanghai Saga,* 168.

181. Biweng, "Shanghai renlichefu," 64.

182. Pal, *Shanghai Saga,* 169–70.

183. Zhu Bangxing et al., *Shanghai chanye yu Shanghai zhigong*, 675.

184. *Shenbao*, December 31, 1874.

185. Shanghaishi chuzu qiche gongsi, *Shanghai chuzu qiche renliche*, 86; Perry, *Shanghai on Strike*, 227n.

186. *Wenhui bao*, October 1, 1946, October 4, 1946, and October 18, 1946. The Spanish seaman was sentenced to one year and three months in jail and the American sailor was judged by the American military court in Shanghai to have acted in "self-defense" and so was declared innocent. See Shanghaishi chuzu qiche gongsi, *Shanghai chuzu qiche renliche*, 109–10; and Tang Hai, *Zang Dayaozi zhuan*, 50.

187. Officially, Shanghai's foreign concessions ended in 1943, but many of the privileges enjoyed by Westerners continued until the Communist takeover in May 1949. Zang was born in 1903; he came to Shanghai and started to pull a rickshaw at age thirteen; see *Wenhui bao*, October 4, 1946. For a complete biography of Zang, see Tang Hai, *Zang Dayaozi zhuan*.

188. Biweng, "Shanghai renlichefu," 60. The translation is in Honig, *Creating Chinese Ethnicities*, 60, cited here with some modifications.

189. Ibid.

190. I-21, August 11, 1995; I-22, August 3, 1995.

191. Krasno, *Strangers Always*, 109.

CHAPTER 3. ESCAPING THE SHANTYTOWN

1. Hence G. E. Miller's well-known and multitranslated book, *Shanghai, the Paradise of Adventurers*.

2. Barber, *Fall of Shanghai*, 17.

3. Honig, *Sisters and Strangers*, 23.

4. Shanghaishi Nanshi quzhi bianzuan weiyuanhui, *Shanghaishi Nanshi quzhi*, 891–914.

5. The cultural value of this architecture in Shanghai is, to varying degrees, recognized by today's Chinese government, and certain measures have been taken for preservation and protection. By 1991, six sites in Shanghai were ranked by the authorities as "Nationally Registered Key Cultural Relics for Protection," fifty-two were ranked as "Municipally Registered Key Cultural Relics for Protection," and eighty-two were ranked as "District Registered Key Cultural Relics for Protection." At a time when the urban structure of Shanghai is undergoing large-scale radical changes, the architecture categorized in these hierarchies may not be demolished for any purpose. Wang Shaozhou, *Shanghai jindai chengshi jianzhu*, 23. Zhang Baogao and Fan Nengchuan, *Shanghai luyou wenhua*, 347.

6. The term *yangfang* can be used to refer to any Western-style architecture, including office buildings, but customarily it referred mainly to residential detached houses.

7. Details of shikumen appear in chapter 4.

8. Until very recently this area was still viewed by the people of Shanghai

as an undesirable rural backwater. By the late 1980s, when mounting pressure on housing had become a most serious social problem in Shanghai, an old folk saying remained valid: "A single room in Puxi [west of the Huangpu River] is better than a whole apartment in Pudong" (*ningyao Puxi yijianfang, buyao Pudong yitaofang*).

9. See "Report of the Housing Committee, 1936–37"; Bureau of Social Affairs, *Standard of Living*, 135–40; Tu Shipin, *Shanghai chunqiu, xia*: 3–7. Wang Shaozhou, *Shanghai jindai chengshi jianzhu*, 73–196; Chen Congzhou and Zhang Ming, *Shanghai jindai jianzhu shigao*, 160–70.

10. I-32.

11. Regarding inner-city slums in twentieth-century America, see Wilson, *Truly Disadvantaged*; and Ward, *Poverty*. In terms of the location of its shantytowns, Shanghai was more like Asian cities such as Calcutta than Latin American cities such as Mexico City. Recent research in the field of urban poverty has corrected the notion that in developing countries the urban poor tend to live on the outskirts of the city. In Mexico, for example, new migrants from the countryside prefer to live as renters in the inner city. The urban peripheral "shantytowns" are inhabited mostly by low-income families who own the property on which they live. In other words, the urban periphery consists of neighborhoods relatively better than the cheap rental accommodations in the central city. An "archipelago" model is more descriptive of the slums there. See Gilbert and Varley, *Landlord and Tenant*, 98–99; Sernau, *Economies of Exclusion*, 99–100.

12. Zhang Jiaqi and Ban Zhiwen, "Shanghaishi penghuqu gaikuang diaocha baogao," 235.

13. Mengyi, "Shanghai de yijiao." Of course, economic status often serves as a decisive measure for the social acceptance of newcomers. Speaking of nineteenth-century Hankou (Hankow), William Rowe notes that people tended to look on merchants as legitimate sojourners but discriminated against "vagrants" (*youmin*, many of whom were shack dwellers) as unwanted outsiders. See Rowe, *Hankow: Conflict and Community*, 298–99.

14. For a detailed discussion of the definition of the homeless, see Peroff, "Who Are the Homeless?"

15. Namely, the International Settlement Shanghai Municipal Police, the French Concession Police, the Nationalist Garrison Command's Military Police, and the Chinese Special Municipality's Public Safety Bureau. See Wakeman, "Policing Modern Shanghai."

16. *Xinwen bao* (Daily news) (Shanghai), January 26, 1932. Here the term "street beggars" referred to those who did not have a regular shelter (or "home") in Shanghai. It was estimated that Shanghai's professional beggars at that time numbered about 20,000.

17. Peroff, "Who Are the Homeless?" 34.

18. Charles Hoch, "Brief History."

19. In China up to the early 1990s, people still referred to getting an urban job as "upward transformation" (*shangdiao*), and to going to the countryside

to work as "downward exile" (*xiafang*) (I-33). On "rural send-downs" in China with a particular focus on the case of Shanghai, see White, *Policies of Chaos*, passim.

20. Normally, for these people the homes, however humble, they had left in their villages were better than the shanties of Shanghai. On China's rural housing, see Knapp, *China's Traditional Rural Architecture*, 108–21; *China's Vernacular Architecture*; and *Chinese House*, 5–49.

21. After 1955 the Communist government pursued an extremely strict household registration (*hukou*) system that successfully prevented rural residents from entering the cities. Although this system contributed to the gradual disappearance of squatter areas in Shanghai, the lure of Shanghai was not diminished. In China's present reform, for the first time in half a century, a huge number of rural residents are entering Shanghai in search of a better life. By the early 1990s, the so-called floating population exceeded 1 million and, like their predecessors some fifty years earlier, many of them stay illegally in those areas that lie between Shanghai proper and its suburbs. See Shanghaishi tongjiju, *Shanghai liudong renkou*, 39–57; *World Journal*, April 29, 1992. On the hukou system see also Tiejun Chen and Mark Selden, "Origins and Social Consequences," and Harry Xiaoying Wu, "Rural to Urban Migration."

22. *Shenbao*, September 24, 1872. Jiangnan, *Jiangnan zaochuan changshi*, 27–30.

23. Shanghai shehui kexueyuan jingji yanjiusuo, *Shanghai penghuqu*, 3.

24. Zhang Zhongli, *Jindai Shanghai chengshi yanjiu*, 53–59, 712–52.

25. Cheng Shi, "Yaoshuilong de gushi," 2–3.

26. Zhu Bangxing et al., *Shanghai chanye*, 91; Shanghai shehui kexueyuan jingji yanjiusuo, *Shanghai penghuqu*, 9.

27. Shanghai shehui kexueyuan jingji yanjiusuo, *Shanghai penghuqu*, 11.

28. I-7, a former resident of Fangualong.

29. The term *penghu* can also refer to the straw-hut occupants themselves, although these occupants were more commonly called *penghu jumin* rather than *penghu*. In Shanghai, "penghu" is an official term referring to straw huts or mat sheds. For a classification of housing types in Shanghai see Shanghaishi tongjiju, *Shanghai tongji nianjian, 1988*, 438, 441.

30. I-1, a former resident of Yaoshuilong.

31. Zhang Jiaqi and Ban Zhiwen, "Shanghai penghuqu," 237.

32. Shanghai shehui kexueyuan jingji yanjiusuo, *Shanghai penghuqu*, 12.

33. Lamson, "Problem," 147–48.

34. Shanghai shehui kexueyuan jingji yanjiusuo, *Shanghai penghuqu*, 10–11.

35. Tu Shipin, *Shanghai chunqiu, xia*: 6.

36. I-6, a former resident of Yaoshuilong.

37. Shanghai's population, taken in triennial censuses, was 2,641,220 in 1927, 3,144,805 in 1930, 3,404,435 in 1933, and 3,814,315 in 1936. Zou Yiren, *Jiu Shanghai renkou*, 90.

38. Shanghai shehui kexueyuan jingji yanjiusuo, *Shanghai penghuqu*, 13.

39. *Shibao*, November 19, 1914; Kuai Shixun, *Shanghai gonggong zujie*, 488–89.

40. Zheng Zuan, "Jindai Zhabei de xingshuai," 418.

41. Chen Gongpu, *Paohuo xia de Shanghai*, 170–87.

42. Lamson, "Problem," 147.

43. Zhu Maocheng, *Diaocha Shanghai gongren*, 8.

44. Bureau of Social Affairs, *Standard of Living of Shanghai Laborers*, 138. Another report of 1936 indicated that average annual rent for sufficient land to erect a straw hut was $10, and $5–6 for land in a less desirable location; see *Shehui ribao*, July 17, 1936.

45. Ibid. See also Zhu Bangxing et al., *Shanghai chanye*, 91.

46. Zhu Maocheng, *Diaocha Shanghai gongren*, 7–8.

47. Shanghai shehui kexueyuan jingji yanjiusuo, *Shanghai penghuqu*, 23–28.

48. Lieu, *Growth*, 172.

49. Benshu bianxiezu, *Zhaojiabang*, 3.

50. Shanghai shehui kexueyuan jingji yanjiusuo, *Shanghai penghuqu*, 17.

51. Ibid., 16–18.

52. See Lu, "Creating Urban Outcasts," figs. 1–10.

53. Shanghai shehui kexueyuan jingji yanjiusuo, *Shanghai penghuqu*, 75–80. I-1; I-5; I-6, March 19, 1989.

54. Tu Shipin, *Shanghai chunqiu, xia*: 6.

55. Chen Gang, *Shanghaigang matou de bianqian*, 39–41.

56. Zhu Maocheng, *Diaocha Shanghai gongren*, 7.

57. Zhang Jiaqi and Ban Zhiwen, *Shanghaishi penghuqu*, 236. See also Tu Shipin, *Shanghai chunqiu, xia*: 6–7.

58. See Lu, "Creating Urban Outcasts," map on p. 567.

59. Xue Yongli, "Jiu Shanghai penghuqu de xingcheng." The following table shows the number of the straw-hut slums in Shanghai in the early 1950s (adapted from *Shanghai penghuqu*, 7):

Households per Slum	Number of Slums
over 2,000	4
1,001–2,000	39
501–1,000	36
301–500	150
200–300	93

60. Ibid. In March 1949, two months before the Communists took over the city, Shanghai's population was 5,455,007. See Zou Yiren, *Jiu Shanghai renkou*, 91.

61. Bandyopadhyay, "Inheritors."

62. Zhou Erfu, *Morning in Shanghai*, 28.

63. Honig, *Sisters and Strangers*, 79–93.

64. I-4.

65. Dongping, "Pinminku fangwen ji."

66. Official statistics in 1936 show that there were 226,718 factory workers in Shanghai at that time, of which 136,665 (60 percent) were women and 27,091 (12 percent) were children. Most of the child workers were between the ages of 12 and 14. There were also a considerable number of child workers who were under 12 years of age; the youngest were only 6 or 7 years old. Feng Ruogu, "Shanghai tonggong nügong zhi shenghuo gaikuang."

67. Cheng Shi, "Yaoshuilong de gushi."

68. Shanghai shehui kexueyuan jingji yanjiusuo, *Shanghai penghuqu*, 5.

69. Honig, "Invisible Inequalities," and *Creating Chinese Ethnicity*, 52.

70. I-5, resident of Yaoshuilong, 1941–83.

71. *Shehui ribao*, July 17, 1936.

72. Currently available Shanghai population statistics indicating native place specify only the province. Shanghai's native-place associations (*tongxianghui*) left about fifteen hundred volumes of documents dated from 1912 to 1959, which are now available in the Shanghai Municipal Archives. However, data on residents' origin below the provincial level (i.e., county or prefecture) is still extremely fragmentary. In any case, no matter where they came from, shantytown dwellers were generally ignored by these associations. Native-place associations were in many ways dominated by the middle and upper classes, and issues related to shantytown dwellers were usually not on their agenda. This is another illustration of the "outcast" status of shantytown squatters. On Shanghai's native-place associations, see Goodman, *Native Place, City, and Nation*.

73. Zhu Bangxing et al., *Shanghai chanye*, 90–91.

74. Shanghai shehui kexueyuan jingji yanjiusuo, *Shanghai penghuqu*, 9–10.

75. The results of this survey are published in Yang Ximeng, *Shanghai gongren shenghuo chengdu de yige yanjiu*.

76. The results of this survey are published in Bureau of Social Affairs, *Standard of Living of Shanghai Laborers*.

77. The bungalow-type, single-story row house is very common in Pudong (the area east of the Huangpu River) and other suburbs of Shanghai. Although structurally similar to the alleyway house—i.e., both have brick walls and tiled roofs—they are decidedly inferior in construction; these houses could not bear the weight of a second story. Yang Ximeng, *Shanghai gongren shenghuo*, 71–72.

78. An official survey of working hours and income of Shanghai's workers in 1930–34 shows that among the sixteen industries surveyed, cotton-spinning workers had the longest working hours and ranked fifteenth in pay. Bureau of Social Affairs, *Wage Rates in Shanghai*, 60.

79. Bureau of Social Affairs, *Standard of Living*, 60.

80. Lamson, "Problem," 148.

81. Zhang Jingyu, *Shehui diaocha: Shenjiahang shikuang*, 59–61; Lamson, "Effect."

82. Luo Zhiru, *Tongjibiao zhong zhi Shanghai*, 86.

83. Bureau of Social Affairs, *Standard of Living*, 14.

84. *Shanghaishi nianjian*, 1947: C:17–C19; Shanghai shehui kexueyuan jingji yanjiusuo, *Shanghai penghuqu*, 64–65.

85. Ibid., 65.

86. Ibid., 15.

87. Ibid., 9–10.

88. Ibid., 64–66.

89. Dongping, "Pinminku fangwen ji."

90. Shanghai tebieshi shehuiju, *Shanghai zhi gongye*.

91. Shanghai shehui kexueyuan jingji yanjiusuo, *Rongjia qiye shiliao*, 1:337.

92. See Honig, *Sisters and Strangers*, especially chapter 5, for details.

93. Shanghai tebieshi shehuiju, *Shanghai zhi gongye*, table 13.

94. Xu Weiyong and Huang Hanmin, *Rongjia qiye fazhan shi*, 276.

95. Shanghaishi fangzhi gongyeju et al., *Yong'an fangzhi yinran gongsi*, 232.

96. Shanghai shehui kexueyuan jingji yanjiusuo, *Rongjia qiye shiliao*, 2:314.

97. Hengfeng, *Ranchang jinxi*, 5, 7–8.

98. *Chinese Economic Journal* 8, no. 2:106–12; Shanghaishi liangshiju, *Zhongguo jindai mianfen gongye shi*, 314; Zhu Bangxing et al., *Shanghai chanye*, 622.

99. Shanghaishi liangshiju, *Zhongguo jindai mianfen gongye shi*, 331.

100. Shanghai shehui kexueyuan jingji yanjiusuo, *Rongjia qiye shiliao*, 1:125.

101. *Shehui ribao*, July 17, 1936.

102. Ibid., 8.

103. Pedicabs were introduced in 1942, partly as a result of the gasoline shortage during the war. They gradually replaced rickshaws and became one of the main forms of transportation within the inner city of Shanghai after 1945. Under a government program, rickshaws, which were increasingly considered "inhuman and unscientific" by the public after World War II, were to be eliminated step by step and replaced by pedicabs. Many rickshaw pullers became pedicab drivers, although rickshaws were not officially abolished until 1956. Tu Shipin, *Shanghai chunqiu, zhong*: 34; Shanghai shehui kexueyuan, *Shanghai penghuqu*, 67.

104. Shanghaishi renmin zhengfu bangongting, *Shanghai shizheng gong-zuo qingkuang tongjitu*, 28.

105. Jiang Siyi and Wu Yuanshu, *Shanghai qibai ge qigai de shehui diao-cha*, 26–33.

106. Darwent, *Shanghai*, 84; *Shanghai Municipal Council Report for the Year 1932 and Budget for the Year 1933*, 211; Peters, *Shanghai Policeman*, 241.

107. Zhang Jiaqi and Ban Zhiwen, "Shanghaishi penghuqu gaikuang diaocha baogao," 235.

108. For a view of these signs, see Pan, *Shanghai,* 56; Tang Zhenchang, *Jindai Shanghai fanhua lu,* 75, 234.

109. Bureau of Social Affairs, *Standard of Living,* 104; Yang Ximeng, *Shanghai gongren shenghuo chengdu,* 35.

110. "Report of the Housing Committee," 101.

111. Shanghaishi wenshi yanjiu guan, *Haishang chunqiu,* 48–49; Wang Yingxia, *Wang Yingxia zizhuan,* 70; Shanghaishi Jing'anqu renmin zhengfu, *Shanghaishi Jing'anqu dimingzhi,* 214.

CHAPTER 4. THE HOMES OF THE LITTLE URBANITES

1. This neglect of the lilong at the popular level has also been reflected in the scholarly literature. Given the importance of this type of house in the development of Shanghai and its significance in the everyday life of the city's people, it is remarkable how little it has been studied. This neglect has been partly corrected by some recent academic research in China, notably the works of Luo Suwen and Zhang Jishun, which treat the shikumen as a legitimate topic for historical research and associate the topic with the broader urban culture of Shanghai (See Luo Suwen, *Shikumen: xunchang renjia;* Zhang Jishun, "Lun Shanghai lilong"). Although still not part of mainstream historiography, this work is part of the very recent trend in the People's Republic to reverse the four decades of neglect of social history. None of this recent work, however, rises above generalities, nor does any of it focus on the structure of everyday life in shikumen neighborhoods. In the English-speaking world, Jeffrey W. Cody has an ongoing research project related to this subject. See his "Residential Real Estate in Republican Shanghai," a paper presented at the international conference on Shanghai at the Shanghai Academy of Social Sciences, Shanghai, August 17–19, 1993.

2. Kuai Shixun, *Shanghai gonggong zujie shigao,* 347; Guo Yuming, *Shanghai xiaodaohui qiyi shi,* 249.

3. Lang, *Shanghai, Considered Socially,* 27; Kuai Shixun, *Shanghai gonggong zujie shigao,* 359.

4. Zou Yiren, *Jiu Shanghai renkou,* 3–4, 90–91.

5. De Jesus, *Historical Shanghai,* 98–99.

6. Zhu Jiancheng, "Jiu Shanghai fangdichan de xingqi," 11; Wang Shaozhou, *Shanghai jindai chengshi jianzhu,* 75; Kuai Shixun, *Shanghai gonggong zujie shigao,* 347.

7. Spencer, "House of the Chinese"; Knapp, *Chinese House,* 5–25.

8. Hu Jianhua, "Songdai chengshi fangdichan guanli jianlun," 29–30.

9. Zhu Jiancheng, "Jiu Shanghai fangdichan de xingqi," 10.

10. Alcock, *Capital of the Tycoon,* 37.

11. Ge Yuanxi, *Huyou zaji,* 14.

12. Shen Bojing and Chen Huaipu, *Shanghaishi zhinan,* 13.

13. Zhang Zhongli and Chen Zengnian, *Shaxun jituan zai jiu Zhongguo,* 34–35.

14. Shen Chenxian, "Nanjing lu fangdichan de lishi."

15. Zhu Jiancheng, "Jiu Shanghai fangdichan de xingqi," 15.

16. Ibid., 14.

17. The following is a list of some top Chinese real estate magnates in Shanghai, all of whom were compradors for Western companies in Shanghai (See Zhu Jiancheng, "Jiu Shanghai de Huaji fangdichan dayezhu"):

Cheng Jinxuan	Comprador of Sassoon and Co.
Zhou Liantang	Comprador of Sassoon and Co.
Bei Runsheng	Comprador, a "pigment magnate"
Yu Qiaqing	Comprador of the Dutch Bank
Zhu Dachun	Comprador of Jardine Matheson and Co. (Yihe)
Chen Binxian	Comprador of Burkill and Sons (Xiangmo)
Ying Zhiyun	Comprador of Tonghe
Wei Tingrong	Comprador of the French Bank
Zhu Ziyao	Comprador of Banque de L'Indo-chine (Tongfang huili Bank)

18. For the convenience of narration, the "Nanking Road area" refers to the British Settlement in its early stage. It centered on Nanking Road and was bounded by the Bund on the east, Tibet Road on the west, the southern bank of Suzhou Creek on the north, and Yangjingbang Creek (later transformed into Avenue Edward VII) on the south. The boundaries of this, the core area of modern Shanghai, were set by the Shanghai Daotai, Lin Gui, and the British consul Rutherford Alcock in November 1848.

19. Shen Chenxian, "Nanjing lu fangdichan de lishi" and "Shanghai zaoqi de jige waiguo fangdichan shang."

20. Shanghaishi tongjiju, *Shanghai tongji nianjian*, 438.

21. Ibid., 438; Shanghai zhuzhai, *Shanghai zhuzhai (1949–1990)*, 147.

22. The terms *lilong* and *longtang* have exactly the same meaning, but there is a slight difference in usage. *Lilong* is used on both formal and informal occasions, while *longtang* is more or less slang. For instance, in post-1949 Shanghai, one of the basic neighborhood organizations based essentially on divisions of alleyway houses was called *"lilong* residents' committees" not *"longtang* residents' committees."

23. Bureau of Social Affairs, *Standard of Living of Shanghai Laborers*, 136. The framework was made of marble or the local red stone produced in Ningbo. Later, in order to reduce costs, these materials were often replaced by bricks. But the term *shikumen* was still popularly used; the name was not thought to fall short of reality, because the word *shi* (stone) in the Shanghai dialect is commonly used to refer to cement and brick.

24. Luo, *Shikumen*, 18.

25. *Shenbao*, September 27, 1872.

26. Bird, *Yangtze Valley and Beyond*, 15, 19.

27. For instance, the dragon and the phoenix were symbols of the emperor and the empress respectively, but a wedding of ordinary people was (and still

is) commonly described by others in complimentary terms as a joining of dragon and phoenix (I-10, March 26, 1989; I-22, August 3, 1995).

28. Zhang Jishun, "Lun Shanghai lilong."

29. For instance, Wagner wrote, "In Shanghai the two-story *li* or alleyway house is the typical housing unit" (*Labor Legislation in China*, 50).

30. Shi Songjiu, *Shanghaishi luming daquan*, 401–673.

31. Zheng Zuan, *Shanghai diming xiaozhi*, 73–74.

32. Shi Songjiu, *Shanghaishi luming daquan*, 540–41.

33. See ibid., 401–673, table of the Names of Alleyway-House Compounds in the City Proper of Shanghai, passim.

34. This is evident in the correspondence of many well-known figures who resided in Shanghai, including Mao Zedong. In a letter dated 1920, Mao told his friend that his address in Shanghai was "Hatong Road, Minhounan Li, number 29." (The letter is preserved in the CCP's First National Congress museum.) In the 1950s, all residential compounds were given a street number.

35. Blaser, *Courtyard House in China*, 5–14; Knapp, *Chinese House*, 11–13.

36. Shanghai zhi zui bianweihui, *Shanghai zhi zui*, 133.

37. Gao Chao, "Shanghai lilong zhuzhai yan'ge," 225–26; Jia You, "Shanghai longtang mian mian guan," 286–87.

38. Wang Shaozhou, *Shanghai jindai chengshi jianzhu*, 81.

39. Chen Congzhou and Zhang Ming, *Shanghai jindai jianzhu shigao*, 163.

40. Wang Shaozhou and Chen Zhimin, *Lilong jianzhu*, 59–60; Chen Congzhou and Zhang Ming, *Shanghai jindai jianzhu shigao*, 163.

41. Wang Shaozhou, *Shanghai jindai chengshi jianzhu*, 77; Chen Congzhou and Zhang Ming, *Shanghai jindai jianzhu shigao*, 160–65.

42. Shanghaishi fangchan guanliju, *Shanghai lilong minju*, 26.

43. Wang Shaozhou, *Shanghai jindai chengshi jianzhu*, 81–83. For twenty detailed samples of these new-style alleyway-house compounds, see Shanghaishi fangchan guanliju, *Shanghai lilong minju*, 97–145.

44. Zhang Zhongli, *Jindai Shanghai chengshi*, 53–59, 712–52.

45. Lanning and Couling, 2:26.

46. Wang Shaozhou and Chen Zhimin, *Lilong jianzhu*, 6–8.

47. Luo Suwen, *Shikumen*, 17.

48. In the less than seventy years from 1865 to 1933, the average land value in the International Settlement had increased twenty-six times, from 1,318 taels per mu to 33,877 taels per mu (1 acre = 6 mu). See Zhang Zhongli and Chen Zengnian, *Shaxun jituan zai jiu Zhongguo*, 35–36.

49. Luo Suwen, *Shikumen*, 21.

50. Shanghaishi Jing'anqu, *Shanghaishi Jing'anqu dimingzhi*, 93; Luo Suwen, *Shikumen*, 21. This alleyway-house compound is still densely populated. It is located to the west of Lane 566 in Xinzha Road, Jing'an District.

51. Shanghaishi fangchan guanliju, *Shanghai lilong minju*, 26. I-28, August 7, 1995.

52. "Report of the Housing Committee," 99.

53. The present-day address of Jianye Li is "Lanes 440, 456, and 496 of Jianguoxi Road." The following description of Jianye Li is based on the author's field study conducted in July 1993. For more information on Jianye Li, see Shanghaishi Xuhuiqu, *Shanghaishi Xuhuiqu dimingzhi*, 32, and 191; Shanghaishi fangchan guanliju, *Shanghai lilong minju*, 84–85.

54. The floor plan described above is the original design. Virtually all houses in Jianye Li had undergone some sort of remodeling to accommodate more rooms and tenants, as I will discuss below.

55. See Yu Shan, "Er fangdong yu dingfei yazu."

56. Ibid.

57. "Report of the Housing Committee, 1936–1937," 99–100. My interpolations (in brackets) are added to indicate the standard local terms for the rooms and tenants.

58. Zhang Zhongli and Chen Zengnian, *Shaxun jituan zai jiu Zhongguo*, 45.

59. "Report of the Housing Committee, 1936–1937," 98.

60. Shen Weibing and Jiang Ming, *Ala Shanghai ren*, 29.

61. Cao Maotang and Wu Lun, *Shanghai yingtan huajiu*, 206–9.

62. Chen Yanlin, *Shanghai dichan daquan*, 337.

63. Kotenev, *Shanghai: Its Mixed Court*, 468.

64. Bao Tianxiao, *Chuanyinglou huiyilu*, 315–16.

65. Jia You, "Shanghai longtang mian mian guan," 102; Xia Lingen, *Jiu Shanghai sanbai liushi hang*, 166.

66. Shanghaishi liangshiju et al., *Zhongguo jindai mianfen gongye shi*, 323–24.

67. Xu Run, *Xu Yuzhai zixu nianpu*, 234.

68. Although geographically Nanjing is located south of the Yangzi River, by custom people of Nanjing origin were often regarded as "half-Subei" people. This may be partly because the Nanjing dialect is sufficiently different from major Jiangnan dialects such as the Suzhou dialect and close to Subei dialects.

69. Honig, *Creating Chinese Ethnicity*, 44–45.

70. I-21, July 14, 1993; I-25, July 16, 1993; I-26, August 6, 1993.

71. Zou Yiren, *Jiu Shanghai renkou bianqian*, 90.

72. Shanghaishi Huangpuqu, *Shanghaishi Huangpuqu dimingzhi*, 211–23.

73. Liu Fengsheng, "Buke siyi de Shanghai yi shi zhu."

74. Wang Weizu, *Shanghaishi fangzu zhi yanjiu*; Yu Shan, "Er fangdong yu dingfei yazu"; Luo Suwen, *Shikumen*, 30–31.

75. Hua Zi, "Erfangdong zhi xinji"; Yu Shan, "Er fangdong yu dingfei yazu"; Du Li, "'Termites' and the Second-Landlords."

76. In January 1930, the name was officially changed to "permanent rental contract" (*yong zu qi*), but the term *daoqi* continued in use until 1949. See Zhang Xiaobo, "Shanghai daoqi kao," 98–100.

77. Ye Shumei, "Shanghai zujie de fangdichan maimai zhidu."

78. Jin Xuan, "Shanghai fangdichan chanquan pingzheng pouxi," 34; Ye Shumei, "Shanghai zujie de fangdichan maimai zhidu," 180.

79. Du Li, "'Baimayi' yu erfangdong," 276.

80. Wang Weizu, *Shanghaishi fangzu zhi yanjiu*, 50392.

81. Ye Shumei, "Shanghai zujie de fangdichan maimai zhidu," 180.

82. Chen Yanlin, *Shanghai dichan daquan*, 327–29.

83. Shanghai jiqiye, *Shanghai jiqiye gongren yundong shi*, 56–57.

84. Shanghai shehui kexueyuan jingji yanjiusuo, *Shanghai Yong'an gongsi*, 190–91.

85. Su Zi, "Shanghai ren," 17.

86. Hua Zi, "Erfangdong zhi xinji."

87. *Shenbao*, March 8, 1948.

88. Wang Weizu, *Shanghaishi fangzu zhi yanjiu*, 50391.

89. I-10, March 20, 1989; I-21, July 14, 1993.

90. Examples of class labeling and political campaigns in the PRC can be found in White, *Policies of Chaos*, 10–15, and passim, on the situations in Shanghai.

91. Xia Yan, *Shanghai wuyan xia*, 88.

92. Ibid.; Biweng, "*Shanghai wuyanxia* jiantao."

93. About 43 square feet (4 square meters) per person was approximately the average dwelling space for the people of Shanghai in the late 1940s. Up to 1990, this ratio was still a cutoff figure for the allocation of houses in Shanghai. Families with floor space below that figure were classified as "households in difficulty" (*kunnan hu*). See Shanghaishi zhufang zhidu, *Shanghai zhufang zhidu gaige*, 75–76.

94. Xiangyu, "Gelou shijing."

95. Yang Ximeng, *Shanghai gongren shenghuo*, 71–73; Bureau of Social Affairs, *Standard of Living of Shanghai Laborers*, 54–56; Zhu Bangxing et al., *Shanghai chanye*, passim.

96. Zhu Bangxing et al., *Shanghai chanye*, passim.

97. Duojiugong, "Shanghai tingzijian jiepou tu."

98. Si Ying, "Tingzijian de shenghuo."

99. Wang Guanquan, *Huainian Xiao Hong*, 63.

100. Zhang Qing, *Tingzijian*, 5.

101. Lu Xun entitled the three collections *Qiejieting zawen* (Essays from the Qiejie pavilion), *Qiejieting zawen erji* (Essays from the Qiejie pavilion, volume 2), and *Qiejieting zawen mobian* (Final essays from the Qiejie pavilion). The expression *Qiejieting* is a pun. The first character, *qie*, forms half of the character *zu*. The second character, *jie*, forms half of a different character also read *jie*. This latter character (*jie*) combined with the character *zu*, forms the word *zujie*, meaning "foreign concession." *Ting* implies a pavilion room. Hence, *Qiejieting* cleverly suggests "a pavilion room in the semiconcession."

Why Lu Xun chose this name had to do with where his home was situated. His residence, Number 9 Dalu Xincun (where he lived from April 1933 to his death in October 1936), was located in Hongkou, at the boundary between the International Settlement and the Chinese district. It was here that some of the controversial "extra-Settlement roads," discussed in chapter 1, had been built. As noted, sovereignty over the areas covered by these roads was ambiguous. Hence, these areas could be called a "semiconcession." The three collections of essays are found in volume 6 of *Lu Xun quanji*.

102. Cited from Zhang Qing, *Tingzijian*, 3.

103. See chapter 6 for details.

104. *Shehui ribao*, October 1, 1934.

105. I-20; I-25, July 29, 1995. See also Jia You, "Shanghai longtang mian mian guan."

106. Shen Deci et al., "Huiyi Datong Daxue," 138.

107. Ou Yuanhui, "Daxia Daxue xiaoshi jiyao," 143–44, 152.

108. Mao Dun, *Wo zouguo de daolu*, 3:196.

109. The bookstores (*shuju*) referred to here were primarily printing houses, but they often had a retail salesroom.

110. Shanghaishi Huangpu quzhi, *Huangpu quzhi*, 1245.

111. Today's address is Lane 1881 of North Sichuan Road. Neishan, the name of the bookstore, is the Chinese pronunciation of the characters for "Uchiyama."

112. Yu Dafu, *Yu Dafu wenji*, 4:221.

113. In 1929, the bookstore was moved to Number 11 Scotte Road (today's Shanyin Road), where it remained until 1949. It was estimated that Lu Xun, whose residence was within a few minutes' walking distance from the bookstore, visited the store more than five hundred times in his later years, usually in the afternoon, and purchased at least a thousand books there. His friendship with Uchiyama allowed him to use the bookstore as a mailing address, for meeting friends, and, at a time when Lu Xun was on the government's blacklist, for refuge. (Lu Xun actually lived on the second floor of the store for a month, from March 19 to April 19, 1930, when a secret warrant for his arrest was issued by the Nationalist government.) Lu Xun's exalted reputation in the PRC led to the bookstore's site being listed as a municipal registered relic on August 26, 1980; and on September 28, 1981, as part of the celebration of the centenary of Lu Xun's birthday, a stone tablet was erected on the site (now a branch of the People's Bank). See Uchiyama, "Rōjin sense"; Lu Xun, *Lu Xun quanji*, 5:166–82; Shanghaishi Hongkouqu renmin zhengfu, *Shanghaishi Hongkouqu dimingzhi*, 368–69.

114. Zhu Lianbao, *Jinxiandai Shanghai chubanye yinxiang ji*, 2 and passim.

115. Yang Hao and Ye Lan, *Jiu Shanghai fengyun renwu*, 111–12. *Fanhua bao* published a number of novels and other works of fiction that are among the important works of twentieth-century Chinese literature, such as Li Boyuan's *Guanchang xianxing ji* (Records of current officialdom), Wu Yuanren's *Hutu shijie* (A muddled world), and Liu E's *Laocan youji* (The travel notes of Laocan).

116. Zhu Lianbao, *Jinxiandai Shanghai chubanye*, 339.

117. *Liangyou*, no. 100 (December 1934).

118. *Shanghai Municipal Police File*, D-627.

119. Wu Guifang, "Jindai Shanghai geming yiji gaishu," 18–19; Gu Yan-pei, "Shanghai Shudian jiuzhi"; Shanghaishi Changningqu, *Shanghaishi Changningqu dimingzhi*, 125, 170.

120. Zhang Qing, "Zhongguo gongchandang"; Shanghaishi Luwanqu, *Shanghaishi Luwanqu dimingzhi*, 215–16; Wu Guifang, *Shanghai fengwu zhi*, 113–17.

121. Ibid.

122. Shanghai yange bianxiezu, *Shanghai de geming yiji*, 7; Shanghaishi Jing'anqu, *Shanghaishi Jing'anqu dimingzhi*, 195; Zheng Chaolin, *Huaijiu ji*, 94–95.

123. Yu Jinghai, "*Xin qingnian* bianjibu jiuzhi"; Wu Guifang, "Jindai Shanghai," 11–12.

124. Wang Meidi, "Zhongguo zuizao"; Shanghaishi Luwanqu, *Shanghaishi Luwanqu dimingzhi*, 146.

125. Shanghaishi Huangpuqu, *Shanghaishi Huangpuqu dimingzhi*, 221. The present-day address of Furun Li is 270 Guizhou Road.

126. Ibid., 250. The present-day address of Baxian Fang is 109 Ninghaixi Road.

127. The present-day address of Qingyuan Li is 288 Beijingdong Road; and of Ruyi Li, 575 Henanzhong Road.

128. Shanghaishi Huangpuqu, *Shanghaishi Huangpuqu dimingzhi*, 207, 210.

129. Ibid., 204–5. The present-day address of Xingren Li is 120 Ningbo Road.

130. Zhang Hong, *Shili yangchang*, 55.

131. Hershatter, "Regulating Sex in Shanghai," 146.

132. Xue Liyong, "Ming-Qing shiqi de Shanghai changji," 154–55.

133. The present-day address of Huile Li is 726 Fuzhou Road.

134. For information on the ranking of prostitutes in Shanghai, see Hershatter, "Hierarchy"; Tang Weikang, "Shili yangchang de changji"; Xue Liyong, "Ming-Qing shiqi de Shanghai changji"; Ping Jinya, "Jiu Shanghai de changji"; Xie Wuyi, "Minchu Shanghai changji yipie"; and Henriot, "From a Throne."

135. Shanghaishi Huangpuqu, *Shanghaishi Huangpuqu dimingzhi*, 277.

136. According to household registration records, by the end of 1948 there were 151 brothels in Huile Li, with 200 registered brothel owners, 587 prostitutes, and 374 servants (*jiyong*). A January 1949 survey reported 171 brothels in the compound, that is, about one-fifth of Shanghai's brothels at that time. See Yang Jiezeng and He Wannan, *Shanghai changji*, 213–21.

137. Shanghaishi Huangpuqu, *Shanghaishi Huangpuqu dimingzhi*, 231. The present-day address of Xiande Li is 539 Xizangzhong Road.

138. Ibid., 266.

139. The name "Great Road" referred to Nanking Road. Thus the street can also be translated as the "Nanking Road of the French Concession." Today this is Jinlingdong Road. Shanghaishi Huangpuqu, *Shanghaishi Huangpuqu dimingzhi,* 267. The present-day address of Shengping Li is 396 Jinlingdong Road.

140. Jia You, "Shanghai longtang mian mian guan."

141. Zhao Yuming, *Zhongguo xiandai guangbo jianshi,* 219–22.

142. The compound was also known as Ji'an Li (Alley of Luck and Peace). It was built in 1929 and contained seventeen two-story shikumen houses. Its current address is Lanes 111–121 North Maoming Road. Shanghai yange bianxiezu, "Shanghai de geming yiji"; Shanghaishi Jing'anqu, *Shanghaishi Jing'anqu dimingzhi,* 148.

143. Shanghai yange bianxiezu, "Shanghai de geming yiji," 10; Shanghaishi Hongkouqu, *Shanghaishi Hongkouqu dimingzhi,* 311. Li was executed by the Guomindang on the eve of the Communists' takeover of Shanghai in May 1949. His devotion to the secret radio station made him a nationally renowned hero and was made the subject of a popular movie, *The Eternal Electric Wave (Yongbu xiaoshi de dianbo).*

144. *Shanghai cidian,* 504.

145. You Youwei, *Shanghai jindai Fojiao jianshi,* 136–37, 171.

CHAPTER 5. BEHIND STONE PORTALS

1. I-15, August 17, 1993.

2. Tian Yuan, *Sanbai liushi hang tushuo,* 162.

3. The custom prevailed in rural areas as well as in large cities like Shanghai, and it continued in Shanghai well into the 1980s. I-15, March 27, 1989; I-18, May 17, 1991.

4. In Yuyao, Zhejiang, for example, a standard nightstool was about two feet high and a little more than one foot in diameter. I-18, May 17, 1991.

5. In many Jiangnan villages, the family toilet (nightstool) was customarily used only by women and children. Men went to the village manure pits. One informant suggested that, as in rural areas, in Shanghai it was regarded as somewhat sissified for a man to use the "honey bucket" at home if a public lavatory was available nearby. I-11, March 20, 1989.

6. City authorities regulated the colors of the cart for the purpose of making them easily distinguishable from other pushcarts. For the regulations on nightsoil carts, see Shanghai tebieshi zhengfu mishuchu, *Shanghai tebieshi shizheng fagui huibian,* 20.

7. Raising a few domestic fowl (chickens were most popular) was common among Shanghai families, particularly in the alleyway houses, where residents ingeniously used spaces like the front courtyard, the roof, the kitchen, and passageways or hallways to put a cage or even a small hut for domestic fowl. Rais-

ing chickens was partly for fun, but more practically for improving the family diet. A homegrown chicken was believed more delicious than one from the market. I-23, I-24.

8. Shanghaishi tongzhiguan, *Shanghaishi zhongyao faling huikan chubian*, 34. Dumping nightsoil into a sewer, as some residents occasionally did when they missed the daily morning collection, was forbidden. It was not wise to do so either, because the pipes of the sewer system were small and easily plugged up.

9. I-26, August 6, 1993.

10. Dingjiu, "Shanghai zhi chen zazouqu."

11. Heppner, *Shanghai Refuge*, 85.

12. In 1986, more than 60 percent of Shanghai families lived in houses without sanitary fixtures. There were about 800,000 nightstools still in use. The number dropped afterward, but by the early 1990s no fewer than 600,000 nightstools were still being used in the city; see Yang Dongping, *Chengshi jifeng*, 320.

The nightsoil carts were gradually eliminated in the 1980s. Instead, a cesspool, sheltered by a brick structure, was dug in the neighborhoods where "honey buckets" were still in use. The cesspool was constructed at the entrance of an alleyway. Residents poured their nightsoil in at designated hours, and a truck (with a huge tank) came daily to pump out the smelly contents and ship it to the countryside.

13. I-14, March 23, 1989.

14. Zhu Menghua, "Jiu Shanghai de sige feipin dawang," 162.

15. Xue Gengshen, "Wo jiechu guo de Shanghai banghui renwu," 105. Although this applied to the pre-1949 era, the source does not indicate the exact time period when this fee was charged. Given the chaotic situation of Chinese currency in the 1940s, the figure "$0.20" (two *jiao*) presumably refers to the value of 20 percent of a silver dollar at the rate current in 1935, when the silver dollar (*yinyuan*) was transferred to the "legal currency" (*fabi*).

16. *Shehui ribao*, October 15, 1936.

17. Xue Gengshen, "Wo jiechu guo de Shanghai banghui renwu," 105.

18. Pan, *Shanghai*, 100.

19. Xue Gengshen, "Wo jiechu guo de Shanghai banghui renwu," 105–6; Zhu Menghua," Jiu Shanghai de sige feipin dawang," 162–63.

20. *Shanghai shenghuo* 1, no. 1 (March 1939): 2. This was a pun, because in Shanghai and many other cities nightsoil was jokingly called "gold."

21. Keeping his hands as clean as possible was not only for the sake of the nightsoil man himself but also, perhaps more important, to prevent soiling the handles of nightstools.

22. A common violation was to empty the nightsoil cart by pouring the excrement into roadside sewers in order to save time. The Heads of Nightsoil, who saw this more as a loss of money than an environment problem, hired private patrols to check for violations. Once caught, a nightsoil man might be fined or fired. *Shehui ribao*, October 15, 1936.

23. Dingjiu, "Shanghai zhi chen zazouqu," 11. Nightstools were so closely associated with the image of Shanghai's alleyways that an author satirically called the alleyway lives of Shanghai the "nightstool civilization" (*matong wenming*); see Mu Mutian, "Longtang."

24. Jiading used to be a county of Jiangsu province. Present-day Jiading is a suburban county of Shanghai municipality. Before the highway between Jiading and Shanghai was built in 1990, however, it was difficult (although not impossible) to make a round-trip in one day.

25. I-17.

26. Yang Dongping, *Chengshi jifeng*, 320. This is a description of the situation in the late 1980s. As mentioned earlier, things were virtually the same in the Republican era.

27. I-21, July 14, 1993.

28. Malone, *New China*, pt. 1, p. 16; *Nusheng* 1, no. 15: 6.

29. The five spices were prickly ash, star aniseed, cinnamon, clove, and fennel.

30. Lu Xun came to Shanghai in October 1927. The present address of his last residence in Shanghai—now a museum in his memory—is Number 9, Dalu Xincun, Shanyin Road. See Yang Jiayou, *Shanghai fengwu gujintan*, 265.

31. Lu Xun, *Lu Xun Quanji*, 6:308–9.

32. Hahn, *China to Me*, 9.

33. See chapter 6 for details.

34. Sergeant, *Shanghai*, caption to figure 34.

35. Tieh, "Street Music of Old Shanghai."

36. Dingjiu, "Shanghai chuxia jietou," 27.

37. I-22, August 3, 1995.

38. Tieh, "More Street Music." A different version of the song of the ginkgo-nut seller can be found in Xu Baohua and Tang Zhenzhu, *Shanghai shiqu fangyan zhi*, 515.

39. Tieh, "More Street Music of Old Shanghai."

40. Ibid.

41. Wei Hui, "Jiu Shanghai jietou de lutian zhiye."

42. Dingjiu, "Shanghai chuxia jietou," 27.

43. *Shanghai Municipal Council Report for the Year 1931 and Budget for the Year 1932*, 130.

44. Tieh, "Street Music of Old Shanghai."

45. "Dizzy sighted" refers to presbyopia.

46. Jiang Liyang, *Haipai yinshi*, 118.

47. *Shanghai shenghuo* 1, no. 5 (July 1937): 38–39; Jiang Liyang, *Haipai yinshi*, 118–19. The word *rehun* (lit., hot and dizzy), meaning "craze," was of Ningbo origin.

48. Wang, *Shanghai Boy*, chapter 2. Wang's unpublished memoir is a fascinating account of the first twenty-two years of his life in Shanghai.

49. Wei Hui, "Jiu Shanghai jietou de lutian zhiye," 295.

50. Tieh, "Street Music of Old Shanghai"; Tian Yuan, *Sanbai liushi hang tushuo*, 89–90.

51. Wang, *Shanghai Boy*, chapter 4. For a similar song, see Xu Baohua and Tang Zhenzhu, *Shanghai shiqu fangyan zhi*, 515–16.

52. Xu Dafeng, "Longtang texie."

53. Zheng Yimei, *Yihai yishao*, 69–72.

54. Lu Dafang, *Shanghaitan yijiu*, 43–44.

55. *Shehui ribao*, November 8, 1936.

56. I-38.

57. Xia Lingen, *Jiu Shanghai sanbai liushi hang*, 2.

58. Lu Xun, *Lu Xun Quanji*, 6:309; Wei Hui, "Jiu Shanghai jietou de lutian zhiye"; Tian Yuan, *Sanbai liushi hang tushuo*, 95, 219.

59. Xu Dafeng, "Longtang texie," 9.

60. Zheng Yimei, *Yihai yishao*, 136.

61. For instance, the child "Three-Hairs" (Sanmao), a protagonist in the famous cartoon series of Zhang Leping, *Records of the Wandering Life of "Three-Hairs"* (*Sanmao liulang ji*), was a newspaper seller. See Zhang Leping, *Zhang Leping's Caricatures*, 42–44, 54–55. See also Zhonggong Shanghai shi-wei xuanchuan bu, *Shanghai min'ge xuan*, for folk songs about child newspaper peddlers.

62. Heppner, *Shanghai Refuge*, 54.

63. I-21, August 11, 1995; I-27, August 10, 1995.

64. I-39. See also the photo in Tata and McLachlan, *Shanghai 1949*, 106; Barz, *Shanghai: Sketches of Present-Day Shanghai*, 43, Tang Zhenchang, *Jindai Shanghai fanhua lu*, 270; Shanghai wenhua chubanshe, *Shanghai zhanggu*, 74.

65. Tian Yuan, *Sanbai liushi hang tushuo*, 155–56.

66. Zou Yiren, *Jiu Shanghai renkou*, 47–50.

67. I-29, August 13, 1996. The Shanghai version of this saying was "The more a man does needlework, the poorer he becomes" (*nan zuo nügong, yuezuo yueqiong*); see Hu Zude, *Huyan*, 11.

68. Tian Yuan, *Sanbai liushi hang tushuo*, 156.

69. I-30, I-33, I-34; Tian Yuan, *Sanbai liushi hang tushuo*, 49, 55, 203–4, 211.

70. Shanghaishi gongshang xingzheng guanli ju and Shanghaishi xiangjiao gongye gongsi, *Shanghai minzu xiangjiao gongye*, 6–7.

71. I-33.

72. I-21, July 14, 1993; I-25, July 15, 1993.

73. The temporary stimulation provided by opium contributed to a widespread belief that the drug was a stimulant, not a depressant.

74. *Shehui ribao*, May 11, 1936.

75. Xia Lingen, *Jiu Shanghai sanbai liushi hang*, 103; *Shehui ribao*, May 11, 1936.

76. *Shehui ribao*, May 11, 1936.

77. Xiao Qian, *Shehui baixiang*, 47–48.

78. Bao Tianxiao, *Shanghai chunqiu*, 2:507.

79. Wei Hui, "Jiu Shanghai jietou de lutian zhiye"; Shanghaishi shifan jiaoyanshi, *Shanghai xiangtu wenhua shi*, 159.

80. I-30, I-31, I-32, I-33. A similar song appears in Tieh, "More Street Music": "Exchange old articles! Have you got something for sale? Any broken bottles and other useless things to part with?"

81. *Tongzhi Shanghai xianzhi, juan 7*.

82. Ch'u, *Local Government*, 150–54; Hsiao, *Rural China*, 82–83; Kuhn, *Rebellion*, 61–62, 100; Naquin and Rawski, *Chinese Society*, 16–17. Ch'u and Hsiao point out that the role of the baojia system has been exaggerated, and that overall the system was ineffective in the Qing. Naquin and Rawski state that "it is unclear if the *baojia* ever functioned as it was supposed to."

83. Wen Juntian, *Zhongguo baojia zhidu*, chapters 23 and 24.

84. Wakeman has argued that the Nationalists' effort to establish a modern police force in Shanghai in the Nanjing decade was chiefly for the purpose of making Shanghai a showcase to demonstrate that the Chinese were capable of running a modern city. See Wakeman, *Policing Shanghai*, 14–15, 288–89.

85. *Shanghaishi nianjian*, 1936: F:110. Feetham, *Report*, vol. 1, pt. 2, pp. 249–50, contains details of the plan.

86. Chen Yanlin, *Shanghai dichan daquan*, 61–63.

87. See Shanghai Municipal Archive, file number Q107.

88. Shanghaishi dang'an guan, *Ri wei Shanghai shizhengfu*, 35, 229, 254.

89. Ibid., 255.

90. Ibid., 229, 257; Gu Sifan, *Shanghai fengwu hua*, 11.

91. Shanghaishi dang'an guan, *Ri wei Shanghai shizhengfu*, 161–62.

92. Ibid., 604–6, 609–11; Tao Juyin, *Gudao jianwen*, 180.

93. Shanghai Municipal Archives, R33, vol. 74, p. 8; vol. 75, pp. 96–97; vol. 221, pp. 6–7; vol. 225, pp. 19–21, 35–36; vols. 226–230. See also Tu Shipin, *Shanghai chunqiu, shang*: 87; Tao Juyin, *Gudao jianwen*, 141–45.

94. Shanghai Municipal Archives, R33, *juan 65*, p. 26.

95. Shanghaishi dang'an guan, *Shanghai jiefang*, 55.

96. Ibid., 10–12.

97. Zhonggong Shanghai shiwei, *Chengshi jiedao banshichu jumin weiyuanhui gongzuo shouce*, 3.

98. On December 31, 1954, the fourth session of the standing committee of the People's Congress passed two pieces of legislation on urban street offices and residents' committees respectively. Street offices were defined by the act as subagencies of city-administered districts, and were to be established in every city-administered district (or, in some cases, cities that were not divided into districts [i.e., small cities] with a population of more than 100,000). Residents' committees were defined as "mass, autonomous residents' organizations" under the guidance of the street offices. (English translations of the full text of these acts are in J. Cohen, *Criminal Process*.)

By August 1955, 129 cities had established street offices and/or residents' committees; in other words, 80 percent of the cities required by the 1954 legislation to establish street organizations had done so. See *Guangming ribao,* August 9, 1955, p. 2.

99. I-30, I-31, I-32, I-33.

100. The Land of Peach Blossoms (*shiwai taoyuan*) was a utopian world created by Tao Yuanming (326–97) in his classic essay "Peach Blossom Spring." It is the Chinese version of the "Garden of Eden," but an earthly paradise (i.e., without religious connotation). For an English translation of Tao's essay, see Lynn H. Nelson and Patrick Peebles, *Classics of Eastern Thought* (New York: Harcourt Brace Jovanovich, 1991), 124–25.

101. See, for example, the "Shanghai Municipal Council Rules with Respect to New Chinese Buildings," *Shanghai Municipal Council Report for the Year 1916 and Budget for the Year 1917,* 56–62. For the regulations on housing and construction in both the International Settlement and the French Concession issued in 1923, see Chen Yanlin, *Shanghai dichan daquan,* appendix, 718–926.

102. Xu Guozhen, *Shanghai shenghuo,* 22.

103. Shanghai shehui kexueyuan shehuixue yanjiusuo, "Shanghai jumin laiyuan diaocha," 18.

104. Whyte and Parish, *Urban Life in Contemporary China,* 17–21; White, *Policies of Chaos,* 88–90.

105. I-34.

106. Huang, *Peasant Economy,* 23.

107. I-27, August 10, 1995; Mao Dun, *Wo zouguo de daolu,* 2:1.

108. In Shanghai slang, there were the so-called upper corners (*shang zhi jiao*) and lower corners (*xia zhi jiao*), which referred to higher-class and lower-class residential areas respectively. The slang reflected more a general social bias or snobbery, so to speak, than an identity based on these "corners." See Shen Weibing and Jiang Ming, *Ala Shanghairen,* 58–65.

109. See Lao-Tzu, *Tao Te Ching,* 80.

110. I-38.

111. On *chōkai* (neighborhood associations) in Tokyo, see Bestor, *Neighborhood Tokyo,* especially pages 66–67, 84–85, 102–21, and 266–67.

112. Literally, "Alley of Abundance and Virtue." This twenty-unit alleyway-house compound was built in 1919 on the boundary between the International Settlement and the French Concession. Its current address is Lanes 8, 18, and 38 of Yunnanzhong Road. In 1989, it housed 261 households, with a total of 837 residents. See Shanghaishi Huangpuqu, *Shanghaishi Huangpuqu dimingzhi,* 282.

113. *Shehui ribao,* November 12, 1929; November 14, 1929; November 16, 1929; December 12, 1929; December 30, 1929.

114. Wang Weizu, *Shanghaishi fangzu zhi yanjiu,* 50500–50501 [or 174].

115. *Jianzhu zhuankan,* no. 1 (June 9, 1934).

116. *Shibao,* January 23, 1943; Wang Jishen, *Shanghai zhi fangdichanye,* 6–7.

117. Wang Weizu, *Shanghaishi fangzu zhi yanjiu,* 50497.

118. "Report of the Housing Committee, 1936–1937," appendix 5; *Jianzhu zhuankan*, no. 1 (June 9, 1934).

119. Dingjiu, "Shanghai shimin shenghuo de zhuanbian"; Jiujun, "Shanghai 'xiaofangzi' cangsang."

120. *Shenbao*, December 29, 1933; January 7, 1934; January 17, 1934; February 20, 1934; June 27, 1934; *Shanghaishi nianjian*, 1935: B:16–18; *Jianzhu zhuankan*, nos. 1–6; *Shehui ribao*, July 21, 1934; *Shishi xinbao*, October 19, 1934.

121. Shanghaishi Jing'anqu, *Shanghaishi Jing'anqu dimingzhi*, 120–21.

122. Sometimes a guojielou was connected to a regular unit to allow one more room for the unit. In more crowded neighborhoods, these floors were also rented out to regular tenants. In fact, because the guojielou had windows on both sides, which of course meant better ventilation and light, and only one guojielou was available in each lane, the guojielou floor or a unit with a guojielou annex was sometimes in demand. Mao Dun recalled that in February 1921 he paid a "deposit" about seven times higher than the market rate to rent a "one-up, one-down" shikumen house with a "spanning-a-lane" annex in Hongxing Fang (Alley of Great Prosperity) in Baoshan Road, Zhabei. See Mao Dun, *Wo zouguo de daolu*, 1:150–51.

123. I-36, I-37.

124. Shen Weibing and Jiang Ming, *Ala Shanghairen*, 32–33.

125. I-28, August 7, 1995; I-29, August 7, 1995; Wu Zaiyang, "Shijiao jiehe diqu jumin shenghuo shangyou zhuduo bubian."

126. The name Red Bean Lane was not real but a literary creation of the author, derived from an ancient poem by the famous Tang poet Wang Wei (701–761), "Red Beans Grow in Southern Country" (*Hongdou sheng nanguo*). "Red beans" are a symbol of homesickness in China.

127. Song Yuehui, "Kuanchang de tianjing hen jimo."

128. The current address of Jingyun Li is Lane 63, Hengbang Road. Mao Dun, *Wo zouguo de daolu*, 2:2–3; Shanghaishi Hongkouqu, *Shanghaishi Hongkouqu dimingzhi*, 236.

129. Lu Xun, *Lu Xun Quanji*, 6:84.

130. *Shehui ribao*, July 24, 1936.

131. Mao Dun, *Wo zouguo de daolu*, 2:3.

132. *Shehui ribao*, July 24, 1936.

133. I-38.

134. A major complaint of people who moved from old alleyway neighborhoods to newly built apartment complexes in recent years was theft. Burglaries were much more frequent in apartment buildings than in lilong houses. See Wu Zaiyang, "Shijiao jiehe diqu jumin shenghuo shangyou zhuduo bubian," 147.

135. Luo Suwen, *Shikumen: xunchang renjia*, 158–71.

136. Xiangyu, "Gelou shijing," 12.

137. Xu Guibao, "Wo de Shanghai shenghuo," 25.

138. Liu Huogong, *Shanghai zhuzhici*, 55.

139. Heppner, *Shanghai Refuge*, 85.

140. Wang Dingjiu, *Shanghai menjing*, section "Lian'ai de menjing," 12–13.

141. I-38, I-39.

142. *Shenbao*, August 9, 1936.

143. *Shanghaitan*, 2:212–13.

144. The name Lin Daiyu was taken from one of the protagonists of the Chinese classic *The Dream of the Red Chamber*. In the story, in Shanghai's first courtesan competition, which was sponsored by *Youxi bao* ("Entertainment Newspaper," edited by the prominent novelist Li Boyuan) in 1897, Lin was selected from among four finalists as Shanghai's number one courtesan: the four were entitled to the accolade "Four Great Attendants of Buddha" (*si da Jin'gang*). See Ping Jinya, "Jiu Shanghai de changji," 166–67.

145. Jiujun, "Shanghai 'xiaofangzi' cangsang."

146. I-29, August 7, 1995; I-30; I-31; I-32.

147. I-34, I-35.

148. The "no tenant without a family" restriction was mainly applied to alleyway houses, especially at the first renting. There was no such restriction in renting an apartment unit. See Xiao Lingjun, *Shanghai changshi*, 47.

149. The present-day address of Jiangyuan Long is Lane 432, Xinchang Road, Huangpu District. The murder made Jiangyuan Long notorious in the city. The residents' committee (*jumin weiyuanhui*, the second layer in the administrative hierarchy of the neighborhood organizations in PRC) there is named after the alleyway compound. See Shanghaishi Huangpuqu, *Shanghaishi Huangpuqu dimingzhi*, 37, 249.

150. Zhao Sufang, "Jiangyuanlong mousha qinfu an." Shanghai's major newspapers all had detailed reports on the case from March to May 1945. The June and July 1945 issues of *Zazhi* magazine published a group of articles sympathetic to Zhou. On September 14, 1945, the Shanghai Higher Court sentenced her to death. Zhou then appealed to the Supreme Court in Nanjing, which on February 20, 1948, reduced the punishment to fifteen years in prison. Zhou lived into the 1990s as a day care worker in the Dafeng Labor Reform Farm in northern Jiangsu province.

151. I-38, I-39.

152. Wei Shaochang, *Yuanyang hudie pai yanjiu ziliao*, 1:178–79, 535–36.

153. People heated the old-type flatiron by placing burning charcoal inside the iron chamber. Periodically they had to blow away the ash in order to keep the charcoal burning.

154. Bao Tianxiao, *Shanghai chunqiu*, 2:695–96.

155. Ibid., 2:696; I-38.

156. Ibid., 2:696.

157. Lu Xun, *Lu Xun Quanji*, 6:99–200.

158. Ibid., 6:213.

159. Li Zhisui, *Private Life*, 493.

CHAPTER 6. BEYOND STONE PORTALS

1. I-10, March 20, 1989; I-13; I-15, March 20, 1989.

2. I-13; I-19, June 30, 1991.

3. I-18, May 17, 1991; I-20.

4. I-13.

5. I-11, March 20, 1989; I-12; I-20.

6. For information on street names of Shanghai (old and new), see Shi Songjiu, *Shanghaishi luming daquan*, 353–92.

7. I-11, I-13, I-17.

8. *Shehui ribao*, June 27, 1936.

9. Shanghaishi shehuiju, *Shanghai zhi shangye*, 183.

10. Zou Yiren, *Jiu Shanghai renkou*, 90.

11. *Gongshang banyuekan* 5, no. 19 (October 1, 1933): 47–48.

12. Bureau of Social Affairs, *Wage Rates in Shanghai*, 60.

13. *Gongshang banyuekan* 5, no. 19 (October 1, 1933): 47.

14. Lu Wenshao, "Benshi mihaoye zhi gaikuang."

15. Shanghaishi gongyong, *Shanghai gongyong shiye*, 25–26, 38–39.

16. Shanghaishi tongjiju, *Shanghai tongji nianjian, 1983*, 320.

17. Bureau of Social Affairs, *Standard of Living of Shanghai Laborers*, 71, 155; Xiao Lingjun, *Shanghai changshi*, 41.

18. Shanghaishi tongjiju, *Shanghai tongji nianjian, 1983*, 320.

19. Wang Chifeng and Qiu Huiyou, "Zenyang taotai Shanghai yibai ling siwan zhi meiqiulu?"

20. Emily Honig has mentioned that lighting the stove was the first thing women workers of Shanghai's cotton mills did in the morning. This was, in fact, a routine morning chore for every household in Shanghai that did not have a gas stove. *Sisters and Strangers*, 136; I-11, March 20, 1989; I-12.

21. Yao Qingshan and Ang Jumin, *Shanghai mishi diaocha*, 3; I-12; I-13.

22. Chen Liang, "Yanzhidian," 14; I-15, March 23, 1989.

23. I-15, March 27, 1989.

24. Regarding the number of stores, see Shanghai xintuo gufen youxian gongsi, *Shanghai fengtu zaji*, 31; quote from *Shehui ribao*, August 15, 1936.

25. Shanghaishi Huangpuqu renmin zhengfu caizheng maoyi bangongshi, *Shanghaishi Huangpuqu shangyezhi*, 472–73. These numbers include both retail and wholesale stores; the source does not specify the numbers in each category. No doubt most of these enterprises were small retail stores. Out of 8,600 stores in 1949, about 1,300 were wholesalers.

26. I-15, March 23, 1989; I-19, June 29, 1991; *Shanghai fengtu zaji*, 31.

27. Note that *A Chinese-English Dictionary* (compiled by Beijing Foreign Language College [Beijing: Commercial Press, 1979]) translates *yi-shi-zhu-*

xing as "food, clothing, shelter and transportation." This was probably to make the translation more idiomatic in English. Or, the translators were puzzled by the original order in Chinese and, assuming that food should be more important than other necessities of life, shifted the order.

28. See *Cihai*, 1915.

29. A slightly different version was *zhi zhong yishan bu zhong ren* (Paying attention only to attire, not to the person). See Xu Guozhen, *Shanghai shenghuo*, 29; Tu Shipin, *Shanghai chunqiu*, pt. 3, p. 16; Leng Xingwu, *Zuixin Shanghai zhinan*, 145.

30. Lu Xun, *Lu Xun Quanji*, 4:563. Lu Xun himself once had an unpleasant experience in the Cathay Hotel, one of the most luxurious hotels on Nanking Road. Dressed in his usual blue cotton gown and rubber shoes, and with hair untidy, Lu Xun went to the hotel to visit a British friend who had a room on the seventh floor. As Lu Xun walked into an elevator in the lobby, the elevator operator, who was supposed to operate the device for every guest, pretended not see him. Lu Xun waited in the elevator for a while, but seeing no other guests walk in he asked the operator to take him "to the seventh floor." The operator looked Lu Xun up and down for a second and then told him, "Get out of here!" Lu Xun had no choice but to take the stairway. Two hours later, when Lu Xun finished his visit and his British friend solicitously walked out with him to the elevators, it happened that the same elevator stopped on that floor. Now the operator, obviously quite embarrassed, served Lu Xun respectfully. Later, when Lu Xun told his friends the story, he seemed amused rather than offended by the event. Indeed, according to convention in the city at the time, the writer's eccentricity, more than the operator's snobbery, was at fault for the incident. See Uchiyama, "Rōjin sensei" ("Lu Xun xiansheng"); Shen Weibing and Jiang Ming, *Ala Shanghairen*, 48.

31. Shen Weibing and Jiang Ming, *Ala Shanghairen*, 20. Here the "beggar" was a representative of all types of poor people, not necessarily mendicants alone; "Western clothing" refers to expensive and formal dress; and "cooking his own rice" implies that the person was not rich enough to hire a maid and therefore had to do all kinds of household chores himself. To the people of Shanghai, this saying conveyed an image of a middle-aged man dressed in a shoddy Western business suit cooking in front of a dirty coal stove.

32. Tu Shipin, *Shanghai chunqiu*, pt. 3, pp. 19–22; Xu Guozhen, *Shanghai shenghuo*, 33–36.

33. A penholder is shaped like an outline of three hills linked together. The center "hill" is the tallest; the other two are lower. Pens (or, more accurately, brushes) can be rested on the "valleys" between the hills. In a pocket flap, the shape is upside-down.

34. Shanghaishi Huangpuqu renmin zhengfu, *Shanghaishi Huangpuqu shangyezhi*, 340–41.

35. Xiong Yuezhi, "Zatan 'Shanghairen.'"

36. Luo Shuang, *"Pouxi" Shanghairen*, 92–95.

37. Shanghaishi Huangpuqu renmin zhengfu, *Shanghaishi Huangpuqu*

Shangyezhi, 346–53; Zhang Baogao and Fan Nengchuan, *Shanghai luyou wenhua*, 210–11.

38. The name "Hongbang" is sometimes misleading, since it literally means "Red Gang," but in truth it had nothing to do with gangs. "Hong" was a mispronunciation of "Feng" (the abbreviated name for Ningbo; many cities in China have an abbreviated, single character name) in the Shanghai dialect (in which "feng" is pronounced "fong"). See Luo Shuang, *"Pouxi" Shanghairen*, 93. Also, "Hongbang" may have a meaning similar to "Fanbang" ("barbarian type"), implying that these were Western-type tailors. For instance, all carpenters (regardless of their native-place origins) who worked for foreign shipyards in nineteenth-century Shanghai were called "Hongbang" carpenters (see Shanghaishi gongshang xingzheng guanliju, *Shanghai minzu jiqi gongye*, 1:59–61). The word "hong," or "red," probably derived from the Chinese notion, which arose in the nineteenth century, that Europeans were "red-haired devils" (*hongmao gui*).

39. Tu Shipin, *Shanghai chunqiu*, pt. 3, pp. 22–24.

40. Ibid., 24.

41. Shanghaishi Huangpuqu renmin zhengfu, *Shanghaishi Huangpuqu shangyezhi*, 329, 332.

42. Ibid., 329–30.

43. See appendix 1, "Patterns of Obtaining Clothing."

44. I-38.

45. Tian Yuan, *Sanbai liushi hang tushuo*, 77–78.

46. This custom had contributed to the popular demand for household sewing machines. During the Mao era, the sewing machine was one of the "Four Bigs" (referring to four highly desired light industrial products: bicycles, wristwatches, radios, and sewing machines), all of which were rationed. I-16; I-38; see also Spence, *Search for Modern China*, 733.

47. Shanghaishi wenshi yanjiu guan, *Haishang chunqiu*, 42.

48. Bao Kanbu, *Shili Yangchang zhongshengxiang*, 60.

49. Tu Shipin, *Shanghai chunqiu*, pt. 3, pp. 20–21.

50. Shen Weibing and Jiang Ming, *Ala Shanghai ren*, 22.

51. *Nüsheng* 1, no. 4: 19.

52. *Shehui ribao*, September 18, 1934.

53. Ibid., September 10, 1934; Wang Dingjiu, *Shanghai menjing*, section "Chi de mingjing," 31, 33–35.

54. Shanghai in the 1940s had about 1,200 wine shops, most of which were family-run small retail businesses. From the late nineteenth century on, the trade had developed into three major types, each with its own trade association: white spirits (distilled from Chinese sorghum), Fen spirit (distilled in Fenyang, Shanxi province), and Shaoxing wine (distilled in Shaoxing, Zhejiang province). Wine was also sold in "soy sauce stores" (*jiangyou dian, zaofang*, or *jiangyuan*). See Shanghaishi Huangpuqu renmin zhengfu caizheng maoyi bangongshi, *Shanghaishi Huangpuqu shangyezhi*, 473–74.

55. Wang Dingjiu, *Shanghai menjing*, section "Chi de menjing," 31.

56. Ibid., 30.

57. *Shehui ribao*, September 12, 1934.

58 Bureau of Social Affairs, *Standard of Living of Shanghai Laborers*, 3; Bureau of Social Affairs, *Wage Rates in Shanghai*, 60, 80; Shen Bojing et al., *Shanghaishi zhinan*, 302–7; Jiang Siyi et al., "Shanghai de qigai," 209.

59. Following are the percentages of household expenditures based on two surveys of working-class families in Shanghai in 1927–1930:

	Survey 1 (November 1927 to October 1928)	Survey 2 (April 1929 to March 1930)
Food	56.0	53.2
Clothing	9.4	7.5
Housing Rent	6.4	8.3
Fuel and Light	7.5	6.4
Miscellaneous	20.6	24.6

Survey 1 did not provide information on how much was spent in restaurants. In Survey 2, 4.8 percent of food expenditures was for meals eaten in restaurants and 1.8 percent for take-out dishes ordered from restaurants. See Bureau of Social Affairs, *Standard of Living of Shanghai Laborers*, 104, 113–14; Yang Ximeng, *Shanghai gongren shenghuo*, 36.

60. *Shanghai shenghuo*, no. 3 (December 15, 1926): 35.

61. Xu Guibao, "Wo de Shanghai shenghuo."

62. I-14, March 23, 1989.

63. Sheng Juncai, "Shanghai shuiluye de bianqian;" *Shehui ribao*, June 27, 1936.

64. See chapter 3 for details.

65. For example, G. William Skinner found that the peasants of Chengdu (Sichuan province) liked to chat in teahouses while Philip Huang found that the teahouse was irrelevant to common peasants on the North China plain. See Skinner, "Marketing and Social Structure in Rural China"; and Huang, *Peasant Economy*, 220–22.

66. Fan Shuzhi, *Ming-Qing Jiangnan shizhen tanwei*, 279–83.

67. Shen Bojing and Chen Huaipu, *Shanghaishi zhinan*, 137.

68. Yang Jiayou, *Shanghai fengwu gujintan*, 237.

69. I-14, March 23, 1989; I-17.

70. I-9; *Shehui ribao*, November 13, 1936.

71. I-9, I-20.

72. I-16; I-14, March 20, 1989; Tang Weikang et al., *Shanghai yishi*, 305.

73. Xia Lingen, *Jiu Shanghai sanbai liushi hang*, 64–65.

74. Shanghaishi Jing'anqu, *Shanghaishi Jing'anqu dimingzhi*, 219. This bathhouse was for men only, but public bathhouses for women had been available in Shanghai since 1912; see Shanghaishi Huangpuqu renmin zhengfu caizheng maoyi bangongshi, *Shanghaishi Huangpuqu shangyezhi*, 670–71.

75. In 1937 at the center of the International Settlement (roughly today's

Huangpu District) there were 24 sizable public bathhouses. The number increased to 29 in 1946; 22 of those bathhouses had, in total, 3,189 seats and employed more than two thousand bath attendants. See Shanghaishi Huangpuqu, *Shanghaishi Huangpuqu shangyezhi,* 671.

76. Gernet, *Daily Life,* 124–25.

77. Fortune, *Three Years' Wanderings,* 266.

78. Ge Yuanxi, *Huyou zaji,* 33. The cost of a bath in 1876 was 70 copper cash (wen) in the luxury section and 35 copper in the economy section. Fortune also recorded the rates in the bathhouse he visited in the early 1840s: 6 copper cash in the economy section and 18 copper cash in the luxury section. He exclaimed about the low prices, "I may mention that one hundred copper cash amount to about 4.5 *d.* of our money; so that the first class enjoy a hot water bath for about one farthing! and the other a bath, a private room, a cup of tea, and a pipe of tobacco for something less than one penny!" Fortune, *Three Years' Wanderings,* 266.

79. Bao Kanbu, *Shili Yangchang zhongshengxiang,* 14–18.

80. Xia Lingen, *Jiu Shanghai sanbai liushi hang,* 64–67.

81. Shanghaishi Huangpuqu, *Shanghaishi Huangpuqu shangyezhi,* 673.

82. Services like "body brushing," "back massages," and "foot cleaning" were usually not available in a laohuzao bathhouse.

83. Qian Nairong, *Shanghai fangyan liyu,* 212; Yiming, *Shanghai shi,* 69.

84. Zhang Chunhai, *Hucheng suishi quge,* 20; *Jiaqing Songjiang fuzhi,* juan 5:4; Ying Baoshi, *Tongzhi Shanghai xianzhi,* juan 1:12.

85. Hu Xianghan, *Shanghai xiaozhi,* 42.

86. Ibid.

87. Read et al., *Shanghai Foods,* 7–35; Jiang Liyang, *Haipai yinshi,* 72–73.

88. Hahn, *China to Me,* 9.

89. Shanghaishi shehuiju, "Shanghaishi renlichefu shenghuo zhuang-kuang diaocha baogaoshu," pt. 2, pp. 44–45; Zhu Bangxing et al., *Shanghai chanye yu Shanghai zhigong,* 675–76.

90. I-11, March 25, 1989; I-18, May 18, 1989.

91. Hauser, *Shanghai: City for Sale,* 79.

92. Jingguan, "Jiuwen shiling," 104–5; Shanghaishi Huangpuqu, *Shanghaishi Huangpuqu dimingzhi,* 141; Wu Shenyuan, *Shanghai zuizao de zhong-zhong,* 82–83.

93. Shanghaishi Huangpuqu, *Shanghaishi Huangpuqu dimingzhi,* 141, 563.

94. Shanghaishi Huangpuqu, *Shanghaishi Huangpuqu shangyezhi,* 429; Hu Xianghan, *Shanghai xiaozhi,* 46; Wu Shenyuan, *Shanghai zuizao de zhongzhong,* 83–84. Some of these markets are still in business in present-day Shanghai.

95. Shanghaishi Huangpuqu renmin zhengfu caizheng maoyi bangongshi, *Shanghaishi Huangpuqu shangyezhi,* 444–45.

96. For instance, the Wuzhou Food Market, a medium-size food market in Hongkou, was built on a spot where a number of food peddlers gathered every

morning. In 1914, it became a regular food market housed in a single-story concrete building. By the late 1940s, the market had 256 food stalls and was surrounded by various types of small stores. The food market served as the center of a fairly busy commercial area. See Shanghaishi Hongkouqu, *Shanghaishi Hongkouqu dimingzhi*, 490.

97. In Jianye Li, for instance, the builder deliberately left an area (where a row of houses could have been built) inside the walled compound as a space to allow peddlers to sell their goods. Gradually an open-air food market emerged there, to the convenience of the residents. Shanghaishi Xuhuiqu, *Shanghaishi Xuhuiqu dimingzhi*, 191.

98. Shanghaishi Hongkouqu, *Shanghaishi Hongkouqu dimingzhi*, 478.

99. Shanghaishi Jing'anqu, *Shanghaishi Jing'anqu dimingzhi*, 338–39. The phrase "upper corner" referred to wealthy residential areas, as opposed to working-class neighborhoods known as "lower corner."

100. Shanghaishi Luwanqu, *Shanghaishi Luwanqu dimingzhi*, 69, 259; Shanghaishi Hongkouqu, *Shanghaishi Hongkouqu dimingzhi*, 485; Shanghaishi Huangpuqu, *Shanghaishi Huangpuqu dimingzhi*, 570.

101. Shanghaishi Hongkouqu, *Shanghaishi Hongkouqu dimingzhi*, 482 and 485.

102. Wu Shenyuan, *Shanghai zuizao de zhongzhong*, 84; Shanghaishi Huangpuqu, *Shanghaishi Huangpuqu shangyezhi*, 430.

103. I-22, July 14, 1993.

104. Sinclair and Wong, *Cultural Shock!* 182.

105. Jiang Liyang, *Haipai yinshi*, 96.

106. An informant who visited her daughter in the United States said she did not enjoy her stay very much because her daughter was quite "Americanized"—in order to keep the house clean the daughter would not allow stir-frying, the mother's favorite type of cooking. I-20.

107. Jiang Liyang, *Haipai yinshi*, 97–98, 101.

108. Bureau of Social Affairs, *Standard of Living of Shanghai Laborers*, 111–14.

109. Chen Da, *Woguo kangRi zhanzheng shiqi shizheng gongren shenghuo*, 320–26.

110. Bernard Read et al., *Shanghai Foods*, 87–101. The list was presented to informants (I-28, I-29, I-34, I-35, I-38) for verification.

111. Shanghaishi Huangpuqu, *Shanghaishi Huangpuqu dimingzhi*, 570; Shanghaishi Luwanqu, *Shanghaishi Luwanqu dimingzhi*, 69; Jiang Liyang, *Haipai yinshi*, 107.

112. After Liberation the local food market became even more important in daily life. Since food peddlers were almost entirely eliminated from the city and numerous foods were put on ration, the food market was virtually the only source for so-called nonstaple food supplies (that is, almost everything except the staple food, grain). For about three decades prior to Deng Xiaoping's economic reform, which diversified food supplies by allowing free markets to operate and peasants to enter the city to sell their products, food markets were al-

ways crowded with people queuing up in front of the various food stalls. A popular saying frequently cited by both the official media and common people revealed the vital importance of the food markets: "To see the [political and economic] situation through the little foods bamboo basket" (*xiaocailan li kan xingshi*). I-18, May 17, 1991; I-36; I-37; I-38.

113. Skinner, "Marketing and Social Structure in Rural China," pt. 1, p. 20.

114. See appendix 1, "Survey Spots and Number of People Surveyed, by Neighborhood" and "Patterns of Shopping Behavior."

115. Shanghaishi Huangpuqu renmin zhengfu, *Shanghaishi Huangpuqu dimingzhi*, 270–71.

116. I-17.

117. I-9; I-10, March 20, 1989; I-11, March 20, 1989; I-12; I-14, March 20, 1989.

118. Shanghaishi Huangpuqu renmin zhengfu, *Shanghaishi Huangpuqu dimingzhi*, 397; Shanghaishi Luwanqu renmin zhengfu, *Shanghaishi Luwanqu dimingzhi*, 191.

119. Zhang Baogao and Fan Nengchuan, *Shanghai luyou wenhua*, 197. See also appendix 1, "Patterns of Shopping Behavior," for the percentages of residents who did most of their shopping at regional commercial centers.

120. Shanghaishi Jing'anqu renmin zhengfu, *Shanghaishi Jing'anqu dimingzhi*, 401–18; Shanghaitong she, *Shanghai yanjiu ziliao*, 224–26; You Youwei, "Shanghai Yufo chansi."

121. Shanghaitong she, *Shanghai yanjiu ziliao, xuji*, 719–24; Shanghaishi Xuhuiqu renmin zhengfu, *Shanghaishi Xuhuiqu dimingzhi*, 95–96.

122. Liu Linsheng, "Caojiadu diaochaji"; Shanghaishi Putuoqu renmin zhengfu, *Putuoqu dimingzhi*, 77–78, 234; Shanghaishi Jing'anqu renmin zhengfu, *Shanghaishi Jing'anqu dimingzhi*, 92; Shanghaishi Changningqu renmin zhengfu, *Changningqu dimingzhi*, 70–71.

123. *Shibao*, January 19, 1914; Zheng Zuan, *Shanghai diming xiaozhi*, 20–23, and "Jindai Zhabei de xingshuai"; Ma Xuexin et al., Shanghai wenhua yuanliu cidian, 204.

124. "Xiahaipu" literally means "lower sea creek." The creek was connected with another branch of the Huangpu River, Shanghaipu (upper sea creek); from Shanghaipu came the name of the town Shanghai. See *Tongzhi Shanghai xianzhi, juan* 1:2.

125. Shanghaishi Hongkouqu renmin zhengfu, *Shanghaishi Hongkouqu dimingzhi*, 141–42; Wang Zheng, "Xiahai miao he Shanghai miao."

126. Lin Xingyuan, "Shanghai de jiu chengyuan"; Zheng Zuan, "Shanghai jiu xiancheng."

127. Wang Yingxia, *Wang Yingxia zizhuan*, 77–78.

128. Shanghaishi wenshi yanjiu guan, *Haishang chunqiu*, 51.

129. *Renmin ribao*, October 21, 1966.

130. This small street has gained some importance in Communist history. In 1920, Mao Zedong lived in House Number 29 of Cihou Nanli (Alley of Benevolence and Kindness, southern section), a lilong compound built in 1910–

12 (and owned by Silas Aaron Hardoon) on Annam Road. The site is now a specially preserved relic. Shanghaishi Jing'anqu renmin zhengfu, *Shanghaishi Jing'anqu dimingzhi,* 243, 214; *Shanghai difangshi ziliao,* 6:37–39.

131. Fei Xichou, *Shanghai xinzhinan,* 133; Shanghaishi Huangpuqu renmin zhengfu caizheng maoyi bangongshi, *Shanghaishi Huangpuqu shangyezhi,* 444–45.

132. Shanghaishi wenshi yanjiu guan, *Haishang chunqiu,* 46–47.

133. I-12.

134. Yuan Jianmin and Hu Jianyu, "Shimin zaocan zhuangkuang lingren danyou."

135. Shen Shanzeng, "Pingchang xin shi dao," 41–42.

136. Xiong Yuezhi, "Zatan 'Shanghai ren.'"

137. Anderson, *Food of China,* 196.

138. *Shehui ribao,* November 3, 1936.

139. Shanghaishi zonggonghui, *Jiefang zhanzheng shiqi,* 246.

140. The general lack of refrigerators in common households was one of the reasons for this custom. In 1989, a survey of 3,000 households that owned a refrigerator showed a low refrigerator-ownership rate before 1980: of the households surveyed, 92.6 percent had first purchased a refrigerator in 1985–89, and 6.6 percent in 1980–84; only .8 percent of the families had owned a refrigerator for more than ten years. See Wu Zaiyang, "Shiqu jumin dianbingxiang zhuanti baogao," 110.

141. Xu Dafeng, "Longtang texie"; I-41.

142. I-9; I-12; I-14, March 20, 1989.

143. Shanghai bowuguan, *Shanghai beike ziliao xuanji,* 365–66; Lu Wenshao, "Benshi mihaoye zhi gaikuang"; Yao Qingshan and An Jumin, *Shanghai mishi diaocha,* 1–6.

144. Sheng Juncai, "Shanghai shuiluye de bianqian"; *Shehui ribao,* June 27, 1936.

145. Sheng Juncai, "Shanghai shuiluye de bianqian."

146. Fang Xiantang, *Shanghai jindai minzu juanyan gongye,* 125; Shanghai baihuo gongsi, *Shanghai jindai baihuo shangye shi,* 28.

147. *Shehui ribao,* November 13, 1936.

148. Jiang Shenwu, "Qingji Shanghai difang zizhi yu ji'erte," 148; Li Cishan, "Shanghai laodong zhuangkuang," 49; *Shehui ribao,* November 3, 1936.

149. Li Cishan, "Shanghai laodong zhuangkuang," 49. In later years, jiangyuan were merged into larger mills. By the late 1940s, Shanghai had 30 jiangyuan, with 1,200 workers (or 40 workers per jiangyuan on average); see Shanghaishi zonggonghui, *Jiefang zhanzheng shiqi,* 246.

150. Lu Wenshao, "Benshi mihaoye zhi gaikuang."

151. *Shehui ribao,* November 13, 1936.

152. Mao Tse-tung, *Selected Works of Mao Tse-tung,* 1:15.

153. *Shehui ribao,* March 19, 1936.

154. Ibid., November 13, 1936.

155. Sheng Juncai, "Shanghai shuiluye de bianqian"; *Shehui ribao*, May 19, 1936.

156. I-12.

157. Kirby, "China Unincorporated."

158. Henriot, *Shanghai, 1927–1937*, chapters 7–9.

159. Kirby, "China Unincorporated"; Wakeman, "Licensing Leisure"; Hershatter, "Regulating Sex in Shanghai."

160. Henriot, *Shanghai, 1927–1937*, 161–64.

161. I-9.

162. Shanghai minshi, *Shanghai minshi tiaojie xiehui baogao*, 2.

163. Henriot, *Shanghai, 1927–1937*, 218.

164. Shanghaishi dang'an guan, *Ri wei Shanghai shizhengfu*, 568.

165. Shanghai minshi, *Shanghai minshi tiaojie xiehui baogao*, 2–4; Xu Piaoping, "Shangjie lingxiu Yu Qiaqing."

166. Tao Juyin, *Gudao jianwen*, 127–128.

167. Yan Esheng, *Shangren tuanti zuzhi guicheng*; Huang Yifeng et al., *Jiu Zhongguo minzu zichan jieji*, 368–69.

168. Shanghai wujin jixie gongsi et al., *Shanghai jindai wujin*, 255; Shanghai baihuo gongsi, *Shanghai jindai baihuo shangye shi*, 28, 278.

169. Bergère, *Golden Age*, 9.

170. Henriot, *Shanghai, 1927–1937*, 163–64.

171. Shanghai shizhengfu mishuchu, *Shanghaishi xingzheng tongji gaiyao*, 81.

172. Sheng Juncai, "Shanghai shuiluye de bianqian."

173. Yiming, *Shanghai shi*, 86.

174. *Shehui ribao*, June 21, 1936; and October 10, 1936.

175. *Shehui yuekan* 2, nos. 7 & 8 (August 5, 1947): 147–48.

176. *Shehui ribao*, November 29, 1936.

177. *Shanghaitan*, 3:107; *Shehui ribao*, November 29, 1936.

178. I-15, March 27, 1989.

179. *Shehui ribao*, August 15, 1936.

180. Ibid., November 29, 1936.

181. Martin, *Shanghai Green Gang*, 64–78, 113–34, 158–89.

182. I-10, March 26, 1989.

183. Jiang Siyi and Wu Yuanshu, *Shanghai qibai ge qigai de shehui diaocha*, 81–83; Jiang Siyi and Wu Yuanshu, "Shanghai de qigai."

CONCLUSION

1. A third category, "bureaucratic capitalism" (referring to the enterprises owned or run by the Nationalist elites), was sometimes added to form what was known as the "Three Mountains" to be overthrown by the revolution. See Mao, *Selected Works*, 3:271–74.

2. Mao Zedong himself well understood this situation: he once referred to

himself as a "big cannon" of ideological slogans and laughed at the idea that anyone would seriously believe them. See Kissinger, *White House Years*, 1062; and "Philosopher and the Pragmatist" (*Newsweek*, March 3, 1997).

3. "Ren wang gaochu zou, shui wang dichu liu," see Zhongguo suyu dacidian, 712.

4. Feng Zikai, *Feng Zikai wenji*, 6:593.

5. In the national calendar, years were dated by their distance from the 1911 revolution; that is, 1912 was designated as the "first year of the republic," 1913 as the "second year of the republic," and so on. But the Gregorian year was often used in tandem with the republican year in calendars and publications (such as newspapers, periodicals, and copyright dates of books). Days and months were counted by the Western calendar.

6. Smith, *Chinese Almanacs*, 41.

7. Originally, "Duanwu" meant "the fifth day (of the fifth month)." The original character *wu* (five) was replaced by a homonym character, *wu* (noon), probably suggesting the bright sun at high noon on a sunny *midsummer's* day (Duanwu usually falls early in June). "Duanyang" may be translated as "sedate sun." See *Cihai*, 1789.

8. *Shanghai shenghuo* 3, no. 1 (January 1939): 4; Shanghaishi gongshang xingzheng guanliju and Shanghaishi fangzhipin gongsi, *Shanghaishi mianbu shangye*, 467; Shanghaishi liangshiju et al., *Zhongguo jindai mianfen gongye shi*, 331.

9. The Western calendar has been called the "public calendar" (*gongli*) since the founding of the People's Republic.

10. Tang Weikang and Du Li, *Hucheng fengsu ji*, 36–39.

11. See *Shanghai shenghuo* 3, no. 2 (February 1939): 3–7, for a detailed report on how the 1939 Chinese New Year was celebrated in the city. Shanghai's foreign communities followed local custom by taking four days off. A foreign resident in Shanghai wrote, "It was the biggest date on the Chinese calendar. Weeks before were spent in preparation. Chinese homes were thoroughly cleaned. Every effort was made to pay up all outstanding debts. The night itself was one continuous wave of popping firecrackers. What interested us most was the ritual surrounding the benign Kitchen God." Carney, *Foreign Devils Had Light Eyes*, 119. See also a "bamboo branch poem" cited in Tang Weikang et al., *Hucheng fengsu ji*, 42.

12. Tang Weikang et al., *Hucheng fengsu ji*, 54–58.

13. Carney, *Foreign Devils Had Light Eyes*, 120.

14. *Jia*, no. 9 (October 1946): 29; I-23.

15. Yulanpen (sometimes simplified as "Lanpen") is a transliteration of the Sanskrit term "Ullambana," which may be literally translated as "save the upside-down [i.e., the suffering]" or, broadly, "salvation."

16. *Shanghai zhoubao* 2, no. 16 (September 14, 1933): 248–49.

17. The Communists inherited the tuanbai institution. For decades, group New Year's calls have been a major activity among officialdom and are publicized in the news media. Sensitive personnel changes among the top leadership

might be divined from the publicized list of officials who participated in the calls. Deng Xiaoping's once-a-year public appearances in his later years, for instance, were deliberately made on this New Year tuanbai occasion.

18. *Shanghai shenghuo* 2, no. 7 (December 1938): 2; 3, no. 1 (January 1939): 2–5.

19. Bird, *Yangtze Valley and Beyond*, 25.

20. Liu Ya'nong, *Shanghai minsu xianhua*, 67.

21. Shanghaishi jiaotong yunshu ju, *Shanghai gonglu yunshu shi*, 19.

22. Ibid., 19–20.

23. Tang Weikang and Du Li, *Hucheng fengsu ji*, 99.

24. Elvin, "Market Towns and Waterways."

25. *Hongzhi Shanghai zhi, juan 1: chengchi*.

26. *Jiaqing Shanghai xianzhi, juan 1: tushuo*.

27. Shanghaishi jiaotong yunshu ju, *Shanghai gonglu yunshu shi*, 20–21.

28. Hu Xianghan, *Shanghai xiaozhi*, 13.

29. In the International Settlement alone, 268 automobile licenses were issued in 1912. By 1927, the number of licenses increased to 5,328; all were for foreign-made cars. Registered wheelbarrows in the Settlement decreased from 6,135 in 1902 to 5,804 in 1910. Still, wheelbarrows remained numerous in Shanghai throughout the Republican period. See Shanghaishi jiaotong yunshu ju, *Shanghai gonglu yunshu shi*, 82–83, 22–23.

30. Pal, *Shanghai Saga*, 167.

31. Wang Yingxia, *Wang Yingxia zizhuan*, 77; also in Shanghaishi wenshi yanjiu guan, *Haishang chunqiu*, 50–51.

32. Wolf, *Urban Village*; Gans, *Urban Villagers*.

33. Perry, *Shanghai on Strike*, 24; Jiangnan, *Jiangnan zaochuan changshi*, 35–36.

34. Honig, *Sisters and Strangers*, 136, 217–24.

35. Buck, *Urban Change in China*, 12, 210.

36. Bestor, *Neighborhood Tokyo*, 39–40.

37. Anderson, *Food of China*, 253.

38. Tang and Shen, *Shanghai shi*, 7; Bergère, "'Other China'"; Murphey, *History of Asia*, 346; Clifford, *Spoilt Children of Empire*, 9.

39. See Yue Zheng, *Jindai Shanghairen shehui xintai*, 5; Shen Weibing and Jiang Ming, *Ala Shanghairen*, 10–14; Luo Shuang, *"Pouxi" Shanghairen*, 100–101; Yang Dongping, *Chengshi jifeng*, 457–81.

40. Xiong Yuezhi, "Zatan 'Shanghairen.'"

41. Yu Qiuyu, *Wenming de suipian*, 206.

42. Quote from Pan Ling, *In Search of Old Shanghai*, 130.

43. Zhang Ailing, *Zhang Ailing wenji*, 4:19–20.

44. In the eyes of many Westerners in Shanghai, the city was not just a place to sojourn but a permanent home. Given the fact that most Chinese Shanghainese had themselves emigrated from elsewhere, the Westerners in the city were in a sense "Shanghainese" of foreign origin.

45. The opening quotation on the stock exchange was known as the *kaipan*

(opening tray) and the closing quotation as the *shoupan* (closing tray). Cheating foreign customers (i.e., giving them an unreasonable price) was thus called *anpan* (hidden tray). Shanghaishi dang'an guan, *Jiu Shanghai de zhengquan jiaoyi*, 49.

46. Qian Nairong, "Shili yangchang hua fangyan"; Luo Shuang, *"Pouxi" Shanghairen*, 106–7; I-24; I-27, August 10, 1995.

47. Zhang Ailing, *Zhang Ailing wenji*, 4:20.

48. Luo Shuang, *"Pouxi" Shanghairen*, 116.

49. *Jiefang ribao*, March 5, 1986.

50. The term "Haipai" was originally created in the late nineteenth century to refer to Shanghai-style painting and Shanghai-style Peking Opera. Later, the term was used in literary circles and figured prominently in a debate in 1933 and 1934 between hinterland-based writers such as Shen Congwen and Shanghai writers. Since the 1930s the terms "Jingpai" and "Haipai" have become broadly defined terms to refer to the general cultural differences between Shanghai and the "hinterlands" (represented by Beijing). For a discussion of the historical background of Jingpai and Haipai, see Yang Dongping, *Chengshi jifeng*, 69–117.

51. Lu Xun, *Lu Xun Quanji*, 6:302.

52. Xu Ke, *Qing bai lei chao*, vol. 37(*xiju*):23.

53. See, for example, Steinhardt, *Chinese Imperial City Planning;* Xiong, "Sui Yangdi and the Building of Sui-Tang Luoyang."

54. Lu Xun, *Lu Xun Quanji*, 6:302.

55. Lee, introduction.

56. Wang Tao, *Wang Tao riji*, 116.

57. Wodusheng, *Huitu Shanghai Zaji, juan* 3:6; *Shenbao*, October 31, 1904.

58. Chen Duxiu, *Duxiu wencun*, 589, 595.

59. Bergère, "'Other China.'"

60. Mao Zedong once used this proverb in one of his poems, "The Capture of Nanjing, April 1949," which was frequently cited during the Cultural Revolution. For both the Chinese original and an English translation, see Barnstone, *Poems of Mao Tse-tung*, 76–77.

61. Shanghaishi Jing'anqu renmin zhengfu, *Shanghaishi Jing'anqu dimingzhi*, 22; Shanghaishi Xuhuiqu renmin zhengfu, *Shanghaishi Xuhuiqu dimingzhi*, 31.

62. Shanghaishi Jing'anqu renmin zhengfu, *Shanghaishi Jing'anqu dimingzhi*, 1–4, 21–24; Shanghaishi Xuhuiqu renmin zhengfu, *Shanghaishi Xuhuiqu dimingzhi*, 31. Similar examples can be found all over the city as recorded in the *dimingzhi* (gazetteers) of various districts published in 1988–1990.

63. The administrative hierarchy in urban industries and commerce in the People's Republic follows this pattern: the municipal council or city government supervises bureaus (*ju*), bureaus supervise corporations (*gongsi*), and corporations supervise factories and stores. Since 1956, there have been two Bu-

reaus of Commerce in Shanghai. The First Bureau of Commerce supervises large commercial enterprises such as major department stores, while the Second Bureau of Commerce supervises small stores.

64. Here, the term "joint state and private operated" refers to a government policy of redemption (or buyout) of private businesses during the 1956 campaign. The government took over private businesses first but promised to pay premiums to the former owners within seven years of the "buyout." This program was extended to ten years in 1963 and suspended in September 1966; owners were never fully paid (Shanghai shehui kexueyuan jingji yanjiusuo, *Shanghai ziben zhuyi gongshangye de shehui zhuyi gaizao,* 224–56).

65. I-18, May 18, 1991; Shanghaishi Huangpuqu renmin zhengfu caizheng maoyi bangongshi, *Shanghaishi Huangpuqu shangyezhi,* 733.

66. I-12.

67. I-13; I-14, March 23, 1989; I-16; I-18, May 17, 1991; I-19, June 29, 1991. A detailed description of the rationing system in urban China (with slight differences from the Shanghai case) is given in Whyte and Parish, *Urban Life in Contemporary China,* 86–90.

68. Shanghai dang'an guan, *Ri wei Shanghai shizhengfu,* 604–12; Tao Juyin, *Gudao jianwen,* 179–90.

69. I-13; I-16; *Jiefang ribao,* August 28, 1955, and September 7, 1955.

70. I-13; I-10, March 26, 1989.

71. To "cut off the tail of capitalism" was a nationwide subcampaign during the Cultural Revolution. Its chief target was the "family plot" (*ziliudi*) in the countryside. In urban areas, small stores became the main target. Xu Jiatun, the former Communist governor of Jiangsu province (and later also the chief Communist representative in Hong Kong, now a dissident exiled in the United States), in his recent memoirs reveals the impact of this slogan in China. See *Xu Jiatun Xianggang huiyilu,* 1:8.

72. I-14, March 23, 1989; I-15, March 23, 1989.

73. I-15, August 21, 1993. For the wages and benefits involved in state and collectively run businesses, see Dangdai Zhongguo congshu bianjibu, *Dangdai Zhongguo,* especially, 66–70, 338–49.

74. I-15, August 17, 1993; I-18, May 18, 1991.

75. *World Journal,* May 20, 1993.

76. Ibid., Dec. 5, 1992, A19.

77. Ibid., March 16, 1993.

78. Shanghaishi tongjiju, *Shanghai: gaige, kaifang yu fazhan,* 118, 137.

79. *World Journal,* May 20, 1993, A2.

80. The figure cited here represents those who registered for a license. It does not include assistants and helpers, who, traditionally, were mostly members of the shopkeeper's family.

81. Shanghaishi tongjiju, *Shanghai: gaige, kaifang yu fazhan,* 53.

82. I-19, June 30, 1991; I-20. Liu died of bronchiectasis in 1992. His widow is now running the business. To "make things alive" (*gaohuo*), or to "make the economy alive" (*gaohuo jingji*), was a popular slogan in China in the 1980s,

suggesting that the centrally planned economy was at a dead end and that China had to find new solutions to keep the national economy alive and active.

83. I-11, I-15, I-19, I-20. The expression "connecting tracks" (*jiegui*) has been used to describe this situation. The term first surfaced in the early 1990s, meaning to keep abreast of advanced economic and technological systems abroad (i.e., connecting "tracks" in China with those in the developed countries). Later it also meant that the skyrocketing inflation had made many commodities as expensive as they were abroad. And, finally, particularly to the older generation, the "track" has been "connected" to the city's controversial past.

84. Jiefang ribao she, *Shanghai jiefang yinian*, 3, 35.

85. *Yehuo shao bu jin, chunfeng chui you sheng,* by the Tang poet Bai Juyi (772–846). This translation is mine. For a complete translation of the poem, see Bynner and Kiang, *Jade Mountain,* 119.

86. In his famous 1992 "inspection tour of the South," Deng Xiaoping made the following comments on Shanghai: "In the areas of talented personnel, technology, and administration, Shanghai has obvious superiority, which radiates over a wide area. Looking back, my one major mistake was not to include Shanghai when we set up the four special economic zones. Otherwise, the situation of reform and opening to the outside in the Yangzi River delta, the entire Yangzi River valley, and even the entire nation would be different." Deng Xiaoping, *Deng Xiaoping wenxuan,* 3:376.

References Cited

Abend, Hallett. *Treaty Ports*. Garden City, N.Y.: Doubleday, Doran, and Company, 1944.

Alcock, Sir Rutherford. *Capital of the Tycoon: A Narrative of a Three Years' Residence in Japan*. New York: Harper and Brothers Publishers, 1863.

Anderson, E. N. *The Food of China*. New Haven: Yale University Press, 1988.

Bandyopadhyay, Raghab. "The Inheritors: Slum and Pavement Life in Calcutta." In *Calcutta: The Living City*, edited by Sukanta Chaudhuri, 78–87. Vol. 2. Oxford: Oxford University Press, 1990.

Bao Kanbu, ed. *Shili Yangchang zhongshengxiang* (A variety of profiles of the people in Shanghai's foreign concessions). Reprint, Beijing: Shumu wenxian chubanshe, 1993.

Bao Tianxiao. *Shanghai chunqiu* (Spring and autumn of Shanghai). 2 vol. 1924, 1926. Reprint, Shanghai: Shanghai guji chubanshe, 1991.

———. *Chuanyinglou huiyilu* (A memoir of the "Bracelet Shadow Tower"). Reprint, Taipei: Wenhai chubanshe, n.d.

Barber, Noel. *The Fall of Shanghai*. New York: Coward, McCann, and Geoghegan, 1979.

Barnstone, Willis, trans. *The Poems of Mao Tse-tung*. In collaboration with Ko Ching-po. New York: Harper and Row, Publishers, 1972.

Barz, R. *Shanghai: Sketches of Present-Day Shanghai*. N.p.: Centurion Printing, n.d.

Benshu bianxiezu [Writing group of the book]. *Zhaojiabang de bianqian* (Vicissitudes of Zhaojiabang). Shanghai: Shanghai renmin chubanshe, 1976.

Bergère, Marie-Claire. "'The Other China': Shanghai from 1919 to 1949." In *Shanghai, Revolution and Development in an Asian Metropolis*, edited by Christopher Howe, 1–34. Cambridge: Cambridge University Press, 1981.

———. *The Golden Age of the Chinese Bourgeoisie, 1911–1937*. Translated by Janet Lloyd. Cambridge: Cambridge University Press, 1986.

Bernhardt, Kathryn. *Rents, Taxes, and Peasant Resistance: The Lower Yangzi Region, 1840–1950*. Stanford, Calif.: Stanford University Press, 1992.

Bestor, Theodore C. *Neighborhood Tokyo*. Stanford, Calif.: Stanford University Press, 1989.

Birch, Cyril, trans. *Stories from a Ming Collection: Translations of Chinese Short Stories Published in the Seventeenth Century*. Bloomington: Indiana University Press, 1958.

Bird, Isabella. *The Yangtze Valley and Beyond*. 1899. Reprint, Boston: Beacon Press, 1987.

Biweng. "*Shanghai wuyanxia* jiantao" (A review of "Under the eaves of Shanghai"). *Shanghai shenghuo* (Shanghai life) 4, no. 8 (August 1940): 34–37.

———. "Shanghai renlichefu" (Rickshaw pullers in Shanghai). *Shanghai shenghuo* (Shanghai life) 4, no. 12 (December 1940): 60–64.

Blaser, Werner. *Courtyard House in China: Tradition and Present*. Basel: Birkhauser, 1979.

A British Resident. *Twelve Years in China: The People, the Rebels, and the Mandarins*. Edinburgh: Thomas Constable and Company, 1860.

Buck, David D. *Urban Change in China: Politics and Development in Tsinan, Shantung, 1890–1949*. Madison: University of Wisconsin Press, 1978.

Bureau of Social Affairs, the City Government of Greater Shanghai, comp. *Standard of Living of Shanghai Laborers*. Shanghai: Chung Hwa [Zhonghua] Book Company, 1934.

———, comp. *Wage Rates in Shanghai*. Shanghai: Commercial Press, 1935.

Bynner, Witter, and Kiang Kang-Hu, trans. *The Jade Mountain: A Chinese Anthology*. New York: Alfred A. Knopf, 1931.

Cai Binxian. "Cong nongcun pochan suo jichulai de renlichefu wenti" (The problem of rickshaw men who were forced to leave the countryside by rural depression). *Dongfang zazhi* (Eastern miscellany) 32, no. 16 (August 1935): 35–43.

Cao Maotang, and Wu Lun. *Shanghai yingtan huajiu* (Reminiscences on Shanghai's movie industry). Shanghai: Shanghai wenyi chubanshe, 1987.

Carney, Dora Sanders. *Foreign Devils Had Light Eyes*. Toronto: Dorset Publishing, 1980.

Chan, Ming K., and Arif Dirlik. *Schools into Fields and Factories: Anarchists, the Guomindang, and the National Labor University in Shanghai, 1927–1932*. Durham, N.C.: Duke University Press, 1991.

Changyong yanyu cidian (A dictionary of frequently used sayings). Compiled and published by Shanghai cishu chubanshe [Shanghai dictionary press], 1987.

Chen Boxi, comp. *Lao Shanghai* (Old Shanghai hands). Shanghai: Taidong shuju, 1919.

Chen Congzhou and Zhang Ming, eds. *Shanghai jindai jianzhu shigao* (A draft history of modern architecture in Shanghai). Shanghai: Sanlian shudian, 1988.

Chen Da. *Woguo kangRi zhanzheng shiqi shizheng gongren shenghuo* (Urban workers' life in China during the War of Resisting Japan). Beijing: Zhong-guo laodong chubanshe, 1993.

Chen Duxiu. *Duxiu wencun* (The writings of Duxiu). Hefei, Anhui: Anhui renmin chubanshe, 1987.

Chen Gang. *Shanghaigang matou de bianqian* (Changes on the docks of Shanghai). Shanghai: Shanghai renmin chubanshe, 1966.

Chen Gongpu. *Paohuo xia de Shanghai* (Shanghai under gunfire). Shanghai: Zhongzheng chubanshe, 1937.

Chen Liang. "Tezhong Shanghai shenghuo" (The special kinds of Shanghai life). *Shanghai shenghuo* (Shanghai life) 4, no. 5 (May 1940): 10–12.

———. "Yanzhidian" (Tobacco and paper stores), *Shanghai shenghuo* (Shanghai life) 4, no. 7 (July 1940): 14–15.

Chen Lizheng, and Yuan Enzhen. *Xinya de licheng* (The history of the Xinya Pharmaceutical Factory). Shanghai: Shanghai Academy of Social Science Press, 1990.

Chen, Tiejun, and Mark Selden, "The Origins and Social Consequences of China's *Hukou* System." *China Quarterly* 139 (September 1994): 644–68.

Chen Yanlin. *Shanghai dichan daquan* (A complete book of Shanghai real estate). Shanghai: Shanghai dichan yanjiusuo, 1933.

Cheng Shi. "Yaoshuilong de gushi" (The story of Yaoshuilong). In *Jiu Shanghai de gushi* (Stories of old Shanghai), 1–10. Shanghai: Shanghai renmin chubanshe, 1974.

Chesneaux, Jean. *The Chinese Labor Movement, 1919–1927*. Translated from the French by H. M. Wright. Stanford, Calif.: Stanford University Press, 1968.

China Handbook Editorial Board, comp. *China Handbook 1950*. New York: Rockport Press, 1950.

China Weekly Review, Shanghai, 1923–37.

Chinese and Japanese Repository, London, 1864–65.

Chinese Economic Journal, published by Bureau of Foreign Trade, Ministry of Industry, Shanghai, 1927–33.

Chouban yiwu shimo (Documents concerning foreign affairs), the Daoguang and Xianfeng Sections. 1930. Reprint, Beijing: Zhonghua shuju, 1979.

Ch'u, T'ung-tsu. *Local Government in China under the Ch'ing*. Cambridge: Harvard University Press, 1962.

Chunshenjun. "Zenyang weichi Shanghai de fanrong" (How to maintain the prosperity of Shanghai). *Shanghai zhoubao* (Shanghai weekly) 1, no. 9 (January 26, 1933).

Cihai (Sea of words). Single-vol. edition. Shanghai: Shanghai cishu chubanshe, 1979.

Claude, Georges. "Neon Tube Lighting." *Transactions of the Illuminating Engineering Society* 8 (1913): 371–78.

Clausen, Soren, and Stig Thogersen. *The Making of a Chinese City: History and Historiography in Harbin*. Armonk, N.Y.: M. E. Sharpe, 1995.

Clifford, Nicholas R. *Spoilt Children of Empire: Westerners in Shanghai and the Chinese Revolution of the 1920s*. Hanover, England: Middlebury College Press, 1991.

Coble, Parks M., Jr. *The Shanghai Capitalists and the Nationalist Government, 1927–1937*. Cambridge: Council on East Asian Studies, Harvard University, 1980.

Cochran, Sherman. *Big Business in China: Sino-Foreign Rivalry in the Cigarette Industry, 1890–1930*. Cambridge: Harvard University Press, 1980.

Cohen, Jerome A. *The Criminal Process in the People's Republic of China, 1949–1963: An Introduction*. Cambridge: Harvard University Press, 1968.

Cohen, Paul A. *Discovering History in China: American Historical Writing on the Recent Chinese Past*. New York: Columbia University Press, 1984.

Commercial Press, comp. *Shanghai zhinan* (Guide to Shanghai). Shanghai: Commercial Press, 1919.

Cowley, Malcolm. *Exile's Return: A Literary Odyssey of the 1920s*. New York: Viking Press, 1951.

Da wanbao (The great evening daily), Shanghai.

Dangdai Zhongguo congshu bianjibu [Editorial office of the *Contemporary China* series], comp. *Dangdai Zhongguo de zhigong gongzi fuli he shehui baoxian* (China today: wages, welfare of staff and workers and social insurance). Beijing: Zhongguo shehui kexue chubanshe, 1987.

Darwent, C. E. *Shanghai: A Handbook for Travellers and Residents to the Chief Objects of Interest in and around the Foreign Settlements and Native City*. 2d ed., rev. and enl. Shanghai: Kelly and Walsh, 1920.

De Jesus, C. A. Montalto. *Historical Shanghai*. Shanghai: Shanghai Mercury, 1909.

Deng Xiaoping. *Deng Xiaoping wenxuan* (Selected works of Deng Xiaoping). Vol. 3. Beijing: Renmin chubanshe, 1993.

Dewey, Evelyn. *The Dalton Laboratory Plan*. New York: E. P. Dutton and Company, 1922.

Dingjiu. "Shanghai zhi chen zazouqu" (Sonata in a jumble in Shanghai's morning). *Shanghai shenghuo* (Shanghai life) 1, no. 4 (June 1937): 11–13.

———. "Shanghai shimin shenghuo de zhuanbian" (Transformation of the life of the people of Shanghai). *Shanghai shenghuo* 2, no. 4 (September 1938): 7–9.

———. "Shanghai chuxia jietou" (Street corners of Shanghai in the early summer). *Shanghai shenghuo* 3, no. 6 (June 1939): 27–29.

Dongfang ribao (The East daily), Shanghai, 1939.

Dongping. "Pinminku fangwen ji" (A record of slum visits). *Xinsheng* (New life) 2, no. 21 (May 1936): 431–32.

Du Li. "'Baimayi' yu erfangdong" (The "termites" and the second landlords). In *Shanghai yishi*, edited by Tang Weikang, Zhu Dailu, and Du Li, 275–84. Shanghai: Shanghai wenhua chubanshe, 1987.

Du Xuncheng. *Minzu ziben zhuyi yu jiu Zhongguo zhengfu (1840–1937)* (National capitalism and the old Chinese government, 1840–1937). Shanghai: Shanghai Academy of Social Sciences Press, 1991.

Duojiugong. "Shanghai tingzijian jiepou tu" (An examination of Shanghai's pavilion rooms). *Shanghai shenghuo* (Shanghai life) 2, no. 2 (July 1938): 1–2.

Dyce, C. M. *The Model Settlement: Personal Reminiscences of Thirty Years' Residence in the Model Settlement Shanghai, 1870–1900*. London: Chapman and Hall, 1906.

Edkins, Joseph. *A Grammar of Colloquial Chinese as Exhibited in the Shanghai Dialect*. 2d ed., cor. 1853. Reprint, Shanghai: Presbyterian Press, 1868.

———. *A Vocabulary of the Shanghai Dialect*. Shanghai: Presbyterian Mission Press, 1869.

Elvin, Mark. "Market Towns and Waterways: The County of Shang-hai from 1480 to 1910." In *The City in Late Imperial China*, edited by William Skinner, 441–73. Stanford, Calif.: Stanford University Press, 1977.

———. "Chinese Cities since the Sung Dynasty." In *Towns in Societies: Essays in Economic History and Historical Sociology*, edited by Philip Abrams and E. A. Wrigley, 79–89. Cambridge: Cambridge University Press, 1978.

Fairbank, John King. *Trade and Diplomacy on the China Coast: The Opening of the Treaty Ports, 1842–1854*. Stanford, Calif.: Stanford University Press, 1969.

Fan Shuzhi. *Ming-Qing Jiangnan shizhen tanwei* (Research on market towns in Jiangnan during the Ming and Qing dynasties). Shanghai: Fudan University Press, 1990.

Fang Fu-an. "Rickshaws in China." *Chinese Economic Journal* 7, no. 1 (July 1930): 796–808.

———. "Shanghai Labor." *Chinese Economic Journal* 7, no. 2 (August 1930): 853–885; no. 3 (September 1930): 989–1012.

Fang Hongkai and Huang Yanpei, comps. *Chuansha xian zhi* (Gazetteer of Chuansha County). Shanghai: Guoguang shuju, 1937.

Fang Xiantang, ed. *Shanghai jindai minzu juanyan gongye* (The modern national cigarette industry in Shanghai). Shanghai: Shanghai Academy of Social Sciences Press, 1989.

Feetham, Richard. *Report of the Hon. Justice Feetham, C. M. G., to the Shanghai Municipal Council*. 3 vols. Shanghai: North-China Daily News and Herald, 1931.

Fei Xichou, ed. *Shanghai xinzhinan* (A new guide to Shanghai). Shanghai: Shengsheng chubanshe, 1939.

Feng Ruogu. "Shanghai tonggong nügong zhi shenghuo gaikuang" (The general situation of the lives of child laborers and woman laborers in Shanghai). *Laogong yuekan* (Labor monthly) 5 (1936): 11–12.

Feng Zikai. *Feng Zikai wenji* (The anthology of Feng Zikai). 7 vols. Hangzhou: Zhejiang wenyi and Zhejiang jiaoyu chubanshe, 1990.

Fewsmith, Joseph. *Party, State, and Local Elite in Republican China: Merchant*

Organizations and Politics in Shanghai, 1890–1930. Honolulu: University of Hawaii Press, 1985.

Finch, Percy. *Shanghai and Beyond.* New York: Charles Scribner's Sons, 1953.

Fluck, Hans-R., Barbara Böke-Fluck, and Zhu Jianhua, eds. *Souvenir from Shanghai: Historical Postcards.* Shanghai: Tongji University Press, 1993.

Forbes, Lieut. F. E. *Five Years in China; From 1842 to 1847. With an Account of the Occupation of the Islands of Labuan and Borneo by Her Majesty's Forces.* London: Richard Bentley, 1848.

Fortune, Robert. *Three Years' Wanderings in the Northern Provinces of China, Including a Visit to the Tea, Silk, and Cotton Countries.* 2d ed. London: John Murray, 1847.

———. *The Tea-Districts of China and India: Two Visits to the Tea Countries of China and the British Tea Plantations in the Himalaya.* 2 vols. London: John Murray, 1853.

Friedrichs, Christopher R. "Capitalism, Mobility, and Class Formation in the Early Modern German City." In *Towns in Societies: Essays in Economic History and Historical Sociology,* edited by Philip Abrams and E. A. Wrigley, 187–213. Cambridge: Cambridge University Press, 1978.

Fu, Poshek. *Passivity, Resistance, and Collaboration: Intellectual Choices in Occupied Shanghai, 1937–1945.* Stanford: Stanford University Press, 1993.

Gamble, Sidney D. *Peking: A Social Survey.* New York: George H. Doran, 1921.

———. *How Chinese Families Live in Peiping.* New York: Funk and Wagnalls, 1933.

Gamewell, Mary Ninde. *The Gateway to China: Picture of Shanghai.* New York: Fleming H. Revell, 1916.

Gans, Herbert J. *The Urban Villagers: Group and Class in the Life of Italian-Americans.* New York: Free Press, 1982.

Gao Chao. "Shanghai lilong zhuzhai yan'ge" (The evolution of alleyway houses in Shanghai). In *Shanghai wenshi ziliao xuanji* (Selected collection of historical materials of Shanghai), edited by Zhongguo renmin zhengzhi xieshang huiyi Shanghaishi weiyuanhui wenshi ziliao weiyuanhui, no. 64 (1990): 222–30.

Gascoyne-Cecil, William, and Florence Cecil. *Changing China.* London: James Nisbet and Company, 1910.

Ge Yuanxi. *Huyou zaji* (Miscellanies on Shanghai sojourn). 1876. Reprint, Shanghai: Shanghai guji chubanshe, 1989.

Gernet, Jacques. *Daily Life in China on the Eve of the Mongol Invasion, 1250–1276.* Stanford, Calif.: Stanford University Press, 1962.

Gilbert, Alan, and Ann Varley. *Landlord and Tenant: Housing the Poor in Urban Mexico.* London: Routledge, 1991.

Gongshang banyuekan (Industry and commerce semimonthly), Shanghai.

Goodman, Bryna. *Native Place, City, and Nation: Regional Networks and Identities in Shanghai, 1853–1937.* Berkeley and Los Angeles: University of California Press, 1995.

Gu Shuping. "Wo liyong Gu Zhuxuan de yanhu jinxing geming huodong" (I used Gu Zhuxuan's protection to conduct revolutionary activities). In *Shanghai wenshi ziliao xuanji* (Selected collection of historical materials of Shanghai), edited by Zhongguo renmin zhengzhi xieshang huiyi Shanghaishi weiyuanhui wenshi ziliao weiyuanhui, no. 54 (1986): 360–66.

Gu Sifan. *Shanghai fengwu hua* (The "genre painting" of Shanghai). Ganxian, Jiangxi: Zhanggong shuju, 1944.

Gu Yanpei. "Shanghai Shudian jiuzhi" (The relic of the Shanghai Bookstore). In *Shanghai difangshi ziliao*, compiled by Shanghaishi wenshiguan, 6: 49–50.

Gu Yanwu. *Ri zhi lu* (Records of knowledge gained day by day). Shanghai: Wanyou wenku, n.d.

Guangming ribao (The bright daily), Beijing.

Guo Chongjie. "Shanghaishi de renliche wenti" (The rickshaw problem in Shanghai). *Shehui banyuekan* (Social semimonthly) 1, no. 1 (September 1934): 11–31.

Guo Yuming. *Shanghai xiaodaohui qiyi shi* (A history of Shanghai's Small Swords rebellion). Shanghai: Zhongguo dabaike quanshu chubanshe, 1993.

Guohuo yuebao (National products monthly), Shanghai, 1924.

Habermas, Jurgen. *The Structural Transformation of the Public Sphere: An Inquiry into a Category of Bourgeois Society*. German original, 1962. Reprint, Cambridge: Massachusetts Institute of Technology Press, 1989.

Hahn, Emily. *China to Me: A Partial Autobiography*. Philadelphia: Blakiston, n.d.

Haishang mingren zhuan bianjibu [Editorial Office of Biographies of Shanghai Celebrities], comp. *Haishang mingren zhuan* (Biographies of Shanghai celebrities). Shanghai: Wenming shuju, 1930.

Hao Yen-P'ing. *The Comprador in Nineteenth Century China: Bridge between East and West*. Cambridge: Harvard University Press, 1970.

Hauser, Ernest O. *Shanghai: City for Sale*. New York: Harcourt, Brace, and Company, 1940.

He Changling and Wei Yuan, eds. *Huangchao jinshi wenbian* (Collected writings on statecraft during the Qing dynasty). 1827. Reprint, Taipei: Shijie shuju, 1964.

Hengfeng yinranchang changshi bianxiezu [Writing group of the history of the Hengfeng dyeing mill]. *Ranchang jinxi—Shanghai Hengfeng Yinranchang shihua* (Past and present in a dyeing mill—a history of the Hengfeng dyeing mill of Shanghai). Shanghai: Shanghai renmin chubanshe, 1966.

Henriot, Christian. *Shanghai, 1927–1937: Municipal Power, Locality, and Modernization*. Translated by Noel Castelino. Berkeley and Los Angeles: University of California Press, 1993.

———. "'From a Throne of Glory to a Seat of Ignominy.'" *Modern China* 22, no. 2 (April 1996): 132–63.

Heppner, Ernest G. *Shanghai Refuge: A Memoir of the World War II Jewish Ghetto*. Lincoln: University of Nebraska Press, 1994.

Hershatter, Gail. *The Workers of Tianjin, 1900–1949.* Stanford, Calif.: Stanford University Press, 1986.

———. "The Hierarchy of Shanghai Prostitution, 1870–1949." *Modern China* 15, no. 4 (October 1989): 463–98.

———. "Regulating Sex in Shanghai: The Reform of Prostitution in 1920 and 1951." In *Shanghai Sojourners,* edited by Frederick Wakeman Jr. and Wenhsin Yeh, 145–85.

———. *Dangerous Pleasure: Prostitution and Modernity in Twentieth-Century Shanghai.* Berkeley and Los Angeles: University of California Press, 1997.

Hoch, Charles. "A Brief History of the Homeless Problem in the United States." In *The Homeless in Contemporary Society,* edited by Richard D. Bingham, Roy E. Green, and Sammis B. White, 16–32. Thousand Oaks, Calif.: Sage Publications, 1987.

Hongzhi Shanghai zhi (Shanghai gazetteer compiled in the Hongzhi period). Compiled by Guo Jing and Tang Jing. 1504. Reprint, Shanghai: Zhonghua shuju, 1940.

Honig, Emily. *Sisters and Strangers: Women in the Shanghai Cotton Mills, 1919–1949.* Stanford, California: Stanford University Press, 1986.

———. "Invisible Inequalities: The Status of Subei People in Contemporary Shanghai." *China Quarterly* (June 1990): 273–92.

———. *Creating Chinese Ethnicity: Subei People in Shanghai, 1850–1980.* New Haven: Yale University Press, 1992.

Hsiao Kung-Chuan. *Rural China: Imperial Control in the Nineteenth Century.* Seattle: University of Washington Press, 1960.

Hu Huanyong, ed. *Zhongguo renkou* (Shanghai fence) (China's Population series, Shanghai volume). Beijing: Zhongguo caizheng jingji chubanshe, 1987.

Hu Jianhua. "Songdai chengshi fangdichan guanli jianlun" (On the management of urban real estate in the Song dynasty). *Zhongguo shi yanjiu* (Research on Chinese history), no. 4 (1989): 24–31.

Hu Pu'an. *Zhonghua quanguo fengsu zhi* (Records of Chinese customs). Various paging. Shanghai: Guangyi shuju, 1923.

Hu Shi. *Hu Shi wencun* (Works of Hu Shi). 4 vols. Taipei: Yuandong tushu gongsi, 1961.

———. *Sishi zishu* (An autobiography at age forty). *Jindai Zhongguo shiliao congkan xuji* (The series of historical materials of modern China), no. 952, edited by Shen Yunlong. N.p: Wenhai chubanshe, n.d.

Hu Xianghan. *Shanghai xiaozhi* (Minor records of Shanghai). 1930. Reprint, Shanghai: Shanghai guji chubanshe, 1989.

Hu Zude. *Huyan* (Popular sayings of Shanghai). 1922. Reprint, Shanghai: Guji chubanshe, 1989.

———. *Huyan waibian* (Popular sayings of Shanghai, additional edition). 1923. Reprint, Shanghai: Guji chubanshe, 1989.

Hua Zi. "Erfangdong zhi xinji" (The calculation of the second landlords). *Shanghai shenghuo* (Shanghai life) 3, no. 1 (January 1939): 16–17.

Huang, Philip C. C. *The Peasant Economy and Social Change in North China.* Stanford, Calif.: Stanford University Press, 1985.

——. *The Peasant Family and Rural Development in the Yangzi Delta, 1350–1988.* Stanford, Calif.: Stanford University Press, 1990.

——. "The Paradigmatic Crisis in Chinese Studies: Paradoxes in Social and Economic History." *Modern China* 17, no. 3 (July 1991): 299–341.

Huang Wei. *Shanghai kaibu chuqi duiwai maoyi yanjiu* (Research on the foreign trade of Shanghai in its early treaty-port era). Shanghai: Shanghai renmin chubanshe, 1979.

Huang Wei and Xia Lingen. *Jindai Shanghai diqu fangzhi jingji shiliao xuanji* (A selected collection of historical materials from local gazetteers on the economy of modern Shanghai). Shanghai: Shanghai renmin chubanshe, 1984.

Huang Yifeng, Jiang Duo, Tang Chuansi, and Xu Dingxin. *Jiu Zhongguo minzu zichan jieji* (The national bourgeoisie in old China). N.p.: Jiangsu guji chubanshe, 1990.

Huxley, Aldous. *Jesting Pilate: An Intellectual Holiday.* New York: George H. Doran, 1926.

Imperial Maritime Customs, comp. *Treaties, Conventions, Etc., between China and Foreign States.* 2 vols. Shanghai: Statistical Department of the Inspectorate General of Customs, 1908.

Isaacs, Harold R. *Five Years of Kuomintang Reaction.* Reprinted from the special May 1932 edition of *China Forum.* Shanghai: China Forum Publishing, 1932.

Ji Kang. *Dageming yilai Shanghai gongren jieji wei zhengqu tongyi tuanjie er douzheng zhong de mouxie qingkuang* (Records on the Shanghai working class that has fought for unification and unity since the Great Revolution [of 1926–27]). Shanghai: Laodong chubanshe, 1951.

Jia (Home), monthly journal, Shanghai.

Jia You. "Shanghai longtang mian mian guan" (Various perspectives on the alleyways of Shanghai). In *Shanghai zhanggu* (Historical anecdotes of Shanghai), edited by Benshe, 89–103. Shanghai: Shanghai wenhua chubanshe, 1982. A slightly different version appears in *Shanghai yishi,* edited by Tang Weikang, Zhu Dalu, and Du Li, 285–93. Shanghai: Wenhua chubanshe, 1987.

Jiang Liyang. *Haipai yinshi* (Shanghai-style food). Shanghai: Shanghai huabao chubanshe, 1991.

Jiang Shenwu. "Qingji Shanghai difang zizhi yu ji'erte" (Local autonomy and guilds in the late Qing). In *Shanghai yanjiu ziliao, xuji* (Research materials on Shanghai, continued), compiled by Shanghaitong she, 143–58. 1939. Reprint, Shanghai: Shanghai shudian, 1984.

Jiang Siyi and Wu Yuanshu. "Shanghai de qigai" (The beggars of Shanghai). *Tianlai* 22, no. 2 (1933): 191–213.

——. *Shanghai qibai ge qigai de shehui diaocha* (A social investigation of seven hundred beggars in Shanghai). 2 parts. Manuscript. Shanghai: Hujiang University, 1933.

Jiangnan zaochuan changshi bianxiezu [Writing group of the history of the Jiangnan Shipyard]. *Jiangnan zaochuan changshi* (A history of the Jiangnan Shipyard). Shanghai: Shanghai renmin chubanshe, 1975.

Jianzhu zhuankan (Journal of architecture), Shanghai.

Jiaqing Shanghai xianzhi (Gazetteer of Shanghai County compiled in the Jiaqing period). Compiled by Wang Datong and Li Linsong. N.p., 1814.

Jiefang ribao (Liberation daily), Shanghai.

Jiefang ribao she [Editorial office of Liberation daily]. *Shanghai jiefang yinian* (The first anniversary of the liberation of Shanghai). Shanghai: Jiefang ribao she, 1950.

Jiefangjun wenyishe [Literature and arts press of the People's Liberation Army], ed. *Nanjing Lu shang Haobalian* (The Good Eighth Company on Nanjing Road). Beijing: Jiefangjun wenyishe, 1963.

Jin Xuan. "Shanghai fangdichan chanquan pingzheng pouxi" (An analysis of real estate title certificates in Shanghai). In *Shanghai wenshi ziliao xuanji* (Selected collection of historical materials of Shanghai), edited by Zhongguo renmin zhengzhi xieshang huiyi Shanghaishi weiyuanhui wenshi ziliao weiyuanhui, no. 64 (1990): 31–38.

Jingguan. "Jiuwen shiling" (Tidbits of the past). In *Shanghai zhanggu* (Anecdotes of Shanghai), edited by Benshe, 104–14. Shanghai: Shanghai wenhua chubanshe, 1982.

Jiujun. "Shanghai 'xiaofangzi' cangsang" (Vicissitudes of Shanghai's "little houses"). *Shanghai shenghuo* (Shanghai life) 1, no. 4 (June 1937): 15–16.

Johnson, Linda Cooke. *Shanghai: From Market Town to Treaty Port, 1074–1858*. Stanford, Calif.: Stanford University Press, 1995.

Johnstone, William Crane, Jr. *The Shanghai Problem*. Stanford, Calif.: Stanford University Press, 1937.

Jones, Susan Mann. "The Ningpo *Pang* and Financial Power at Shanghai." In *The Chinese City between Two Worlds*, edited by Mark Elvin and G. William Skinner, 73–96. Stanford, Calif.: Stanford University Press, 1974.

Kirby, William C. "China Unincorporated: Company Law and Business Enterprise in Twentieth-Century China." *Journal of Asian Studies* 54, no. 1 (February 1995): 43–63.

Kissinger, Henry A. *White House Years*. Boston: Little, Brown, and Company, 1979.

Knapp, Ronald G. *China's Traditional Rural Architecture: A Cultural Geography of the Common House*. Honolulu: University of Hawaii Press, 1986.

——. *China's Vernacular Architecture: House Form and Culture*. Honolulu: University of Hawaii Press, 1989.

——. *The Chinese House: Craft, Symbol, and the Folk Tradition*. Hong Kong: Oxford University Press, 1990.

Kotenev, A. M. *Shanghai: Its Mixed Court and Council.* Shanghai: North-China Daily News and Herald, 1925.

Krasno, Rena. *Strangers Always: A Jewish Family in Wartime Shanghai.* Berkeley, Calif.: Pacific View Press, 1992.

Kuai Shixun. *Shanghai gonggong zujie shigao* (A draft history of the Shanghai International Settlement). Shanghai: Shanghai renmin chubanshe, 1980.

Kuhn, Philip A. *Rebellion and Its Enemies in Late Imperial China: Militarization and Social Structure, 1796–1864.* Cambridge: Harvard University Press, 1970.

Lamson, H. D. "The Effect of Industrialization upon Village Livelihood." *Chinese Economic Journal* 9, no. 4 (October 1931): 1025–82.

———. "The Problem of Housing for Workers in China." *Chinese Economic Journal* 11, no. 2 (August 1932): 139–162.

Lang, H. *Shanghai, Considered Socially.* Shanghai: Kelly and Walsh, 1875.

Lanning, G., and S. Couling. *The History of Shanghai.* 2 vols. Shanghai: Kelly and Walsh, 1921.

Lao-Tzu. *Tao Te Ching.* Translated by Stephen Addiss and Stanley Lombardo. Indianapolis: Hackett Publishing, 1993.

Lee, Tahirih V. Introduction to "Coping with Shanghai: Means of Survival and Success in the Early Twentieth Century—a Symposium." *Journal of Asian Studies* 54, no. 1 (February 1995): 3–18.

Lei Jingdun. *Shanghai Yangshupu renlichefu diaocha* (Survey of rickshaw pullers in Yangshupu, Shanghai). Manuscript. Shanghai: Hujiang University, 1930.

Leng Xingwu. *Zuixin Shanghai zhinan* (The most up-to-date guide to Shanghai). Shanghai: Shanghai wenhua yanjiu she, 1946.

Leung Yuen-sang. *The Shanghai Taotai: Linkage Man in a Changing Society, 1843–90.* Honolulu: University of Hawaii Press, 1990.

Lewis, Oscar. *Five Families: Mexican Case Studies in the Culture of Poverty.* New York: Basic Books, 1959.

———. *La Vida: A Puerto Rican Family in the Culture of Poverty—San Juan and New York.* New York: Vintage Books, 1965.

———. *A Study of Slum Culture: Backgrounds for La Vida.* New York: Random House, 1968.

Li Cishan. "Shanghai laodong zhuangkuang" (Labor conditions in Shanghai). *Xin qingnian* (New youth) 7, no. 6 (May 1920): 56–83.

Li Shulei. *Dushi de qianxi* (The changes of the city). Changchun, Jilin: Shidai chubanshe, 1993.

Li Zhisui. *The Private Life of Chairman Mao: The Memoirs of Mao's Personal Physician.* New York: Random House, 1994.

Liangyou (Fine companion), monthly pictorial, Shanghai, 1926–45.

Lieu, D. K. *The Growth and Industrialization of Shanghai.* Shanghai: China Institute of Pacific Relations, 1936.

Lin Xingyuan, "Shanghai de jiu chengyuan" (Shanghai's old city wall). In

Shanghai fengwuzhi (Records of Shanghai scenery), edited by Wu Guifang, 29–33. Shanghai: Shanghai wenhua chubanshe, 1985.

Lin Yutang. *My Country and My People*. New York: Halcyon House, 1938.

Ling Yan, Wang Zhenmin, Yang Lizhen, and Zhong Rongkui. *Shanghai jizhen* (Market towns of Shanghai). N.p., 1984 (restricted publication).

Link, Perry E. *Mandarin Ducks and Butterflies: Popular Fiction in Twentieth-Century Chinese Cities*. Berkeley and Los Angeles: University of California Press, 1981.

Liu Fengsheng. "Buke siyi de Shanghai yi shi zhu" (The inconceivable clothing, food, and housing of Shanghai). *Shenghuo* (Life) 2, no. 3 (November 1926): 17.

Liu Huogong. *Shanghai zhuzhici* (The "bamboo poems" of Shanghai). Shanghai: Diaolong chubanbu, 1925.

Liu Linsheng. "Caojiadu diaochaji" (A record of a survey of Caojiadu). In *Yuehan niankan* (The yearbook of St. John's University), 3–10. Shanghai: St. John's University, 1921.

Liu Meijun. "Shanghai nanzi shenghuo zhier—Haishang xinshi yugong" (Men's life in Shanghai, part two—a new type of Mr. Hermit in Shanghai). *Nüsheng banyuekan* (Women's voice semimonthly) 1, no. 15 (1932): 4–5.

Liu Ya'nong. *Shanghai minsu xianhua* (Survey of Shanghai folklore). Taipei: Chinese Association for Folklore, n.d.

Lu Dafang. *Shanghaitan yijiu* (Records of life in Shanghai). Taipei: Shijie shuju, 1980.

Lu Fen. *Shanghai shouzha* (Personal records on Shanghai). Shanghai: Wenhua shenghuo chubanshe, 1941.

Lu, Hanchao. "Arrested Development: Cotton and Cotton Markets in Shanghai, 1350–1843." *Modern China* 18, no. 4 (October 1992): 468–99.

———. "Away from Nanking Road: Small Stores and Neighborhood Life in Modern Shanghai." *Journal of Asian Studies* 54, no. 1 (February 1995): 92–123.

———. "Creating Urban Outcasts: Shantytowns in Shanghai, 1920–1950." *Journal of Urban History* 21, no. 5 (July 1995): 563–96.

———. "Becoming Urban: Mendicancy and Vagrants in Modern Shanghai." *Journal of Social History*. Forthcoming.

———. "'Shanghai Tudi Zhangcheng' yanjiu" (Research on the Shanghai Land Regulations). In *Shanghaishi yanjiu* (Research on the history of Shanghai), by Qiao Shuming et al., 100–145.

Lu Wenshao. "Benshi mihaoye zhi gaikuang" (The general conditions of Shanghai's rice stores). In *Shanghai minshi wenti* (The issue of people's food in Shanghai), compiled by Shanghaishi liangshi weiyuanhui [The grain food committee of Shanghai], 133–34. Shanghai: Shanghaishi shehuiju, 1931.

Lu Xun. *Diary of a Madman and Other Stories*. Translated by William A. Lyell. Honolulu: University of Hawaii Press, 1990.

———. *Lu Xun Quanji* (The complete works of Lu Xun). Beijing: Renmin wenxue chubanshe, 1991.

Luo Shuang. *"Pouxi" Shanghairen* (Analyzing Shanghainese). Beijing: Zhongguo shehui chubanshe, 1995.

Luo Suwen. *Shikumen: xunchang renjia* (Shikumen: Ordinary homes). Shanghai: Shanghai renmin chubanshe, 1991.

Luo Xiaowei and Wu Jiang, comps. *Shanghai longtang* (Shanghai alleys). Shanghai: Shanghai People's Fine Arts Publishing House, 1997.

Luo Zhiru. *Tongjibiao zhong zhi Shanghai* (Shanghai as shown in statistical tables). Nanjing: Zhongyang yanjiuyuan, 1932.

Lynch, A. J. *The Rise and Progress of the Dalton Plan: Reflections and Opinions after More Than Three Years' Working of the Plan.* New York: D. Appleton and Company, 1927.

Ma Xuexin, Cao Junwei, Xue Liyong, and Hu Xiaojing, eds. *Shanghai wenhua yuanliu cidian* (A dictionary of the cultural origins of Shanghai). Shanghai: Shanghai shehui kexueyuan chubanshe, 1992.

MacPherson, Kerrie. *A Wilderness of Marshes: The Origins of Public Health in Shanghai, 1843–1983.* Oxford: Oxford University Press, 1987.

Malone, Col. C. L'Estrange. *New China: Report of an Investigation.* 2 parts. London: Independent Labour Party Publication Department, 1926.

Mao Dun. *Wo zouguo de daolu* (The roads I have walked). 3 vols. Hong Kong: Joint Publishing Company [Sanlian chubanshe], 1981.

Mao Tse-tung. *Selected Works of Mao Tse-tung.* 4 vols. Peking (Beijing): Foreign Languages Press, 1965–75.

Mao Tun [Mao Dun]. *Midnight.* Chinese original, 1933. Reprint, Peking: Foreign Language Press, 1957.

Martin, Brian G. *The Shanghai Green Gang: Politics and Organized Crime, 1919–1937.* Berkeley and Los Angeles: University of California Press, 1996.

Maybon, Ch.B., and Jean Fredet. *Histoire de la Concession Française de Changhai* (A history of the French concession of Shanghai). Paris: Librairie Plon, 1929.

McElderry, Andrea Lee. *Shanghai Old-Style Banks (Ch'ien-chuang), 1800–1935.* Ann Arbor: Center for Chinese Studies, University of Michigan, 1976.

McIntosh, Gilbert. *Useful Phrases in the Shanghai Dialect.* Shanghai: Presbyterian Mission Press, 1916.

Mengyi. "Shanghai de yijiao" (A corner of Shanghai). *Renyan zhoukan* (Hearsay weekly) 1, no. 6 (March 24, 1934): 123–24.

Miller, G. E. *Shanghai, The Paradise of Adventurers.* New York: Orsay Publishers, 1937.

Miller, Samuel C., and Donald G. Fink. *Neon Signs.* New York: McGraw-Hill, 1935.

Morse, Hosea Ballou. *The International Relations of the Chinese Empire.* 3 vols. London: Longmans, Green, and Company, 1910–18.

Mote, F. W. "The Transformation of Nanking, 1350–1400." In *The City in Late Imperial China,* edited by G. William Skinner, 101–53. Stanford, Calif.: Stanford University Press, 1977.

Mu Mutian. "Longtang—Shanghai difang sumiao zhier" (Alleyways: Literary sketches of the local life of Shanghai, number 2). *Liangyou*, no. 10 (October 1935): 27.

Murphey, Rhoads. *Shanghai: Key to Modern China*. Cambridge: Harvard University Press, 1953.

————. *A History of Asia*. New York: HarperCollins Publishers, 1992.

Nanjing shifan xueyuan zhongwenxi [Department of Chinese, Nanjing Normal College], comp. *"Nihongdeng xia de shaobing" zhuanji* (A special collection of research materials on the drama "Sentries under Neon"). N.p., 1979.

Naquin, Susan, and Evelyn S. Rawski. *Chinese Society in the Eighteenth Century*. New Haven: Yale University Press, 1987.

Ni Xiying. *Shanghai*. Hong Kong: Zhonghua shuju, 1938.

Nie Baozhang. *Zhongguo maiban zichan jieji de fasheng* (The origin of the comprador class in China). Beijing: Zhongguo shehui kexue chubanshe, 1979.

North China Daily News, Shanghai.

North China Herald, weekly, Shanghai.

Nüsheng (The voice of women semimonthly), Shanghai.

Ou Yuanhui. "Daxia Daxue xiaoshi jiyao" (A concise record of Daxia University). In *Shanghai wenshi ziliao xuanji* (Selected collection of historical materials of Shanghai), edited by Zhongguo renmin zhengzhi xieshang huiyi Shanghaishi weiyuanhui wenshi ziliao weiyuanhui, no. 59 (1988): 143–58.

Pal, John. *Shanghai Saga*. London: Jarrolds, 1963.

Pan Guang, ed. *The Jews in Shanghai*. Shanghai: Shanghai Pictorial Publishing House, 1995.

Pan Ling. *In Search of Old Shanghai*. Hong Kong: Joint Publishing, 1982.

————. *Old Shanghai: Gangsters in Paradise*. Hong Kong: Heinemann Asia, 1984.

Pan, Lynn, ed., with Xue Liyong and Qian Zonghao. *Shanghai: A Century of Change in Photographs: 1843–1949*. Hong Kong: Hai Feng Publishing, 1993.

Parkhurst, Helen. *Education on the Dalton Plan*. New York: E. P. Dutton and Company, 1922.

Peroff, Kathleen. "Who Are the Homeless and How Many Are They?" In *The Homeless in Contemporary Society*, edited by Richard D. Bingham, Roy E. Green, and Sammis B. White, 33–45. Thousand Oaks, Calif.: Sage Publications, 1987.

Perry, Elizabeth J. *Shanghai on Strike: The Politics of Chinese Labor*. Stanford, Calif.: Stanford University Press, 1993.

Peters, E. W. *Shanghai Policeman*. London: Rich and Cowan, 1937.

Ping Jinya. "Jiu Shanghai de changji" (Prostitutes of old Shanghai). In *Jiu Shanghai de yan du chang* (Opium, gambling, and prostitution in old Shanghai), edited by Shanghai wenshiguan, 159–71. Shanghai: Baijia chubanshe, 1988.

Pott, F. L. Hawks. *A Short History of Shanghai.* Shanghai: Kelly and Walsh, 1928.

Powell, John B. *My Twenty-five Years in China.* New York: Macmillan, 1945.

Pullers' Mutual Aid Association of Shanghai. *Statistical Report on the Work of the Pullers' Mutual Aid Association of Shanghai, August 1936 to July 1937.* Shanghai: n.p., 1937.

———. *Annual Report of Pullers' Mutual Aid Association of Shanghai, from August 1937 to July 1938.* Shanghai: n.p., 1938.

Qian Nairong. *Shanghai fangyan liyu* (The local dialect and slang of Shanghai). Shanghai: Shanghai Academy of Social Sciences Press, 1989.

———. "Shili yangchang hua fangyan" (The local dialects in Shanghai's foreign concessions). *Dang'an yu lishi* (Archives and History), no. 4 (1989): 69–72.

Qiao Shuming, Yang Qimin, Wang Pengcheng, Zheng Zuan, and Lu Hanchao. *Shanghaishi yanjiu* (Research on the history of Shanghai). Shanghai: Xuelin chubanshe, 1984.

Rankin, Mary Backus. *Elite Activism and Political Transformation in China: Zhejiang Province, 1865–1911.* Stanford, Calif.: Stanford University Press, 1986.

Read, Bernard E., Lee Wei Yung, and Ch'eng Jih Kuang. *Shanghai Foods.* 2d ed. Special Report Series, no. 8. Shanghai: Chinese Medical Association, 1940.

Renmin ribao (People's daily), Beijing.

"Report of the Housing Committee, 1936–1937." *Municipal Gazette of the Council for the Foreign Settlement of Shanghai,* vol. 30, no. 1653 (March 30, 1937).

Reynolds, Douglas R. *China, 1898–1912: The Xinzheng Revolution and Japan.* Cambridge: Council on East Asian Studies, Harvard University Press, 1993.

Ricsha Committee. "Report of the Ricsha Committee." *Municipal Gazette of the Council for the Foreign Settlement of Shanghai* (February 13, 1934): 57–100.

Ross, James R. *Escape to Shanghai: A Jewish Community in China.* New York: Free Press, 1994.

Rowe, William T. *Hankow: Commerce and Society in a Chinese City, 1796–1889.* Stanford, Calif.: Stanford University Press, 1984.

———. *Hankow: Conflict and Community in a Chinese City, 1796–1895.* Stanford, Calif.: Stanford University Press, 1989.

———. "The Public Sphere in Modern China." *Modern China* 16, no. 3 (July 1990): 309–29.

Rozman, Gilbert, ed. *The Modernization of China.* New York: Free Press, 1981.

Schoppa, R. Keith. *Chinese Elites and Political Change: Zhejiang Province in the Early Twentieth Century.* Cambridge: Harvard University Press, 1982.

Schurmann, Franz. *Ideology and Organization in Communist China.* Berkeley and Los Angeles: University of California Press, 1966.

Seagrave, Sterling. *The Soong Dynasty.* New York: Harper and Row, 1986.

Seidensticker, Edward. *Low City, High City: Tokyo from Edo to the Earthquake.* New York: Alfred A. Knopf, 1983.

Sergeant, Harriet. *Shanghai: Collision Point of Cultures, 1918–1939.* New York: Crown Publishers, 1990.

Sernau, Scott. *Economies of Exclusion: Underclass Poverty and Labor Market Change in Mexico.* Westport, Conn.: Praeger, 1994.

Shanghai baihuo gongsi [Shanghai General Merchandise Company], Shanghai shehui kexueyuan, jingji yanjiusuo [Institute of Economics, Shanghai Academy of Social Sciences], and Shanghaishi gongshang xingzheng guanliju [Shanghai Municipal Bureau of Industry and Commerce], comps. *Shanghai jindai baihuo shangye shi* (A history of the general merchandise business in modern Shanghai). Shanghai: Shanghai Academy of Social Sciences Press, 1988.

Shanghai bowuguan [Shanghai Museum], comp. *Shanghai beike ziliao xuanji* (Selections of stelae materials of Shanghai). Shanghai: Shanghai renmin chubanshe, 1980.

Shanghai cidian (A dictionary of Shanghai). Shanghai: Fudan University Press, 1989.

Shanghai Civic Association. *Statistics of Shanghai.* Shanghai: Commercial Press, 1933.

Shanghai fangzhi gongren yundong shi bianxiezu [The writing group of A History of the Labor Movement in Shanghai's Textile Industries]. *Shanghai fangzhi gongren yundong shi* (A history of the labor movement in Shanghai's textile industries). Beijing: Zhonggong dangshi chubanshe, 1991.

Shanghai jiqiye gongren yundong shi bianshen weiyuanhui [Committee for the history of the labor movement in Shanghai's machinery industry]. *Shanghai jiqiye gongren yundong shi* (A history of the labor movement in Shanghai's machinery industry). Beijing: Zhonggong dangshi chubanshe, 1991.

Shanghai Mercury, ed. *Shanghai, 1843–1893: The Model Settlement, Its Birth, Its Youth, Its Jubilee.* Shanghai: Shanghai Mercury Office, 1893.

———, ed. *Shanghai by Night and Day.* Shanghai: Shanghai Mercury Office, 1902.

Shanghai minshi tiaojie xiehui [Coordination council for people's food in Shanghai]. *Shanghai minshi tiaojie xiehui baogao, 1939.12–1941.6* (A report of the coordination council for people's food in Shanghai, December 1939 to June 1941). Shanghai: n.p., 1941.

Shanghai Municipal Archives, Shanghai.

Shanghai Municipal Council Report for the Year 1916 and Budget for the Year 1917. Shanghai: Office of the North-China Daily News and Herald.

Shanghai Municipal Council Report for the Year 1931 and Budget for the Year 1932. Shanghai: Kelly and Walsh.

Shanghai Municipal Council Report for the Year 1932 and Budget for the Year 1933. Shanghai: Kelly and Walsh.

Shanghai Municipal Police Files. Microfilms from the U.S. National Archives.

Shanghai renlicheye tongye gonghui [Shanghai rickshaw trade union]. *Shang-*

hai gongbuju gaige renliche jiufen zhenxiang (The true nature of the disputes over the Shanghai Municipal Council's reform of the rickshaw trade). Shanghai: Shanghai renlicheye tongye gonghui, 1934.

Shanghai renmin chubanshe [Shanghai people's publishing house], comp. *Qingdai riji huichao* (A collection of personal diaries from the Qing period). Shanghai: Shanghai renmin chubanshe, 1982.

Shanghai shehui kexueyuan jingji yanjiusuo [Institute of Economics, Shanghai Academy of Social Sciences]. *Shanghai penghuqu de bianqian* (Changes in the squatter areas of Shanghai). Shanghai: Shanghai renmin chubanshe, 1962.

————. *Shanghai ziben zhuyi gongshangye de shehui zhuyi gaizao* (The socialist reform of Shanghai's capitalist industries and commerce). Shanghai: Shanghai renmin chubanshe, 1980.

————. *Shanghai Yong'an gongsi de chansheng, fazhan he gaizao* (The birth, development, and transformation of the Shanghai Yong An Company). Shanghai: Shanghai renmin chubanshe, 1981.

————. *Jiangnan zaochuanchang changshi* (A history of the Jiangnan Shipyard). N.p.: Jiangsu renmin chubanshe, 1983.

————, comp. *(Maoxin, Fuxin, Shenxin xitong) Rongjia qiye shiliao* (Historical materials of the Rong family enterprises). 2 vols. Shanghai: Shanghai renmin chubanshe, 1962, 1980.

————, comp. *Liu Hongsheng qiye shiliao* (Historical materials of the Liu Hongsheng enterprises). 3 vols. Shanghai: Shanghai renmin chubanshe, 1981.

————, comp. *Shanghai jindai wujin shangye shi* (A history of the hardware trade in modern Shanghai). Shanghai: Shanghai Academy of Social Sciences Press, 1990.

Shanghai shehui kexueyuan lishi yanjiusuo [Institute of History, Shanghai Academy of Social Sciences], comp. *Wusi yundong zai Shanghai shiliao xuanji* (Selected historical materials of the May Fourth Movement in Shanghai). Shanghai: Shanghai renmin chubanshe, 1960.

————, comp. *Shanghai xiaodaohui qiyi shiliao huibian* (Collection of historical materials on the Shanghai Small Sword Uprising). 1958. Reprint, Shanghai: Shanghai renmin chubanshe, 1980.

————, comp. *"Ba yi san" kangzhan shiliao xuanbian* (Selected historical materials of the August 13 war of resistance). Shanghai: Shanghai renmin chubanshe, 1986.

Shanghai shehui kexueyuan shehuixue yanjiusuo [Institute of Sociology, Shanghai Academy of Social Sciences], comp. "Shanghai jumin laiyuan diaocha" (An investigation on the origins of Shanghai city residents). Manuscript, 1990.

Shanghai shenghuo (English title printed on cover: Shanghai guide), journal published by Shanghai lianhua guanggao gongsi, 1939–41.

Shanghai shenghuo (Shanghai life), monthly journal published by Shanghai shenghuo she, 1926–27.

Shanghai shizhengfu mishuchu [Office of the secretary of the Shanghai Municipal Government], comp. *Shanghaishi xingzheng tongji gaiyao, Zhonghua Minguo shiba niandu* (The key statistics of Shanghai municipal administration in 1929). Shanghai: Shanghai shizhengfu, 1930.

Shanghai tebieshi shehui ju [Social Bureau of the Shanghai Special Municipality]. "Yiqian sibai yu youmin wenhua de jieguo" (A survey of fourteen hundred—odd vagrants). *Shehui yuekan* 1, no. 4 (April 1929): 1–6.

———. *Shanghai zhi gongye* (The industry of Shanghai). Shanghai: Zhonghua shuju, 1930.

Shanghai tebieshi zhengfu mishuchu [Office of the Secretary of the Shanghai Special Municipal Government], comp. *Shanghai tebieshi shizheng fagui huibian* (A collection of the municipal laws and regulations of the Shanghai Special Municipality). Shanghai: n.p., 1928.

Shanghai wenhua chubanshe [Shanghai cultural publishing house], ed. *Shanghai zhanggu* (Shanghai anecdotes). Shanghai: Shanghai wenhua chubanshe, 1982.

Shanghai wujin jixie gongsi [Shanghai hardware and machinery company], Shanghaishi gongshang xingzheng guanliju [Shanghai municipal bureau of industry and commerce], Shanghai shehui kexueyuan jingji yanjiusuo [Institute of Economics, Shanghai Academy of Social Sciences], comps. *Shanghai jindai wujin shangye shi* (A history of the hardware trade in modern Shanghai). Shanghai: Shanghai Academy of Social Sciences Press, 1990.

Shanghai xinbao (Shanghai newspaper), Shanghai, 1862.

Shanghai xintuo gufen youxian gongsi, comp. *Shanghai fengtu zaji* (Miscellany on local conditions and customs in Shanghai). Shanghai: Shanghai xintuo gufen youxian gongsi, 1932.

Shanghai yan'ge bianxiezu [Writing group of the Evolution of Shanghai]. "Shanghai de geming yiji" (Revolutionary relics in Shanghai). In *Shanghai difangshi ziliao*, compiled by Shanghaishi wenshiguan, 6:6–10.

Shanghai yanjiu zhongxin [Shanghai Research Center] and Shanghai renmin chubanshe [Shanghai People's Publishing House], eds. *Shanghai 700 nian* (The seven hundred years of Shanghai). Shanghai: Shanghai renmin chubanshe, 1991.

Shanghai zhi zui bianweihui (Editorial committee of the Most, the Earliest, and the Number Ones in Shanghai). *Shanghai zhi zui* (The most, the earliest, and the number ones in Shanghai). Shanghai: Shanghai renmin chubanshe, 1990.

Shanghai zhoubao (Shanghai weekly), Shanghai, 1933.

Shanghai zhuzhai (1949–1990) bianjibu [Editorial office of the Dwellings of Shanghai (1949–1990)]. *Shanghai zhuzhai (1949–1990)* (The dwellings of Shanghai, 1949–1990). Shanghai: Shanghai kexue puji chubanshe, 1993.

Shanghaigang shihua bianxiezu [Writing group of the History of the Port of Shanghai]. *Shanghaigang shihua* (A history of the port of Shanghai). Shanghai: Shanghai renmin chubanshe, 1979.

Shanghaishi Changningqu renmin zhengfu [Government of Changning District of Shanghai], comp. *Changningqu dimingzhi* (A gazetteer of Changning District of Shanghai). Shanghai: Xuelin chubanshe, 1988.

Shanghaishi chuzu qiche gongsi dangshi bianxiezu [Writing group for the Party History of the Shanghai Taxi Company]. *Shanghai chuzu qiche renliche gongren yundong shi* (A history of the labor movement among Shanghai's taxi drivers and rickshaw pullers). Beijing: Zhonggong dangshi chubanshe, 1991.

Shanghaishi dang'an guan [Shanghai Municipal Archive], comp. *Ri wei Shanghai shizhengfu* (The puppet Shanghai municipal government under the Japanese occupation). Beijing: Dang'an chubanshe, 1986.

————, comp. *Shanghai jiefang* (The liberation of Shanghai). Beijing: Dang'an chubanshe, 1989.

————, comp. *Jiu Shanghai de zhengquan jiaoyi* (The stock exchange of old Shanghai). Shanghai: Shanghai guji chubanshe, 1992.

————, comp. *Zhuiyi — Jindai Shanghai tushi* (Recollections: A history of modern Shanghai in documentary photographs). Shanghai: Shanghai guji chubanshe, 1996.

Shanghaishi fangchan guanliju [Shanghai Municipal Bureau of Real Estate]. *Shanghai lilong minju* (Shanghai's alleyway houses). Beijing: Zhongguo jianzhu gongye chubanshe, 1993.

Shanghaishi fangzhi gongyeju [Shanghai Municipal Bureau of Textile Industry] and Shanghai mianfangzhi gongye gongsi [Shanghai Cotton Textile Company], comps. *Yong'an fangzhi yinran gongsi* (The Yong'an Textile and Dyeing Company). Beijing: Zhonghua shuju, 1964.

Shanghaishi gong'anju huzhengchu [Household Registration Division of the Shanghai Municipal Public Security Bureau], comp. *Shanghaishi renkou ziliao huibian* (A collection of materials on the population of Shanghai). Shanghai: Shanghaishi gong'anju, 1984.

Shanghaishi gongshang xingzheng guanliju [Shanghai Municipal Bureau of Industry and Commerce] and Shanghaishi diyi jidian gongyeju jiqi gongye shiliaozu [Group for Historical Materials of the Shanghai Number One Machinery and Electric Bureau], comps. *Shanghai minzu jiqi gongye* (The national manufacturing industry in Shanghai). 2 vols. Beijing: Zhonghua shuju, 1979.

Shanghaishi gongshang xingzheng guanliju [Shanghai Municipal Bureau of Industry and Commerce] and Shanghaishi fangzhipin gongsi [Shanghai Municipal Bureau of Textile Products], comps. *Shanghaishi mianbu shangye* (The cotton cloth trade in Shanghai). Beijing: Zhonghua shuju, 1979.

Shanghaishi gongshang xingzheng guanliju [Shanghai Municipal Bureau of Industry and Commerce] and Shanghaishi xiangjiao gongye gongsi [The Shanghai Municipal Bureau of Rubber Industry], comps. *Shanghai minzu xiangjiao gongye* (The national rubber industry in Shanghai). Beijing: Zhonghua shuju, 1979.

Shanghaishi gongshang xingzheng guanliju [Shanghai Municipal Bureau of

Industry and Commerce] and Zhongguo fangzhipin gongsi Shanghaishi gongsi [The Shanghai Bureau of the Chinese Textile Company], comps. *Shangye zibenjia shi zenyang canku boxue dianyuan de — jiu Shanghai Xiedaxiang choubu shangdian de Diangui* (How commercial capitalists exploited shop assistants cruelly—the *Store Rules* of the Xiedaxiang Silk and Cotton Cloth Store in old Shanghai). Shanghai: Shanghai renmin chubanshe, 1966.

Shanghaishi gongyong shiye guanliju [Shanghai Municipal Bureau of Public Utilities], comp. *Shanghai gongyong shiye* (Public utilities of Shanghai). Shanghai: Shanghai renmin chubanshe, 1991.

Shanghaishi Hongkouqu renmin zhengfu [Government of Hongkou District of Shanghai], comp. *Shanghaishi Hongkouqu dimingzhi* (A gazetteer of Hongkou District of Shanghai). Shanghai: Shanghai Academy of Social Sciences Press, 1989.

Shanghaishi Huangpu quzhi bianzuan weiyuanhui [Editorial committee of The Local Records of Huangpu District], comp. *Huangpu quzhi* (The local records of Huangpu District). Shanghai: Shanghai Academy of Social Sciences Press, 1996.

Shanghaishi Huangpuqu renmin zhengfu [Government of Huangpu District of Shanghai], comp. *Shanghaishi Huangpuqu dimingzhi* (A gazetteer of Huangpu District of Shanghai). Shanghai: Shanghai Academy of Social Sciences Press, 1989.

Shanghaishi Huangpuqu renmin zhengfu caizheng maoyi bangongshi [Office of Finance and Trade of the government of Huangpu District of Shanghai], comp. *Shanghaishi Huangpuqu shangyezhi* (A gazetteer of commerce in Huangpu District of Shanghai). Shanghai: Shanghai kexue jishu chubanshe, 1995.

Shanghaishi jiaotong yunshu ju [Shanghai Municipal Bureau of Transportation], ed. *Shanghai gonglu yunshu shi* (A history of roads and transportation in Shanghai). Vol. 1. Shanghai: Shanghai Academy of Social Sciences Press, 1988.

Shanghaishi Jing'anqu renmin zhengfu [Government of Jing'an District of Shanghai]. *Shanghaishi Jing'anqu dimingzhi* (A gazetteer of Jing'an District of Shanghai). Shanghai: Shanghai Academy of Social Sciences Press, 1988.

Shanghaishi liangshiju [Shanghai Municipal Bureau of Food Grains], Shanghai gongshang xingzheng guanliju [Shanghai Municipal Bureau of Industry and Commerce], Shanghai shehui kexueyuan jingji yanjiusuo jingjishi yanjiushi [Economic History Division of the Institute of Economics, Shanghai Academy of Social Sciences], comps. *Zhongguo jindai mianfen gongye shi* (A history of the flour industry in modern China). Beijing: Zhonghua shuju, 1987.

Shanghaishi Luwanqu renmin zhengfu [Government of Luwan District of Shanghai]. *Shanghaishi Luwanqu dimingzhi* (A gazetteer of Luwan District of Shanghai). Shanghai: Shanghai Academy of Social Sciences Press, 1990.

Shanghaishi Nanshi quzhi bianzuan weiyuanhui [Editorial committee of The Local Records of Nanshi District], comp. *Shanghaishi Nanshi quzhi* (The local records of Nanshi District). Shanghai: Shanghai Academy of Social Sciences, 1997.

Shanghaishi nianjian (Shanghai year book), 1935–37, 1946–48.

Shanghaishi Putuoqu renmin zhengfu [Government of Putuo District of Shanghai], ed. *Shanghaishi Putuoqu dimingzhi* (A gazetteer of Putuo District of Shanghai). Shanghai: Xuelin chubanshe, 1988.

Shanghaishi renmin zhengfu bangongting [Office of the Shanghai Municipal Government]. *Shanghai shizheng gongzuo qingkuang tongjitu* (Statistic charts of Shanghai municipal administration). Shanghai: n.p., 1950.

Shanghaishi renmin zhengfu mishuchu [Office of the Secretary of the Shanghai Municipal Government]. *Yijiu sijiu nian Shanghaishi zonghe tongji* (Comprehensive statistics of Shanghai in the year 1949). Shanghai: n.p., 1950.

Shanghaishi shehuiju [Shanghai Municipal Bureau of Social Affairs], comp. "Shanghaishi renlichefu shenghuo zhuangkuang diaocha baogaoshu" (Report of an investigation into the living conditions of Shanghai rickshaw men). 3 parts. *Shehui banyuekan* (Social semimonthly) 1, nos. 1, 3, 4 (1934): no. 1, 99–113; no. 3, 37–50; no. 4, 45–57.

———. "Shanghai de gongzi tongji" (Wage statistics of Shanghai). *Guoji laogong tongxun* 5, no. 8 (August 1938): 1–129.

———. *Shanghai zhi shangye* (Commerce of Shanghai). 1935. Reprint, Taipei: Wenhai chubanshe, n.d.

Shanghaishi shifan jiaoyanshi [Office for the Normal School Education in Shanghai], comp. *Shanghai xiangtu wenhua shi* (A history of Shanghai native culture). N.p: Shanghaishi shifan jiaoyanshi, 1990.

Shanghaishi tongjiju [Shanghai Municipal Bureau of Statistics], comp. *Shanghai tongji nianjian, 1983* (Shanghai statistics annual, 1983). Shanghai: Shanghai renmin chubanshe, 1984.

———, comp. *Shanghai: gaige, kaifang yu fazhan* (Shanghai: Reform, openness, and development). Shanghai: Sanlian shudian, 1988.

———, comp. *Shanghai tongji nianjian, 1988* (Shanghai statistics annual, 1988). Shanghai: Shanghai renmin chubanshe, 1988.

———, comp. *Shanghai liudong renkou* (The Floating Population in Shanghai). N.p.: Zhongguo tongji chubanshe, 1989.

———, comp. *Shanghai tongji nianjian, 1989* (Shanghai statistics annual, 1989). Shanghai: Shanghai renmin chubanshe, 1989.

Shanghaishi tongzhiguan [Shanghai Municipal History Institute]. *Shanghaishi zhongyao faling huikan chubian* (First edition of a collection of important municipal laws and regulations of Shanghai). Shanghai: Zhonghua shuju, 1937.

Shanghaishi wenshi yanjiu guan [Shanghai Institute of Culture and History], comp. *Haishang chunqiu* (Historical narratives on Shanghai). Shanghai: Shanghai shudian, 1992.

Shanghaishi wenshiguan [Shanghai Culture and History Institute], comp. *Shanghai difangshi ziliao* (Materials on the local history of Shanghai). 6 vols. Shanghai: Shanghai Academy of Social Sciences Press, 1982–88.

Shanghaishi Xuhuiqu fangchan guanliju, comp. *Shanghai Xuhui zhuzhai* (Dwellings in Xuhui District, Shanghai). N.p.: Wuzhou chuanbo chubanshe, 1995.

Shanghaishi Xuhuiqu renmin zhengfu [Government of Xuhui District of Shanghai], comp. *Shanghaishi Xuhuiqu dimingzhi* (A gazetteer of Xuhui District of Shanghai). Shanghai: Shanghai Academy of Social Sciences Press, 1989.

Shanghaishi zhufang zhidu gaige lingdao xiaozu bangongshi [Office of reforming the Shanghai housing system], comp. *Shanghai zhufang zhidu gaige* (Reforming the housing system of Shanghai). Shanghai: Shanghai renmin chubanshe, 1991 (restricted version).

Shanghaishi zonggonghui [General Labor Union of Shanghai], comp. *Jiefang zhanzheng shiqi Shanghai gongren yundong shi* (A history of the labor movement in Shanghai during the War of Liberation). Shanghai: Yuandong chubanshe, 1992.

———, comp. *KangRi zhanzheng shiqi Shanghai gongren yundong shi* (A history of the labor movement in Shanghai during the War of Resistance). Shanghai: Yuandong chubanshe, 1992.

Shanghaitan heimu (Shady deals in Shanghai). 4 vols. Beijing: Guoji wenhua chuban gongsi, 1992. Originally compiled by Qian Kesheng and published in 1917 by *Shanghai shishi xinbao* (Shanghai current affairs daily) under the title *Shanghai heimu huibian* (A collection of shady deals in Shanghai).

Shanghaitong she [Office of old Shanghai hands], comp. *Shanghai yanjiu ziliao* (Research Materials on Shanghai). Shanghai: Zhonghua shuju, 1936.

———, comp. *Shanghai yanjiu ziliao, xuji* (Research Materials on Shanghai, continued). Shanghai: Zhonghua shuju, 1939.

Shehui ribao (Social Daily News), Shanghai, 1934–36.

Shehui yuekan (Social monthly), Shanghai, 1929–30 and 1946–48.

Shen Bojing and Chen Huaipu. *Shanghaishi zhinan* (Guide to Shanghai). Shanghai: Zhonghua shuju, 1933.

Shen Chenxian. "Nanjing lu fangdichan de lishi" (A history of the real estate of Nanking Road). In *Shanghai wenshi ziliao xuanji* (Selected collection of historical materials of Shanghai), edited by Zhongguo renmin zhengzhi xieshang huiyi Shanghaishi weiyuanhui wenshi ziliao weiyuanhui, no. 64 (1990): 18–30.

———. "Shanghai zaoqi de jige waiguo fangdichan shang" (A few foreign real estate merchants in early "treaty port" Shanghai). In *Shanghai wenshi ziliao xuanji* (Selected collection of historical materials of Shanghai), edited by Zhongguo renmin zhengzhi xieshang huiyi Shanghaishi weiyuanhui wenshi ziliao weiyuanhui, no. 64 (1990): 129–40.

Shen Deci, Fang Jishi, Wang Huaichang, and Dong Dichen. "Huiyi Datong Daxue" (Recalling Datong University). In *Shanghai wenshi ziliao xuanji* (Selected collection of historical materials of Shanghai), edited by Zhongguo renmin zhengzhi xieshang huiyi Shanghaishi weiyuanhui wenshi ziliao weiyuanhui, no. 59 (1988): 137–42.

Shen Ji, Dong Changqing, and Gan Zhenhu, comp. *Zhongguo mimi shehui* (China's secret society). Shanghai: Shanghai shudian, 1993.

Shen Shanzeng. "Pingchang xin shi dao" (A common heart is the Way). In *Shengming zhi shu changlu* (Evergreen is the tree of life), edited by Shanghaishi renkou pucha bangongshi [Office of Census, Shanghai Municipality], 37–44. Beijing: Zhongguo tongji, 1992.

Shen Weibing and Jiang Ming. *Ala Shanghairen* (We are Shanghainese). Shanghai: Fudan University Press, 1993.

Shen Ximeng, Mo Yan, Lu Xingchen. *Nihongdeng xia de shaobing* (Sentries under neon lights). Beijing: Jiefangjun wenyishe, 1963.

Shenbao (Shanghai daily). Shanghai, 1872–1949.

Sheng Juncai. "Shanghai shuiluye de bianqian" (Changes in Shanghai's hot-water services). *Shehui yuekan* (Social monthly) 2, no. 3 (1930): 1–11.

Shi Songjiu, ed. *Shanghaishi luming daquan* (A guide to Shanghai street names). Shanghai: Shanghai renmin chubanshe, 1989.

Shibao (Times), Shanghai, 1914.

Shijie ribao (World Journal), New York.

Shishi xinbao (Current affairs daily), Shanghai, 1934.

Si Ying. "Tingzijian de shenghuo" (Life in the pavilion room). *Shanghai shenghuo* 1, no. 1 (March 1937): 24–25.

Siao, Yu. *Mao Tse-tung and I Were Beggars.* Syracuse, N.Y.: Syracuse University Press, 1959.

Sima Qian. *Shiji* (Historical records). Beijing: Zhonghua shuju, 1959.

Sinclair, Kevin, with Iris Wong Po-yee. *Cultural Shock! China: A Guide to Customs and Etiquette.* Portland, Ore.: Graphic Arts Center Publishing, 1990.

Skinner, G. William. "Marketing and Social Structure in Rural China." 3 parts. *Journal of Asian Studies* 24, nos. 1–3 (1964–1965): 33–44; 195–228; 363–99.

———. "Introduction: Urban and Rural in Chinese Society." In *The Chinese City in Late Imperial China,* G. William Skinner, 253–73. Stanford, Calif.: Stanford University Press, 1977.

Smith, Richard J. *Fortune-Tellers and Philosophers: Divination in Traditional Chinese Society.* Boulder, Colo.: Westview Press, 1991.

———. *Chinese Almanacs.* Hong Kong: Oxford University Press, 1992.

Song Rulin and others, comps. *Jiaqing Songjiang fuzhi* (Gazetteer of Songjiang prefecture compiled in the Jiaqing period). 84 *juan,* 40 vols. N.p., 1818.

Song Yuehui. "Kuanchang de tianjing hen jimo" (The spacious courtyard is very lonely). *Xinmin wanbao* (New people's evening news) (December 23, 1994).

Spence, Jonathan D. *The Search for Modern China.* New York: W. W. Norton and Company, 1990.

Spencer, J. E. "The House of the Chinese." *Geographical Review* 37 (1947): 254–73.

Steinhardt, Nancy Schatzman. *Chinese Imperial City Planning.* Honolulu: University of Hawaii Press, 1990.

Stephens, Thomas B. *Order and Discipline in China: The Shanghai Mixed Court, 1911–27.* Seattle: University of Washington Press, 1992.

Strand, David. *Rickshaw Beijing: City People and Politics in the 1920s.* Berkeley and Los Angeles: University of California Press, 1989.

Su Zi. "Shanghairen" (Shanghai people). *Shanghai shenghuo* (Shanghai life) 3, no. 11 (1939): 17–19.

Tang Hai. *Zhongguo laodong wenti* (Chinese labor issues). Shanghai: Guanghua shuju, 1927.

Tang Hai. *Zang Dayaozi zhuan* (A biography of Zang Dayaozi). Hong Kong: Haiyang shuwu, 1947.

Tang Weikang. "Shili yangchang de changji" (Prostitution in Shanghai's foreign concessions). In *Shanghai yishi,* edited by Tang Weikang, Zhu Dailu, and Du Li, 261–74. Shanghai: Wenhua chubanshe, 1987.

Tang Weikang and Du Li. *Hucheng fengsu ji* (Records of the customs of Shanghai). Shanghai: Shanghai huabao chubanshe, 1991.

———. *Shanghai zujie 100 nian* (A century of foreign concessions in Shanghai). Shanghai: Shanghai huabao chubanshe, 1991.

Tang Weikang, Zhu Dailu, and Du Li, eds. *Shanghai yishi* (Shanghai anecdotes). Shanghai: Wenhua chubanshe, 1987.

Tang Zhenchang, ed. *Jindai Shanghai fanhua lu* (Records of the prosperity of modern Shanghai). Hong Kong: Commercial Press, 1993.

Tang Zhenchang and Shen Hengchun, eds. *Shanghai shi* (History of Shanghai). Shanghai: Shanghai renmin chubanshe, 1989.

Tao Juyin. *Gudao jianwen* (Shanghai during the solitary island period). Shanghai: Shanghai renmin chubanshe, 1979.

Tata, Sam, and Ian McLachlan. *Shanghai 1949: The End of an Era.* London: B. T. Batsford, 1989.

Thorbecke, Ellen. *Shanghai.* Shanghai: North-China Daily News and Herald, 1941.

Tian Yuan. *Sanbai liushi hang tushuo* (The 360 callings as illustrated by pictures). Changsha, Hunan: Hunan shaonian ertong chubanshe, 1991.

Tian Zhongchu. "NanSong Lin'an fangwu zulin shulue" (On the housing rental in Lin'an [Hangzhou] in the Southern Song dynasty), *Shilin* (History circles) 3 (1994): 8–12.

Tieh, Tim Min. "Street Music of Old Shanghai." Manuscript, 1940.

———. "More Street Music of Old Shanghai." Manuscript, 1980.

Tu Shipin. *Shanghai chunqiu* (Annals of Shanghai). Hong Kong: Zhongguo tushu bianyiguan, 1968. Originally published in Shanghai in 1948 under the title *Shanghaishi daguan* (Overview of Shanghai).

Uchiyama Kanzou (Neishan Waizao). "Rōjin sense" ("Lu Xun xiansheng") (Mr. Lu Xun). *Yiwen* (Translation monthly) 2, no. 3 (November 1936): 35–44.

Vermeer, Eduard B. "New County Histories: A Research Note on Their Compilation and Value." *Modern China* 18, no. 4 (October 1992): 438–67.

Wagner, Augusta. *Labor Legislation in China.* Peking: Yenching University, 1938.

Wakeman, Frederic, Jr. "Policing Modern Shanghai." *China Quarterly,* no. 115 (September 1988): 408–40.

———. "Licensing Leisure: The Chinese Nationalists' Attempt to Regulate Shanghai, 1927–49." *Journal of Asian Studies* 54, no. 1 (February 1995): 19–42.

———. *Policing Shanghai, 1927–1937.* Berkeley and Los Angeles: University of California Press, 1995.

———. *The Shanghai Badlands: Wartime Terrorism and Urban Crime, 1937–1941.* Cambridge: Cambridge University Press, 1996.

Wakeman, Frederic, Jr., and Wen-hsin Yeh, eds. *Shanghai Sojourners.* Berkeley, Calif.: Institute of East Asian Studies, 1992.

Waley, Paul. *Tokyo: Now and Then, an Explorer's Guide.* New York: Weatherhill, 1984.

Wang Chifeng and Qiu Huiyou. "Zenyang taotai Shanghai yibai ling siwan zhi meiqiulu?" (How to get rid of Shanghai's 1.04 million coal stoves?). *Jiefang ribao* (Liberation daily), March 31, 1990.

Wang Delin. "Gu Zhuxuan zai Zhabei faji he kaishe Tianchan Wutai" (Gu Zhuxuan rose to power in Zhabei and opened the Tianchan Theater). In *Shanghai wenshi ziliao xuanji* (Selected collection of historical materials of Shanghai), edited by Zhongguo renmin zhengzhi xieshang huiyi Shanghaishi weiyuanhui wenshi ziliao weiyuanhui, no. 54 (1986): 357–59.

Wang Dingjiu. *Shanghai menjing* (The key to Shanghai). Shanghai: Zhongyang shudian, 1937.

Wang Dunqing. "You Jiangbei zhimindi ji" (Record of travel in a Jiangbei colony). *Shanghai shenghuo* (Shanghai life), no. 3 (December 15, 1926): 17–19.

Wang, George Zhengwen. *Shanghai Boy.* Manuscript, 1991.

Wang Guanquan, ed. *Huainian Xiao Hong* (Cherishing the memory of Xiao Hong). Harbin: Heilongjiang renmin chubanshe, 1981.

Wang Hongquan, Jiang Xiefu, and Yao Bingnan. *Pudong jingu daguan* (Pudong's past and present). Beijing: Kexue jishu wenxian chubanshe, 1992.

Wang Jishen. *Shanghai zhi fangdichanye* (The real estate business in Shanghai). Shanghai: Shanghai jingji yanjiusuo, 1944.

Wang Meidi. "Zhongguo zuizao de Qingniantuan zhongyang jiguan jiuzhi" (The relic of China's earliest headquarters of the Communist Youth

League). In *Shanghai difangshi ziliao,* compiled by Shanghaishi wen-shiguan, 6:43–45.

Wang Shaozhou. *Shanghai jindai chengshi jianzhu* (Modern urban architecture in Shanghai). N.p.: Jiangsu kexue jishu chubanshe, 1989.

Wang Shaozhou and Chen Zhimin. *Lilong jianzhu* (Architecture of alleyway houses). Shanghai: Shanghai kexue jishu wenxian chubanshe, 1987.

Wang Tao. *Wang Tao riji* (The diary of Wang Tao). Compiled by Fang Xing and Tang Zhijun. Beijing: Zhonghua shuju, 1987.

———. *Yingru zazhi* (Miscellaneous records on Shanghai). 1875. Reprint, Shanghai: Shanghai guji chubanshe, 1989.

Wang Wei. *Shanghai neimu* (Inside stories of Shanghai). Shanghai: Zazhi chubanshe, n.d.

Wang Weizu. *Shanghaishi fangzu zhi yanjiu* (Research on house rent in Shanghai). Reprint of a 1933 manuscript. Taipei: Chengwen chuban gongsi, 1977.

Wang Yingxia. *Wang Yingxia zizhuan* (Autobiography of Wang Yingxia). Taipei: Zhuanji wenxue chubanshe, 1990.

Wang Zheng. "Xiahai miao he Shanghai miao" (Xiahai temple and Shanghai temple). In *Shanghai difangshi ziliao,* compiled by Shanghaishi wen-shiguan, 1:219–23.

Wang Zhong and Hu Renfeng, comps. *Fahuaxiang zhi* (Gazetteer of Fahua village). N.p.: Tangzhijing Hushi, 1922.

Ward, David. *Poverty, Ethnicity, and the American City, 1840–1925.* New York: Cambridge University Press, 1989.

Wasserstrom, Jeffrey. *Student Protests in Twentieth Century China: The View from Shanghai.* Stanford: Stanford University Press, 1991.

Weber, Max. *The City.* New York: Free Press, 1958.

Wei, Betty Peh-T'i. *Shanghai: Crucible of Modern China.* Oxford: Oxford University Press, 1987.

———. *Old Shanghai.* Hong Kong: Oxford University Press, 1993.

Wei Hui. "Jiu Shanghai jietou de lutian zhiye" (The open-air professions in the streets of old Shanghai). In *Shanghai yishi,* edited by Tang Weikang, Zhu Dailu, and Du Li, 294–98. Shanghai: Wenhua chubanshe, 1987.

Wei Shaochang and Wu Chenghui, eds. *Yuanyang hudie pai yanjiu ziliao* (Research materials on the School of Mandarin Ducks and Butterflies). Shanghai: Shanghai wenyi chubanshe, 1984.

Wen Juntian. *Zhongguo baojia zhidu* (The baojia system of China). 1935. Reprint, Taipei: Commercial Press, 1976.

Wenhui bao (Wenhui daily), Shanghai, 1946.

White, Lynn T., III. *Policies of Chaos: The Organizational Causes of Violence in China's Cultural Revolution.* Princeton, N.J.: Princeton University Press, 1989.

Whyte, Martin King, and William L. Parish. *Urban Life in Contemporary China.* Chicago: University of Chicago Press, 1984.

Wilson, William Julius. *The Truly Disadvantaged: The Inner City, the Underclass, and Public Policy.* Chicago: University of Chicago Press, 1987.

Wodusheng. *Huitu Shanghai zaji* (Pictorial Shanghai miscellanies). Shanghai: n.p., 1905.

Wolf, Stephanie Grauman. *Urban Village: Population, Community, and Family Structure in Germantown, Pennsylvania, 1683–1800.* Shanghai: North-China Daily News and Herald, 1936.

Woodhead, H. G. W., ed. *The China Year Book, 1936.* Reprint, Nendeln/Liechtenstein: Kraus-Thomson Organization, 1969.

Wright, Arnold. *Twentieth Century Impressions of Hongkong, Shanghai, and Other Treaty Ports of China: Their History, People, Commerce, Industries, and Resources.* London: Lloyd's Greater Britain Publishing, 1908.

Wright, Tim. "Shanghai Imperialists versus Rickshaw Racketeers: The Defeat of the 1934 Rickshaw Reforms." *Modern China* 17, no. 1 (January 1991): 76–111.

Wu Guifang. *Gudai Shanghai shulue* (A narrative of ancient Shanghai). Shanghai: Shanghai jiaoyu chubanshe, 1980.

———. "Jindai Shanghai geming yiji gaishu" (A survey of revolutionary relics in modern Shanghai). In *Shanghai difangshi ziliao,* compiled by Shanghaishi wenshiguan, 6:11–31.

———, ed. *Shanghai fengwu zhi* (Records of Shanghai scenery). Shanghai: Shanghai wenhua chubanshe, 1985.

Wu, Harry, and Carolyn Wakeman. *Bitter Winds: A Memoir of My Years in China's Gulag.* New York: John Wiley and Sons, 1994.

Wu, Harry Xiaoying. "Rural to Urban Migration in the People's Republic of China." *China Quarterly* 139 (September 1994): 669–98.

Wu Peichu. "Jiu Shanghai waishang yinhang maiban" (The compradors of foreign banks in old Shanghai). In *Shanghai wenshi ziliao xuanji* (Selected collection of historical materials of Shanghai), edited by Zhongguo renmin zhengzhi xieshang huiyi Shanghaishi weiyuanhui wenshi ziliao weiyuanhui, no. 56 (1987): 72–111.

Wu Shenyuan. *Shanghai zuizao de zhongzhong* (The origins of a variety of things in Shanghai). Shanghai: East China Normal University Press, 1989.

Wu Zaiyang. "Shijiao jiehe diqu jumin shenghuo shangyou zhuduo bubian" (There are still a lot of inconveniences for the residents who live in the immediate suburban areas). In *Shanghai chengshi shehui jingji diaocha baogaoji, 1990* (Reports on the social and economic conditions of Shanghai, 1990), edited by Shanghaishi chengshi shehui jingji diaochadui [Team for Investigating Social and Economic Conditions of Shanghai], 145–48. Shanghai: n.p., 1990.

———. "Shiqu jumin dianbingxiang zhuanti baogao" (A special report on the use of refrigerators among the residents of urban Shanghai). In *Shanghai chengshi shehui jingji diaocha baogaoji, 1990* (Reports on the social and economic conditions of Shanghai, 1990), edited by Shanghaishi chengshi shehui jingji diaochadui [Team for Investigating Social and Economic Conditions of Shanghai], 109–14. Shanghai: n.p., 1990.

Xi Wei. "Shanghai shehui de pouxi" (An analysis of Shanghai society). *Shehui zhoubao* (Society weekly) 1, no. 4 (May 1934): 70–72.

Xia Lingen. *Jiu Shanghai sanbai liushi hang* (The three hundred and sixty professions in old Shanghai). Shanghai: East China Normal University Press, 1989.

Xia Yan. *Shanghai wuyan xia* (Under the eaves of Shanghai). Beijing: Zhongguo xiju chubanshe, 1957.

Xiangyu. "Gelou shijing" (Ten views from a loft). *Shanghai shenghuo* (Shanghai life) 2, no. 3 (August 1938): 11–13.

Xiao Lingjun. *Shanghai changshi* (General knowledge about Shanghai). Shanghai: Jingwei shuju, 1937.

Xiao Qian, ed. *Shehui baixiang* (All aspects of society). Taipei: Taiwan Shangwu yinshu guan, 1992.

Xie Wuyi. "Minchu Shanghai changji yipie" (A glance at Shanghai's prostitutes in the early Republican period). In *Jiu Shanghai de yan du chang* (Opium, gambling, and prostitution in old Shanghai), edited by Shanghai wenshiguan [Shanghai Institute of Culture and History], 172–75. Shanghai: Baijia chubanshe, 1988.

Xin qingnian ("La jeunesse"; New youth), Shanghai.

Xin Zhonghua zazhi she [Editorial office of the New China Magazine], ed. *Shanghai de jianglai* (The future of Shanghai). Shanghai: Zhonghua shuju, 1934.

Xinwen bao (News daily), Shanghai.

Xiong, Victor Cunrui. "Sui Yangdi and the Building of Sui-Tang Luoyang." *Journal of Asian Studies* 52, no. 1 (February 1993): 66–89.

Xiong Yuezhi. "Zatan 'Shanghairen'" (On "Shanghainese"). *Haishang wentan* (Shanghai literary forum) (published monthly by Shanghaishi zuojia xiehui [Shanghai Association of Professional Writers]), June 1994.

Xu Baohua and Tang Zhenzhu. *Shanghai shiqu fangyan zhi* (A gazetteer of the dialect of the Shanghai proper). Shanghai: Shanghai jiaoyu chubanshe, 1988.

Xu Dafeng. "Longtang texie" (A feature article on the alleyways). *Shanghai shenghuo* 3, no. 4 (April 1939): 9–11.

Xu Gongsu and Qiu Jinzhang. "Shanghai gonggong zujie zhidu" (The system of the Shanghai International Settlement). In *Shanghai shi ziliao congkan: Shanghai gonggong zujie shigao* (Collection of Shanghai historical materials: Draft history of the Shanghai International Settlement), 1–297. 1933. Reprint, Shanghai: Shanghai renmin chubanshe, 1980.

Xu Guibao. "Wo de Shanghai shenghuo" (My life in Shanghai). *Shanghai shenghuo* no. 2 (November 15, 1926): 23–26.

Xu Guozhen. *Shanghai shenghuo* (Shanghai life). Shanghai: Shijie shuju, 1933.

Xu Jiatun. *Xu Jiatun Xianggang huiyilu* (A memoir of Hong Kong by Xu Jiatun). 2 vols. Hong Kong: Lianhebao youxian gongsi, 1993.

Xu Ke. *Qing bai lei chao* (Assorted collection of anecdotes of the Qing). Shanghai: Commercial Press, 1917.

Xu Piaoping. "Shangjie lingxiu Yu Qiaqing" (Yu Qiaqing, the leader of the business circles). In *Jiu Shanghai fengyun renwu* (Men of the hour in old Shanghai), edited by Yang Hao and Ye Lan, 124–34. Shanghai: Shanghai renmin chubanshe, 1989.

Xu Run. *Xu Yuzhai zixu nianpu* (An auto-chronicle of Xu Yuzhai). 1910. Reprint, Taipei: Shihuo chubanshe, 1977.

Xu Weiyong and Huang Hanmin. *Rongjia qiye fazhan shi* (A history of the Rong family enterprises). Beijing: Renmin chubanshe, 1985.

Xu, Xiaoqun. "State and Society in Republican China: The Rise of Shanghai Professional Associations, 1912–1937." Ph.D. diss., Columbia University, New York, 1993.

Xu Xinwu, ed. *Zhongguo jindai saosi gongyeshi* (A history of the silk-reeling industry in modern China). Shanghai: Shanghai renmin chubanshe, 1990.

Xu Zongcai and Ying Junling. *Changyong suyu shouce* (Handbook of everyday folk adages). Beijing: Beijing yuyan xueyuan chubanshe, 1985.

Xue Gengshen. "Wo jiechu guo de Shanghai banghui renwu" (The Shanghai gang members I have known). In *Shanghai wenshi ziliao xuanji* (Selected collection of historical materials of Shanghai), edited by Zhongguo renmin zhengzhi xieshang huiyi Shanghaishi weiyuanhui wenshi ziliao weiyuanhui, no. 54 (1986): 87–107.

Xue Liyong. "Ming-Qing shiqi de Shanghai changji" (Shanghai's prostitutes in the Ming-Qing period). In *Jiu Shanghai de yang du chang* (Opium, gambling, and prostitution in old Shanghai), edited by Shanghai wenshiguan, 150–58. Shanghai: Baijia chubanshe, 1988.

Xue Yongli. "Jiu Shanghai penghuqu de xingcheng" (The formation of shantytowns in old Shanghai). In *Shanghai wenshi ziliao xuanji* (Selected collection of historical materials of Shanghai), edited by Zhongguo renmin zhengzhi xieshang huiyi Shanghaishi weiyuanhui wenshi ziliao weiyuanhui, no. 64 (1990): 231–39.

Yan Esheng. *Shangren tuanti zuzhi guicheng* (Regulations of merchant organizations). Shanghai: Shanghaishi shanghui, 1936.

Yang Dongping. *Chengshi jifeng: Beijing he Shanghai de wenhua jingshen* (Urban monsoon: The cultural spirits of Beijing and Shanghai). Beijing: Dongfang chubanshe, 1994.

Yang Hao and Ye Lan, eds. *Jiu Shanghai fengyun renwu* (Men of the hour in old Shanghai). Shanghai: Shanghai renmin chubanshe, 1987.

Yang Jiayou. *Shanghai fengwu gujintan* (Historical narratives on the scenery and relics of Shanghai). Shanghai: Shanghai shudian, 1991.

Yang Jiayou and He Mingyun. *Ta qiao gujin tan* (A historical talk on pagodas and bridges). Shanghai: Shanghai huabao, 1991.

Yang Jiezeng and He Wannan. *Shanghai changji gaizao shihua* (A history of transforming the prostitutes of Shanghai). Shanghai: Sanlian shudian, 1988.

Yang, Martin. *A Chinese Village: Taitou, Shantung Province*. New York: Columbia University, 1945.

Yang Peiming. "Kang Youwei zai Shanghai de yusuo" (Kang Youwei's residences in Shanghai), *Jiefang ribao* (Liberation daily), August 10, 1993.

Yang Ximeng. *Shanghai gongren shenghuo chengdu de yige yanjiu* (A study of the standard of living of Shanghai laborers). Beiping [Beijing]: Shehui diaochasuo, 1930.

Yao Qingshan and Ang Jumin. *Shanghai mishi diaocha* (Investigation of the Shanghai rice market). Shanghai: Shehui jingji diaochasuo, 1935.

Ye Shumei. "Shanghai zujie de fangdichan maimai zhidu" (The real estate market system in Shanghai's foreign concessions). In *Shanghai difangshi ziliao*, compiled by Shanghaishi wenshiguan, 3:177–82.

Yeh, Wen-hsin. *The Alienated Academy: Culture and Politics in Republican China, 1919–1935*. Cambridge: Council on East Asian Studies, Harvard University Press, 1990.

———. "Progressive Journalism and Shanghai's Petty Urbanites: Zou Taofen and the Shenghuo Enterprise, 1926–1945." In *Shanghai Sojourners*, edited by Frederic Wakeman Jr. and Wen-hsin Yeh, 186–238. Berkeley, Calif.: Institute of East Asian Studies, 1992.

———. "Corporate Space, Communal Time: Everyday Life in Shanghai's Bank of China." *American Historical Review* 100, no. 1 (February 1995): 97–122.

Yi'an zhuren. *Hujiang shangye shijing ci* (Poems on commerce and city scenery of Shanghai). 4 *juan*. Shanghai: n.p., 1906. Lithographic printing.

Yiming. *Shanghai shi* (History of Shanghai). Reprint, Taipei: Guangwen shuju, 1983.

Ying Baoshi and others, comps. *Tongzhi Shanghai xianzhi* (A gazetteer of Shanghai County compiled in the Tongzhi period). 34 *juan*. Shanghai: n.p., 1882.

You Youwei. "Shanghai Yufo chansi, Longhua gusi, Jing'an gusi jinxi tan" (The past and present of Shanghai's Yufo temple, Longhua temple, and Jing'an temple). In *Shanghai difangshi ziliao*, compiled by Shanghaishi wenshiguan, 6:229–42.

———. *Shanghai jindai Fojiao jianshi* (A concise history of Buddhism in modern Shanghai). Shanghai: East China Normal University Press, 1988.

Yu Dafu. *Night of Spring Fever and Other Writings*. Beijing: Panda Books, 1984.

———. *Yu Dafu wenji* (Anthology of Yu Dafu). Guangzhou: Huacheng chubanshe, 1984.

Yu Jianhua. *Zhongguo huihua shi* (A history of Chinese painting). 2 vols. Shanghai: Commercial Press, 1937.

Yu Jinghai. "*Xin qingnian* bianjibu jiuzhi" (The relic of the editorial office of the New Youth). In *Shanghai difangshi ziliao,* compiled by Shanghaishi wenshiguan, 6:46–48.

Yu Ling. *Yu Ling juzuo xuan* (Selected plays of Yu Ling). Beijing: Renmin wenxue chubanshe, 1979.

Yu Qiuyu. *Wenming de suipian* (The crushed bits of civilization). Shenyang: Chunfeng wenyi chubanshe, 1994.

Yu Shan. "Er fangdong yu dingfei yazu" (The second landlords and rent deposits). In *Shanghai wenshi ziliao xuanji* (Selected collection of historical materials of Shanghai), edited by Zhongguo renmin zhengzhi xieshang huiyi Shanghaishi weiyuanhui wenshi ziliao weiyuanhui, no. 64 (1990): 43–48.

Yuan Jianmin and Hu Jianyu. "Shimin zaocan zhuangkuang lingren danyou" (The conditions of the city people's breakfast are worrisome). In *Shanghai chengshi shehui jingji diaocha baogaoji, 1991* (Reports on the social and economic conditions of Shanghai, 1991), edited by Shanghaishi chengshi shehui jingji diaochadui [Team for Investigating Social and Economic Conditions of Shanghai], 210–15. Shanghai: n.p., 1991.

Yuan, L. Z. *Sidelights on Shanghai.* Shanghai: Mercury Press, 1934.

Yue Zheng. *Jindai Shanghairen shehui xintai* (The social mentality of modern Shanghainese). Shanghai: Shanghai renmin chubanshe, 1991.

Zhang Ailing. *Zhang Ailing wenji* (A collection of Zhang Ailing's writings). 4 vols. Hefei, Anhui: Anhui wenyi chubanshe, 1992.

Zhang Baogao and Fan Nengchuan, eds. *Shanghai luyou wenhua* (Shanghai Tourism Culture). Shanghai: Shanghai shudian, 1992.

Zhang Biwu. "Zhu gongguan de baoche fu" (The rickshaw man of the Zhu residence). *Xingsheng banyue kan* (The "sound of the heart" bimonthly) 1, no. 4 (February 7, 1923).

Zhang Chunhai. *Hucheng suishi quge* (The seasonal folk songs of Shanghai). In *Shanghai zhanggu congshu* (Compendium of anecdotes about Shanghai). Ca. 1840. Reprint, Shanghai: Zhonghua shuju, 1936.

Zhang Hong. *Shili yangchang: bei chumai de Shanghai tan* (The foreign concession: The sold Shanghai). Shanghai: Shanghai renmin chubanshe, 1991.

Zhang Jiaqi and Ban Zhiwen. "Shanghaishi penghuqu gaikuang diaocha baogao" (Report of a survey of the general condition of shack settlements in Shanghai). In *Youguan Shanghai ertong fuli de shehui diaocha* (Investigation of social welfare for children in Shanghai), edited by Chen Renbing, 235–57. Shanghai: Shanghai ertong fuli cujinhui, 1948.

Zhang Jingyu. *Shehui diaocha, Shenjiahang shikuang* (A social survey of Sung-Ka-Hong). Brown-in-China Monograph, no. 1. Shanghai: Commercial Press, 1924.

Zhang Jishun. "Lun Shanghai lilong" (On the alleyway houses of Shanghai), *Shanghai yanjiu luncong* (Papers on Shanghai Studies), no. 9: 59–77. Shanghai: Shanghai Academy of Social Sciences, 1993.

Zhang Leping. *Zhang Leping's Caricatures.* Shanghai: Shaonian ertong chubanshe, 1993.

Zhang Qing. *Tingzijian: yiqun wenhuaren he tamen de shiye* (The pavilion rooms: A group of literati and their careers). Shanghai: Shanghai renmin chubanshe, 1991.

———. "Zhongguo gongchandang diyici quanguo daibiao dahui huizhi he daibiao sushe" (The relics of the first national congress of the Chinese Communist Party and the lodging accommodations for its participants). In *Shanghai difangshi ziliao,* compiled by Shanghaishi wenshiguan, 6:32–36.

Zhang Xiaobo. "Shanghai Daoqi kao" (An empirical study of title deeds sealed by the Daotai). In *Shanghai difangshi ziliao,* compiled by Shanghaishi wenshiguan, 2:98–107.

Zhang Zhongli, ed. *Jindai Shanghai chengshi yanjiu* (Research on modern Shanghai city). Shanghai: Shanghai renmin chubanshe, 1990.

Zhang Zhongli and Chen Zengnian. *Shaxun jituan zai jiu Zhongguo* (The Sassoons in old China). Beijing: Renmin chubanshe, 1985.

Zhao Puchu. "Kangzhan chuqi de Shanghai nanmin gongzuo" (Working with refugees in Shanghai in the early stage of the War of Resistance), *Dangshi ziliao congkan* (Series of materials on party history), no. 2. Shanghai: Shanghai renmin chubanshe, 1981.

Zhao Sufang. "Jiangyuanlong mousha qinfu an" (The case of a husband's murder in the Alleyway of the Sauce and Pickle Shop). In *Shencheng jiuyue — Shanghaitan shida ming'an* (Old lawsuits in Shanghai: Ten best-known legal cases), edited by Xin Zhiniu, 56–72. Shanghai: Fudan University Press, 1991.

Zhao Yuming. *Zhongguo xiandai guangbo jianshi* (A concise history of broadcasting in modern China). N.p.: Zhongguo guangbo dianshi chubanshe, 1995.

Zheng Chaolin. "Chen Duxiu zai Shanghai zhuguo de difang" (Chen Duxiu's residences in Shanghai). *Dang'an yu lishi* (Archives and History), no. 16 (April 1989): 63–65.

———. *Huaijiu ji* (Recollections of the past). Beijing: Dongfang chubanshe, 1995.

Zheng Tianyi and Xu Bin. *Yan wenhua* (The tobacco culture). Beijing: Zhongguo shehui kexueyuan, 1992.

Zheng Yimei. *Shanghai jiuhua* (Stories about Shanghai). Shanghai: Shanghai wenhua chubanshe, 1957.

———. *Yihai yishao* (A scoop of water in the sea of literature). Tianjin: Tianjin guji chubanshe, 1994.

Zheng Zuan. "Jindai Zhabei de xingshuai" (The rise and decline of modern Zhabei). In *Shanghaishi yanjiu erji* (Research on the history of Shanghai, second volume), edited by Tang Zhenchang and Shen Hengchun, 414–18. Shanghai: Xuelin chubanshe, 1988.

———. *Shanghai diming xiaozhi* (A moderate gazetteer of Shanghai). Shanghai: Shanghai Academy of Social Sciences Press, 1988.

————. "Shanghai jiu xiancheng" (The old county seat of Shanghai). In *Shanghaishi yanjiu* (Research on the history of Shanghai), by Qiao Shuming et al., 77–99.

Zhenhua. "Shanghai de matou xiaogong" (Shanghai's dock coolies). *Shanghai shenghuo* (Shanghai life) 1, no. 1 (March 1937): 21–23.

Zhonggong Shanghai Hualian shangxia weiyuanhui [CCP Committee at the Hualian Shopping Mall]. *Shanghai Yong'an gongsi zhigong yundong shi* (History of labor movement in Shanghai's Wing On [Yong'an] Department Store). Beijing: Zhongguo dangshi chubanshe, 1991.

Zhonggong Shanghai shiwei bangongting shiquzu [Urban Division of the CCP Shanghai Municipal Committee], comp. *Chengshi jiedao banshichu jumin weiyuanhui gongzuo shouce* (Working handbook for urban street offices and residents' committees). Shanghai: Shanghai renmin chubanshe, 1988.

Zhonggong Shanghai shiwei xuanchuan bu [Propaganda Bureau of the CCP Shanghai Municipal Committee], ed. *Shanghai min'ge xuan* (A collection of the folk songs of Shanghai). Shanghai: Xinwenyi chubanshe, 1958.

Zhongguo kexueyuan Shanghai jingji yanjiusuo [Shanghai Institute of Economics, the Chinese Academy of Science], Shanghai shehui kexueyuan jingji yanjiusuo [Institute of Economics, Shanghai Academy of Social Sciences], eds. *Nanyang xiongdi yancao gongsi shiliao* (Historical materials of the Nanyang Brothers Tobacco Company). Shanghai: Shanghai renmin chubanshe, 1958.

Zhongguo renmin yinhang Shanghaishi fenhang jinrong yanjiushi [The Banking Research Office of the Shanghai Branch of the People's Bank of China], comp. *Shanghai qianzhuang shiliao* (Historical materials of Shanghai's Chinese banks). Shanghai: Shanghai renmin chubanshe, 1978.

Zhongguo renmin zhengzhi xieshang huiyi Shanghaishi weiyuanhui wenshi ziliao weiyuanhui [Committee on Cultural and Historical Materials, Shanghai Branch of the Chinese People's Political Consultative Conference]. *Shanghai wenshi ziliao xuanji* (Selected collection of historical materials of Shanghai). Shanghai: Shanghai renmin chubanshe, 1986, 1987, 1988, 1990.

Zhongguo suyu dacidian (A grand dictionary of Chinese folk adages). Shanghai: Shanghai cishu chubanshe, 1989.

Zhou Erfu. *Morning in Shanghai*. Translated by A. C. Barnes. Beijing: Foreign Language Press, 1962.

Zhu Bangxing, Hu Lin'ge, and Xu Sheng. *Shanghai chanye yu Shanghai zhigong* (Industries and workers in Shanghai). Shanghai: Shanghai renmin chubanshe, 1984. Originally published by Yuandong chubanshe, in Hong Kong, in 1939.

Zhu Jiancheng. "Jiu Shanghai de Huaji fangdichan dayezhu" (The Chinese big real estate investors of old Shanghai). In *Shanghai wenshi ziliao xuanji* (Selected collection of historical materials of Shanghai), edited by Zhongguo renmin zhengzhi xieshang huiyi Shanghaishi weiyuanhui wenshi ziliao weiyuanhui, no. 64 (1990): 14–17.

————. "Jiu Shanghai fangdichan de xingqi" (The rise of real estate markets in old Shanghai). In *Shanghai wenshi ziliao xuanji* (Selected collection of historical materials of Shanghai), edited by Zhongguo renmin zhengzhi xieshang huiyi Shanghaishi weiyuanhui wenshi ziliao weiyuanhui, no. 64 (1990): 10–13.

Zhu Lianbao. *Jinxiandai Shanghai chubanye yinxiang ji* (A record of the presses in modern and contemporary Shanghai). Shanghai: Xuelin chubanshe, 1993.

Zhu Maocheng [M. Thomas Tchou]. *Diaocha Shanghai gongren zhuwu ji shehui qingxing jilue* (Outlines of Report on Housing and Social Conditions among Industrial Workers in Shanghai). Shanghai: Industrial Department, National Committee, YMCA of China, 1926.

Zhu Menghua. "Jiu Shanghai de sige feipin dawang" (Four "Kings of Waste" of old Shanghai). In *Shanghai difangshi ziliao*, compiled by Shanghaishi wenshiguan, 3:157–63.

Zhu Zijia. *Huangpu Jiang de zhuolang* (The turbid breakers of the Huangpu River). Hong Kong: Wuxingji shubaoshe, 1964.

Zou Yiren. *Jiu Shanghai renkou bianqian de yanjiu* (Research on population change in old Shanghai). Shanghai: Shanghai renmin chubanshe, 1980.

Glossary and Index

Ah Jin (Lu Xun character), 241–42

Ah Q, 8

Airen 愛仁 (love and benevolence), 145

Alcock, Sir Rutherford, 33–34, 365n18

Alley factories, 173

Alley schools, 169, 173, 175

Alleyway cleaning fee, 229

Alleyway guards, 229

Alleyway houses: as *baojia* unit, 219, 221; as category of residential dwellings, 110; compared to single-story bungalow, 362n77; dwelling space in, 158, 168, 368n93; floor plans, 146–50, 148 fig. 13, 151–56, 367n54; front yards of, 243, 245, 245 fig. 29; garden, 58, 112–13; as homes of little urbanites, 2, 63–64; living rooms of, 243–45, 245 fig. 29; name for, 143, 356n22; new-style, 112–13, 150–51, 158, 226, 228, 249, 366n43; origins of, 33, 142, 339n34; ownership of, 164; and real estate market, 142; rent for, 137; sanitary facilities and amenities in, 150; shrinkage of, 150, 151, 152; types of, 112–13; used as stores, 113 fig. 8, 173, 243–44. *See also* Alleyway-house compounds; *Shikumen*

Alleyway-house compounds: addresses of, 146, 366n34; bookstores and presses in, 175–77; broadcasting stations in, 184; Buddhist temples in, 185; craftspeople in, 215; entertainment establishments in, 182–84; entrance to, 70 fig. 4, 144; financial institutions in, 181–82; front-row units, 173, 243–44, 245 fig. 29; government intervention in, 221–22; increase in size of, 152; lacked sanitary fixtures, 189, 190 fig. 19, 191; lanes of, 152, 154, 155 fig. 15, 244 fig. 28; layout of, 244 fig. 28; libraries in, 212; location of, 42 fig. 1; love affairs in, 233–38; mixture of residence and commerce in, 173–74, 215, 314; morning scene in, 197–98; names for, 145–46, 147 fig. 12; native place of residents, 223; neglect of, 138, 364n1; neighborhood relations in, 146, 222, 224–25, 229–33; nostalgia for, 230; occupations of residents, 223; privacy in, 233, 235; quarreling in, 21, 239–42; seamstresses in, 212–13; stability and mobility in, 145, 222–23; survey in, 323–28; theft infrequent in, 233, 377n134; typical scenes of, 13; used by Communist Party, 177–81, 184. *See also* Peddlers

American Church Mission, 29

American Settlement, 29, 33, 35, 36, 139. *See also* International Settlement

Compositors:	G & S Typesetters, Inc.
	Birdtrack Press
Display:	Aldus
Text:	10/13 Aldus
Printer and binder:	BookCrafters, Inc.